Hong Kong
Macau & Canton
a travel survival kit

Robert Storey

Hong Kong, Macau & Canton – a travel survival kit
6th edition

Published by
Lonely Planet Publications
Head Office: PO Box 617, Hawthorn, Vic 3122, Australia
Branches: PO Box 2001A, Berkeley, CA 94702, USA and London, UK

Printed by
Colorcraft Ltd, Hong Kong
Script: typeset by Literary Photo-Typesetting & Printing Co, Hong Kong

Photographs by
Jim Hart (JH)
Roger Hunter (RH)
Richard I'Anson (RI)
Graham Imeson (GI)
Ian McQueen (IMcQ)
Paul Steel (PS)
Robert Storey (RS)
Tony Wheeler (TW)
Front cover: Street scene, Hong Kong Island (Hong Kong Tourist Authority)

First Published
1978

This Edition
May 1992

Although the authors and publisher have tried to make the information as accurate as possible, they accept no responsibility for any loss, injury or inconvenience sustained by any person using this book.

National Library of Australia Cataloguing in Publication Data

Storey, Robert
Hong Kong, Macau & Canton – a travel survival kit.

[6th ed.].
Includes index
ISBN 0 86442 142 7.

1. Hong Kong – Description and travel – Guidebooks. 2. Macau – Description and travel – Guidebooks.
3. Canton (China) – Description and travel – Guidebooks. I. Clewlow, Carol. Hong Kong, Macau & Canton
II. Title. (Series: Lonely Planet travel survival kit).

915.12504

text & maps © Lonely Planet 1992
photos © photographers as indicated 1992

Robert Storey

Devoted mountain climber and computer nerd, Robert has had a number of distinguished careers, including monkeykeeper at a zoo and slot machine repairman in a Las Vegas casino. After running out of money while travelling, Robert finally got a decent job as an English teacher in Taiwan. Robert then diligently learned Chinese, wrote Lonely Planet's *Taiwan – a travel survival kit* and became a respectable citizen and pillar of the community. With his Las Vegas past still in his blood, Robert was lured into a Macau casino and massage parlour during one crazed weekend, and was thus inspired to update the previous edition of this book so he could pay his way back to Taiwan. Now safely at home, Robert has devoted the rest of his life to serious pursuits such as studying Chinese calligraphy and writing a computer program that will allow him to win at the roulette tables.

Robert has worked as co-author on the following Lonely Planet books: *China – a travel survival kit, North-East Asia on a shoestring, South-East Asia on a shoestring* and *Indonesia – a travel survival kit.*

From the Author

I am deeply grateful to a number of local residents in Hong Kong, Macau and Canton who generously donated their time and energy to help me research this book. In Hong Kong, special thanks go to Andre & Patrick De Smet, Stanley Mo, Anna Lee and Ron Gluckman. In Macau, I am indebted to Astrid Lau and William Chan for their assistance. My contacts in Canton, survivors of the Cultural Revolution, prefer to remain anonymous, but I am especially grateful to them. Also thanks to Polly Pang of Hong Kong for help with the Chinese calligraphy.

From the Publisher

The first edition of this book was researched and written by Carol Clewlow. Since then it has gone through several incarnations under the influence of a number of people. The second edition was updated by Jim Hart, with a Canton section added by an Australian student who had lived and studied in China for some time. The third and fourth editions were updated by Alan Samalgalski. The fifth and sixth editions were major rewrites done by Robert Storey.

This 6th edition of *Hong Kong, Macau & Canton* was edited at the Lonely Planet office in Australia by Tom Smallman, Katie Cody, Kay Waters, Jeff Williams and Colin Cairnes, and Alan Tiller helped with the proofing. Felicia Zhang proofed the Chinese script. Margaret Jung was responsible for mapping, illustrations, design and cover design. Thanks also to Dan Levin for his help with computers.

We've had a number of letters carrying useful information from people 'out there', particularly now that China has opened up – even the odd letter from Chinese in the People's Republic. With thanks to everyone, and with apologies to anyone who's been left out, we'd like to mention:

Rose Allender, Mike Archbold (USA), Giles Aublin (F), Nick Bamber, Kenneth Hughes Berry (UK), R B Bunker, Kevin Burke (IRL), Alan Cassels (C), Miss J

K Charrington (UK), Frank Cheung (HK), Giles Chong (HK), Digby Christian (AUS), John Coomber, Shelly Cox (USA), Fiona Cronin (IRL), John Cross (USA), Wayne Dennisovich, Bill Farrelly, Cecilia Fenery (UK), Oona Gleeson, David L Green (UK), Lance Hartland (UK), Mark Hunter (AUS), Bruce Hayes, Roger Hunter (AUS), Klaus Kimpel (D), Chris Lambert, Sam Lau (HK), Troy May (NZ), Danny McCann (C), E Meyer (USA), Todd Miller, Bryan Murphy, Kay Nellins (UK), Clive Noffke, Andrew Olson, Mrs Marion Parrott (UK), Ed & Philippa Peters, Gary Phelan (Ire), David Phillips (UK), Jean-Luc Praz (CH), William Ramsden (UK), Dario Regazzoni, T N Shane, Rebecca Shaw (UK), Angela Slezak (USA), Louise Smith (UK), Ian Stone (UK), Duke Thornley (C), Hans Verhoef (NL), Virginia Warfield (UK), A S Watson (C), Arthur Brent Williams (USA)

AUS – Australia, C – Canada, CH – Switzerland, D – Germany, F – France, HK – Hong Kong, IRL – Ireland, NL – Netherlands, NZ – New Zealand, UK – United Kingdom, USA – United States of America,

Warning & Request

No place in the world changes more rapidly than Hong Kong. Every time you turn around, the local street market becomes a shopping mall, a cheap youth hostel changes into a 60-storey skyscraper, and even the beach is transformed into 'reclaimed land'. In Hong Kong they build like there's no tomorrow – and perhaps there won't be after 1997. In the meantime we'd like to hear from you.

Your letters will be used to help update future editions and, where possible, important changes will also be included as a Stop Press section in reprints.

All information is greatly appreciated and the best letters will receive a free copy of the next edition, or any other Lonely Planet book of your choice.

Contents

MACAU

CANTON

Map Legend

BOUNDARIES

— · — · — · —	.... International Boundary
— · · — · · —	.... Internal Boundary
++++++++++++++	.... National Park or Reserve
- - - - - - - - -	.... The Equator
· · · · · · · · · · · · · · ·	.... The Tropics

SYMBOLS

◉ NEW DELHI	.... National Capital
● BOMBAY	.... Provincial or State Capital
● Pune	.... Major Town
• Borsi	.... Minor Town
■	.... Places to Stay
▼	.... Places to Eat
≜	.... Post Office
✈	.... Airport
i	.... Tourist Information
◖	.... Bus Station or Terminal
66	.... Highway Route Number
♣ ✝ ✝	...... Mosque, Church, Cathedral
∴	.... Temple or Ruin
✛	.... Hospital
☀	.... Lookout
▲	.... Camping Area
⊓	.... Picnic Area
⌂	.... Hut or Chalet
▲	.... Mountain or Hill
	.... Railway Station
	.... Road Bridge
	.... Railway Bridge
⇒ ⇐	.... Road Tunnel
↦ ↤	.... Railway Tunnel
	.... Escarpment or Cliff
⌣	.... Pass
	.... Ancient or Historic Wall

ROUTES

————————	.... Major Road or Highway
- - - - - - - - - - -	.... Unsealed Major Road
————————	.... Sealed Road
- - - - - - - - -	..... Unsealed Road or Track
══════════	.... City Street
++++++++++++++	.... Railway
—■—◉—■—	.... Subway
· · · · · · · · · · · · · ·	.... Walking Track
- - - - - - - - - - -	.... Ferry Route
+++++++++	.... Cable Car or Chair Lift

HYDROGRAPHIC FEATURES

	.... River or Creek
	.... Intermittent Stream
	.... Lake, Intermittent Lake
	.... Coast Line
	.... Spring
	.... Waterfall
	.... Swamp
	.... Salt Lake or Reef
	.... Glacier

OTHER FEATURES

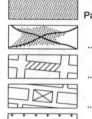

Park, Garden or National Park

.... Built Up Area

... Market or Pedestrian Mall

.... Plaza or Town Square

.... Cemetery

Note: not all symbols displayed above appear in this book

Introduction

Hong Kong is the last British-occupied corner of China, the final chapter of a colonial saga that began over 150 years ago and will end when the colony is handed back to its former owner in 1997.

Most people think of Hong Kong as an island. It is, but not just one. There are 236 islands plus a chunk of mainland bordering the Chinese province of Guangdong – a mere dot on the map compared to the rest of China. Much of it is uninhabited while other parts, especially Hong Kong Island itself, are among the most densely populated areas in the world.

Hong Kong Island is the heart of it all, and the oldest part in terms of British history (the British acquired it in 1841). The centre of Hong Kong Island is the business district of

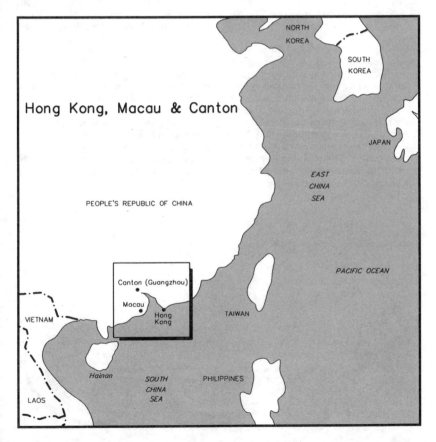

Central where the greater part of the colony's business life goes on. New office blocks, and the rents, shoot up almost daily to accommodate the ever-growing financial elite who want to be part of the Asian Wall St.

From Central it's a seven-minute ferry ride across one of the world's great harbours to the Kowloon Peninsula on the mainland. At the tip of Kowloon is the shopping and tourist ghetto of Tsimshatsui, and beyond that are the high-rise commercial and industrial estates.

Beyond Kowloon lie the New Territories, which include not only the mainland area bordering China but also the other 235 islands which make up Hong Kong. Together the New Territories form the bulk of Hong Kong territory.

Why go to Hong Kong? Contrary to popular belief, it's more than just a place to buy a duty-free musical wristwatch. Hong Kong is one of the world's great trading ports and provides an eye-opener on how to make the most from every sq km, since space is Hong Kong's most precious commodity.

Although very Westernised, Hong Kong still supports an almost intact traditional Chinese culture. This is in sharp contrast to the rest of the mainland where the old culture was attacked and weakened by the Cultural Revolution of the 1960s. There are quiet, empty hills where you can walk for an afternoon and barely see another person, and there are remote villages where the locals still lead rural lives that have changed little over many generations.

Most travel agents and package tours allow a week at the most for visiting Hong Kong – enough time for a whistle-stop tour of a half-dozen attractions plus the obligatory shopping jaunt. But if you give yourself longer and make the effort to get out of Central and Tsimshatsui, you will find a lot more. Hong Kong is only the start.

An hour's hydrofoil ride away is the 500-year-old Portuguese colony of Macau. To the north of Hong Kong and adjoining the New Territories is the special economic zone of Shenzhen where the People's Republic of China has been packing foreign money into development schemes designed to help modernise the entire country. Another special economic zone, Zhuhai, is adjacent to Macau and has turned into a Mediterranean-style resort playground for Hong Kong Chinese.

Northwards up the Pearl River is Canton, the chief city of Guangdong province – a curious mixture of Hong Kong as it was 50 years ago and the new directions China is taking.

HONG KONG

Facts about Hong Kong

HISTORY

'Albert is so amused at my having got the island of Hong Kong', wrote Queen Victoria to King Leopold of Belgium in 1841. But while her husband could see the funny side of this apparently useless little island off the south coast of China, considerably less amused was the British Foreign Secretary, Lord Palmerston. He considered the acquisition of Hong Kong a massive bungle by Captain Charles Elliot, Britain's Superintendent of Trade in China, who had negotiated the deal. 'A barren island with hardly a house upon it!', he raged in a letter to the unfortunate Elliot.

Western Traders

The story of Hong Kong really begins upriver, in the city of Canton, where the British had begun trading with China on a regular basis in the late 17th century.

The British were not the first Westerners on the scene, as regular Chinese contact with the modern European nations began in 1557 when the Portuguese were given permission to set up base in nearby Macau. Jesuit priests also arrived and, in 1582, were allowed to establish themselves at Zhaoqing, a town north-west of Canton. Their scientific and technical knowledge aroused the interest of the Imperial Court and a few priests were permitted to reside in Beijing.

The first trade overtures from the British were rebuffed by the Chinese, but Canton was finally opened to trade with Europeans in 1685. From then on British ships began to arrive regularly from the East India Company bases on the Indian coast, and traders were allowed to establish warehouses (factories) near Canton as a base to export tea and silk.

From the end of the 17th century the British and French started trading regularly at Canton, followed by the Dutch in 1729, the Danes and Swedes in 1731 and the USA in about 1785.

Even so, the opening of Canton was an indication of how little importance was placed on trade with Western 'barbarians'. Canton was considered to exist on the edge of a wilderness far from Nanjing and Beijing, which were the centres of power under the isolationist Ming (1368-1644) and Qing (1644-1911) dynasties. As far as the Chinese were concerned, only the Chinese Empire was civilised and the people beyond its frontiers were barbarians. China was the Middle Kingdom, therefore other nations had to approach her as inferiors and accept vassalage or pay tribute. The Qing could not have foreseen the dramatic impact which the Europeans were about to have on the country.

In 1757 the fuse to the Opium Wars was lit when, by imperial edict, a Canton merchants' guild called the Co Hong gained exclusive rights to China's foreign trade, paid for with royalties, fees, kickbacks and bribes.

Numerous restrictions were forced on the Western traders: they could reside in Canton from about September to March only; they were restricted to Shamian Island on Canton's Pearl River, where they had their factories; and they had to leave their wives and families downriver in Macau (although not all found this a hardship). Also, it was illegal for foreigners to learn Chinese or to deal with anyone except the Co Hong. The traders complained about the restrictions and the trading regulations which changed daily. Nevertheless trade flourished, mainly in China's favour because the tea and silk had to be paid for in cash (usually silver).

Trade in favour of China was not what the Western merchants had in mind and in 1773 the British unloaded a thousand chests at Canton, each containing almost 70 kg of Bengal opium. The intention was to balance, and eventually more than balance, their purchases of Chinese goods. The Chinese taste for opium, or 'foreign mud' as it was called, amounted to 2000 chests a year by the turn of the 19th century.

Emperor Dao Guang, alarmed at the drain of silver from the country and the increasing number of opium addicts, issued an edict in 1796 totally banning the drug trade. But the foreigners had different ideas, and with the help of the Co Hong and corrupt Cantonese officials the trade continued. By 1816 yearly imports totalled 5000 chests.

Opium Wars & After

Two decades later, in 1839, opium was still the key to British trade in China and the emperor appointed Lin Zexu as Commissioner of Canton with orders to stamp out the opium trade once and for all. The British Superintendent of Trade, Captain Charles Elliot, was under instructions from Lord Palmerston, the British Foreign Secretary, to solve the trade problems with China.

It took Lin just a week to surround the British in Canton, cut off their food supplies and demand they surrender all the opium in their possession. The British stuck it out for six weeks until they were ordered by their own Captain Elliot to surrender 20,000 chests of opium – an act which earned him their undying hatred. Lin then had the 'foreign mud' destroyed in public at the small city of Humen by the Pearl River.

Having surrendered the opium, Captain Elliot tried unsuccessfully to negotiate with Lin's representative. The British then sent an expeditionary force to China under Rear Admiral George Elliot (a cousin of Captain Charles Elliot), to extract reprisals, secure favourable trade arrangements and obtain the use of some islands as a British base.

The force arrived in June 1840, blockaded Canton and then sailed north, occupying or blockading a number of ports and cities on the coast and the Yangtze River, ultimately threatening Beijing itself. The emperor, alarmed, lost confidence in Lin and authorised Qi Shan to negotiate with the two Elliots whom he persuaded to withdraw from northern China. Captain Elliot (replacing Admiral Elliot who had become ill) continued nego-

tations in Canton and, in January 1841, after further military actions and threats, forced Qi Shan to agree to the Convention of Chuan Bi. The convention was repudiated by both sides. Qi Shan, it is said, was hauled back to Beijing in chains for selling out the emperor. If Palmerston could have given Elliot the same treatment, he probably would have done so. He believed the empire had been sold short, and curtly informed Elliot that he was to be replaced by Sir Henry Pottinger. Despite the British repudiation of the treaty, their Commodore Gordon Bremmer led a contingent of naval men ashore and claimed Hong Kong Island for Britain on 26 January 1841.

Elliot did not wait for Pottinger. In late February he successfully attacked the Bogue forts, took control of the Pearl River and laid seige to Canton, withdrawing in May after extracting $6 million and other concessions from the Canton merchants.

Pottinger arrived in August 1841 with a powerful force and sailed north, seizing Xiamen (Amoy) on 26 August, Dinghai on 1 October and Ningbo on 13 October. In May 1842 further reinforcements arrived from India and the British continued, taking Wusong (16 June), Shanghai (19 June) and Jingjiang (21 July). With Nanjing (Nanking) under immediate threat, the Chinese were forced to accept the Treaty of Nanking which, among other things, officially ceded the island of Hong Kong to the British 'in perpetuity'.

That wasn't the end of the fighting. In 1856 war broke out again over the interpretation of earlier treaties and over the boarding of a British-owned merchant ship, the *Arrow*, by Chinese soldiers searching for pirates. French troops joined the British in this war and the Russians and Americans lent naval support. The war was brought to an end by the Treaty of Tientsin, which permitted the British to establish diplomatic representation in China.

In 1859 a flotilla carrying the first 'British Envoy & Minister Plenipotentiary' to Beijing attempted to force its way up the Bei He (Bei River), contrary to Chinese requests

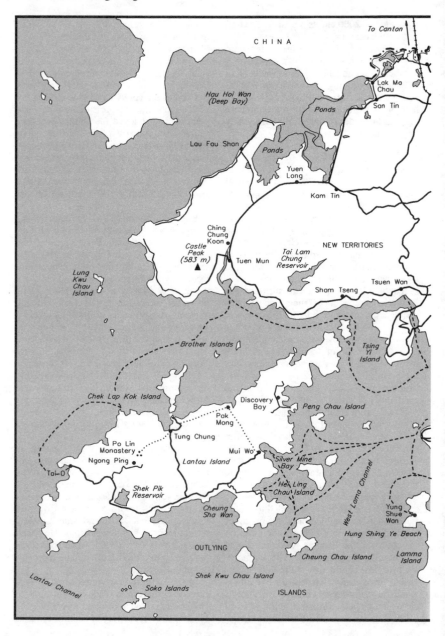

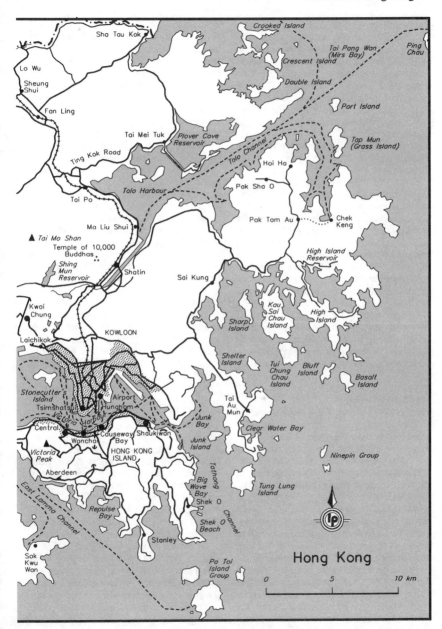

Hong Kong

and warnings. It was fired upon by the Chinese forts on the two shores and sustained heavy losses. With this excuse, a combined British and French force invaded China and marched on Beijing. Another treaty, the Convention of Peking (Beijing), was forced on the Chinese. Along with other concessions, this ceded to the British the Kowloon Peninsula (the area of mainland adjacent to Hong Kong Island and as far north as what is now Boundary Rd) plus Stonecutters Island just off the western coast of the peninsula.

Hong Kong made its last land grab in a moment of panic 40 years later when China was on the verge of being parcelled out into 'spheres of influence' by the Western powers and Japan, all of which had sunk their claws into the country. The British army felt it needed more land to protect the colony, and in June 1898 the Second Convention of Peking presented Britain with what is known as the New Territories on a 99-year lease, beginning 1 July 1898 and ending in 1997.

Despite a shaky start in the latter half of the 19th century and in the early 20th century, Hong Kong flourished as a trading centre and became an intermediary between China and the rest of the world.

War & Revolution

Prior to WW II Hong Kong began a gradual shift away from trade to manufacturing. This move was hastened by the civil war in China during the 1920s and '30s and by the Japanese invasion of the country in the '30s as Chinese capitalists fled with their money to the safer confines of the British colony. The crunch finally came during the Korean War when the US embargo on Chinese goods threatened to strangle the colony economically. In order to survive, the colony had to develop service industries such as banking and insurance, as well as manufacturing.

When the Communists came to power in China in 1949 many people were sure that Hong Kong would soon be overrun. Militarily, it would have been a simple matter: the Communists could have overrun Hong Kong in less time than it takes to make fried rice. However, while the Communists denounced the 'unequal treaties' which created a British territory on their soil, they made no military moves to threaten Hong Kong.

Even without force, the Chinese could simply have ripped down the fence on the border and sent the masses to peacefully settle on Hong Kong territory. In 1962 China actually staged what looked like a trial run for this and sent 70,000 people across the border in a couple of weeks.

In 1967, at the height of the Cultural Revolution, Hong Kong again seemed doomed when riots inspired by the Red Guards rocked the colony. Several bombs were detonated. On 8 July 1967 a militia of 300 Chinese crossed the border with automatic rifles, killed five policemen and penetrated three km into the New Territories before pulling back. The governor, David Trench, kept an aircraft at Kai Tak Airport on standby in case he and his family had to flee the colony.

Property values in Hong Kong fell sharply and so did China's foreign exchange earnings as trade and tourism ground to a near halt. Perhaps it was the loss of foreign exchange that sobered China, for by the end of '67 order was restored.

Now it seems unthinkable that China would want to do anything to undermine the economy of Hong Kong. China International Trust & Investment Corporation (CITIC) – the People's Republic overseas investment arm – has bought heavily into the colony's hotels, banks and department stores. Hong Kong is estimated to be the source of approximately 30% of China's foreign exchange. It could in fact be more than that, given the amount of investment and know-how which flows across the border from Hong Kong to the People's Republic.

At the same time, Hong Kong relies on China's goodwill, as a great deal of Hong Kong's food and water comes from just across the border. Also, Hong Kong's unique position as the gateway to China accounts for a lot of the trade and tourism that passes through the colony.

The 1997 Blues

Hong Kong and China need each other. Yet the problem faced by both the British and the Chinese was the colony's fate when the lease on the New Territories expires in 1997. At that time the Chinese border would theoretically move south as far as Boundary Rd on the Kowloon Peninsula, taking in the whole colony except for Hong Kong Island, Stonecutters Island and Kowloon, which would no longer be viable when severed from most of the population.

If it were purely a problem of economics, Hong Kong should take over China in 1997. For the Chinese, the problem is not economics, but keeping face. Hong Kong is the last survivor of a period of foreign imperialism on Chinese soil (Macau being a somewhat different story) and a symbol of the humiliation of China by Japan and the Western powers in the late 19th and early 20th centuries.

After the Opium Wars the Chinese were forced to pay large war indemnities, permit Western diplomats to take up residence in Beijing and allow freedom of movement to missionaries. Other powers seized Chinese territory or territory controlled by the

The ceremony following the signing of the Sino-British Joint Declaration in 1984 after the British had agreed to hand Hong Kong back to China in 1997.

Chinese, such as Vietnam. The defeat of the Japanese in WW II and the subsequent defeat of the Kuomintang by the Communists finally cleared out the foreign armies, but China still had to deal with problems left over from the civil war and foreign imperialism. One problem was Taiwan, where the Kuomintang fled after their defeat on the mainland, and the other was Hong Kong.

In September 1984 the British agreed to hand the entire colony – lock, stock and skyscrapers, including Kowloon and Hong Kong Island – back to China in 1997. An alternative was to divide the colony leaving each side with a useless piece, and Britain hanging on to a colony which, arguably, it did not want. Some have said that Britain should have just shut up about the whole issue, forcing China to seek a Macau-style solution – allow the British to continue running Hong Kong with no formal agreement. However, the British were keen to have something on paper, and now they've got it.

The agreement, enshrined in a document known as the Sino-British Joint Declaration, theoretically will allow Hong Kong to retain its present social, economic and legal systems for at least 50 years after 1997. Hong Kong will cease to be a British colony and will become a Special Administrative Region (SAR) of China. The Chinese catch phrase for this is 'One country, two systems', whereby Hong Kong will be permitted to retain its capitalist system after 1997 while across the border the Chinese continue with a system which they label socialist. As the secretary-general of the Communist Party, Jiang Zemin, succinctly put it:

According to the principle of 'One country, two systems', China practises socialism, Hong Kong practises capitalism. The well water should not interfere with the river water.

As a follow-up to the joint declaration, in 1988 Beijing published *The Basic Law for Hong Kong*, a hefty document of what is essentially a constitution. The Basic Law permits the preservation of Hong Kong's legal system and guarantees the right of property and ownership; allows Hong Kong residents to retain the right to travel in and out of the colony; permits Hong Kong to remain as a free port and to continue its independent membership of international organisations; and guarantees continuing employment after 1997 for the colony's civil servants (both Chinese and foreigners, including the police). The rights of assembly, free speech, association, travel and movement, correspondence, choice of occupation, academic research, religious belief and the right to strike are all included.

However, there's a great deal of scepticism about China's promises to allow Hong Kong to run most of its affairs after 1997. Beijing has has made it abundantly clear that it will not allow Hong Kong to establish its own democratically elected government, not even on a municipal level. Although some low-level officials will be chosen by election, Hong Kong's new leaders are to be appointed. The Basic Law provides Beijing with options to interfere in Hong Kong's internal affairs to preserve public order, public morals or in the interests of national security. Beijing has also stated that Britain must remove its Gurkha battalion, which will be replaced by the People's Liberation Army (PLA).

Hong Kong's fledgling pro-democracy movement has denounced the Basic Law as a 'basic flaw', and Britain is accused of selling out the best interests of Hong Kong people in order to keep good relations with China. The pro-democracy movement in the People's Republic of China reached its zenith in the latter half of May, 1989, when about one million people took part in protests in and around Beijing's Tiananmen Square. Hong Kong responded with its own demonstrations, with 500,000 people marching through the streets of Hong Kong supporting democracy. On 4 June, the PLA gave its response: tanks were sent into Tiananmen Square, protestors were gunned down and a wave of arrests followed.

In Hong Kong, more than one million people attended rallies to protest the massa-cre in Beijing. Confidence plummeted – the Hong Kong stock market fell 22% in one day and a great deal of capital headed to safer havens overseas. In 1991, Beijing shattered confidence again by indicating it might rescind Hong Kong's recently passed Bill of Rights.

Of course, not all Hong Kongers have to become citizens of the People's Republic in 1997 if they don't want to. Hong Kong is a capitalist enclave and those with the money can buy their way out just as other capitalists can buy their way in. Highly educated Chinese – business management staff, engineers and computer programmers – will also have little difficulty emigrating. Ironically, the outward migration of money and talent could turn ominous predictions about Hong Kong's future into a self-fulfilling prophecy.

Many countries are positively encouraging the trade in passports as they try to benefit from the scramble of money and talent that's been heading out of Hong Kong. Some South American countries simply sell passports. After the Beijing massacre, there has been a notable increase in the number of Hong Kong residents applying for emigration to Third World countries, but most would prefer to resettle in the richer and more secure Western nations.

Canada and Australia have reaped a bonanza of foreign investment by offering passports to those with the necessary funds or job skills. The USA has a similar programme, but requires a US$1 million investment, which not every Hong Konger can come up with. After much debate, Britain decided it would grant immigration status to just 50,000 Hong Kong families, mostly valuable civil servants.

It was hoped that granting the right of abode to these families would convince them to stay put in Hong Kong, since British citizenship would give them protection. However, Beijing sabotaged that by saying it might not recognise their British passports and would instead treat them as Chinese citizens.

Mainland Chinese have also used Hong Kong as a stepping stone for immigration to the West. In 1990, the defection of Xu Jiatun to the USA (via Hong Kong) sent shock waves through the Communist Party. He was director of the Hong Kong branch of Xinhua News Agency (Beijing's unofficial embassy to the colony) and was the highest ranking Chinese official ever to defect to the West.

In its brief 160 years Hong Kong has been transformed. What was originally a 'barren island with hardly a house upon it' is now a highly developed city-state. Ultimately, Hong Kong's fate will be determined by the political drama that is now unfolding in China.

And what of the opium trade that started it all? It folded by mutual consent in 1907, by which time the trading companies had diversified sufficiently to put their sordid pasts behind them without fear of financial ruin. Ironically, Hong Kong now has a serious heroin problem, with about 38,000 addicts – a constant reminder of the colony's less than creditable beginnings.

GEOGRAPHY

Hong Kong's 1070 sq km is divided into four main areas – Kowloon, Hong Kong Island, the New Territories and the Outlying Islands, with most tourists visiting only the first two areas.

Kowloon is a peninsula on the northern side of the harbour. The southern tip of this peninsula (Tsimshatsui), the biggest tourist area, is where most of the hotels are. Kowloon proper only includes the land south of Boundary Rd, a mere 12 sq km. North of Boundary Rd is New Kowloon which is part of the New Territories.

Hong Kong Island covers 78 sq km or just 7% of Hong Kong's land area. The island is on the southern side of the harbour and is the main business area, with numerous tourist hotels and sightseeing spots. Towering above the skyscrapers is the Peak, Hong Kong's premier scenic viewpoint.

The New Territories occupy 980 sq km, or 91% of Hong Kong's land area, and are north of Kowloon and south of the Chinese border. Foreign visitors rarely make the effort to visit the New Territories even though they have much to offer. About one-third of Hong Kong's population lives here.

The Outlying Islands refers to any island apart from Hong Kong Island. Officially, the

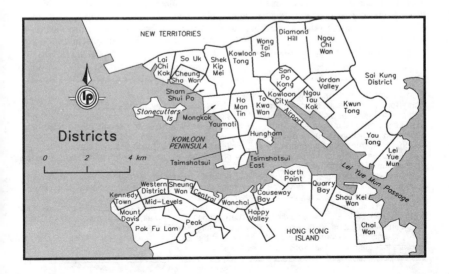

Outlying Islands are part of the New Territories and make up about 20% of Hong Kong's total land area. There are actually 235 islands. Some are tiny rocks, but the largest one, Lantau Island, is nearly twice the size of Hong Kong Island. Many tourists never make it to these islands, which is a shame since they offer a taste of tranquil village life quite unlike Hong Kong's crowded urban jungle. With the exception of Cheung Chau, all of the outlying islands are sparsely inhabited.

Within these four main areas are numerous subdivisions. Hong Kong Island can be divided into Central, Wanchai, Causeway Bay, Quarry Bay and so on, while Kowloon can be divided into Tsimshatsui, Yaumati, Mongkok, Hunghom, etc. (See the Districts map.)

CLIMATE

Hong Kong is perched on the south-eastern coast of China just a little to the south of the Tropic of Cancer. Although this puts the colony on much the same latitude as Hawaii or Calcutta, the climate is not tropical. This is because the huge land mass of Asia generates powerful blasts of cold arctic wind that blow from the north in winter. In summer, the seasonal wind (monsoon) reverses and blows from the south bringing hot, humid tropical air.

Winter is chilly. It never snows or freezes, but it's cold enough to require a warm sweater or coat. Many travellers arrive at Kai Tak Airport in shorts and T-shirt, totally unprepared. Winter weather also tends to be windy and frequently cloudy. Not much rain falls, but when it does, it's usually a chilly, depressing drizzle that lasts for days on end. Because of a low cloud ceiling, the mountains are often shrouded in mist, which means it isn't too good for visiting the Peak and other scenic outlooks. Winter weather usually continues into March and often ends abruptly when the Siberian wind stops blowing.

Autumn, from October until early December, is the best time to visit. The weather is generally sunny and comfortable. Typhoons sometimes occur in October, but not often, and November usually has ideal weather.

Spring is a short season in Hong Kong, but it's also a good time to visit. It's generally warm by the end of March and stays pleasant until the end of May. In March or April, an occasional wind will swoop out of the north and send temperatures plummeting for a few days. Big thundershowers become more frequent as June approaches. June tends to be the wettest month, with the beginning of the summer monsoon. The Chinese call this the plum rain.

Summer is hot and humid. The weather is sunny, but big thundershowers can occur suddenly.

Hong Kong's Environment

Hong Kong is an urbanised, consumer-oriented, throw-away society. In the past, little or no attention was paid to environmental protection, but the concept is beginning to take root, albeit slowly. Some 40% of the total land area is devoted to country parks, which provide scenic hiking areas and watershed protection. In 1991, the Hong Kong government agreed to spend HK$2.6 billion (US$333 million) on environmental programmes. This includes funding the Environmental Protection Department (EPD) with a staff of 840 persons. The bulk of the funds will go for programmes to improve waste disposal and curb water pollution.

A fairly recent proposal was to rehabilitate privately owned stone quarries, which have badly scarred the hillsides of Hong Kong. The government proposes to give the quarry operators economic incentives to resurface and reforest areas which have been mined.

In spite of these mildly hopeful signs, Hong Kong's increasing population and growing standard of living will probably lead to more environmental degradation. The new airport project promises to wreak havoc on Lantau Island, which up till now has been Hong Kong's garden spot.

An international environmental group, Friends of the Earth, now has a Hong Kong chapter. It appears that they have their work cut out for them. ■

Temperature & Rainfall

Month	Jan	Feb	Mar	Apr	May	Jun	Jul	Aug	Sep	Oct	Nov	Dec
Temp °C	15.8	15.9	18.5	22.2	25.9	27.8	28.8	28.4	27.6	25.2	21.4	17.6
Rain mm	23	48	67	162	317	376	324	391	300	145	35	27

Typhoons

Typhoon is the Chinese word for 'big wind'. Hong Kong's worst typhoon struck on 2 September 1937 when more than 1000 junks (boats) sank and about 2500 people drowned. Also, two dozen or so ocean-going ships were grounded as winds of 267 km per hour lashed the colony. Fortunately this doesn't happen very often and, in this age of weather satellites, typhoons no longer arrive without warning.

Typhoons can hit as early as May, but the typical typhoon season is from mid-July to mid-October. A November typhoon is very rare. Typhoons vary in size from tropical storms to severe super-typhoons. If the typhoon just brushes past Hong Kong, it will bring a little rain and wind that might only last for half a day. If it scores a direct hit, the winds can be deadly and it may rain for days on end.

Typhoons are really not much fun even if you are safely entrenched in a hotel room. You can't go outside during a bad typhoon and most businesses shut down. Sitting around a hotel with nothing to do might not be the worst fate, but if the electric power is cut it can be rather miserable.

With no lights, air-conditioner or electric fan, hotel rooms quickly lose their charm, especially as you can't open a window for ventilation when there is a 200 km per hour wind blowing. You may find yourself without water if the electric pumps that build up water pressure are out of operation for more than a few hours. Given these possibilities, it would be prudent to stock up on food, water, candles, matches and a torch if a big typhoon is heading your way. A battery-operated radio or tape player helps to pass the time. Keep extra batteries on hand.

When a typhoon becomes a possibility, warnings are broadcast continuously on TV and radio. Signal one goes out when there is a tropical storm centred within 800 km of Hong Kong. This is followed by signals three and eight, by which time offices are closed and everyone goes home while there is still public transport. Even at this stage, heavy rain, accompanied by violent squalls, may occur. There used to be other in-between signals with consecutive numbers, but this got too confusing so a simplified system was introduced, hence the odd jumps in the numbering.

Signals nine and 10 are rare. Nine means that the storm is expected to increase significantly in strength. Ten means that hurricane-force winds are expected. This signal indicates that the centre of the storm will come close to Hong Kong.

Warning bulletins are broadcast at two minutes to every hour and half-past every hour whenever any of the signals eight, nine or 10 are displayed. If you are without a radio, or miss a bulletin, there is a number you can call (☎ 8351473).

Signals are hoisted at various vantage points throughout Hong Kong, particularly on both sides of the harbour. There's also a system of white, green and red lights. See the telephone directory for details.

GOVERNMENT

Hong Kong is not a democracy, and the Chinese seem determined to make sure it doesn't become one. Hong Kong is a British colony, and after 1997 it seems likely to become a Chinese one.

Heading Hong Kong's administration is a governor who presides over meetings of both the Executive Council (EXCO) and the Legislative Council (LEGCO).

Hong Kong Coat of Arms

The Executive Council is technically the main policy-making body of the government. It's composed of top-ranking officials such as the attorney general and the commander of the British armed forces in the colony, together with other members who are appointed either by the governor or on the instructions of the British government. On the next rung down is the Legislative Council, which frames legislation, enacts laws and controls government expenditure.

The Urban Council is in charge of the day-to-day running of services in Hong Kong Island and Kowloon. This council is concerned with street cleaning, garbage collection, food hygiene, hawkers' licences and the like. The council has 30 members, 15 appointed by the Governor and the rest elected by a franchise of about one million people. In the New Territories, the Regional Council has much the same function as the Urban Council.

On the next rung down are the District Boards, set up in 1982 to give Hong Kong residents a degree of control over their local area. The boards consist of government officials and elected representatives from the local area. The problem is that these boards have little (if any) real power. As a result there is much apathy – the seats are sought after by a small number of candidates who are voted in by the small proportion of the electorate who bothered to register to vote.

Staff in all government departments and other areas of administration are under the umbrella of the Hong Kong Civil Service which employs 173,000 people, of whom about 3500 are expatriates filling nearly all the top policy-making positions. Of the 60-odd government departments, 50 are headed by expatriates. The officer corps in the 27,000-strong police force also has a high proportion of expatriates.

However, it has been decided to stop recruiting British professionals for top administrative posts and to replace them gradually with Chinese in preparation for handing over the colony to China in 1997. The Joint Declaration decrees that expatriates cannot be heads of major government departments or deputy heads of some departments; below these levels, however, expatriates may still be employed after China takes over.

In spite of occasional criticism, the colonial government is generally efficient and mostly free of corruption.

It wasn't always so. Hong Kong's police and civil service were riddled with corruption until the 1970s when the British established the Independent Commission Against Corruption (ICAC). To prosecute a case, the commission only needs to show that the civil servant has wealth disproportional to his or her income – it's not necessary to prove where the income came from. Not only can the defendant be imprisoned, but also must turn over the ill-gotten gains to the Hong Kong government. After 1997, many believe that corruption will once again reign supreme, just as it does in China.

The Chinese Communist Party (CCP) has a long history in Hong Kong, going back at least to 1949 when the Communists came to power in China and formed the People's Republic of China (PRC). Officially the CCP is called the Hong Kong Macau Work Committee (HMWC) and has always been headed by the director of the PRC's Xinhua news agency's Hong Kong branch, which is Beijing's official mouthpiece in the colony.

Members of the HMWC include top Xinhua officials, representatives of major PRC-based commercial organisations and so on.

Another connection between Hong Kong and China is the 50 or so Hong Kong delegates to the National People's Congress (or NPC, China's rubber-stamp parliament) and to that other peculiar body, the Chinese People's Political Consultative Conference (CPPCC). The job of the CPPCC delegates seems to be to confer and consult among each other and provide an image of a united front between China, Macau, Hong Kong and Taiwan.

The NPC has 16 Hong Kong delegates, all top people from banking, business, commerce, education, trade unions, media and other professional walks of life – and all reliably pro-Beijing. The purpose of having prominent Hong Kong residents on powerless bodies like the NPC and CPPCC is lost in the mysterious world of Chinese politics, but presumably it creates an image of support for a Chinese takeover.

ECONOMY

Hong Kong was originally established solely to serve the needs of traders, and to a large extent the colony remains dominated by business. Regarded by some as a paragon of the virtues of capitalism, Hong Kong is a hard-working, competitive, money-oriented society. Its economic policies are a capitalist's dream: free enterprise and free trade, low taxes, a hard-working labour force, a modern and efficient seaport and airport, excellent worldwide communications, and a government famous for its hands-off approach to private business.

Generally, the trend is towards capital-intensive rather than labour-intensive industries, with a corresponding upward shift in wages and living conditions. But for the time being manufacturing is the most important industrial sector. The largest proportion of Hong Kong's exports go to the USA (45%). Other large export markets are in China, Britain, Germany, Japan, Canada, Australia and Singapore.

Manufacturing is the mainstay of Hong Kong's economy, with perhaps as much as 90% of its manufactured goods being exported. With an official unemployment rate around 2%, Hong Kong suffers from a labour shortage which, together with rising labour costs, has induced many investors to relocate factories to China to take advantage of cheap land and labour. A great deal of investment has poured into Shenzhen, just across the border.

In stark contrast to most other Asian states which have populations engaged mainly in agricultural production, Hong Kong has a very small agricultural base with only about 9% of the total land area suitable for crop farming, and this is decreasing due to urbanisation. Less than 2% of the total population is engaged in agriculture or fishing, and even these small numbers will no doubt decline.

Most food is imported, although Hong Kong's farming and fishing industries are efficient. Hong Kong has a sizeable ocean fishing industry which employs about 29,000 people working 5000 fishing vessels. However, most of Hong Kong's food supply is imported, almost half from China.

In fact, because of its limited natural resources, Hong Kong depends on imports for virtually all of its requirements, including consumer goods, raw materials, equipment and fuel. Hong Kong even imports its water – more than 50% is pumped from China. To pay for all these imports, Hong Kong has to generate enough foreign exchange through exports, tourism and overseas investments.

Only about 350,000 people of the 2.5 million workforce are unionised, which appears to suit Hong Kong capitalists as much as it does the Chinese government. It's argued that the PRC believes that a strong independent union movement could become the focus of mass political discontent and upset the 'stability and prosperity' of the colony which is of such great importance to China.

The living standards and wages of most people in Hong Kong are much higher than those in China and most other Asian countries, barring Japan and Singapore. While China's per capita income is around US$400, Hong Kong's is about US$11,000 or more a year and growing fast.

Maximum personal income tax is no more than 15%, company profits tax does not exceed 16.5% and there are no capital gains or transfer taxes. But the money is not evenly spread and the government supports only meagre spending on social welfare. Nevertheless, even people at the bottom of Hong Kong's economic ladder are better off than the bulk of China's citizens.

There are great extremes of living conditions, with thousands of people living in shanty-town housing. Despite the massive housing estates you see in the New Territories (more than two million Hong Kongers live in government-subsidised housing), about 6% of Hong Kong's residents live in squatter huts. These tin shacks, precariously perched on hillsides, are easy prey for fires and typhoons. Even these shacks don't always come free. Symptomatic of too many people and too little space, there is a brisk (though illegal) trade in the sale of squatter huts. Daily police patrols to prevent the construction of new huts may be relieving the symptoms, if not the underlying problem.

Hong Kong's importance to China is manifold. For the first three decades after the Communist takeover in China in 1949, China was largely content to sell Hong Kong foodstuffs, raw materials and fuel. Hong Kong bought the produce and in return provided China with a large proportion of its foreign-exchange earnings, as it continues to do. Chinese investments in Hong Kong property, manufacturing and service industries amount to possibly a third of all direct foreign investment in the colony. Of course, China is not the the only country with a profound interest in what happens to Hong Kong after 1997. The Japanese have also invested enormous assets in Hong Kong.

About half of all livestock exported by China goes to Hong Kong while Chinese factories trying to upgrade their tools and equipment make Hong Kong their first shopping stop because the colony can produce, or arrange to import, whatever is needed. Taiwan businesses trade with China through Hong Kong intermediaries.

Apart from Western tourists, Hong Kong is a favourite destination of visitors from China. More than 200,000 Chinese citizens travel legally to Hong Kong every year.

POPULATION

Hong Kong's official population is about 5.8 million, although with all the foreigners and transients, it is probably closer to six million, making Hong Kong one of the most densely populated places in the world. The overall density of the population works out to about 5000 people per sq km, but this figure is rather deceiving since there is an extremely wide variation in density from area to area. Some urban areas have tens of thousands of people per sq km, stacked in multi-block high-rise housing estates, while many areas are genuinely rural. Many of the Outlying Islands are totally uninhabited.

PEOPLE

About 98% of Hong Kong's population is ethnic Chinese, most of whom have their origins in China's Guangdong Province. About 60% of the population were born in the colony. About 37% of the population lives in Kowloon, 22.3% on Hong Kong Island and the rest in the New Territories and Outlying Islands.

If any groups can truly claim to belong to Hong Kong, they are the Tankas, the nomadic boat people who have fished the local waters for centuries, and the Hakkas, who farmed the New Territories long before Charles Elliot thought about running the Union Jack up a flagpole. The Hakka are a distinct group which emigrated from north to south China centuries ago to flee persecution. Hakka means guest. Hakka women can be recognised in the New Territories by their distinctive spliced-bamboo hats with wide brims and black cloth fringes.

The other 2% of the population is made up of foreigners, mainly Westerners and other Asians. Americans (15,000) and British (14,000 excluding the armed forces) are the largest groups of Westerners, followed by Australians (9000) and Canadians (9000). Of the resident non-Chinese Asians, the two largest groups are the Filipinos (39,000) and the Indians (16,000). There are also sizeable communities of Pakistanis, Japanese, Thais, Indonesians, Malaysians, Koreans, Dutch, Germans, Portuguese and French.

A very touchy issue is what will happen in 1997 to 'foreigners' who were born in Hong Kong and hold Hong Kong passports. Some are half or quarter Chinese, but Beijing has indicated that citizenship can only be endowed on those Hong Kongers 'of Chinese descent'. In other words, racial purity is the deciding factor, not place of birth. Some countries, such as India, have indicated they will accept back their citizens even if these people were born in Hong Kong and never set foot in the home country. The issue of just what will happen to people of 'mixed blood' has not been fully settled.

One of the larger non-Chinese Asian groups in the colony is the 4500-man Gurkha battalion. These Nepalese soldiers have served in the British army since 1817 and Hong Kong has been their headquarters since 1971. Guarding the border against the entry of illegal immigrants from China has been the main reason for Britain's continued recruitment of these troops from Nepal, which bring in close to US$15 million a year for Nepal (a significant slice of that country's foreign exchange earnings). No one knows what will happen to the Gurkha force if its job in Hong Kong is taken over by the Chinese army in 1997.

The colony's huge Chinese population is largely a product of the events in China in the first half of this century. In 1851 the colony's population was a mere 33,000.

The Qing Dynasty collapsed in 1911 and during the 1920s and '30s the wars between the Kuomintang, the warlords, the Communists and the Japanese caused Chinese to flee to the safer confines of Hong Kong. By 1931 there were 880,000 people living there. When full-scale war between China and Japan erupted in 1937 (the Japanese having occupied Manchuria several years before) and after Canton fell in 1938, another 700,000 people fled to Hong Kong.

The Japanese attacked the colony on 8 December 1941, the same day as the attack on Pearl Harbour, and occupied it for the next 3½ years. Mass deportations of Chinese civilians, aimed at relieving the colony's food shortage, reduced the population to 600,000 by 1945 but the displaced people began returning after the war. When Chiang Kaishek's Kuomintang forces were defeated by the Communists in 1949, another 750,000 followed, bringing the total population to about 2½ million.

During the 1950s, '60s and '70s there was a varying flow of immigrants (they're no longer called refugees) across the border from China. In two years alone at the end of the 1970s, the population rose by a quarter of a million as a result of Chinese immigration, some of it legal but most of it not.

Hong Kong has also been a destination for more than 100,000 Vietnamese boat people, several thousand of whom have been allowed to stay in the colony while the majority have been taken in by other countries. Those who arrived in Hong Kong after July 1982 have been installed at closed centres – effectively prisons which they are not allowed to leave until they can be resettled in another country. This system of closed centres was designed to end boat peoples' attraction to Hong Kong, but it hasn't worked.

In 1990, with Vietnam's cooperation, the Hong Kong authorities tried forced repatriation. This worked wonders – the inflow of refugees slowed to a trickle. After vigorous objections from the USA, the policy of forced repatriation was dropped, and Vietnamese refugees once again flooded into Hong Kong. However, in late 1991 forced repatriations resumed.

EDUCATION

Hong Kong's education system closely follows the British model. Primary education is free and compulsory. At secondary level students begin to specialise, some going into a college preparatory programme while others select vocational education combined with apprenticeships.

At tertiary level, education is fiercely competitive. Practically all Chinese parents push their children hard to go to university. The result is that there are not nearly enough university places to meet demand. Only about 5% of students who sit university entrance exams actually gain admission. This is less of a problem for wealthy families who simply send their children abroad to study.

Hong Kong has three universities. Hong Kong University, established in 1911, is the oldest and has about 8500 students. The campus is on the western side of Hong Kong Island in the Mid-Levels area. The language of instruction is English.

The Chinese University of Hong Kong is at Ma Liu Shui in the New Territories. It was officially established in 1963 on a beautiful campus. Enrolment is 7700 students.

The newest is Hong Kong University of Science & Technology, which admitted its first students in 1991. The campus is in the south-east of the New Territories.

Another of Hong Kong's small collection of degree mills is the Open Learning Institute, which started operations in 1989. Based on Britain's Open University, this school caters to working adults by offering evening and weekend classes leading to a degree. Most of the students stuudy business management.

Hong Kong Polytechnic was established in 1972 in the Hunghom area and has 7800 students. City Polytechnic of Hong Kong has 4800 students and is soon to move to a permanent campus in Kowloon Tong. Hong Kong Baptist College, a private school in Kowloon Tong with 2600 students, receives some government support.

ARTS
Dance
Lion Dances Chinese festivals are never sombre occasions – when the religious rites are over at any festival there is generally a lion dance, some opera or a show by a visiting puppeteer.

Celebrations in Chinatowns throughout the world have made the lion dance synonymous with Chinese culture. There is no reason why it should be. The lion is not indigenous to China and the Chinese lion is a strictly mythical animal.

Now lion dances display kung fu movements. The lion dancers, young men in their teens or early 20s, learn the dance at an early age and usually belong to local associations or national organisations. Shopkeepers often give money to the lion dancers to come inside and dance around the shop for a few minutes to bring some good fortune to the business.

Music
Hong Kong's home-grown variety of music consists of soft-rock love melodies. The songs are sung in Cantonese and are collectively known as 'Canto-Pop'. Pop songs sung in Mandarin are also imported from Taiwan and sometimes even mainland China. Most Chinese find Western-style hard rock, heavy metal and punk too harsh and grating.

Theatre Arts
Chinese Opera Few festivals are complete without an opera performance. There are probably more than 500 professional opera performers in Hong Kong and hundreds of amateur groups, so no local function has difficulty booking an act. Chinese opera is a world away from the Western variety. It is a mixture of singing, speaking, mime, acrobatics and dancing that often goes on for five or six hours.

There are three types of Chinese opera performed in Hong Kong. Top of the line among Chinese culture buffs is reckoned to be the Beijing variety, a highly refined style which uses almost no scenery but a variety of traditional props. More 'music hall' is the Cantonese variety, usually with a 'boy meets girl' theme, and often incorporating modern and foreign references. The most traditional is Chaozhou (Chiu Chow), now the least performed of the three. It is staged almost as it was in the Ming Dynasty, with stories from

Chaozhou legends and folklore, and always containing a moral.

Chinese operas are staged infrequently. For details check with the Hong Kong Tourist Association (HKTA).

Puppets Puppets are the oldest of the Chinese theatre arts and the country has produced some of the finest puppetry in the world. You can see rod, glove, string and shadow puppets. The rod puppets, visible only from waist up, are fixed to a long pole with short sticks for hand movements. The puppets are made from camphorwood and the important characters have larger heads than the minor roles.

Shadow puppets are found in China as well as in Java, Thailand, Malaysia, India and (presuming some of the puppeteers managed to escape murder by the Khmer Rouge) in Cambodia. The Chinese puppets, made from leather, cast shadows on to a silk screen. The skills of the puppeteer are passed on from the parents, and the performances relate tales of past dynasties.

CULTURE
Traditional Lifestyle
Face Having 'big face' is synonymous with prestige, and prestige is important in the Orient. All families, even poor ones, are expected to have big wedding parties and throw around money like water, in order to gain face.

Much of the Chinese obsession with maximalism is really to do with gaining face, not material wealth. Owning nice clothes, a big car (even if you can't drive), a piano (even if you can't play it), imported cigarettes and liquor (even if you don't smoke or drink), will all cause one to gain face. Therefore, when taking a gift to a Chinese friend, try to give something with snob appeal such as a bottle of imported liquor, perfume, cigarettes or chocolate. This will please your host and help win you points in the face game.

The whole concept of face seems very childish to Westerners and most never learn to understand it, but it is important in the Orient.

Chinese Zodiac Astrology has a long history in China and is integrated with religious beliefs. As in the Western system of astrology, there are 12 zodiac signs. However, unlike the Western system, your sign is based on the year rather than the month in which you were born. Still, this is a simplification. The exact day and time of birth is also carefully considered in charting an astrological path.

If you want to know your sign in the Chinese zodiac, look up your year of birth in the chart. It's a little more complicated than that though, because Chinese astrology goes by the lunar calendar. The Chinese Lunar New Year usually falls in late January or early February, so the first month will be included in the year before.

Chinese Zodiac

Snake	1917	1929	1941	1953	1965	1977	1989
Horse	1918	1930	1942	1954	1966	1978	1990
Sheep	1919	1931	1943	1955	1967	1979	1991
Monkey	1920	1932	1944	1956	1968	1980	1992
Rooster	1921	1933	1945	1957	1969	1981	1993
Dog	1922	1934	1946	1958	1970	1982	1994
Pig	1923	1935	1947	1959	1971	1983	1995
Rat	1924	1936	1948	1960	1972	1984	1996
Ox/Cow	1925	1937	1949	1961	1973	1985	1997
Tiger	1926	1938	1950	1962	1974	1986	1998
Rabbit	1927	1939	1951	1963	1975	1987	1999
Dragon	1928	1940	1952	1964	1976	1988	2000

It is said that the animal year chart originated when Buddha commanded all the beasts of the earth to assemble before him. Only 12 animals came and they were rewarded by having their names given to a specific year. Buddha also decided to name each year in the order in which the animals arrived – the first was the rat, then the ox, tiger, rabbit and so on.

Fortune Tellers Having your fortune told can be fun. It can also be dangerous. The danger is the psychological problems that can occur when someone's fortune is bleak.

One good friend of mine was told that she would die by the age of 23. Three fortune tellers made the same prediction. She became very depressed and nearly gave up trying to live. It almost became a self-fulfilling prophecy, but the last time I saw her she was 26 and still very much alive. She swears that she will never see another fortune teller again.

How did three fortune tellers manage to make the same alarming prediction? Quite simply, they used the same methods. For example, one line on your palm is your life line – a short one indicates a short life. Other lines indicate the number of spouses, children, your health, wealth and happiness. Also, astrologers use the same reference works when charting an astrological path. Some people do their own fortune telling at home using the Chinese Almanac – a sort of annual horoscope.

Hong Kong has many fortune tellers, most of whom congregate near temples. The Wong Tai Sin Temple in Kowloon is particularly fertile ground for finding a fortune teller. But if you decide, as many tourists do, to take the plunge and find out what fate has in store for you, keep my warning in mind.

Geomancy In Chinese it's called *fung shui* – literally 'wind water' – the art (or science if you prefer) of manipulating or judging the environment. If you want to build a house or find a suitable site for a grave then you call in a geomancer. Without fung shui an apartment block cannot be built, highways cannot be laid, telephone poles cannot be erected

and trees cannot be chopped down. Trees may have a spirit living inside, and for this reason some villages and temples in the New Territories still have fung shui groves to provide a place for the good spirits to live.

Businesses that are failing may call in a geomancer. Sometimes the solution is to move the door or a window. If this doesn't do the trick, it might be necessary to move an ancestor's grave. The location of an ancestor's grave is an especially serious matter. If the grave is in the wrong spot, or facing the wrong way, then there is no telling what trouble the spirits might cause. If a geomancer is not consulted, and the family of the deceased suddenly runs into an episode of bad luck, then it's time to see a Taoist priest who knows how to deal with the ghosts who are causing all the trouble.

Construction of Hong Kong's underground Mass Transit Railway began with an invocation by a group of Taoist priests who paid respects to the spirits of the earth whose domain was about to be violated.

Taboos
Red Ink Don't write a note in red ink. If you want to give someone your address or telephone, write in any colour but red. Red ink conveys a message of unfriendliness.

Killer Chopsticks Leaving chopsticks sticking vertically into the bowl is a bad omen. This resembles incense sticks in a bowl of ashes, a sure death sign.

Avoiding Offence
Clothing Hong Kong is a fashion-conscious city. The Chinese generally judge a person by their clothing far more than a Westerner would. Still, Hong Kong is cosmopolitan – they've seen it all, so you can get away with wearing almost anything. Revealing clothing is OK – shorts, miniskirts and bikinis (at the beach only) are common. However, nude bathing at beaches is a definite no-no.

Although Hong Kongers are usually tolerant when it comes to dress, there is one exception – flip-flop sandals (thongs). Flip-flops are OK to wear in your hotel room or maybe the corridor of your hotel, but not in its lobby and most definitely not outdoors (except around a swimming pool or beach). Many restaurants and hotels will not let you in the door wearing them. Many Westerners ignore this unwritten rule, and although the police won't arrest you for wearing thongs in public, you will be looked upon with contempt.

Ironically, sandals are perfectly acceptable. The difference between sandals and thongs is the strap across the back of the ankle. As long as the strap is there, it's OK. No strap, and you're dressed indecently.

Handling Paper Always hand a piece of paper to somebody using both hands. This shows respect. This is especially true if that person is somebody important, like a public official, your landlord or a business associate. If you only use one hand, you will be considered rude.

Sport
Taichichuan & Martial Arts Slow motion shadow boxing, or taichichuan, is popular now in Western countries, but it has been popular in China for centuries. It is basically a form of exercise, but it's also an art and is one form of Chinese martial arts *(wushu)*.

Taichichuan is very popular among old people and also with young women who believe it will help keep their bodies beautiful. The movements are supposed to develop the breathing muscles, promote digestion and improve muscle tone. A modern innovation is to perform taichichuan movements to the thump of disco music supplied by a portable cassette tape player.

Kung fu differs from taichichuan in that the former is performed at much higher speed and with the intention of doing bodily harm. Kung fu also often employs weapons. Taichichuan is not a form of self-defence but the movements are similar to kung fu.

RELIGION
In Chinese religion now, Taoism, Confucianism and Buddhism have become inextricably entwined. Ancestor worship and ancient animist beliefs have also been incorporated into the religious milieu.

In Hong Kong there are many Buddhist temples and monasteries, of which the most famous is the Po Lin Monastery on Lantau Island. The Temple of 10,000 Buddhas at Shatin and at the Mui Fat Monastery are both in the New Territories. In all, there are about 360 Buddhist and Taoist temples, shrines and monasteries in Hong Kong.

Buddhism
Siddartha Buddhism was founded in India in the 6th century BC by Siddhartha Gautama of the Sakya clan.

Siddhartha was a prince brought up in luxury, but he became discontented with the physical world when he was confronted with the sights of old age, sickness and death. He despaired of finding fulfilment on the physical level, since the body was inescapably subject to these weaknesses.

Around the age of 30 Siddhartha broke from the material world and sought 'enlightenment' by following various yogic disciplines. After several failed attempts he devoted the final phase of his search to intensive contemplation. One evening as he sat beneath a banyan tree, he slipped into a deep meditation and emerged having achieved enlightenment. His title Buddha means 'the awakened' or 'the enlightened one'.

Buddha founded an order of monks and preached his ideas for the next four decades until his death around 480 BC. To his followers he was known as Sakyamuni, the 'silent sage of the Sakya clan', because of the unfathomable mystery that surrounded him. It is said that Gautama Buddha was not the only Buddha, but the fourth, and is not expected to be the last.

Buddhist Philisophy The cornerstone of Buddhist philosophy is the view that all life is suffering. Everyone is subject to the traumas of birth, sickness, decrepitude and death; to what they most dread (an incurable disease or an ineradicable personal weakness); and to separation from what they love. The cause of suffering is desire – specifically the desires of the body and the desire for personal fulfilment. Happiness can only be achieved if these desires are overcome, and this requires following the 'eightfold path'. By following this path the Buddhist aims to attain *nirvana*.

Volumes have been written in attempts to define nirvana; the *sutras* (discourses of the Buddha) simply say that it's a state of complete freedom from greed, anger, ignorance and the various other 'fetters' of existence.

The first limb of the eightfold path is 'right understanding': the recognition that life is suffering, that suffering is caused by desire for personal gratification and that suffering can be overcome. The second limb is 'right mindedness' – cultivating a mind free from sensuous desire, ill will and cruelty. The remaining limbs require that one refrains from abuse and deceit; that one shows kindness and avoids self-seeking in all actions; that one develops virtues and curbs passions; and that one practises meditation.

The many varieties of Buddhist meditation use mental exercises to penetrate deep into the psyche where it is believed the real problems and answers lie, and to achieve a personal experience of the verities of existence.

Buddha wrote nothing, and the writings that have come down to us date from about 150 years after his death. By the time these texts came out, divisions had already appeared within Buddhism. Some writers tried to emphasise Buddha's break with Hinduism, while others tried to minimise it. At some stage Buddhism split into two major schools: *Theravada*, or 'doctrine of the elders', school (also called Hinayana, or 'little vehicle' by non-Theravadins) and *Mahayana*, or 'big vehicle' school.

The Theravada school holds that the path to nirvana is an individual pursuit. It centres on monks and nuns who make the search for nirvana a full-time profession. This school maintains that people are alone in the world and must tread the path to nirvana on their own – Buddhas can only show the way. The Theravada school is the Buddhism of Sri Lanka, Burma (Myanmar), Thailand, Laos and Cambodia.

The Mahayana school holds that since all existence is one, the fate of the individual is linked to the fate of others. The Buddha did not just point the way and float off into his own nirvana, but continues to offer spiritual help to others seeking nirvana. The Mahayana school is the Buddhism of Vietnam, Japan, Tibet, Korea, Mongolia and China.

The outward difference between the two schools is the cosmology of the Mahayana school. Mahayana Buddhism is replete with innumerable heavens, hells and descriptions of nirvana. Prayers are addressed to the Buddha, combined with elaborate ritual. There are deities and Bodhisattvas (a rank of supernatural beings in their last incarnation before nirvana). Temples are filled with images such as the future Buddha Maitreya, often portrayed as fat and happy over his coming promotion, and Amitabha, a saviour who rewards the faithful with admission to a sort of Christian paradise. The ritual, tradition and superstition that Buddha rejected came tumbling back in with a vengeance.

In Tibet and in areas of Gansu, Sichuan and Yunnan a unique form of the Mahayana school is practised, Tantric or Lamaist Buddhism (*lǎmā jiào* in Mandarin). Tantric Buddhism, often called Vajrayana ('thunderbolt vehicle') by its followers, has been practised since the early 7th century AD and is heavily influenced by Tibet's pre-Buddhist Bon religion, which relied on priests or shamans to placate spirits, gods and demons.

Generally speaking, it is much more mystical than other forms of Buddhism, relying heavily on *mudras* (ritual postures), *mantras* (sacred speech), *yantras* (sacred art) and secret initiation rites. Priests called *lamas* are believed to be reincarnations of highly evolved beings; the Dalai Lama is the supreme patriarch of Tibetan Buddhism.

Buddhism in China Buddhism developed in China during the 3rd to 6th centuries AD. It was probably introduced by Indian merchants who took Buddhist priests with them on their land and sea journeys to China. Later, an active effort was made to import Buddhism into China.

In the middle of the 1st century AD the religion had gained the interest of the Han Emperor Ming, who sent a mission to the west; the mission returned in 67 AD with Buddhist scriptures, two Indian monks and images of the Buddha. Centuries later, other Chinese monks like Xuan Zang journeyed to India and returned with Buddhist scriptures which were then translated from the original Sanskrit to Chinese – a massive job involving Chinese as well as foreign scholars from central Asia, India and Sri Lanka.

Buddhism spread rapidly in the north of China where it was patronised by various ruling invaders, who in some cases had been acquainted with the religion before they came to China. Others patronised the Buddhist monks because they wanted educated officials who were not Confucians. In the south, Buddhism spread more slowly, carried down during Chinese migrations

from the north. There were several periods in which Buddhists were persecuted and their temples and monasteries sacked and destroyed, but the religion survived. To a people constantly faced with starvation, war and poverty its appeal probably lay in the doctrines of reincarnation and nirvana which it had borrowed from Indian Hinduism.

Buddhist monasteries and temples sprang up everywhere in China, and played a similar role to the churches and monasteries of medieval Europe. Monasteries were guesthouses, hospitals and orphanages for travellers and refugees. With gifts obtained from the faithful, they were able to amass considerable wealth, which enabled them to set up moneylending enterprises and pawn shops. These pawn shops were the poor man's bank right up to the mid-20th century.

Taoism

Originally a philosophy, Taoism evolved into a religion. Unlike Buddhism, which was imported from India, Taoism is truly a Chinese home-grown religion and second only to Confucianism in its influence on Chinese culture. While Buddhism is found throughout East Asia, Taoism is seldom practised by non-Chinese.

The philosophy of Taoism originated with Laoze (Laotse), who lived in the 6th century BC. Very little is known about Laoze and some have questioned whether or not he existed. His name simply means the old one. Laoze is believed to have been the custodian of the imperial archives for the Chinese government and Confucius is supposed to have consulted him.

Laoze (or someone else) left behind a record of his beliefs, a slim volume entitled the *Dao De Qing*, or *The Way and its Power*. It is doubtful that Laoze ever intended his philosophy to become a religion. Chang Ling is more or less credited with formally establishing the Taoist religion in 143 BC.

Understanding Taoism is not simple. The word *tao*, pronounced 'dao', means 'the way'. It is considered indescribable, but might be interpreted as the guiding path, the

truth or the principle of the universe. It is not a god, saviour, statue or object of any kind.

One of the main principles of Taoism is the concept of *wuwei*, or 'doing nothing'. A quote, attributed to Laoze, 'Do nothing, and nothing will not be done', emphasises this principle. The idea is to remain humble, passive, nonassertive and noninterventionist. Qian Sima, a Chinese historian who lived from 145 BC to 90 BC, put it in another way: 'Do not take the lead in planning affairs or you may be held responsible'.

Nonintervention or 'live and let live' ideals are the keystones of Tao. Harmony and patience are needed, and action is obtained through inaction. Taoists like to note that water, the softest substance, will wear away stone, the hardest substance. This runs directly contrary to Western notions about taking action and getting things done quickly.

Just as there have been different interpretations of Tao, there have been different interpretations of *De*, 'the power', which has led to three distinct kinds of Taoism in China.

The first holds that the power of Tao is philosophical and that the philosophical Taoist, by reflection and intuition, orders their life in harmony with the way of the universe. In this way they achieve the understanding or experience of Tao.

The second holds that the power of the universe is basically psychic in nature and that by practising yoga-like exercises and meditation some individuals can become receptacles for Tao and can radiate a healing, calming and psychic influence.

The third form holds that the power of the universe is the power of gods, magic and sorcery.

Unlike philosophical Taoism, which has many Western followers, Chinese Taoism is a religion. It has been associated with alchemy and the search for immortality, which partly led Taoists to often attract the patronage of Chinese rulers before Confucianism gained the upper hand.

It's arguable that only philosophical Taoism actually takes its inspiration from the *Dao De Qing*, and that all the other labels under which Taoism has been practised attached themselves to the book as they developed, using the name of Laoze to give them respectability and status.

As time passed, Taoism increasingly became wrapped up in the supernatural, self-mutilation, hot coal dances, witchcraft, fortune telling and magic. All this is evident if you visit a Taoist temple during the ghost month or certain other religious festivals.

Confucianism

Without a doubt, Confucius is regarded as China's greatest philosopher and teacher. The philosophy of Confucius has been borrowed by Japan, Korea, Vietnam and other neighbours of China. Confucius never claimed to be a religious leader, prophet or god, but his influence has been so great in China that Confucianism is regarded as a religion by many.

Confucius (551 BC to 479 BC) lived through a time of great chaos known as the Warring States Period. He emphasised devotion to parents and family, loyalty to friends, justice, peace, education, reform and humanitarianism. Confucius was a great reformer and humanitarian. He preached the virtues of good government. His philosophy led to China's renowned bureaucracy and the system of civil service and university entrance examinations, where a person gained position through ability and merit rather than through noble birth and connections.

Confucius preached against such evils as corruption, war, torture and excessive taxation. He was the first teacher to open his school to all students on the basis of their eagerness to learn rather than their noble birth and ability to pay for tuition.

The philosophy of Confucius is most easily found in the *Lunyu* or the *Analects of Confucius*. Many quotes have been taken from these works, the most famous perhaps being the Golden Rule. The Western version of this rule is 'Do unto others as you would have them do unto you'. The Confucian version is written in the negative, 'Do not do unto others what you would not have them do unto you'. The Chinese who are influ-

View from Victoria Peak (PS)

Top: Tram (Streetcar), Central, Hong Kong Island (RI)
Left: Another Star Ferry crosses Hong Kong Harbour (JH)
Right: For a more elevated view, take the Peak Tram (JH)

enced by Confucius and the Tao are not so aggressive as to wish to 'do unto' anybody.

The glorification of Confucius began only after his death, but eventually his ideas permeated every level of Chinese society – government offices presupposed a knowledge of the Confucian classics and spoken proverbs trickled down to the illiterate masses.

During the Han Dynasty (206 BC to 220 AD), Confucianism effectively became the state religion. In 130 BC, Confucianism was made the basic discipline for training government officials, and remained so until almost the end of the Qing Dynasty in 1911.

In 59 AD, sacrifices were ordered for Confucius in all urban schools. In the 7th and 8th centuries, during the Tang Dynasty, temples and shrines were built to him and his original disciples. During the Song Dynasty the Analects of Confucius became the basis of all education.

Although Confucius died 2500 years ago, his influence remains strong in China. The Chinese remain solidly loyal to friends, family and teachers. The bureaucracy and examination system still thrives and a son is almost universally favoured over a daughter. It can be said that much of Confucian thought has become Chinese culture as we know it.

Chinese Religion Now

On a daily level the Chinese are much less concerned with the high-minded philosophies and asceticism of Buddha, Confucius or Laoze than they are with the pursuit of worldly success, the appeasement of the dead and the spirits, and the seeking of hidden knowledge about the future.

The most important word in the Chinese popular religious vocabulary is *joss*, meaning 'luck'. The Chinese are too astute to leave something as important as luck to chance. Gods have to be appeased, bad spirits blown away and sleeping dragons soothed to keep joss on your side. No house, wall or shrine is built until an auspicious date for the start of construction is chosen and the most propitious location is selected. Incense has to be burned, gifts presented and prayers said to appease the spirits who might inhabit the future construction site.

Integral parts of Chinese religion are death, the afterlife and ancestor worship. At least as far back as China's Shang Dynasty (16th century to 11th century BC) there were lavish funeral ceremonies involving the interment of horses, carriages, wives and slaves. The more important the person, the more possessions and people had to be buried with him on the grounds that he required them in the next world. The deceased had to be kept happy because his powers to inflict punishments or to grant favours greatly increased after his death.

Even now a Chinese funeral can be a lavish event. First there's the clash of cymbals and the moan of oboes (most unmelodic to Western ears). Next comes the clover-shaped coffin and grief-stricken mourners, some paid to weep and many wearing ghost-like outfits with white hoods. A fine spread of roast pigs and other foods, not to be eaten but offered to the gods for the one gone beyond, accompanies the funeral.

A grave site is chosen on the side of hills with a good view for the loved one who must lie there. At the grave the mourners burn paper models of material treasures like cars and boats, as well as bundles of paper money, to ensure that the dead person is getting the good things of the first life in the great beyond. Just as during the Shang Dynasty when the dead continue to look after the welfare of the living, the living continue to take care of the dead.

Chinese Temples

The three basic types of Chinese temples are Buddhist, Taoist and Confucian.

Taoist temples seem the most common and are mainly small, except for a few really large ones. They are easily identified by bright colours, dragons and riotous celebrations complete with lion dances, firecrackers and the burning of ghost money. On occasion there are exorcism ceremonies, fortune telling and people possessed by ghosts. There are no monks or nuns, but there is often a Taoist priest and temple caretaker.

Buddhist temples are comparatively rare and much more sedate. Less colourful, but no less beautiful, the temples tend to be built on mountainsides whenever possible and some are very large. There are usually monks and/or nuns in residence who tend the gardens surrounding the temple. A common feature are statues of elephants by the temple entrance.

Confucian temples are the least common. These are very quiet and no monks reside on the grounds. The only ceremony occurs once a year to celebrate the birthday of Confucius.

There is also a good deal of mixing of Chinese temples, especially between Taoism and Buddhism. The Chinese like to hedge their bets, and Buddhist statues appear right next to Taoist deities in many Hong Kong temples.

There is no set time for prayer and no communal service except for funerals. Worshippers enter the temple whenever they want to make offerings, pray for help or give thanks.

At Taoist temples it's common to find stalls selling joss sticks (incense) or spirals of incense which are suspended from the ceiling and burn for two weeks. Ghost money is also on sale. The temple keeper and/or a medium attached to the temple charges for interpreting fortune papers, numbered to correspond with sticks of wood. The worshipper shakes these in a cylindrical box called a *chim*, until one falls out.

Another way of getting advice from the gods is tossing *sing pui*, two pieces of wood with irregular sides which indicate a positive or negative response to a question. Such forms of fortune telling are direct appeals to the gods for knowledge about the future – the fall of the fortune sticks or the sing pui is regarded as the voice of the gods.

Temples often have shelves filled with the 60 *tai sue* – the gods in charge of each year of the Chinese calendar, and worshippers make offerings to the god of the year in which they were born.

Chinese Gods

Chinese religion is polytheistic, having many divinities. Every Chinese house has its kitchen or house god, and trades have their gods too. Students worship Wan Chung, the deified scholar. Shopkeepers pray to Tsai Shin, god of riches. Numerous temples in Hong Kong and Macau are dedicated to certain gods or goddesses. Following are some of the important local divinities.

Tin Hau Queen of Heaven and Protector of Seafarers, she is one of the most popular goddesses in Hong Kong. In Macau she is known as Ah Ma, or Mother, and in Taiwan she is known as Ma Jo, or Ancestress. In Singapore she is Ma Chu Po, or Respected Great Aunt because many fishing people dedicate their children to her.

In Hong Kong Tin Hau has about 250,000 fishing people as followers and there are about two dozen temples dedicated to her dotted around the colony. The most famous is the Tai Miu (Great Temple) at Joss House Bay near Fat Tong Mun. Others are on Cheung Chau Island, at Sok Kwu Wan on Lamma Island, on Market St in Kowloon's Yaumati district, on Tin Hau Temple Rd in Causeway Bay and at Stanley village on the southern coast of Hong Kong Island.

Tin Hau is a classic case of the deification of a real person.

Born on an island in Fujian Province between 900 AD and 1000 AD, the story goes that she went into a trance and dreamt that a storm would destroy all the boats in the fishing fleet. Running down the beach she stared fixedly at her father's boat, which became the only one saved. It is said that in her trance Tin Hau saw that the storm had already hit, that the fleet was in trouble and that in spirit she lead her brothers to safety.

After her death the cult of Tin Hau spread along the coast of China and she became the patron goddess of fishing people. The story continues that in the 11th century two members of her family were shipwrecked on Tung Lung Island at what is now Hong Kong and built a temple for her. Their descendants were responsible for building the original temple at Joss House Bay in 1266. Kublai Khan, the Mongol emperor of China, named her Tin Hau, or Queen of Heaven, in 1278 – possibly a political move to curry favour with the southern Chinese.

Kuanyin The Buddhist equivalent of Tin Hau, primarily a Taoist deity, is Kuanyin, the Goddess of Mercy, who stands for tenderness and compassion for the unhappy lot of mortals. She is also known as Kwun Yum, and as Kuan Iam in Macau. Kuanyin temples are at Repulse Bay and Stanley on Hong Kong Island. There are some in Macau also.

Kuanti Soldiers pray to Kuanti, the red-faced God of War. Prior to his deification, Kuanti was a great warrior who lived at the end of the Han Dynasty (206 BC to 220 AD) and is worshipped not only for his might in battle but because he is the embodiment of right action, integrity and loyalty. The life of Kuanti is told in an old Chinese legend called 'The Story of the Three Kingdoms'.

A cult developed around Kuanti after his death, and by the 7th century Buddhists had adopted him. In the 12th century he was ennobled by the emperor as a Faithful & Loyal Duke and then as a Magnificent Prince & Pacifier. In 1594 he was made a god by the Ming Emperor Wan Li, who gave him the title of Supporter of Heaven & Protector of the Kingdom. Since then he has been worshipped as the God of War.

However, Kuanti is not a cruel tyrant delighting in battle and the slaying of enemies. Rather, he can avert war and protect people from its horrors.

Kuanti is revered not only by soldiers. He is also the patron god of restaurants, pawn shops and literature, as well as the Hong Kong police force and secret societies such as the Triad organisations.

Kuanti temples are at Tai O on Lantau Island and the Man Mo (literally, 'civil and military') Temple on Hollywood Rd, Hong Kong Island.

Pak Tai Like all gods for special localities, Pak Tai keeps an eye out for his area, Cheung Chau Island.

Like Kuanti, Pak Tai is a military protector of the state and there are various stories about his origins. One is that he lived around 2000 BC and was responsible for introducing flood control and drainage systems. Another is that he was placed at the head of a heavenly army to fight two monsters who were ravaging the earth, and having destroyed them was made the First Lord of Heaven. He also holds the title of Emperor of the North, and north being associated with death he is, therefore, overlord of the realms of the dead.

Since Chinese ancestors are the spiritual guardians of their descendants, Pak Tai is the Guardian of Society. When chaos reigns and there is destruction he is believed to descend from heaven to restore peace and order.

On the island of Cheung Chau, Pak Tai is revered as a life-giver, having intervened to end a plague which hit the island at the end of the last century. A large temple on Cheung Chau, the Temple of Jade Vacuity, is dedicated to him.

Tam Kung This god is worshipped only along a small stretch of the southern Chinese coast which includes Macau and Hong Kong. One theory is that he was actually the last emperor of the Southern Song Dynasty (1127 AD to 1279 AD) which was overrun by Kublai Khan's Mongol armies. The emperor was a boy of eight or nine years and is now worshipped under the pseudonym of Tam Kung.

The story goes that the boy emperor and his retinue paused on the Kowloon Peninsula during their flight from the Mongols and that for some reason he came to be worshipped as a god. A temple for Tam Kung can be seen in Coloane Village in Macau.

Wong Tai Sin This god watches over the housing settlement of the same name in Kowloon. Wong Tai Sin had a meteoric rise to success in the colony, having been brought to Hong Kong in 1915 by a man and his son who came from Guangdong Province carrying a painting of him. They installed the painting and an altar in a small temple in Wanchai. A temple was built in Kowloon in 1921 and his popularity grew.

One story says that Wong Tai Sin is a deified shepherd boy while others hold that he may originally have been worshipped as Huang Di, the mythical yellow emperor and one of the oldest gods of China, but that he has come down in status.

Other Religions

Hong Kong has a cosmopolitan population and many religious denominations, other than the traditional Chinese ones, are represented.

Christianity Christian missionaries have been active in Hong Kong and have won many converts among the Chinese. Christians are estimated to number about 500,000 in Hong Kong – about 274,000 Roman Catholics with the rest Protestants, the latter broken up into about 50 different denominations and sects including Lutherans, Baptists, Quakers and Mormons.

A list of all the colony's churches can be found in the yellow pages. Church services are advertised in Saturday's edition of the *South China Morning Post*.

Sikhism The Sikhs, from the Punjab province of north-west India, are distinguished by their beards and uncut hair wrapped in turbans. They first came to Hong Kong as part of the British Armed Forces in the 19th century. Because of their generally strong physique, they comprised a large segment of the Hong Kong police force before WW II. (Colonial powers often used foreigners who would make no alliances with the local population: the British used Gurkhas to patrol Hong Kong's border with China; and before WW II the French area of Shanghai was

policed by Vietnamese.) The Sikh temple is at 371 Queen's Rd East, Wanchai, where religious services are held every Sunday morning.

Islam There are about 50,000 followers of Islam in Hong Kong. More than half are Chinese, while the rest are from Pakistan, India, Malaysia, Indonesia and the Middle East. The oldest mosque in the colony is the Jamia Mosque on Shelley St, Hong Kong Island, built around the turn of the century and rebuilt in 1915. The newest Islamic landmark is the imposing Kowloon Central Mosque on Nathan Rd, near the intersection with Cameron Rd.

Hinduism There are about 10,000 Hindus in the colony. Their temple is on Wong Nai Chung Rd, Happy Valley, and several Hindu festivals are observed there. The temple is also used for meditation, yoga and teaching, and often has visiting swamis and gurus. Religious music and recitals are performed every Sunday morning and Monday evening.

Judaism Hong Kong's Jewish community worships on Friday evening, Saturday morning and on Jewish holidays at the Synagogue Ohel Leah in Robinson Rd, Mid-Levels, Hong Kong Island. The buildings here include a rabbi's residence and a recreation club for the 1000 people in the congregation.

LANGUAGE

While the Chinese have about eight main dialects, about 70% of the population of China speaks the Beijing dialect (commonly known as Mandarin) which is the official language of the People's Republic. In China it's referred to as *pǔtōnghuà* or 'common speech' and the Chinese government set about popularising it in the 1950s. For details see the Facts about Canton chapter. Hong Kong's two official languages are English and Cantonese. Cantonese is a southern Chinese dialect spoken in Canton and the surrounding Guangdong Province, Hong Kong and Macau.

While in Hong Kong Cantonese is used in everyday life, English is the prime language of commerce, banking and international trade, and is also used in the law courts.

Mandarin is also fairly common in Hong Kong, mainly because of the large number of refugees from China. Also, with China set to take over Hong Kong in 1997, the importance of Mandarin can only increase. Cantonese might be useful to learn if you're going to take up permanent residence in Hong Kong, but otherwise Mandarin is *the* dialect to study.

You can get along fine in Hong Kong without a word of Cantonese. Some expatriates live there for years and, despite good intentions when they first arrive, never learn the language.

The Spoken Language

Cantonese differs from Mandarin as much as English differs from Spanish. Speakers of both dialects can read Chinese characters, but a Cantonese speaker will pronounce many of the characters differently from a Mandarin speaker. For example, when Mr Ng from Hong Kong goes to Beijing the Mandarin-speakers will call him Mr Wu. If Mr Wong goes from Hong Kong to Fujian Province the character for his name will be read as Mr Wee, and in Beijing he is Mr Huang.

To add to the confusion, Chinese is a tonal language – the difference in intonation being a deciding factor in the meaning of a word. If you get the tones mixed, you can say something entirely different from what was intended. There are only four basic tones in Mandarin but Cantonese has about nine (linguists argue about the exact number). Written Chinese has many thousands of characters, but there are only a few hundred syllables with which to pronounce them, so the tones are used to increase the number of word sounds available.

The large number of tones in Cantonese causes much difficulty for foreigners who want to study the language. Mandarin is usually considered significantly easier to learn because there are only four tones to struggle with.

The Written Language

Written Chinese has about 50,000 pictographs or characters which symbolise objects or actions. About 5000 are in common use and you need about 1500 minimum to read a newspaper. Although each character has meaning, it does not necessarily represent an entire word, but rather a syllable of a word. Most Chinese words consist of two or three characters. As an example, the Chinese word for 'flower' is composed of a single character *(huā)*, but must be combined with two more characters to form the word for 'granite' *(huā gāng yàn)*.

All Chinese use mostly the same characters though the Cantonese have invented some which are not understood by Mandarin speakers. All Chinese can read the same newspaper (with some difficulty), but Mandarin speakers could not read a Cantonese menu since there are so many special characters dealing with food. Cantonese and Mandarin speakers also pronounce all the characters differently. To add more complexity, some Cantonese words require two characters to write whereas saying the same thing in Mandarin might require three characters.

There is another complication. In the 1950s, the Chinese government introduced a system of simplified characters in an effort to make the written script easier to learn and increase literacy in the country. Unfortunately, apart from China, only Singapore has adopted these simplified forms. The result is that many of the characters you'll see in Hong Kong are written quite differently from the same ones in China. The simplified characters, which should have made Chinese easier to learn, have actually made it more difficult for students since they often end up having to study both systems.

In Hong Kong, Chinese characters can be read from left to right, right to left, or top to bottom. The Chinese government has been trying to get everyone to read and write from left to right.

Romanisation

One difficulty which Westerners have in Hong Kong is pronouncing the romanised place and street names properly. Apart from the problem of getting the tone right, the system of romanisation used for Cantonese is highly misleading.

For example, the letter 'k' is pronounced as a 'g' and the letter 't' is pronounced as a 'd'. If you pronounce romanised street names the way they look to an English speaker, the Chinese probably won't understand you. Ironically, other English speakers may understand some of your botched attempts to speak Cantonese because they have been similarly misled.

The People's Republic uses a romanisation system known as *pinyin* which, while very accurate once you learn its peculiarities, only works for the Mandarin dialect. You cannot use it to romanise Cantonese. An explanation of the pinyin system is in the Language section of the Facts about Canton chapter.

Learning Chinese

If you want to study Chinese seriously, the Chinese University in Hong Kong offers regular courses in Cantonese and Mandarin. Classes can be arranged through the New Asia Yale in China language institute, associated with the university. Several people who completed the course have told me that it is well worth it.

There are three terms a year – one 10-week summer term and two regular 15-week terms. The summer course costs HK$6000 and the regular terms cost HK$9000. Unfortunately, the university does not provide dormitories, so you must make your own living arrangements.

Although I am certain that Hong Kong is a great place to learn Cantonese, I can't recommend it for learning Mandarin. The local accent in Hong Kong is very nonstandard and you'll probably find a vast difference between what the teachers speak in the classroom and what you hear in street conversations. Unless you are fortunate enough to be living with a Chinese family which has recently moved to Hong Kong from Beijing, you will probably be frustrated when trying to practise your newly acquired vocabulary. If you are determined to learn good spoken Mandarin, your best bet is to study in either Taiwan or Beijing.

Language Footnote

While Hong Kong's expatriate community tries to speak the Queen's English, some Chinese words have been incorporated into the local vernacular. *Taipan* means a 'big boss', usually in a large company, which is referred to as a *hong. Godown* means 'warehouse'. An *amah* is 'servant', usually a woman who babysits and takes care of the house. A *cheongsam* is a fashionable, tight-fitting Chinese dress with a slit up the side.

Foreigners are often referred to as *gwailo* – a Chinese word which literally means 'ghost man' but which is usually translated as 'foreign devil'. It used to have a negative connotation, but these days many foreigners call themselves gwailo without giving it a second thought.

The word *shroff*, frequently used in Hong Kong, is not derived from Chinese – it's an Anglo-Indian word meaning 'cashier'. ■

Facts for the Visitor

VISAS & EMBASSIES

For most visitors to Hong Kong a passport is all that's required.

UK citizens (or Commonwealth citizens who were born in the UK or in Hong Kong) can normally stay for up to 12 months without a visa, and it is possible to stay longer. Australians, Canadians and New Zealanders and other Commonwealth citizens do not require a visa for visits of up to three months. Citizens of most Western European countries are permitted to stay for three months without a visa, depending on which country they're from. Americans can stay for one month without a visa.

Officially, visitors have to show that they have adequate funds for their stay and that they have an onward ticket or a return ticket to their own country. In practice, this rule is seldom enforced. The only visitors who must rigidly obey these rules are those who hold passports from the People's Republic. Visitors from other developing and Communist countries may also be questioned.

Visitors are not permitted to take up employment, establish any business or enrol as students. If you want to enter for employment, education or residence you must have a work visa unless you are a UK citizen, and even then you officially have to show means of support in Hong Kong.

If you do need a visa, apply at any British embassy, consulate or high commission.

Visa Extensions

In Hong Kong, inquire at the Immigration Department (☎ 8246111), 2nd floor, Wanchai Tower Two, 7 Gloucester Rd, Wanchai, Hong Kong Island.

Foreign Embassies in Hong Kong

Below are some of the diplomatic missions in Hong Kong. There's a complete list in the Yellow Pages under Consulates. Some of the small countries are represented by honorary consuls who are normally business people employed in commercial firms – so it's advisable to phone beforehand to find out if they're available.

Australia
    23rd & 24th floors, Harbour Centre, 25 Harbour Rd, Wanchai (☎ 5731881)
Austria
    14th floor, Diamond Exchange Building, 8-10 Duddell St, Central (☎ 5222388)
Burma (Myanmar)
    Room 2421-2425, Sung Hung Kai Centre, 30 Harbour Rd, Wanchai (☎ 8913329)
Canada
    11th-14th floors, Tower One, Exchange Square, 8 Connaught Place, Central (☎ 8104321)
China
    Visa Office of the Ministry of Foreign Affairs, 5th floor, Lower Block, 26 Harbour Rd, Wanchai (☎ 8353794)
Denmark
    Room 2402B, Great Eagle Centre, 23 Harbour Rd, Wanchai (☎ 8936252)
Finland
    Room 1818, Hutchison House, Central (☎ 5255385)
France
    26th floor, Admiralty Centre, Tower Two, 18 Harcourt Rd, Admiralty (☎ 5294351)
Germany
    21st floor, United Centre, 95 Queensway, Admiralty (☎ 5298855)
India
    Room D, 16th floor, United Centre, 95 Queensway, Central (☎ 5275821)
Indonesia
    6-8 Keswick St, Causeway Bay (☎ 8904421)
Israel
    Room 702, Tower Two, Admiralty Centre, 18 Harcourt Rd, Central (☎ 5296091)
Italy
    Room 805, Hutchison House, 10 Harcourt Rd, Central (☎ 5220033)
Japan
    24th floor, Bank of America Tower, 12 Harcourt Rd, Central (☎ 5221184)
Korea (South)
    5th floor, Far East Finance Centre, 16 Harcourt Rd, Central (☎ 5294141)
Malaysia
    24th floor, Malaysia Building, 50 Gloucester Rd, Wanchai (☎ 5270921)

Nepalese Liaison Office
> c/o HQ Brigade of Gurkhas, HMS Tamar, Prince of Wales Building, Harcourt Rd, Central (☎ 8633253, 8633111). Office hours are from 10 am to noon, Monday to Friday.

Netherlands
> Room 301, 3rd floor, China Building, 29 Queen's Rd, Central (☎ 5225120)

New Zealand
> Room 3414, Jardine House, Connaught Rd, Central (☎ 5255044)

Norway
> Room 1401, AIA Building, 1 Stubbs Rd, Wanchai (☎ 3749253)

Pakistan
> Room 307, Asian House, 1 Hennessy Rd, Wanchai (☎ 5274623)

Philippines
> 21st floor, Wah Kwong Agent Centre, 88 Queen's Rd, Central (☎ 8100183)

Portugal
> 10th floor, Tower Two, Exchange Square, Central (☎ 5225488)

Singapore
> Room 901, 9th floor, Tower One, Admiralty Centre, 18 Harcourt Rd, Admiralty (☎ 5272212)

South Africa
> 27th floor, Sunning Plaza, 10 Hysan Ave, Causeway Bay (☎ 5773279)

Spain
> 8th floor, Printing House, 18 Ice House St, Central (☎ 5253041)

Sri Lanka
> 8th floor, Loke Yew Building, 50-52 Queen's Rd, Central (☎ 5238810)

Sweden
> Room 804, Hong Kong Club Building, Chater Rd, Central (☎ 5211212)

Switzerland
> Room 3703, Gloucester Tower, The Landmark, 11 Pedder St, Central (☎ 5227147)

Taiwan
> Chung Hwa Travel Service, 4th floor, East Tower, Bond Centre, 3 Queensway, Central, (☎ 5258315)

Thailand
> 8th floor, Fairmont House, 8 Cotton Tree Drive, Central (☎ 5216481)

UK
> c/o Overseas Visa Section, Hong Kong Immigration Department, 2nd floor, Wanchai Tower Two, 7 Gloucester Rd, Wanchai (☎ 8246111)
>
> c/o British Council, Ground floor, Easey Commercial Building, 255 Hennessy Rd, Wanchai (☎ 8315138). The British Council is the closest thing the UK has to an embassy in Hong Kong.

USA
> 26 Garden Rd, Central (☎ 5239011)

DOCUMENTS

Visitors to all parts of the colony are required to carry proof of identification. Residents are expected to carry ID cards at all times, but visitors are advised to carry any sort of identification which includes a personal photograph, such as a driving licence.

The Chinese are very impressed by namecards, so bring some along. Alternatively, make use of the namecard machines found in the Kowloon-Canton Railway (KCR) stations, the Outlying Islands Ferry Pier, and elsewhere. For HK$25 you get 40 cards, which you design yourself.

CUSTOMS

Even though Hong Kong is a duty-free port, there are still items on which duty is charged. In particular, there are high import taxes on cigarettes, alcohol, perfume and toilet water. The duty-free allowance for visitors is 200 cigarettes (one carton), one litre of alcohol, 60 ml of perfume and 250 ml of toilet water. Apart from these limits there are no other import tax worries, so you can bring in reasonable quantities of almost anything without paying taxes or obtaining permits.

Of course, you can't bring in anything which is illegal in Hong Kong; this includes fireworks. Hong Kongers returning from Macau and China are often vigorously searched for this reason. Needless to say, firearms and other lethal weapons cannot be brought into Hong Kong without special permits.

Most importantly, dope is strictly prohibited. It makes no difference whether it's heroin, opium or marijuana – the law makes no distinction. If customs officials find dope or the equipment for smoking it in your possession, you can expect to be arrested immediately. Being a foreigner doesn't get you off the hook. Depending on the quantity found, the sentence for possession or smuggling of narcotics can be several years' jail in addition to large fines. You should have some sympathy for the enormous job that customs officials must perform. As well as air passengers, more than 700 ships a day pass through Hong Kong's harbour. It's obvious that not all ships can be inspected. One customs official told me that the biggest problems are with ships from South-East Asia (carrying heroin) and from the USA (smuggling guns and ammunition). This is in addition to small speedboats from China bringing guns, drugs and illegal immigrants.

MONEY

As Asia's leading financial centre, Hong Kong is one of the easiest places to cash travellers' cheques, replace stolen cheques and have money wired to you. There are no exchange control regulations and money can be freely transferred into and out of Hong Kong. There is no foreign currency black market. Banks and moneychangers can exchange all major trading currencies and many minor ones as well.

Avoid changing money at the airport! At the time this book was being researched, the moneychangers at the airport were giving an exchange rate of US$1 to HK$7.36, equivalent to a 5.6% commission.

Banks give the best exchange rates. Hong Kong banks take all the legal holidays, both Chinese and Western, which can be a problem during long holidays like the Chinese New Year and Easter.

The best exchange rates I've found were at the Wing Lung Bank, 4 Carnarvon Rd, Tsimshatsui, next to the New Astor Hotel. The Hang Seng Bank is also famous for giving excellent rates, and for changing many odd currencies that other banks won't touch, such as Macau patacas. The main Tsimshatsui branch of Hang Seng Bank is at 18 Carnarvon Rd. The small branches in the MTR stations do not change money.

The Hongkong Bank gives relatively poor rates for a bank, and in addition tacks on a HK$20 service charge for each transaction.

Licensed moneychangers are abundant in tourist areas like Tsimshatsui. Their chief advantage is that they stay open on Sunday, holidays and late into the evening when banks are closed. They charge no commission but give lousy exchange rates equivalent to a 5% commission. These rates are clearly posted. The moneychangers stand in booths behind bars and unbreakable glass, not so much to protect themselves from robbers as from irate tourists.

Bargain with moneychangers just as you

do with shopkeepers. I've never been cheated by a Hong Kong moneychanger. They've always given me whatever rate was agreed on beforehand. But if you don't ask first, they will always give you the lousy posted rate.

The only other place that you can change money is at the big hotels. Generally, the rates are very unfavourable.

Before the actual exchange is made, the moneychanger is required by law to give you a form to sign clearly showing the amount, exchange rate and any service charges.

The credit cards accepted by most places are American Express, Bank Americard (Visa), Carte Blanche, Diners Club, JCB, MasterCard and Air Travel. Major charge and credit cards are accepted by many restaurants and shops in Hong Kong.

Some shops may try to add a surcharge to the cost of the item if you charge your purchase against your card. This is not an acceptable practice although I have some sympathy for the shops. The credit card companies normally charge shops a commission on each purchase, up to 5%, but they insist that this charge not be passed on to the customer for the obvious reason that it would hurt the credit-card business. To get around this, many shops say that there is no commission charged if you use a credit card, but there is a 5% discount if you pay cash.

Currency

When making a large purchase, like a camera, many shops will accept payment in US dollars (and sometimes other currencies) but may give you slightly less than the official rate. For most of your everyday needs, however, you'll have to pay in Hong Kong dollars (HK$).

The Hong Kong dollar is divided into 100 cents. There are different banknote designs in circulation, although the notes are interchangeable.

Bills are issued in denominations of HK$10 (green), $50 (blue), HK$100 (red), HK$500 (brown) and HK$1000 (yellow). Coins are issued in denominations of HK$5,

HK$2, HK$1, 50 cents, 20 cents and 10 cents.

Exchange Rates

Since 1983, the Hong Kong dollar has been rigidly tied to the US dollar at a rate of US$1 equals HK$7.8. However, the Hong Kong dollar is permitted to float within a very narrow range of this level. The following exchange rates were current at the time of researching this book.

A$1	=	HK$6.07
C$1	=	HK$6.78
Y1 (China)	=	HK$1.47
DM1	=	HK$4.59
Y100 (Japan)	=	HK$5.68
G1 (Netherlands)	=	HK$4.07
NZ$1	=	HK$4.59
Kr1 (Sweden)	=	HK$1.27
SFr1 (Switzerland)	=	HK$5.46
UK£1	=	HK$13.66
US$1	=	HK$7.79

Costs

Hong Kong is certainly not cheap – it's a result of the continuing economic boom. Nevertheless, you can still find beds for around HK$40, but it takes effort to find a double room for less than HK$100 these days.

On the other hand, food is reasonably priced – you can keep the eating bill down to HK$40 a day if you eat fast food or buy your own from supermarkets. Transport is cheap and amazingly efficient.

The main way to cut costs is to control yourself – shopping in Hong Kong can be addictive. Many people find all those cameras and electronic goodies on sale to be irresistible and suddenly decide they need to buy all sorts of things they don't need at all!

Tipping

The good news is that historically the Chinese never had the habit of tipping. The bad news is that Westerners have introduced this vulgar custom to Hong Kong. You should feel no obligation to tip taxi drivers (they make plenty as it is), but it's almost mandatory to tip hotel porters (bellhops) at least HK$10. If you make use of the porters at the airport, HK$1 per suitcase is normally expected.

Fancy hotels and restaurants stick you with a mandatory 10% service charge which is supposedly your tip. Nevertheless, many waiting and hotel-cleaning staff expect more, especially from free-spending tourists. It is said that Japanese tourists are the best tippers, Westerners the worst. Let your conscience be your guide. If you think the service was great, you might want to leave them something. Otherwise don't bother − there's no need to reward rotten service.

Bargaining

Bargaining is expected in Hong Kong, but some people turn it into an exercise in East-West relations, a test of one-upmanship. Some tourists operate on the theory that you can always get the goods for half the price originally quoted. My philosophy is that if you can bargain something down to half price, then you shouldn't buy in that shop anyway because they were trying to rip you off in the first place. If they're that crooked, they will probably find other ways to cheat you, like selling electronics with missing components, or a secondhand camera instead of a new one. In an honest shop, you shouldn't be able to bargain more than a 10% discount, if they'll bargain at all.

Many stores, especially department stores, put price tags on their goods and won't bargain at all. If no prices are marked, bargaining becomes essential. If you really dislike bargaining (it can get tiresome), your best bet is to shop in the New Territories where prices are usually marked.

WHEN TO GO

Anytime is OK, but summer is the peak season, which means higher airfares and sometimes a shortage of hotel rooms. This is not to mention the hot and humid weather. The Chinese New Year is also a crunch time, and ditto for Easter. The ideal time is autumn, when the weather is at it's best and tourists relatively scarce.

WHAT TO BRING

As little as possible. Many travellers try to bring everything, including the kitchen sink. Keep in mind that you can and will buy things in Hong Kong and elsewhere, so don't burden yourself with a lot of unnecessary junk.

That advice having been given, there are some things you will want to bring from home. But the first thing to consider is what kind of bag you will use to carry all your goods.

Backpacks are the easiest type of bag to carry and a frameless or internal-frame pack is the easiest to manage on buses and trains. Packs that close with a zipper can usually be secured with a padlock. Of course, any pack can be slit open with a razor blade, but a padlock will usually prevent pilfering by hotel staff and baggage handlers at airports.

A daypack can be handy. Leave your main luggage at the hotel or left-luggage room in the train stations. A beltpack is OK for maps, extra film and other miscellanea, but don't use it for valuables such as your travellers' cheques and passport, as it's an easy target for pickpockets.

If you don't want to use a backpack, a shoulder bag is much easier to carry than a suitcase. Some cleverly designed shoulder bags can double as backpacks by rearranging a few straps. Forget suitcases.

Inside? Lightweight and compact are two words that should be etched in your mind when you're deciding what to bring. Saw the handle off your toothbrush if you have to − anything to keep the weight down! You only need two sets of clothes − one to wear and one to wash. You will, no doubt, be buying clothes along the way − you can find some real bargains in Hong Kong, Macau and China. However, don't believe sizes − 'large' in Asia is often equivalent to 'medium' in the West. Asian clothing manufacturers would be wise to visit a Western tourist hotel to see what 'large' really means.

Nylon running or sports shoes are best −

comfortable, washable and lightweight. If you're going to be in cold weather, buy them oversized and wear them with heavy woollen socks − it's better than carrying a pair of boots. A pair of flip-flop sandals (thongs) are useful footwear for indoors and shower rooms.

A Swiss army knife (even if not made in Switzerland) comes in handy, but you don't need one with 27 separate functions. Basically, you need one small sharp blade, a can opener and bottle opener − a built-in magnifying glass or backscratcher isn't necessary.

The secret of successful packing is plastic bags or nylon 'stuff bags' − they keep things not only separate and clean but also dry.

Below is a checklist of things you might consider packing, but don't feel obligated to pack everything on this list − you can buy all these things in Hong Kong.

If you're planning on working or studying abroad, it could be helpful to have copies of transcripts, diplomas, letters of reference and other professional qualifications.

A final thought: airlines do lose bags from time to time − you've got a much better chance of it not being yours if it is tagged with your name and address *inside* the bag as well as outside. Other tags can always fall off or be removed.

TOURIST OFFICES
Local Tourist Offices
The enterprising Hong Kong Tourist Associ-

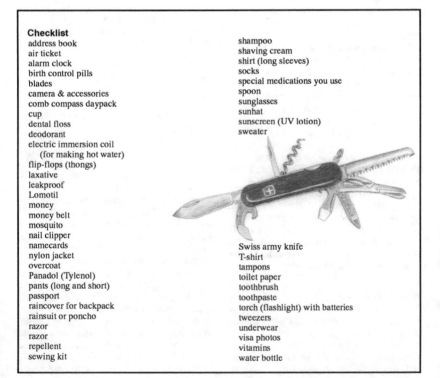

Checklist
address book
air ticket
alarm clock
birth control pills
blades
camera & accessories
comb compass daypack
cup
dental floss
deodorant
electric immersion coil
    (for making hot water)
flip-flops (thongs)
laxative
leakproof
Lomotil
money
money belt
mosquito
nail clipper
namecards
nylon jacket
overcoat
Panadol (Tylenol)
pants (long and short)
passport
raincover for backpack
rainsuit or poncho
razor
razor
repellent
sewing kit

shampoo
shaving cream
shirt (long sleeves)
socks
special medications you use
spoon
sunglasses
sunhat
sunscreen (UV lotion)
sweater

Swiss army knife
T-shirt
tampons
toilet paper
toothbrush
toothpaste
torch (flashlight) with batteries
tweezers
underwear
visa photos
vitamins
water bottle

ation (HKTA) is definitely worth a visit. They're efficient and helpful and have reams of printed information, free or fairly cheap.

You can call the HKTA hotline (☎ 8017177) from 8 am to 6 pm daily. Shopping advice and inquiries on HKTA members can be obtained by phone (☎ 8017278), from 9 am to 5 pm Monday to Friday, and from 9 am to 12.45 pm on Saturday.

The HKTA office at Kai Tak Airport operates a hotel booking service for people with no place to stay. They don't deal with the real cheapies but they will probably find you a room at a reasonable budget-priced hotel or maybe at the YMCA or YWCA. If you arrive very late at night it can be worth spending a bit more than your usual budget for the first night to avoid hauling heavy bags around the streets, especially as many of the smaller places don't open their doors after midnight. You'll find HKTA offices at:

Kowloon
Star Ferry Terminal, Tsimshatsui. Open from 8 am to 6 pm Monday to Friday, and from 9 am to 5 pm weekends and holidays.
Buffer Hall, Kai Tak Airport. Open 8 am to 10.30 pm daily. Information provided for arriving passengers only.

Central, Hong Kong Island
Shop 8, Basement, Jardine House, 1 Connaught Place. Open from 8 am to 6 pm weekdays, and from 8 am to 1 pm on Saturday. Closed on Sunday and holidays.
Head Office, 35th floor, Jardine House, 1 Connaught Place (☎ 8017111). This is a business office – not for normal tourist inquiries.

Overseas Reps

Australia
Level 5, 55 Harrington St, The Rocks, Sydney (☎ (02) 2512855, outside Sydney (008) 251071)

Canada
347 Bay St, Suite 909, Toronto, Ontario M5H 2R7 (☎ (416) 3662389)

France
38 Ave George V, 75008, Paris (entree 53 Rue Francois 1er, 7 etage) (☎ (01) 47203954)

Germany
Weisenau 1, D-6000 Frankfurt am Main (☎ (069) 722841)

Italy
Casella Postale 620, 00100 Roma Centro (☎ (06) 6869112)

Japan
4th floor, Toho Twin Tower Building, 1-5-2 Yurakucho, Chiyoda-ku, Tokyo 100 (☎ (03) 35030735)
4th floor, Hong Kong & Shanghai Bank Building, 6-1 Awaji-machi 3-chome, Chuo-ku, Osaka 541 (☎ (06) 2299240)

New Zealand
PO Box 2120, Auckland (☎ (09) 5213167)

Singapore
10 Collyer Quay, 13th floor, 13-08 Ocean Building, Singapore 0104 (☎ 5323668)

UK
5th floor, 125 Pall Mall, London, SW1Y 5EA (☎ (071) 9304775)

USA
333 North Michigan Ave, Suite 2400, Chicago, Illinois 60601-3966 (☎ (312) 7823872)
5th floor, 590 Fifth Ave, New York, NY 10036-4706 (☎ 212 8695008)
10940 Wilshire Blvd, Suite 1220, Los Angeles, CA 90024 (☎ (213) 2084582)
360 Post St, Suite 404, San Francisco, CA 94108 (☎ (415) 7814582)

USEFUL ORGANISATIONS

The Hong Kong Information Services Department (☎ 8428777) is on the Ground, 1st, 4th, 5th and 6th floors of Beaconsfield House, 4 Queen's Rd, Central. They can answer specific questions or direct you to other government agencies that can handle your inquiry. It's best to try the HKTA before resorting to the Information Services Department.

Since the likelihood of getting ripped off by shopkeepers is high, it's good to know about the the Hong Kong Consumer Council (☎ 7363322). The main office is in China Hong Kong City, Canton Rd, Tsimshatsui, Kowloon. It has a complaints and advice hot line (☎ 7363636) and an Advice Centre (☎ 5411422) at 38 Pier Rd, Central, near the Outlying Islands Ferry Pier.

The Royal Asiatic Society (RAS) (☎ 5510300), GPO Box 3864, is dedicated to helping its members or visitors learn more about the history and culture of Hong Kong. The RAS organises lectures and field trips, operates a lending library and puts out publications of its own. The RAS was founded in London in 1823 and has branches in several Asian countries.

St John's Cathedral Counselling Service (☎ 5257202) provides help to all those in need.

If you're interested in doing business in Hong Kong, you might want to consult the Hong Kong Chamber of Commerce (☎ 5237177), 902 Swire House, 9-25 Chater Rd, Central.

BUSINESS HOURS & HOLIDAYS

Office hours are Monday to Friday from 9 am to 5 pm, and on Saturday from 9 am to noon. Lunch hour is from 1 to 2 pm; many offices simply shut down and lock the door at this time. Banks are open Monday to Friday from 9 am to 4.30 pm and do not close for lunch – on Saturday they are open from 9 am to 12.30 pm.

Stores and restaurants that cater to the tourist trade keep longer hours, but almost nothing opens before 9 am. Even tourist related businesses shut down by 9 or 10 pm, and many will close for major holidays, especially Chinese New Year.

Western and Chinese culture combine to create an interesting mix of holidays. Trying to determine the exact date of each holiday is a bit tricky since two calendars are used in Hong Kong – the Gregorian solar calendar and the Chinese lunar calendar. The two calendars do not correspond exactly because a lunar month is only 28 days. To keep the two calendars from becoming totally out of harmony, an extra month is added to the lunar calendar once every 30 months. The result is that the Lunar New Year, the most important Chinese holiday, can fall anywhere between 21 January and 28 February on the Gregorian calendar.

Many of the Chinese festivals go back hundreds, perhaps thousands, of years, their true origins often lost in the mists of time. The reasons for each festival vary and you will generally find there are a couple of tales to choose from. The Hong Kong Tourist Association's free leaflet, *Chinese Festivals & Special Events*, will tell you the exact dates that festivals are celebrated.

New Year

The first weekday in January is a public holiday.

Chinese (Lunar) New Year

The first, second and third day of the Chinese New Year are public holidays. Almost everything closes but you won't starve in the tourist areas. The first day of the first moon usually falls at the end of January or the beginning of February.

The festival is a family one, with little for the visitor to see. For the new year, houses are cleaned, debts paid off and feuds, no matter how bitter, are ended – even if it's only for the day. Pictures of gods are pasted around the front doors of houses to scare off bad spirits, along with messages of welcome on red paper to encourage the good ones.

By tradition, everyone asks for double wages. The garbage collector, the milkman and so on get *lai see* ('lucky money') in red envelopes as tips, which are good reasons for the traditional Chinese New Year greeting *kung hey fat choi* – literally 'good wishes, good fortune'.

It costs double to get your hair cut in the week leading up to the New Year. Even cinemas put their prices up.

It's not the time to go to China, as hordes of Hong Kong people cram the trains and every other form of transport to get there.

It is worth seeing the huge flower fairs where, on the night before New Year's Day, the Chinese buy lucky peach blossoms, kumquat trees and narcissi from the hundreds of flower sellers. Victoria Park in Causeway Bay, Hong Kong Island, is the place to go for this, although it's jam-packed. Other than that, there isn't much else to see at Chinese New Year. You might catch a lion dance in a street, but if not, you will certainly see one specially laid on in the top tourist hotels.

Lantern Festival

Also known by its Chinese name Yuen Siu, this is not a public holiday but is more interesting than the Chinese Lunar New Year. At the end of the new year celebrations – customarily the 15th day of the first moon (middle or end of February) – lanterns in traditional designs are lit in homes, restaurants and temples. Out in the residential areas, you'll see people carrying lanterns through the streets. The Lantern Festival is also a holiday for lovers.

Easter

In Hong Kong, Easter is a three-day public holiday starting from Good Friday and running through to Easter Sunday. Although many Westerners don't realise it, the date of Easter is fixed by the lunar calendar, falling somewhere in March or April.

Ching Ming

Celebrated at the beginning of the third moon, usually in April, Ching Ming is very much a family affair. It is a time for visiting graves, traditionally to call up ancestors to ask if they are satisfied with their descendants. Graves are cleaned and food and wine left for the spirits, while incense and paper money are burned for the dead. Some people follow the custom of pasting long strips of red and white paper to the graves to indicate that the rituals have been performed. The festival is thought to have its origins during the Han period about 2000 years ago, when ancestors' tombs were swept, washed and repaired.

Ching Ming, a public holiday, is not a particularly good time to visit Hong Kong, though not nearly so bad as the Chinese New Year. Many people take a three or four-day holiday. Banks and many other businesses close for Ching Ming, public transport is extremely crowded and the border crossing into China turns host to a near riot.

Tin Hau Festival

While not a public holiday, this is one of Hong Kong's most colourful occasions. The Taoist festival is traditionally held on the 23rd day of the third moon, usually in May, and about three weeks after Ching Ming. Tin Hau, patroness of fishing people, is one of the colony's most popular goddesses.

Junks on the water are decorated with flags and sail in long rows to Tin Hau temples around the colony to pray for clear skies and good catches. Often her image is taken from the temple and paraded through the streets. Shrines from the junks are carried to the shore to be blessed by Taoist priests.

The best place to see the festival and the fortune telling, lion dances and Chinese opera that follow is at the site of Tin Hau's best known temple, the Tai Miu Temple in Joss House Bay. It's not accessible by road and is not on the normal ferry route but at festival time the ferry company puts on excursion trips, which are usually packed.

Another main Tin Hau temple is at Sok Kwu Wan on Lamma Island. The Tin Hau temple at Stanley on the south coast of Hong Kong Island was built before the mid-18th century and is the oldest building standing in Hong Kong.

Cheung Chau Bun Festival

The Bun Festival of Tai Chiu is held in May on Cheung Chau Island, traditionally on the sixth day of the fourth moon. Precise dates are decided by village elders on the island about three weeks before it starts. A Taoist festival, it is one of the festival calendar highlights, and there are three or four days of religious observances.

While not a public holiday, it is definitely worth getting to Cheung Chau for. See the Cheung Chau section in the Outlying Islands chapter for more information on the Bun Festival.

Birthday of Lord Buddha

Also referred to as the Bathing of Lord Buddha, this festival is celebrated on the eighth day of the fourth moon, usually in late May. It's not a public holiday and, like most Buddhist festivals, it's rather more sedate than Taoist holidays.

The Buddha's statue is taken from monasteries and temples and ceremoniously bathed in water scented with sandalwood, ambergris (a waxy substance secreted from the intestine of a sperm whale and often found floating in the sea), garu wood, turmeric and aloes (a drug used for clearing the bowels, made from the fleshy, spiny-toothed leaves of the aloe tree). Afterwards the water is drunk by the faithful, who believe it has great curative powers.

While Lantau Island is the best place to observe this event because of its many Buddhist monasteries, most people visit only Po Lin, the largest and best known of the monasteries. Extra ferries operate for the crowds.

The New Territories has several good Buddhist temples worth visiting at this time, such as the Temple of Ten Thousand Buddhas in Shatin or the Miu Fat Monastery at Lam Tei.

Dragon Boat Festival

A main public holiday, *Tuen Ng* — Double Fifth (fifth day, fifth moon) or the Dragon Boat Festival — is normally held in June. It's a lot of fun despite the fact that it commemorates the sad tale of Chu Yuan

Chu Yuan was a 3rd-century BC poet-statesman who hurled himself into the Mi Lo River in Hunan Province to protest against the corrupt government. The people who lived on the banks of the river raced to the scene in their boats in an attempt to save him but were too late. Not unmindful of his sacrifice, the people later threw dumplings into the water to keep the hungry fish away from his body.

Traditional rice dumplings are still eaten in memory of the event and dragon boat races are held in Hong Kong, Kowloon and the outlying islands. See the races at Shaukiwan, Aberdeen, Yaumati, Tai Po and Stanley, and on Lantau and Cheung Chau islands. The boats are rowed by teams from Hong Kong's sports and social clubs. International dragon boat races are held at Yaumati.

Queen's Birthday

This public holiday is normally held on a Saturday in June. The Monday after is also a public holiday.

Birthday of Lu Pan, Master Builder

Legends say that Lu Pan was born around 507 BC and later deified. A master architect, magician, engineer, inventor and designer, Lu Pan is worshipped by anyone connected with the building trade. Ceremonies sponsored by the Builders' Guilds are held at Lu Pan Temple in Kennedy Town, Hong Kong Island. The celebration occurs around mid to late-July. It's a minor holiday.

Maidens' Festival

This is a minor holiday and you might not even notice anything special taking place. Also known as the Seven Sisters' Festival, this celebration for girls and young lovers is held on the seventh day of the seventh moon (about mid-August).

This festival has its origins in an ancient Chinese story about two celestial lovers, Chien Niu the cowherd and Chih Nu the spinner and weaver. One version says that they became so engrossed in each other that they forgot their work. As a punishment for this, the Queen of Heaven decided that they should be separated from each other by being placed on either side of a river which she cut through the heavens with her hairpin. The King of Heaven took pity on the lovers and said they could meet once a year, but provided no bridge across the river, so magpies (regarded as birds of good omen) flocked together, spread their wings and formed a bridge so the two lovers could be reunited.

At midnight on the day of this festival prayers are offered by unmarried girls and young men to Chien Niu and Chih Nu. Prayers are also directed to Chih Nu's six sisters who appear in another version of the story. The main offerings made to the seven sisters are cosmetics and flowers.

Ghost Month

On the first day of the seventh moon (late August or early September), the gates of hell are opened and the ghosts are free for two weeks to walk the earth. On the 14th day, called the Yue Lan Festival, ghosts receive offerings of food from the living before returning down below.

Paper cars, paper houses and paper money are burnt, and once this occurs these goodies become the property of the ghosts.

People whose relatives suffered a violent death are particularly concerned to placate the spirits. Many people will not swim, travel, get married, move house or indulge in other risky activities during this time.

The ghost month is an excellent time to visit Taoist temples in Hong Kong, as these are usually packed with worshippers burning incense and making offerings. There are also lots of Cantonese opera performances – presumably to give the ghosts one good night out before they go back down below for another year. This is not a public holiday, so there aren't any problems with crowded buses and trains.

Liberation Day
Celebrated on the last Monday in August, this public holiday commemorates the liberation of Hong Kong from Japan after WW II. The preceding Saturday is also a public holiday.

Mid-Autumn (Moon) Festival
The Mid-Autumn Festival is held in September, on the 15th night of the eighth moon. Because the festival begins at night, the day after is a public holiday.

Although the observance of the moon is thought to date back to much earlier times, today the festival recalls an uprising against the Mongols in the 14th century when plans for the revolution were passed around in cakes.

Moon cakes are still eaten and there are many varieties – all delicious. The various fillings include coconut, dates, nuts, lotus, sesame seeds and sometimes an egg.

Everyone heads for the hilltops, where they light special lanterns with candles inside and watch the moon rise. The Peak Tram is crammed, as is all transport to the New Territories, where hillsides abound. For young couples, it's a romantic holiday – a time to be together and watch the moon.

Birthday of Confucius
Confucius' birthday is in early October and religious observances are held by the Confucian Society in the Confucius Temple at Causeway Bay. It's a minor holiday that usually passes unnoticed by most Hong Kongers.

Cheung Yeung Festival
While not an especially interesting occasion, the Cheung Yeung Festival is a public holiday.

The story goes that back in the Eastern Han Dynasty (in the first two centuries AD), an old soothsayer advised a man to take his family away to a high place for 24 hours to avoid disaster. When the man returned to his village he found every living thing had been destroyed and only he and his family had survived.

Many people head for the high spots again to remember the old man's advice. The Cheung Yeung Festival is held in mid to late October.

Christmas & Boxing Day
Christmas (25 December) and the day after (Boxing Day) are, of course, public holidays.

CULTURAL EVENTS
There are literally hundreds of cultural events throughout the year, but the exact dates vary. The HKTA publishes a complete schedule every month. If you want to time your visit to Hong Kong to coincide with a particular event, it would be wise to contact the HKTA beforehand. A brief rundown of important annual events includes:

HK Arts Festival – an assortment of exhibitions and shows usually held in January.
Orientation Competition – sponsored by the Urban Council, this event is usually staged in January in Tai Tam Country Park.
HK Festival Fringe – the Fringe Club supports upcoming artists and performers from Hong Kong and elsewhere. This three-week festival occurs from late January to February.
HK Golf Open – this is held at the Royal Hong Kong Golf Club, usually in February.
HK International Marathon – organised by the Hong Kong Amateur Athletic Association, this major event is held in Shatin, usually in March.
HK Food Festival – sponsored by the HKTA and usually held in March.
HK International Film Festival – organised by the Urban Council, this event usually occurs in March or April.
HK International Handball Invitation Tournament – organised by the Hong Kong Amateur Handball Association, this event is in March or April.
Sotheby's Auction – this usually occurs in April.

International Dragon Boat Festival – usually falling in June, the international festival is usually held the week after the Chinese dragon boat races.

Davis Cup – this tennis tournament is usually held in July.

International Arts Carnival – this unusual summer festival promotes performances by children's groups. The carnival usually falls in July or August.

Asian Regatta – organised by the Hong Kong Yachting Association, this event usually occurs in October.

Festival of Asian Arts – this is one of Asia's major international events, attracting performers from Australia as well as nearby countries. This festival usually occurs in October or November.

Cultural Centres

The main venue for cultural events is the shiny new Hong Kong Cultural Centre (☎ 7342009), 10 Salisbury Rd, Tsimshatsui, Kowloon. The Philharmonic Orchestra and Chinese Orchestra, among others, have regular performances here. Big events like rock concerts are held at the Hong Kong Coliseum (☎ 7659234), 9 Cheong Wan Rd, Hunghom, Kowloon, a 12,500-seat indoor facility next to the Kowloon-Canton Railway (KCR) station. A few performances are also booked at the Ko Shan Theatre (☎ 3342331) on Ko Shan Rd, Hunghom, Kowloon.

On Hong Kong Island, the main centre for cultural events is the Hong Kong Academy for the Performing Arts (☎ 8231505), 1 Gloucester Rd, Wanchai. Just across the street is the Hong Kong Arts Centre (☎ 8230230), 2 Harbour Rd, Wanchai. Some groups book performances at City Hall Theatre (☎ 5233800), right next to the Star Ferry Terminal in Central. Queen Elizabeth Stadium (☎ 5756793), 18 Oi Kwan Rd, Wanchai, is the site for both sporting events and large rock concerts.

There are three big cultural centres in the New Territories: Shatin Town Hall (☎ 6942503), 1 Yuen Ho Rd, Shatin; Tuen Mun Town Hall (☎ 4527308), 3 Tuen Hi Rd, Tuen Mun; Tsuen Wan Town Hall (☎ 4939143), 72 Tai Ho Rd, Tsuen Wan.

POST & TELECOMMUNICATIONS
Postal Rates

Local Mail Rates for Hong Kong mail are as follows:

Weight Not Over	Letters & Postcards	Printed Matter
30 g	HK$0.80	HK$0.70
50 g	HK$1.40	HK$0.80
100 g	HK$2.00	HK$1.20
250 g	HK$3.00	HK$2.00
500 g	HK$6.00	HK$3.50
1 kg	HK$12.00	HK$4.60

International Airmail The Hong Kong postal service divides the world into two distinct zones. Zone 1 is China, Japan,

Taiwan, South Korea, South-East Asia, Indonesia and India. Zone 2 is everywhere else. The rates are as follows:

Letters & Postcards	Zone 1	Zone 2
first 10 g	HK$1.80	HK$2.30
each additional 10 g	HK$1.00	HK$1.10
Printed Matter		
first 10 g	HK$1.20	HK$1.70
each additional 10 g	HK$0.60	HK$0.80

International Surface Mail The postal service also divides the world in two parts, but not the same zones as for airmail. Area 1 is China, Macau and Taiwan. Area 2 is all other countries. The rates for Area 2 are as follows:

Weight Not Over	Letters & Postcards	Printed Matter	Small Packet
30 g	HK$1.70	HK$1.60	HK$3.70
50 g	HK$3.00	HK$2.50	HK$3.70
100 g	HK$4.00	HK$3.50	HK$3.70
250 g	HK$8.00	HK$6.50	HK$7.50
500 g	HK$15.50	HK$11.50	HK$13.00
1 kg	HK$27.00	HK$19.00	HK$22.00
2 kg	HK$44.00	HK$27.00	HK$28.00

Sending Mail
On the Hong Kong Island side, the General Post Office (GPO) is on your right as you alight the Star Ferry. On the Kowloon side, the most convenient post office is at 10 Middle Rd, east of the Ambassador Hotel and Nathan Rd, Tsimshatsui. Another good post office (and less crowded) is in the basement of the Albion Plaza, 2-6 Granville Rd, just off Nathan Rd, Tsimshatsui. All post offices are open Monday to Saturday from 8 am to 6 pm, and are closed on Sunday and public holidays.

Allow five days for delivery of letters, postcards and aerogrammes to the UK and the USA. Speedpost reduces delivery time by about half. Sea mail is slow, so allow from six to 10 weeks for delivery to the UK and the USA.

Receiving Mail
There are poste-restante services at the GPO and other large post offices. Mail will be held for two months. Simply address an envelope c/o Poste Restante, GPO Hong Kong, and it will go to the Hong Kong Island side. If you want letters to go to the Kowloon side, they should be addressed to Poste Restante, 10 Middle Rd, Tsimshatsui, Kowloon.

Telephone
All calls within Hong Kong are local calls, and local calls from private phones are free. There are free public phones in the arrival area of the airport. Otherwise, public pay phones cost HK$1 per local call. You can find public phones in the airport, ferry terminals, post offices and hotel lobbies. On the street they are relatively rare.

Dial 108 for directory inquiries. To check the time and temperature dial 1852.

If you want to phone overseas, it's cheapest to use an IDD (International Direct Dialling) telephone. You can place an IDD call from most phone boxes, but you'll need a stack of HK$5 coins handy if your call is going to be anything but very brief. An alternative is to buy a 'Phonecard', which comes in denominations of HK$50, HK$100 or HK$250. You can find Phonecards in shops, on the street or at a Hong Kong Telecom office. There are two Hong Kong Telecom offices: at 10 Middle Rd, Tsimshatsui, and at Room 102A, Tower One, Exchange Square, Central. They are open 24 hours a day, including holidays.

To make an IDD call from Hong Kong, first dial 001, then the country code, area code and number. If calling to Hong Kong from abroad, the country code is 852.

If you go to Hong Kong Telecom, there are three options for overseas phone calls: operator-connected calls, paid in advance with a minimum of three minutes; international direct dialling (IDD) which you dial yourself after paying a deposit – the unused portion of your deposit is refunded; and reverse charges, which require a small deposit refundable if the charge is accepted or if the call doesn't get through. The cost of long-distance calls is listed in the Business Telephone Directory. The more conveniently located Hong Kong Telecom offices are:

Mercury House, 3 Connaught Rd, Central. It's open 24 hours a day, including public holidays.

GPO Building, Connaught Place, Central. Open Monday to Friday from 10 am to 6 pm, and Saturday from 10 am to 3 pm.

Hong Kong Airport, Terminal Building, Kai Tak Airport, Kowloon. Open from 8 am to 11 pm daily, including public holidays, fax 7216486.

Hermes House, 10 Middle Rd, Tsimshatsui, Kowloon. Open 24 hours a day, including public holidays.

Ocean Terminal, 1st floor, Room 102, Tsimshatsui, Kowloon. Open from 7.30 am to midnight every day, including public holidays.

New Mercury House, 22 Fenwick St, Wanchai, Hong Kong. Open Monday to Friday from 8 am to midnight, and Saturday from 8 am to 3 pm.

Phone Directories There are more phone directories than you would expect! Currently, there are four types: the Yellow Pages Buying Guide (three volumes, all bilingual); the Yellow Pages Commercial & Industrial Guide (one volume, English only); the Business Telephone Directory (one volume each in English and Chinese); and Residential Directories (three volumes each in English and Chinese).

If you're staying any length of time in the colony, you should at least pick up the Business Telephone Directory and the Yellow Pages Buying Guide. If you're looking for a job in a particular line of work, you might want to get the Yellow Pages Commercial & Industrial Guide since it would list such things as modelling or advertising agencies.

Fax, Telex & Telegraph

All your telecommunication needs can be taken care of at Hong Kong Telecom. To send a one-page fax (A4 size) they charge HK$10 within Hong Kong; HK$30 for South-East Asia; HK$35 to Australia, New Zealand, Canada, USA and UK; and HK$45 to all other countries. For HK$10 per page, you can also receive a fax here. Be sure the sending party puts your name and your Hong Kong telephone number on the top of the page.

Most large hotels offer their guests international phone, telex and fax services at the cost of a 10% service charge.

TIME

Hong Kong Standard Time is eight hours ahead of Greenwich Mean Time. Hong Kong does not have daylight-saving time.

When it is noon in Hong Kong it is also noon in Singapore and Perth; 2 pm in Sydney; 8 pm the previous day in Los Angeles; 11 pm the previous day in New York; and 4 am in London.

ELECTRICITY

The standard is 220 V, 50 Hz (cycles per second) AC, which is near enough as makes no difference to Europe and Australia. Appliances designed for 110 V will quickly burn out, although some have a switch for dual operation. If you're determined to use 110-V appliances, you can buy a transformer which will step down the voltage. Also, luxury tourist hotels often have razor outlets with multi-fittings to suit different plugs and voltages.

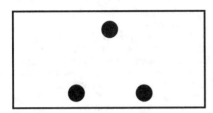

In Hong Kong, the electric outlets are designed to accommodate three round prongs. Inexpensive plug adapters are widely available in Hong Kong appliance stores and supermarkets. However, these adapters are only meant to solve the problem of incompatible plug designs – they are not meant to be used as transformers! If you ignore this warning and plug a 110-V appliance into a 220-V outlet, keep a fire extinguisher handy.

Apart from needing the right voltage, a few electric motors need the right frequency of current to work properly. For example, your 60 Hz clock will run slow on 50 Hz current, but it shouldn't harm the motor.

LAUNDRY

There is no need to hide your dirty laundry as there are plenty of places in Hong Kong which will clean it cheaply. Many hotels, even the cheap youth hostels, have a laundry service. If they don't, just ask where one is. Prices are normally HK$22 for three kg. If it is less than three kg, you still pay the same, so you might want to throw your clothes together with a friend's.

Two convenient laundry services in Tsimshatsui include Carlye Steam Laundry, Golden Crown Court, 66-70 Nathan Rd, and Purity Laundry, 25 Chungking Arcade, Chungking Mansions, 30 Nathan Rd.

WEIGHTS & MEASURES

The international metric system is in official use in Hong Kong. In practice, traditional Chinese weights and measures are still common. For those of you who still use imperial measurements there is a conversion table near the back of this book.

If you want to shop in the local markets, become familiar with Chinese units of weight. Things are sold by the *leung*, which is equivalent to 37.5 grams, or in *catty*, where one catty is about 600 grams. There are 16 leung to the catty.

Gold is sold by the *tael* which is exactly the same as a leung, and you will find many banks selling gold in Hong Kong. The Chinese have a long history of putting their wealth into gold as they generally have little faith in paper money. The rapid inflation that China has experienced in the past makes it easy to understand why.

BOOKS & MAPS

There are many good books about Hong Kong. Of course, these are most easily purchased in Hong Kong, but you may be able to get a bookstore in your home country to order them too.

History

The classic history of Hong Kong is *A History of Hong Kong* (Oxford University Press, London, 1958) by G B Endacott, which has everything you ever wanted to know about Hong Kong and more.

Maurice Collin's *Foreign Mud* (Faber & Faber, UK, 1946) tells the sordid story of the Opium Wars. Another version of the same story is *The Opium War* by the Foreign Language Press in Peking.

One of Hong Kong's most famous journalists was Richard Hughes, a reporter for the London *Sunday Times* and later for the *Far Eastern Economic Review.* His best known book about Hong Kong is *Borrowed Time, Borrowed Place*. He also wrote *Foreign Devil – Thirty Years of Reporting in the Far East*.

The Hong Kong Guide, 1893, while out of date, makes fascinating reading. It's available as a reprint.

The Taipans – Hong Kong's Merchant Princes (Oxford University Press, Hong Kong, 1981) tells the story of the Westerners or Taipans ('big managers') who profiteered during the Opium Wars.

A prolific writer and respected magistrate, Austin Coates wrote *Whampoa – Ships on the Shore* (South China Morning Post, 1980). This is a history of the Hong Kong & Whampoa Dock Company, which was formed in 1863 and was the first great company to be founded in Hong Kong. Coates also wrote *Myself a Mandarin*.

Coffee-Table Books

There are many large, beautiful books that often include good information along with photographs and sketches.

The government's annual report is entitled *Hong Kong 1990, Hong Kong 1991*, etc. In addition to the excellent photographs, the text is a gold mine of information about the government, politics, economy, history, arts and just about any other topic relevant to Hong Kong. It is widely available in bookshops as well as at the Government Publications Centre. For a coffee-table book, the price of HK$45 is dirt cheap.

Hong Kong, part of the series of Insight Guides by Apa Productions, has outstanding photographs and very readable text.

Fragrant Harbour by John Warner has many early photographs of Hong Kong.

The Taipan Traders by Anthony Lawrence is one of the Formasia series of books. A large sketchbook, it depicts many portraits by Asia's finest painters. *Great Cities of the World – Old Hong Kong* is another interesting Formasia book.

Hong Kong Illustrated, Views & News 1840-1890, compiled by John Warner, is a large sketchbook and history of the colony.

Hong Kong by Ian Lloyd & Russell Spurr is a good pictorial and part of the series of Times Editions.

Politics

The Other Hong Kong Report (Chinese University Press) is a fascinating and somewhat cynical rebuttal to the government's optimistic annual report. It's a hard-hitting collection of essays by people who don't see Hong Kong through rose-coloured glasses.

Fiction

Certainly the most famous fiction set in Hong Kong is *The World of Suzie Wong* by Richard Mason. Written in 1957, it still makes an excellent read; the movie was filmed in Hong Kong in 1960.

The marathon-length *Tai-Pan* by James Clavell will certainly help pass away your idle hours, although it's not a very realistic version of Hong Kong's early days of ships and traders. The sequel to *Tai-Pan* is another epic-length book, *Noble House*. If you've read Clavell's other blockbuster novel, *Shogun* (about Japan), you've got the idea.

Also set in Hong Kong and China are Robert Elegant's *Dynasty* (McGraw-Hill, UK, 1977) and *Mandarin* (Hamish Hamilton, UK, 1983).

Triad by Derek Lambert (Hamish Hamilton, London) is a violent fictional account of the Chinese underworld.

Humour

Larry Feign doesn't pull any punches with his poignant political cartoons which have graced the pages of the *South China Morning Post* and the *Hong Kong Standard*. His best works have been released in a series of books published by Macmillan (HK) Ltd. Some titles to look for include *The World of Lily Wong* and *The Adventures of Superlily*.

Guides

There are some special-interest guidebooks which you might want to look into if you're staying in Hong Kong for a while.

The US Chamber of Commerce publishes *Living in Hong Kong*, somewhat useful for those planning a long stay.

The book, *Associations, Clubs, Institutes and Societies in Hong Kong*, published by the HKTA, has a self-explanatory title.

If you're looking for obscure consulates (how about Lesotho, Monaco or St Kitts?), the Government Publications Centre publishes *Consular Posts, Officially Recognised Representatives and Bodies Established under the Sino-British Joint Declaration*.

The Best of Hong Kong & Macau, compiled and edited by Harry Rolnick, is a connoisseur's guide to the restaurants, nightclubs, discos and even shoe-repair shops in Hong Kong.

Lonely Planet publishes other guides to the region, including *North-East Asia on a shoestring, South-East Asia on a shoestring, China – a travel survival kit* and *Mandarin Chinese Phrasebook*.

Religion

Jonathan Chamberlain's *Chinese Gods* (Long Island Publishers, Hong Kong, 1983) is a very readable account of the nature of Chinese religion – a mixture of Buddhism, Taoism and Confucianism with animist beliefs and ancestor worship.

Another enlightening book is Frena Bloomfield's *The Book of Chinese Beliefs* (Arrow Books, London, 1983) which deals with a range of Chinese religious beliefs regarded by Westerners as superstition.

Chinese Temple Festivals (South China Morning Post, Hong Kong, 1983) by Ralph P Modder, is a rundown of the origins and beliefs associated with the main Chinese religious festivals celebrated in Hong Kong. Temple festivals are listed but Modder's book is far more comprehensive.

Extras

The *Journal of the Royal Asiatic Society* is published every year by the RAS (☎ 5510300), GPO Box 3864, Hong Kong. Each volume delves into different topics, everything from history to flora & fauna.

Hong Kong Country Parks by Stella L Thrower is an excellent government publication if you want to hike in the backwaters of Hong Kong.

The Occult World of Hong Kong by Frena Bloomfield may fascinate you or give you nightmares.

If you want to socialise with the masses then you might want to read *How to Play Mahjong* (David McKay Books) by Marcia Hammer.

Bookshops

There are several excellent bookshops in Hong Kong. One of the biggest and best is Swindon Books (☎ 3668001), 13 Lock Rd, Tsimshatsui, which has a wide selection of books on most topics. It also has a smaller branch on the 3rd floor, Ocean Terminal, Tsimshatsui.

Times Books (☎ 3110301) gives its address as Shop C, 96 Nathan Rd, but the entrance is around the corner on Granville Rd in Tsimshatsui. It's also a large store with a complete collection and has a branch (☎ 7226583) in Tsimshatsui East at the Houston Centre, lower ground floor, Shop No LG-23. Another Times Books shop (☎ 5258797) is at Hutchison House, Shop G-31, Central, Hong Kong Island. Hutchison House is at the corner of Murray Rd and Lambeth Walk.

Wanderlust Books (☎ 5232042), 30 Hollywood Rd, Central, Hong Kong Island, is well worth visiting for its collections of travel books, maps and books about Hong Kong. The staff is extremely helpful and friendly, a rarity in Hong Kong bookshops. At the corner of Hollywood Rd and Shelley St, it's reached after a steep walk from the Central Market area.

There is a South China Morning Post Bookshop (☎ 5221012) at the Star Ferry Terminal on Hong Kong Island. They have another branch on the 3rd floor of Ocean Terminal in Tsimshatsui.

Peace Book Company (☎ 3672201), 35 Kimberly Rd, Tsimshatsui, is an excellent store and has many books about China.

The Chung Hwa Book Company (☎ 7825054), 450 Nathan Rd, Yaumati, has a good selection of books and maps. It stocks many books in Chinese as well as in other languages.

Not to be overlooked is the Government Publications Centre in the GPO building next to the Star Ferry Terminal. It undoubtedly has the best collection of Hong Kong maps and produces some handy books about the economy, ecology, history and transport system of Hong Kong.

Libraries

The main library is at City Hall, City Hall High Block, Central, just a block to the east of the Star Ferry Terminal. However, they will not let you make photocopies of anything which is copyrighted (which means just about everything). As a result, most of their reference books have pages ripped out of them by frustrated students.

The American Library (☎ 5299661), 1st floor, United Centre, 95 Queensway, Admiralty, has good research facilities and *does* allow you to make photocopies.

Maps

There are a couple of good maps of Hong Kong worth picking up. Some of the best city maps are the *Kowloon Street Plan* and its sister the *Hong Kong Street Plan*, which you can buy in the bookshops for HK$10 each. These are very detailed with keys to main buildings and streets.

Even more detailed and highly recommended is a small atlas called the *Hong Kong Guide – Streets & Places*, which has complete maps and an index of all the buildings and streets in Hong Kong. It's a government publication and can be bought at the Government Publications Centre in the GPO building next to the Star Ferry on Hong Kong Island. It's also sold at the Survey & Mapping Office, Buildings & Lands Department, 382 Nathan Rd, Yaumati, Kowloon, near Kansu St. Many bookshops also carry it.

If you intend walking on the islands, it's a good idea to get the *Countryside* series of maps, also available from the Government Publications Centre in the GPO building on Hong Kong Island.

The map most people use is the freebie put out by the HKTA and private sponsors. It's covered with advertisements but is very good for finding your way around the lower Kowloon and Hong Kong city areas.

MEDIA
Newspapers & Magazines

Hong Kong is the leading information and news centre in Asia. The colonial government has the power to censor newspapers and occasionally uses it to avoid upsetting China. In 1989, a documentary entitled *Mainland China 1989* was censored because it was likely 'to seriously damage good relations with other territories'. The power of censorship, nonetheless, is used very sparingly in Hong Kong. What will happen after 1997 is the big question on every publisher's mind.

The two main local newspapers are the *South China Morning Post* and the *Hong Kong Standard*. Both are of reasonably good quality and are certainly a lot better than the scandalous tabloids produced in many Western countries.

Three international newspapers produce Asian editions which are printed in Hong Kong. These are the *Asian Wall Street Journal, USA Today* and the *International Herald Tribune*, which is put together by the *New York Times* and the *Washington Post* for readers outside the USA.

There are many magazines published in Hong Kong, but the most outstanding is the *Far Eastern Economic Review*, which focuses on news throughout Asia. *Asiaweek* is also published in Hong Kong, as well as the Asian editions of *Time* and *Newsweek*.

Radio & TV

Radio Television Hong Kong (RTHK) operates three stations: RTHK (Radio 3) at AM 567 and 1584 kHz, and FM 97.9 and 106.8 mHz; RTHK (Radio 4) at 97.6 and 98.9 mHz FM; RTHK (Radio 6) with the BBC World Service relay at AM 675 kHz. Commercial Radio (CR) is at AM 864 kHz. The British Forces Broadcasting Service (BFBS) is at FM 93.1, 96.6, 102 and 104.8 mHz. The English-language newspapers publish a daily guide to radio programmes.

Hong Kong's TV stations are run by two companies, Television Broadcasts Ltd (TVB) and Asia Television Ltd (ATV). Each company operates one English-language and one Cantonese-language channel, making a total of four stations in Hong Kong. The two English stations are TVB Pearl (channel 3) and ATV World (channel 4). The two Cantonese stations are called TVB Jade (channel 1) and ATV Home (channel 2). The programme schedule is listed daily in the English-language newspapers.

Since people in Macau also read Hong Kong newspapers, programmes from the Macau station (TdM) are listed, but the signal is too weak to be received in Hong Kong. TdM has wanted to broadcast to Hong Kong for years, but the Hong Kong government has strenuously objected, claiming that this would cause interference. Many suspect the real reason is that Hong Kong's two stations would prefer not to have any competition.

FILM & PHOTOGRAPHY

Almost everything you could possibly need in the way of film, camera and photographic accessories is available in Hong Kong, usually at cheaper prices than you'd pay at home.

HEALTH
Predeparture Preparations

No vaccinations are required provided you are coming from a noninfected area.

If you have been to an infected place within the past 14 days of your arrival in Hong Kong, a cholera vaccination is necessary. However, health requirements change so it is best to check the rules before travelling.

If you need vaccinations while in Hong Kong, the Port Health office can give you a low-cost jab for cholera and typhoid. They occasionally stock other vaccines depending on which epidemics are ravaging this part of Asia. Port Health has two branch offices: Kowloon (☎ 3683361), Room 905, Government Offices, Canton Rd, Yaumati; Hong Kong Island (☎ 5722056), 2nd floor, Centre Point Building, 181-185 Gloucester Rd, Wanchai.

Health Insurance Hong Kong has no national health service and all medical treatment has to be paid for by the patient. Fortunately, Hong Kong is reasonably safe and you aren't likely to catch any serious infectious diseases. Still, if you do a lot of travelling, it would be prudent to take out a travel insurance policy which covers you for medical expenses, including additional costs incurred if you have to fly home unexpectedly.

Medical Kit Many travellers like to put together a small, straightforward medical kit with any necessary medicines, anti-diarrhoeal drugs (Lomotil, Imodium), a laxative, tweezers (for removing splinters), plasters, antiseptic, acetominophen (Panadol, Tylenol, etc) and a thermometer.

Basic Rules
Food & Water Hong Kong is a very healthy place and no special precautions are needed. Chinese cooking relies heavily on fresh ingredients so the food is fairly safe, even from the street stalls despite their dubious appearance.

The government says it's perfectly safe to drink Hong Kong's tap water. Traditions die hard, however, and most Chinese will boil it anyway because they always did so in China (for good reason). On some of the outlying islands the water is still taken from wells and could conceivably be contaminated, but even this is a rare occurrence.

Medical Problems & Treatment
Skin Diseases While Hong Kong is a fairly healthy place, various skin diseases, caused by the hot, humid climate, are a common summertime affliction. None of these minor ailments are life-threatening, but they can cause considerable discomfort.

The most common skin problems are jock itch (a fungal infection near the groin), athlete's foot (a fungal infection known to the Chinese as Hong Kong feet), contact dermatitis (caused by a necklace or watch-band rubbing the skin) and prickly heat (caused by excessive sweating). All these ailments thrive under hot, moist conditions. Prevention and treatment is often a matter of good hygiene.

For fungal infections, bathe at least twice daily and use lots of soap. For athlete's foot, get an old toothbrush and scrub between the toes, then thoroughly dry your feet before dressing. For jock itch, standing in front of an electric fan is a good way to get completely dry. Dust the affected area with an antifungal powder such as *Desenex, Tinactin* or *Mycota*. It's even more effective if you use both an antifungal ointment and a powder. There are many brands — just look for an ointment or powder containing undecylenic acid and zinc undecylenate.

For jock itch, wear light cotton underwear or no underwear at all if the condition gets serious. Wear the lightest outer clothing possible when the weather is really hot and humid. Wearing open-toed sandals will often solve the problem of athlete's foot.

Treat contact dermatitis by removing the offending necklace, bracelet or wristwatch. Avoid anything that chafes the skin, such as tight clothing, but especially elastic.

You probably have prickly heat if your skin develops what appears as little painful red pin pricks. This is the result of excessive sweating blocking the sweat ducts and causing inflammation. The treatment is to dry and cool the skin. Bathe often, keep dry and use talcum powder.

A cool environment will definitely help. Hong Kong is one of the most heavily air-conditioned places on earth, and even though you might prefer sleeping with just an electric fan, paying a little more for a room with air-conditioning room might be well worth the expense if you have a skin problem.

Tuberculosis The infection rate for TB is surprisingly high in Hong Kong. More than 7000 cases are reported annually. While there is no reason to be unduly alarmed, if you're travelling with children it might be wise to have them vaccinated. These days, nearly all children in Hong Kong are immunised at birth. (See the Health section in the Canton Facts for the Visitor chapter.)

Hepatitis More than 1500 cases of hepatitis are reported in Hong Kong annually, but the unreported number of cases is probably several times that. Also, many cases are probably first contracted in China. Hepatitis is not a serious problem in Hong Kong, so don't dwell on it. (See the Health section in the Canton Facts for the Visitor chapter.)

Sexually Transmitted Diseases Sexual contact with an infected sexual partner spreads these diseases. While abstinence is the only 100% preventative, using condoms is also effective. Gonorrhoea and syphilis are the most common of these diseases; sores, blisters or rashes around the genitals, discharges or pain when urinating are common symptoms. Symptoms eventually disappear completely but the disease continues and cancause severe problems in later years. The treatment of gonorrhoea and syphilis is by antibiotics.

There are numerous other sexually transmitted diseases, for most of which effective treatment is available. However, there is no cure for herpes and there is also currently no cure for AIDS. Using condoms is the most effective preventative.

Hospitals Public hospitals charge low fees, but Hong Kong residents pay less than foreign visitors. Private doctors usually charge reasonable fees, but fees vary and it pays to make some inquiries first. Most large hotels have resident doctors.

Hong Kong has a shortage of dentists and fees are consequently very high. If the next stop on your itinerary is Taiwan, you might want to wait because the cost for dental treatment is much lower there.

Most pharmacies in Hong Kong are open 9 am to 6 pm, with some until 8 pm. Watson's has branches all over Hong Kong and can supply most pharmaceutical needs.

Public hospitals include: Queen Elizabeth Hospital (☎ 7102111), Wylie Rd, Yaumati,

Kowloon; Princess Margaret Hospital (☎ 7427111), Lai Chi Kok, Kowloon; and Queen Mary Hospital (☎ 8179463), Pokfulam Rd.

There are some excellent private hospitals in Hong Kong, but their prices reflect the fact that they must operate at a profit. Some of the better private hospitals in Hong Kong include:

Adventist
    40 Stubbs Rd, Wanchai, Hong Kong Island (☎ 5746211)
Baptist
    222 Waterloo Rd, Kowloon Tong (☎ 3374141)
Canossa
    1 Old Peak Rd, Mid-Levels, Hong Kong Island (☎ 5222181)
Grantham
    125 Wong Chuk Hang Rd, Deep Water Bay, Hong Kong Island (☎ 5546471)
Hong Kong Central
    1B Lower Albert Rd, Central, Hong Kong Island (☎ 5223141)
Matilda & War Memorial
    41 Mt Kellett Rd, The Peak, Hong Kong Island (☎ 8496301)
St Paul's
    2 Eastern Hospital Rd, Causeway Bay, Hong Kong Island (☎ 6906008)
St Teresa's
    327 Prince Edward Rd, Kowloon (☎ 7119111)

Herbal Medicine Western visitors to Hong Kong often become so engrossed buying cameras and electronic goods that they never realise Hong Kong is well known for something else – herbal medicine.

Nearby Canton is less expensive for buying Chinese medicines, but in Hong Kong there are more chemists who can speak English, and Hong Kong's prices really aren't much higher. Also, in Hong Kong it's easier to find everything you want in one place and there's less problem with counterfeit medicines.

Many Westerners never try Chinese medicine because they either know nothing about it or simply don't believe in it. Prominent medical authorities in the West often dismiss herbalists as no better than witch doctors. The ingredients, which may include such marvellous things as snake gall bladder or powdered deer antlers, will further discourage potential non-Chinese customers. Also, even for true believers, there is a bewildering variety of herbs available on the shelves of any Chinese pharmacy, and many Westerners are baffled as to where to start.

Having experimented with Chinese medicine for several years, I'm convinced that it has something to offer, but several warnings are in order. Chinese herbalists have all sorts of treatments for stomach aches, headaches, colds, flu and sore throat. They also have herbs to treat long-term problems like asthma. Many of these herbs seem to work. Whether or not Chinese medicine can cure more serious illnesses like cancer and heart disease is much more uncertain. All sorts of overblown claims have been made for herbal medicines, especially by those who make and sell them. Some gullible Westerners have persuaded themselves that Chinese doctors can cure any disease. A visit to any of China's hospitals will quickly shatter this myth.

In general, Chinese medicine works best for the relief of unpleasant symptoms (pain, sore throat, etc) and for some long-term conditions which resist Western medicines, such as migraine headaches, asthma and chronic backache. But for acute life-threatening conditions, such as a heart attack, it's best to see a Western doctor.

When reading about the theory behind Chinese medicine, the word 'holistic' appears often. Basically, this means that Chinese medicine seeks to treat the whole body rather than focusing on a particular organ or disease.

Using appendicitis as an example, a Chinese doctor may try to fight the infection using the body's whole defences, whereas a Western doctor would simply cut out the appendix. While the holistic method sounds great in theory, in practice the Western technique of attacking the problem directly often works better. In the case of appendicitis, surgery really is a more reliable treatment than taking herbs. On the other hand, in the case of migraine headaches, herbs might prove more effective than Western painkillers.

Another point to be wary of when taking herbal medicine is the tendency of some manufacturers to falsely claim that their product contains numerous potent and expensive ingredients. For example, some herbal formulas may list rhinoceros horn as an ingredient. Rhinoceros horn, widely acclaimed by herbalists as a cure for high temperature (fever, sweating and hot flushes) is so rare and extremely expensive that it is practically impossible to buy. Any formula listing rhinoceros horn may, at best, contain water buffalo horn. In any case, the rhino is a rare and endangered species, and you will not wish to hasten its extinction by demanding rhino horn products.

One benefit of Chinese medicine is that there are generally few side-effects. Compared to a drug like penicillin which can produce allergic reactions and other serious side-effects, herbal medicines are fairly safe. Nevertheless, herbs are still medicines, and not candy. There is no need to gobble herbs if you're feeling fine to begin with. Allergic reactions to herbs are not unknown and some herbs are even mildly toxic, which can result in liver damage if you take them for too long (months or years).

Before shopping for herbs, keep in mind that in Western medicine, doctors talk about broad-spectrum antibiotics, such as penicillin, which are good for treating a range of infections. But for many illnesses, a specific antibiotic might be better for a specific type of infection. The same is true in Chinese medicine. A broad-spectrum remedy such as snake gall bladder may be good for treating colds, but there are many different types of colds. The best way to treat a cold with herbal medicine is to see a Chinese doctor and get a specific prescription. Otherwise, the herbs you take may not be the most appropriate for your condition.

If you visit a Chinese doctor, you might be surprised by what he or she discovers about your body. For example, the doctor will almost certainly take your pulse and then may tell you that you have a slippery pulse

or perhaps a thready pulse. Chinese doctors have identified more than 30 different kinds of pulses. A pulse could be empty, prison, leisurely, bowstring, irregular or even regularly irregular.

The doctor may then examine your tongue to see if it is slippery, dry, pale, greasy, has a thick coating or maybe no coating at all. The doctor, having discovered that you have wet heat, as evidenced by a slippery pulse and a red greasy tongue, will prescribe the proper herbs for your condition.

High Fever Shinshyue Dan Granules *(xiñ xŭe dān)*. This is a very bitter mixture, so if you can't stand the taste, load the granules into empty gelatin capsules.

Sore Throat A good brand is Superior Sore Throat Powder *(hóu fēng sǎn)*.

Headache Nothing works better than *piān tóu tòng wán*.

Phlegm Coughing and spitting up phlegm is a national pastime in China. The Chinese manufacture expectorants and decongestants from the gall bladder of snakes. Among the choices are Sanshetan Chuanpeimo *(sān shé dǎn chūan bèi mò)*.

Diarrhoea Berberine hydrochloride *(huáng liǎn sù)* is highly effective.

Women's Tonic To help with anaemia and menstrual problems, try *sì wù tāng*.

Liniments Highly fragrant, these oils feel hot when applied to the skin. Use liniment to treat headaches, stomach aches, backaches and almost anything else. Just rub the oil on wherever it hurts, but be careful about getting it into the eyes or mouth. There are dozens of popular brands on the market. Some good Hong Kong brands are White Flower Oil *(bái huā yóu)*, Regal Medicated Oil & Embrocation *(qū fēng yóu)* and Po Sum On. In China, look for *qīng liáng yóu* and *fēng yóu*. Rubbing this stuff on the back, neck and shoulders is great even if you're not sick.

Salves These are similar to liniments but are not as strong. The most famous brand is Tiger Balm.

Plaster For sprains and sore muscles, try a sticky dog-skin plaster *(gǒu pí gāo yào)* which is not made from dog skin nowadays. A popular brand is 701 gao.

Many Chinese medicines are powders that come in vials. Typically, you take one or two vials a day. Some of these powders taste OK, but others are very bitter and difficult to swallow. If you can't tolerate the taste, you may want to buy some empty gelatine capsules and fill them yourself with the powder.

A good place to purchase herbal medicines is Yue Hwa Chinese Products Emporium at the corner of Nathan Rd and Jordan Rd in Yaumati. If you can't find the medicines listed, then explain your condition to a Chinese chemist and ask for a recommendation. They consider this part of their job.

There are plenty of books available to learn more about Chinese medicine. One of the easiest to understand is *The Web That Has No Weaver: Understanding Chinese Medicine* (Congdon & Weed, New York) by Ted J Kaptchuk.

If you want a more advanced text, *The Theoretical Foundations of Chinese Medicine* (MIT Press, Cambridge, Mass) by Manfred Porkert is good. However, the author has been criticised for introducing many Latin terms which make the book more difficult to read.

There are some old classics dealing with Chinese medicine. One of the best known is *The Treasures of Chinese Medicine (běn cǎo gāng mù)*, written in the 16th century. Another ancient reference is *The Yellow Emperor's Classic of Internal Medicine (huángdì nèijīng sūwén)* which was first published around 2600 BC.

Acupuncture Can you cure people by sticking needles into them? The Chinese think so and they've been doing it for thousands of years. Now the technique of acupuncture is gaining popularity in the West. In recent years, many Westerners have made the pilgrimage to China either to seek treatment or to study acupuncture. Canton is a particularly popular place for both patients and students who want to learn more about this ancient medical technique.

Getting stuck with needles might not sound pleasant, but if done properly it doesn't hurt. Knowing just where to insert the needle is crucial. Acupuncturists have identified more than 2000 insertion points, but only about 150 are commonly used.

The exact mechanism by which acupuncture works is not fully understood. The Chinese talk of energy channels or meridians which connect the needle insertion point to the particular organ, gland or joint being treated. The acupuncture point is sometimes quite far from the area of the body being treated. Acupuncture is even used to treat impotency, but I've never wanted to ask just where the needle is inserted.

Among acupuncturists there are different schools of thought. The most common school in China is called the Eight Principles School. Another is the Five Elements School.

As with herbal medicine, the fundamental question asked by potential acupuncture patients is: 'Does it work?'. The answer has to be: 'That depends'. It depends on the skill of the acupuncturist and the condition being treated. Like herbal medicine, acupuncture tends to be more useful for those who suffer from long-term conditions (like chronic headaches) rather than sudden emergencies (like an acute appendicitis).

There are times when acupuncture can be used for an immediate condition. For example, some major surgical operations have been performed using acupuncture as the only anaesthetic (this works best on the head). In this case, a small electric current (from batteries) is passed through the needles. This is a good example of how Western medicine and Chinese medicine can be usefully combined.

While some satisfied patients give glowing testimonials about the prowess of acupuncture, others are less impressed. The only way to really find out is to try it.

While acupuncture itself is probably harmless, one should not forget that AIDS can be spread easily by contaminated needles. In Western countries, the use of disposable acupuncture needles has become routine, but this is not the case in China. If you're going to experiment with acupuncture, first find out if the doctor has disposable needles. If not, it is possible for you to buy your own needles and bring them to the doctor when you need treatment. Of course, you must find out if the doctor is willing. Also, you need to consult with the doctor to find out what size and gauge of needles you should buy. There are many varieties, and the doctor may not be willing to use whatever you just happen to purchase.

Unfortunately, you can't depend on finding acupuncture needles readily available in Canton. China's inefficient factories cannot produce them fast enough to meet demand. There is a perpetual needle shortage in Canton because so many foreigners buy them. Hong Kong has a main acupuncture supply house called Mayfair Medical Supplies (☎ 7303256), 35 Austin Rd, Yaumati. They have some acupuncture reference books. Other suppliers could be found by looking in the Yellow Pages Commercial/Industrial Guide under Medical Equipment & Supplies.

The following organisations could be worth checking: Chinese Acupuncture Association (☎ 5457640), 10th floor, Flat E, Lyndhurst Building, 29 Lyndhurst Terrace, Central; International Acupuncture Institute (☎ 3888836), Room 1113A, Champion Building, 301-309 Nathan Rd, Yaumati.

EMERGENCY

For emergency services – police, fire or

ambulance – dial ☎ 999. These calls are free, even from pay phones. When the operator answers, say which of the three services you need. To report a crime (nonemergency) call the police hotline (☎ 5277177).

WOMEN TRAVELLERS

While Hong Kong poses no special dangers for women, unpleasant incidents can occur. And like anything else in Hong Kong, sex is a business. One woman traveller had this to report:

A young Chinese man came to the Traveller's Hostel looking for an English girl who was after some modelling work. He asked me if I wanted some extra money, offering me escort/film work. I replied 'No' as I was returning home shortly and didn't need money. However, as he persisted and offered me HK$1000 for an evening solely as an escort, I agreed, with the other girl, to meet him the next evening. He turned out to be working as a pimp for Chinese 'high-class' customers. OK, I should have known better. I left as soon as possible amid threats from him and an Indian boss, and quite frankly I was really frightened. My friend who was interested in modelling stayed, but soon found out that the entire business was just to find European girls to have sex with Chinese men.

I was old enough and had money enough in Hong Kong to refuse these people who were obviously hoping to intimidate or force us into working for them, but I think some people would be too scared to say no, as they were extremely persistent!

I had gone to see this man, Mr Chan, out of idle curiosity and ended up very frightened! I'd like other women to be warned, as they tried very hard to conceal the true nature of their business and Mr Chan is extremely charming and pleasant to start with. They obviously know where to find female travellers (we were approached in the kitchen of the Traveller's Hostel)!

I was really taken in, but having travelled through Asia and Central America I thought I was pretty good at spotting trouble. Please be warned!

DANGERS & ANNOYANCES
Rudeness

'Give us your money and get the hell out!', seems to be the motto of many Hong Kong shopkeepers and hotel owners. The biggest complaint of travellers is that Hong Kong people are often appallingly rude, pushy and impatient. This impression partly results from the fact that most foreigners deal mainly with people in the tourist trade rather than the typical Hong Kong resident. However, this is a thin excuse. Sales clerks in Taiwan, Korea, Japan or the Philippines are generally cheerful and friendly, but this is seldom the case in Hong Kong. The HKTA is aware of the problem, and has attempted to educate people to smile and say 'hello' and 'thank you'. Unfortunately, their efforts have been less than stunningly successful.

It's not just tourists who complain. Many indigenous Hong Kongers also feel that their home town is far less friendly than it should be. This doesn't mean that you will never encounter a hospitable person in Hong Kong. Within this sea of frowning faces, there are smiles. You might even meet someone who will be polite, helpful, friendly and generous and not expect anything in return. Sadly, such experiences are all too rare, especially if you're a only a short-term visitor.

Crime

In a form of poetic Chinese justice, the colony's initial opium-based founding has rebounded and Hong Kong now has a serious dope problem. There are an estimated 38,000 drug addicts in Hong Kong, 90% of whom are male. While the women addicts mostly finance their habit through prostitution, the men resort to more aggressive crimes such as pickpocketing, burglary and robbery. The effect on travellers is that you have to be careful with your valuables.

It is generally safe, however, to walk around at night, but it's best to stick to well-lit areas. Tourist districts like Tsimshatsui are heavily patrolled by the police and there is little danger of violent crime, though pickpocketing can occur anywhere. Crime is very rare on the outlying islands such as Lamma and Lantau.

Much of the problem has its roots in Hong Kong's notorious Triads. At one time the Triads, or secret societies, may have been a positive influence in China. It is said they opposed the corrupt and brutal Manchu (Qing) Dynasty and aided the revolution that brought down the Manchus in 1911. Unfortunately, the Triads that exist now are the Chinese equivalent of the Mafia. They are involved in illegal gambling, protection rackets, the smuggling of drugs and weapons, prostitution and loan sharking.

WORK
Visas
Stretching the cash? Legally speaking, there are only three groups of foreigners who do not need employment visas for Hong Kong: UK citizens, British passport holders or registered British subjects. Such people are granted a 12-month stay on arrival, after which extensions are merely a formality.

As for foreign nationals, including Australians, Americans and Canadians, to work in Hong Kong you must get an employment visa from the Hong Kong Immigration Department before you arrive.

Applications for employment visas can be made to any British embassy or British consular or diplomatic office. If you arrive in Hong Kong as a visitor and get a job, you will have to leave the colony, apply for a visa and return when it is obtained. Americans are normally granted a six-month work visa. Extensions should be applied for a month before the visa expires. There are stiff penalties for employers who hire foreigners illegally.

Finding a Job
As for finding a job, it's true that many travellers stop off in Hong Kong to pick up work. The place is full of people who stopped for a few months to replenish the coffers and are still there 15 years later. Success in finding work depends largely on what skills you have. Professional people such as engineers, computer programmers and accountants will have no problem landing a job, especially now that Hong Kong's well-educated class is emigrating in droves to Canada, Australia and elsewhere.

Those who do not possess rare high-technology skills are at a distinct disadvantage. A Hong Kong boss can employ a first-class bilingual Chinese secretary for half the wage that her Western counterpart would ask. This is the same for mechanics, electricians, sales clerks, bank tellers and most other jobs that don't require a university degree. If you're a professional, try registering with some of the Hong Kong personnel agencies. Also check the classified sections of the *South China Morning Post* and the *Hong Kong Standard*.

Qualified teachers with British passports, or a British spouse, could try applying to the British Council (☎ 8315138), Ground floor, Easey Commercial Building, 255 Hennessy Rd, Wanchai, for full or part-time teaching posts (including teaching English).

It's fairly easy to pick up work teaching conversational English. Pay is around HK$50 per hour, and you may find yourself doing a lot of commuting between part-time jobs. Teaching English is not always as easy as it sounds. If your students are good, it can be a pleasure, but if their English is very poor, teaching them can be both boring and frustrating. However, it does provide one opportunity to meet local people.

If you're fluent in one or more foreign languages then you might get work as a translator. You can find such companies listed in the Yellow Pages Buying Guide under Translators & Interpreters.

Occasionally Westerners can find work standing around as extras in Hong Kong movies (long hours and little pay). Some people even try busking, but this does not seem to be highly lucrative.

Modelling is another possibility for both men and women. Modelling agencies are listed in the Yellow Pages Commercial & Industrial Guide.

Bar and waiting jobs are other options. There are numerous British and Australian-style pubs and bars in the colony and people passing through Hong Kong often get jobs at one of these.

For females, paid babysitting is an option. Contact Rent-a-Mum (☎ 8179799), 88B Pokfulam Rd, Hong Kong Island.

There is no legal minimum wage in Hong Kong, so you must reach an agreement on salary before you begin any job.

Top: Night view of Central, Hong Kong Island (RH)
Left: Looking west along Queensway, Central, Hong Kong Island (PS)
Right: Street scene in Sheung Wan, Hong Kong Island (RI)

Top: Hong Kong Harbour (GI)
Bottom: Hong Kong Harbour at sunset (RH)

One form of employment which requires no work visa, but which is not recommended, is smuggling. The idea is that you cart a bagful of goodies – such as one watch, one Walkman, one camera, one diamond ring or some other valuable item to a place such as South Korea where imports of such foreign-made goods are heavily taxed or prohibited. Customs often won't hassle you if you're not carrying too much. Westerners are employed by professional smugglers who are usually Hong Kong Chinese.

The theory is that the customs people are less likely to stamp the goodies on a Western passport, thus requiring you to exit with them. Once you pass customs, you hand the goods to an accompanying Hong Kong Chinese, who then zips off to sell them. You either get a fee for this service and go back to Hong Kong to do it again, or else you've gained yourself a free air ticket to South Korea or Taiwan and saved some money. These small-time smuggling expeditions are commonly known as milk runs and the travellers who carry the goods are called mules.

It all sounds very benign, but the risks increase dramatically when you go for the big time. When I was in Hong Kong, a traveller living in Chungking Mansions was solicited to smuggle seven kg of gold into Nepal and was offered US$2000 for his trouble. He got caught and was given four years in prison. Another traveller I met got caught at Seoul Airport wearing three mink coats under his jacket. He was fined and given two months in jail before being booted out of the country. Furthermore, smuggling to South Korea and Taiwan has fallen off dramatically as those countries have liberalised their protected economies.

ACTIVITIES

Hong Kong may not have downhill skiing, but the city offers plenty of ways to keep fit and have fun at the same time.

Anyone who is serious about sports should contact the South China Athletic Association (SCAA) (☎ 5776932), Caroline Hill Rd, Causeway Bay, Hong Kong Island. The SCAA has numerous indoor facilities such as bowling, tennis, ping pong (table tennis) tables, an exercise room, yoga classes, karate classes and others. Membership costs HK$40, but visitors can join for HK$10 per month.

Hong Kong's largest sporting facility is the Jubilee Sports Centre (☎ 6023810), near the Fo Tan KCR Station, Shatin, New Territories. They have a huge indoor and outdoor sporting complex.

Billiards & Snooker

Most of the venues for billiards and snooker are in Tsimshatsui East. Among the better known places are the Peninsula Billiard Club (☎ 7390638), 3rd floor, Peninsula Centre, and the Castle Billiards Club (☎ 3679071), Houston Centre.

On Hong Kong Island, Trinity House, on the corner of Wanchai Rd and Heard St, Wanchai, seems to be a local hot spot for billiards. There are three billiards clubs here: Centre Billiard Saloon (☎ 5738221); Dai Wai Sze Billiard Saloon (☎ 8339903); and Trinity Billiard Saloon (☎ 8343709).

Bowling

In Kowloon, the most popular bowling venue for foreigners is the 1st floor of the Mariners' Club, 11 Middle Rd, Tsimshatsui.

Good lanes can be found at Fourseas Bowling Centre (☎ 5670703), Cityplaza Shopping Centre, Tai Koo Shing, Quarry Bay. Take the MTR to Tai Koo Station.

Cycling

There are bicycle paths in the New Territories mostly around Tolo Harbour. The paths run from Shatin to Tai Po and continue up to Tai Mei Tuk. You can rent bicycles in these three places, but it's very crowded on weekends. On a weekday you may have the paths to yourself.

The Hong Kong Cycling Association (☎ 5733861) can be contacted at Room 1013, Queen Elizabeth Stadium, 18 Oi Kwan Rd, Wanchai. Or try the Hong Kong Cyclist Club (☎ 7207788), 1st floor, 267 Lai Chi Kok Rd, Shamshuipo, Kowloon.

A good shop to buy bicycles, parts and accessories is Flying Ball Bicycle Company (☎ 3813661), 201 Tung Choi St, Mongkok, Kowloon.

Diving

Diving enthusiasts can contact the Sea Dragon Skin Diving Club (☎ 8912113), GPO Box 10014, Hong Kong. The YMCA also has diving classes.

Golf

There are four golf courses in Hong Kong. On weekends, forget it. On weekdays, the Royal Hong Kong Golf Club (RHKGC) permits visitors. Of course, you have to pay green fees and hire equipment. The RHKGC has two venues: the cheaper one is at Deepwater Bay (☎ 8127070) on the south side of Hong Kong Island, and charges HK$250 for 18 holes or HK$400 for the whole day. Operating hours are 9.30 am to 2.30 pm from May to August, and 9.30 am to 1.30 pm from September to April. The RHKGC course at Fanling (☎ 6701211) in the New Territories. charges HK$1000 for 18 holes. The course is open from 7 am to 6 pm.

The Discovery Bay Golf Club (☎ 9877271) on Lantau Island is open Monday to Friday, from 8 am to 3.15 pm, and charges HK$600 for 18 holes.

The Clearwater Bay Golf & Country Club (☎ 7195936) is in the Sai Kung Peninsula in the New Territories. The course is open Monday to Friday from 7.30 am to 6 pm. Green fees are HK$1000, but you can book a special Sports & Recreation Tour through the HKTA. The tour costs HK$260 plus another HK$600 for use of the facilities. This permits you to play table tennis, swim or use the saunas and jacuzzi in addition to playing golf.

Hiking

Although trekking in Hong Kong is less challenging than the Nepal Himalaya, some basic equipment is necessary. Most important is a full water bottle. Other useful items include food, a rainsuit, sunhat, toilet paper, maps and compass. Boots are not really necessary but running shoes are preferred over flip-flop sandals (thongs). If you're prone to getting blisters, take some plasters (band-aids). Of course, just how much equipment you decide to drag along depends on how far you plan to walk.

Good maps will save you a lot of time and trouble. Check out the *Countryside* series of maps available from the Government Publications Office in the GPO near the Star Ferry Terminal on Hong Kong Island.

Serious walkers should remember that the high humidity during spring and summer is tiring. November to March are the best months for strenuous treks. At high elevations, like at the youth hostel at Ngong Ping on Lantau, it can get very cold so it's essential to bring warm clothes and even a down sleeping bag if you're staying the night.

The sun can be merciless, so a sunhat and/or UV lotion are useful. There is little shade here because there are few trees on the slopes of Hong Kong's mountains. Hong Kong is believed to have had more trees at one time, but massive tree cutting by settlers as long ago as the Song Dynasty (960 AD to 1279) stripped the hills bare causing soil erosion. One effect of this is that landslides still occur during heavy rainstorms – another hazard to hikers.

Very few hiking areas in Hong Kong are dangerous, but there have been several injuries and some deaths. The victims are mostly inexperienced walkers taking foolish risks. It is wise to stick to the established trails and heed the signs saying 'Steep and Seasonally Overgrown' or 'Firing Range'.

Snakes are not a serious problem and are rarely encountered. If you see a snake, the best thing to do is to walk away from it. Most snakes fear creatures larger than themselves, including humans, and will try to avoid you. Most people get bitten when they attempt to beat a snake with a stick.

Mosquitoes are a nuisance, so a good mosquito repellent is essential. Autan is a popular brand of repellent available from Watson's and other Hong Kong drugstores. Mosquito coils (incense) are also effective when you're sitting in one place, but should not be used inside a tent or any other enclosed area as they are a fire hazard and the smoke contains a poison that isn't particularly good for your lungs.

Hiking in Hong Kong has become so popular that many trails are very crowded on weekends, so try to schedule your walks during weekdays.

To contact hiking clubs, call the Federation of Hong Kong Hiking & Outdoor

Activities Groups (☎ 7800077), 2nd floor, Front Portion, 61 Shantung St, Yaumati.

Horse Racing

Gambling is deeply ingrained in Chinese culture, though, to be fair, it was the British who introduced horse racing to Hong Kong.

Apart from mahjong games and the twice-weekly Mark Six Lottery which raises money for the government, racing is the only form of legal gambling in Hong Kong. This is why Macau is so popular with the gambling-addicted Chinese. The first horse races were held in 1846 at Happy Valley on Hong Kong Island, and became an annual event. Now there are about 65 meetings per year at two tracks and about 450 races in all. The newer and larger track is at Shatin in the New Territories: it has seats in an air-conditioned enclosure and can accommodate up to 70,000 people.

The HKTA has Come Horseracing tours to Happy Valley and Shatin. Each costs HK$350 and includes entrance to the visitors' box inside the members' enclosure of the Royal Hong Kong Jockey Club (RHJKC), bus fare and lunch or dinner. Inquire at the HKTA offices. You can go there yourself and get in for HK$50. You must be aged 18 years or over to enter, and you may need to show your passport.

The racing season is from late September to June. Normally, races at Shatin are held on Saturday from 1 to 6 pm. At Happy Valley, races are normally on Wednesday evening from about 7 to 11 pm. However, this schedule isn't followed religiously. Sometimes extra races are held on Sunday or holidays. Check with the HKTA in late September or early October to get the schedule for the forthcoming season.

Betting is organised by the RHKJC. Many types of betting combinations are available. One combination is the Quinella (picking the first two horses) or Double Quinella (picking the first two horses from two specific races). There is also the Treble (picking the winner from three specific races) or the Six-Up (out of the day's six races, pick the first or second in each race).

Jogging

If you'd like a morning run with spectacular views, nothing beats the path around Victoria Peak on Harlech and Lugard Rds. Almost as spectacular is the jog along Bowen Rd, which is closed to traffic and runs in an east-west direction in the hills above Wan chai. There is a running track in Victoria Park in Causeway Bay, Hong Kong Island.

A popular place to run is the Promenade which runs along the waterfront in Tsim shatsui East. The problem here is that it's not a very long run, but the views are good and it's close to many of the hotels.

The Hong Kong International Marathon is held on the second day of the Chinese New Year. The Coast of China Marathon is held in March. Contact the HKTA or the Hong Kong Amateur Athletic Association, Room 913, Queen Elizabeth Stadium, 18 Oi Kwan Rd, Wanchai.

Lawn Bowling

Victoria Park in Causeway Bay has facilities for lawn bowling. These are open on weekdays in the afternoon only, but all day on weekends.

Sauna & Massage

The art of massage has a long history in China. Sauna baths are popular in Hong Kong and many bath houses offer a good massage service. During the chilly winter season there is probably no better way to relax. The legitimate places are suitable for both men and women. The saunas tend to be crowded in the evenings. Prices typically range from around HK$100 to HK$170 per hour, but ask first. The high-priced places are mainly found in Tsimshatsui East.

Many less respectable establishments offer additional services. The legitimate saunas are listed in the Yellow Pages Buying Guide under Baths. The questionable ones are listed under Massage or Escort – the advertisements make interesting reading even if you never make use of their services.

Skating

The best ice-skating rink in Hong Kong is on

the 1st floor of Cityplaza-Two (☎ 8854697), Cityplaza Shopping Centre, 18 Tai Koo Shing Rd, Quarry Bay. The easiest way to get there is to take the MTR to the Tai Koo Station.

If you are interested in ice dancing or ice hockey, contact the Hong Kong Ice Activities Association (☎ 8910476), B8-9/F, Causeway Bay Centre, just off of Yee Wo St, Causeway Bay.

If you prefer wheels to blades, Rollerworld at Cityplaza Shopping Centre can accommodate you. Take the MTR to the Tai Koo Station. There's also a roller rink in Kowloon's Telford Gardens shopping mall.

Squash & Tennis

Public squash courts tend to be crowded, especially in the evening. One place to go is the Hong Kong Squash Centre (☎ 8690611), 23 Cotton Tree Drive, Central, next to Hong Kong Park. Book in advance. There are squash courts in the Queen Elizabeth Stadium, Wanchai. There are tennis courts at King's Park, Yaumati. In the New Territories, you can play squash and tennis at the Jubilee Sports Centre (☎ 6023810), near the Fo Tan KCR Station, Shatin.

Spectators may be interested in the Hong Kong Open Tennis Championship, held every September. In October, there's the Hong Kong Tennis Classic in Victoria Park.

Swimming

Except for Kowloon and the north side of Hong Kong Island, there are good beaches spread throughout the colony. The most accessible beaches are on the south side of Hong Kong Island, but excellent beaches can be found on Lantau Island, Lamma Island and in the New Territories. See those chapters for details. The longest beach in Hong Kong is Cheung Sha on Lantau Island.

Expect the beaches to be chock-a-block on weekends and holidays. On weekdays, it's not bad at all. All beaches controlled by the Urban Council or the Urban Services Depart ment are patrolled by life-savers. A red flag means the water is too rough for swimming and a blue flag means it's unsafe for children

and weak swimmers. At most of the beaches you will find toilets, showers, changing rooms, refreshment stalls and sometimes restaurants. The usual life-saving hours are from 9 am to 6.30 pm on weekdays. On weekends at the more popular and bigger beaches, life-saving hours are extended from 8 am to 7.30 pm.

Hong Kong's Urban Council operates 13 public swimming pools. During school-term weekdays the pools are nearly empty so this is the best time to go. There's a pool in Kowloon Park, Tsimshatsui, and Victoria Park, Causeway Bay.

Table Tennis & Badminton

It's widely acknowledged that the Chinese are the best table tennis players in the world. It's not so widely known that they are also badminton enthusiasts. The Queen Elizabeth Stadium, 18 Oi Kwan Rd, Wanchai, has facilities for badminton and table tennis. Ditto for the South China Athletic Association (☎ 5776932), Caroline Hill Rd, Cause way Bay.

Taichichuan & Martial Arts

If you want to participate in taichichuan with a group, or if you just want to watch, you must get up early. The Chinese traditionally do this exercise at the crack of dawn. Parks are the place to go. The most popular park for Taichichuan is Victoria Park in Causeway Bay, Hong Kong Island. Other popular venues include the Zoological & Botanical Gardens in Central, and Kowloon Park in Tsimshatsui.

Contact the Hong Kong Taichi Association (☎ 3954884), 11th floor, 60 Argyle St, Mongkok, Kowloon. You can also try the following associations:

Chinese Martial Arts Association
    9th floor, Flat A & B, 687 Nathan Rd, Mongkok, Kowloon (☎ 3944803)
Judo Association
    Room 902, Queen Elizabeth Stadium, 18 Oi Kwan Rd, Wanchai (☎ 8913879)
Karatedo Association
    Room 1006, Queen Elizabeth Stadium, 18 Oi Kwan Rd, Wanchai (☎ 8919705)

Taekwondo Association
   Room 1004, Queen Elizabeth Stadium, 18 Oi
   Kwan Rd, Wanchai (☎ 8912036)

Waterskiing

If you've got money to burn, try waterskiing for a mere HK$250 or so per hour. Call the Deep Water Bay Speedboat Company (☎ 8120391).

Windsurfing

It is possible to hire windsurfing equipment at most public beaches. Beach resorts in the Sai Kung area of the New Territories are good for this. Ditto for Tungwan Beach on Cheung Chau Island, and Stanley Main Beach on the south side of Hong Kong Island. The rental fees are from HK$40 to HK$60 per hour.

Yachting & Sailing

This is not exactly an inexpensive activity either. If you can afford it, contact the Hebe Haven Yacht Club (☎ 7199682), Hirams Highway, Pak Sha Wan, Sai Kung, New Territories. Alternatively, there's the Royal Hong Kong Yacht Club (☎ 8322817), Kellett Island, Causeway Bay.

HIGHLIGHTS

The trip on the Peak Tram to Victoria Peak has been practically mandatory for visitors since it opened in 1888. A 30-minute ride on a sampan through Aberdeen Harbour is equally exciting. Lunch at a good dim sum restaurant is one of the great pleasures of the Orient, and of course, shopping is what Hong Kong is all about.

ACCOMMODATION

If you're looking for dirt-cheap accommodation, Hong Kong is no paradise. High land prices mean high prices for tiny, cramped rooms. Even though new hotels are constantly being built, demand always seems to exceed supply. Still, you can usually find a room without too much hassle, although this can be difficult during peak holiday times like Chinese New Year and Easter.

The HKTA runs a hotel booking counter at the airport, and while they won't find you a rock-bottom hovel, they will do their best to get you something. This can be especially useful if you arrive at night since the cheapies are more likely to be full by then and it's no joy carting your luggage around the streets looking for elusive beds at midnight. Many won't open the door at that hour even if they have got a bed.

Camping Camping is generally permitted next to Hong Kong Youth Hostel Association (HKYHA) youth hostels in remote areas, where you will be permitted to use their toilet and washroom facilities.

Also, several government and independent campsites on Lantau Island are listed in a HKTA camping leaflet.

HKYHA Hostels The Hong Kong Youth Hostels Association (☎ 7881638), Room 225, Block 19, Shek Kip Mei Estate, Kowloon, sells IYHF cards for HK$60. They can also give you a members handbook which shows the locations of the hostels and explains the regulations in excruciating detail, including that you can't bring guns or heroin into the hostel − just in case you weren't sure. Their office is inconveniently located in a hideous housing estate near the Shek Kip Mei MTR Station.

The hostels charge HK$25 a night for a dormitory bed, which is by far the cheapest place to sleep in Hong Kong. The hostels close between 10 am and 4 pm, and it's lights out at 11 pm. Similar to youth hostels in other countries, you are required to use a special IYHF sleeping sheet (you can buy or rent these at the hostels) and you must do a few simple cleaning chores. Advance booking is required for some hostels and this can be done by either writing, telephoning or going to the head office.

Guesthouses This is where most budget travellers wind up staying. They are most numerous in dilapidated buildings in the Tsmishatsui area or in some parts of Hong Kong Island. Expect to pay around HK$40 for a dormitory bed. They often have private rooms too, which range in price from HK$100 up to HK$300 depending on the standard of accommodation. Usually, two people can share a room for little or no extra cost.

One thing to be cautious about are touts who hang around the bus stop at the airport and offer cheap rooms. Sometimes they really do have good, cheap rooms, but you can't be sure until you actually see it. The problem is that if you go with them, see the room and decide that you don't like it, you might be faced with demands to pay HK$50 or more 'service charge' for the trouble they took to guide you from the airport. To avoid this problem, make it clear before you even get on the bus that you won't pay them anything if the room is not to your liking.

Hotels Mid-range hotels start at around HK$350 and go up to around HK$650. There are plenty of hotels in this range, including the YMCA.

You can get as much as a 40% discount at mid-range and luxury hotels if you book through certain travel agencies. One agency offering this service is Traveller Services (☎ 3674127, fax 3110387), 7th floor, 57 Peking Rd, Tsimshatsui.

Luxury hotels are easy to find in Hong Kong. The HKTA's Hotel Guide lists all the main places. If you haven't made a reservation, you might as well use the HKTA booking office at Kai Tak Airport to make sure you have a room and don't have to drag your luggage around in a long, frustrating search.

You can be reasonably sure that any luxury hotel has whatever you need. About the only thing you need to consider is whether or not you like the location.

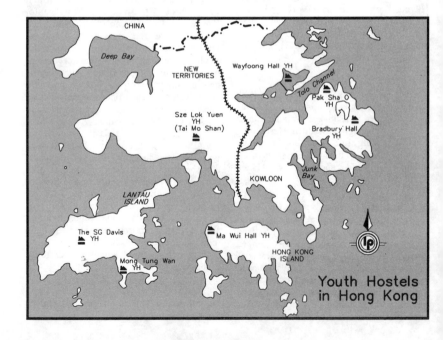

Youth Hostels in Hong Kong

Tsimshatsui East is the newest and most modern area and fairly close to the airport. Nearby Tsimshatsui is OK but older and a bit more tattered. On the Hong Kong Island side, there are several big hotels in the heart of Central (such as the Hilton) and a lot more further east in Wanchai and Causeway Bay.

If you stay in any proper hotels you will find a 10% service charge and a 5% government tax added to your bill, but you won't be troubled with either in the cheap places.

Rentals A long stay basically means a month or more. Many hotels offer big discounts for monthly rentals.

Not to be overlooked are the hotels on Lamma, Cheung Chau and Lantau islands – many of these are amazingly cheap if rented by the month, but very expensive for short-term stays. There are also flats and small houses available for rent on these islands. Cheung Chau has the largest community of expatriates in the outlying islands, but Lamma comes a close second. Lantau Island has a large expatriate community at Discovery Bay, connected to Central by hoverferry. Typical rent in the outlying islands is around HK$3000 for a flat. Equivalent accommodation in Kowloon or Hong Kong Island would cost around HK$7000.

The most expensive areas to live on Hong Kong Island are the Mid-Levels, the Peak, and the south side of the island, particularly Stanley. Rents in all these areas are nothing short of outrageous. Many Westerners who can afford such accommodation don't pay for it – their company does.

Some Westerners have moved out to the New Territories towards Tuen Mun, Shatin and Tsuen Wan. The problem here is commuting. Rush-hour traffic in Hong Kong grinds to a halt, but it's tolerable if you take the MTR, KCR or a ferry. Nevertheless, expect all forms of public transport to be packed during rush hour.

An important factor in determining the cost of rent is the age of a building. Usually the younger the apartment block the higher the rents. Since even moderate Hong Kong rents are still high by international standards, most single people share flats.

One little trick that many gwailos have discovered is that practically all Chinese have a strong fear of anything associated with death. Consequently, apartments with views overlooking cemeteries are always cheaper and almost always rented by foreigners.

Flats are generally rented exclusive of rates and unfurnished. However, you can easily find inexpensive rattan and bamboo furnishings.

If you are stuck for accommodation, 'leave' flats are worth investigating. Employees on contract are rewarded every couple of years with long holidays and usually rent their flats out while they are away. The usual duration is three months, during which time you are responsible for the rent and the wages of the amah (servant). Occasionally, people even offer the flat rent-free with just the amah's wages to pay, in order to have someone keep an eye on the place. Nice work if you can get it. Leave flats are listed under a separate heading in the classified advertisements of the *South China Morning Post*.

The best place to look for flats is in the classified sections of the *South China Morning Post* or the *Hong Kong Standard*, the two morning papers. Having a Chinese person to check the Chinese-language newspapers can be a tremendous help.

Then of course there are the real estate agents. Look in the Yellow Pages Buying Guide under Estate Agents.

If you're lucky enough to be moving to Hong Kong on contract you'll probably have your hotel room paid for you while you flat-hunt. That's the custom in Hong Kong and if that isn't in your contract then you haven't negotiated very well.

Residential burglaries are a problem in Hong Kong, so keep security in mind. A steel door helps and many places have bars on the windows. Change the locks when you move in. A building with security guards is best, but this is a luxury you have to pay for.

FOOD

Hong Kongers will tell you that their city has the best food in the world, an assertion you may wind up agreeing with if you visit some of Hong Kong's better restaurants.

Unfortunately, eating well in Hong Kong is no longer cheap, although with effort you can still get a good Chinese meal for a few dollars. A lot depends on the surroundings. If you're willing to eat from pushcarts and street stalls, you can save a bundle. In Hong Kong's seated restaurants you'll find that Chinese food isn't much cheaper than Western food, mainly because a high proportion of the price of a restaurant meal goes to pay for the space occupied by the customer's bottom.

Even though Hong Kong is justly famous for its Chinese food, a lot of travellers find themselves eating a lot more Big Macs than they originally intended. Cost is one reason, as fast food is significantly cheaper than a good Chinese meal. Another reason is that after a few months in Asia many Western travellers find that they can't stand the sight of one more noodle.

The strangest explanation (also truthful) for eating fast food concerns the attitude of the restaurants. Most Chinese restaurants only list Western food in the English menu and list Chinese food in Chinese only. Unable to decipher the Chinese menu, frustrated travellers turn to the English menu and end up eating hot dogs and spaghetti, while the Chinese at adjacent tables feast on Peking duck, egg rolls and steamed dumplings.

Finding top-notch Chinese restaurants is easy, but if you're on a budget it's worthwhile exploring the *dai pai dongs*, the cheap street stalls from which you can buy excellent food for just a few dollars. There are no menus to struggle with, so just point to what you want.

Several good books on eating out in Hong Kong are available at any of the English-language bookstores. The *South China Morning Post* publishes the *Post Guide to Hong Kong Restaurants*, and there is also *The Best of Hong Kong & Macau* by Harry Rolnick. The trouble with such books is that they date very quickly. Listed places go bust or are under new management (with a consequent deterioration in service) and new places open all the time.

The HKTA's *Official Guide to Shopping, Eating Out and Services* in Hong Kong is updated annually and is free. Ask at any HKTA office for a copy. The association also has a free pamphlet called *Gourmet Dining in Hong Kong*, and it will sell you a copy of the *Visitors' Guide to Chinese Food in Hong Kong*, which lists many dishes with both English names and Chinese characters.

Chinese Cooking

Over many centuries the Chinese have perfected their own unique style of cooking which they regard as a fine art. Being a large country, China can be divided into many geographical areas, each with its own style of cooking, and the ingredients used tend to reflect what is available in that region.

For example, northern China is suitable for raising wheat, so noodles, dumplings and other wheat-based dishes are most common. In the south, where the climate is warm and wet, rice dominates as the basic staple. Coastal areas are where seafood is best. The Sichuan area, where spices grow well, is famous for fiery hot dishes.

However, it is not only geography that determines which ingredients are used. Tradition and culture play a part. The Cantonese, the least squeamish among the Chinese, are known for their ability to eat virtually anything. While most Chinese would never think of eating a dog, you'll find dogs, cats and rats on the menu in Canton.

In Hong Kong, the government doesn't permit eating what Westerners regard as pets, but this just drives many Hong Kongers across the border on weekends in search of a good meal. Most Westerners won't admit it publicly, but many who live in Hong Kong also join the weekend dog-eating expeditions to Canton. There are some illegal dog-meat restaurants in the New Territories, but these understandably maintain a low profile and you'll need the assistance of a local resident to find them.

While you won't find German shepherd or French poodle being served up in Hong Kong, there are plenty of other delicacies made with more mundane ingredients like pork, duck and fish. If you don't eat meat you can still survive.

Etiquette

Chinese meals are social events. Typically, four or five people eat together at the same table. The idea is to order many dishes (at least one dish per person) and then share. The Chinese think nothing of sticking their chopsticks right into the communal dish. This is one reason why hepatitis is still rampant in Hong Kong (even worse in China). You may prefer to use a serving spoon.

Apart from the communal dishes, everyone gets an individual bowl of rice or small soup bowl. Proper etiquette demands that you hold the bowl near your lips and shovel the contents into your mouth with chopsticks (or a spoon for soup).

As an alternative to holding the bowl up to your mouth, place a spoon in your left hand and the chopsticks in the right, then push the food on to the spoon. Then use the spoon as you normally would. Chinese food is never eaten with a knife or fork.

If the food contains bones, spit them out on to the tablecloth or, if you want to be extra polite, into a separate bowl (most people use the tablecloth). You needn't use a napkin (serviette) to hide the spitting out of bones. As you'll discover, Chinese people generally leave a big mess when they finish eating. Restaurants know this and are prepared – they change the tablecloth after each customer leaves.

Soup is usually eaten at the end of a meal, rather than at the beginning as Westerners do. The Chinese only occasionally eat dessert – fruit is preferred. Men often smoke after meals. This is almost entirely a male activity as practically no Chinese women smoke, at least not in public.

The 'bill' in Chinese is *mai dan*. You can expect a big fight over who pays the bill – not that people want to avoid paying, just the opposite. Everybody tries to pay for every-

one else. It's an amusing scene – each person insisting that they should pay while trying to stuff money into the hands of the bewildered waitress.

Chopsticks

If you're planning a trip to Hong Kong or China, you'd be wise to practise with chopsticks before you leave home. You know you're becoming proficient when you can pick up a peanut and deliver it to your mouth without dropping it. Hold the chopsticks between the thumb and the forefinger, resting them on the index finger, and move them up and down like pincers. The illustration may help.

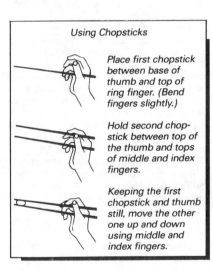

Using Chopsticks

Place first chopstick between base of thumb and top of ring finger. (Bend fingers slightly.)

Hold second chopstick between top of the thumb and tops of middle and index fingers.

Keeping the first chopstick and thumb still, move the other one up and down using middle and index fingers.

Sauces & Spices

It's not unusual for a meal to be served with small dishes filled with various sauces. The most popular with Cantonese food is hot mustard sauce. If they don't put it on the table, you can ask for it.

I've never seen salt shakers in a Chinese restaurant unless they also served Western food, but they sometimes have pepper. Often you will find several small bottles on the table containing soy sauce, vinegar and sesame oil. Most Westerners like the soy sauce, but the vinegar and sesame oil is definitely an acquired taste. The Chinese often mix all three together. The vinegar, usually a very dark colour, is easily confused with the soy sauce, so taste some first before dumping it on your food. Actually, the Chinese don't dump sauces on their food, but prefer to pour some into a separate dish and dip the food into it.

Banquets

The Chinese love banquets and look for any opportunity to have one. Weddings are the most obvious occasions to warrant a feast, but banquets can be held almost anytime, even for funerals.

You might find yourself invited to a banquet if you do business in Hong Kong or if a friend gets married. You'd be well advised not to eat anything all day before the banquet. When the banquet begins, you may at first be disappointed – it will seem as if there isn't enough food on the table. Nevertheless, eat slowly to avoid feeling satisfied because one course will follow another. You will often be urged to eat more and more no matter how full you are. About 10 to 12 courses is considered normal at a banquet.

The host will often apologise that the magnificent food is 'so poor' and that 'there is not enough'. You are not supposed to agree! The correct response is to say: 'Oh, the food is wonderful, the best I ever had' (even if it's lousy).

There is plenty of toasting between courses. The host raises a glass and says *gam bei* (literally 'dry glass') which basically means 'bottoms up!'. You do not have to empty your glass, just take small sips, especially since Chinese liquor is powerful. Some people who can't handle strong alcohol fill their glass with tea instead. However, you definitely must go along with the toast – it would be most rude to sit and not drink something when a toast is made.

Dim Sum

One of the big rewards of coming to Hong Kong is the opportunity to indulge in a dim sum binge. Dim sum is a uniquely Cantonese dish served only for breakfast or lunch, but never dinner. The term dim sum means a snack. If the characters are translated literally, dim sum means 'to touch the heart'. The act of eating dim sum is usually referred to as yum cha, which literally means 'to drink tea', since this is always served with dim sum meals.

Eating dim sum is a social occasion and something you should do in a group. If you're travelling by yourself, try to round up three or four other travellers for a dim sum lunch. Of course, you can eat dim sum by yourself, but the problem is that dim sum consists of many separate dishes which are meant to be shared. You can't simply order a plate of dim sum. Having several people to share with you means you can try many different dishes.

Dim sum delicacies are normally steamed in a small bamboo basket. Typically, each basket contains four identical pieces, so four people would be an ideal number for a dim sum meal. You pay by the number of baskets

---

Rice

The Chinese don't ask 'Have you eaten yet?'. Instead they say 'Have you eaten rice yet?'. Rice is an inseparable part of Chinese culture – the key to survival in their long history.

Among older, more conservative Chinese, wasting rice is practically a sin. Leaving half a bowl of uneaten rice is most improper. Don't order more rice than you can eat, and eat what you do order. They'd rather you waste the Peking duck than waste the rice, despite rice being much cheaper.

At banquets, eat little or no rice. Rice at banquets is considered a filler, and if you're eating a 12-course meal you'll soon become too full with seven courses yet to come. ∎

you order. The baskets are stacked up on pushcarts and rolled around the dining room.

You don't need a menu, just stop the waiter or waitress and choose something from the cart, and it will be marked down on your bill. Don't try to order everything at once. Each pushcart has a different selection, so take your time and order many different dishes from different carts. It's estimated that there are about 1000 dim sum dishes. Usually dim sum is not expensive – HK\$25 per person is about average for a good meal.

Dim sum restaurants are normally brightly lit and very large, rather like eating in an aircraft hanger. Nevertheless, it can get very crowded, especially at lunch time.

The restaurants normally open about 7.30 am and close about 3 pm. Arriving after lunch is probably not a good idea as the best food will be gone. Experienced dim sum connoisseurs say late morning, at 10.30 am or 11 am, is the ideal time to arrive. Since dim sum restaurants can get very crowded at the noon rush hour, especially on Sunday and holidays, a reservation is advisable. In the evening, when dim sum is no longer served, these restaurants often become nightclubs.

The HKTA produces a useful small book called *Guide to Dim Sum Delights in Hong Kong* which costs HK\$5. It has a colour photo of each dish and shows the name in English, romanised Chinese and in Chinese characters.

Cooking Styles

Each province of China has its own style of cooking. Not surprisingly, in Hong Kong Cantonese food dominates. Also popular are Chaozhou (Chiu Chow), Hakka, Beijing (Peking), Shanghai and Sichuan (Szechuan) food.

Beijing (Peking) & Shandong These cooking styles, which come from one of the coldest parts of China, use heaps of spices to warm the body. Bread and noodles are often used instead of rice. The chief speciality is Peking duck, of which the crisp skin is the prized part.

Another popular dish, beggar's chicken, is supposedly created by a beggar who stole the emperor's chicken and then had to bury it in the ground to cook it. The chicken is stuffed with mushrooms, pickled Chinese cabbage, herbs and onions, then wrapped in lotus leaves, sealed in clay and baked all day in hot ashes.

Another speciality is a Mongolian barbecue – assorted barbecued meats and vegetables mixed in a hotpot.

Cantonese This is southern Chinese cooking with lots of steaming, pot boiling and stir frying. Cantonese is the most widely eaten Chinese food in Hong Kong. It also uses the least amount of oil. It's lightly cooked and not as highly spiced as the other main styles. It includes lots of vegetables, roast pork, chicken, steamed fish and fried rice. *Congee* is a thick Cantonese rice porridge that most Westerners find tasteless.

Specialities are abalone, shark's fin soup (very expensive), roast pig and a snake dish known as Dragon's Duel Tiger which is a combination of wild cat and snake meat. Pigeon is a Cantonese speciality served in various ways, including with lemon or oyster sauce, but the gourmet's delight is plain roast. Since the Cantonese live next to the sea and Hong Kong is surrounded by water there's also plenty of seafood.

Incidentally, you do not find fortune cookies in Cantonese or any other real Chinese cuisine. They are a foreign invention. Thousand-year-old (also known as 100-year-old) eggs are a Cantonese speciality – these are duck eggs soaked in a chemical solution for several days and not a thousand years. This turns the white of the egg green and the yolk a greenish-black. In the old days, these eggs were made by soaking them in horse urine. Most Westerners say these eggs smell and taste like ammonia.

Chaozhou (Chiu Chow) This is a Han-Chinese ethnic group which used to earn a living from the sea and had homes around the port of Shantou in south-eastern China. Now the group has spread throughout South-

East Asia. Chaozhou cooking uses many different sauces and is inclined to be a bit oily. Garlic and vinegar sauce are favourites. Seafood figures prominently, especially steamed lobster, deep-fried shrimp balls, crab-meat balls and steamed eel. Since it's been influenced by Cantonese cooking, vegetables are used abundantly. Goose and duck are other Chaozhou specialities.

Chaozhou meals start and finish with a small cup of a dark, bitter tea known as Iron Buddha — one to get the stomach ready, the other to calm it down. It's a type of *oolong* tea and is thought to aid digestion. It's also known as the Iron Goddess of Mercy or *Tit Kwun Yum*.

Hakka This cuisine is a mixture of Cantonese and Shanghai styles and was developed by the Hakka peasants who have been farming the New Territories since long before Queen Victoria's day. The Hakka were originally northern Chinese who migrated south over the centuries, hence the amalgam of styles in their cooking.

Their efforts to use every part of the animal result in such delicacies as chicken-blood soup and braised fish lips. Stuffed duck (deboned through the neck and stuffed with rice, lotus seeds and chopped meat) is a Hakka speciality.

Shanghai This cuisine uses lots of chilli and spices, and is heavier and oilier than either Beijing or Cantonese food. Given the fact that Shanghai is a main port, it's not surprising that seafood plays an important role. Eels are popular, as is drunken chicken — the bird is cooked in *shaoshing*, a potent Chinese wine which tastes a bit like warm sherry. Also try the cold meat-and-sauce dishes, ham-and-melon soup, bean curd with brown sauce, braised meatballs, deep-fried chicken and pork ribs with salt and pepper.

The big speciality of Shanghai food is the strange, hairy crab which arrives in September or October and keeps the gourmets happy for three months or so. The crabs are eaten for the roes and are beyond the price of most shoestring travellers.

Sichuan (Szechuan) This, the hottest of the categories, is characterised by the heavy use of spices and peppers. The *mapo dofou*, or spicy bean curd, is a Sichuan classic. Other specialities include frogs' legs, smoked duck, shrimps with salt and garlic, dried chilli beef, bears' paws braised in brown sauce and fish in spicy bean sauce. Sichuan food also features noodles and beautiful, warm bread.

Vegetarian Hong Kong is a good place for vegetarian Chinese food. Even if you are not a vegetarian it is worth giving one of the excellent vegetarian restaurants a try.

Vegetarian food is based on soybean curd (tofu) — but the Chinese do some miraculous things with it. 'Fish' can be made by layering pieces of dried bean curd or can be fashioned from mashed taro root. Not only do they make it taste like any food you could think of, they make it look like it as well. *Lo lun chai* is a delicious mixed vegetable dish, a meal in itself. Try also the noodle and bean-curd dishes, congee, fried spring rolls, sweet-and-sour and sweet corn soup.

Other Asian Food Many Asian people apart from Chinese live in Hong Kong and many of them have found it profitable to go into the restaurant business. The cosmopolitan atmosphere assures you of plenty of ethnic food from various countries in the region. Indian restaurants are particularly abundant and you won't have trouble finding just about any Asian cuisine, from Korean *bulgogi* (barbecue) and *kimchi* (a spiced and fermented cabbage dish) to an Indonesian *satay* (kebabs with peanut sauce) or *gado gado* (salad with prawn crackers and peanut sauce).

Japanese food is never cheap. A Japanese meal will cost at least double what you'd spend for a similar level of service in a Chinese restaurant. It is interesting to speculate why. A lot of Japanese come to Hong Kong, and since they are used to paying exorbitant prices anyway, perhaps local restaurateurs want to make them feel at home.

When eating Japanese food, take a credit card or a suitcase full of cash!

The flood of refugees from Vietnam is a tragic episode, and new arrivals continue to place an unwanted responsibility on Hong Kong. However, thousands of the refugees, especially those who came earlier, have obtained legal residence status and operate the many excellent Vietnamese restaurants throughout Hong Kong.

Western Hong Kong is a cosmopolitan city and you can expect some of the best that the West has to offer. French, Italian, Mexican or whatever you desire will probably be available, but prices will be high. Expect to pay considerably more than you would for a good Chinese meal.

Fast Food No matter what negative feelings you might have about fast food, after two months or more in China, the sight of rice and noodles becomes intolerable for many travellers, who find themselves dreaming of milkshakes and French fries.

If you were expecting to find McDonald's and other fast-food chains in Hong Kong chock full of Westerners, then you're in for a surprise. Most of the customers are Chinese. The Chinese attach no stigma to eating fast food. On the contrary, McDonald's and Kentucky Fried enjoy a prestigious reputation in the Orient. Hanging out at McDonald's is considered chic.

The Chinese have their own versions of fast food, some of which isn't bad at all.

DRINKS
Tea
You can drink as much tea as you like free of charge in any Chinese restaurant. On the other hand, coffee is seldom available except in Western restaurants or coffee shops, and is never free.

When your teapot is empty and you would like a refill, signal this by taking the lid off the pot. To thank the waiter or waitress for pouring your tea, tap your fingers on the table. You needn't say thank you. The finger-tapping is only done for tea, not for when food is brought.

There are three main types of tea: green or unfermented; *bolay* or fermented, also known as black tea; and *oolong*, which is semi-fermented. There are many varieties of tea. Jasmine tea *(heung ping)* is a blend of tea and flowers which is always drunk straight, without milk or sugar. Most of the tea is imported from China, but some comes from India and Sri Lanka. Hong Kong has only one tea plantation (at Ngong Ping on Lantau Island) which is basically a tourist attraction.

Alcohol
In free market Hong Kong, you can easily find most major brands of imported alcohol. Excellent beer is available everywhere, and San Miguel even has a brewery in Hong Kong. However, alcohol is heavily taxed and therefore not really cheap.

What the Chinese generally call wine is not really wine at all – it's hard liquor, more like whisky or rum. Many of these wines are brewed from grains like rice, sorghum and millet. To the Western palate, they more closely resemble petrol. *Siu hing* is a rice-based wine, the fiery *go leung* is distilled from sorghum and *mao tai* is made from millet. More closely resembling wine is *ng ka pay* which has a sweet taste and is made with herbs. The Chinese seldom dilute their alcohol – they drink it just as it comes from the bottle.

You may have an opportunity to see the finger game, a type of drinking game in which the loser is obliged to empty his glass ('his' is appropriate as women seldom play).

Happy Hour Obviously, if you enjoy drinking, the cheapest way to do it is to get a bottle of Chinese rice wine, preferably in a brown paper sack, and sit in Kowloon Park to finish it off. If you prefer a more cheerful atmosphere, there is another low-cost option. During certain hours of the day, several bars, discos and nightclubs give substantial discounts on drinks. Some places give you drinks for half-price during happy hour, while others let you buy one drink and give you the second one free. Usually, happy hour is in the late afternoon or early evening. If you enter a bar during happy hour, make note of the time when it ends. Otherwise, you may linger too long and wind up paying more than you expected.

ENTERTAINMENT

In Hong Kong, you get what you pay for. This applies as much to entertainment as it does to shopping. Outside of sitting around Chungking Mansions and smashing cockroaches with a rolled up newspaper, most forms of amusement require money.

Fortunately, if your needs are simple, it doesn't have to cost a lot. You can get at least a few hours of free or almost free nightlife by exploring the street stalls, the dai pai dongs, which are usually bustling with activity from about 8 to 11 pm. There are plenty of cheap snacks from pushcarts for about HK$2, and occasionally you will be entertained by a Cantonese opera performing on a makeshift stage in the street.

Harbour cruises can be taken day or night, but these are not cheap. See the Tours section in the Getting Around chapter.

The Saturday and Sunday English-language newspapers usually have a weekend entertainment insert which lists nightspots. Also have a look at the *Dining and Nightlife* pamphlet published by the HKTA. The pamphlet only gives you a vague idea of what a place is like, but it lists many with a telephone number, address and operating hours.

Pubs Since British influence has been substantial in Hong Kong, it's not surprising that British-style pubs are plentiful, especially in the tourist areas. Often the owners are British or Australian, and you can expect authentic decor, meat pies, darts and sometimes Aussie bush bands. Overall, Tsimshatsui is best for pubs, but there are plenty on the Hong Kong Island side too.

Girlie Bars How does it feel to be legally mugged in Hong Kong? Anyone can find out just by visiting one of the many sleazy-

looking topless bars along Peking Rd (and adjacent streets) in Tsimshatsui.

Be wary of places where an aggressive tout, sometimes female, stands at the front door, grabs your arm and tries to push, pull and persuade you to go inside. The tout is usually saying: 'Take a look, take a look'.

Very likely there will be signs on the front door promising 'Drinks Only HK$25' and naughty pictures to stimulate interest. If you go inside, you can expect the following:

A cocktail waitress, usually topless and often wearing nothing but knickers, will serve you a drink. She will probably be friendly and chat for a few minutes. It will be one of the most expensive conversations of your life, because after a pleasant five-minute chat you will be presented with a bill for about HK$400.

When you protest, they will undoubtedly point to the tiny sign 'prominently' posted on the wall behind a vase which informs you of the HK$400 service charge for talking to the waitress. If you balk at paying this fee, don't be surprised if two muscular thugs suddenly happen to be standing by your elbows. Rumour has it that these heavies are connected with Hong Kong's notorious Triads. The bars accept travellers' cheques.

If you really want to be waited on by almost-naked women you should realise that it will cost you. Don't think that you can quietly sit in the back of the room, sip their beer and get out for HK$25. That just doesn't happen (unless you're a card-carrying member of the Triads).

For those who have money to burn, many places will let customers 'buy the girl out' and have her as an escort for the rest of the evening. This does not necessarily imply anything sexual. Typically this costs about HK$1000.

If the customer would like the escort to perform any additional recreational services, the price is by negotiation. The bar is not involved. I have it on good information (not personal experience) that HK$2000 is the minimum charge. And in this era of the AIDS epidemic, you may get even more than you paid for.

Karaoke Not many foreigners get into this, but the Chinese love it. The word *karaoke* ('empty orchestra') was borrowed from Japanese. Basically, members of the audience take turns singing, while the background music and words are supplied by a video. Most of the songs are in Chinese, but they have English too. The Chinese love singing and if you visit a karaoke bar you will certainly be asked to perform. No matter how badly you sing, you will undoubtedly receive polite applause. If your singing is truly awful, however, for the sake of international relations don't subject the audience to more than one song.

Cinema Hong Kong produces many of its own films, many of which have English subtitles even though the sound track is in Cantonese or Mandarin. Hong Kong is especially famous for kung fu epics such as the Bruce Lee series. Unfortunately, Bruce Lee has died and a lot of what is produced now doesn't come up to the high standards he set. Some other stars, like Jackie Chan, have tried to take his place, but no one has yet managed to make their films so realistic-looking.

Most of the present crop of kung fu films depict super heroes with supernatural abilities who fly through the air, jump over buildings and heal dying people with 10 seconds of *qigong* (kung fu meditation).

Nevertheless, Hong Kong does occasionally come up with a good local film, often a drama from Chinese history or a heartbreaking love story. Hong Kong's leading movie companies are Shaw Brothers (with their huge Movietown studios on Clearwater Bay Rd in the New Territories) and Golden Harvest, which started the Bruce Lee series. Hong Kong films are exported to overseas Chinese communities all over the world, and many are shown in Taiwan and China too.

Western films are very popular, particularly violent US movies featuring psycho pathic killers. Most major Western films will play in Hong Kong, but it is never certain that you will see the whole movie. There is a tendency to cut movies, in part because Hong Kong does have a mild form of film censorship, but largely because cinema owners find it more profitable to shorten the films to get one or two extra showings a day (plus a few advertisements).

Young people in Hong Kong are crazy about the movies. Theatres tend to be jam packed and it is often necessary to buy your ticket a day in advance if you want a seat. Your ticket will have an assigned seat number and you are expected to sit only there. Choose where you want to sit when you buy your ticket. Of course, all the good seats sell quickly. Ticket prices are between HK$23 and HK$33.

To find out what's on at the cinemas, look in the *South China Morning Post* or the *Hong Kong Standard* which list English-language movies, show times and telephone numbers. Unfortunately, no addresses are listed. In fact, the papers give no clue as to what part of town the theatre is in.

Video Game Arcades If you have an urge to test your skills at Space Invaders or Martian Masher, check out one of the ubiquitous video arcades.

Mahjong If you walk down the side streets of Hong Kong, sooner or later you are bound to hear the rattle of mahjong pieces. Mahjong is so popular in Hong Kong that there are licensed mahjong centres where you can meet other players and gamble all day. Hong Kong is a good place to play mahjong, but you should realise that there is a lot of local talent and that you'll be up against the pros. If you want to visit a mahjong centre, get a Chinese person to take you.

Illegal Gambling There are plenty of illegal private poker matches in Hong Kong. The real hard-core gambling addicts attend dog fights and (I kid you not) cricket fights.

Concerts, Culture & Events Pick up the *South China Morning Post* and look in the index for the Arts page. This is where you'll find a daily section called 'What's on Today' which gives a good rundown on art exhibitions, film festivals, opera, meetings, concerts, beauty pageants, lion dances and so on. The Saturday edition of the *Hong Kong*

Standard has a special insert called 'Buzz' which lists everything of entertainment value happening in Hong Kong, including a subsection called Special Events which mentions cultural activities.

The HKTA, the Urban Council and the Arts Centre also have programmes, information about which can be obtained from the Arts Centre or HKTA offices.

The HKTA has a publication entitled *Culture* which includes a monthly schedule of events such as performances by Cantonese opera troupes, piano recitals, Fujianese puppet shows, Chinese folk singers and exhibits of Chinese watercolours.

For a calendar of main events during the year see the Cultural Events section earlier in this chapter.

To find out more about the avant-garde cultural scene, contact the Fringe Club (☎ 5217251), 2 Lower Albert Rd, Central, which should have the latest information on the annual Hong Kong Festival Fringe – a four-week event which includes everything from drama and dance to mime and street shows. The Fringe Club has a small theatre, painting studio, exhibition area, a bar and pottery workshop.

THINGS TO BUY

As the HKTA so proudly points out, Hong Kong is a shopper's paradise. Actually, prices are not as low as many tourists imagine. Imported goods like Japanese-made cameras and electronic gadgets can be bought for roughly the same price in many Western countries. What makes Hong Kong shine, however, is the variety – if you can't find it in Hong Kong, it probably doesn't exist. It's almost as if Hong Kong were one gigantic shopping mall.

That said, there are bargains to be had on locally manufactured products. Clothing, footwear and luggage are especially cheap in Hong Kong – maybe only one-quarter the price you would pay at home. Goods from the People's Republic are sometimes cheaper in Hong Kong than in China!

The HKTA is your best source of information. They publish a handy little booklet called *Shopping* with recommended shops that are HKTA members. They publish a number of special interest pamphlets such as the *Shopping Guide to Video Products* and *Shopping Guide to Jewellery*.

Duty Free

'Duty free' is just a slogan. Hong Kong is a duty-free port, and the only imported goods on which duty is paid are alcohol, tobacco, perfumes, cosmetics, cars and some petroleum products. Although many shops in Hong Kong display a big sign proclaiming 'Duty-Free Goods' there is little reason to bother with them as they cater mostly to a Japanese clientele who are already accustomed to being ripped off.

There is only one duty-free shop worth visiting in Hong Kong – the liquor and tobacco shop in Kai Tak Airport which you can find after passing through immigration and the security check (metal detectors). The other so-called duty-free shops in the check-in area of the airport are no different from the shops in downtown Hong Kong. Indeed, they are more expensive. So if you want to buy some duty-free cigarettes and liquor, you can do so a few minutes before you board your flight. Many airlines also sell duty-free liquor, tobacco and perfume on board the aircraft.

Guarantees

Be careful when buying in Hong Kong. There are too many cases of visitors being sold defective equipment. Many retailers won't honour warranties and there is quite a bit of pirating of brand names. Some dealers offer a local guarantee card and occasionally an international one for better brands of goods.

Every guarantee should carry a complete description of the item (including model and serial numbers) as well as the date of purchase, the name and address of the shop it was purchased from and the shop's official stamp.

A common practice is to sell grey-market equipment (ie imported by somebody other than the official local agent). Such equipment may have no guarantee even if it is an international brand name.

If you buy goods such as cameras and electronic equipment at discount prices, then make sure – if you really do need the latest model – that the model hasn't been superseded. Also find out whether the guarantee is affected by the discount. The agent or importer can tell you this. Contacting an agent is a good way of obtaining a detailed explanation of what each model actually does, rather than relying on the shopkeeper's advice. The HKTA *Shopping* guide has a list of sole agents and their phone numbers in the back of the pamphlet.

Always check prices in a few shops, take your time and return to a shop several times if necessary. Don't buy anything expensive in a hurry and always get a manufacturer's guarantee that is valid worldwide. When comparing prices, on cameras for example, make sure you're comparing not only the same camera body but also the same lenses and any other accessories.

Refunds & Exchanges

Many shops will exchange goods if they are defective, or in the case of clothing, if the garment simply doesn't fit. Be sure to keep receipts and go back to the store as soon as possible.

Forget about refunds. They are almost never given in Hong Kong. This applies to deposits as well as final payment. If you put a deposit on something, don't ever expect to see that money again.

Rip-Offs

Caveat emptor, or 'let the buyer beware', are words which should be securely embedded in your mind while shopping in Hong Kong, especially during that crucial moment when you hand over the cash.

Rip-offs do happen. While most shops are honest, there are plenty which are not. The longer you shop in Hong Kong, the more likely it is that you'll run into a shopkeeper who is nothing but a crook. It would be wise to learn how to recognise the techniques of rip-off artists in order to avoid them.

The HKTA recommends that you only shop in stores which display the HKTA membership sign. This sounds like great advice except that the vast majority of stores are not HKTA members. If you're going to purchase many expensive items, then perhaps it is worth seeking out HKTA members. Most shoppers will probably find this restriction too limiting.

The most common way to cheat tourists is to overcharge. In the tourist shopping districts of Tsimshatsui and Causeway Bay, you'll rarely find price tags on anything. Checking prices in several stores therefore becomes essential. However, shopkeepers know that tourists compare prices in several locations before buying, so they will often quote a reasonable price on a big ticket item, only to get the money back by overcharging on small items or accessories. You may be quoted a reasonable price on a camera, only to be gouged on the lens cap, neck strap and flash.

Some dishonest shopowners are even more sneaky. They sometimes remove vital components that should have been included free (like the connecting cords for the speakers on a stereo system) and demand more money when you return to the shop to get them.

You should be especially wary if they want to take the goods into the back room to 'box it up'. This provides ample opportunity to remove essential items that you have already paid for. The camera case, usually included free with most cameras, will often be sold as an accessory. Another tactic is to replace some of the good components with cheap or defective ones. Only later will you discover that the 'Nikon' lens turns out to be a cheap no-name brand. When it's time to put your equipment in the box, it's best if you do it yourself.

Another sneaky ploy is to knowingly sell defective merchandise. Your only safeguard is to inspect the equipment carefully before handing over the cash.

Also be alert for signs of wear and tear – the equipment could be secondhand. Whatever you do, insist on getting an itemised receipt. You should avoid handing over the cash until you have the goods in hand and they've written a receipt.

There is really no reason to put a deposit on anything unless it is being custom-made for you, like a fitted suit or a pair of eyeglasses. Some shops might ask for a deposit if you're ordering a very unusual item that they wouldn't normally stock, but this isn't a common practice.

Here are a few experiences of dissatisfied customers:

They took a deposit and demanded an extra $800 for the camera when I came for delivery...used abusive language and started fist fights.

I signed a receipt for a US$200 disc player. They had another receipt underneath the first one and produced a $30 record player when they went to put the disc player in a box. So I ended up with a $30 record player which cost $200 − and a receipt for a record player (switched!).

Couldn't be worse. They try to provoke you! To start a fight...

Getting Help

There isn't much you can do if a shop simply overcharges. On the other hand, if you discover that the goods are defective or something is missing, return to the shop immediately taking the goods and receipt with you. Sometimes it really is an honest mistake and they will clear the problem up at once. Honest shopkeepers will give you an exchange on defective goods or replace missing components. On the other hand, if the shop intentionally cheated you, expect a bitter argument.

If you feel that you were defrauded, don't expect any help from the police. There is an unfortunate lack of consumer protection in Hong Kong, though there are a few agencies that might be able to help you.

The first place to try is the HKTA (☎ 8017111) on the 35th floor of Jardine House, 1 Connaught Place, Central. If the shop is one of their members they can lean on them heavily. If not, they can at least advise you on who to contact for more help.

Another place to try is the Hong Kong Consumer Council (☎ 7363322) main office in China Hong Kong City, Canton Rd, Tsimshatsui, Kowloon. It has a complaints and advice hot line (☎ 7363636) and an Advice Centre (☎ 5411422) at 38 Pier Rd, Central, near the Outlying Islands Ferry Pier.

As a last desperate measure, you can take matters into your own hands. By this I don't mean you should punch the shopkeeper, which might help you feel better but is illegal. It is entirely legal to stand outside the shop and tell others about your experience. Some pickets have successfully gotten back their money after driving away other customers. However, this can be an exhausting way to spend your time in Hong Kong and results are by no means guaranteed.

Fake Goods

Watch out for counterfeit brand goods. Fake labels on clothes is the most obvious example, but there are fake Rolex watches, fake Gucci leather goods, fake herbal medicines and even some fake electronics. Obviously, there's more risk buying electronic goods than buying clothes or luggage.

Fortunately, Hong Kong's customs agents have been cracking down hard on the fake electronics and cameras. One customs agent assured me that they had solved the problem of counterfeit Walkmans. If you discover that you've been sold a fake brand-name watch or electronic item, it would be worth your while to contact the police or customs as this is definitely illegal.

Beware of factory rejects. Antiques and jewellery are also problem areas.

Shipping Goods

Goods can be sent home by post, and some stores will package and post the goods for you, but events are usually more certain when you do it yourself. If you take the goods out of Hong Kong in your luggage, you should be warned that Kai Tak Airport is strict about size and weight limitations. The price for overweight baggage can be high − sometimes 1% of the 1st-class air fare for each kg.

You don't necessarily have to ship goods by post. United Parcel Service (UPS) offers services from Hong Kong to 40 other countries. It ships by air and accepts parcels weighing up to 30 kg. UPS (☎ 7353535) has an office in the World Finance Centre, Canton Rd, Tsimshatsui.

In Hong Kong, there are many shipping companies that transport larger items by sea freight. One of the biggest is Orient Consolidation Service (☎ 3687206), 13th floor, Albion Plaza, 2-6 Granville Rd, Tsimshatsui. Many others are listed in the Yellow Pages Commercial & Industrial Guide under Freight Forwarding or Freight Consolidating.

If you want to ship heavier goods by air, there are many air cargo companies. Most have offices at Kai Tak Airport. Among the better known companies are Jacky Maeder (☎ 7159611) and DHL (☎ 7658111).

Shopping Hours

There are no hard and fast shopping hours in Hong Kong, but generally, shops in the four main shopping areas are open as follows: Central and Western districts from 10 am to 6 pm; Causeway Bay and Wanchai from 10 am to 10 pm; Tsimshatsui, Yaumati and Mongkok from 10 am to 9 pm; and Tsimshatsui East from 10 am to 7.30 pm. Causeway Bay is the best part of town for late-night shopping.

Most shops are open seven days a week, although a few of the larger department stores are closed on Sunday. Some of the Japanese department stores are open Sunday and are closed on a given weekday. Street markets are open every day and well into the night (with the exception of the Jade Market in Kowloon which is open from 10 am to 3.30 pm). Almost everything closes for two or three days during the Chinese New Year holiday period.

Cheapest Places to Shop

Nontourist Shopping Malls If you really want to get a good price with a minimum of bargaining, hassling and dealing with rude shop owners, do yourself a favour and get away from the whole Tsimshatsui tourist scene. There are several large shopping malls where local Hong Kong residents buy goods. You will find price tags on almost every item and bargaining is unnecessary. Prices are cheaper outside the tourist zone simply because rents are so much lower – the savings in rent gets passed down to the customer.

One of the most accessible shopping malls is Cityplaza on Hong Kong Island. Take the MTR to Tai Koo Station. The exit from the MTR takes you into Cityplaza.

One of the most impressive shopping malls in Hong Kong is the Shatin New Town Plaza in the New Territories. Take the MTR to Kowloon Tong Station, then transfer to the Kowloon-Canton Railway (KCR) and get off at Shatin Station. From there you can walk right into the mall. If you need some exercise, bring along your swimsuit because the mall has one of the largest indoor swimming pools in Hong Kong.

With a little more effort, you can visit the Tuen Mun Town Plaza in the north-west part of the New Territories. The fastest way to get there is to take the hoverferry to Tuen Mun (30 minutes) from Central. Catch the hoverferry from Blake Pier, west of the Star Ferry Pier. When you arrive at the Tuen Mun Ferry Pier, take the Light Rail Transit (LRT) to the town centre. The shopping mall is three buildings interconnected by ramps. This is Hong Kong's largest shopping centre and, it is claimed, the largest in Asia.

Although there are no shopping malls as such, Mongkok in Kowloon is an excellent neighbourhood to buy almost anything. The shops spread out in every direction from Nathan Rd near Mongkok MTR Station.

Street Markets The reason why Hong Kong women look so chic despite the fact that many of them receive peasant wages is that it is possible to buy just about anything in the street markets and clothing alleys.

They can be found at Temple St in Yaumati and Tung Choi St in Mongkok. These sell clothes, cassettes, watches, ballpoint pens with built-in digital clocks, radios, knives, cheap jewellery, naughty postcards, potions, lotions and false teeth, among hundreds of other items.

Street markets and alleys have cheaper prices than the shops, but because of the largely Chinese clientele clothes sizes are mainly small. To complicate matters, you can't try on garments such as trousers before you buy. You're also taking a chance on quality. Most of the time you can ignore monograms as Hong Kong is monogram mad and makes excellent reproductions of fashion luggage, handbags and clothes as well as copies of labels.

Factory Outlets The best luck I had with clothes was at Leighton Textiles Company Ltd (☎ 7465349), 868 Cheung Sha Wan Rd, Laichikok. Take the MTR to Laichikok. Leighton Textiles is on the ground floor across the street from the station. Be fore-warned that this is not a glamorous neighbourhood – it's mostly factories and warehouses.

Always check purchases carefully for defects as factory outlets rarely give refunds or exchanges. Some will accept credit cards, but most won't. If they do accept credit cards, they'll often offer a discount if you pay cash, so be sure to ask.

If you're going to spend some time hunting down factory outlets, it's essential that you get the *Complete Guide to Hong Kong Factory Bargains* by Dana Goetz, widely available from bookstores throughout Hong Kong. The book gives a thorough rundown on what's available and where to find it.

A wide range of goods is available from factory outlets, such as jewellery, carpets, camphorwood chests, leatherware, silks, shoes, handbags, ceramics and imitation antique pieces.

What to Buy

Custom-Made Clothes Tailors exist in profusion. There are plenty of listings in the Yellow Pages Buying Guide. Some require that you buy their material, while others will let you bring your own. The more time you

give the tailor, the more fittings you will have and the better the outcome is likely to be.

Jade Watch out for jade fakes. The deep-green colour associated with some jade pieces can be achieved with a dye pot, as can the white, green, red, lavender and brown of other pieces. Green soapstone and plastic can be passed off as jade too.

Most so-called Chinese jade sold in Hong Kong comes from South Africa, New Zealand, Australia and the USA. One trick of jade merchants is to sell a supposedly solid piece of jade jewellery which is actually a thin slice of jade backed by green glue and quartz.

It is said that the test for jade is to try scratching it with a steel blade – real jade will not scratch. Another story is that water dropped on real jade will form droplets if the stone is genuine.

There are two varieties of jade: jadeite and nephrite, both different minerals. While the colour green is usually associated with jade, the milk-white shade is also highly prized. Shades of pink, red, yellow, brown, mauve and turquoise come in between and can also be produced using artificial dyes.

The circular disc with a central hole worn around many necks in Hong Kong represents heaven in Chinese mythology. In the old days, amulets and talismans of jade were worn by Chinese court officials to denote rank, power and wealth. One emperor was reputed to have worn jade sandals, and another gave his favourite concubine a bed of jade.

Jewellery If you don't know what to look for when buying good jewellery, don't expect any great success as there's plenty of fake stuff around.

Hong Kong has a reputation for being a cheap place for gems and gold, although this isn't exactly true. What is cheap is the labour which turns the gems and gold into wearable jewellery.

The cost of gold is tied to world markets and fluctuates accordingly. The marking of gold items is *not* mandatory in Hong Kong.

The only legal requirement is that any marking should be accurate. The HKTA requires its members to mark any gold or gold-alloy item they display or sell with the fineness of the gold or gold-alloy and with the identity of the manufacturer or retailer.

There are large numbers of jewellery shops in the streets of Tsimshatsui and in the large hotels and shopping arcades. But watch out! Green transparent agate, shipped from Burma (Myanmar), is indistinguishable from emerald to the tourist's naive eye. Less valuable stones turn up in shops under exotic names, so that a plain garnet, pretty as it is, becomes an Arizona ruby, yellow quartz is flogged off as topaz and speckled quartz becomes Indian jade.

Computers Hong Kong is a popular place to buy personal computers. While prices are competitive, it is also important to pay careful attention to where you buy and what you buy. Computers are expensive and prone to breakdowns, so finding a shop with a good reputation for honesty is vital. Before leaving Hong Kong it's also important to run the computer continuously for several days to make sure it is free of defects.

You may have your own ideas about what kind of computer you want to buy, but I'd recommend sticking to a name-brand laptop computer such as Toshiba or Sharp. A portable computer (as opposed to a desktop machine) is a whole lot easier to transport home, and if it's a name-brand computer, it will probably be good quality. If it does break down, parts and service will be easier to find. Be certain you have an international guarantee unless you're planning to be in Hong Kong during the first year you own the machine.

Many shops will be happy to sell you a generic (no name) desktop computer, IBM-PC compatible and custom designed to whatever configuration you desire. Buying a generic computer isn't a bad idea, but it entails risks. My first computer was one of these generic models and it had to be repaired many times. The shop was honest and did the repairs free of charge, but this wouldn't have been possible if I had taken the machine abroad. Generic computers do not have international guarantees and I cannot recommend that you buy one in Hong Kong unless the price in your home country is significantly higher.

Some Hong Kong computer shops still sell pirated computer software, although the authorities have cracked down on this. Bear in mind that besides being illegal, pirated programs often contain computer viruses (there is one called 'AIDS' and wearing a condom offers no protection whatsoever).

Electronics Remember that most electrical appliances in Hong Kong are designed to work with 220 V. Also, Hong Kong's standard plug design, which uses three round prongs, is not used in other countries. Plugs are easily changed, however, or you can buy an adapter in Hong Kong. If they can't supply you with the correct adaptor, ask the store to change the plug for you, which they should do free of charge.

Buying a TV (including the handheld Sony Watchman) is fraught with risks and not recommended unless you know what you're doing. The reason has to do with the numerous incompatible broadcasting standards for TV. The most common standards are PAL (used in Hong Kong, Australia, New Zealand, UK), SECAM (France) and NTSC (Canada, Japan, USA). Unfortunately, there are additional complications. A PAL standard TV bought in Hong Kong may not work for you even if your home country uses PAL because the stations might be adjusted to different frequencies.

If you're interested in purchasing a video tape recorder, you have the same problem – a video tape recorder must be compatible with your TV. You can't connect a PAL video player to an NTSC TV or vice versa. Also, the video player won't work if it uses a frequency different from that used by your TV set, although this problem can be adjusted by a technician (for a fee). The same is true of video cameras – they must be compatible with the video-tape player and TV with which they will be used.

Don't expect the sales people in the stores to know all about international TV and video compatibility. Their job is only to make a sale and few of them have the technical knowledge to advise you. Of course, if you live in Hong Kong and don't plan to take the equipment abroad, there is no problem.

Ivory Ivory jewellery and ornaments were big sellers in Hong Kong, fuelling the demand for tusks and contributing to the slaughter of Africa's already depieted elephant population. In 1989, the Hong Kong government stopped the import of raw ivory after the USA, Japan and Western European nations banned the import of all ivory products. You may still find some carved ivory products around, but most likely your own country will prohibit you from bringing it back home. The elephants have made such a big comeback, though, that there is now a movement under way to resurrect the legal ivory trade.

Diamonds The Diamond Importers Association (☎ 5235497), Room 1102, Parker House, 72 Queen's Rd, Central, will give you a list of members who offer a fair price and a guarantee. If you just want to look, they might be able to make an appointment for you with a retailer or cutting factory.

Antiques & Curios How do you tell a real Ming vase from a fake when the cracks and chips and age discolouration have been cleverly added? Hong Kong factories quite legitimately turn out antique replicas. Many dealers state when a piece is a reproduction and some even restrict their sales to these items. Unfortunately, others do not particularly feel the necessity to tell the customers/ suckers.

The Tang Dynasty ran from 618 AD to 906, the Song Dynasty from 960 to 1279, the Ming Dynasty from 1368 to 1644 and the Qing Dynasty from 1566 to 1911. So a Qing vase might only be 78 years old, which in Western terms would hardly qualify as an antique. Basically, if you don't know what to look for or who to buy from, the serious purchase of antiques is not for the tourist on a stopover!

There are still many beautiful items to buy in Hong Kong, including fine examples of Chinese art and craft – not necessarily antique, which doesn't matter as long as you don't pay antique prices.

If you want to take home a genuine piece of ancient China – carving, figurine or whatever – then it would probably be best to stick to the People's Republic-owned Chinese Arts & Crafts Stores where at least you'll know you're getting exactly what you pay for.

The annual International Asian Antiques Fair is held in Hong Kong.

Getting There & Away

AIR
Hong Kong is the major gateway to China and much of East Asia. Consequently, international air service is excellent and competition keeps fares relatively cheap when compared to neighbouring countries.

Air Tickets
It's useful to see what's available and become familiar with airline ticketing jar gon. One of the best sources of information is the monthly magazine *Business Traveller* which is available in a British and Hong Kong version. They're available from news-stands in most developed countries, or direct from 60/61 Fleet St, London EC4Y 1LA, UK, and from 13th floor, 200 Lockhard Rd, Hong Kong.

You will have to choose between buying a ticket to Hong Kong only and then making other arrangements when you arrive, and buying a ticket allowing various stopovers around Asia. For example, such a ticket could fly you from Sydney to London with stopovers in Denpasar, Jakarta, Hong Kong, Bangkok, Calcutta, Delhi and Istanbul.

There is a host of other deals which travel agents will offer in order to sell you a cheaper ticket. Fares will vary according to your point of departure, the time of year, how direct the flight is and how flexible you can be. Whatever you do, buy air tickets from a travel agent. The airlines don't deal directly in discount tickets, only the travel agents do. Also, always make sure you understand how the fare works and what conditions and restrictions apply to the tickets you intend to buy.

Air fares are seasonal with the lowest being in winter and the highest in summer. However, the winter/summer issue becomes obscured when you're flying between the northern and southern hemispheres. Furthermore, the Chinese New Year is also peak season.

Normal Economy-Class Tickets Despite the name, these are usually not the most economical way to go though they do give you maximum flexibility and the tickets are valid for 12 months. Also, if you don't use them they are fully refundable as are unused sectors of a multiple ticket.

Bucket Shop Tickets At certain times of year and/or on certain sectors, many airlines fly with empty seats. This isn't profitable. It's more cost-effective for them to fly full even if that means having to sell a certain number of tickets which have been drastically discounted. They do this by off-loading them onto certain agents which are commonly known as 'bucket shops'. The agents, in turn, sell them to the public at reduced prices. These tickets are often the cheapest you will find. Their availability varies widely and you not only have to be flexible in your travel plans but you have to be quick off the mark once the advertisements for them appear in the press.

Most of the bucket shops are reputable organisations but there will always be the occasional fly-by-night operator who sets up shop, takes your money and then either disappears or issues you with an invalid or unusable ticket – luckily, these agents are rare. Be sure to check what you are buying before you hand over the money.

Bucket shops advertise in newspapers and magazines and there's a lot of competition and different routes available so it's best to telephone first before rushing round there. Naturally, they'll advertise the cheapest available tickets but, by the time you get there, those may be sold for the date on which you want to leave and you might be looking at something slightly more expensive if you cannot wait.

APEX Tickets APEX (Advance Purchase Excursion) tickets are sold at a discount but will lock you into a rigid schedule. Such tickets must be purchased two or three weeks ahead of departure, do not permit stopovers and may have minimum and maximum stays as well as fixed departure and return dates. Unless you definitely must return at a certain time, it's best to purchase APEX tickets on a one-way basis only. There are stiff cancellation fees if you decide not to use your APEX ticket.

Round-the-World Tickets These are usually offered by an airline or combination of airlines, and let you take your time (six months to a year) moving from point to point on their routes for the price of one ticket. The main restriction is that you have to keep moving in the same direction; a drawback is that because you are usually booking individual flights as you go, and can't switch carriers, you can get caught out by flight availabilities, and have to spend more or less time in a place than you want.

Student Discounts Some airlines offer student discounts on their tickets of between 20% to 25% to student card holders. The same often applies to anyone under the age of 26. These discounts are generally only available on ordinary economy-class fares. You wouldn't get one, for instance, on an APEX or a Round-the-World ticket since these are already discounted.

Children's Fares Airlines usually carry babies up to two years of age at 10% of the relevant adult fare — a few may carry them free of charge. Reputable international airlines usually provide nappies (diapers), tissues, talcum and all the other paraphernalia needed to keep babies clean, dry and half-happy. For children between the ages of four and 12 the fare on international flights is usually 50% of the regular fare or 67% of a discounted fare. These days most fares are likely to be discounted.

Frequent Flyer Frequent-flyer plans have proliferated in recent years and are now offered by most airlines, even some budget ones. Basically, these allow you a free ticket if you chalk up so many km with the same airline. The plans aren't always as good as they sound — some airlines require you to acquire and use all your frequent-flyer credits within one year or you lose the lot. Sometimes you find yourself flying on a particular airline just to get frequent-flyer credits, but the ticket is considerably more expensive than one you might have gotten from a discount airline without a frequent-flyer bonus.

When you purchase the ticket, be sure to give the travel agent or airline your frequent-flyer membership number. A common complaint seems to be that airlines 'forget' to record your frequent-flyer credits when you fly with them — save all your ticket receipts and be prepared to push if no bonus is forthcoming. This applies as much to big name 'reputable' airlines as well as to dinky Third World ones.

Back-to-Front Tickets Avoid these! A back-to-front ticket is best explained by example — if you want to fly from Japan (where tickets are expensive) to Hong Kong (where tickets are cheap), you can pay by cheque or credit card and have a friend or travel agent in Hong Kong mail the ticket to you. The problem is that the airlines have computers and will know that the ticket was issued in Hong Kong rather than Japan, and they will refuse to honour it. Consumer groups have filed lawsuits over this practice with mixed results, but in most countries the law protects the airlines, not consumers. In short, you must be physically present in the country where the ticket was issued.

To/From the USA

There are some very good open tickets which remain valid for six months or one year (opt for the latter), but don't lock you into any fixed dates of departure. For example, there are cheap tickets between the US west coast and Hong Kong with stopovers in Japan, Korea and Taiwan for very little extra money — the departure dates can be changed and you have one year to complete the journey. However, be careful during the peak season (summer and Chinese New Year) because seats will be hard to come by unless reserved months in advance.

Usually, and not surprisingly, the cheapest fare to a particular country is offered by a bucket shop owned by someone who originates from that country. San Francisco is the bucket shop capital of the USA, although some good deals can be found in Los Angeles, New York and other cities. Bucket shops can be found through the Yellow Pages or the major daily newspapers. Those listed in both roman and oriental scripts are invariably discounters. A more direct way is to wander around San Francisco's Chinatown where most of the shops are located – especially in the Clay St and Waverly Place area. Many of these are staffed by recent arrivals from Hong Kong and Taiwan who speak little English. Inquiries are best made in person.

It's not advisable to send money (even cheques) through the post unless the agent is very well established – some travellers have reported being ripped off by fly-by-night mail-order ticket agents.

Council Travel is the largest student travel organisation, and though you don't have to be a student to use them, they do have specially discounted student tickets. Council Travel has an extensive network in all major US cities and is listed in the telephone book.

One of the cheapest and most reliable travel agents on the west coast is Overseas Tours (☎ (800) 3238777 in California, (800) 2275988 elsewhere), 475 El Camino Real, Room 206, Millbrae, CA 94030. Another good agent is Gateway Travel (☎ (214) 9602000, (800) 4411183), 4201 Spring Valley Rd, Suite 104, Dallas, TX 75244 – they seem to be reliable for mail-order tickets.

The cheapest fares through these agents are on Korean Air, the Taiwan-based China Airlines (CAL) and Philippine Airlines (PAL), which cut up to 30% on published APEX fares and 60% on full economy-class fares. One-way trips usually cost 35% less than a round trip. Discount fares on KAL quoted in 1991 from either Los Angeles or San Francisco to Hong Kong one-way/return were US$458/719. United Airlines has some cheap fares, but you should note that their open tickets are usually only valid for six months rather than one year.

From Hong Kong, one-way fares to the US west coast start from about US$398. Return tickets begin at US$795. Fares to New York start from about US$500 one way, US$962 return.

To/From Canada
Travel CUTS is Canada's national student travel agency and has offices in Vancouver, Victoria, Edmonton, Saskatoon, Toronto, Ottawa, Montreal and Halifax. You don't have to be a student to use their services.

Getting discount tickets in Canada is much the same as in the USA. Go to the travel agents and shop around. In Vancouver try Kowloon Travel, Westcan Treks and Travel CUTS.

To/From the UK
British Airways, British Caledonian, Cathay Pacific and other airlines fly from London to Hong Kong. Air-ticket discounting has been a long-running business in the UK and it's wide open. The various agents advertise their fares and there is nothing under-the-counter about it at all. To find out what's going, there are a number of magazines in Britain which have good information about flights and agents. These include: *Trailfinder*, free from the Trailfinders Travel Centre in Earl's Court, and *Time Out* and *City Limits*, the London weekly entertainment guides widely available in the UK.

Discount tickets are almost exclusively available in London. You won't find your friendly travel agent out in the country offering cheap deals. The danger with discounted tickets in Britain is that some of the 'bucket shops' (as ticket-discounters are known) are unsound. Sometimes the backstairs over-the-shop travel agents fold up and disappear after you've handed over the money and before you've got the tickets. Get the tickets before you hand over the cash.

Two reliable London bucket shops are

Trailfinders in Earl's Court; and STA Travel, which has several offices.

You can expect a one-way London to Hong Kong ticket to cost from around UK£250, and a return ticket around UK£450. London ticket discounters can also offer interesting one-way fares to Australia with a Hong Kong stopover from around UK£520.

For tickets purchased in Hong Kong, typical one-way fares direct to Britain and Europe start at about US$410, and return fares are exactly double.

To/From Europe

The Netherlands and Belgium are good places for buying discount air tickets. In Antwerp, WATS has been recommended. In the Netherlands, NBBS is a reputable agency.

In Zurich try SOF Travel and Sindbad. In Geneva try Stohl Travel.

Good deals can be obtained on Aeroflot, the Polish airline LOT and the Rumanian airline Tarom, but none of these flies into Hong Kong. The closest they come is Bangkok or Beijing. Be aware that most East European airlines have a reputation for poor safety and lost luggage.

To/From Australia

Australia is not a cheap place to fly out of, and air fares between Australia and Asia are expensive considering the distances flown. However, there are a few ways of cutting the cost.

Among the cheapest regular tickets available in Australia are the advance purchase fares. The cost of these tickets depends on your departure date from Australia. The year is divided into 'peak' (expensive) and 'low' (cheaper) seasons; peak season is December to January.

It's possible to get reductions on the cost of advance purchase and other fares by going to the student travel offices and/or other travel agents in Australia that specialise in cheap air tickets.

If you book through such an agent, the advance-purchase fares from Melbourne to

Hong Kong are around A$500 one way and A$900 return, flying with Cathay Pacific.

The weekend travel sections of papers like the *Age* (Melbourne) or the *Sydney Morning Herald* are good sources for travel information. Also look at *Student Traveller*, a free newspaper published by STA Travel, the Australian-based student travel organisation which now has offices worldwide. STA Travel has offices all around Australia (check the phone directory) – and you definitely do not have to be a student to use them.

Also well worth trying is Flight Centres International (☎ (03) 6700477) at 386 Little Bourke St, Melbourne. They have other branches in Melbourne, and in Sydney (☎ (02) 2332296) and Brisbane (☎ (07) 2299958, 2299211).

For tours and package deals contact Access Travel (☎ (02) 2411128), 5th floor, 58 Pitt St, Sydney. Apart from tours running through Hong Kong and China, they also organise tours on the Trans-Siberian Railway, including a possible side tour to Mongolia.

From Hong Kong, one-way fares to Australia's east coast flying into Melbourne, Sydney or Brisbane start from about US$628 one way, US$948 return.

To/From New Zealand

Air New Zealand flies from Auckland to Hong Kong. In the 'peak' season a return excursion ticket costs around NZ$1900, and in the 'low' season it's NZ$1550. You have to pay for your ticket at least 21 days in advance and spend a minimum of six days overseas.

Cathay Pacific also flies from Auckland to Hong Kong using Air New Zealand carriers. In 'peak' season a one-way excursion ticket from Auckland to Hong Kong is around NZ$1500. An advance-purchase return excursion ticket is around NZ$1900. As with the Air New Zealand excursion ticket, a minimum of six days must be spent overseas.

To/From other Asian Countries

To/From China Prices are exactly the same whether you buy the ticket in China or Hong

Kong. One-way fares to Hong Kong from Beijing are US$218; from Shanghai, US$154; and from Canton, US$38. Return fares are exactly double.

To/From Indonesia Garuda Airlines has direct flights from Jakarta to Hong Kong, and from Denpasar to Hong Kong via Jakarta. Cheap discount air tickets out of Indonesia can be bought from travel agents in Jakarta and in Kuta Beach, Bali.

In Jakarta, one of the cheapest travel agents I've found is Seabreeze Travel (☎ 326675), JalanJaksa 43. There are several other travel agents on Jalan Jaksa, but none quoted fares as low as Seabreeze Travel. Travel International (☎ 330103), in the President Hotel on Jalan Thamrin, is also a good place for cheap tickets, asi is Vayatour (☎ 3100720) next door to Travel International.

There are numerous airline ticket discounters around Kuta Beach – several on the main strip, Jalan Legian. You can also buy discount tickets in Kuta for departure from Jakarta.

From Hong Kong, the cheapest one-way/return tickets to Jakarta cost US$282/ 450. A round trip to Denpasar is much higher at US$545.

To/From Japan Expensive! If you have to buy a ticket in Japan there are often advertisements for specialist travel agents in the English-language papers and magazines aimed at resident foreigners. Council Travel (☎ (03) 35817581) has an office at the Sanno Grand Building, Room 102, 14-2 Nagata-cho, 2-chome, Chiyoda-ku, Tokyo 100. STA (☎ (03) 32211733) is at Sanden Building, 3-5-5 Kojimachi, Chiyoda-ku, Tokyo.

For tickets purchased in Hong Kong, the cheapest one-way/return fares to Tokyo are US$240/360.

To/From Singapore A good place for buying cheap air tickets in Singapore is Airmaster Travel Centre. Also try STA Travel. Other agents advertise in the *Straits Times* classified columns.

For tickets purchased in Hong Kong, the lowest one-way/return airfares cost US$185/ 320.

To/From South Korea The best deals are available from the Korean International Student Exchange Society (KISES) (☎ (02) 7339494), Room 505, YMCA Building, Chongno 2-ga, Seoul. Quoted fares from Seoul to Hong Kong are one way/return US$220/385. In Hong Kong, the lowest prices available to Seoul are US$220/270 one way/return.

To/From Taiwan Taiwan is not especially cheap for tickets, but some of the best deals can be found at Jenny Su Travel Service (☎ (02) 5951646), 10th floor, 27 Chungshan N Rd, Section 3, Taipei. The cheapest one-way/return tickets are around US$180/220, but these are often heavily booked. From Hong Kong, the best deals going are US$125/153.

To/From Thailand In Bangkok, Student Travel in the Thai Hotel is helpful and efficient.

For tickets bought in Hong Kong, one-way/return fares start at US$135/224.

Airline Offices

Listed are some of the airlines which fly into Hong Kong, along with the addresses of ticketing offices on both sides of the harbour. The reservation and reconfirmation telephone number (Res) is followed by the flight information telephone number (Info). A few airlines have only one telephone number.

Air France
    Room 2104, Alexandra House, 7 Des Voeux Rd Central, Hong Kong (☎ Res 5248145, Info 7696662)
Air India
    10th floor, Gloucester Tower, Central (☎ Res 5221176, Info 7696558)
Air Lanka
    Room 52, 2nd floor, Admiralty Centre, Tower II, Central (☎ Res 5299708, Info 7697183)
Air Mauritius
    1512 Melbourne Plaza, 33 Queen's Rd, Central (☎ 5231114)

Air New Zealand
Suite 902, 3 Exchange Square, 8 Connaught Place, Central (☎ Res 8458063, 5249041)
Air Niugini
Room 705, Century Square, 1-13 D'Aguilar St, Central (☎ Res 5242151, Info 7477888)
Alitalia
Room 2101, Hutchison House, 10 Harcourt Rd, Central (☎ Res 5237047, Info 7696448)
All Nippon
Room 2512, Pacific Place Two, 88 Queensway, Admiralty (☎ Res 8107100, Info 7698606)
British Airways
30th floor, Alexandra House, 7 Des Voeux Rd Central (☎ Res 8680303, Info 8680768)
Room 112, Royal Garden Hotel, 69 Mody Rd, Tsimshatsui East (☎ Res 3689255, Info 7698571)
CAAC (Civil Aviation Administration of China)
Ground floor, 17 Queen's Rd, Central, Hong Kong Island
Ground floor, Hankow Centre, 4 Ashley Rd, Tsimshatsui (☎ Res 8610322)
Canadian Airlines International
Ground floor, Swire House, 9-25 Chater Rd, Central (☎ Res 8683123, Info 7697113)
Cathay Pacific
Ground floor, Swire House, 9-25 Chater Rd, Central
Room 11th floor, Room 1126, Ocean Centre, Tsimshatsui
Shop 109, 1st floor, Royal Garden Hotel, 69 Mody Rd, Tsimshatsui East (☎ Res 7471888, Info 7477888)
China Airlines (Taiwan)
Ground floor, St George's Building, Ice House St, Central (☎ Res & Info 8682299)
G5-6 Tsimshatsui Centre, Tsimshatsui East (☎ Res 3674181, Info 7698391)
Dragonair
1843 Swire House, 9-25 Chater Rd, West Wing, Central (☎ 8108055)
Garuda Indonesia
2nd floor, Sing Pao Centre, 8 Queen's Rd, Central (☎ Res 8400000, Info 5229071)
Japan Air Lines
20th floor, Gloucester Tower, 11 Pedder St, Central (☎ Res 5230081)
Harbour View Holiday Inn, Mody Rd, Tsimshatsui East (☎ Res 3113355, Info 7696534)
Japan Asia
20th floor, Gloucester Tower, 11 Pedder St, Central (☎ Res 5218102)
KLM Royal Dutch Airlines
Room 701-5 Jardine House, 1 Connaught Place, Central (☎ 8228111)

Korean Air
Ground floor, St George's Building, Ice House St, Central (☎ Res 5235177)
11th floor, South Seas Centre, Tower II, 75 Mody Rd, Tsimshatsui East (☎ Res 3686221)
G12-15 Tsimshatsui Centre, Salisbury Rd, Tsimshatsui East (☎ 3686221)
Lauda (Austria)
M1, New Henry Housse, 10 Ice House St, Central (☎ Res 5246178, Info 7697107)
Lufthansa German Airlines
6th floor, Landmark East, 12 Ice House St, Central (☎ Res 8682313, Info 7696560)
Malaysian Airline System
Room 1306, Prince's Building, 9-25 Chater Rd, Central (☎ Res 5218181, Info 7697967)
Northwest Airlines
29th floor, Alexandra House, 7 Des Voeux Rd Central, Central (☎ 8104288)
G34A-37A, Lock Rd, Hyatt Regency Hotel, Tsimshatsui
Philippine Airlines
Room 603, West Tower, Bond Centre, Central (☎ Res 5249216)
Room 6, Ground floor, East Ocean Centre, 98 Granville Rd, Tsimshatsui East (☎ Res 3694521, Info 7698111)
Qantas
Room 1422, Swire House, 9-25 Chater Rd, Central (☎ Res 5242101, Info 5256206)
Royal Brunei Airlines
Room 1406, Central Building, 3 Pedder St, Central (Res c/o Cathay Pacific, ☎ 7471888)
Royal Nepal Airlines
Room 704, Sun Plaza, 28 Canton Rd, Tsimshatsui (☎ Res 3699151, Info 7212180)
Singapore Airlines
Ground floor, Alexandra House, 7 Des Voeux Rd, Central (☎ Res 5202233)
Ground floor, Wing On Plaza, Tsimshatsui East
South African Airways
c/o Jardine Airways, 30th floor, Alexandra House, Central (☎ Res 8773277, Info 8680768)
c/o Jardine Airways, Room 112, The Royal Garden Hotel, 69 Mody Rd, Tsimshatsui East
Swissair
8th floor, Tower II, Admiralty Centre, Central (☎ Res 5293670, Info 7698864)
Thai International
Shop 124, 1st floor, World Wide Plaza, Central (☎ 5295601)
Shop 105-6, The Omni Hong Kong Hotel, 3 Canton Rd, Tsimshatsui (☎ 5295601)
United Airlines
29th floor, Gloucester Tower, Central
Ground floor, Empire Centre, Mody Rd, Tsimshatsui East (☎ Res 8104888)

To/From the Airport

There are four airport buses. Two go to Kowloon and the other two go to Hong Kong Island. The buses have plenty of room for luggage. Touts at the bus stop often try to persuade backpackers to come with them to guest houses. You can take their namecards, but it's best not to go with them because they will then often insist that you are obligated to stay at their place since they guided you into town.

Bus No A1 goes to Tsimshatsui on the Kowloon side and follows a circular route. It runs down Chatham Rd, then turns onto Cameron Rd, then turns down Nathan Rd (the main artery of Tsimshatsui) and onto the Star Ferry Terminal. It then runs through Tsimshatsui East and back to the airport. The first bus starts at 7 am and the last bus leaves the airport at midnight. They are supposed to run every 15 minutes, though my experience has been that 20 minutes is more likely. The fare is HK$8 and no change is given on the bus.

Bus No A2 goes to Hong Kong Island via the Cross-Harbour Tunnel. It stops at all the main hotels in the Wanchai, Central and Sheung Wan districts. The bus goes down Gloucester Rd in Wanchai, and stops near the following hotels: China Harbour View, Evergreen Plaza, Furama, Victoria, Harbour, Harbour View International, Hilton, Luk Kwok, Mandarin Oriental, New Harbour and Ramada Inn. The bus turns around at the Macau Ferry Pier and follows the same route back to the airport. Service begins at 6.50 am and the last bus departs the airport at midnight. The fare is HK$12 and a bus is supposed to run every 15 minutes.

Bus No A3 takes a circular route through Causeway Bay in Hong Kong Island. The first bus is at 6.55 am and the last one leaves the airport at midnight. It should run once every 15 minutes and the fare is HK$12. The bus stops near these hotels: Caravelle, Excelsior, Lee Gardens and Park Lane Radisson.

Traffic jams are common during rush hour so start out early to avoid missing your flight. The Cross-Harbour Tunnel is a bottleneck, so if you're coming from Hong Kong Island during peak hour, you might want to cross the harbour by MTR (Mass Transit Railway) or ferry, then take the A1 bus.

LAND

To/From Europe

From Europe, you can reach Hong Kong by rail, though most travellers following this route also tour China along the way. Don't take this rail journey just to save money – a direct flight from Europe to Hong Kong works out to be about the same price. The idea is to get a glimpse of the Russia, Mongolia and China along the way.

It's a long haul. The most commonly taken routes are from Western Europe to Moscow, then on to Beijing via the Trans-Manchurian or Trans-Mongolian Railway. From Beijing, there are trains to Canton, and from there express trains to Hong Kong. The minimum time needed for this rail journey (one way) is 10 days, although most travellers will spend at least a month in China before finally arriving in Hong Kong.

There are three routes: the Trans-Siberian, Trans-Manchurian and Trans-Mongolian. The Trans-Siberian route goes from Moscow to Nakhodka (near Vladivostok) from where you can get a ship to Japan or Hong Kong. By taking this route you don't pass through China. The Trans-Manchurian goes from Moscow to Beijing and bypasses Mongolia, saving the need to get a Mongolian visa. The Trans-Mongolian runs from Moscow to Beijing via Mongolia.

For the latest information, contact specialist agencies or national tourist agencies such as Intourist (Russia). Several readers have recommended Scandinavian Student Travel Service (SSTS), 117 Hauchsvej, 1825 Co penhagen V, Denmark. Lonely Planet's *China – a travel survival kit* and *North-East Asia on a shoestring* provide more details. For more depth, there's the *Trans-Siberian Rail Guide* (Bradt Publications, UK, 1987) by Robert Strauss, and the *Trans-Siberian Handbook* (Trailblazer, The Old Mansse, Tower Rd, Hindhead, Surrey, GU26 6SU, UK) by Bryn Thomas.

It can be hard to book this trip during the

summer peak season. Travel agents in Europe say that it's even difficult to get a September booking in April! Off-season shouldn't be a problem, but plan as far ahead as possible.

The cost for a simple Moscow to Beijing economy ticket is US$530. For some strange reason, it's less than half that from Beijing to Moscow. If you want to go from Beijing to Moscow, you can book the ticket in Hong Kong at Monkey Business (☎ 7231376), 4th floor, E-Block, Flat 6E, Chungking Mansions, Tsimshatsui, Kowloon.

SEA

Considering the renowned beauty of Hong Kong Harbour, it's a pity so few people can arrive by ship. The days of cheap passage on a cargo ship are mostly over. Of course, there are luxurious passenger ships making cruises of the Far East, but these are anything but cheap. About the only cheap ships are those coming from China, such as the popular Shanghai/Hong Kong cruise.

LEAVING HONG KONG

If you have an onward ticket, remember to reconfirm your departing flight when you arrive in Hong Kong or the computer will probably give away your seat. You can reconfirm at the airport or by telephone.

On all flights, carry-on hand baggage must be able to fit in a space no larger than 22½ cm x 35 cm x 55 cm. This limit is strictly enforced by security guards.

If you need a pushcart to haul luggage around the airport, these are available only on the ground floor (the arrival area). There are none in the departure area, where the carts are really needed. So go downstairs, grab a cart and take it upstairs in the lift. People have complained about this for years, but to no avail.

Cathay Pacific offers a 'CityCheck' (☎ 7477888) early check-in service on both the Hong Kong and Kowloon sides. You can check in the day before departure, or for the same day if it's at least three hours before departure. It's a useful service since you can get rid of your bags and get a first choice of seats. On Hong Kong Island, CityCheck is available on the 4th floor, Shop 403, The Mall, Pacific Place, 88 Queensway, Admiralty. In Kowloon, CityCheck is on the Lower Ground floor, China Hong Kong City, Canton Rd, Tsimshatsui.

Travel Agents

Adam Smith would be pleased by the free-wheeling capitalist competition which keeps ticket prices in Hong Kong among the lowest in the world.

Many Hong Kong travel agents hesitate to sell you the cheapest ticket available. This is not always because they want to squeeze more money out of you. Airlines have cheap special deals, but the number of such seats may be limited, and there are often severe restrictions. With the cheapest tickets, you often have to pay the travel agent first and then pick up the ticket at the airport. Nevertheless, these cheap tickets may be worth the extra trouble. If you want the cheapest flight, tell the agent, and then make sure you understand what restrictions, if any, apply.

One of the cheapest travel agents on Hong Kong Island is Travel Expert (☎ 5432770, fax 5447055), Room 708, Haleson Building, 1 Jubilee St, Central. You could also try their Kowloon office (☎ 3670963), Room 803, Metropole Building, 57 Peking Rd, Tsimshatsui.

The travel agent that I often use in Hong Kong is Traveller Services (☎ 3674127, fax 3110387), Room 704, Metropole Building, 57 Peking Rd, Tsimshatsui.

Phoenix Services (☎ 7227378) in Room B, 6th floor, Milton Mansion, 96 Nathan Rd, Tsimshatsui, is scrupulously honest and gets rave reviews from travellers.

Many travellers still use the Hong Kong Student Travel Bureau (☎ 7303269), Room 1021, 10th floor, Star House, Tsimshatsui. However, they are no longer especially cheap, although you can get a discount with an ISIC card. Still, they might be worth a try. They have several branch offices: Argyle Centre (☎ 3900421), Room 1812, 688 Nathan Rd, Mongkok; Wing On Central Building (☎ 8107272), Room 901, 26 Des

Voeux Rd, Central; and Circle Plaza
(☎ 8339909), 11th floor, 499 Hennessy Rd,
Causeway Bay.

Another agent to try is Travel Expert Ltd.
It has one office (☎ 5432770) at Room 708,
Haleson Building, 1 Jubilee St, Central,
Hong Kong Island; and another (☎ 3670963)
at Room 803, Metropole Building, 57
Peking Rd, Tsimshatsui, Kowloon.

Rip-Offs Be careful when you buy tickets –
rip-offs do occur. It happens less now than it
used to, but Hong Kong has long been
plagued with bogus travel agents and the fly-
by-night operations that appear shortly
before peak holiday seasons and dupe customers into buying nonexistent airline seats
and holiday packages. One way to tell is to
see if they are listed in the telephone book,
since fly-by-night operations don't stay
around long enough to get listed.

One trick to look out for is requests for a
nonrefundable deposit on an air ticket, as
when you come to pay the balance the agent
might tell you the price of the ticket has risen.
A popular trick of these operators is to accept
a deposit for a booking, then when you go to
pick up the tickets they say that the flight is
no longer available, but that there is another
flight which costs 'X' dollars more.

It is best not to pay a deposit, but rather
to pay for the ticket in full and get a receipt
clearly showing that there is no balance due,
and that the full amount is refundable if no
ticket is issued. Tickets are normally issued
the next day after booking, but for the really
cheap tickets, you must pick these up yourself at the airport.

If you think you have been ripped off, and
the agent is a member of the HKTA, the
organisation can apply some pressure (and
apparently has a fund to handle cases of
outright fraud). Even if an agent is a member
of the HKTA he does not have to comply
with any set of guidelines.

Since mid-1985 all travel agencies offering outward-bound services must be
licensed. A fund was also set up to compens-
ate cheated customers. It could be worth
inquiring about if you get ripped off.

Departure Tax
There is an airport departure tax of HK$150
for adults, but it's free if you can persuade
them that you're under 12 years of age.

Getting Around

Hong Kong is small and crowded, which makes public transport the only practical way to move people. Consequently, public transport is cheap, fast, widely used and generally efficient. It is mostly privately owned and operates at a profit.

If you want to master all the intricacies of Hong Kong's complex system of buses, minibuses, trams and ferries, pick up the book *Public Transport in Hong Kong – A Guide to Services* published by the transport department. This guide describes the routes in excruciating detail. Indeed, the worst thing about the book is that it inundates you with information, some of it confusing. Unfortunately, it doesn't contain maps. The guide can be purchased from the Government Publications Centre adjacent to the GPO near the Star Ferry Terminal on Hong Kong Island.

BUS

The extensive bus system offers a bewildering number of routes that will take you anywhere you want to go in Hong Kong.

Figuring out which bus you want may take some effort. One useful fact is that any bus number ending with the letter K (78K, 69K, etc) means that the route connects with a KCR station. Similarly, bus numbers ending with M (51M, 68M, etc) go to the MTR stations. Those ending with R are recreational buses and normally run on Sunday, public holidays or for special events like the races at Happy Valley. Buses with an X are express.

CMB & KMB Buses

The China Motor Bus Company (CMB) operates the blue-and-white buses on Hong Kong Island, and the Kowloon Motor Bus Company (KMB) runs the red-and-cream buses in Kowloon.

The HKTA has a useful free brochure listing bus numbers and fares from Tsim shatsui and Central to various places of interest in the New Territories, Hong Kong Island and Kowloon.

Most buses run from about 6 am until

bus/tram	from	to	every (mins)	trip (mins)	cost
Hong Kong Island					
tram	Central	Sai Wan Ho	2-7	40	HK$1.00
6	Central	Stanley	10-20	40	HK$4.50
7	Aberdeen	Central	6-10	30	HK$3.00
14	Sai Wan Ho	Stanley	20-30	40	HK$4.50
70	Central	Aberdeen	4-10	25	HK$2.80
73	Stanley	Aberdeen	15-30	30	HK$4.50
New Territories					
bus	from	to	every (mins)	trip (mins)	cost
51	Tsuen Wan	Kam Tin	15-25	50	HK$3.600
54	Yuen Long	Kam Tin	7-12	20	HK$1.40
60M	Tsuen Wan	Tuen Mun	7-15	36	HK$3.60
75K	Tai Po	Tai Mei Tuk	12-30	26	HK$2.40
77K	Kam Tim	Sheung Shui	12-20	25	HK$3.00
92	Choi Hung	Sai Kung	6-15	38	HK$2.60

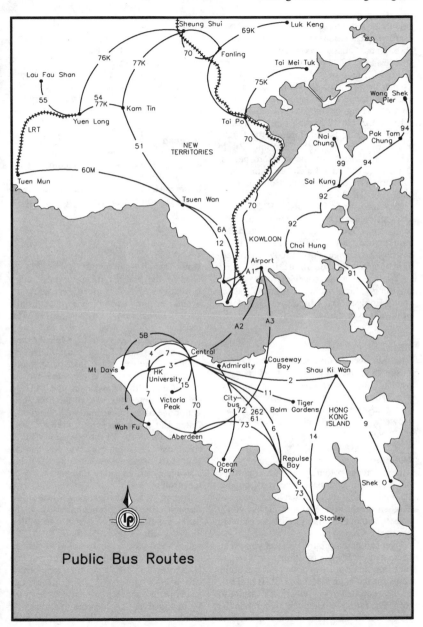

Public Bus Routes

midnight, but Nos 121 and 122 are 'Cross-Harbour Recreation Routes' which operate through the Cross-Harbour Tunnel every 15 minutes from 12.45 to 5 am. Bus No 121 runs from Macau Ferry Pier on Hong Kong Island, then through the tunnel to Chatham Rd in Tsimshatsui East before continuing on to Choi Hung on the eastern side of the airport. Bus No 122 runs from North Point on Hong Kong Island, through the Cross-Harbour Tunnel, onto Chatham Rd in Tsimshatsui East and the northern part of Nathan Rd and on to Laichikok in the north-western part of Kowloon. Both of these buses cost HK$6.50.

Bus fares range from about HK$1.80 for the short routes to HK$9 for the longest route in the New Territories. Drop the exact fare into the box next to the driver as you board the bus. No change is given so keep a collection of coins with you all the time.

When you want to get off just yell out anything – the drivers usually don't speak much English. The Chinese say *yau lok* if you want to be correct.

Citybus

These are special, luxurious, air-con, express buses which usually go nonstop between two points. They do cost more, though. For travellers, the most popular Citybus is the one going to Ocean Park which costs HK$8. However, these buses also go from Central to the various housing estates.

Minibus

This is a cream-coloured bus with a red stripe down the side and usually seats 14 people. Its final destination is written in Chinese and English on the sign at the front, but you'll have to squint to see the English squeezed in above the Chinese.

You can hail a minibus just as you do an ordinary taxi. It will stop almost anywhere to pick you up or put you down, but not at the stops for the large KMB and CMB buses or in the restricted zones where it's unsafe to stop. The fares are not much higher than the large buses and they aren't nearly as crowded. You are not allowed to stand on a minibus so they won't pick up more passengers than they have seats.

Fares range from HK$2 to HK$6, and you pay when you get off; they usually can give change. Minibuses to the New Territories can be picked up at the Jordan Rd Ferry Pier in Kowloon.

Maxicab

Maxicabs are like minibuses, but have a green stripe and operate on fixed routes and stop at designated places. Fares, which cost between HK$1 and HK$8, vary according to distance. You pay when you get on and no change is given.

TRAIN
Mass Transit Railway (MTR)

One of the world's most modern metro systems, the MTR is clean, fast and safe. Trains run every two to four minutes from 6 am to 1 am daily on three lines (see the MTR map).

The cheapest fare is HK$3, while the most expensive is HK$7. For short hauls, the MTR is more expensive than other public transport. If you want to cross the harbour from Central to Tsimshatsui, the MTR is about five times the price of the Star Ferry with none of the view, and only marginally faster. But if you go further, like to Tsuen Wan in the New Territories, the MTR is considerably faster than a ferry and a bus and almost the same price. Also, the MTR has air-con, which you may find worth paying for in summer.

Riding the MTR is dead easy – just follow the signs. Everything is automated, from the ticket vending machines to the turnstiles. Ticket machines take HK$5, HK$2, HK$1 and 50-cent pieces but do not give change, so feed in the right amount. If you put in a HK$5 coin for a HK$4 ticket the next person gets a HK$1 discount! There are change machines that accept coins only – notes must be changed at the information desks or minibanks. Once you pass through the turn-

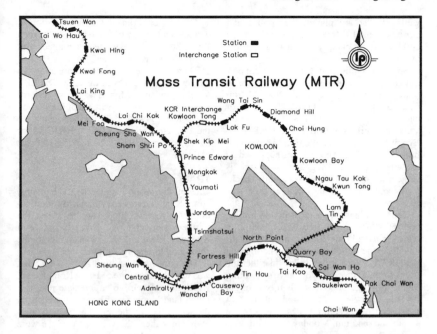

Mass Transit Railway (MTR)

stiles, you only have 90 minutes to complete the journey or the ticket becomes void.

The MTR uses 'smart tickets' with a magnetic coding strip on the back. When you pass through the turnstile, the card is encoded with the station identification and time. At the other end, the exit turnstile sucks in the ticket, reads where you came from, the time and how much you paid, and lets you through if you pass the test.

You can't buy return tickets, but there are 'Common Stored Value Tickets' for making multiple journeys. These are available in denominations of HK$50, HK$100 and HK$200, and are definitely worthwhile if you use the MTR frequently. They can also be used on the Kowloon-Canton Railway except for Lo Wu Station (the Chinese border station). Actually, the HK$50 ticket is the best buy because you benefit from the 'last ride bonus' – no matter how little the value remaining on the ticket, you don't have to pay extra for the final ride when the ticket

is used up. The single-journey MTR tickets must be used the same day, so it's no good buying one to use tomorrow. You can buy these tickets at the minibanks in the MTR stations.

There's also a 'tourist ticket' – better known as the 'sucker ticket' – which is valid for HK$20 worth of travel but costs HK$25! As small compensation, you get to keep the ticket as a souvenir.

Children aged two or under can travel free and there are special child/student tickets which are much cheaper than adult prices. These can only be used by children aged three to 11.

Passengers aged 12 or over can only use the child/student tickets if they are students carrying a Hong Kong Student Travel Card – an International Student Identity Card (ISIC) is not acceptable. You might be tempted to buy a child/student ticket to save money, after all, how can the machine know you aren't a student? However, the MTR is well patrolled by plainclothes police and closed-circuit TV. If you're spotted buying a child/student ticket, you may have some explaining to do.

Smoking, eating and drinking are not permitted in the MTR stations or on the trains (makes me wonder about all those Maxim Cake Shops in the stations). The fine for eating or drinking is HK$1000, while smoking will set you back HK$2000. Busking, selling and soliciting are also prohibited activities. You are not supposed to carry large pieces of luggage, but 'large' is subject to interpretation. Apparently, backpacks and suitcases are OK – at least I've never been hassled.

There is a passenger information hotline (☎ 7500170) and a free MTR pamphlet which is useful only for the map. It's available from the station information booths and the HKTA. There are no toilets in either the trains or the stations. If you leave something on the train and nobody steals it, you might be able to reclaim your goods at the lost property office at Admiralty Station between 11 am and 6.45 pm, Monday to Saturday.

Kowloon-Canton Railway (KCR)

This line runs from Kowloon to the China border at Lo Wu. Most trains terminate at the border but special express trains run all the way through to Canton. You can change from the MTR to the KCR at the Kowloon Tong Station. If you buy a stored value or tourist ticket for the MTR you can also use it on the KCR for every station but Lo Wu. You are not supposed to ride up to Lo Wu Station unless you have a visa for China.

The KCR is a good way to get to various parts of the New Territories. (See the New Territories chapter.)

Light Rail Transit (LRT)

The latest addition to the alphabet soup of Hong Kong trains is the LRT. This is rather like a modern air-con version of the tram. The LRT runs on the road surface and stops at designated stations. It's also much faster than the tram, at times reaching a maximum speed of 70 km/h.

The LRT only runs in the New Territories, connecting the city of Tuen Mun with Yuen Long, but may be extended to connect with the MTR and KCR.

There are five LRT lines connecting the various small suburbs in the area. The LRT terminal in Tuen Mun is at the hoverferry pier, from where you can reach Central on Hong Kong Island in 30 minutes. Fares on the LRT are from HK$2.40 to HK$3.50 for adults, or from HK$1.20 to HK$1.80 for children.

TRAM

One of the world's great travel bargains, Hong Kong's trams are tall, narrow, double-decker streetcars that trundle along the northern side of Hong Kong Island from Kennedy Town to Shaukiwan and along the short loop to Happy Valley.

The tram line was built in 1904 on what was then the shoreline of Hong Kong Island, which should help you appreciate just how much land Hong Kong has reclaimed from the sea. Although the tram has been in operation since then, the vehicles you see were built in the 1950s and 1960s.

The trams are not fast but they are cheap and fun. For a flat fare of HK$1 (dropped in a box beside the driver when you leave – no change) you can go as far as you like, whether it's one block or the end of the line. Trams operate between 5.45 am and 12.25 am.

Try to get a seat at the front, upstairs window to enjoy a first-class view of life in Hong Kong while rattling through the crowded streets. If you don't get a seat, like during the rush hours, the ride is not so good. The HKTA's free fact sheet, *Tram Tour*, lists sights along the route.

TAXI

In Kowloon and Hong Kong Island, taxis are red with silver tops. In the New Territories they are green with white tops. In Lantau, the colour code is blue.

The New Territories taxis are cheapest but they are not permitted to pick up or put down passengers in Kowloon or Hong Kong

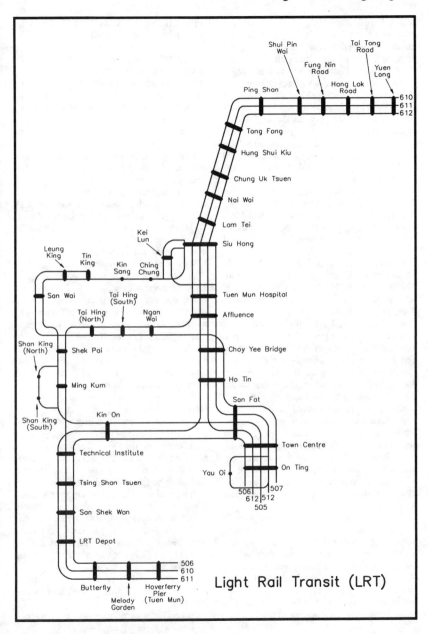

Light Rail Transit (LRT)

Island. It's often hard to get taxis during rush hour, when it rains or during shift changes (around 4 pm). Taxis are also in great demand after midnight since public transport stops by then. There are no extra late-night charges and no extra passenger charges.

When a taxi is available, there should be a red 'For Hire' sign displayed in the windscreen and the 'Taxi' sign on the roof will be lit up at night.

The flagfall in Hong Kong and Kowloon is HK$8 for the first two km and an extra 90 cents for every additional 0.25 km. In the New Territories the flagfall is HK$7 for the first two km and 80 cents for every additional 0.25 km. There is a luggage fee of HK$2 per bag but not all drivers insist on this. Most drivers carry very little change (to prevent robberies), so keep a supply of coins and HK$10 bills.

If you go through the Cross-Harbour Tunnel you'll be charged an extra HK$20. The toll is only HK$10, but the driver is allowed to assume that he won't get a fare back so you have to pay. You are also charged an extra HK$3 for the Aberdeen Tunnel and an extra HK$3 for the Lion Rock Tunnel which goes to Shatin in the New Territories. Finally, there is a HK$1 extra charge for a radio call. If you have any doubts, there is a card on the inside of the doors explaining these charges. There is no charge for the tunnel under Kai Tak Airport.

All taxis have a card on which the top 50 destinations are listed in Cantonese, English and Japanese – very useful since a lot of the taxi drivers don't speak English. Even if the card doesn't list your specific destination, it will certainly have some nearby place. The card is usually kept above the driver's sun visor.

If you feel a taxi driver has ripped you off, get the licence number and call the police hotline (☎ 5277177) to lodge a complaint with the relevant details about when, where and how much. It's unlikely you'll need to. Getting a taxi licence is extremely difficult and it can be easily revoked if the driver breaks the rules. The number of licences is limited and they are obtained through competitive bidding. The last time I checked the going rate was HK$600,000.

CAR & MOTORBIKE
Road Rules
Driving is on the left side of the road, the same as Australia and Britain but the opposite to China. Seat belts must be worn by the driver and all front-seat passengers. The police are strict and there are draconian fines for traffic violations.

Driving in crowded Hong Kong has been made deliberately expensive in order to discourage it. For a local resident to get a driving licence, he or she must take an expensive driving course and wait about 18 months. The motor vehicle import tax is 100% and the petrol tax is more than 100%. Vehicle registration (based on engine size) averages about HK$8000 annually and liability insurance is compulsory.

As for foreigners, anyone over the age of 18 with a valid driving licence from their home country, or an international driving permit, can drive in Hong Kong for up to 12 months. If you're staying longer, you'll need a Hong Kong licence. To get one, apply to the Transport Department Licensing Division (☎ 5261577), 41st floor, Wanchai Tower II, 7 Gloucester Rd, Wanchai. A driving test is not required.

Rental
The best advice that I can give about renting a car is don't! Except for touring some of the backwaters in the New Territories, a car saves no time at all. The MTR doesn't have to stop for traffic lights and taking the bus will often be faster than driving. The reason is that parking in the city is a nightmare, and it's likely that you'll have to park so far away from your destination that the time you saved will be used up walking to and from the car park. Hong Kongers who own cars mainly do so to gain face, not because they have any need for a motor vehicle. Expatriates with fragile egos also buy cars for the same reason. Another point to consider is the expense.

Several car-hire companies provide a

variety of cars for self-drive or chauffeur-driven rental. You'll find their addresses and phone numbers in the Yellow Pages Buying Guide under Motorcar Renting & Leasing. Also look in the classified advertisements of the newspapers.

You normally get unlimited km at no extra cost and discounts if you rent for a week or more. Many car-rental outlets and the big hotels offer a chauffeur-driven service, but using this service for one day could easily cost more than your hotel room.

Motorbikes seem impossible to rent, but can be bought if you're staying long enough. They are not very popular.

BICYCLE
Bicycles are not recommended for the steep streets and impatient traffic of Hong Kong Island or for the traffic of Kowloon either, but they are suitable for some parts of the New Territories and the outlying islands. There are places on Lantau and on Cheung

Chau where you can hire bicycles for a few hours or for the whole day. This is the same for Shatin and Tai Po in the New Territories.

WALKING
Despite the concrete, glass and steel, Hong Kong presents plenty of good opportunities for walking.

There are many interesting city walks around Hong Kong Island and Kowloon, as well as more rural walks on the outlying islands and in the New Territories, some of which are described in the relevant chapters.

Also useful is the HKTA free leaflet *Six Walks*. One 50-km walk twists and winds across the length of Hong Kong Island from Shek-O to Victoria Peak, with the 3.5 km Peak circuit walk as the starting or finishing stretch.

Selected Walks in Hong Kong by Ronald Forrest and George Hobbins describes walks of varying lengths in all regions.

TRAVELATOR
Though not yet in operation, Hong Kong's latest transport scheme is attracting widespread attention. Officially dubbed the 'Hillside Escalator Link', this novel system looks like something out of a science-fiction movie. Basically, the system consists of escalators and moving walkways, called 'travelators', elevated above the street level.

One of Hong Kong's long-standing problems is that many well-to-do residents live in the Mid-Levels, the lower portion of the Peak, but work in the skyscraper forest below. The roads are narrow and the distance is more vertical than horizontal, which means that walking involves a strenuous climb to get back home. The result is a rush hour nightmare of bumper-to-bumper taxis, minibuses and private cars. The Hillside Escalator Link aims to solve this problem by getting people out of their vehicles entirely.

The Link will be about 800 metres long when it is operational, hopefully by late 1993, and there is a possibility of expanding the system later. Other cities are watching with interest. Score another first for Hong Kong.

BOAT

Hong Kong ferries are cheaper and almost always faster than the bus. As long as you are not prone to seasickness, these are also loads of fun. There are also boats to the Outlying Islands.

Inter-Island Ferries

Star Ferry Practically every visitor takes a ride on the Star Ferry which is also an essential mode of transport for commuters. The ferry runs between Central (Hong Kong Island) and Tsimshatsui (the lower tip of Kowloon). When the weather is clear, the harbour views are stunning.

The service runs seven days a week from 6 am to 11.30 pm and is continuous. You never have to wait more than a few minutes to take the seven-minute trip. All of the ferries have names like *Morning Star, Evening Star, Celestial Star, Shining Star,* etc.

There are two fares: lower deck costs HK$1 per trip and upper deck is HK$1.20 per trip. The coin-operated turnstiles do not give change. You can get change from the ticket window if you take the upper deck, but the lower deck does not have a ticket window.

The top deck is less crowded and gives a different perspective than bottom deck, and has both a smoking and non-smoking section. I personally prefer the lower deck for photography purposes, but it's worth the extra 20c to go top deck at least once.

Pickpockets do a brisk business on the Star Ferry when it's crowded. Signs on the ferry warn about this. The problem has been reduced by undercover police who specialise in catching pickpockets, but it still pays to be careful with your cash.

Another Star Ferry This one goes from Central to Hunghom (near the KCR station in Tsimshatsui East). Unless you're going directly from Central to Hunghom KCR Station, you probably won't use this ferry. It's good to know about it so you don't get on it by mistake!

Other Cross-Harbour Ferries Other cross-harbour ferries include those between Wanchai and Jordan Rd in Kowloon, between Wanchai and Hunghom close to the KCR station, and between Hunghom and North Point. There's also a vehicular ferry between Jordan Rd and Central, but you probably won't use it.

Kaido These are small to medium-sized ferries which can make short runs like the trip from Aberdeen to Lamma Island.

A *sampan* is a motorised launch which can only accommodate a few people. A sampan is too small to be considered seaworthy, but can safely zip you around typhoon shelters like Aberdeen Harbour.

Bigger than a sampan, but small than a kaido, is a *walla walla*. These operate as water taxis on Victoria Harbour. Sailors normally take a walla walla to and from their ships anchored in the harbour.

Outlying Islands Ferry

Ferries to Lantau, Peng Chau and Cheung Chau depart from the Outlying Islands Ferry Pier. Ferries to Lamma Island depart from the adjacent Central Harbour Ferry Pier. (See the Outlying Islands chapter.)

Hoverferry

Hoverferries are about twice as fast as conventional boats. Inside they are luxurious with aircraft-type seats (no one stands) and air-conditioning. They are exciting to ride in but are not for the faint hearted!

Hoverferries are not particularly smooth. When the water is rough, they go bouncing along the surface like a stone skipping across a pond. If you're prone to seasickness, don't get on a hovercraft after eating a big plate of greasy pork chops and lasagna. You won't have the option of getting rid of this unpleasant mess over the side as the windows on hoverferries don't open.

The hovercraft you'll mostly use go to the outlying islands and depart from Government Pier, just to the west of the Outlying Islands Ferry Pier. There is also a hoverferry to Discovery Bay on Lantau Island, departing from Blake Pier. See the Outlying Islands chapter.

A hoverferry also goes from Blake Pier to Tuen Mun in the New Territories. It takes 30 minutes and is the fastest way to reach the western part of the New Territories from Central.

If you want a short ride, a hoverferry to Central departs from Tsimshatsui East every 20 minutes from 10 am to 5 pm. Board at the Promenade, which is east of the New World Hotel and very close to Tsimshatsui Centre on Salisbury Rd.

RICKSHAW

This was once the main means of public transport in Hong Kong. Rickshaws were invented by an American Baptist missionary in Japan in 1871 and quickly caught on in Hong Kong.

That was then and this is now – rickshaws are just for photograph-taking. Licences to operate a rickshaw have not been issued for many decades and the remaining drivers are in their 70s. You have to bargain the fare with them. For only a photograph they'll ask at least HK$20 but you can often get them down to HK$10. The fare escalates dramatically if you ask them to take you any distance, even around the block. Agree on the fare first and ignore demands for more. If the rickshaw drivers try to cheat you, threaten to call the police.

TOURS

There are so many tours available it's impossible to list them all. You can get one to just about anywhere in Hong Kong. Some popular destinations include the Sung (Song) Dynasty Village, Ocean Park, Stanley, the Outlying Islands or the duck farms in the New Territories.

Tours can be booked through the HKTA, travel agents, large tourist hotels or directly from the tour company. If you're a student, the HKSTB offers discounts of HK$10 or HK$20 on the cost of the tours. Here's a sample of what's on:

Watertours
There are more than a dozen of these popular tours, covering such diverse places as Victoria Harbour and Cheung Chau Island. Book these trips through a travel agent or call Watertours (☎ 5254808). Costs vary enormously according to which tour you take.

Harbour Cruises
These are offered by the Star Ferry Company, and you book at the Star Ferry Pier. There are both day and evening cruises. They cost HK$80 to HK$120 for adults, HK$60 for children.

Tram Dim Sum Tours
You ride a tram, sample dim sum and explore the city. Book at the Star Ferry Pier. It costs HK$97 for adults, HK$80 for children.

Come Horse-Racing Tour
You get to sit in the Visitors' Box of the Members' Enclosure of the Royal Hong Kong Jockey Club. A Western lunch or dinner is thrown in. The tours follow the racing season, and you must be 18 or older to participate. It costs HK$350 and the tour is conducted by the HKTA.

Cultural Diversions Tour

Held at the Hong Kong Cultural Centre, the tour covers Chinese acrobatics, folk dances, songs and magic shows, and ends with an eight-course banquet. It costs HK$290 for adults, HK$240 for children aged six to 15 and the tour is conducted by the HKTA.

Heritage Tour

This covers major historical sights, including Lei Cheng Uk, a 2000-year-old burial chamber. It costs HK$250 and the tour is conducted by the HKTA.

Housing Tour & Home Visit

You visit two public housing estates and see how the people live. You get to visit a family's apartment, a rest home and a large Taoist temple. It costs HK$180 for adults and HK$140 for children under 16. The tour is conducted by the HKTA.

Land Between Tour

This popular tour covers the New Territories. It costs HK$260 for adults, HK$210 for children under 16 and the tour is conducted by the HKTA.

Sports & Recreation Tour

You get to use the facilities at the Clearwater Bay Golf & Country Club. This tour includes the golf course, jacuzzi, swimming pool, sauna, tennis courts, etc. A free meal is thrown in. The cost is HK$260 for the tour, plus HK$600 for use of the facilities. The tour is conducted by the HKTA.

Yum Sing Night on the Town

This self-guided tour has two options. The Grand Package costs HK$130, and includes a coupon for drinks at a pub, bar or nightclub, and one coupon for a drink at a disco. All cover charges are waived. The Deluxe Package costs HK$380 and includes a drink and an hour of chatting with a hostess at a high-class girlie bar. This tour is sponsored by the HKTA!

Kowloon 九龍

The name Kowloon is thought to have originated when the last emperor of the Song Dynasty passed through the area during his flight from the Mongols. He counted eight peaks on the peninsula and commented that there must therefore be eight dragons there – but was reminded that since he himself was present there must be nine.

Kowloon means nine dragons and is derived from the Cantonese words *kau* for nine and *loong* for dragon. Now Kowloon is a mere 12 sq km of high-rise buildings extending from the Tsimshatsui waterfront at the tip of the peninsula to as far north as Boundary St.

TSIMSHATSUI 尖沙咀
Hong Kong's tourist ghetto lies at the very tip of the Kowloon Peninsula in Tsimshatsui. About one sq km of shops, restaurants, pubs, topless bars charging rip-off prices, fast-food places and camera and electronics stores are clustered on either side of Nathan Rd.

Clock Tower 鐘樓
Adjacent to the Star Ferry Terminal and the new Hong Kong Cultural Centre, the clock tower is all that remains of a railway station that once existed at the tip of the Kowloon Peninsula. The railway station – the southern terminal of the present KCR – was built in 1916 and torn down in 1978. The old station was a colonial-style building with columns, but was too small to handle the volume of passenger traffic. The new station, where many travellers begin their journey to China, is a huge, modern building at Hunghom to the north-east of Tsimshatsui.

Hong Kong Cultural Centre 文化中心
Adjacent to the Star Ferry Pier, the Hong Kong Cultural Centre (☎ 7342009) is one of Hong Kong's landmarks. The complex includes a concert hall able to seat 2200 people and a cinema that accommodates 1800, an arts library, two restaurants and a garden. On the south side of the building is a viewing area where you can admire Victoria Harbour, also known as Hong Kong Harbour.

Space Museum 太空館
This is the peculiar building shaped like half a golf ball at 10 Salisbury Rd, adjoining the Hong Kong Cultural Centre. It's divided into three parts: the Planetarium (Space Theatre), an Exhibition Hall and a Hall of Solar Sciences devoted to exhibitions about the sun.

Exhibits include a lump of moon rock, models of rocket ships, telescopes, time lines and videos of moon walks – all very educational and worth a look. The Mercury space capsule piloted by Scott Carpenter in 1962 is displayed.

Opening times for the Exhibition Hall and the Hall of Solar Sciences are Monday, Wednesday, Thursday and Friday from 2 to 9.30 pm; Saturday from 1 to 9.30 pm and Sunday and public holidays from 10.30 am to 9.30 pm. Admission is free.

The Planetarium has seven shows each day (except Tuesday), some in English and some in Cantonese, but headphone translations are available for all shows. Check times with the museum. Admission to the Planetarium is HK$20, or HK$13 for students and seniors (over 60). The museum is closed on Tuesday. They have a number (☎ 7212361) for inquiries. Telephone reservations (☎ 7349009) are valid until one hour before the show.

Star House 星光行
This building occupies a prime piece of turf right next to the Star Ferry Bus Terminal. Astronomical rents are charged for ground floor shops; the shops recover their money through the constant flow of tourists. Watson's Drugstore is the cheapest place around here to buy film which you might need for photographing the harbour. Most of the stores inside the arcade are overpriced,

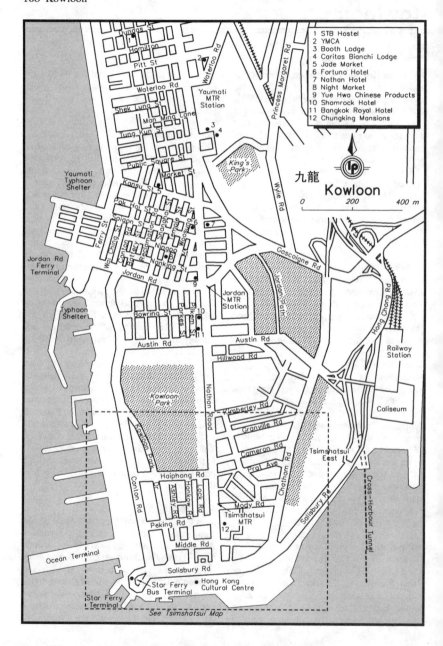

1 STB Hostel
2 YMCA
3 Booth Lodge
4 Caritas Bianchi Lodge
5 Jade Market
6 Fortuna Hotel
7 Nathan Hotel
8 Night Market
9 Yue Hwa Chinese Products
10 Shamrock Hotel
11 Bangkok Royal Hotel
12 Chungking Mansions

九龍
Kowloon

0   200   400 m

but check out Chinese Arts & Crafts (owned by the People's Republic).

Ocean Terminal 海運大廈

Just around to the left from Star House, the long building jutting out into the harbour is the Ocean Terminal. Luxury cruise-ship passengers come ashore here, and to meet their needs the terminal and adjoining Ocean Centre are crammed with very ritzy shops in endless arcades. Not the place for cheap souvenir hunting but interesting for a stroll. On the waterfront is a small park built on a pier, which has benches and good views of the harbour.

Peninsula Hotel 半島酒店

One of Hong Kong's most prestigious landmarks, the Peninsula used to be *the* place to stay in Hong Kong. It's on Salisbury Rd and was once right on the waterfront, but land reclamation has extended the shoreline south another block.

Before WW II it was part of a chain of prestigious hotels across Asia where everybody who was anybody stayed. The list included Raffles in Singapore, the Taj in Bombay and the Cathay (now called the Peace) in Shanghai.

Given the age of the hotel and the expensive real estate it occupies, rumours occasionally surface that it will be torn down to make way for yet another 40-storey cigar box. Fortunately, the Peninsula has no trouble making money despite the high prices for rooms. As long as it remains a profitable venture, it will most likely continue to grace Hong Kong's skyline.

The hotel's lobby offers high-ceilinged splendour. It is worth paying the extra for a cup of coffee or a beer here to enjoy the rarefied atmosphere and to spot people spotting other people. The rich and famous are said to stay here, but if so, they don't hang around the lobby.

Nathan Rd 彌敦道

The main drag of Kowloon, Nathan Rd was named after the governor around the turn of this century, Sir Matthew Nathan. It was promptly renamed Nathan's Folly because in those times Kowloon was sparsely populated and such a wide road was unnecessary. The trees that once lined the street are gone and some would say that the folly has remained.

Now the lower end of the road is known as the Golden Mile, which refers to both the price of real estate here and also its ability to suck money out of tourist pockets.

Kowloon Park 九龍公園

Shrinking Park might be a better name for this place. I remember a time when the park bordered Nathan Rd and was filled with trees, flowers, joggers and strolling couples. Those days are gone. Now the park is hidden behind Yue Hwa's Park Lane Store on Nathan Rd and new concrete blocks on Austin Rd. Most tourists staying in nearby hotels are not aware that the park exists.

Just as well, because the park is so artificial that it might as well be indoors. Some recent creations include the Sculpture Walk, a grotesque outdoor 'art gallery' made up of metal tubes. Other highlights include the aviary, a space-age indoor sports hall, fountains, concrete plazas, a museum and other intrusions. The multiple swimming pools are perhaps the best feature of this place, but they're packed on weekends. There are still a few magnificent old trees left in the park, but just wait, they'll get those too. Personally, I liked the park better before the authorities 'improved' it. Admission is free. The park is open daily from 6.30 am to 11.30 pm.

Museum of History 香港博物館

Located inside Kowloon Park on Nathan Rd this museum (☎ 3671124) covers all of Hong Kong's existence, from prehistoric times to the present. It contains a large collection of 19th and early 20th-century photographs of the city.

The museum is open Monday to Thursday and Saturday from 10 am to 6 pm, and Sunday and public holidays from 1 to 6 pm. It is closed on Friday and admission is free. Enter from Haiphong Rd on the south side of the park.

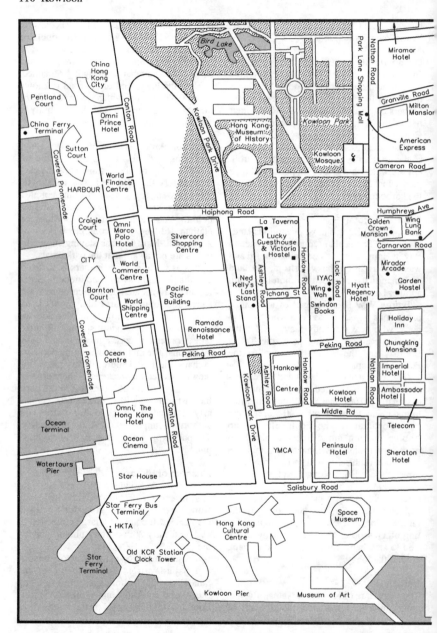

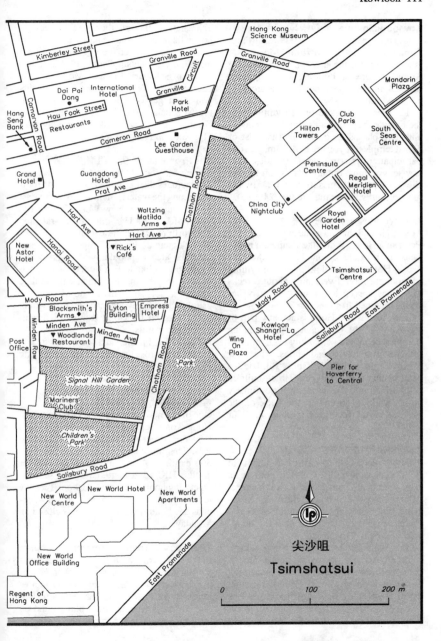

尖沙咀
Tsimshatsui

Kowloon Mosque 回教禮拜堂

Near the intersection of Nathan and Cameron Rds, the Kowloon Mosque & Islamic Centre is the largest mosque in Hong Kong. The present building was completed in 1984 and occupies the site of a previous mosque built in 1896.

The mosque is interesting to admire from the outside, but you can't simply wander in and take photos as occurs in Buddhist or Taoist temples. If you are a Muslim, you can participate in their religious activities. Otherwise, you must obtain permission to visit the mosque. Permission isn't always granted, but you can inquire (☎ 7240095).

New World Hotel 新世界酒店

You might call this place the antithesis of the Peninsula Hotel. While the Peninsula maintains an air of old, colonial charm, the New World Hotel is a shining, glittering symbol of modernisation. Everything about it reeks of newness – even the ground it's built on has been reclaimed from the sea.

The New World Hotel is actually part of the New World Centre, a large shopping complex complete with many excellent restaurants, nightclubs and shops. The New World Centre is at 22 Salisbury Rd. Hidden right behind it is the Regent Hotel, built on piles driven into the sea floor. It's definitely worth walking around to the back of the Regent Hotel for the excellent harbour views.

TSIMSHATSUI EAST 尖沙咀東部

This big piece of land east of Chatham Rd didn't even exist until 1980. Built entirely on reclaimed land, Tsimshatsui East is a cluster of shopping malls, hotels, theatres, restaurants and nightclubs. Everything is new – there are none of the old, crumbling buildings of nearby Tsimshatsui.

Tsimshatsui East caters to Hong Kong's middle class and nouveaux riches. Oddly, foreigners are relatively few. It's interesting to speculate on why this is. Perhaps the sight of all those shiny buildings makes visitors think the area is horribly expensive. Actually, prices are about the same as in Tsimshatsui, though there are no budget hotels like Chungking Mansions.

The area has one very good shopping mall, the Tsimshatsui Centre, 66 Mody Rd, between Salisbury Rd and Mody Rd. Of course, if you're looking for real bargains you must get completely away from the tourist zone and go where the locals shop – Shatin in the New Territories or Cityplaza (Tai Koo) on Hong Kong Island.

The Promenade 尖沙咀海濱公園

Some of the best things in life are free, and this includes the Promenade – the wide footpath along the waterfront in Tsimshatsui East on the south side of New World Centre. The views of Victoria Harbour are first-rate and it's worth repeating the trip at night. Races are held here during the Dragon Boat Festival. The area is popular with joggers and Chinese who like to fish right off the Promenade, despite the less than immaculate water. I'm not sure what they do with the fish caught, but if anyone eats it, that would partly account for Hong Kong's high incidence of hepatitis.

From the Promenade, you can take a hoverferry across the harbour to Hong Kong Island.

Hong Kong Science Museum 香港科學博物館

One of the newest attractions in the city, the Hong Kong Science Museum (☎ 7323232) is at the corner of Chatham and Granville Rds. This multilevel complex houses over 500 exhibits. Admission costs HK$25 for adults, HK$15 for students and seniors. Operating hours are from 1 to 9 pm Tuesday to Friday, and from 10 am to 9 pm on weekends and holidays. The museum is closed on Monday.

Whampoa Garden Commercial Complex

In the middle of a high-rise housing estate is the Whampoa, a full-sized concrete model of a luxury cruiser. The 'ship' is 100 metres long and four decks tall. Inside is a restaurant, shops, a cinema and a playground on the top deck. The basement also harbours

Top: Vanishing Hong Kong - an amah and a letter writer (IMcQ)
Bottom: Another disappearing trade - the rickshaw (IMcQ)

Top: A busy wharf, Kowloon (GI)
Bottom: Crowded waterways, Aberdeen, Hong Kong Island (GI)

more shops and a car park. The concrete ship was built by one of Hong Kong's largest companies – Hutchison Whampoa.

The Whampoa is little bit off the beaten tourist track, but not difficult to reach. It's at the corner of Shung King and Tak Fung Sts in the Hinghom district, a little to the north-east of the KCR station in Tsimshatsui East. It's actually easiest to reach from the Hong Kong Island side because you can take the Star Ferry to the Hunghom Ferry Pier, or else the ferry from Wanchai to Hunghom. From the pier it's only about a 10-minute walk to the east. The 'ship' is next to Whampoa Garden, one block from the waterfront.

YAUMATI 油蔴地

Immediately north of Tsimshatsui – and indistinguishable from it – is the Yaumati district. Its chief attraction is the Jade Market, the Temple St night market and the Chinese emporiums along Nathan Rd.

There are many interesting walks to take along the streets between Jordan Rd and Kansu St. These include Canton Rd (ivory and mahjong shops), Saigon St (a street market) and Ning Po St (paper items such as kites and paper houses, and luxury items for the dead).

Worth checking out is the Yaumati Typhoon Shelter just to the west of Ferry St. Built in 1915 after a disastrous typhoon, it is one of Hong Kong's big three typhoon shelters. The other two are Aberdeen Harbour and Cheung Chau. Thousands of people live here permanently on boats. The area was once famous for its floating brothels, but these no longer compete with the land-based businesses.

Jade Market 玉器市場

The Jade Market is at the junction of Reclamation and Kansu Sts under the overpass in the Yaumati district, just to the west of Nathan Rd. It's open daily between 10 am and 3.30 pm, but go early as you may find the sellers packing up and leaving at about 1 pm. It's more for the Chinese than for tourists, but you can get some good deals here. Be sure to bargain hard.

To get there take bus No 9 from the Kowloon Star Ferry Bus Terminal, get off at Kowloon Central Post Office and walk down to the intersection of Kowloon and Reclamation Sts. Coming from Hong Kong Island, take the MTR and get off at either Jordan or Yaumati MTR stations.

Tin Hau Temple 天后廟

On Market St, a block or two to the north of the Jade Market, is a sizable Tin Hau temple, dedicated to the patron goddess of seafarers. See the Religion section in the Facts About Hong Kong chapter. The temple is open daily from 7.30 am to 8.30 pm.

Temple St 廟街

The liveliest night market in the city, Temple St (and Shanghai St which runs parallel to it) is the place to go for cheap clothes, cheap food, watches, footwear, cookware and everyday items. It's geared more towards men's clothes than women's. Temple St is at its best in the evening from about 8 to 11 pm when it's clogged with stalls and people. All of the streets have lots of small shops worth looking into.

MONGKOK 旺角
Tung Choi St 通菜街

Mongkok is a good shopping area, and Tong Choi St is the liveliest street market in Hong Kong. This market is supposed to feature women's clothing, but in fact you can find just about anything here.

Bird Market 雀鳥市場

The most exotic sight in Mongkok is the Bird Market. It's on Hong Lok St, an obscure alley on the south side of Argyle St, two blocks west of Nathan Rd. In crowded Hong Kong, few people keep dogs or cats, but birds are highly prized as pets, especially if they can sing. Aside from the hundreds of birds on display, large bags of live grasshoppers are for sale. The birds seem to live pretty well: the Chinese use chopsticks to feed the grasshoppers to their feathered friends, the bird cages are elaborately carved from teak and bamboo, and the water and food dishes are made from ceramic.

NEW KOWLOON 新九龍
North of Kowloon proper is an area of about 30 sq km known as New Kowloon, which includes places such as Sham Shui Po, Laichikok and Kwun Tong. Strictly speaking, these places are part of the New Territories but people tend to include them in Kowloon in everyday usage. Boundary St marks the border between Kowloon and the New Territories, and this would have become the new border in 1997 had Great Britain and China failed to reach an agreement on Hong Kong's future.

Wong Tai Sin Temple 黃大仙廟
This very large and active Taoist temple was built in 1973 and is adjacent to the Wong Tai Sin housing estate. It is dedicated to the god of the same name. The image of the god in the main temple was brought to Hong Kong from China in 1915 and was originally installed in a temple in Wanchai until it was moved to the present site in 1921. For information on Wong Tai Sin see the Religion section in the Facts About Hong Kong chapter, and for a useful description of the temple, building by building, get a free copy of the HKTA *Wong Tai Sin* fact sheet.

On Sunday afternoon the temple is crowded with worshippers burning joss sticks and making offerings of plates of food. Some bring their own carefully prepared dishes, others buy oranges from the numerous fruit stalls that engulf the entrance. The incense is burned, the offerings are made (but not left, since the gods can't be all that hungry and no-one wants good food to go to waste) and the fortune sticks are cast.

Adjacent to the temple is an arcade filled with about 150 booths operated by fortune tellers. Some of them speak good English, so if you really want to know what fate has in store for you, this is your chance to find out. Just off to one side of the arcade is a small open area where you can look up and get a magnificent view of Lion Rock, one of Hong Kong's prominent landmarks.

Getting to the temple is easy. Take the MTR to the Wong Tai Sin Station then follow the signs in the station to come out in front of the temple.

The temple is open daily from 7 am to 5 pm. The busiest times are around the Chinese New Year, on Wong Tai Sin's birthday on the 23rd day of the eighth lunar month, during the seventh lunar month (the ghost month) and most Sundays.

Sung (Song) Dynasty Village 宋城
The village was once part of Laichikok Amusement Park before it was hyped up as an authentic re-creation of a Chinese village from 10 centuries ago.

It's a type of Chinese Disneyland-supermarket where craftspeople and other villagers walk around in period costumes, engaging in Song Dynasty (960 AD to 1279) pursuits such as fortune-telling, blacksmithing, woodcarving and getting married.

Candy and pastries can be bought with coupons made to look like Song money, but if you want a kimono, paperweight or other souvenir from the village shop you'll have to have 20th-century cash.

Beneath the Restaurant of Plentiful Joy lies Hong Kong's largest wax museum, which houses figures of people from Chinese history.

The Sung Dynasty Village is big with tour groups, but individuals are admitted from 10 am to 8.30 pm daily. Admission costs HK$95. It drops to HK$75 on weekends and public holidays between 12.30 and 5 pm.

You can get there either by bus or MTR. From the Kowloon Star Ferry Bus Terminal take bus No 6A, which terminates near the Sung Dynasty Village.

From Hong Kong Island, take the vehicular ferry to the Jordan Rd Ferry Terminal, then catch bus No 12 to the park. Alternatively, you can take the MTR but you'll have to do more walking: take the MTR to Mei Foo Station. From there head north along Lai Wan Rd and turn left at the junction with Mei

Lai Rd. Continue down Mei Lai Rd, at the end of which is the Sung Dynasty Village.

Lei Cheng Uk Museum & Han Tomb
李鄭屋村古墓

The Han Tomb at 41 Tonkin St, Lei Cheng Uk Estate, is a branch of the Museum of History. The site is an actual late Han Dynasty (25 AD to 220) burial vault. The tomb and tiny museum are in Sham Shui Po, a district of New Kowloon immediately north of Boundary St.

The Han Tomb is Hong Kong's earliest historical monument. It was discovered in 1955 when workers were levelling the hillside in preparation for a housing estate. The tomb consists of four barrel-vaulted brick chambers in the form of a cross, around a domed, central chamber. The tomb, estimated to be more than 1600 years old, is behind the museum and encased in a concrete shell for protection.

The tomb is open daily (except Thursday) from 10 am to 1 pm, and from 2 to 6 pm. On Sunday and public holidays it's open from 1 to 6 pm. Admission is 10c.

To get there, take bus No 2 from the Kowloon Star Ferry Bus Terminal and get off at Tonkin St. The nearest MTR station is Cheung Sha Wan, a five-minute walk from the tomb.

PLACES TO STAY – BOTTOM END
Chungking Mansions

There is probably no other place in the world like *Chungking Mansions*, the bottom-end accommodation ghetto of Hong Kong. It's a huge high-rise dump at 30 Nathan Rd in the heart of Tsimshatsui.

For years there has been much talk about tearing down Chungking Mansions because it's an eyesore and a fire trap, but the cost would be huge and the Hong Kong government tends to take a 'hands off' approach to private enterprise. More than likely, the demise of Chungking Mansions will come when someone decides to put up the money to buy the place, tear it down and put up a new high-rise luxury hotel.

Chungking Mansions is chock full of dormitories and cheap guesthouses, some amazingly filthy and others surprisingly good. If you're travelling budget class, there is a very good chance that you'll wind up staying here, though there are many other cheap alternatives.

The entrance to Chungking Mansions is a shopping arcade facing Nathan Rd. Wander around and you will find lifts labelled A to E. There are only two tiny overworked lifts for each 17-storey block. Long lines form in front of the lifts in A and B blocks. It's often faster to walk up the stairs if you think you can cope with up to 17 storeys.

Despite the dilapidated state of the building, most of the little hotels are OK – generally clean and often quite comfortable, though rooms are the size of closets. The Mansions is a good place to eat cheaply too, with several low-priced restaurants, many run by Indians and Pakistanis. The ground floor is also filled with shops selling everything imaginable.

The places listed here are just a sample of what's available. There are more than 100 guesthouses in Chungking Mansions, far too many to name them all, and every month new ones open and old ones close. Prices are only a guide and vary with the season, peaking in summer and during certain holidays such as Easter.

Bargaining is certainly possible when business is slack. You can often negotiate a cheaper price if you stay a long time, but never do that the first night. Stay one night and find out how you like it before handing over two weeks' rent. Once you pay, there are no refunds.

If you want to check out Chungking Mansions' guesthouses other than those listed here, just stand in the lobby with your luggage. There are plenty of touts who will approach you with offers for cheap rooms.

Dormitories There are now only a few places in Chungking Mansions still offering dormitories, though there are dormitories elsewhere in Tsimshatsui (see the following Other Cheapies section).

The ever-popular *Travellers' Hostel* (☎ 3687710), A Block, 16th floor, is a Chungking Mansions landmark. It has mixed dormitory accommodation for HK$38 a bed. Double rooms without/with bath cost HK$80/130. They have metal lockers and good security, and the hostel was completely renovated recently. The management also operates a cheap beachside hostel at Ting Kau in the New Territories. See the Places to Stay section of the New Territories chapter for details.

Sky Guesthouse, A Block, 3rd floor, won't win any contests for cleanliness but it's one of the cheapest places in Hong Kong, with dormitory beds for HK$35. Another advantage is that it's a short walk up the stairs, so you can avoid the horrible lift queues in A Block.

Friendship Travellers' House (☎ 3110797), B Block, 6th floor, has mixed dormitory accommodation for HK$35 a night. Although rather cramped, it's popular with travellers. Single rooms range from HK$80 to HK$140.

A Block This has the most guesthouses, offering a wide selection in both price and quality. The only drawback is the frequent long queues to get into the lifts. You may find yourself using the stairs more than you expected, which wouldn't be so terrible except that the stairwells are incredibly filthy and the cockroaches show no fear. Still, A Block is the happy hunting ground for cheap accommodation and you are likely to find yourself staying there.

Super Guesthouse (☎ 3683767), 17th floor, is a quiet place with big double rooms for HK$180. The manager does not live on the premises, so you must first go to the 12th floor, flat A5, to book a room. One advantage of staying here is that you can easily go on the roof at night and admire Hong Kong's spectacular skyline.

Park Guesthouse (☎ 3681689), 15th floor, has singles from HK$80 to HK$100 and doubles from HK$100 to HK$120. With a private bath, doubles are from HK$160 to HK$180. It's clean, has air-con and is friendly. Also on the 15th floor is *Ocean Guesthouse* (☎ 7213255), which has singles with shared/private bath for HK$80/150.

New Grand Guesthouse (☎ 3686520), 14th floor, has singles from HK$100 to HK$150, and doubles from HK$140 to HK$240.

Ashoka Guesthouse (☎ 7244646), 13th floor, is a little bit dumpy-looking but relatively cheap. Singles/doubles are HK$90/100.

Peking Guesthouse (☎ 7238320), 12th floor, has very friendly management and is very clean. Highly recommended. All rooms have air-con and singles run from HK$120 to HK$260.

Lucky Guesthouse (☎ 3687414), on the 11th floor, has doubles with shared bath for HK$130.

New International Guesthouse (☎ 3692613), 11th floor, has singles with shared/attached bath for HK$90/160. Doubles range from HK$110 to HK$300 with a private bath, air-con, TV and a personal refrigerator. It has a laundry service and is clean and friendly.

New Mandarin Guesthouse (☎ 3661070), 8th floor, is clean and has singles from HK$90 with a shared bath to HK$130 with a private bath, air-con and TV.

Sun Ying Guesthouse (☎ 3688094), 8th floor, is run by a very friendly woman who keeps clean rooms. Singles cost HK$100 with air-con and TV or HK$130 for a double.

Tom's Guesthouse (☎ 7224956), 8th floor, has singles and doubles from HK$120 to HK$140. More expensive rooms have a private bath. The management was positively rude on my last visit.

New Asia Guesthouse (☎ 7240426), 8th floor, is clean and has singles with shared/attached bath for HK$80/110. They can do laundry and serve inexpensive meals and drinks.

Welcome Guesthouse (☎ 7217793), 7th floor, is the one I'd go for in this block. Run by a very friendly man, rooms are HK$90 a single with a shared bath or HK$120 to HK$160 with a private bath, TV and air-con. They run a laundry service and can arrange visas for China. One traveller, taken with the place, said: 'When I got back from China and found them all full, I took a bed next to the entranceway just so I could stay there'.

Double Seven Guesthouse (☎ 7230148), 7th floor, has singles from HK$90 to HK$140 with air-con and rooms from HK$100 have a private bath. This place offers good value for money.

London Guesthouse (☎ 7245000), 6th floor, is friendly and clean and has singles from HK$85 to HK$180 with TV and air-con. All rooms have telephones.

Chungking House (☎ 3665362), 4th & 5th floors, while not very friendly, is the most classy place in Chungking Mansions with prices to match. Singles/doubles cost HK$230/322. All rooms have private bath. Rooms can even be booked at the HKTA office at Kai Tak Airport.

B Block This block has almost as many guesthouses as A Block, so you may still have to queue for the lifts. The stairwells support a rather large amount of wildlife, including a rare species of aggressive cockroach which is indigenous to this region of

Chungking Mansions. Be grateful for the stray cats as they keep the rats in check.

Starting from the top, the dilapidated-looking *Asia Guesthouse* (☎ 3668879), 17th floor, has singles/doubles at HK$80/100, complete with thundering TVs. They cater mainly to Indians but will take Westerners.

New Regent Guesthouse (☎ 3112525), 16th floor, is run by a very friendly Chinese woman who keeps the place spotlessly clean. Singles cost HK$110, and large, bright double rooms are HK$160.

Carlton Guesthouse (☎ 7210720), 15th floor, has singles for HK$90 and doubles for HK$130. A very clean, very tidy place with friendly people, it caters mainly to a Pakistani clientele, but will take Westerners.

New Washington Guesthouse (☎ 3665798), 13th floor, is friendly, clean and popular. Doubles range from HK$100 to HK$160.

Grandway Guesthouse (☎ 3675565), 12th floor, is a quiet and clean place, but the people who run it are consistently unfriendly towards Westerners. Nevertheless, it is worth trying if you can't find anything else. Singles cost HK$110 with air-con and TV and doubles cost HK$120.

Hong Kong Guesthouse (☎ 7237842), 11th floor, has singles for HK$120 and doubles for HK$180 with TV and air-con.

Kowloon Guesthouse, (☎ 3699802), 10th floor, has singles from HK$90 to HK$100 and caters mostly to an African clientele.

Grand Guesthouse (☎ 3686520), 9th floor, has doubles with a private bath for HK$150. The place looks rather dirty.

Lumbini Guesthouse, 8th floor, caters to a mostly Pakistani clientele. Doubles are HK$120 to HK$150.

Jinn's Ti Guesthouse (☎ 3670203), 7th floor, looks relatively clean and has rooms for HK$150.

Tin Tin Guesthouse (☎ 7392271), 5th floor, offers singles from HK$70 to HK$90.

Harbour Guesthouse (☎ 7212207), 4th floor, is clean, bright and friendly. Doubles cost HK$150 with air-con and a private bath.

C Block The one great advantage of staying in C Block is that there are no queues for the lifts. Also, the stairwells and hallways are much cleaner than elsewhere in Chungking Mansions.

The reason for this is that C Block has few guesthouses and is mostly a residential area. Thus your choice of accommodation is limited. Also, the guesthouses are small, usually with four or five rooms, so you won't

have many opportunities to meet other travellers. Lastly, several places don't have air-con, which is no problem in winter but can be uncomfortable in summer. But, if you value cleanliness and can't tolerate the lifts in A or B blocks, C Block might be for you.

Tom's Guesthouse (☎ 3679258), 16th floor, is clean and quiet and has singles for HK$80 and doubles for HK$120 to HK$130. The manager lives here and is very friendly.

Garden Guesthouse (☎ 3680981), 16th floor, has singles with private bath for HK$160. The rooms are small but clean and have TV and air-con.

Berlin Guesthouse (☎ 3691944), 14th floor, has singles/doubles for HK$70/110. It's a small place and the owner lives on the premises. He keeps it very clean, speaks good English and is friendly.

Garden Guesthouse (☎ 3687414), 7th floor, is not to be confused with the hotel of the same name on the 16th floor. This guesthouse is new and clean, and charges HK$150 for a room with private bath.

New Brother's Guesthouse (☎ 7240135), 6th floor, is very clean and has singles for HK$120 and doubles from HK$140 to HK$180. Every room has a TV and air-con.

Centre Point Inn (☎ 3685974), 3rd floor, has singles/doubles for HK$120/140 with shared bath. Large singles/doubles with private bath are HK$260/310. This place looks a little tattered around the edges but has a huge lobby.

D Block This part of Chungking is almost as tattered and dirty as A and B blocks. It rates third in terms of the number of guesthouses, and you sometimes have to queue for the lifts.

Four Seas Guesthouse (☎ 3687469), 15th floor, is basic but friendly. Singles cost HK$100 and doubles cost HK$120.

Guangzhou Guesthouse (☎ 7241555), 13th floor, is not particularly friendly, but has OK singles from HK$90 to HK$110, or HK$140 for a double with air-con.

Broadway Inn (☎ 3680081), 10th floor, looks like a nice place. Singles/doubles cost HK$100/120.

New Shanghai Guesthouse, 8th floor, has singles for HK$90 and doubles for HK$120 to HK$150.

Royal Plaza Inn (☎ 3671424), 5th floor, is one of the better places in D Block. They have singles for HK$160 and doubles for HK$190 with a private bath.

Dragon Garden (☎ 3116644), 5th floor, has doubles with a private bath for HK$150.

China Town (☎ 7213546), 3rd floor, is one of the fancier places in D Block but prices are high at HK$220 with shared bath and HK$250 with private bath.

Princess Guesthouse, 3rd floor, is cheap at HK$100/120 for singles/doubles. The management is friendly.

E Block Like C Block, this area is a backwater which is fairly clean and quiet, and has relatively few guesthouses. There are no long queues for the lifts.

Shan-E-Punjab Guesthouse (☎ 7233138), 17th floor, caters to Indians but will rent to anyone. It looks nice and has doubles for HK$140 with air-con.

Far East Guesthouse (☎ 3681724), 14th floor, has doubles from HK$100. Rooms are clean and have a telephone, TV and air-con.

Home Town Guesthouse (☎ 7238229), 10th floor, is one of the fanciest places in Chungking Mansions. The rooms are absolutely beautiful and are carpeted, but prices are high. Doubles cost HK$280 with air-con, phone and private bath. This place also has an entrance from D Block.

Sheraton Guesthouse (☎ 3687981), 3rd floor – no relation to another rather larger Sheraton establishment further down Nathan Rd – has singles with air-con for HK$90 and doubles for HK$110.

Other Cheapies

There are a few privately run hostels and guesthouses of the Chungking genre, mostly in the streets nearby. You may want to try these just to avoid the stigma of having to say: 'I'm staying in Chungking Mansions'.

The *International Youth Accommodation Centre (IYAC)* (☎ 3663419), 6th floor, 21A Lock Rd, Tsimshatsui, is very popular. Dormitory beds cost HK$40 and the dorms have air-con. On the ground floor is an excellent and inexpensive coffee shop and restaurant.

Golden Crown Guesthouse (☎ 3691782) Golden Crown Mansion, 5th floor, 66-70 Nathan Rd, Tsimshatsui, has dormitory beds for HK$40, singles range from HK$80 to HK$220 and doubles cost from HK$130 to HK$220. *London Guesthouse* (☎ 3681740) is next door, where singles and doubles start at HK$120 and go up to about HK$240 for three people. Also on the 5th floor, hidden in the back, is the spotlessly clean and highly recommended *Wah Tat Guesthouse* (☎ 3666121) where singles/doubles cost HK$120/150.

Victoria Hostel (☎ 3120621), 1st floor, 33 Hankow Rd, Tsimshatsui, is one of the nicest hostels in Hong Kong. There are several dormitories. The cheaper ones have no air-con and cost HK$40. Dorms with air-con cost HK$51. This place has a lot of useful amenities, including a kitchen, lockers and IDD card phones. The same management also operates the *Victoria Guesthouse* (☎ 3668508), 2nd floor, 4 Minden Ave, Tsimshatsui, where there are private rooms starting from HK$140.

Lucky Guesthouse (☎ 3670342) is a very popular place with travellers. It's on the 3rd floor, 33 Hankow Rd, Tsimshatsui. The dormitory beds cost HK$38 a night.

Club Hostel (☎ 3800782), 3rd floor, 714 Shanghai St, in Mongkok, has been highly recommended. Dormitory accommodation costs HK$45, while private rooms range from HK$90 to HK$110.

Around the corner from Chungking Mansions is the *Garden Hostel* (☎ 7218567). It's in Mirador Arcade, 58 Nathan Rd, but it's easier to find if you enter from Mody Rd. Turn right as you come out of the main entrance to Chungking and then right at the first street (Mody Rd). On the left side of the street you see an obvious sign. Enter the stairwell and go to the 3rd floor. Accommodation costs HK$38 a night in an air-con dormitory.

The *STB Hostel* (☎ 3321073), operated by the Hong Kong Student Travel Bureau, costs HK$50 in the dormitory, HK$250 to HK$300 for twins. Clean and well managed, it's on the 2nd floor at Great Eastern Mansion, 255-261 Reclamation St, Mong kok, on the corner of Reclamation and Dundas Sts, just west of the Yaumati MTR Station.

Mirador Arcade, 58 Nathan Rd, is like a scaled-down version of Chungking Mansions, but considerably cleaner. It's on Nathan Rd between Mody Rd and Carnarvon Rd, one block north of Chungking. Places to try at the Mirador include *First Class Guest-*

house (☎ 7224935), 16th floor, where single rooms cost HK$100 and doubles are HK$120 to HK$150.

My personal favourite in this building is *Man Hing Lung Guesthouse* (☎ 7220678) on the 14th floor. Immaculate singles/doubles are HK$160; if you're a single traveller, the management can find you a roommate and you pay HK$80 each. They have fancier rooms on the 15th floor at HK$200/240 for doubles/triples. All rooms have private bath, air-con and TV. Also clean and well managed is the *Kowloon Hotel* (☎ 3112523), on the 10th and 13th floors, with room prices ranging from HK$120 to HK$200, all with private bath.

Lee Garden Guesthouse (☎ 3672284) is on the 8th floor, D Block, 36 Cameron Rd, close to Chatham Rd. All rooms have air-con and TV. Doubles with shared/private bath cost HK$150/250. This place has a very friendly manager.

Tourists Home (☎ 3112622) is on the 6th floor, G Block, Champagne Court, 16 Kimberley Rd. Singles range from HK$180 to HK$200, and doubles from HK$200 to HK$220 with a private bath.

The *Lyton Building*, 32-40 Mody Rd, has several good guesthouses. There are four blocks with separate lifts, but none of these are labelled as in Chungking Mansions, so look at the directory next to each lift. *Lyton House Inn* (☎ 3673791) on the ground floor is very quiet and has small but clean rooms with private baths. Doubles cost HK$150 or HK$200 with air-con. On the 6th floor of the north-eastern block is *Tourist House* (☎ 7218309), which has rooms with private bath for HK$180.

The *New Lucky Mansions*, 300 Nathan Rd (near Jordan Rd), Yaumati, is in a better neighbourhood than most of the guesthouses. There are many places here to choose from. A good deal is *Nathan House* (☎ 7801302), 10th floor, where rooms range from HK$110 to HK$150.

YMCA International House (☎ 7719111, fax 3885926), 23 Waterloo Rd, Yaumati, has some cheap rooms with shared bath for HK$125 for men only. The majority of their rooms are rented to both men and women, but these are expensive at HK$420 to HK$560.

The *YWCA* (☎ 7139211, fax 7611269) is inconveniently located on Man Fuk Rd near Pui Ching and Waterloo Rds in Mongkok. It's up a hill behind a Caltex petrol station. Relatively cheap rooms for women only are HK$190. Other single rooms are HK$300, and twins cost from HK$380 to HK$410.

PLACES TO STAY – MIDDLE

You can get as much as 40% off at some mid-range and luxury hotels by booking your room through a local travel agency. One agent offering this service is Traveller Services (☎ 3674127, fax 3110387), 7th floor, 57 Peking Rd, Tsimshatsui.

Guesthouses

Star Guesthouse (☎ 7238951) is on the 6th floor at 21 Cameron Rd. Immaculately clean rooms with private bath and TV cost HK$250. This is the place I'd go for in this price range. The manager, Charlie Chan, is extremely helpful and friendly.

China Guesthouse (☎ 3111322), 2nd floor, Lyton Building, North-East Block, 44 Mody Rd, Tsimshatsui, has air-con and is very clean. Single/double rooms are HK$200/220. However, the rooms are tiny, there is a common bath and no TV. For this much money you would expect at least a private bath. In the same building on the 6th and 7th floors, South-East Block, is *Frank House* (☎ 7244113), where double rooms without/with private bath are HK$250/350. In the same building, 3rd floor, North-West Block, is the *Raja Guesthouse* (☎ 7396877), which has good singles/doubles for HK$250/300.

The Salvation Army runs a place called *Booth Lodge* (☎ 7719266), 11 Wing Sing Lane, Yaumati, where doubles/twins are HK$374/462. Just around the corner is *Caritas Bianchi Lodge* (☎ 3881111), 4 Cliff Rd, Yaumati, where doubles range from HK$405 to HK$465.

Hotels

There are plenty of excellent mid-range hotels. Some places to consider include:

Bangkok Royal Hotel, 2-12 Pilkem St, Yaumati (take the MTR to Jordan Station), singles HK$350, twins HK$410 to HK$580 (☎ 7359181, fax 7302209)

Concourse Hotel, 20-46 Lai Chi Kok Rd, Mongkok (take MTR to Prince Edward Station), doubles/twins HK$600/1000 (☎ 3976683, fax 3813768)

Imperial Hotel, 30-34 Nathan Rd, Tsimshatsui, singles HK$500 to HK$620, doubles/twins HK$580/880 (☎ 3662201, fax 3112360)

International Hotel, 33 Cameron Rd, Tsimshatsui, singles HK$380 to HK$680, twins HK$500 to HK$880 (☎ 3663381, fax 3695381)

King's Hotel, 473-473A Nathan Rd, Yaumati, singles HK$340, doubles/twins HK$400/430 (☎ 7801281, fax 7821833)

Mariner's Club, 11 Middle Rd, Tsimshatsui, singles/doubles HK$330/390 (☎ 3688261)

Nathan Hotel, 378 Nathan Rd, Yaumati, singles HK$550, doubles/twins HK$600/700 (☎ 3885141, fax 7704262)

Shamrock Hotel, 223 Nathan Rd, Yaumati, singles HK$450 to HK$480, twins HK$520 to HK$700 (☎ 7352271, fax 7367354)

YMCA, 41 Salisbury Rd, Tsimshatsui, twins HK$560 (☎ 3692211, fax 7399315)

PLACES TO STAY – TOP END

Luxury hotels are easy to find and the HKTA's *Hotel Guide* makes the task even easier.

Ambassador, 26 Nathan Rd, Tsimshatsui, doubles/twins HK$880/1580 (☎ 3666321, fax 3690663)

Eaton, 380 Nathan Rd, Yaumati (take the MTR to Jordan Station), singles HK$800 to HK$1120, twins HK$880 to HK$1200 (☎ 7821818, fax 3858132)

Empress, 17-19 Chatham Rd, Tsimshatsui, singles HK$750 to HK$950, twins HK$800 to HK$1000 (☎ 3660211, fax 7218168)

Fortuna, 355 Nathan Rd, Yaumati (take the MTR to Jordan Station), singles HK$550, twins HK$850 to HK$1000 (☎ 3851011, fax 7800011)

Grand, 14 Carnarvon Rd, Tsimshatsui, singles HK$660 to HK$940, twins HK$720 to HK$1000 (☎ 3669331, fax 7237840)

Grand Tower, 627-641 Nathan Rd, Mongkok, singles HK$730 to HK$960, twins HK$790 to HK$1050 (☎ 7890011, fax 7890945)

Guangdong, 18 Prat Ave, Tsimshatsui, doubles/twins HK$770/990 (☎ 7393311, fax 7211137)

Holiday Inn Golden Mile, 46-52 Nathan Rd, Tsimshatsui, singles HK$800, doubles/twins HK$1100/1650 (☎ 3693111, fax 3698016)

Holiday Inn Harbour View, 70 Mody Rd, Tsimshatsui East, singles HK$1150 to HK$2050, twins HK$1250 to HK$2150 (☎ 7215161, fax 3695672)

Hyatt Regency, 67 Nathan Rd, Tsimshatsui, doubles/twins HK$1330/1930 (☎ 3111234, fax 7398701)

Kimberley, 28 Kimberley Rd, Tsimshatsui, doubles/twins HK$780/1100 (☎ 7233888, fax 7231318)

Kowloon, 19-21 Nathan Rd, Tsimshatsui, singles HK$790 to HK$930, twins HK$820 to HK$980 (☎ and fax 3698698)

Kowloon Shangri-La, 64 Mody Rd, Tsimshatsui East, singles HK$1600 to HK$2500, twins HK$1750 to HK$2650 (☎ 7212111, fax 7238686)

Metropole, 75 Waterloo Rd, Mongkok (take the KCR to Mongkok Station), doubles/twins HK$760/1220 (☎ 7611711, fax 7610769)

Miramar, 130 Nathan Rd, Tsimshatsui, singles HK$1400 to HK$1800, twins HK$1600 to HK$2000 (☎ 3681111, fax 3691788)

New Astor, 11 Carnarvon Rd, Tsimshatsui, doubles/twins HK$780/980 (☎ 3667261, fax 7227122)

New World, 22 Salisbury Rd, Tsimshatsui, singles HK$1300 to HK$1600, twins HK$1400 to HK$1750 (☎ 3694111, fax 3699387)

Nikko, 72 Mody Rd, Tsimshatsui East, singles HK$1350 to HK$2350, twins HK$1500 to HK$2500 (☎ 7391111, fax 3113122)

Omni,The Hong Kong Hotel, Harbour City, 3 Canton Rd, Tsimshatsui, singles HK$750 to HK$1500, twins HK$1150 to HK$2250 (☎ 7360088, fax 7360011)

Omni Marco Polo, Harbour City, Canton Rd, Tsimshatsui, doubles/twins HK$1200/1350 (☎ 7360888, fax 7360022)

Omni Prince, Harbour City, Canton Rd, Tsimshatsui, doubles/twins HK$1200/1350 (☎ 7361888, fax 7360066)

Park, 61-65 Chatham Rd South, Tsimshatsui, singles HK$800 to HK$1000, doubles and twins HK$900 to HK$1100 (☎ 3661371, fax 7397259)

Peninsula, Salisbury Rd, Tsimshatsui, twins HK$2150 to HK$3000 (☎ 3666251, fax 7224170)

Prudential, 222 Nathan Rd, Tsimshatsui, twins HK$700 to HK$900 (☎ 3118222, fax 3114760)

Ramada Inn, 73-75 Chatham Rd South, Tsimshatsui, twins HK$950 to HK$1200 (☎ 3111100, fax 3116000)

Ramada Renaissance, 8 Peking Rd, Tsimshatsui, twins HK$1350 to HK$2200 (☎ 3113311, fax 3116611)

Regal Meridien, 71 Mody Rd, Tsimshatsui East, singles HK$950 to HK$1680, twins HK$1280 to HK$1680 (☎ 7221818, fax 7236413)

Regal Airport, Sa Po Rd, Kowloon (next to airport), singles HK$1100 to HK$1500, twins HK$1200 to HK$1600 (☎ 7180333, fax 7184111)

Regent, Salisbury Rd, Tsimshatsui, twins HK$1560 to HK$2400 (☎ 7211211, fax 7394546)

Royal Garden, 69 Mody Rd, Tsimshatsui East, twins HK$1200 to HK$1800 (☎ 7215215, fax 3699976)

Royal Pacific, China Hong Kong City, 33 Canton Rd, Tsimshatsui, twins HK$880 to HK$1850 (☎ 7361188, fax 7361212)

Sheraton, 20 Nathan Rd, Tsimshatsui, singles HK$1100 to HK$2050, twins HK$1200 to HK$2200 (☎ 3691111, fax 7398707)

Stanford, 112 Soy St, Mongkok, singles HK$620, twins HK$750 to HK$840 (☎ 7811881, fax 3883733)

Windsor, 39-43A Kimberley Rd, Tsimshatsui, twins HK$890 to HK$1090 (☎ 7395665, fax 3115101). Owned by the People's Republic of China.

PLACES TO EAT
Breakfast

The window of the *Wing Wah Restaurant* (☎ 7212947) is always filled with great-looking cakes and pastries. It's at 21A Lock Rd near Swindon's Bookstore and the Hyatt Regency. Either take it away or sit down with some coffee. Prices are very reasonable. Good and inexpensive Chinese food is also served.

A very similar place with cakes, coffee and other delicacies is the nearby *Kam Fat Restaurant* at 11 Ashley Rd.

Deep in the bowels of the MTR stations you can find *Maxim's Cake Shops*. There is one in every MTR station except Tin Hau and North Point. The cakes and pastries look irresistible, but don't sink your teeth into the creamy delights until you're back on the street as it is prohibited to eat or drink anything in the MTR stations or on the trains – HK$1000 fine if you do.

There is an excellent chain of bakeries around Hong Kong with the name *St Honore Cake Shop*. There's no English sign on their stores but you'll soon recognise their ideogram. You can find one at 221 Nathan Rd,

Yaumati, and a much smaller one at 1A Hanoi Rd, Tsimshatsui.

As you face the entrance to the Star Ferry, about 50 metres over to your left is *Tropicana Pastries*, which is top notch. This store opens and closes with the ferry service, from about 6 am to 11.30 pm.

If you're up very early before most places open, *7-Eleven* operates 24 hours a day and serves microwaved breakfasts.

Fast Food

Oliver's has two stores in Tsimshatsui: one in Ocean Centre and another at China Hong Kong City on Canton Rd, the place where you catch the ferries to China. It's a great place for breakfast – HK$10 for bacon, eggs and toast. The sandwiches are equally excellent, though it gets crowded at lunch time.

The *Spaghetti House* continues to get rave reviews from all who eat there, but it's sometimes so crowded that you have to queue to get in. Branches of this restaurant in Tsimshatsui can be found at: 3B Cameron Rd; 1st floor, 57 Peking Rd; 6-6A Hart Ave; and 1st floor, 38 Haiphong Rd.

Fairwood Fast Food is a large Hong Kong chain, and if the big plastic clown face on the door doesn't make you feel like throwing up, it's a great place to catch a quick meal. Prices are low and they do mixed Western and Chinese food. They have a branch at 6 Ashley Rd, Tsimshatsui.

Ka Ka Lok Fast Food Shop does quick meals that you take away in a styrofoam box. In Tsimshatsui, there's one at 32B Mody Rd but the entrance is on Blenheim Ave, a tiny side street. You can also find one at 16A Ashley Rd, but again it's on a side street that runs between Ashley Rd and Hankow Rd, parallel to (and north of) Peking Rd. Another Ka Ka Lok is at 235 Temple St, Yaumati.

Another home-grown fast-food chain is *Café de Coral*. They do a combination of Chinese and Western fast food. As is usual in Hong Kong, hot dogs and tuna sandwiches are on the English menu, and all the good Chinese food is listed in Chinese only. In Tsimshatsui, you can find Café de Coral just off Nathan Rd at 2 Granville Rd. There is another in Harbour City and more just about everywhere else you'd care to look.

You know what to expect at Pizza Hut, 1st floor, Hanford House, 221C-D Nathan Rd, Yaumati. There is another *Pizza Hut* in the Tsimshatsui Centre, 66 Mody Rd, Tsimshatsui East.

There's a *McDonald's* on practically every street corner, alley and arcade in Tsimshatsui. Late-night restaurants are amazingly scarce in Hong Kong, so it's useful to know that two McDonald's in Tsimshatsui, at 21A-B Granville Rd and 12 Peking Rd, operate 24 hours a day.

The Colonel spreads his wings at *Kentucky Fried Chicken*, 2 Cameron Rd, Tsimshatsui, and at 241 Nathan Rd, Yaumati.

Chinese Food

Tsimshatsui's Chinese restaurant alley is Hau Fook St which does not appear on the HKTA tourist map. Easy to find, it's the tiny street between Cameron Rd and Granville Rd. Walking north on Carnarvon Rd, pass Granville Rd and it's the first alley on your right. Unfortunately, most of these places do not have English menus.

Street Stalls The cheapest place to enjoy authentic Chinese cuisine is the *Temple St Night Market* in Yaumati. It starts at about 8 pm and begins to fade at 11 pm.

Dim Sum & Cantonese Dim sum is normally served from around noon to 3 pm, but a few places have it available for breakfast. From about 5 pm until the late hours it's standard Cantonese fare. One of my favourites is *Ocean City Restaurant* (☎ 3699688),

Level 3, New World Centre, 18 Salisbury Rd, Tsimshatsui. They have dim sum breakfasts and the prices are moderate. Some of the less-expensive dim sum restaurants are:

Canton Court, Guangdong Hotel, 18 Prat Ave, Tsimshatsui (☎ 7393311)
Dragon Feast Seafood, 5th floor, Lifung Tower, China Hong Kong City, 33 Canton Rd, Tsimshatsui (☎ 7360688)
Fook Follow, UG2, Chinachem Golden Plaza, 77 Mody Rd, Tsimshatsui East (☎ 3116889)
Harbour View Seafood, 3rd floor, Tsimshatsui Centre, 66 Mody Rd, Tsimshatsui East (☎ 7225888)
Heichinrou Restaurant, 2nd floor, Sun Plaza, 28 Canton Rd, Tsimshatsui (☎ 7217123)
International, 3rd floor, Good Hope Building, 612 Nathan Rd, Mongkok (☎ 3320531)
Jade Garden, 4th floor, Star House, 3 Salisbury Rd, Tsimshatsui (☎ 7306888)

Beijing (Peking) If you like lots of dumplings, steamed bread, duck and noodles, try these places:

Beijing Restaurant, 34-36 Granville Rd, Tsimshatsui (☎ 3669968)
China Garden, 1st floor, 45-47 Carnarvon Rd, Tsimshatsui (☎ 3660408)
North China Peking Seafood, 2nd floor, Polly Commercial Building, 21-23 Prat Ave, Tsimshatsui (☎ 3116689)
Peking Garden, 3rd floor, Star House, 3 Salisbury Rd (☎ 3687879)
1st floor, Empire Centre, 68 Mody Rd, Tsimshatsui East (☎ 3687879)
Peking Restaurant, 1st floor, 227 Nathan Rd, Yaumati (☎ 7301315)
Spring Deer, 1st floor, 42 Mody Rd, Tsimshatsui (☎ 7233673)
Sun Hung Cheung Hing, 1st floor, Kimberley Plaza, 45-47 Kimberley Rd, Tsimshatsui (☎ 3677933)

Shanghai For eels or drunken chicken it's the *Great Shanghai* (☎ 3668158), 1st floor, 26 Prat Ave, Tsimshatsui. Next door at No 24 is the *Shanghai Restaurant* (☎ 7397083)

The *Wu Kong Shanghai* (☎ 3667244), Basement, Alpha House, 27 Nathan Rd, Tsimshatsui, is also good.

Sichuan (Szechuan) The *Lotus Pond* (☎ 7308688), Shop 007, Ground floor, Phase IV, Harbour City, 15 Canton Rd, Tsimshatsui, serves the type of spicy dishes that bring tears to the eyes. Also popular is *Prince Court* (☎ 7303100), Shop 115-116 Sutton Court, Harbour City, 9 Canton Rd, Tsimshatsui.

Chaozhou (Chiu Chow) To taste this saucy but rather oily style of cooking in which seafood and vegetables predominate, try any of the following:

Capital, 3rd floor, Chinachem Golden Plaza, 77 Mody Rd, Tsimshatsui East (☎ 3669979)

Chiuchow Garden, 2nd floor, Tsimshatsui Centre, 69 Mody Rd, Tsimshatsui East (☎ 3688772)

City Chiuchow, 1st floor, East Ocean Centre, 98 Granville Rd, Tsimshatsui East (☎ 7236226)

Eastern Palace, 3rd floor, Omni The Hong Kong Hotel, Shopping Arcade, Harbour City, Canton Rd, Tsimshatsui (☎ 7306011)

Golden Island Bird's Nest, 3rd & 4th floors, 25-31 Carnarvon Rd, Tsimshatsui (☎ 3695211)

2nd floor, East Half, Star House, 3 Salisbury Rd, Tsimshatsui (☎ 7366228)

New Golden Red, Ground floor, 13-15 Prat Ave, Tsimshatsui (☎ 3666822)

Hakka One of the best Hakka restaurants is *New Home Restaurant* (☎ 3665876) at 19-20 Hanoi Rd, Tsimshatsui. Dim sum is served in the morning and afternoon.

Vegetarian *Bodhi* (☎ 7392222), Ground floor, 56 Cameron Rd, Tsimshatsui, is one of Hong Kong's biggest vegetarian restaurants with several branches: 36 Jordan Rd, Yaumati; 32-34 Lock Rd, Tsimshatsui; 8 Granville Rd, Tsimshatsui; and 56 Cameron Rd, Tsimshatsui.

You can also try *Pak Bo Vegetarian Kitchen* (☎ 3671257), Ground floor, 20 Austin Ave, Tsimshatsui.

Other Asian Food

Filipino The *Mabuhay* (☎ 3673762), 11 Minden Ave serves good Filipino and Spanish food.

Indian The greatest concentration of cheap Indian and Pakistani restaurants is in Chungking Mansions on Nathan Rd. A meal of curried chicken and rice, or curry with chapattis and dahl, will cost HK$20 per person.

Start your search for Indian food on the ground floor of the arcade. The bottom of the market belongs to *Kashmir Fast Food* and *Lahore Fast Food*. These open early, so you can have curry, chapattis and heartburn for breakfast.

Upstairs in Chungking Mansions are many other places with better food and a more pleasant atmosphere. Prices are still low, with set meals from HK$28 to HK$35. Highly rated by travellers is *Kashmir Club* (☎ 3116308), 3rd floor, A Block, which even offers free home delivery. The food is outstanding and cheap at *Taj Mahal Club Mess* (☎ 7225454), 3rd floor, B Block. This place has air-con and is very comfortable, at least by Chungking Mansions standards. On the 6th floor of B Block is the highly recommended *Centre Point Club* (☎ 3661086). Yet another cheap and good place is the *Delhi Club Mess* (☎ 3681682), 3rd floor, C Block. You'll find that D Block also has a mess of restaurants, including the *New Madras Mess* on the 16th floor, and the *Southern India Club Mess* on the 3rd floor.

Moving out of Chungking Mansions, and therefore up-market, you can find numerous good Indian restaurants in Tsimshatsui including:

Bukhara Tandoori, 2nd floor, Sheraton Hong Kong Hotel, 20 Nathan Rd (☎ 3691111, ext 3921)

Gaylord, 1st floor, Ashley Centre, 23-25 Ashley Rd (☎ 7241001)

Koh-I-Noor, 1st floor, 3-4 Peninsula Apartments, 16C Mody Rd (☎ 3683065)

New Dehli, Mezzanine, 52 Cameron Rd (☎ 3664611)

Surya, 34-38 Mody Rd (☎ 3669902)

Woodlands, 8 Minden Ave (☎ 3693718)

Indonesian The *Rijsttafel* (☎ 3761230), at Han Hing Mansion, 38 Hankow Rd, Tsimshatsui, is a good place to enjoy a 'rijsttafel', (literally, a 'rice table') – a Dutch-influenced Indonesian meal consisting of lots of individual dishes with rice.

Japanese If you want to find cheap Japanese food, make it yourself. Japanese restaurants charge Japanese prices. You can economise slightly by looking for one which is not inside a big hotel or financial high-rise office building. If you can afford the ticket, consider the following:

Ah-So, 159 Craigie Court, World Finance Centre, Harbour City, Canton Rd, Tsimshatsui (☎ 7303392)
Banka, Grand Tower Hotel, 627-641 Nathan Rd, Mongkok (☎ 7890011, ext 211)
Fukui, Hotel Fortuna, 351-361 Nathan Rd, Yaumati (☎ 3851011)
Kotobuki, Flat A & B, 1st floor, Good Result Building, 176 Nathan Rd, Tsimshatsui (☎ 3682711)
Matsuzaka, UG23-28 South Seas Centre, 75 Mody Rd, Tsimshatsui East (☎ 7243057)
Nadaman, Shangri-La Hotel, 64 Mody Rd, Tsimshatsui East (☎ 7212111)
Sagano, Hotel Nikko, 72 Mody Rd, Tsimshatsui East (☎ 7391111)
Sui Sha Ya, Ground floor, 9 Chatham Rd, Tsimshatsui (☎ 7225001)
Unkai, Sheraton Hotel, 20 Nathan Rd, Tsimshatsui (☎ 3691111, ext 2)

Korean There are several excellent Korean restaurants in Tsimshatsui. A good one is *Seoul House* (☎ 3673675), 35 Hillwood Rd.

Another place is *Manna*, a chain restaurant with outlets at 83B Nathan Rd (☎ 7212159); Lyton Building, 32B Mody Rd (☎ 3674278); and 6A Humphrey's Rd (☎ 3682485).

Two other places are the *Arirang* (☎ 7303667), 9 Sutton Court, Harbour City, Canton Rd, and *Korea House* (☎ 3675674), Empire Centre, 68 Mody Rd, Tsimshatsui East.

Malaysian The *Singapore Restaurant*, 23 Ashley Rd, Tsimshatsui, is a great bargain. Excellent Malaysian, Chinese and Western food for about HK$45 for a set dinner. The only problem is that you might have to queue to get in.

Kuala Lumpur Restaurant (☎ 3670863) at 12 Observatory Rd, Tsim shatsui, serves Malay dishes as well as European and Chinese food.

Good rice and curry dishes are served at moderate prices at *Nam Ah* (☎ 3660118), 27 Ashley Rd, Tsimshatsui. They also serve

Singapore noodles – thin rice noodles stir-fried with vegetables, shrimp and chicken, and mixed with curry. Hot stuff!

Thai Thai food is devastatingly hot but excellent. A reasonably priced and good Thai restaurant is *Royal Pattaya* (☎ 3669919), 9 Minden Aven, Tsimshatsui. Also good is *Sawadee* (☎ 7225577), 1 Hillwood Rd, Tsimshatsui.

Vietnamese One excellent place is *Café de La Paix Vietnamese Cuisine* (☎ 7212095) at 17 Hillwood Rd. Also highly recommended is *Golden Bull* (☎ 3694617), Level 1, 17 New World Centre, Salisbury Rd. Another good place is *Mekong* (☎ 3113303), 2 Kimberley Rd.

Western Food

Italian A great Italian restaurant is *Valentino* (☎ 7216653) at 16 Hanoi Rd, and also at 115 Chatham Rd South. Also highly rated is *La Taverna* (☎ 3691945), Astoria Building, 36-38 Ashley Rd.

Pizza World (☎ 3692688), Ground floor, New World Centre, 22 Salisbury Rd, is extremely popular and has the best salad bar in Hong Kong – the large salad for HK$25 is a meal in itself.

French At 7B Hanoi Rd the *New Marseille* (☎ 3665732) is good value, with French/Chinese food and a cheap set dinner. Moderately expensive but good is *Au Trou Normand* (☎ 3668754), 6 Carnarvon Rd, Tsimshatsui. Slightly cheaper is *Napoleon Grill* (☎ 3686861), Princess Wing, Hotel Miramar, 130 Nathan Rd, Tsimshatsui. Along similar lines is the *Taipan* (☎ 7360088), Omni The Hong Kong Hotel, Harbour City, 3 Canton Rd, Tsimshatsui.

Kosher *Beverley Hills Deli* (☎ 3698695), Level 2, Shop 55, New World Centre, Salisbury Rd, is where you'll find gefilte fish and lox. It's good, but *not* cheap.

American *Mariners' Club* (☎ 3688261), 11 Middle Rd, serves good food at very reasonable prices. *Rick's Café* (☎ 3672939), Basement, Enterprise Centre, 4 Hart Ave, serves oddly named sandwiches and drinks, as well as Mexican-style snacks.

The *San Francisco Steak House* (☎ 7357576), 101 Barnton Court, Harbour City, Canton Rd, Tsimshatsui, serves steak and lobster, baked potatoes, jumbo onion rings and toasted garlic bread.

Pleasant and economical set meals can be found at *Top Saints Restaurant & Lounge* (☎ 3663105), 1 Minden Ave, Tsimshatsui.

Supermarkets If you're on a tight budget, or you're just so tired of restaurants that you can't stand the sight of another noodle, buy something and cook it yourself. Maybe you'd just like to sit back with some yoghurt or cheese while reading the morning newspaper. Supermarkets in Hong Kong provide an abundant selection and are very cheap.

Close to Chungking Mansions is *Wellcome Supermarket*, inside the Dairy Farm Creamery (an ice-cream parlour) at 74-78 Nathan Rd. The location is good, but it's cramped and crowded inside.

There is a much bigger and better *Wellcome Supermarket* on the north-western corner of Granville and Carnarvon Rds.

The Silvercord Shopping Centre at 30 Canton Rd has a good basement *Park'n Shop Supermarket* with nice wide aisles so you don't have to climb over other people and shopping carts – a rare find in Hong Kong. There's another *Park'n Shop* on the 3rd floor of the Ocean Terminal, 3 Canton Rd (near the Star Ferry Terminal).

The *Wellcome Supermarket* on Waterloo Rd, near the corner with Nathan Rd, Yaumati, is convenient if you're staying in the Waterloo Rd YMCA.

You must visit the supermarket in the basement of *Yue Hwa Chinese Products*, 301 Nathan Rd, Yaumati (on the north-western corner of Nathan and Jordan Rds), even if you don't want to buy any food. It has absolutely everything, including many Western products, but also many exotic goods from China such as tea bricks and flattened chickens.

ENTERTAINMENT
Night Markets
The biggest night market and the one most popular with tourists is the Temple St market in Tsimshatsui. The market gets going about 8 pm and closes around midnight.

Another big market is at Tung Choi St in Mongkok. However, this market is geared more towards selling clothing and operates mostly in the daytime.

Pubs, Bars & Discos
Ned Kelly's Last Stand (☎ 3660562), 11A Ashley Rd, open from 11.30 am to 2 am, became famous as a real Australian pub complete with meat pies. Now it is known mainly for its jazz band.

Schnurrbart (☎ 7239827), Winner Building, 6 Hart Ave, is said to have the best beer in Hong Kong. Just next door is *Rick's Cafe* (☎ 3672939), Basement, 4 Hart Ave.

The *Waltzing Matilda Arms* (☎ 3688046), 12-14 Hart Ave, Tsimshatsui, sounds like a typical Aussie pub but actually is a gay bar which may, or may not, be what you want. Incidentally, homosexuality is illegal in Hong Kong, though the police don't waste their time peeking into bedrooms.

Blacksmith's Arms (☎ 3696696), 16 Minden Ave, Tsimshatsui, is a British-style pub with darts and barstools. Similar decor can be found at *Friar Tuck* (☎ 7303298), Room 053, World Shipping Centre, Harbour City, 7 Canton Rd, Tsimshatsui.

Fancy a German beer? Then head to the *Biergarten* (☎ 7212302) at 8 Hanoi Rd, Tsimshatsui.

There are eight Chinese bars, most of them good, at Chatham Court, an obscure alley adjacent to Austin Ave near the intersection with Chatham Rd South. One of these bars is considered a gay bar – *The Wall* (☎ 7230350), 8 Chatham Court. The others are straight.

A truly authentic Aussie pub is the ever-popular *Kangaroo Pub & Windjammer Restaurant* (☎ 7238293), 11A Chatham Rd.

Another popular place for Aussies is *Harry's Bar* (☎ 7236060) at 6-8A Prat Ave.

They do food and are open from 10 am until 2 am.

Canton Disco (☎ 7350209), Sutton Court (north tower), World Finance Centre, Canton Rd, moves from 9 pm until 4 am in the main disco and features singers in the private bar from 11.30 pm. A happy hour is held from 2.30 to 6.30 pm.

If you'd like something else, try *Someplace Else* (☎ 3691111 ext 5), the bar in the Sheraton Hotel, 20 Nathan Rd. It features good singers and Mexican food.

The 3rd floor of the *Mariners' Club* (☎ 3688261), 11 Middle Rd, is where you'll find the *China Coast Bar & Lounge*, which has darts, a good atmosphere and good, cheap food.

Another place that gets good reviews from travellers is the *Schooner Pub* (☎ 3682623), Leader Commercial Building, 54-56 Hillwood Rd. It's known for its good food in the daytime and for being a lively place at night. Hillwood Rd is a good street for restaurants and nightlife in general.

The *White Stag* (☎ 3661951), 72 Canton Rd, Tsimshatsui, has British pub atmosphere, good food and beer. Nearby is *Porky's* (☎ 3668441), at 76 Canton Rd, Tsimshatsui.

Girlie Bars

Many of these places make a habit of cheating foreigners with hidden extra 'service charges'. See the Entertainment section in the Facts for the Visitor chapter for details.

A few girlie bars won't cheat the customer at all, but their prices are high, as the lineup of Mercedes and Rolls Royces outside the door will suggest. They offer live music, featuring Filipino bands. These high-class girlie bars prefer to be known as 'hostess clubs'. Most of these places are in Tsimshatsui East.

A very popular place is *Club Volvo* (☎ 3692883), New Mandarin Plaza, 14 Science Museum Rd, Tsimshatsui East, open from 3 pm to 4 am. To have a drink and sit and watch the show will cost around HK$500. Figure on another HK$500 for a girl to sit with you and talk. In the same

league is the *Metropolitan* (☎ 3111111), Chinachem Golden Plaza, 77 Mody Rd, Tsimshatsui East.

Also worth considering is *Club De Hong Kong* (☎ 3686070), Tsimshatsui Centre, Tsimshatsui East.

The only other club worth mentioning is the *China City Night Club* (☎ 7230388), 4th floor, Peninsula Centre, 67 Mody Rd, Tsimshatsui East, open from 3 pm to 3 am. Again, it costs HK$500 at the minimum.

Club Deluxe (☎ 7210277), L-301, New World Centre, Salisbury Rd, Tsimshatsui, is open from 9 pm to 3 am and features, among other things, an indoor waterfall.

There are many other girlie bars in Tsimshatsui advertising cheap drinks for HK$25 or so, but most will hit the customer with about HK$300 or more in mandatory 'service charges'.

Cinemas

The more popular English-language cinemas in Kowloon include:

Astor, 380 Nathan Rd, Yaumati (☎ 7811833)
Broadway, 6 Sai Yeung Choi St, Mongkok (☎ 3325731)
Chinachem, Chinachem Golden Plaza, 77 Mody Rd, Tsimshatsui East (☎ 3113000)
Harbour City I, World Shipping Centre, Canton Rd, Tsimshatsui (☎ 7356915)
Harbour City II, World Commerce Centre, Canton Rd, Tsimshatsui (☎ 7308910)
Liberty, 26A Jordan Rd, Tsimshatsui (☎ 3666148)
London, 219 Nathan Rd, Yaumati (☎ 4522123)
Ocean, Harbour Centre, 3 Canton Rd, Tsimshatsui (☎ 7305444)
Rex, 242 Portland St, Mongkok (☎ 3963110)
Washington, 92 Parkes St, Tsimshatsui (☎ 7710405)

The *Space Museum* (☎ 7212361) near the Star Ferry Terminal in Tsimshatsui also shows good films.

Video Game Arcades

A popular place is the *Silver Star Amusement Game Centre*, 27 Lock Rd. Nearby is *Game World* at 38 Hankow Rd.

THINGS TO BUY

Oh yeah, shopping, I guess some people

come to Hong Kong for that. In Tsimshatsui, you don't have to look for a place to shop – the shopping comes to you. People are constantly trying to stuff advertisements into your hands. About every third person on Nathan Rd comes up behind you and yells 'Copy watch!' in your ear – if you need a fake Rolex that will probably stop running in a week's time, this is the place to get it.

Prices are lower and the pace is more relaxed at the Temple St night market in Yaumati. It tends to carry more men's clothing than women's, but you can find most anything here.

The streets between Nathan Rd and Chatham Rd are good for cheap clothes. Check out Giordano's, Golden Crown Mansion, 66-70 Nathan Rd.

In Tsimshatsui there is a factory outlet for gems called Chaumont (☎ 3687331), 10th floor, 57 Peking Rd, open from 10 am to 1 pm and from 2 to 7 pm, Monday to Saturday.

Tourist Shopping Malls

Don't overlook the shopping complexes, touristy though they may be. Prices are not necessarily higher than along Nathan Rd, and you can bargain in shopping malls just as you can elsewhere in Tsimshatsui. Also, the malls are interesting tourist attractions in themselves.

In the tourist zone of Tsimshatsui, there are three big complexes in a row on Canton Rd: Ocean Terminal near the Star Ferry, Ocean Centre and Harbour City. Across the street at 30 Canton Rd is Silvercord. The New World Centre is on Salisbury Rd, adjacent to the New World Hotel.

In Tsimshatsui East, the biggest mall is Tsimshatsui Centre at 66 Mody Rd (between Salisbury and Mody Rds).

Chinese Emporiums

Yue Hwa Park Lane Shopper's Boulevard is on Nathan Rd just north of the Kowloon Mosque. It's the two-storey block that looks like the world's longest garage and is much less interesting than the main store at Jordan Rd.

The People's Republic owns Chinese Arts & Crafts, which has three branches in Tsimshatsui: New World Centre, Salisbury Rd; the Silvercord Shopping Centre, 30 Canton Rd, near the corner of Haiphong Rd; and in the touristy Star House, at the corner of Salisbury and Canton Rds. There is another branch in Yaumati at 233-239 Nathan Rd. Everything has price tags and no bargaining is necessary.

Chung Kiu Chinese Products Emporium at 530 Nathan Rd, Yaumati, is also well known for arts and crafts.

Department Stores

My favourite store in Hong Kong is the main branch of Yue Hwa Chinese Products Emporium at 301 Nathan Rd, Yaumati (on the corner of Nathan and Jordan Rds). In spite of the name, it has a wide assortment of practical everyday products, as well as some Chinese exotica like herbal medicines.

Wing On is an up-market Hong Kong department store with three branches in Kowloon: 361 Nathan Rd, Yaumati; 620 Nathan Rd, Mongkok; and Wing On Plaza, Mody Rd, Tsimshatsui East. Another Hong Kong department store is Sincere, 83 Argyle St, Mongkok. Lane Crawford has a store in Ocean Terminal.

There are a few Japanese stores in Tsimshatsui: Mitsukoshi, corner of Peking Rd and Canton Rd; Isetan at 20 Nathan Rd in the Sheraton Hotel shopping mall; and *Tokyu* in the New World Centre, Salisbury Rd.

Electronics & Appliances

Mongkok is the best neighbourhood for all this stuff. Starting from Argyle St and heading south, explore all the side streets running parallel to Nathan Rd, such as Tung Choi St, Sai Yeung Choi St, Portland St, Shanghai St, Reclamation St and Canton Rd. In this area you can buy just about everything imaginable.

Cameras

Tsimshatsui is a lousy neighbourhood for buying photographic equipment. It's amazing that there aren't more homicides when you consider the way they blatantly cheat tourists. You'll do better to visit the shopping malls such as Cityplaza in Quarry Bay or New Town Plaza in Shatin.

From my own experience, the best luck I've had buying cameras in Tsimshatsui was at the Kimberley Camera Company (☎ 7212308), Champagne Court, 16 Kimberley Rd. They actually put price tags on their equipment. Even without bargaining, their prices were lower than I could bargain for on Nathan Rd. They also sell used equipment.

Computers
The Silvercord Shopping Centre, 30 Canton Rd, is a huge complex with dozens of computer shops. Most of these are on the lower ground floor (LG). This is definitely the best place to go because of the wide selection of equipment.

The computer on which this book was written was purchased from PC People (☎ 7398007), Shop No LG-16 & 17, Silvercord Shopping Centre (ask for Andy). I've bought several pieces of equipment there over the years and have always found their prices to be the best, plus they honour the warranty. Another shop that earns high marks for honesty and low prices is Reptron Computer Ltd (☎ 3661721), Shop No LG-47. They specialise mostly in components but also sell complete computers and seem to be more technically competent than other shops in Silvercord.

A store to avoid in Silvercord is Sunlite Computer Shop, LG-52, where they charge 20% to 500% higher than elsewhere, especially on accessories.

They told me that the printer I wanted to buy could run on both 220 V and 110 V, but in fact it could only run on 220 V. I had to bargain vigorously to get a fair price; then they tried to charge extra for components which were supposed to be included free with the equipment. To top it off, I was subjected to a barrage of obscene verbal abuse when I pointed out the high prices. This is from personal experience: I would rate this as the worst shop I've ever done business with in Hong Kong.

The Golden Shopping Centre, Basement, 146-152 Fuk Wah St, Sham Shui Po, has the best collection of computers, accessories and components in Hong Kong. To get there, take the MTR to the Sham Shui Po Station. It's easy to get lost in this neighbourhood, so before you exit the station, keep your eyes open for signs in the MTR pointing to the way. If you reach the proper exit you'll be facing the shopping centre, which is on the corner of Kweilin St and Fuk Wah St. If you can't find it, go back down into the MTR and look again for the signs.

Opticians
Nathan Rd is lined with opticians charging high prices for low quality, but the rude service is free. I always get my spectacles made on the 3rd floor of Yue Hwa Chinese Products, 301-309 Nathan Rd, Yaumati (on the north-western corner of Nathan and Jordan Rds).

Hong Kong Island 香港島

The commercial heart of Hong Kong pumps away on the northern side of Hong Kong Island, where banks and businesses, high-rise apartment blocks and hotels cover a good part of its 78 sq km.

From the Star Ferry the island looks unbelievably crowded, and on the lower levels it certainly is, but from 400 metres up on the Peak you realise how much space is left.

As well as moving up the hill for more building space, Hong Kong keeps on moving out. Reclamation along the harbour edge continues to add the odd quarter km every so often, and buildings once on the waterfront are now several hundred metres back. Some of the reclaimed land has been used for new roads to accommodate the traffic which has swamped the old narrow streets.

The south side of Hong Kong Island has a completely different character than the north. For one thing, there are some fine beaches here, and the water is actually clean enough to swim in. The best beaches are at Big Wave Bay, Deep Water Bay, Shek O, Stanley and Repulse Bay. Expensive villas are perched on the hillsides, and the impression is more like the French Riviera rather than crowded Hong Kong. Unfortunately, huge, multistorey apartment blocks have been going up in recent years, though it still has a long way to go before it overtakes Kowloon.

It's easy to circumnavigate the island by public transport, starting from Central and taking a bus over the hills to Stanley, then heading clockwise along the coast back to the Star Ferry Terminal.

CENTRAL 中環

Central is most people's first impression of Hong Kong Island since it's where the Star Ferry lands. As you leave the ferry terminal, immediately on your right is the General Post Office, in front of which is the towering Jardine House with its distinctive port hole windows.

Hong Kong Museum of Art 香港藝術館

This museum (☎ 5224127) has a collection of Chinese art and antiquities and is housed on the 10th and 11th floors of City Hall (High Block), just a couple of minutes' walk from the Star Ferry Terminal.

Included in the collection are paintings, calligraphy, rubbings, ceramics, bronze pieces, lacquerware, jade, cloisonné, papercuts and embroidery.

The extensive ceramics collection contains pieces from almost every period in Chinese history. The historical picture collection includes more than 800 paintings, prints, drawings, lithographs and engravings recording Sino-British contacts in the 18th and 19th centuries. There is also a large number of paintings, sculptures and prints by contemporary artists from Hong Kong and other parts of Asia. Special exhibitions are shown throughout the year.

The museum is open daily from 10 am to 6 pm, except Thursday when it's closed. On Sundays and public holidays the opening hours are 1 to 6 pm. Admission is free.

Statue Square 皇后廣場

To reach the main part of Central you have to cross Connaught Rd. Straight ahead as you leave the Star Ferry is the pedestrian underpass which surfaces at the side of Statue Square. On the east side of the square is the Hong Kong Club, the last bastion of the British Empire. Half of Statue Square is also on the other side of Chater Rd where you can see the old Supreme Court Building, the 74-storey Bank of China (the tallest building in Hong Kong, owned by the People's Republic) and the Hong Kong & Shanghai Bank Building.

Hong Kong & Shanghai Bank Building
香港滙豐銀行

At the far end of Statue Square (at Des Voeux Rd, along which the trams run) you come face to face with the Hong Kong & Shanghai

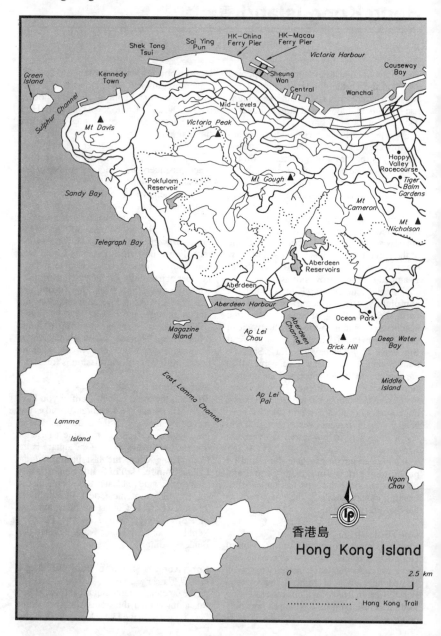

香港島
Hong Kong Island

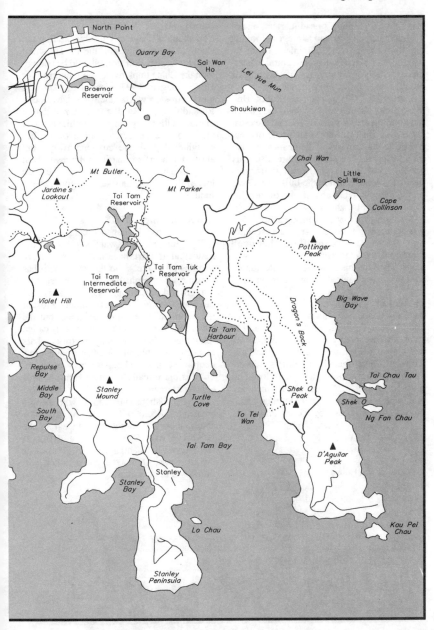

Banking Corporation's headquarters, one of the most expensive and strangest looking buildings in the world. Opinions differ on whether this place is an architectural masterpiece or a monstrosity, but it certainly is unique and definitely worth visiting.

Locals call this place the 'Robot Building', and it's easy to see why – the guts of the building are all visible. That is, the escalators and lifts (elevators) are made of clear plastic so you can see all the gears and other moving parts. The stairwells are also only walled in with glass, affording dizzying views to workers inside the building. Obviously, people who are afraid of heights should apply elsewhere.

Definitely try to visit it during office hours when you can go inside and ride the escalator up to the bank on the first floor. They don't mind tourists wandering in. Indeed, they're all prepared for this as souvenir postcards are sold inside the bank at the information desk.

Li Yuen St 利源街

Actually this is two streets: Li Yuen St East and Li Yuen St West, which run parallel to each other between Des Voeux Rd, Central, and Queen's Rd, Central, opposite the Lane Crawford Department Store. Both streets are actually narrow alleys and are closed to motorised traffic. These two lanes are crammed with shops selling clothing, handbags, fabrics and just about everything else.

Central Market 中央市場

You shouldn't have any trouble finding the Central Market – just sniff the air. The smell from the fish section alone should be enough to make China think twice about taking over Hong Kong in 1997. Central Market is a large four-storey affair between Des Voeux Rd and Queen's Rd. It's more a zoo than a market, with everything from chickens and quail to eels and crabs, alive or freshly slaughtered. Fish are cut lengthways, but above the heart so that it continues to beat and pump blood around the body. There are lots of little restaurants serving good, cheap food.

Lan Kwai Fong 蘭桂坊

This is a narrow L-shaped street running off of D'Aguilar St. Lan Kwai Fong is not of any historical importance, nor does it have temples or markets. On the contrary, it has become what might best be described as a playground for yuppie stockbrokers and other well-moneyed social climbers. Most of the yuppie clientele are foreigners, but the Chinese who come here are invariably called 'chuppies'. There are many overpriced bars and eating establishments. Just what attracts people to Lan Kwai Fong is a mystery to me, but this place really is where Hong Kong's chic Westerners hang out.

If you wish to rub elbows with people wearing HK$2000 tieclips and alligator shoes, then you might want to eat in the Beverly Hills Deli, or sip a drink at Hemingway's Champagne Bar, Scotties or the Brasserie. Or maybe you'd rather give Lan Kwai Fong a miss.

Government House

Government House 督憲府

On Upper Albert Rd, opposite the Zoological & Botanic Gardens, is Government House, residence of the Governor of Hong Kong. It's closed to the public except for one day in March when the azaleas are in bloom. At this time the place is swamped with locals and tourists.

The original sections of the building date back to 1858. Other features were actually built to Japanese designs during the war, when Japan occupied the colony and the Japanese governor wanted to establish a residence and administrative centre worthy of his role.

Zoological & Botanical Gardens
動植物公園

The gardens are home to statues, hundreds of species of birds, exotic trees, plants and shrubs. Among the statues is one of the innovative Sir Arthur Kennedy, the first governor to invite Chinese to government functions. If you go to the gardens at about 8 am the place will be packed with Chinese toning up with a bit of shadow-boxing on their way to work. The gardens are divided by Albany Rd, with the botanics and the aviaries in the first section, off Garden Rd, and the zoologicals in the other. Admission is free.

The gardens are at the top end of Garden Rd, which leads up from behind the Hilton Hotel – an easy walk, but you can also take bus Nos 3 or 12 to the stop in front of the Jardine House on Connaught Rd. The bus takes you along Upper Albert and Caine Rds on the northern boundary of the gardens. Get off in front of the Caritas Centre (at the junction of Upper Albert and Caine Rds) and follow the path uphill to the gardens.

Hong Kong Park 香港公園

Just behind the city's tallest skyscraper, the Bank of China, Hong Kong Park is one of the most unusual parks in the world. It was deliberately designed to look anything but natural. Rather, the park emphasises synthetic creations such as its fountain plaza, Conservatory (greenhouse), aviary, artificial waterfall, Indoor Games Hall, Visual Arts Centre, playground, viewing tower, museum and Taichi Garden. For all that, the park is beautiful in its own weird way, and makes for dramatic photography with a wall of skyscrapers on one side and mountains on the other.

Within the park is the **Flagstaff House Museum** (☎ 8690690), the oldest Western-style building still standing in Hong Kong, dating from the mid-19th century. Enter from Cotton Tree Drive. The museum houses a Chinese teaware collection, including pieces dating from the Warring States period (475-221 BC) to the present. The museum is open daily except Wednesday, from 10 am to 5 pm and is closed on several public holidays. Admission is free. Bus Nos 3, 12, 23, 23B, 40 and 103 all go this way. Get off at the first stop on Cotton Tree Drive.

SHEUNG WAN 上環

West of Central (on the right as you come off the Star Ferry) is Sheung Wan (the Western District), which once had something of the feel of old Shanghai about it. The comparison is a bit forced now since much of old Sheung Wan has disappeared under the jack-hammers of development, and old stairway streets once cluttered with stalls and street sellers have been cleared away to make room for more new buildings or the MTR. Nevertheless the area has plenty of interest and is worth exploring.

Just to the west of Central Market is about where Central and Sheung Wan merge. Here you can find **Wing On St**, also known as Cloth Alley since it's filled with sellers of all kinds of fabrics. Then there is **Wing Sing St**, famous for its variety of eggs, including the 1000-year-old ones (which aren't 1000 years old but certainly smell like it). Finally, there are the two **Kwong Yuen Sts** (East and West) where the flag and banner makers sit sewing.

These streets run between Des Voeux Rd and Queen's Rd, Central (Kwong Yuen St runs between Wing Lok St and Queen's Rd), which is a big shopping area. Look out for the traditional bridal stores with everything

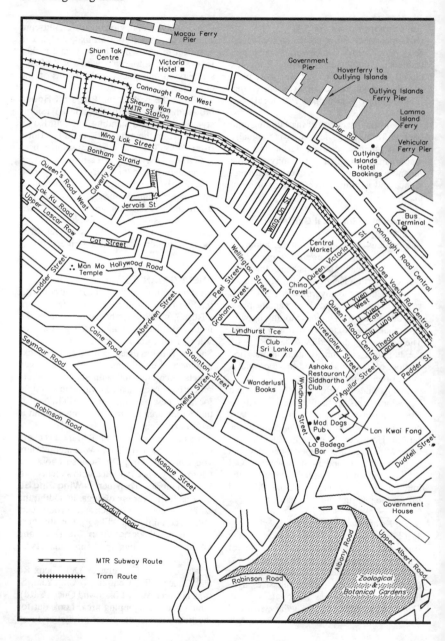

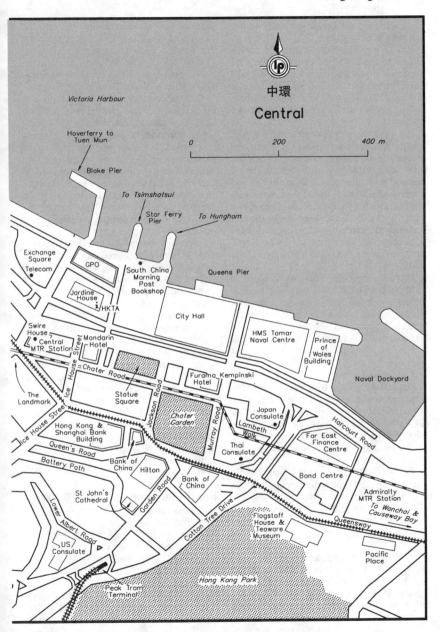

中環
Central

0   200   400 m

Victoria Harbour

Hoverferry to Tuen Mun

Blake Pier

To Tsimshatsui

Star Ferry Pier

To Hunghom

Exchange Square Telecom

GPO

South China Morning Post Bookshop

Queens Pier

Jardine House

HKTA

City Hall

HMS Tamar Naval Centre

Prince of Wales Building

Swire House

Central MTR Station

Mandarin Hotel

Chater Road

Furama Kempinski Hotel

Naval Dockyard

The Landmark

Statue Square

Chater Garden

Japan Consulate

Ice House Street

Lambeth Walk

Far East Finance Centre

Harcourt Road

Hong Kong & Shanghai Bank Building

Jackson Road

Murray Road

Thai Consulate

Queen's Road

Battery Path

Bank of China

Hilton

Bank of China

Bond Centre

Admiralty MTR Station

To Wanchai & Causeway Bay

St John's Cathedral

Lower Albert Road

Garden Road

Cotton Tree Drive

Flagstaff House & Teaware Museum

Queensway

US Consulate

Peak Tram Terminal

Hong Kong Park

Pacific Place

for a wedding, the ornate jewellery shops, and the silk emporiums.

Past Wing Sing St, Queen's Rd curves around to the left to be called Queen's Rd West, but if you go straight ahead you will be on Bonham Strand East. Veer left opposite Kwong Yuen St for Jervois St. Down here and along Hillier St you will find **snake shops**.

Eating snake is considered good for your health. The more venomous the snake, the greater its reputation as a cure-all. Cobras are a favourite. Little old ladies drink the blood because they think it will cure arthritis and rheumatism. Some men do the same because they believe it's an aphrodisiac. During one visit a snake vendor grabbed me by the arm and excitedly started proclaiming the virtues of his product. I don't know why he picked on me – maybe I looked like I needed the stuff.

From Queen's Rd, head south, uphill to **Hollywood Rd**. This street has several funeral shops selling everything for the best-dressed corpses, as well as wreath and coffin makers. It is also full of furniture shops with antiques of all kinds, from the genuine article to modern reproductions made before your very eyes.

Cat St used to be famous in Hong Kong for its arts and crafts, but the street has disappeared under an urban renewal project. The arts and crafts dealers are now at the **Cat St Galleries**, Casey Building, Lok Ku Rd. The galleries contain five floors of arts and crafts, antiques and souvenirs, plus an exhibition hall and auction room.

Possession St is a small lane, but its name recalls that somewhere around here the flag was planted for Britain after Captain Elliot did his deal with Qi Shan. The area just to the west of Possession St is known as Possession Point.

Man Mo Temple 文武廟

This temple, at the corner of Hollywood Rd and Ladder St, is one of the oldest and most famous in Hong Kong. The Man Mo – literally meaning civil and military – is dedicated to two deities. The civil deity is a Chinese

statesman of the 3rd century BC and the military deity is Kuanti, a soldier born in the 2nd century AD and now worshipped as the God of War. (See the Religion section in the Facts about Hong Kong chapter.) Kuanti is also known as Kwan Tai or Kwan Kung.

Outside the entrance are four gilt plaques on poles which are carried at procession time. Two plaques describe the gods being worshipped and the others request quietness and respect, and warn menstruating women to keep away. Inside the temple are two antique chairs shaped like houses used to carry the two gods at festival time. The coils suspended from the roof are incense cones burnt by worshippers. A large bell on the right is dated 1846 and the smaller ones on the left, 1897.

The exact date of the temple's construction has never been agreed on, but it's certain it was already standing when the British arrived to claim the island as their own. The present Man Mo Temple was renovated in the middle of the last century.

The area around the Man Mo Temple was used extensively for location shots in the film *The World of Suzie Wong*. The building to the right of the temple was used as Suzie's hotel. Ironically, the real hotel in the novel (the Luk Kwok, alias the Nam Kok) was in Wanchai, several km to the east.

The extremely steep flight of steps next to the temple is Ladder St. Once it was crammed with stalls and shops selling everything, but the stall owners were cleared away. Ladder St is well over 100 years old and probably the best example of old Hong Kong remaining.

HONG KONG UNIVERSITY 香港大學

West of Sheung Wan takes you through Sai Ying Pun and Shek Tong Tsui districts to Kennedy Town, a residential and harbour district at the end of the tram line. The chief attraction of Shek Tong Tsui is Hong Kong University's Fung Ping Shan Museum.

Fung Ping Shan Museum 馮平山博物館
This museum (☎ 8592114) houses collections of ceramics and bronzes, plus a lesser

number of paintings and carvings. The bronzes are in three groups: Shang and Zhou Dynasty ritual vessels; decorative mirrors from the Warring States Period to the Tang, Song, Ming and Qing (Ching) dynasties; and Nestorian crosses from the Yuan Dynasty (the Nestorians were a Christian sect which arose in Syria, and at some stage found their way to China, and probably during the Tang Dynasty).

A collection of ceramics includes Han Dynasty tomb pottery and recent works from the Chinese pottery centres of Jingdezhen and Shiwan in the People's Republic.

The museum is in Hong Kong University, 94 Bonham Rd. Take bus No 3 from Edinburgh Place (adjacent to city hall), or bus Nos 23 or 103 coming from Causeway Bay, and get off at Bonham Rd, opposite St Paul's College. The museum is open Monday to Saturday from 9.30 am to 6 pm, and is closed on Sunday and several public holidays. Admission is free.

VICTORIA PEAK 太平山頂

If you haven't been to the Peak, as it's usually called, then you haven't been to Hong Kong. Every visitor tries to make the trip, and for good reason – the view is one of the most spectacular in the world. It's also a good way to get Hong Kong into perspective. It's worth repeating the Peak trip at night – the illuminated view is something else.

The Peak has been *the* place to live ever since the British moved in. The Taipans built their summer houses there to escape the heat and humidity (it's usually about 5°C cooler than down below), although they spent three months swathed in mist for their efforts. It's still the most fashionable place to live in Hong Kong, but the price of real estate is astronomical.

At the top of the tram line at 400 metres elevation is the **Peak Tower**, a type of scenic shopping mall. The place is built like an iceberg, one-third above ground and two-thirds below, and can withstand winds of up to 270 km per hour. High-powered binoculars on the lower balcony cost HK$1 for a few minutes – worth every cent. Inside the

tower you can find all sorts of overpriced shops peddling everything from ice cream to T-shirts. Upstairs is the Peak Tower Restaurant, noted for its dim sum.

When people refer to the Peak, they generally mean the Peak Tower and surrounding residential area. Victoria Peak is the actual summit, about half a km to the west and 140 metres higher. You can walk around Victoria Peak easily without exhausting yourself. Harlech and Lugard Rds encircle it. Harlech Rd is on the south side of the peak while Lugard Rd is on the north slope. Together these form a loop. For those who would rather run, not walk, this makes a spectacular jogging route.

You can walk from the restaurant to the remains of the **old governor's mountain lodge** near the summit (550 metres elevation). The lodge was burnt to the ground by the Japanese during WW II, but the gardens remain and are open to the public. The views are particularly good and there is a toposcope identifying the various geographical features you can see.

For a downhill hike you can walk about two km from the Peak to Pok Fu Lam Reservoir Rd, which leaves Peak Rd near the car park exit. This goes past the reservoir to the main Pok Fu Lam Rd where you can get the No 7 bus to Aberdeen or back to Central.

Another good walk is down to Hong Kong University. First walk to the west side of Victoria Peak by taking either Lugard or Harlech Rds. After reaching Hatton Rd on the west side of Victoria Peak, follow it down. The descent is very steep but the path is obvious.

If you're going to the Peak, you should go by the Peak Tram – at least one way. The tram terminal is in Garden Rd, Central, behind the Hilton Hotel, 650 metres from the Star Ferry Terminal. There is a free shuttle bus between the Star Ferry and the Peak Tram terminals during business hours. The tram trip takes about eight minutes and costs HK$8 one way, or HK$14 round trip (discounts for children under 12). The tram operates every day from 7 am to midnight, and runs about every 10 minutes with three

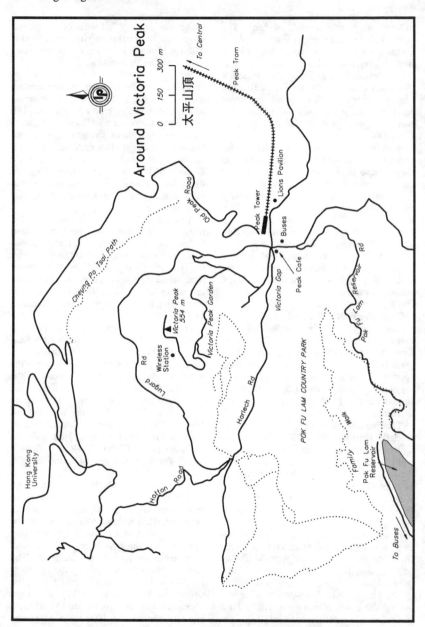

Around Victoria Peak

太平山頂

0   150   300 m

stops along the way. Avoid going on a Sunday when there tends to be long queues.

Running for more than a century, the tram has never had an accident – a comforting thought if you start to have doubts about the strength of the cable. In 1885 everyone thought the Honourable Phineas Kyrie and William Kerfoot Hughes were quite crazy when they announced their intentions of building a tramway to the top, but it opened three years later, wiping out the scoffers and the sedan chair trade in one go. Since then the only occurrences which stopped the tram were WW II and the violent rainstorms of 1966 which washed half the track down the hillside.

Alternatively, bus No 15 from the Central Bus Terminal will take you on a 40-minute trip around the perilous-looking road to the top. Buses cost HK$3.80 and depart from the Central Bus Station underneath Exchange Square in Central. Minibus No 1 leaves from the HMS *Tamar* building, on the eastern side of City Hall and charges HK$4 for the trip to the Peak.

HONG KONG TRAIL 港島徑
For those who would like a real challenge, it is possible to walk the entire length of Hong Kong Island. Start from the Peak, then go down to the hills near Aberdeen. The trail then zigzags across the ridgetops all the way to Shek O in the south-eastern corner of Hong Kong Island. It's not likely that you'll want to do the entire hike in one day, though it is possible if you're very fit.

If you intend to do this hike, it would be wise to purchase the map *Hong Kong Trail* published by the Country Parks Authority (CPA). Another map worth picking up is *Countryside Series Sheet No 1: Hong Kong Island* which shows many details of the streets and topography not on the hiking map. Both maps are available from the Government Publications Centre next to the GPO on Hong Kong Island.

WANCHAI 灣仔
Heading east from Central brings you to Hong Kong's famed Wanchai district. In all the tourist-brochure hype, Wanchai is still inseparable from the name of Suzie Wong –

not bad considering that the book dates back to 1957 and the movie to 1960. Although Wanchai had a reputation during the Vietnam War as a seedy red-light district, these days you can bring grandma and the kids.

Instead of brothels and girlie bars Wanchai is being taken over by high-rise office blocks spreading out from Central; but a walk down Lockhart Rd will give you a wisp of what it was like when the place was really jumping. You can still find plenty of topless bars, massage parlours and tattooists, but you don't need an appointment anymore. Further along Lockhart Rd towards Causeway Bay, the area turns into a tourist shopping district that rivals Tsimshatsui in Kowloon.

Hong Kong Arts Centre 香港藝術中心
Also in the Wanchai district is the Arts Centre (☎ 8230200) on Harbour Rd. The Pao Sui Loong Galleries are on the 4th and 5th floors of the centre and international and local exhibitions are held year round with the emphasis on contemporary art. Opening hours are 10 am to 8 pm daily. Admission is free. It's easy to get there on the MTR to the Wanchai Station.

Police Museum 警隊博物館
This museum (☎ 8496018), at 27 Coombe Rd, emphasises the history of the Royal Hong Kong Police Force, which was formed in 1844. Intriguingly, the museum also houses a Triad Societies Gallery.

Operating hours are Wednesday to Sunday from 9 am to 5 pm, and Tuesday from 2 to 5 pm. It's closed on Mondays and admission is free.

You can get there on bus No 15 from Central. Get off at the intersection of Peak and Stubbs Rds.

Museum of Chinese Historical Relics 文物展覽館
This museum (☎ 5742692) houses cultural treasures from China unearthed in archaeological digs. Two special exhibitions each year focus on artefacts from specific provinces.

The museum is on the 1st floor, Causeway

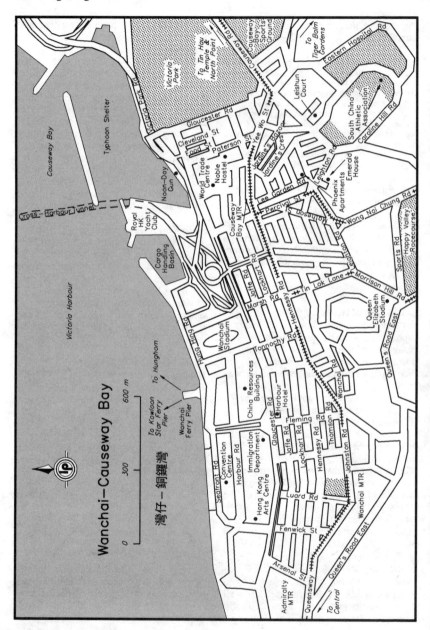

Wanchai—Causeway Bay

灣仔—銅鑼灣

Centre, 28 Harbour Rd, Wanchai. Enter from the China Resources Building. Operating hours are from 10 am to 6 pm. Admission is HK$20 for adults. From Central, take bus Nos 10A, 20, 21 or 104.

CAUSEWAY BAY 銅鑼灣

Catch the tram which goes through Wanchai and let it take you to Causeway Bay. The old Causeway Bay – Tung Lo Wan in Chinese, meaning Copper Gong Bay – has almost disappeared through reclamation. This area was the site of a British settlement in the 1840s and was once a godown (warehouse) area for merchants and a harbour for fishermen. A lot of this area has been reclaimed from swamp and the bottom of the harbour.

Causeway Bay is one of Hong Kong's top shopping and nightlife areas. Many of the big Japanese department stores are here, mostly clustered around the Hotel Excelsior and Park Lane Radisson (both famous for discos).

Jardine Matheson 怡和有限公司

Hong Kong's largest and most powerful *hong* (big company) set up shop in Causeway Bay in 1844, after moving its headquarters from Macau. Now Jardine Matheson's head office resides in the World Trade Centre next to the Hotel Excelsior.

The area is still full of company names and memorials. Percival St, which crosses Hennessy Rd, is named after Alexander Percival, a relative of Sir James Matheson who joined the firm in 1852 and ended up a partner. Matheson St leads off it. Hennessy Rd becomes Yee Wo St, Yee Wo being the name under which Jardine Matheson traded in Shanghai.

Jardine Matheson bought heavily in the first land sale in the colony in 1841. It bought a large tract of land on what was then the waterfront at Causeway Bay and hewed a whole township out of the rock. It built godowns, offices, workshops, a slipway, homes and messes for employees. All that remains of the East Point establishment is an old gateway with a couple of plaques. You'll find it up a side-street from Yee Wo St. It's

still owned by Jardine Matheson but is now full of modern warehouses.

Two streets to the right (south) behind Yee Wo St are Jardine's Bazaar and Jardine's Crescent, names which recall the old firm. A Chinese bazaar used to held on the first street. Things haven't changed much. The area still has Chinese provision stores, herb stores and cooked-food stalls. Jardine's Crescent has a market which is very good for cheap clothes. Between Jardine's Bazaar and Crescent is the short Fuk Hing Lane, an interesting shopping alley with good, inexpensive leather handbags, silk scarves, Chinese padded jackets and well-cut jeans.

Nearby Pennington St has a good Chinese medicine shop, pawn shops and herbal tea houses. Irving St, off Pennington St, is well known for its soy sauce and wine shops. Russell St, off Percival St, has an all-day fresh-food market.

Typhoon Shelter 避風塘

Causeway Bay's waterfront is a mass of junks and sampans huddling in the typhoon shelter. The land jutting out is Kellett Island, which was actually an island until a causeway was built to it in 1956. Further land reclamation turned it into a peninsula. Now it's the headquarters of the Royal Hong Kong Yacht Club. The Cross-Harbour Tunnel comes up here too.

Noon-Day Gun 午炮

The best known landmark in Causeway Bay is probably the noon-day gun – a recoil mounted three-pounder built by Hotchkiss in Portsmouth in 1901. It stands in a small garden in front of the Excelsior Hotel on Gloucester Rd and is fired daily at noon. Exactly how this tradition started is unknown.

One story claims that Jardine Matheson either fired it to wish bon voyage to a departing managing director or to welcome an incoming ship. The navy got so enraged that their function had been usurped (or because an ordinary person got a salute reserved for officials) that they told Jardine's to fire the gun every day as punishment.

Noel Coward made the gun famous with his

satirical 1924 song *Mad Dogs and Englishmen* about colonists who braved the heat of the noon-day sun while the locals stayed indoors:

In Hong Kong they strike a gong,
and fire a noon-day gun,
To reprimand each inmate who's
in late.

Jardine's executives stand around the gun on New Year's Eve and fire it off at midnight, to the applause of a colonial gathering.

Food St 食街
Between the Excelsior Hotel and the end of Gloucester Rd is Food St, a modern arcade of restaurants of varied ethnic persuasions. Have a look but don't expect a banquet-like selection of traditional Chinese fare – you're more likely to find the place crowded with Hong Kong Chinese having a family excursion to eat Western. However, there are some really good Chinese places here.

Victoria Park 維多利亞公園
Victoria Park, between Causeway Rd and Victoria Park Rd, is a large playing field built on reclaimed land. Football matches are played on weekends and the Urban Services League puts on music and acrobatic shows. Early in the morning it is a good place to view the slow-motion choreography of taichichuan practitioners. Victoria Park becomes a flower market a few days before the Chinese New Year, and it's also worth a visit for the Lantern Festival (see the Facts about Hong Kong chapter). Other events in the park include the Hong Kong Tennis Classic and the Hong Kong International Kart Grand Prix.

Causeway Bay Sports Ground
銅鑼灣運動場
This is the most popular sports ground in Hong Kong and home of the Chinese Recreation Club. The sports ground is on the south side of Causeway Rd, just south of Victoria Park. Among the public facilities are areas to play football, volleyball, badminton and tennis.

Tin Hau Temple 天后廟
One more thing worth a look in Causeway Bay is a tiny Tin Hau temple on Tin Hau Temple Rd (at the junction with Dragon Rd), on the east side of Victoria Park (near the Tin Hau MTR Station). Before reclamation, the temple to the seafarers' goddess stood on the waterfront. An old bell inside dates back to the 15th century. The temple itself is about 200 years old.

Tiger Balm Gardens 虎豹別墅
Not actually in Causeway Bay but in the adjacent Tai Hang District are the famous (infamous?) Tiger Balm Gardens, also known as the Aw Boon Haw Gardens. A pale relative of the better known park of the same name in Singapore, Hong Kong's Tiger Balm Gardens are three hectares of grotesque statuary in appallingly bad taste. These concrete gardens were built at a cost of HK$16 million (and that was in 1935!) by Aw Boon Haw, who made his fortune from the Tiger Balm cure-everything medication. Aw is widely described as having been a philanthropist, though perhaps his millions could have been put to a more philanthropic use.

Sad to say, the gardens are wilting – the paint is peeling and the concrete statues crumbling, making the place look all the more grotesque. If you haven't seen the larger Tiger Balm Gardens in Singapore then this place is worth visiting!

The gardens are just off Tai Hang Rd, within walking distance of Causeway Bay, or take bus No 11 from the Admiralty MTR Station. They are open daily from 10 am to 4 pm. Admission is free.

HAPPY VALLEY 快活谷
There are two horse-racing tracks in Hong Kong – one at Shatin in the New Territories and the other at Happy Valley. The racing season is from late September to May. For details, see the Activities section in the Facts for the Visitor chapter of this book.

Getting to Happy Valley is easy. A tram which is marked Happy Valley runs from Central.

QUARRY BAY 鰂魚涌
The main attraction of Quarry Bay is the Cityplaza Shopping Centre, one of Hong Kong's finest. Although not normally considered a tourist attraction, it has much to recommend it. For one thing, shopping is much more pleasant once you get out of the tourist zones. Shops have price tags on merchandise and there is no bargaining, yet prices are generally lower than you could bargain for in Tsimshatsui.

Even if you don't want to buy anything, Cityplaza has other amenities: it's the only shopping mall in Hong Kong with an ice skating rink; its Tivoli Terrace cafe is one of the nicest in town; and it has a good dim sum place, the Cityplaza Palace Restaurant.

To get to Cityplaza, take the MTR to Tai Koo Station from where there is an exit which leads directly into the shopping mall.

SHEK O 石澳
Shek O, on the south-east coast, has one of the best beaches on Hong Kong Island. All around Shek O are homes that belong to Hong Kong's wealthy entrepreneurial class, but many of the best homes are protected by walls which are cleverly hidden by landscape gardening. Shek O is a prestigious place to live, though the Peak still ranks as number one in terms of snob appeal.

To get to Shek O, take the MTR to Shaukiwan, and from Shaukiwan take bus No 9 to the last stop, which is Shek O.

Big Wave Bay, another excellent beach, is two km to the north of Shek O, but there is no public transport. It does make a nice walk, passing the Shek O Country Club and Golf Course along the way.

STANLEY 赤柱
This is the trendy, out-of-town gwailo place to live, on the south-east side of the island just 15 km as the crow flies from Central. Once the village was indeed a village. About 2000 people lived here when the British took over in 1841, making it one of the largest settlements on the island at the time. The British built a prison near the village in 1937

– just in time to be used by the Japanese to intern the expatriates.

Now it's used as a maximum-security prison. Hong Kong's contingent of British troops is housed in Stanley Fort at the southern end of the peninsula, which is off-limits to the public.

There is an OK beach (not as crowded as the one at Repulse Bay) at Stanley Village. The **Stanley Market** dominates the town and on weekends it's wall-to-wall tourists. The market is open from 10 am to 7 pm, sells clothes, furniture, household goods, hardware, foodstuffs and imitation designer jeans.

Because of the expatriate community there's a British-style pub, the *Smuggler's Inn* (☎ 8138852) at 90A Stanley Main St, near the intersection with Stanley Market Rd.

Stanley has a **Tin Hau temple** which dates back to 1767. On one of the walls hangs the skin of a tiger killed by Japanese soldiers outside the temple. The temple is on a corner of Stanley Main St, approaching Ma Hang Village.

Further up from the Tin Hau temple is the **Kuanyin (Kwun Yum) Temple** in Ma Hang Village. Kuanyin is the Goddess of Mercy and the temple contains a six-metre statue of her. The statue is sheltered by a pavilion specially built in 1977 following a claim by a woman and her daughter that they'd seen the statue move and a bright light shine from its forehead...Maybe Stanley isn't such a dull place?

From Stanley you can take bus No 73A to **St Stephen's Beach** a bit further down the coast. Both Stanley and St Stephen's beaches have all the usual facilities. The cemetery at St Stephen's Beach is for military personnel who have died since the British occupation of Hong Kong and during WW II. The oldest graves date from 1843.

Getting There & Away
To get to Stanley from Central take bus No 6 or express bus No 260 from the Central Bus Terminal under Exchange Square in Central. Fares are HK$3 for the ordinary bus and

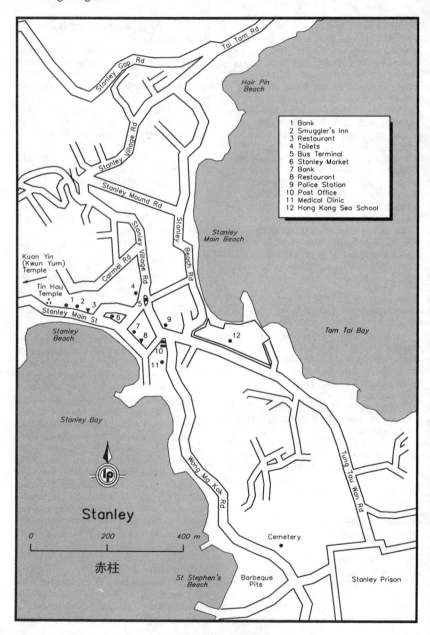

Tai Tarn Rd

Hair Pin Beach

Stanley Gap Rd

Stanley Village Rd

Stanley Mound Rd

Stanley Main Beach

1 Bank
2 Smuggler's Inn
3 Restaurant
4 Toilets
5 Bus Terminal
6 Stanley Market
7 Bank
8 Restaurant
9 Police Station
10 Post Office
11 Medical Clinic
12 Hong Kong Sea School

Kuan Yin (Kwun Yum) Temple

Tin Hau Temple

Carmel Rd

Stanley Village Rd

Stanley Beach Rd

Stanley Main St

Stanley Beach

Tam Tai Bay

Stanley Bay

Stanley

0   200   400 m

赤柱

Wong Ma Kok Rd

Tung Tau Wan Rd

Cemetery

St Stephen's Beach

Barbeque Pits

Stanley Prison

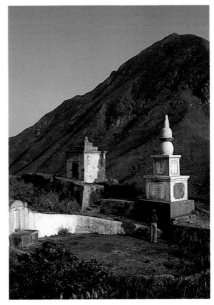

Top: Aberdeen Harbour, Hong Kong Island (PS)
Left: Junk under construction, Cheung Chau (TW)
Right: Near Po Lin Monastery, Lantau (TW)

Top, Left & Right: At the Po Lin Monastery, Lantau (TW)

HK$4.80 for the express bus. The bus to Stanley takes a very scenic trip down Tai Tam Rd to the reservoir, then along the coast at Tai Tam Bay. Along the way you pass Turtle Cove, a small but pretty beach. If you're coming from Shaukiwan (eastern terminus of the tram), take bus No 14 down to Stanley. Bus No 73 connects Stanley with Repulse Bay.

REPULSE BAY 淺水灣

The prime attraction is the beach and, if you're into it, one of the biggest McDonald's in Hong Kong. In fact, the beach attracts so many people on hot weekends you're just about swimming in suntan lotion. To find even a niche in the sand you have to get there early. Otherwise the place looks OK from the road and makes a scenic drive. You could also walk down the coast a bit to Middle Bay and South Bay, about 10-minute and 30-minute walks respectively.

To reach Repulse Bay from Central, take bus Nos 6 or 61 from the Central Bus Terminal just to the west of the Star Ferry. The No 6 bus carries on to Stanley. Bus No 73 connects Repulse Bay with Stanley and Aberdeen.

OCEAN PARK 海洋公園

Next around the coast is Deep Water Bay, now famous for Ocean Park, opened in 1976. Although generally advertised as an oceanarium or a marine world, the emphasis is on the fun fair with its roller coaster, space wheel, octopus, swinging ship and other astronaut-training machines. There's also a sensurround cinema housed in a 20-metre-high dome. Ocean Park has to rate as one of the best theme parks in the world.

The complex is built on two levels connected by a seven-minute cable car ride, and looks down on Deep Water Bay below. At the park entrance are landscaped gardens with a touch-and-feed section where kids can pet tame llamas, goats, calves and kangaroos. I never saw such cooperative kangaroos in Australia, not even in a zoo, and I wonder how the Chinese managed this. Perhaps the kangaroos were given prefrontal lobotomies.

Chinese arts like kung fu, opera and so on are often staged in the gardens. There's an exotic bird section too. There are several theatres where penguins, whales, sea lions, monkeys and other animals perform. Bring a pen and paper to write down the various showtimes – these are displayed on a noticeboard at the entrance but there is no hand-out available.

Right at the rear entrance to Ocean Park is the Middle Kingdom, a sort of Chinese cultural village representing 13 dynasties. The village has temples, pagodas, traditional street scenes and Middle Kingdom employees dressed in the fashionable outerwear of ancient China.

Entrance fees are HK$140 (discounts for children). Opening hours are 10 am to 6 pm Monday through Saturday, and 9 am to 6 pm on Sunday and holidays. Get there early because there's much to see. It's best to go on weekdays since weekends are very crowded.

Getting There & Away

The cheapest way to get to Ocean Park from Central is to take bus No 70 (HK$2.80) from the Central Bus Terminal (under Exchange Square, near Star Ferry) and get off at the first stop after the tunnel. From there it's a 10-minute walk. Slightly more expensive is minibus No 6 from the Central Bus Terminal (HK$5), but it does not run on Sunday and holidays. Most expensive is the air-con Ocean Park Citybus, which leaves Admiralty MTR Station (underneath Bond Centre) every half-hour from 9 am (HK$8).

Bus No 73 connects Ocean Park with Aberdeen to the west and Repulse Bay and Stanley to the east.

WATER WORLD 水上樂園

Adjacent to the front entrance of Ocean Park is Water World, a collection of swimming pools, water slides and diving platforms. Water World is open during summer (June, July, August) from 10 am to 10 pm. During May, late September and October it is open from 10 am to 5 pm. Admission for adults is HK$60. Hours are shorter and prices reduced in the other months, and it's closed from late November to the end of March, though the rest of Ocean Park remains open. From the Central Bus Terminal in Exchange Square (Central), take bus No 70 and get off at the first stop after the tunnel, then follow the signs to Ocean Park. Alternatively, take minibus No 6 from the Central Bus Terminal (HK$5), but it does not run on Sunday and holidays. You can also take the Ocean Park Citybus from Bond Centre, Admiralty, but it's very important that you get off at the first stop, which is the front entrance of Ocean Park. The second stop is the rear entrance of Ocean Park, which is far away from Water World.

ABERDEEN 香港仔

Hong Kong's top tourist attraction apart from the Peak is Aberdeen, where nearly 6000 people live or work on junks anchored in the harbour. Also moored in the harbour are three palace-like floating restaurants, sightseeing attractions in themselves.

Sampan tours of Aberdeen Harbour are inexpensive and definitely worth it. The price should run at about HK$35 per person, though you can bargain a little. If you're with a group, you can charter a sampan for about HK$100 for 30 minutes, or maybe less if you bargain hard. If you are by yourself, just hang out by the harbour as the old women who operate the boats will leap on you and try to get you to join a tour. Some travellers take a free harbour tour by riding the boat out to the Jumbo Floating Restaurant and then riding back.

On one side of the harbour is the island of Ap Lei Chau. The island used to be not much more than a junk-building centre, but now it's covered with housing estates. The walk across the bridge to Ap Lei Chau affords good views of the harbour.

At the junction of Aberdeen Main Rd and Aberdeen Reservoir Rd is a Tin Hau temple built in 1851.

Getting There & Away
A tunnel linking Aberdeen with the northern side of Hong Kong Island provides rapid

access to the town. From the Central Bus Terminal in Exchange Square, take bus No 7 or No 70 to Aberdeen. Bus No 7 goes via Hong Kong University, and No 70 goes via the tunnel. Bus No 73 from Aberdeen will take you along the southern coast to Ocean Park, Repulse Bay and Stanley.

PLACES TO STAY – BOTTOM END
Hostels
On top of Mount Davis, not far from Kennedy Town is the *Ma Wui Hall* youth hostel (☎ 8175715). This place gets rave reviews from travellers, mainly because it's very clean, quiet, has great views of the harbour and costs only HK$25 per night. It's a bit out of the way, but that's the price you pay to escape the coffin-sized sweatboxes in Chungking Mansions. There are cooking facilities and secure lockers. The hostel has more than 100 beds and is closed between 10 am and 4 pm.

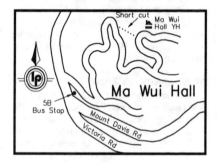

Take bus Nos 5B, 47 or 77 and get off at Felix Villas (the 5B terminal) on Victoria Rd. From the bus stop, walk back 100 metres. Look for the YHA sign and follow the unnamed motorable road – there is a shortcut (with a sign) halfway up the hill. The walk from the bottom up to the hostel takes from 20 to 30 minutes.

If you come from the airport, take the A2 bus to Central, then change to the 5B or 47 bus. Bus No 5B runs from Paterson St in Causeway Bay to Felix Villas. Bus No 47

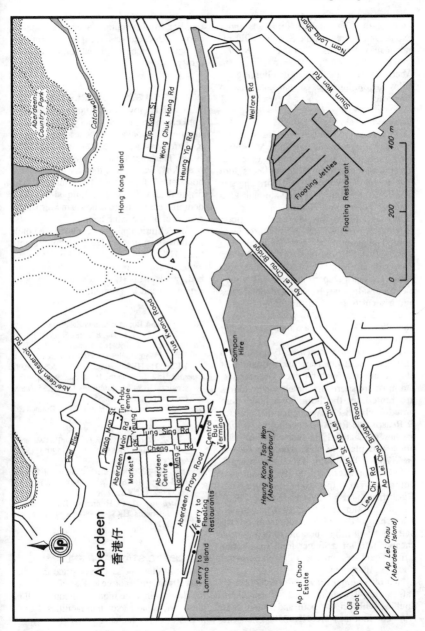

starts at the Central Bus Terminal, under Exchange Square near the Star Ferry Terminal. You're least likely to use bus No 77, which runs from the Western District to Aberdeen. If you can't handle climbing the hill with your luggage, you can take a taxi to the hostel.

Guesthouses

Leishun Court at 116 Leighton Rd is Causeway Bay's answer to Chungking Mansions. The building houses a number of cheap guesthouses, mostly on the lower floors. *Fuji House* (☎ 5779406), 1st floor, charges HK$150 for a room with private bath. *Villa Lisboa Hotel* (☎ 5765421) and *Cannes House* (☎ 8902736) are also on the 1st floor.

Noble Hostel (☎ 5766148) has three locations. The main office – where you check in – is at Flat C1, 7th floor, 37 Paterson St, Paterson Building, Causeway Bay, just above Daimaru Department Store. It's very clean and safe – they have locked metal gates and a security guard in the lobby. Singles/doubles are HK$190/240 with shared bath, and HK$290 with private bath. It's highly recommended.

The *Phoenix Apartments*, 70 Lee Garden Hill Rd, Causeway Bay, has a number of elegant and reasonably-priced guesthouses, but most are short-time hotels where rooms are rented by the hour. One hotel here proudly advertises 'Avoidance of Publicity & Reasonable Rates'. Nevertheless, as long as they've changed the sheets recently, it's not a bad place to stay. The *Sunrise Inn* (☎ 5762419) on the 1st floor charges HK$128 for overnight or HK$58 for two hours. Moving up-market, the *Hoi Wan Guest House* (☎ 5777970), 1st floor, Flat C has plush rooms and friendly management. They charge HK$280 for a room with private bath, but you might be able to negotiate a cheaper rate for a longer term (or shorter term). There are numerous other places in the Phoenix Apartments.

Nearby is *Emerald House* (☎ 5772368), 1st floor, 44 Leighton Rd, where clean doubles with private bath and round beds (I'm not kidding) are HK$250. Enter the building from Leighton Lane just around the corner. Guesthouses are plentiful in this section of Leighton Rd, but some are pretty grotty.

PLACES TO STAY – MIDDLE

Wanchai is now pretty tame and you're unlikely to accidentally find yourself checking into a brothel as did the lead character in Richard Mason's novel *The World of Suzie Wong*. The hotel mentioned in that novel, the *Nam Kok*, was in fact the *Luk Kwok*, a real hotel at 67 Gloucester Rd, Wanchai. The original *Luk Kwok* has long since been demolished, but there is now a modern highrise hotel by the same name.

For definition purposes, mid-range hotels are those costing over HK$200 but no more than HK$600. Couples looking to save money should specify that they want one bed, since twins (two beds) are both more expensive and less romantic.

Bonham, 50-54 Bonham Strand East, Sheung Wan, twins HK$400 (☎ 5442882, fax 5443922)

China Merchants, 160-161 Connaught Rd West, Sheung Wan, singles HK$560 to HK$800, twins HK$620 to HK$850 (☎ 5596888, fax 5590038)

Emerald, 152 Connaught Rd West, Sheung Wan, singles HK$470, doubles/twins HK$570/690 (☎ 5468111, fax 5590255)

Garden View International House, 1 MacDonnell Rd, Central, twins HK$480 to HK$580 (☎ 8773737, fax 8456263)

Harbour View International, 4 Harbour Rd, Wanchai, doubles/twins HK$560/700 (☎ 5201111, fax 8656063)

Harbour, 116-122 Gloucester Rd, Wanchai, Singles HK$460 to HK$620, twins HK$600 to HK$900 (☎ 5748211, fax 5722185)

New Harbour, 41-49 Hennessy Rd, Wanchai, doubles/twins HK$600/880 (☎ 8611166, fax 8656111)

PLACES TO STAY – TOP END

Hotels in this category have price tags that start from just above HK$600 and rise rapidly towards the moon. Obviously, all of these places have excellent facilities. Hotels in this category include:

China Harbour View, 189-193 Gloucester Rd, Wanchai, doubles/twins HK$700/1200, (☎ 8382222, fax 8380136)

City Garden, 231 Electric Rd, North Point (take the MTR to Tin Hau Station), singles HK$800 to HK$1050, twins HK$900 to HK$1150 (☎ 8872888, fax 8871111)

Conrad, Pacific Place, 88 Queensway, Admiralty, doubles/twins HK$1500/2600 (☎ 5213838, fax 5213888)

Easton Valley, 1A Wang Tak St, Happy Valley (the nearest MTR station is Causeway Bay), doubles/twins HK$1100/1500 (☎ 5749922, fax 8381622)

Evergreen Plaza, 33 Hennessy Rd, Wanchai, doubles/twins HK$950/1050 (☎ 8669111, fax 8613121)

Excelsior, 281 Gloucester Rd, Causeway Bay, doubles/twins HK$1050/1600 (☎ 8948888, fax 8956459)

Furama Kempinski, 1 Connaught Rd, Central, doubles/twins HK$1500/1750 (☎ 5255111, fax 8459339)

Grand Hyatt, 1 Harbour Rd, Wanchai, doubles/twins HK$1620/2300 (☎ 8611234, fax 8611677)

Grand Plaza, 2 Kornhill Rd, Quarry Bay (take the MTR to Tai Koo Station), singles HK$760 to HK$1480, twins HK$860 to HK$1480 (☎ 8860011, fax 8861738)

Hilton, 2 Queen's Rd, Central, singles HK$1360 to HK$1860, twins HK$1440 to HK$1970 (☎ 5233111, fax 8452590)

JW Marriot, Pacific Place, 88 Queensway, Admiralty, doubles/twins HK$1750/2050 (☎ 8108366, fax 8450737)

Island Shangri-La, Pacific Place, 88 Queensway, Admiralty, doubles/twins HK$1700/2600 (☎ 8773838, 5218742)

Lee Gardens, Hysan Ave, Causeway Bay, doubles/twins HK$900/1800 (☎ 8953311, fax 5769775)

Luk Kwok, 72 Gloucester Rd, Wanchai, singles HK$860 to HK$1060, twins HK$960 to HK$1160 (☎ 8662166, fax 8662622)

Mandarin Oriental, 5 Connaught Rd, Central, doubles/twins HK$1500/2400 (☎ 5220111, fax 8106190)

New World Harbour View, 1 Harbour Rd, Wanchai, singles HK$1350 to HK$1750, twins HK$1600 to HK$1900

Park Lane, 310 Gloucester Rd, Causeway Bay, doubles/twins HK$1100/1900 (☎ 8903355, fax 5767853)

Ramada Inn, 61-73 Lockhart Rd, Wanchai, doubles/twins HK$950/1200 (☎ 8611000, fax 8656023)

Victoria, Shun Tak Centre, 200 Connaught Rd, Sheung Wan, doubles/twins HK$1450/2050 (☎ 5407228, fax 8583398)

PLACES TO EAT
Breakfast

St Honore Cake Shop has a branch at 116C Percival St, Causeway Bay, and 80 Johnston Rd, Wanchai.

For a quick breakfast, there are food windows adjacent to the Star Ferry that open shortly after 6 am.

Fast Food

Fairwood Fast Food is my favourite in the fast-food race, and it's easy to find — just look for the big smiling clown face. There are branches at: 165 Wanchai Rd, Wanchai; 9 Cannon St, Causeway Bay; 24 Connaught Rd, Central.

Highly recommended is *Oliver's Super Sandwiches*, which has several outlets: 2nd floor, Prince's Building, 10 Chater Rd, Central; Shop 104, Tower Two, Exchange Square, 8 Connaught Place, Central; Shop A, Ground floor, Fleet House, 38 Gloucester Rd, Wanchai; Kiosk 8, 1st floor, Fast Food Centre, Cityplaza 2, Tai Koo, Quarry Bay.

Spaghetti House has great Italian submarine sandwiches and pizza. The food is cheap and the place is extremely popular. They have four branches on Hong Kong Island: Hay Wah Building, 85B Hennessy Rd, Wanchai; LG floor, 10 Stanley St, Central; 5 Sharp St East, Causeway Bay; 433 King's Rd, North Point.

For take-away food, there is a *Ka Ka Lok* at 476 Jaffe Rd in Causeway Bay.

Maxim's is a well-known Hong Kong chain of fast-food restaurants. They do passable Chinese food, but the eggs and sausages look as if they've been spray-painted on to the plate. As you face the entrance to the Star Ferry on Hong Kong Island, there is a Maxim's off to your right. There is a larger one at the corner of Percival St and Leighton Rd in Causeway Bay, and also one at 36 Queen's Rd, Central.

Café De Coral has numerous branches: 122 Queen's Rd, Central; 186 Connaught Rd West, Sheung Wan; 76 Johnston Rd, Wanchai; 8 King's Rd, Causeway Bay.

Pizza Hut needs no introduction. You can find it at B38, Basement 1, Edinburgh Tower,

The Landmark, 17 Queen's Rd, Central; 4th & 5th floors, Goldmark Jardine Bazaar, Yee Wo St, Causeway Bay; Shop 214-216 City plaza, Tai Koo, Quarry Bay; Shop A, Ground floor, Beach Centre, 33 Beach Rd, Repulse Bay.

If finger lick'n chicken is what you have in mind, the Colonel beckons to you at *Kentucky Fried Chicken*, 6 D'Aguilar St, Central, or at 40 Yee Wo St, Causeway Bay. *McDonald's* raises its arches at the Hang Cheong Building, 5 Queen's Rd, Central; CC Wu Building, 302-308 Hennessy Rd, Wanchai; and at 46 Yee Wo St, Causeway Bay.

Chinese Food
Street Market A small night market called the *Poor Man's Nightclub* sets up in the car park on the west side of the Macau Ferry Terminal from about 8 to 11 pm. You can get very good noodles for a couple of dollars and there's no language barrier, just point to whatever looks good.

Dim Sum & Cantonese Dim sum is relatively cheap, but it's served for lunch only. A few restaurants have breakfast dim sum. In the evening, they roll out more expensive Cantonese fare such as pigeon, snake and shark's fin soup. You can easily find expensive Cantonese restaurants in big tourist hotels, but all of the following places are in the lower price range:

Asiania, 1st floor, Asian House, 1 Hennessy Rd, Wanchai (☎ 5282121)
Blue Ocean, 9th floor, Aberdeen Marina Tower, 8 Shum Wan Rd, Aberdeen (☎ 5559415)
Broadway Seafood, Hay Wah Building, 73-85B Hennessy Rd, Wanchai (☎ 5299233)
Cityplaza Palace, Room 310, Cityplaza, Phase Two, Tai Koo, Quarry Bay (☎ 5670330)
Diamond 265-275 Des Voeux Rd, Sheung Wan (☎ 5444921)
Dragon Court Seafood, China Merchants Hotel, 160 Connaught Rd West, Sheung Wan (☎ 5596888)
Emerald Court, Emerald Hotel, 152 Connaught Rd West, Sheung Wan (☎ 5468111)

Jade Garden, 1st floor, Swire House, 9-25 Chater Rd, Central (☎ 5239966)
Shop 5, Lower Ground floor, Jardine House, 1 Connaught Place, Central (☎ 5245098)
North Point Fung Shing, Ground floor, 62-68 Java Rd, North Point (☎ 5784898)
Ping Shan, 28 Beach Rd, Repulse Bay (☎ 8127485)
Ruby, 1st floor, Hong Kong Mansions, 1 Yee Wo St, Causeway Bay (☎ 5776222)
Tai Woo, 15-19 Wellington St, Central (☎ 5245618)
Tsui Hang Village, 2nd floor, New World Tower, 16-18 Queen's Rd, Central (☎ 5242012)
Tung Yuen Seafood, 3rd floor, Tai Yau Building, 181 Johnston Rd, Wanchai (☎ 8336116)
Victoria City Seafood, 2D, Sun Hung Kai Centre, 30 Harbour Rd, Wanchai (☎ 8919938)

Beijing (Peking) & Shandong For a relatively cheap meal with good food try the inappropriately named *New American Restaurant* (☎ 5750458), Ground floor, 177-179 Wanchai Rd, Wanchai.

Make a reservation for the *Peking Garden Restaurant* (☎ 5777231), Excelsior Hotel Shopping Arcade, Causeway Bay, and you will be rewarded with nightly demonstrations of noodle making. There is another branch of the *Peking Garden* (☎ 5266456) in the basement, Alexandra House, 6 Ice House St, Central.

Another is *Hong Kong Chung Chuk Lau* (☎ 5774914), 30 Leighton Rd, Causeway Bay. Also try the *King Heung* (☎ 5771035), 59-65 Paterson St, Causeway Bay.

You can pass the evening slowly sipping your shark's fin soup at the *Prosperous Restaurant* (☎ 8811656), 46 Leighton Rd, Causeway Bay.

Floating Restaurants There are three floating restaurants moored in Aberdeen Harbour, all specialising in seafood. Dinner in such a place will cost about HK$150 depending on what you order. Top of the line is *Jumbo Floating Restaurant* (☎ 5539111), which also serves relatively cheap dim sum from 7.30 am to 5 pm. Nearby is the *Tai Pak Floating Restaurant* (☎ 5525953) and *Sea Palace* (☎ 8148955). Another alternative is to take an evening kaido from Aberdeen to Sok Kwu Wan on Lamma Island where seafood is somewhat cheaper.

Shanghai *Dim Sum Burger* (☎ 5777199), Shop 3, Kingston Building, 4 Kingston St, Causeway Bay, doesn't sell burgers, just good Shanghai food. They serve Shanghai-style dim sum from 7 am to almost midnight.

Also popular is the *Shanghai Garden* (☎ 5238322), Shop G30, 115-124 & 126 Hut chison House, 10 Harcourt Rd, Central. Another *Shanghai Garden* (☎ 5779996) is on the 1st floor, Hennessy Centre, 500 Hennessy Rd, Causeway Bay.

Shanghai Grand Restaurant (☎ 8906828) serves up eels and marinated yellow fish. It's on the 4th floor, Island Shopping Centre, 1 Great George St, Causeway Bay.

Sichuan (Szechuan) No prizes for guessing the speciality of *Red Pepper* (☎ 5768046), at 7 Lan Fong Rd, Causeway Bay. Other well-known Sichuan restaurants are as follows:

Cleveland, Ground floor, New Town Mansion, 6 Cleveland St, Causeway Bay (☎ 5763876)
Jun Jun, Flat C, Ground floor, Causeway Bay Mansion, 48 Paterson St, Causeway Bay (☎ 5778362)
Pep'n Chilli, Shop F, Ground floor, 12-22 Blue Pool Rd, Happy Valley (☎ 5738251)
Sichuan Garden, 3rd floor, Gloucester Tower, the Landmark, 11 Pedder St, Central (☎ 5214433)
Shop 4, The Mall, Pacific Place, 88 Queensway, Admiralty (☎ 8458433)
Sze Chuan Lau, 466 Lockhart Rd, Causeway Bay (☎ 8919027)

Chaozhou (Chiu Chow) Chaozhou restaurants are excellent. Some to try include the following:

Chiuchow Garden, Basement, Jardine House, 1 Connaught Place, Central (☎ 5258246)
3rd floor, Vicwood Plaza, 199 Des Voeux Rd, Sheung Wan (☎ 5445199)
2nd floor, Hennessy Centre, 500 Hennessy Rd, Causeway Bay (☎ 5773391)
Kornhill, Ground floor, Kornhill Plaza, 1 Kornhill Rd, Quarry Bay (☎ 8854461)
Manning, 1st floor, Asian House, 1 Hennessy Rd, Wanchai (☎ 5297669)
Paterson, Shop A, Ground floor, Towning Mansion, 50-56 Paterson St, Causeway Bay (☎ 5776891)
Pepper Garden, 6th & 7th floors, Hong Kong Arts Centre, 2 Harbour Rd, Wanchai (☎ 5272883)

Vegetarian If you want a non-meat option, one of the best-known vegetarian restaurants in town is the *Wishful Cottage* (☎ 5735645), Ground floor, 336 Lockhart Rd, Causeway Bay. They serve delicious vegetarian dim sum at lunch time.

Vegi Food Restaurant (☎ 8906660), Ground floor, Highland Mansions, 8 Cleveland St, Causeway Bay, has a sign warning you not to bring meat or alcohol onto the premises. If you're carrying a meatloaf and bottle of Johnny Walker in your backpack, you'd better check it at the door.

One of Hong Kong's biggest Chinese vegetarian restaurants is *Bodhi* (☎ 5732155), Ground floor, 388 Lockhart Rd, Causeway Bay.

Other Asian Food

Burmese For Burmese food, you can try the *Rangoon Restaurant* (☎ 8921182), Ground floor, 265 Gloucester Rd, Causeway Bay

Indian Indian food is plentiful and popular in Hong Kong. Highly recommended is the *Ashoka* (☎ 5249623), 57 Wyndham St, Central, or the nearby *Bombay Palace* (☎ 5270115), Shop C1, Ground floor, Far East Finance Centre, 16 Harcourt Rd, Admiralty. Also worth trying is the *Viceroy of India* (☎ 5727227), 2nd floor, Sun Hung Kai Centre, 30 Harbour Rd, Wanchai. Moving down-market, there is the *Shalimar* (☎ 8952108), Ground floor, 13 Irving St, Causeway Bay. Also reasonably priced is the *Maharaja* (☎ 5749838), 222 Wanchai Rd, Wanchai. *Siddharth Club* (☎ 5254117) at 57 Wyndham St, is equally impressive.

Club Sri Lanka (☎ 5266559), in the basement of 17 Hollywood Rd (almost at the Wyndham St end), has great Sri Lankan curries. Their fixed-price all-you-can-eat deal is a wonderful bargain.

Indonesian For Indonesian food try the *Shinta* (☎ 5278780), 1st floor, Kar Yau Building, 36 Queen's Rd East, Wanchai. There's the *Indonesia Padang Restaurant* (☎ 5761828), 85 Percival St, Causeway Bay.

Japanese Eating Japanese cuisine can quickly lead to bankruptcy, but if you've got deep pockets, you might want to try some of the following:

Benkay, Basement 1, Gloucester Tower, the Landmark, 11 Pedder St, Central (☎ 5213344)

Kanetanaka, 22nd floor, East Point Centre, 545-563 Hennessy Rd, Causeway Bay (☎ 8336018)

Hooraiya, Shop D, Ground floor, Welcome Mansion, 58-64 Paterson St, Causeway Bay (☎ 5771183)

Momoyama, Shop 15, LG floor 3, Jardine House, 1 Connaught Place, Central (☎ 8458773)

Nanbantei Yakitori, Ground & 1st floors, 52-54 D'Aguilar St, Central (☎ 5267678)

Okahan, Ground floor, Lee Gardens Hotel, 33 Hysan Ave, Causeway Bay (☎ 5766188)

Sakuraya, Flat A, Florida Mansion, Ground floor, 9-11 Cleveland St, Causeway Bay

Sui Sha Ya, 1st floor, Lockhart House, 440 Jaffe Rd, Causeway Bay (☎ 8381808)

Yorohachi, Ground floor, 6 Lan Kwai Fong, Central (☎ 5241251)

Korean Korean food is fiery hot, but tasty and relatively cheap. There is a *Korea House* restaurant (☎ 5440007), in the Korea Centre Building, 19th floor, 119-121 Connaught Rd, Central. It has great views of Hong Kong's glittering night skyline. Also worth visiting is *Koreana* (☎ 5775145), Kingston Mansion, 1 Paterson St, Causeway Bay.

Malaysian If you like Malaysian food, try the *Malaya* (☎ 5251675), 15B Wellington St, Central. It has Western food too, but it's considerably more expensive.

Thai Like Korean food, Thai cuisine is often spicy hot but good. You can sample it at the *Royal Thai* (☎ 8322111), G12, Elizabeth House, 250 Gloucester Rd, Causeway Bay. Also excellent is *Supatra's* (☎ 5218027), 46 D'Aguilar, Central.

Vietnamese A very nice Vietnamese restaurant is *Saigon Beach* (☎ 5297823), at 66 Lockhart Rd, Wanchai. Also excellent is the reasonably priced *Yin Ping* (☎ 8329038), 24 Cannon St, Causeway Bay. Slightly up-market is *Vietnam City* (☎ 8336882), 3rd floor, Elizabeth House, 250 Gloucester Rd, Causeway Bay.

Western

Italian You can try the pleasantly relaxed *Rigoletto's* (☎ 5277144) at 16 Fenwick St in Wanchai. Pizza and lasagna is tantalising at *La Bella Donna* (☎ 5279907), 1st floor, Shui On Centre, 6-8 Harbour Rd, Wanchai. Another good place is *La Taverna* (☎ 5228904), 1st floor, Shun Ho Tower, 24-30 Ice House St, Central.

French Wine, cheese, the best French bread and bouillabaisse can be found at *Le Tire Bouchon* (☎ 5235459), Ground floor, 9 Old Bailey St, Central. Other French delicacies can be sampled at the *Barcelona* (☎ 5779633), Ground floor, Prospect Mansion, 68 Paterson St, Causeway Bay.

Kosher *Beverley Hills Deli* (☎ 8015123), Basement, 2-3 Lan Kwai Fong, Central, caters to Hong Kong's yuppie class.

Mexican *Casa Mexicana* (☎ 5665525), Ground floor, Victoria Centre, 15 Watson Rd, North Point, has excellent food and great atmosphere, but is not cheap. The outstanding Sunday buffet costs HK$120. The mariachi bands are Filipinos, but they're first rate.

Continental *Jimmy's Kitchen* (☎ 5265293), Basement, South China Building, 1 Wyndham St, Central, serves a variety of Western dishes. Prices are moderately expensive.

American The *Fountainside* (☎ 5264018), Shop 6-7, Ground floor, The Landmark, 16 Des Voeux Rd, Central, has a cafe atmosphere and New York cuisine. The food is fairly expensive but good at the *California* (☎ 5211345), 24 Lan Kwai Fong, Central.

Self-Catering

If you're tired of the high prices in the restaurants, give Hong Kong's markets a try. Small convenience stores even have frozen dim sum and a microwave oven to heat it up.

If you've got a place to cook, you can try the local fresh-food markets and supermarkets.

Fresh-Food Markets Every neighbourhood has its local market. The biggest in the city is the Central Market on Queen's Rd, between Jubilee and Queen Victoria Sts, Central. There are three floors of meat, vegetables, fish and poultry. The daily prices are posted on a large notice board. If you can speak some Chinese, you might get a better deal, though generally they won't try to cheat you even if you have a foreign face.

Supermarkets A *Park'n Shop* is across from the Central Market on Jubilee St near Queen's Rd, Central. Another *Park'n Shop* is at 18 Johnston Rd and there's a *Wellcome Supermarket* at 26 Johnston Rd, Wanchai.

ENTERTAINMENT
Pubs, Bars & Discos
In Central there are many business pubs in the office buildings, some of which offer good food and drinks.

The *Mad Dogs Pub* (☎ 5252383), 33 Wyndham St, Central, is just off the trendy Lan Kwai Fong. It's a big two-floor Australian-style pub serving some light food but no meals.

The *Jockey Pub* (☎ 5261478) is at 108A Swire House, 11 Chater Rd, Central. Open from 11 am to 11 pm, it's a fairly quiet pub during the day, with dancing at night.

The *Bull & Bear* (☎ 5257436), Ground Floor, Hutchison House, 10 Harcourt Rd, Central, is a British-style pub and gets pretty lively in the evenings. It opens from 8 am to 10.30 am, and again from 11 am to midnight.

Nineteen 97 (☎ 8109333), Cosmos Building, 8-11 Lan Kwai Fong, Central, is a restaurant and disco. An increasingly popular venue, but it has a cover charge.

For good beer, visit *Schnurrbart* (☎ 5234700) in the Winner Building on D'Aguilar St, Central.

Joe Bananas (☎ 5291811), 23 Luard Rd, Wanchai, has become a trendy nightspot and has no admission charge, but you may have to queue to get in. Happy hour is from 11.30

am until 9 pm when the disco party gets started.

Also in Wanchai at 54 Jaffe Rd, just west of Fenwick Rd, is the *Wanchai Folk Club* (☎ 8611621), a very pleasant little folk-music pub with beer and wine at regular prices. It's also known as *The Wanch*.

Crossroads (☎ 5272347), 42 Lockhart Rd, Wanchai, attracts a young crowd. Dancing is from 9 pm to 4 am. There is a cover charge, but one drink is included.

DD II (☎ 5235863), 38-44 D'Aguilar St, Central, is a trendy disco open from 10 pm to 4 am.

The *California* (☎ 5211345), 24-26 Lan Kwai Fong, Central, is the most expensive bar mentioned in this book. Open from noon to 1 am, it's a restaurant by day, but there's disco dancing and a cover charge Wednesday to Sunday night from 5 pm onwards.

Girlie Bars
It will cost a bundle to visit any of these places. *Club Celebrity* (☎ 5755601), 1st floor, 175-191 Lockart Rd, Wanchai, is open from 3 pm to 3 am. *Mandarin Palace* (☎ 5756551), 24-28 Marsh Rd, Wanchai, is open from 6 pm to 3 am. *New Tonnochy Nightclub* (☎ 5754376) at 1-5 Tonnochy Rd, Wanchai, is open from 6 pm to 3 am and is named after the old Tonnochy, once famous for its ballroom dancing.

Cinema
For real film fanatics, some cultural organisations show films occasionally. *Alliance Française* (French Institute) (☎ 5277825) at 123 Hennessy Rd, Wanchai, is one place to try. Also contact the *Goethe Institute* (German Cultural Centre) (☎ 5270088), 14th floor, Hong Kong Arts Centre, 2 Harbour Rd, Wanchai.

Another place to check out is Studio One, The Film Society of Hong Kong Ltd (☎ 8453339), 2 Arbuthnot Rd, Central.

English-language cinemas include the following:

Cathay, 125 Wanchai Rd, Wanchai (☎ 8335677)

Cine-Art, Sun Hung Kai Centre, 30 Harbour Rd,
Wanchai (☎ 8384820)
Columbia Classics, Great Eagle Centre, 23 Harbour
Rd, Wanchai (☎ 5738291)
Imperial, 29 Burrows St, Wanchai (☎ 5737374)
Isis, 7 Moreton Terrace, Causeway Bay (☎ 5773496)
Jade, Paterson St, Causeway Bay (☎ 5771011)
Lee, 27 Percival St, Causeway Bay (☎ 8954433)
Palace, 280 Gloucester Rd, Causeway Bay
(☎ 8951500)
Park, 180 Tunglowan Rd, North Point (☎ 5704646)
Pearl, Paterson St & Great George St, Causeway Bay
(☎ 5776352)
President, 517 Jaffe Rd, Causeway Bay (☎ 8331937)
Queen's, Luk Hoi Tung Building (rear entrance), 31
Queen's Rd, Central (☎ 5227036)
State, 291 King's Rd, North Point (☎ 5706241)
Sunbeam, 423 King's Rd, North Point (☎ 5632959)
UA Queensway, Pacific Place One, Admiralty
(☎ 8690372)

THINGS TO BUY

Central is the big tourist shopping district on
Hong Kong Island, closely followed by
Admiralty, Wanchai and Causeway Bay, but
prices are slightly lower in the non-touristy
neighbourhoods. The most glitzy tourist
shopping mall in Hong Kong is at Pacific
Place, 88 Queensway, Admiralty.

In Central the clothing alleys run between
Queen's Rd and Des Voeux Rd. One alley
sells only buttons and zips, while another,
Wing On St, known to the locals as Cloth
Alley, sells materials. Li Yuen St sells
costume jewellery, belts, scarves and shoes.
Another street is devoted almost exclusively
to handbags and luggage, and yet another to
sweaters, tights, underwear and denims.

Your best bet may be to go out to
Cityplaza, the huge shopping mall in Quarry
Bay. It's nice to see price tags for a change.
Get off the MTR at the Tai Koo Station and
you'll find the mall right in front of you. A
good shop in here is Broadway which does
electronics and photo supplies – cheap prices

and they actually smile (well, sometimes at
least).

Chinese Emporiums

Check out the Hong Kong Exhibition Centre
in the China Resources Building at 26
Harbour Rd, Wanchai, opposite the ferry pier
– on the 3rd and 4th floors of the low block
and on the 5th floor of the main block of the
building (open 10 am to 7 pm). Goods manufactured in Hong Kong and from other
countries are also exhibited. The China
Resources Artland on the ground and 1st
floors (open 10 am to 7 pm) sells just about
every variety of artwork from China, including paintings, porcelain, jewellery and silk.

Department Stores

These are not very cheap, so if you're
looking for bargains, look elsewhere. Hong
Kong's original Western-style department
store is Lane Crawford which has its main
branch in the Lane Crawford House, 70
Queen's Rd, Central.

Hong Kong Chinese department stores in
the Central district include Wing On with
branches at 211 and 26 Des Voeux Rd;
Dragon Seed, 39 Queen's Rd; and Sincere,
173 Des Voeux Rd.

Japanese department stores are heavily
concentrated in Causeway Bay. These
include Daimaru at the corner of Paterson
and Great George Sts, Matsuzakaya at 6
Paterson St and Sogo at 545 Hennessy Rd.

Auctions

Serious antique buyers should check out the
auction houses. Two good ones are Lammert
Brothers (☎ 5223208), 9th floor, Malahon
Centre, 10 Stanley St, Central, and Sotheby's
Hong Kong Ltd (☎ 5248121), 9th floor,
Lane Crawford House, 70 Queen's Rd,
Central.

The New Territories 新界

The New Territories is Hong Kong's bedroom. About one-third of Hong Kong's population lives in the New Territories, mostly in appropriately named new towns, most of which have been constructed since 1972.

Everything north of Boundary St on the Kowloon Peninsula up to the China border is the New Territories. This land was leased from China in 1898 for 99 years. The lease covers not only the New Territories, but all the Outlying Islands except tiny Stonecutters Island off the west coast of Kowloon.

Excluding the Outlying Islands, the New Territories make up 70% of Hong Kong's total land area. With the expiration of the lease in 1997, China could have legally taken all this back, plus the outer islands. Instead, they're getting back all Hong Kong.

Since its inception, the New Towns Programme has consumed more than half the government's budget, with a lot of that money spent on land reclamation, sewage, roads and other infrastructure projects. About 60% of the new housing units have been built by the government.

The population of the New Territories has mushroomed from fewer than half a million in 1970 to the present two million, and is expected to reach 3.5 million by the year 2000.

The biggest impediment to growth in the New Territories used to be the lack of good transportation. This changed dramatically in 1982 with the opening of the MTR Tsuen Wan Line. In the same year, the KCR underwent a major expansion when the system was electrified and double-tracked.

The LRT system opened in 1988 and hoverferries now connect Tuen Mun to Central, reducing commuting time to just 30 minutes. However, fewer people in the New Territories need to commute to Kowloon and Hong Kong Island now because many industries are moving into the New Territories to take advantage of the cheaper land.

Only a small percentage of visitors to Hong Kong take the time to visit the New Territories. This is a shame since it has a character very different from the bustling commercial districts of Kowloon and Hong Kong Island. The New Territories is large – larger than Hong Kong Island, Kowloon and Lantau combined. You can see a lot of the New Territories in one day, but not all of it. Still, any effort you make to see this part of Hong Kong will be very rewarding.

The area in the very northern part of the New Territories, within one km of the China border, is a closed area which is fenced and well marked with signs. Sometimes the fence has large holes in it, usually created by would-be immigrants from China. Holes or not, don't be tempted to walk inside the

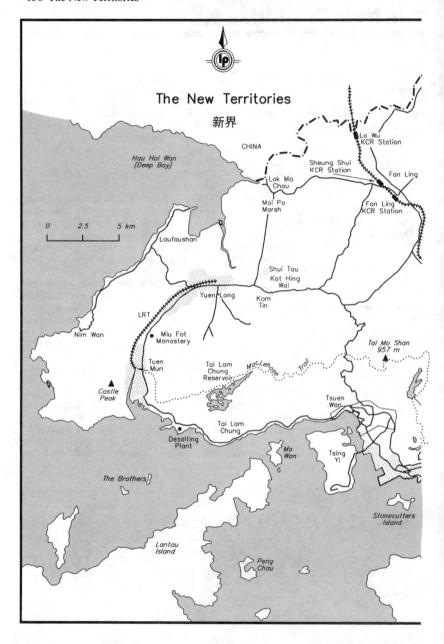

The New Territories

新界

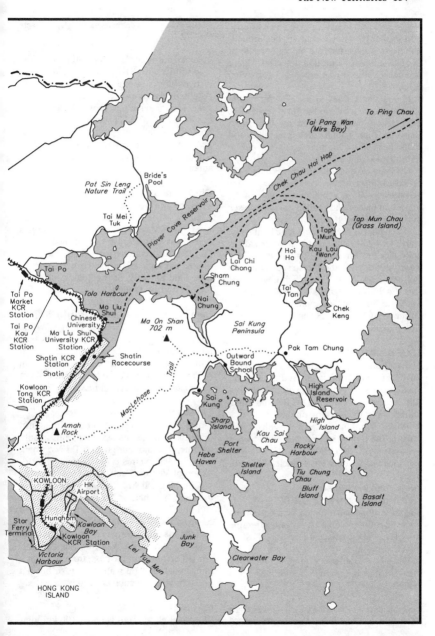

closed area just to have a look, even briefly. You probably won't see any police around, but the area is well-staked out with the latest in high-technology motion detectors. There is a heavy fine for entering this forbidden zone.

If you don't want to hassle with public transport, take a tour to the New Territories. The HKTA can book you on the 'Land Between Tour' which takes four hours and costs HK$260. Do it yourself by public transport for about HK$60.

Do yourself a favour and pick up the map called *Countryside Series Sheet No 2: New Territories – West*, which covers most of the important places you're likely to want to see in the New Territories.

If you plan to visit the Sai Kung Peninsula, map No 4 *Sai Kung & Clearwater Bay* is helpful. Few foreigners visit Plover Cove Reservoir, but if you'd like to see it, map No 5 *North-East New Territories* covers this area. Each of these maps cost HK$10 and is available from the Government Publications Office next to the GPO in Central, Hong Kong Island.

TSUEN WAN 荃灣
The easiest place to reach in the New Territories, Tsuen Wan is an industrial and residential area just to the north-west of Kowloon. Simply take the MTR to the Tsuen Wan Station, the last stop on the line.

Tsuen Wan is a major development scheme and by 1993 it is expected to have a population of 890,000, half of which is expected to be employed in Tsuen Wan itself.

Yuen Yuen Institute & Western Monastery 圓玄學院
The main attraction in Tsuen Wan is the Yuen Yuen Institute, which is a Taoist temple complex, and the adjacent Buddhist Western Monastery.

The monastery is very quiet, but the Yuen Yuen Institute is extremely active during festivals.

I was fortunate to visit during the ghost month when people were praying and burning ghost money, and when cymbals were crashing and worshippers were chanting.

To reach the monastery and temple complex, take Minibus No 81 from Shiu Wo St which is two blocks south of the MTR station. Alternatively, take a taxi, which is not expensive. The monastery is about 1½ km to the north-east of the MTR station. It would be possible to walk except that there seems to be no way for a pedestrian to get across Cheung Pei Shan Rd, which is basically a super highway.

Chuk Lam Sim Yuen 竹林禪院
This is another monastery and temple complex in the hills north of Tsuen Wan. The Yuen Yuen Monastery is better, so give this one a miss unless you are a dedicated temple fan. The instructions for getting there are almost the same as for the Yuen Yuen Institute. Find Shiu Wo St (two blocks south of the MTR station) and take minibus No 85.

Sam Tung Uk Museum 三棟屋博物館
The museum is an old Hakka village. Within the museum grounds are eight houses plus an ancestral hall. The museum is a five-minute walk to the east of the Tsuen Wan MTR Station and is open from 9 am to 4 pm daily except Tuesday. Admission is free.

TAI MO SHAN 大帽山
Hong Kong's highest mountain is not Victoria Peak, as many tourists mistakenly assume. That honour goes to Tai Mo Shan, which at 957 metres is nearly twice the elevation of Victoria Peak.

Climbing Tai Mo Shan is not extremely difficult, but there is no Peak Tram to the summit. To reach the mountain, take bus No 51 from the Tsuen Wan MTR Station. The bus heads up Route Twisk ('Twisk' is derived from Tsuen Wan Into Shek Kong). Get off at the top of the pass, from where it's uphill on foot. You walk on a road but it's unlikely you'll encounter traffic.

MACLEHOSE TRAIL 麥理浩徑
The MacLehose Trail is about 100 km long

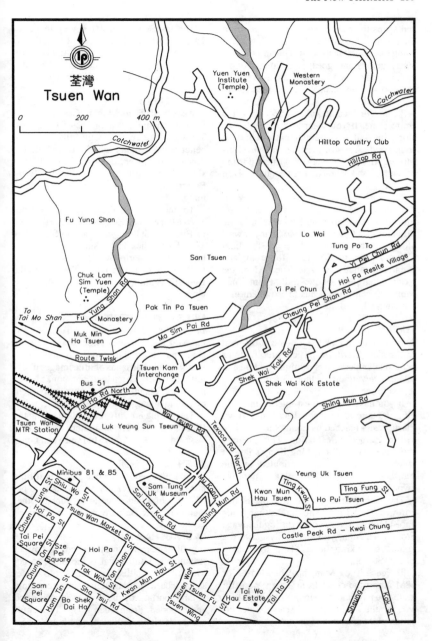

and spans the New Territories. It runs from Tuen Mun in the west to Pak Tam Chung (Sai Kung Peninsula) in the east. The trail follows the ridgetops and goes over Hong Kong's highest peak, Tai Mo Shan, and also passes close to Ma On Shan, Hong Kong's fourth highest peak.

There are breathtaking views along the entire route. If you want to hike anywhere along this trail, it's essential that you buy the countryside series of maps on the New Territories. Map No 2 covers the western portion of the trail and Map No 4 covers the eastern section.

The easiest access is from Tsuen Wan. Take bus No 51M to the top of Route Twisk. From here you have the choice of heading off to the east (towards Tai Mo Shan) or west along the MacLehose Trail to Tai Lam Country Park, the Tai Lam Reservoir and eventually all the way to Tuen Mun, the western terminus of the trail. From Tuen Mun you can catch a bus to Kowloon or a hoverferry to Central.

TUEN MUN 屯門

This is the main new town in the north-west of the New Territories. There are no slums here, just endless rows of high-rise housing estates. Nevertheless, there are interesting things to see.

If you have the slightest interest in shopping, be sure to visit the Tuen Mun Town Plaza, easily reached by taking the LRT line to the Town Centre Station. This gigantic shopping mall will be Hong Kong's largest when completed. It's dominated by the Yaohan Department Store, a Japanese-owned chain.

The Ching Chung Koon Temple is just north of Tuen Mun. This interesting, huge Taoist temple is very active during festivals. From Tuen Mun, you can easily get to the temple by taking the LRT to the Ching Chung Station.

To reach Tuen Mun, take bus No 68 or 68M along the coast from Tsuen Wan. En route you pass another Hong Kong high-tech wonder, the world's largest seawater desalination plant at Lok An Pai.

The fastest and most fun way to get to Tuen Mun is by hoverferry. These depart from the Blake Pier in front of the GPO on Hong Kong Island. The ride takes 30 minutes and lets you off at the LRT terminal.

CASTLE PEAK 青山

Just west of Tuen Mun is Castle Peak, a rugged mountain that reaches 583 metres. The views are great, though I liked it much better before China Light & Power built the Castle Peak Power Station on the south-west side of the mountain. Nearby **Butterfly Beach** on Castle Peak Bay is good for swimming.

To get to Castle Peak, take a bus from Tuen Mun to Shek Kok Tsui, or take the LRT to Butterfly Station and walk to Shek Kok Tsui. From Shek Kok Tsui follow the trail that heads due north towards the summit. Get to Butterfly Beach by taking the LRT to the Butterfly Station, then walking a short distance.

MIU FAT MONASTERY 妙法寺

In Lam Tei, a few km north of Tuen Mun, is the Miu Fat Buddhist Monastery. The top floor has three large golden statues of Buddha plus thousands of little images clinging to the walls. Often there are monks inside the temple chanting. Try not to disturb them by taking photographs with a flash.

The temple is easily reached by taking the LRT to Lam Tei. The monastery is on Castle Peak Rd, between Tuen Mun and Yuen Long.

YUEN LONG 元朗

There isn't anything special here, but it's the last stop on the LRT line so you have to get off. It's not a bad place to eat lunch. Other than that, there isn't any reason to linger.

LAUFAUSHAN 流浮山

If you're interested in oyster beds and oyster restaurants, Laufaushan is the place to go. Most of the shellfish are turned into oyster sauce, a basic ingredient in Chinese cooking. A large portion of the oysters is also dried and exported. From Yuen Long, it's an out-and-back trip to Laufaushan on bus No 55.

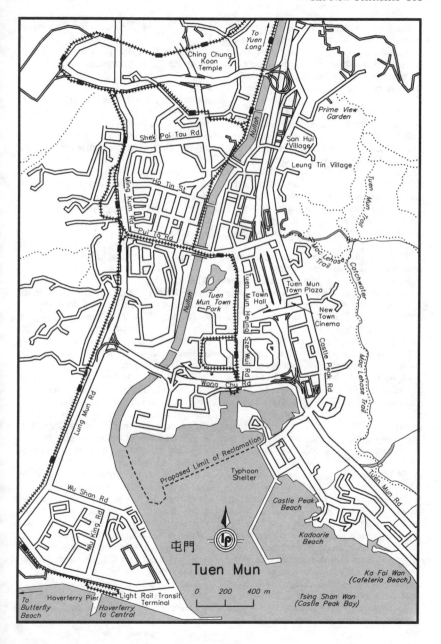

To Yuen Long

Ching Chung Koon Temple

Prime View Garden

Shek Pai Tau Rd

San Hui Village

Leung Tin Village

Ho Tin St

Ming Kum Rd

Pui To Rd

Nullah

Tuen Mun Trail

Mac Lehose Trail

Catchwater

Tuen Mun Town Park

Tuen Mun Heung Sze Wui Rd

Town Hall

Tuen Mun Town Plaza

New Town Cinema

Mac Lehose Trail

Castle Peak Rd

Wong Chu Rd

Lung Mun Rd

Proposed Limit of Reclamation

Typhoon Shelter

Tuen Mun Rd

Castle Peak Beach

Wu Shan Rd

Kadoorie Beach

Wu King Rd

屯門

Ka Fai Wan (Cafeteria Beach)

Tuen Mun

0   200   400 m

To Butterfly Beach

Hoverferry Pier

Light Rail Transit Terminal

Hoverferry to Central

Tsing Shan Wan (Castle Peak Bay)

Just how long Laufaushan retains its rural charm remains to be seen. Right next to Laufaushan is the oyster-raising community of Tin Shui Wai, the site of a soon-to-be-built town with 35-storey housing estates. Enjoy the oysters while you can.

MAI PO MARSH 米埔

If you're a bird-watching aficionado, the 300-hectare Mai Po Marsh in the north-west part of the New Territories is one of the few places in Hong Kong where you can see your feathered friends (besides on the dinner plate at the Temple St night market). Most of the birds are migratory, which means the marsh is at its best in the spring and autumn. Winter is also not too bad, but the birds are fewest during summer. Over 250 species have been identified.

The good news is that this is a protected area. The bad news is that, unless you have connections, you must join an organised tour to be allowed in. There are two four-hour tours (morning and afternoon) on Wednesday, Thursday, Saturday and Sunday. The tour costs a steep HK$480 per person for a minimum of two persons, and HK$180 for a minimum of 10 persons. The tour price includes the admission fee, a guide and transport. Tours can be booked up to four months in advance with Jetway Express Ltd (☎ 3695591, fax 7243151), 704 Houston Centre, Tsimshatsui East, Kowloon.

Bird-watchers are advised to bring their own binoculars, cameras, walking shoes or boots, and not to wear bright clothing.

KAM TIN 錦田

The small town of Kam Tin contains two walled villages – Kat Hing Wai and Shui Tau. Most tourists go to Kat Hing Wai, so if you aren't fond of souvenir stalls go to Shui Tau – it's bigger and more interesting anyway.

Other walled villages in the colony are Kat Hing Wai, Kam Tsin Wai and Shek Tsin Wai. The walled villages are one of the last reminders that once the villagers were faced with marauding pirates, bandits and soldiers.

To reach Kam Tin and the two walled villages (Kat Hing Wai and Shui Tau), take

bus No 54 from Yuen Long Bus Terminal at Kik Yeung Rd (off Castle Peak Rd). You can also reach Kam Tin from Tsuen Wan by taking bus No 51 over scenic Route Twisk.

Kat Hing Wai 吉慶圍

Just off the main road is this tiny 500-year-old village, walled sometime during the Ming Dynasty (1368 AD to 1644). It's really one small street with a maze of dark alleyways leading off it. The high street is packed with souvenir sellers. You are expected to give a donation of HK$1 when you enter the village. Put the money into the coin slot by the entrance.

You can take photographs of the Hakka women in their black traditional dress, but first agree on a fee. Most of them are anxious to model as long as you pay. Between HK$2 and HK$4 is usually sufficient.

Shui Tau 水頭

To reach Shui Tau get off bus No 54 on the outskirts of Kam Tin and walk down the road to the left. The 17th-century village is famous for its carved roofs, ship-prow decorated with stone fish and dragons. Tiny traditional-style Chinese houses huddle inside Shui Tau's walls.

The village is the home of the Tang clan who have lived there for centuries. They were high-ranking public servants in the imperial court of China in the 19th century. The ancestral hall in the middle of the village is used as a school in the morning but was originally built as a place for the clan to worship its forebears.

Their ancestors' names are listed on the altar in the inner hall and on the long boards down the side. The stone fishes on the roof of the entrance hall represent husband and wife and are there for good luck. Soldiers painted on the doors guard the entrance.

The Tin Hau temple on the outskirts of the town was built in 1722. Its enormous bell weighs 106 kg.

You will find Shui Tau quiet and the locals friendly. It's definitely worth a look and there are a number of beer stalls scattered around.

SHEUNG SHUI 上水

This is where you can get on the KCR. From Yuen Long or Kam Tin, take bus No 77K. Buy a ticket and take the train just one station south to Fan Ling. A stored value ticket or tourist ticket from the MTR can be used on the KCR.

FAN LING 粉嶺

The main attraction in this town is the **Fung Ying Sin Kwun Temple**, a Taoist temple for the dead. The ashes of the departed are deposited here in what might be described as miniature tombs with a photograph on each one. It's an interesting place to look around, but be respectful of worshippers.

Easy to find, the temple is opposite Fan Ling KCR Station.

TAI PO 大埔

Another of the residential and industrial new towns, Tai Po is home to many of Hong Kong's high-tech industries. There isn't much which is special about the town, but one worthwhile activity is to hire a bicycle and ride to Plover Cove Reservoir and/or the Chinese University in Ma Liu Shui. Although there is an inland route, follow the coastal route along Tolo Harbour for the best views.

Bicycle rentals are easy to find around the Tai Po Market KCR Station. Definitely do this trip on a weekday, as on weekends and holidays thousands of Chinese descend on the place with the same idea. At these times, bikes are scarce, the rates are higher and the road is crowded with cyclists.

Hong Kong Railway Museum
鐵路博物館

The Railway Museum, an old railway station built in 1913 and recently restored, is also at Tai Po. The museum features old trains dating back to 1911 and exhibits explaining the historical background of local railway development.

To reach the museum from Tai Po Market KCR Station walk for between 10 and 15 minutes to the north-west. The museum is near the railway tracks on On Fu Rd and

there are a few signs pointing the way. No bus goes directly there so a taxi would be best. The museum is open daily (except Tuesday) from 9 am to 4 pm. Admission is free.

Man Mo Temple 文武廟

Like the Man Mo Temple in Sheung Wan, Hong Kong Island, this place is dedicated to two Taoist deities representing the pen and the sword. The temple is on Fu Shin St, about 200 metres from the railway museum.

Tai Ping Carpet Factory 太平地氈

If you're a carpet enthusiast, you can visit this large factory (☎ 6565161). Guided tours are offered Monday to Thursday from 2 to 4 pm by appointment only.

Plover Cove Reservoir 船灣淡水湖

If you're trying to see the New Territories in one day, you won't have time for this place. Plover Cove Reservoir is good hiking and cycling country. If you make the effort to come here, you'll probably want to spend a full day.

Plover Cove Reservoir was completed in 1968. Prior to its construction Hong Kong often faced critical water shortages and water rationing was common. The reservoir was built using a very unusual technique: rather than build a dam across a river (Hong Kong has few rivers that amount to anything), a dam was built across the mouth of a bay. The seawater was then pumped out and fresh water was pumped in, mostly from China.

The **Pat Sin Leng Nature Trail** is an excellent walk. The trail begins near the Country Park Visitor Centre at Tai Mei Tuk and ends near Bride's Pool. Public transport is at both ends of the trail. The walk is only five km with an elevation gain of 300 metres. The scenery is good, but the place gets packed on weekends unless a typhoon comes along and clears out the tourists.

If you want to do more strenuous walking, detour to the nearby summit of Wong Leng, which is more than 600 metres high, then continue on to Hok Tau Reservoir and the Country Parks Management Centre at Hok

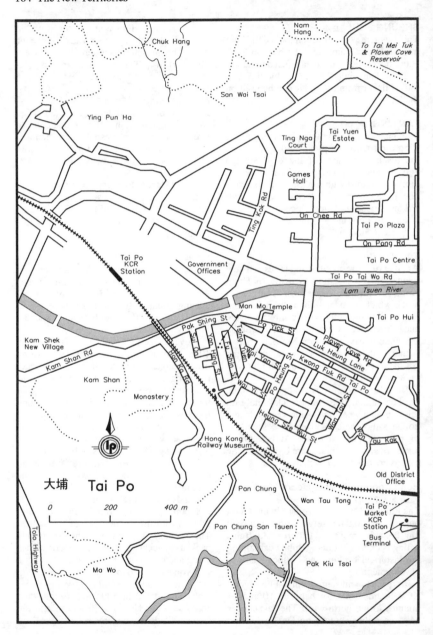

大埔 Tai Po

Tau Wai. The distance from Tai Mei Tuk to Hok Tau Wai is 12 km and takes about four hours. You can camp at Hok Tau Wai or walk another 1.5 km to Shau Tau Kok Rd, then catch a bus to Fan Ling and a train to Kowloon.

To reach Plover Cover Reservoir, catch bus No 75K from the Tai Po KCR Station and take it all the way to the last stop at Tai Mei Tuk. On Sunday and public holidays Bus 75R goes on to Bride's Pool.

If you're going to hike in the Plover Cover Reservoir area be sure to pick up the HKTA *Countryside Series Sheet No 5: North-East New Territories*.

TAI PO KAU 大埔滘

This forest reserve between Tai Po KCR Station and the Chinese University is one of the few places in Hong Kong that has real trees. It's a great place to get away from the crowds, even on weekends. To get there, take bus No 72A which runs from Tai Wai to Tai Po Industrial Estate. Get off at the stop before Shatin.

CHINESE UNIVERSITY 中文大學

Ma Liu Shu is home to the Chinese University, established in 1963. The university has a most beautiful campus and is certainly worth a visit.

Inside the campus, the Institute of Chinese Studies has an interesting art gallery (☎ 6952218) which houses local collections as well as those from museums in China. There's an enormous exhibit of paintings and calligraphy by Guangdong artists from the Ming period to modern times, as well as a collection of 2000-year-old bronze seals and a large collection of jade flower carvings.

The gallery is open weekdays and Saturday from 10 am to 4.30 pm, and on Sunday and public holidays from 12.30 to 4.30 pm (closed on some public holidays). Admission is free.

You can easily reach the Chinese University by taking the KCR to Ma Liu Shui University Station. A free bus outside the station runs through the campus to the top of the hill. It's easiest to take the bus uphill and then walk back down to the station. Near the top of the hill is a student cafeteria – a good, cheap place for lunch.

SHATIN 沙田

In a long, narrow valley, Shatin is a new town built mostly on reclaimed land that was a big mudflat just a few years ago. Unlike some of the other new towns, Shatin is both a desirable place to live and an attractive town for tourists to visit.

Shatin is sure to grow larger in the years ahead. In addition to the Lion Rock Tunnel, a second tunnel to Kowloon (Tate's Cairn Tunnel) is in construction and a third tunnel is being bored through the mountain to reach Tsuen Wan.

Shatin is easy to get to by taking the KCR to Shatin Station.

Ten Thousand Buddha Monastery 萬佛寺

There are in fact 12,800 miniature statues of Buddha inside the monastery's main temple. Built in the 1950s, it sits on a hillside about 500 metres to the west of the Shatin New Town Plaza. You can get there only by walking because even a taxi cannot negotiate the 400-odd steps up to the temple. The trail starts from Shatin KCR Station – just ask anyone to point the way. The temple complex is open from 8 am to 6.30 pm.

From the main monastery area, walk up some more steps to find a smaller temple housing a gold-plated monk who died in 1965 at the age of 87. He was the founder of the monastery. His body was encased in gold leaf and is now on display behind a glass case. It is considered polite to put a donation in the box next to the display case to help pay for the temple's upkeep.

Che Kung Miu 車公廟

This is a small, Taoist temple about 1½ km to the south-east of Shatin KCR Station. It's not nearly as interesting as some of the larger Taoist temples (such as Wong Tai Sin in Kowloon) so don't be afraid to give it a miss. It is very popular with the Chinese though, especially on holidays.

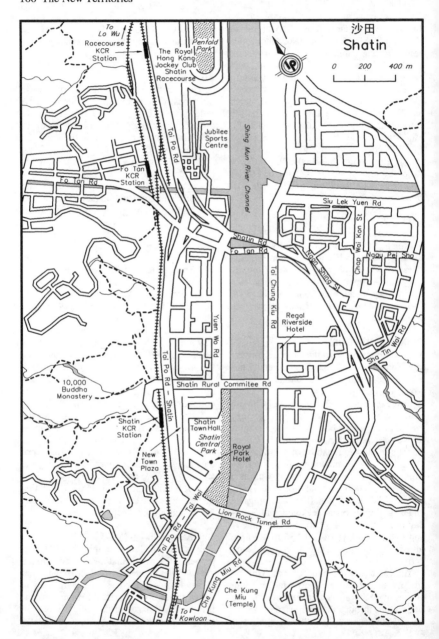

沙田
Shatin

0   200   400 m

To
Lo Wu

Racecourse
KCR
Station

The Royal
Hong Kong
Jockey Club
Shatin
Racecourse

Penfold
Park

Shing Mun River Channel

Jubilee
Sports
Centre

Fo Tan
KCR
Station

Fo Tan Rd

Tai Po Rd

Siu Lek Yuen Rd

Chap Wai Kon St

Ngau Pei Sha

Shatin Rd

Fo Tan Rd

Ngan Shing St

Tai Chung Kiu Rd

Sha Tin Wai Rd

Yuen Wo Rd

Regal
Riverside
Hotel

10,000
Buddha
Monastery

Tai Po Rd – Shatin

Shatin Rural Commitee Rd

Shatin
KCR
Station

New
Town
Plaza

Shatin Town Hall

Shatin
Central
Park

Royal
Park
Hotel

Tai Po Rd – Tai Wai

Lion Rock Tunnel Rd

Che Kung Miu Rd

Che Kung
Miu
(Temple)

To
Kowloon

As you enter the temple grounds, be prepared to be mugged by little old women who excitedly stuff red pieces of paper with Chinese characters into your hands and then demand money for them. With the help of a Chinese friend, I was able to discern that the papers are a type of blessing. The women will insist that 'the more money you give, the more blessing you will receive'. Unfortunately, they prove to be insatiable, as 'the more you give, the more they want'. The best bet is to keep your hands in your pockets and run past them quickly, as they won't follow you inside the temple.

From Tai Wai KCR Station, you can walk to the temple. Bus 80K from Shatin KCR Station stops near Che Kung Miu. A taxi ride from the station would also be inexpensive.

Shatin Racecourse 沙田

Shatin is the site of Hong Kong's second racecourse, opened in 1980 after seven years in the making at a cost of HK$500 million. It was financed by the introduction of night racing at Hong Kong Island's Happy Valley racecourse.

In the centre of the racetrack is the interesting eight-hectare Penfold Park, open to the public most days except on race days, Mondays and the day following public holidays.

You can get to the racecourse by taking the KCR to either Fo Tan or Racecourse stations.

Amah Rock 望夫石

It may just be a rock, but like many Chinese landmarks, a local legend has grown up around it.

The story goes that for many years a fisherman's wife, with her baby on her back, climbed to this vantage point to watch for her husband's return. The husband never came back and the gods took pity on her and transported her to heaven with a lightning bolt which left a rock in her place.

As you take the train south towards Kowloon, you can spot Amah Rock out the left side up on the hillside after passing the Tai Wai KCR Station but before the train enters the tunnel.

New Town Plaza 新城市廣場

Many Hong Kongers flock to Shatin on weekends to shop at the New Town Plaza, one of the biggest shopping malls in Hong Kong. The New Town Plaza is adjacent to the Shatin KCR Station. Inside the plaza is a huge indoor swimming pool, roller rink and bowling alley.

Adjacent to the New Town Plaza is a well-stocked public library, the largest in the New Territories. Many cultural events are held in the adjoining Shatin Town Hall.

SAI KUNG PENINSULA 西貢半島

The last great chunk of land in the New Territories which is still relatively unspoilt, the Sai Kung Peninsula is a playground for hikers, campers, swimmers and boating enthusiasts. Some of the best swimming beaches are on the Sai Kung Peninsula, where windsurfing equipment can also be hired.

The peninsula is largely undeveloped, and those who care about Hong Kong's environment would like to keep it that way. Meanwhile, real estate agents look at all those virgin beaches devoid of villas and lick their chops.

Sai Kung Town 西貢

The only town of any significant size in the area, Sai Kung Town was mainly a marketplace for farming and fishing communities in the area. Now it is beginning to be infected with that dreaded disease – creeping condominiums – but the town still retains much of its charm.

To get there, take the MTR to Choi Hung Station, then catch bus No 92 to Sai Kung Town.

Hebe Haven 白沙灣

Bus No 92 to Sai Kung Town passes the small bay of Hebe Haven (*Pak Sha Wan*), the yachting centre of the New Territories. The Hebe Haven Yacht Club is here.

If you're not a yachting buff, catch a

sampan to the tiny peninsula across the bay to swim off the sandy beach. The beach is excellent and the sampan trip should be only a couple of dollars. Alternatively, walk out to the peninsula from Sai Kung Town, a distance of about 2½ km each way.

Ma On Shan 馬鞍山

At 702 metres, Ma On Shan is the fourth highest peak in Hong Kong, only surpassed by Tai Mo Shan in the New Territories and two peaks on Lantau Island (Lantau Peak and Sunset Peak).

Ma On Shan (the mountain) is not to be confused with Ma On Shan (the village). Ma On Shan village is to become yet another new town, complete with a row of high-rise housing estates and shopping malls.

Access to Ma On Shan is by the Mac-Lehose Trail. The trail does not actually go over the summit, but comes very close and the spur route to the peak is obvious. This is a steep, strenuous climb. You can walk from Ma On Shan (mountain) down to Ma On Shan (the new town) and get a bus to Shatin, then head back to Kowloon by train.

Get to the MacLehose Trail by walking from Sai Kung Town or get closer to the peak by taking bus No 99 from Sai Kung Town. The bus runs along Sai Sha Rd. To find the right bus stop, let the driver know you want to climb Ma On Shan.

Pak Tam Chung 北潭涌

This is the easternmost bus terminal in the Sai Kung Peninsula. It's also the eastern terminus of the MacLehose Trail. You can get to Pak Tam Chung on bus No 94 from Sai Kung Town.

Along the way, the bus passes **Tai Mong Tsai** where there is an Outward Bound school (☎ 7924333). Outward Bound is an international organisation that teaches wilderness survival. If you're interested in the school's activities, you can ring them.

From Pak Tam Chung you can walk to **High Island Reservoir**. The reservoir, opened in 1978, used to be a channel of the sea. Both ends were blocked with dams and

the seawater was pumped out, then fresh water pumped in.

While in Pak Tam Chung, visit the **Sai Kung Country Parks Visitor Centre** which has excellent maps, photographs and displays of the area's geology, fauna & flora. The centre is open every day from 9 am to 5 pm.

From Pak Tam Chung, it's a 25-minute walk south along a trail to find the **Sheung Yiu Folk Museum**, a restored Hakka village typical of those found in Hong Kong in the 19th century. The museum is open daily, except Tuesday, from 9 am to 4 pm. Admission is free.

If you want to explore the north shore of the Sai Kung Peninsula, bus No 94 continues from Pak Tam Chung to Wong Shek Pier in Tai Tan.

TOLO HARBOUR 大埔海

From Ma Liu Shui, ferries cruise through Tolo Harbour to Tap Mun Chau (Grass Island) and back again, calling in at various villages on the way. Stops may include Kau Lau Wan, Chek Keng, Tai Tan, Lai Chi Chong, Sham Chung and Shap Sze Hung.

Only one ferry a day makes all these stops and departs from Ma Liu Shui at 3.15 pm. Consult the current ferry timetable to be sure. The timetable is available from the Hong Kong & Yaumati Ferry Company (HYF) (☎ 5423081), Central Harbour Services Pier, 1st floor, Pier Rd, Hong Kong Island.

Tap Mun Chau is an interesting island to visit, though the transportation there is inconvenient. See the Outlying Islands chapter.

CLEARWATER BAY 清水灣

Clearwater Bay is in the most south-eastern corner of the New Territories and, as the name implies, has brilliant, clear-blue water. It certainly stands in sharp contrast to nearby Junk Bay which, as the name implies, has plenty of junk floating in it.

Clearwater Bay is beautiful and has one of the best beaches in Hong Kong. It's very popular – in fact too popular, as on a hot summer weekend it's standing room only. If someone were to faint, they would never hit the ground, but would just be pushed around by the crowd until the beach closed.

Naturally the beauty of Clearwater Bay has not gone unnoticed by Hong Kong's well-to-do class. Mediterranean-style villas have sprouted on the hillsides and there is now a Clearwater Bay Country Club, complete with golf course, squash and tennis courts, jacuzzi, badminton, etc.

Junk Bay, just a stone's throw from Clearwater Bay, is to be the site of another huge new town housing project. A new tunnel is to be built across Junk Bay, which will make Clearwater Bay much more accessible. Development pressure is sure to follow, though perhaps sanity will prevail and Clearwater Bay will be preserved, much like Stanley on Hong Kong Island.

There are some country parks on the peninsula and some decent trails, but serious hikers desiring a strenuous walk should look elsewhere in the New Territories.

One of Hong Kong's leading movie companies is Shaw Brothers which has its huge Movietown studios on Clearwater Bay Rd. To visit the studios, phone the company's public relations office.

Clearwater Bay is easily accessible. Take the MTR to Choi Hung Station. From there, walk to the nearby bus terminus and catch bus No 91 which goes all the way to Clearwater Bay.

PLACES TO STAY
Private Hostels

Travellers' Hostel (☎ 3687710), Chungking Mansions, 16th floor, A Block, Tsimshatsui, also operates a *Beachside Hostel* (☎ 4919179) at Ting Kau near Tsuen Wan, opposite Tsing Yi Island. Dorm beds at the hostel cost HK$30 a night. A private room with shared/private bath costs HK$80/120. You get there by taking the MTR to Tsuen Wan, then minibus No 96 or 96M. It's hard to find this place if you've never been there, so ring them up first and they'll send someone to meet you.

YHA Hostels

Sze Lok Yuen (☎ 4888188) is on Tai Mo Shan Rd. Beds cost HK$25 and tent camping is permitted. A YHA card is needed to stay there. Take the No 51 bus (Tsuen Wan Ferry Pier – Kam Tin) at Tsuen Wan MTR Station and alight at Tai Mo Shan Rd. Follow Tai Mo Shan Rd for about 45 minutes, then turn on to a small concrete path on the right-hand side which leads directly to the hostel. This is a good place from which to climb Tai Mo Shan, Hong Kong's highest peak. Because of the high elevation, it can get amazingly cold at night, so be prepared.

Wayfoong Hall is another YHA hostel. It was being rebuilt at the time of this writing, so currently has no telephone number. The name might also be changed in the future. The hostel is at the base of Plover Cove Reservoir on Ting Kok Rd, just a few hundred metres south of Tai Mei Tuk. Take the KCR train to Tai Po Station, then take bus No 75K to Tai Mei Tuk and follow the access road with the sea on your right side.

Pak Sha O (☎ 3282327) charges HK$25 a bed and also permits tent camping. A YHA card is needed. Take bus No 92 from the Choi Hung Estate bus terminal and get off at the Sai Kung Town terminal. From Sai Kung Town, take Bus No 94 towards Wong Shek Pier, but get off at Ko Tong village. From there, find Hoi Ha Rd and a road sign 30 metres ahead showing the way to Pak Sha O.

Also on the Sai Kung Peninsula is *Bradbury Hall* (☎ 3282458), in Chek Keng. From Choi Hung Estate bus terminal, take bus No 92 to the Sai Kung bus terminal. From Sai Kung Town, take bus No 94 to Yellow Stone Pier, but get off at Pak Tam Au. There's a footpath at the side of the road leading to Chek Keng village. The hostel is right on the harbour just facing the Chek Keng Pier. An alternative route is to take the ferry from Ma Liu Shui (adjacent to the Chinese University KCR Station) to Chek Keng Pier.

Hotels

Shatin has some good hotels, but none is cheap. The *Regal Riverside* (☎ 6497878), Tai Chung Kiu Rd, has singles from HK$750 to HK$1000 and twins from HK$850 to HK$1100. The *Royal Park* (☎ 6012111, fax 6013666), 8 Pak Hok Ting St, Shatin, has doubles for HK$850 to HK$1100.

One of the newest hotels in Hong Kong is the *Kowloon Panda Hotel* (☎ 4091111, fax 4091818), Tsuen Wah St, Tsuen Wan, where double rooms go for HK$700 to HK$900.

Outlying Islands 離島

Take away Hong Kong Island itself and you've still got 235 other islands. Together the Outlying Islands make up about 20% of the total land area of Hong Kong. Officially, they are part of the New Territories, except for tiny Stonecutters Island which is part of Kowloon.

While many of the islands are little more than uninhabited rocks, occasionally seen above sea level, Lantau Island is actually larger and higher than Hong Kong Island.

Cheung Chau Island is fast developing into another Honolulu or Surfers Paradise, yet many of the islands are largely unspoilt. Free of motor vehicles, noise and the congestion of the city, the Outlying Islands have a totally different character from tourist ghettos such as Tsimshatsui and Central. Unfortunately, few travellers take the time to visit Hong Kong's peaceful backwaters.

Cars are prohibited on all the Outlying Islands except Lantau, where a special vehicle permit is required.

Only seven of the Outlying Islands are served by public ferries, so you probably won't visit the many other islands unless you can afford to charter a boat. Many of the remote islands are popular destinations for Hong Kong's fleet of yachts, where boat owners often participate in such prohibited pastimes as nude swimming and sunbathing.

Just a few decades ago, almost all the habitable islands had permanent settlements supported mostly by the fishing industry. Now many of these villages have become ghost towns, the inhabitants lured away by the promise of wealth in the nearby glittering city.

Orientation & Information

If you intend to do a major hike, it would be wise to equip yourself with the excellent *Countryside* series of maps produced by the Crown Lands & Surveys Office. The essential map for the Outlying Islands is called *Countryside Series Map No 3: Lantau &*
Islands. Another useful map is *Lantau Trail*. The maps are cheap and can be bought at the Government Publications Office in the General Post Office block near the Star Ferry Terminal on Hong Kong Island.

Accommodation

In Central, at the ferry pier for departures to Lamma Island, is the Outlying Islands Holiday Flats Booking Office (☎ 5413357). Actually, the 'office' is just a small booth between the two newsstands. The signs identifying this booth are in Chinese only, but photographs of bedrooms prominently displayed make it obvious. If you book a room through this office, you'd better get them to write down the address and directions to your hotel or flat in Chinese so you can actually find the place.

Getting There & Away

The main Outlying Islands are linked to Hong Kong by regular ferry services – not primarily for tourists but for locals who work on the mainland and live on the islands. The ferries are comfortable and ridiculously cheap, and many have an air-con top deck. They all have a basic bar serving drinks and snacks.

Most of the ferries leave from the Government Pier or from the Outlying Islands Ferry Pier, which are side by side several hundred metres west of the Hong Kong Star Ferry Terminal.

Hoverferries are also available but cost at least twice as much as the conventional ferries and go twice as fast. They're also twice as much fun, but are definitely not for those prone to seasickness! Eat lightly or take a plastic bag.

If you're going to use the ferries a lot, pick up a timetable from the HKTA. If you want information about the boats to Discovery Bay, Tap Mun (Grass Island) or Ping Chau, you can get the latest timetables from the Hong Kong & Yaumati Ferry Company

(HYF) office (☎ 5423081) at the Central Harbour Services Pier, 1st floor, Pier Rd.

If you want to catch breakfast on Hong Kong Island while waiting for the ferry, the *Seaview Restaurant*, upstairs in the Outlying Islands Ferry Pier, does a mean dim sum.

The islands are popular with Hong Kong residents – in fact too popular! On weekends the ferries become so crowded that it's a wonder they don't sink. As soon as business offices close on Saturday afternoon there is a mad rush for the boats. The fares are also higher on weekends and the beaches are practically standing room only. Many hotels charge double or triple rates during weekends, and that's if you can find a room!

Always keep at least HK$20 worth of change with you, but preferably more. For some ferries you can buy the ticket from a booth, but for others you must put the exact fare into a turnstile as you do for the Star Ferry. You can also buy return tickets.

If your time is limited, Watertours (☎ 5254808) runs trips to the islands.

Cheung Chau 長洲

Only 2.5 sq km in size, Cheung Chau is 10 km west of Hong Kong, off the south-east tip of Lantau. Despite the small size, it's the most populous of the Outlying Islands with 20,000 residents. Cheung Chau means 'long island' in Cantonese.

Archaeological digs have shown that Cheung Chau, like Lamma and Lantau, was inhabited in prehistoric times. The island had a thriving fishing community 2500 years ago and a reputation for piracy from the year dot – probably started by the earliest Cantonese and Hakka settlers who supplemented their incomes with piracy and smuggling.

When Canton and Macau opened up to the West in the 16th century the island was a perfect spot from which to prey on passing ships stacked with goodies. The infamous and powerful pirate Cheung Po Tsai is said to have had his base there during the 18th century.

Now the piracy and smuggling have gone and about 40,000 people now live on the island – about 10% on junks and sampans anchored offshore. Fishing is still an important industry for a large number of the island's inhabitants, and the place is noted for its fine seafood.

There are several interesting temples on the island, the most important being the Pak Tai Temple which is the focus of the annual Cheung Chau Bun Festival.

There are a couple of OK beaches on the island. Overlooking the largest beach is Cheung Chau's tallest building, the six-storey Warwick Hotel, which may be a portent of abominations to come. The island is getting crowded, but there are still a few unspoilt headlands where you can get away from the claustrophobia of Hong Kong Island. Because of the crowded situation, the island can no longer supply its own drinking water, so it's brought in by an undersea pipeline from Lantau.

While Cheung Chau is not for serious walkers, it's ideal if you like concrete paths through lush vegetation and butterflies to spot along the way. The island is packed with missionary schools, churches, retreats and youth centres of every denomination and has built up a fair-sized community of gwailos who have escaped from the rat-race and high rents on Hong Kong Island.

The Cheung Chau typhoon shelter is one of the big three in Hong Kong. The other two are Aberdeen Harbour and Yaumati. Besides offering a protected harbour, thousands of people live here permanently on boats.

There is no traffic noise on the island. In fact, there is no motorised transport other than a few tiny cargo tractors with lawn mower engines. Cheung Chau is extremely popular with the locals, especially on weekends and holidays when it becomes a circus.

Cheung Chau Village 長洲村
No longer a village but a small town, the main built-up area on the island is along the narrow strip at the centre of the two headlands that make up the dumb-bell-shaped

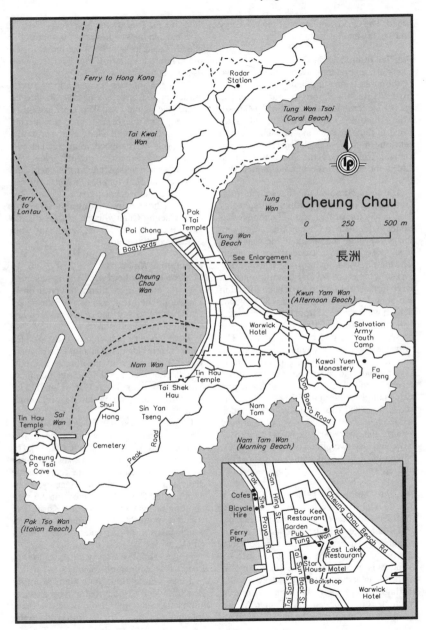

Cheung Chau

長洲

island. The waterfront is a bustling place any time of day and late into the night.

Pak Tai Temple 北帝廟

There are several temples on the island, two of the most interesting being on the waterfront. To find them, turn to your left as you get off the ferry and walk up Kwok Man Rd. You will come to the Pak Tai Temple dedicated to the god Pak Tai – see the Religion section in the Facts About Hong Kong chapter. The temple is the oldest on the island and is the focus of the famous annual Bun Festival.

The story goes that the first settlers from Guangdong province in China brought Pak Tai, protector of fisherfolk (among other things) with them to Cheung Chau. Carrying the god through the village in the year 1777 is supposed to have scared away a plague. The temple was built six years later.

The temple has several historic relics. A large iron sword said to have been forged in the Song Dynasty (960 AD to 1279) stands here. It was recovered from the sea by a local fisherman more than 100 years ago and was presented to the god by the islanders. The sword is regarded as a symbol of good luck and its disappearance from the temple several years ago caused great consternation on the island. The person who took it was kind enough to return it when he realised the concern he had caused. There is a wooden sedan chair, made in 1894, which was used to carry Pak Tai around the island on festival days, and also two pillars depicting dragons, hewn out of hunks of granite at the turn of the century.

Tin Hau Temples 天后廟

The several Tin Hau temples, dedicated to the patron goddess of fishermen, indicate the important role fishing has played on this island. One Tin Hau temple is at the southern end of the Cheung Chau village waterfront. Another is at Saiwan on the south-western tip of the island – walk here or take a kaido (village ferry) near the Hong Kong & Yaumati Ferry Company (HYF) pier. A third temple is to the north of the Pak Tai Temple.

Cheung Po Tsai Cave 張保仔洞

This cave in the south-western corner of the island is said to have been the hiding place of the infamous pirate, Cheung Po Tsai, who used Cheung Chau as a base.

The cave area has become a local tourist attraction and there is a nearby Cheung Po Tsai Cave picnic area. The glorification of Cheung Po Tsai seems ironic, considering that he had a reputation for extreme brutality, having ruthlessly robbed, murdered and tortured many innocent people. Near the maniac's cave and picnic area is one of the island's Tin Hau temples, which you can easily visit at the same time.

Reach the cave by walking almost two km from Cheung Chau village, or take a kaido to the pier at Saiwan. From Saiwan the walk is less than 200 metres.

Beaches & Walks

Most of the northern headland is deserted, with not much more than a reservoir on it. The central and southern parts of the island are most interesting, and can be covered in a couple of hours by foot.

From the ferry pier, follow Tung Wan Rd to the eastern side of the island. This is where you'll find **Tung Wan**, the biggest and most popular, but not the best, beach on the island. The best part of Tung Wan is at the far southern end. It's possible to hire windsurfers.

Continuing past the six-storey Warwick Hotel brings you to what is generally referred to as Afternoon Beach. At the end of the beach is a footpath which takes you uphill past the small Kuanyin (Kwun Yum) Temple dedicated to the Goddess of Mercy. Continue up the footpath and look for the sign pointing the way to the **Fa Peng Knoll**. The concrete footpath soon becomes a dirt track which takes you past quiet, tree-shrouded villas.

From the knoll you can walk down to Don Bosco Rd (again look for the sign) which will take you to **Nam Tam Wan** (Morning Beach), which is rocky but good for swimming. If you ignore Don Bosco Rd and continue straight down you will come to the intersection of Peak and Kwun Yum Wan Rds. Kwun Yum Wan Rd will take you to Cheung Chau village.

Peak Rd is the main route to the island's cemetery, one of the most popular burial places in Hong Kong. You'll pass several pavilions on the road, built for coffin bearers who have to sweat their way along the hilly climb to the cemetery.

Once at the cemetery it's worth dropping down to **Pak Tso Wan**, otherwise known as Italian Beach – a sandy, unspoilt, quiet spot which is good for swimming.

Peak Rd continues to Saiwan, a little village on the south-western bulge of the island.

Bun Festival 飽山節

The festival takes its name from the bun towers – bamboo scaffolding covered with edible buns. The towers can be up to 20 metres high.

If you go to Cheung Chau a week or so before the festival you'll see these huge bamboo towers being built in the courtyard of the Pak Tai Temple.

In previous times, at an appointed hour, hundreds of people would scramble up the bun towers to fetch one of the holy buns for good luck. It was believed that the buns higher up would bring better luck, so naturally it got to be something of a riot as everyone headed for the top. This sounds like a recipe for disaster and indeed, a serious accident occurred in 1978. Now the buns are handed out and no one is allowed to climb up to fetch their own.

The third day of the festival (a Sunday) is the most interesting due to a procession with floats, stilt walkers and people dressed as legendary characters. Children in amazingly colourful costumes are one of the prime attractions.

Most fascinating are the 'floating children' who are carried through the streets on poles, although they appear to be floating over the crowd. In fact, they are cleverly strapped into metal supports hidden under their clothes. The supports include built-in footrests and a padded seat for the child. On Pak She St, a few doors down from the Pak Tai Temple, is a photo exhibition of the floating children. One of the supports for carrying the floating children is displayed.

During the celebrations several deities are worshipped, including Tin Hau, Pak Tai and Hung Hsing (the God of the South) – all significant to people who make their living from the sea. Homage is also paid to Tou Tei, the God of the Earth, and to Kuanyin, the Goddess of Mercy.

Offerings are made to the spirits of all the fish and animals whose lives have been sacrificed to provide food, and during the four days of worship no meat is eaten. A priest reads a decree calling on the villagers to abstain from meat-eating so that no animal will be killed on the island during festival time.

The festival is unique to Cheung Chau and its origins are not really known. One popular theory is that the ceremony is to appease the ghosts of those killed by pirates, who otherwise would bring disasters such as typhoons to the island.

The Bun Festival is held over four days in May. Accommodation in Cheung Chau is heavily booked at this time. The stacks of extra ferries laid on for the festival are always packed. Still, it's worth making the journey if you can.

Places to Stay

There are several good places to stay, but prices escalate dramatically on weekends unless you book for a long term, like a month.

As you exit the ferry pier, right in front of you and a little to the left are numerous tables and booths displaying photographs of various rooms for rent. Practically none of the people who operate these booths speak English, but if you can make yourself understood, it's possible to find a cheap room. Some of these people rent out rooms in their own flat, while others will rent you a whole flat or villa for yourself. Prices vary wildly, but at the lower end it's HK$140 on weekdays, and HK$500 on weekends. You can negotiate cheaper rates for a longer term.

The best cheap place to stay is the *Star*

House Motel (☎ 9812186) at 149 Tai Sun Bak St. Double rooms start at HK$120 on weekdays and run to between HK$600 and HK$700 a night on weekends.

The *Warwick Hotel* (☎ 9810081, fax 9819174) is a luxury resort, a six-storey eyesore on Tung Wan Beach. Doubles cost HK$805 on a weekday and HK$1127 on a weekend, plus a 10% service charge and 5% tax. The hotel has a good Cantonese and Western restaurant.

Places To Eat

Like most islands around Hong Kong, seafood is the local speciality but you won't have any trouble finding other types of Chinese food. In the morning many restaurants along the waterfront serve dim sum.

As you get off the ferry, turn to your left and head about 200 metres up the street. Here you'll find numerous sidewalk cafes. Prices are low, and you can sit here by the waterfront and watch the world go by as you eat.

Two restaurants offering good food and low prices are *Bor Kee* and *East Lake*, on Tung Wan Rd just east of the Garden Pub. Both are popular with local expatriates. During summer evenings, they set up outdoor tables and the place takes on the atmosphere of an open-air party.

There are a couple of restaurants on the eastern waterfront overlooking Tung Wan Beach.

From the cargo pier, you can take a free sampan (the one with the flag) to the *Floating Restaurant*. Fishing communities have their wedding parties there.

Entertainment

There is only one real nightlife spot, the *Garden Cafe/Pub* (☎ 9814610), 84 Tung Wan Rd, just west of the Bor Kee Restaurant. It's a friendly place and always packed with gwailos. This is the only place on the island which serves European food, but it's rather expensive. Fortunately, the drinks there are reasonably priced.

There's a bar at the Warwick Hotel, but it's high-priced and doesn't attract much of a following among the expatriate community.

Getting There & Away

The Outlying Islands Ferry Pier in Hong Kong has almost 20 departures a day to Cheung Chau. The earliest ferry departs at 6.25 am and the last departure is at 11.30 pm. On your return, the earliest ferry departs Cheung Chau at 5.45 am and the last leaves at 10.30 pm. The trip takes one hour. On weekdays, the fare is HK$6.50 in ordinary class, and HK$10 in deluxe (air-con cabin). On weekends, the fare jumps to HK$10 for ordinary and HK$18 for deluxe.

There is also a ferry service from Cheung Chau to Peng Chau via Chi Ma Wan and Mui Wo (both on Lantau Island). The first ferry leaves Cheung Chau at 5.35 am and the last at 10.15 pm. There are about nine departures per day but some skip Chi Ma Wan or Mui Wo or both, or only go as far as Mui Wo.

Getting Around

Apart from walking you can hire bikes on the island − useful for getting around the built-up area but probably not much use further afield, where it's all uphill. Bicycles can be hired from the shop right on the western waterfront near the northern end of Praya St.

A good map of the island is available from a small book and stationery shop on Tai Sun Back St, a few doors to the south of Star House Motel. The government's *Countryside* series of maps *(Map No 3: Lantau and Islands)* also cover Cheung Chau.

Lamma 南丫島

Also known as Pok Liu Chau, Lamma is the least developed of the large islands. About 13 sq km in size, Lamma supports a population of about 3000, compared with more than one million residents on Hong Kong Island. Lamma is believed to be one of the first settled of Hong Kong's islands.

Most Hong Kong Chinese find it hard to imagine why anyone would want to live on Lamma Island. As they see it, living on Lamma is not convenient − no nightlife, movie theatres, shopping centres, etc.

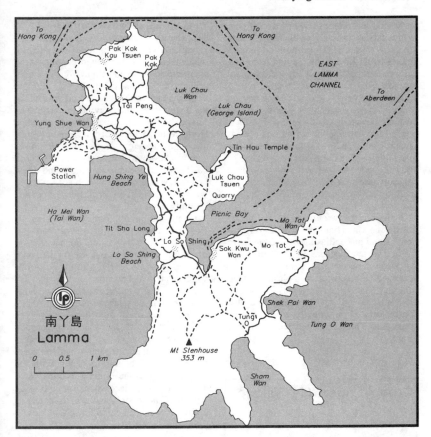

To Hong Kong

To Hong Kong

EAST
LAMMA
CHANNEL

To Aberdeen

Pak Kok
Kau Tsuen
Pak Kok

Luk Chau Wan

Luk Chau
(George Island)

Tai Peng

Yung Shue Wan

Tin Hau Temple

Power Station

Hung Shing Ye Beach

Luk Chau Tsuen

Quarry

Ha Mei Wan
(Tai Wan)

Picnic Bay

Mo Tat Wan

Tit Sha Long

Lo So Shing

Sok Kwu Wan

Mo Tat

Lo So Shing Beach

Shek Pai Wan

Tung O

Tung O Wan

南丫島
Lamma

0   0.5   1 km

Mt Stenhouse
353 m

Sham Wan

However, many expatriates are more than happy to put up with the inconvenience of tranquil village life. There is a small but devoted Western community on Lamma which has fled Hong Kong's sky-high rents and urban congestion. A large proportion are journalists, artists, musicians, or just beach-combers, but there are also bankers, attorneys and office workers. Ironically, the foreigners have become some of the staunchest defenders of Lamma's traditional way of life. Unfortunately, they have had much to defend against.

Plans to build an oil refinery on Lamma

were dropped in 1973 after a lot of heated opposition. Instead, Hongkong Electric constructed a huge coal-fired power station on the north-west coast of the island. The two enormous smoke stacks are clearly visible from Hong Kong Island. Meanwhile, on the south-eastern side of the island, the hillsides around Sok Kwu Wan are slowly being quarried away. Patrons at the bayside seafood restaurants can admire the quarry and adjacent cement plant while dining on crabs and prawns.

Vigorous objections were raised by local residents at the time these schemes were proposed, but 'progress' won out over environmental concerns. Given the fact that there are more than 200 uninhabited islands around Hong Kong which could have been reduced to rubble without anyone complaining, just why Lamma was singled out for such development is a mystery to many.

Fortunately, enough of Lamma is still unspoilt to make it worth visiting. The island is good for walking and swimming and is a favourite weekend mooring spot for gwailo junks. It's also a fishing port and you can get good seafood on both ends of the island, particularly at Sok Kwu Wan.

Yung Shue Wan 榕樹灣

The larger of the two townships on Lamma, Yung Shue Wan (Banyan Tree Bay) is still a pretty small place. Plastic was the big industry here a few decades ago, when people worked at home and almost everyone sprayed a vast assortment of plastic parts for toys and other goods. The plastics industry has vanished and now restaurants and other tourist-related businesses are the main employers. There is a small Tin Hau temple here.

Yung Shue Wan to Sok Kwu Wan

The most interesting way to see Lamma Island is to walk between these two villages, which takes a little more than an hour. At the southern end of Yung Shue Wan is a sign pointing to the Lamma Youth Hostel. Follow the signs and you will soon find yourself in the countryside on an obvious, paved track.

The first developed place you reach is **Hung Shing Ye Beach** which is very nice although the view of the nearby power station takes some getting used to. The beach has lifeguards, a small restaurant and a few hotels. It would be a pleasant place to stay on weekdays, though on weekends the crowds multiply rapidly.

Continuing south from Hung Shing Ye Beach, the path climbs steeply until it reaches a Chinese-style pavilion near the top of the hill. This is a nice place to relax, with fine views of the power station. From this vantage point it becomes obvious that the island is mostly hilly grassland and large boulders with very few trees.

Continuing south from the pavilion, you soon come to a ridge where you can look down at Sok Kwu Wan. It's a beautiful sight until you notice the quarry and adjacent cement works. The trail forks here with one branch going to the Lamma Youth Hostel. The hostel isn't a place where foreigners stay – it's for Chinese only and is used mainly as a summer weekend camp for school kids.

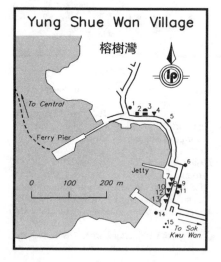

1	Public Library
2	Man Lai Wah Hotel
3	Post Office
4	Man Fung Seafood Restaurant
5	The Island Bar
6	Hong Kong Shanghai Bank
7	Capital Restaurant
8	Man Kee Restaurant
9	Lamma Vacation House
10	Sau Kee Restaurant
11	The Corner Bar
12	Lamcombe Restaurant
13	Tai Hing Restaurant
14	The Waterfront Bar
15	Tin Hau Temple

As you follow the path down to Sok Kwu Wan, keep your eyes open for dogs. Although it's illegal to have an unleashed and unmuzzled dog in Hong Kong, the rules are largely ignored here. The dogs are mostly friendly but some are fond of taking a bite out of tourism. If you are bitten, get a good look at the dog and then call the police. They may be able to track down the dog and the owner, who will have to pay your medical expenses plus a fine.

Before you reach Sok Kwu Wan, there is a path on your right that heads west over the island's narrow saddle to **Lo So Shing Beach**. Like Hung Shing Ye, this is a developed beach with lifeguards and other modern amenities.

Sok Kwu Wan 索罟灣

Although it's only a small settlement, Sok Kwu Wan (Picnic Bay) supports about a dozen or more excellent waterfront seafood restaurants.

There's a Tin Hau temple as you enter the township from Lo So Shing. From Sok Kwu Wan you can head back to Hong Kong on the ferry or do some more walking.

The small harbour at Sok Kwu Wan is filled with floating fish farms which are rafts from which cages are suspended. Some people live on the rafts or on boats anchored in the harbour, but others work on the rafts and commute by rowboat to their homes in the village.

The South-East

If you'd like a clean and uncrowded beach (on weekdays), it's worthwhile making the 20-minute walk from Sok Kwu Wan to **Mo Tat Wan Beach** along a path that runs by the coast. Mo Tat Wan is good for swimming but has no lifeguards. You can also get there on a kaido, but these are infrequent – they start at Sok Kwu Wan, stop at Mo Tat Wan and then continue on to Aberdeen.

There are a couple of good remote beaches down in the south-east – **Tung O Wan** and **Sham Wan**. These are relatively isolated and do not have lifeguards or other modern facil-

ities. Get to them by the path which leads south from Mo Tat Wan.

Mt Stenhouse

Most of the southern part of the island consists of the 353-metre-high Mt Stenhouse which you can walk to the top of. The climb up and back takes no more than two hours, but the paths are rough and not well-defined, so be prepared for a climb. The coastline around here is rocky and it's hard to find somewhere good to swim.

Places to Stay

There are two places to stay in Yung Shue Wan, and several beachside hotels at Hung Shing Ye. The nicest hotel in Yung Shue Wan is the *Man Lai Wah Hotel* (☎ 9820220) near the ferry pier. Singles and doubles cost HK$250 on weekdays and HK$350 on weekends. All rooms have air-con and a private bath. The management speaks English.

The *Lamma Vacation House* (☎ 9820427) is at 29 Main St in Yung Shue Wan. Its smallest rooms are HK$180 on weekdays or HK$450 on weekends.

At Hung Shing Ye beach there is the *Wing Yuen Hostel* (☎ 9820222), currently the cheapest place to stay on Lamma. Rooms cost HK$160 on weekdays, HK$330 on Saturday and holidays, and HK$200 on Sunday. Rates drop dramatically for long-term rentals: HK$850 for a week and HK$2000 for a month. Intriguingly, rooms cost HK$50 for one hour.

Also at Hung Shing Ye is the classy and expensive *Concerto Inn* (☎ 8363388). Rooms in the bachelor/deluxe suites cost HK$476/616 Monday to Friday, and HK$680/880 on weekends.

Still another place at Hung Shing Ye is *Han Lok Yuen* (☎ 9820608) where double rooms start at HK$300.

Places to Eat

Yung Shue Wan has a string of good seafood restaurants along Main St. Close to the ferry pier is the *Man Fung Seafood Restaurant* which has a nice view of the harbour. Further down Main St are the *Capital, Man Kee, Lee Garden, Sau Kee, Lamcombe* and *Tai Hing* restaurants. Most of these places have English menus if you ask for them.

An evening meal at Sok Kwu Wan is the most fun, and a good way to end a trip to the island. The restaurants are in a row along the waterfront. Some have interesting names like the *Lamma Hilton* and *Lamma Regent*. A few years ago these buildings were little more than shacks, but now they are modern buildings, an indication of the money that the island has since come by.

If you haven't noticed it by now, Hong Kong people like to eat, and they are particularly fond of seafood. A steady convoy of kaidos brings customers to Sok Kwu Wan every evening from Hong Kong Island.

Entertainment

The large number of expats on the island supports three pubs in Yung Shue Wan which become quite busy from about 6 pm onwards. The *Island Bar* is where the real old-timers hang out. The *Corner Bar* is the party place for singles, backpackers and anyone else who happens through. The *Waterfront Bar* is the 'yuppie pub' – it certainly looks flashy and attracts Lamma's trendy professionals.

Paul Chen operates the 'Man Room', a 10-minute walk from Yung Shue Wan on the path to Hung Shing Ye beach. It's a store, not a pub, but on Sunday it becomes an impromptu all-day drinking party.

Getting There & Away

Ferries from Hong Kong Island to Lamma leave from the Central Harbour Pier adjacent to the Outlying Islands Ferry Pier, and kaidos leave from Aberdeen Harbour.

There are 12 ferry departures a day from Hong Kong Island to Yung Shue Wan. On weekdays and Saturday the earliest ferry leaves at about 6.50 am and the last at about 11.20 pm. On Sunday and public holidays the earliest departure is at 8.15 am and the last at 11.20 pm. Returning from Yung Shue Wan, on weekdays and Saturday the first departure is at 6.25 am and the last at 10.35

pm. On Sunday and public holidays the first departure is at about 8.15 am and the last at 10.35 pm. The fare is HK$6.

There are seven departures a day from Central to Sok Kwu Wan, some of which go via Yung Shue Wan. On weekdays and Saturday the first ferry departs Central at 8 am and the last at 11 pm. On Sunday and public holidays the first departure is at 7.30 am and the last at 11 pm. Returning from Sok Kwu Wan, on weekdays and Saturday the first departure is at 6.50 am and the last at 10 pm. On Sunday and public holidays the first is at about 8.20 am and the last at about 10 pm. Fares are HK$6.

The best way to see Lamma is to catch a ferry to the north and hike for an hour to Sok Kwu Wan where you can catch the ferry back to Hong Kong. Otherwise pick up the regular Sok Kwu Wan-Aberdeen kaido service.

From Aberdeen there are five kaidos a day to Mo Tat Wan and Sok Kwu Wan. This service is mostly geared to bringing Hong Kongers over for dinner at the seafood restaurants. Kaidos return from Sok Kwu Wan to Aberdeen at 3, 5, 6.30 and 9.30 pm.

Getting Around

Like Cheung Chau, the island has no motorised traffic except for some carts used to haul seafood to the restaurants. There is one road on Lamma but it doesn't go anywhere. A concrete path links the two main villages, Yung Shue Wan in the north and Sok Kwu Wan in the south, but elsewhere there are mostly overgrown dirt trails. You can walk from Yung Shue Wan to Sok Kwu Wan.

Lantau 大嶼山

Lantau means 'broken head' in Cantonese, but it also has a more appropriate name, Tai Yue Shan (Big Island Mountain). The island certainly is big – 142 sq km, nearly twice the size of Hong Kong Island. Amazingly, fewer than 10,000 people live here, compared with Hong Kong's population of over a million.

Most of those 10,000 are concentrated in just a couple of centres along the coast, mainly because the interior is so mountainous – on a clear day, Lantau Peak can be seen from Macau.

Lantau is believed to have been inhabited by primitive tribes before being settled by the Han Chinese. The last Song Dynasty emperor passed through here in the 13th century during his flight from the Mongol invaders. He is believed to have held court in the Tung Chung Valley, which takes its name from a hero said to have given his life for the emperor. He's still worshipped on the island by the Hakka people who believe he can predict the future.

Over the years Lantau acquired a reputation as a base for pirates, and is said to have been one of the favourite haunts of the famous 18th-century pirate Cheung Po Tsai. The island was also important to the British as a trading post long before they became interested in Hong Kong Island.

Lantau is the home of several important monasteries, including the Trappist Monastery and the Buddhist Po Lin Monastery. The Po Lin was rebuilt several years ago but lately it's become a Disneyland in miniature rather than a place of quiet retreat. On a hill above the monastery is the largest outdoor Buddha statue in the world. Let's hope they don't add a ferris wheel.

Many people find it amazing that Lantau has so far escaped the development schemes which have turned Hong Kong Island into a skyscraper jungle. In contrast, more than 50% of Lantau has been preserved as country parks. Unfortunately, the pressure from developers is beginning to be felt, especially in the coastal areas. One development scheme is Discovery Bay in the north-eastern part of the island, where matchbox high-rises now compete for a view of the sea.

Unfortunately, Discovery Bay is the least of Lantau's problems. The darkest cloud over Lantau's pristine environment is the new international airport on Chek Lap Kok Island, just off the north coast of Lantau. This will involve chopping off the tops of nearby mountains and using the rubble to fill in the sea. Lantau will then be linked to the New Territories by bridges, with a six-lane high way and a high-speed train which will reach Hong Kong Island via a third cross-harbour tunnel. There is no question that this will cause Lantau's economy to boom and turn it into another Hong Kong Island. The airport project is not without its opponents, among them China, which is nervous about the estimated price tag of HK$60 billion (US$7.7 billion). This is enough to deplete Hong Kong's coffers by 1997, when China takes over the colony. The airport proposal set off a flurry of high-level discussions between China and Britain, which broke down into acrimonious accusations that sent the Hong Kong stock-market plummeting. The project, however, was finally approved and construction will have already begun by the time you read this.

Mui Wo (Silvermine Bay) 梅窩

Mui Wo (Five Petal Flower) is often called Silvermine Bay by Westerners because of the old silver mines which were once on the outskirts of the settlement.

This is where the ferries from Hong Kong Island arrive and where you can catch buses to other parts of the island. There's a swimming beach, but the water tends to be murky and frequently choked with floating plastic bags. However, the views are fine, there are opportunities for walking and the township's not a bad place for seafood restaurants. About a third of Lantau's population lives in the township and surrounding hamlets.

Bicycles can be hired on weekends generally in front of the Silvermine Bay Beach Hotel, but these are mainly useful around the village as the island is large and extremely mountainous.

Trappist Haven Monastery
熙篤會神學院

North-east of Mui Wo is the Trappist Haven Monastery. The Trappist order was established by a French clergyman, Armand de Rance, in 1644 and gained a reputation as one of the most austere orders of the Roman Catholic church. The Lantau order was

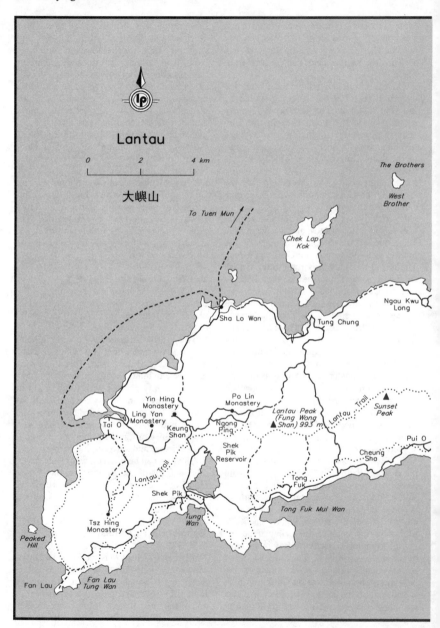

Lantau

大嶼山

0   2   4 km

To Tuen Mun

The Brothers

West Brother

Chek Lap Kok

Ngau Kwu Long

Sha Lo Wan

Tung Chung

Yin Hing Monastery

Po Lin Monastery

Lantau Peak (Fung Wong Shan) 993 m

Sunset Peak

Lantau Trail

Ling Yan Monastery

Tai O

Keung Shan

Ngong Ping

Shek Pik Reservoir

Pui O

Cheung Sha

Lantau Trail

Shek Pik

Tong Fuk

Tsz Hing Monastery

Tung Wan

Tong Fuk Mui Wan

Peaked Hill

Fan Lau

Fan Lau Tung Wan

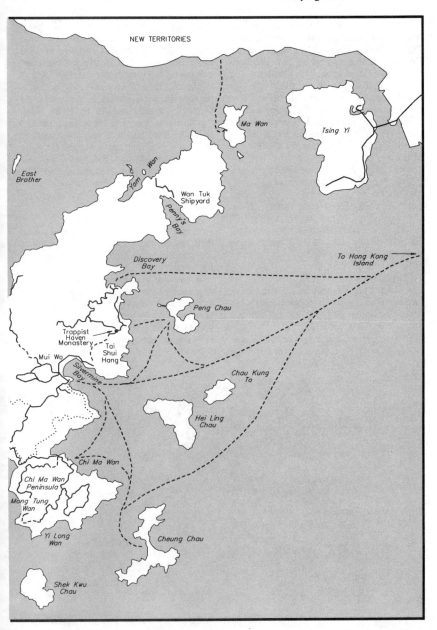

established in Beijing. The Lantau monks run a dairy farm and sell the milk locally. Trappist Haven Milk can be bought in Hong Kong. You can spend the night in the monastery (see Places to Stay for details).

The monastery is not for those who like nightlife, as the monks have all taken a vow of silence and there are signs asking visitors to keep their radios and cassette players turned off and to speak in low tones. If it's a carnival you're after then try the Po Lin Monastery on a weekend.

You can get to the monastery by taking a ferry to Peng Chau and then crossing over to the monastery on its kaido, which meets every ferry from Hong Kong. From the monastery you can walk over the hills on the trail to Mui Wo. It takes about an hour and there are good views across Lantau and back to Peng Chau and Hong Kong.

Po Lin Monastery 寶蓮寺

Perched 500 metres up in the western hills of Lantau in the Ngong Ping region, the Po Lin (Precious Lotus) Monastery is a Buddhist retreat-cum-fairground.

It's a large temple complex of mostly new buildings with the simpler, older buildings tucked away behind them (the original temple was built in 1921). From here the warm hand of friendship is offered not just to tourists but also to local film and television companies who frequently use it as a set.

On a hill above the monastery is the largest outdoor **Buddha statue** in the world, 34 metres high and financed by Hong Kong Buddhists at a cost of more than HK$20 million. There has been one concession to good taste – the statue is not the fat, jolly Buddha often portrayed in tacky souvenir shops. The Birthday of Buddha, around May, is a good time to be here (see Business Hours & Holidays in the Facts About Hong Kong chapter).

Whatever you do, don't visit on a weekend. It's flooded by day-trippers with their radios and families, so you're more likely to trip over a dinky toy than a meditating monk.

Because this is a Buddhist monastery, visitors are requested to observe some decorum in dress and behaviour. It is prohibited to bring meat on the grounds – hard-core carnivores who smuggle in chicken wings in their bags should take note.

You can stay overnight at the monastery

Po Lin Monastery

(see Places to Stay for details) or the nearby youth hostel and tea gardens. Many people who spend the night do so to climb nearby Lantau Peak.

The monastery has a good reputation for its vegetarian food. Some people find it bland, but apparently you get what the monks eat. In the monastery's large canteen HK$25 gets you a big plate of spring rolls, mushrooms, vegetables and rice.

There is a steady stream of buses from Mui Wo to the monastery. Catch bus No 2 from the ferry pier, the first departing at 8.20 am and the last at 6.50 pm. The first bus down from Ngong Ping departs at 7 am and the last at 7.20 pm. The fare is HK$7.20 on weekdays and Saturday, HK$11.60 on Sunday and holidays. The views going up are superb.

Lantau Tea Gardens 昂坪茶場
Beside the Po Lin Monastery are the Lantau Tea Gardens, the only tea gardens in Hong Kong. The tea bushes are in sad shape, but that hardly matters – the emphasis is on commercial tourism. There are horses for hire, and sitting on one for 10 minutes to get your photo taken costs HK$40; 30 minutes of riding is HK$120; one hour is HK$250, and you are supposed to ride with a mini mum group size of three persons. The tea plantation also operates an outdoor skating rink which is in incredibly bad condition and is deserted on weekdays, but can be noisy with screaming kids on weekends. Skate rentals cost HK$15 per hour. You can also spend the night here.

Lantau Peak 鳳凰山
Also known as Fung Wong Shan, at 933 metres this mountain is the second highest peak in Hong Kong. Only Tai Mo Shan in the New Territories is higher. The views from the summit of Lantau Peak are stunning and on a clear day it is possible to see Macau. Unfortunately, a number of moral cretins have trashed the summit with plastic wrappers, styrofoam lunch boxes and drink cans.

The easiest way to make the climb is to spend the night at the Po Lin Monastery, tea gardens or the S G Davis Youth Hostel. Get up at the crack of dawn and head for the summit. Many climbers get up earlier and try to reach the summit to see the sunrise, which appears to be a big deal for the Chinese. Personally, I think climbing this peak in the dark is a good way to get yourself killed – it is very steep in parts. The trail begins just east of the tea plantation and there is an information board there.

Lantau Trail 鳳凰徑
This footpath, 70 km long, runs the whole length of the island along the mountain tops and then doubles back along the coast. At a normal pace, the estimated walking time for the entire route (not allowing for rests) is 23½ hours. Unless you're a marathon runner you probably won't cover it in one day, though no doubt someone will try it.

A more realistic approach is to do the middle section of the trail (the highest and most scenic part) which goes over Lantau Peak and is easily accessible from the Po Lin Monastery at Ngong Ping. From Ngong Ping to Mui Wo via Lantau and Sunset peaks is 17½ km and is estimated to take at least seven hours by foot.

The western part of the trail – along the south-western coast of Lantau – is also very scenic.

Equip yourself with food, water, rain gear and UV (sunblock) lotion. Start out early, allowing yourself plenty of time to reach civilisation or a campsite.

If you're going to walk on this route, it would be wise to pick up the *Lantau Trail* map published by the Country Parks Authority and available from the Government Publications Office next to the GPO in Central, Hong Kong Island.

Tai O 大澳
This is the largest single settlement on the island. A hundred years ago, along with Tung Chung village, Tai O was an important trading and fishing port, exporting salt and fish to China. The salt pans are still there but are almost unused. The locals make a living from duck farming, fishing, rice growing, processing salt fish and making shrimp

paste. Free-spending tourists also contribute to the economy.

Tai O is built partly on Lantau and partly on a tiny island a few metres from the shore – two women pull a rope-drawn boat across the creek. This ferry service could easily be replaced with a modern bridge but no one wants to as the ferry is one of the most photographed spots in town. The cost of the ferry is 30c.

A few of the old-style village houses still stand, but most are being replaced by modern concrete block houses. There are still many stilt houses on the waterfront as well as other shanties, including houseboats that haven't set sail for years and have been extended in such a way that they never could again. It's an interesting place but there are some pretty powerful odours from the fish-processing industry. The village is famous for its seafood, and has several seafood restaurants. The local temple is dedicated to the God of War, Kuanti.

There are at least 28 buses a day from Mui Wo to Tai O on weekdays, the first departing Mui Wo at about 6 am and the last at about 12.30 am. Take bus No 1. The ride takes 45 minutes and costs HK$5.70 weekdays, HK$8.70 on Sunday and holidays. Getting from Ngong Ping to Tai O can be a hassle – the No 2 bus from Ngong Ping will drop you off at the intersection of the mountain road and the main highway, from where you must get bus No 1. Unfortunately, this latter bus is often full and won't stop. The alternative is to walk, which takes about one hour, but at least it's downhill all the way.

On Saturday afternoon, Sunday and holidays, there is a ferry from Central to Tuen Mun in the New Territories, which then continues on to Sha Lo Wan on the north side of Lantau and finally terminates at Tai O before heading back. Check the HYF ferry timetable for details.

Tung Chung 東涌

This relatively flat farming region is centred around the village of Tung Chung on the northern shore of Lantau. There are several Buddhist establishments in the upper reaches of the valley, but the main attraction is the 19th-century Tung Chung Fort which still has its old cannon pointing out to sea. The fort dates back to the early 19th century when Chinese troops were garrisoned on Lantau. The area was used as a base by the infamous pirate Cheung Po Tsai.

Relatively few tourists come here because of the poor transportation. This will change when the new airport is completed and Tung Chung becomes another Kowloon-style housing estate. You can walk from the Ngong Ping tea gardens down to Tung Chung in two hours and then take the bus back. It's about five km. Otherwise hike from Mui Wo to Tung Chung – this takes about 4½ hours, wandering through old Hakka villages before reaching the coast and the farming settlement. Hiking from Tai O to Tung Chung takes about five hours.

There are five or six buses per day from Mui Wo to Tung Chung, the first at about 9.35 am and the last at about 6.50 pm. The bus costs HK$5.10 on weekdays, and HK$7.70 Sunday and holidays.

Cheung Sha Beach & Tong Fuk
長沙海灘，塘福

Buses head to the Po Lin Monastery from Mui Wo along the road that hugs the southern coast. There are long stretches of good beaches (with occasional good surf) from Cheung Sha to Tong Fuk on the south coast of Lantau. Both are major tourist-beach centres. There is also a medium-security prison in Tong Fuk – at least it's a scenic prison.

Numerous buses run from Mui Wo to Cheung Sha and Tong Fuk, the first at about 6 am and the last at 7.40 pm. Bus Nos 1 and 2 both go to Tong Fuk, but bus No 3 only goes as far as Cheung Sha before turning north to Tung Chung.

Shek Pik Reservoir 石壁水塘

At Tong Fuk the bus starts to go inland along the Shek Pik Reservoir (completed in 1963) which provides Lantau with its drinking water. Underwater pipes also supply Cheung Chau and parts of Hong Kong Island with fresh water from this reservoir. It's considered a pretty place, with forest plantations and picnic spots, but a notorious maximum-security prison spoils the view. There are several buses daily from Mui Wo to Shek Pik, the first at about 8.15 am and the last at about 9 pm. You can also take the Ngong Ping bus, or walk down from Ngong Ping.

Discovery Bay 愉景灣
Discovery Bay has been discovered by real estate developers who are trying to turn it into a forest of luxury condominiums, just like the more appropriately named Repulse Bay on Hong Kong Island.

High-speed ferries commute between Discovery Bay and Central in is about 30 minutes. You might want to come here to see what the future holds for Lantau unless Hong Kong is swept with a sudden wave of environmental awareness.

To get to Discovery Bay from Central, catch the ferry from Blake Pier, just a stone's throw west of the Star Ferry Pier.

Fan Lau 分流
Fan Lau on the south-western tip of Lantau has a couple of very good beaches and another old fort, very overgrown but with a good view. From Tai O village, it's a couple of hours' clamber along the coastal section of the Lantau Trail.

Chi Ma Wan 芝蔴灣
Chi Ma Wan, the peninsula in the south-east, takes its name from the large prison there. Chi Ma Wan also has a closed centre, a camp housing boat people from southern Vietnam who arrived in Hong Kong after July 1982. There is at least one other closed centre in Hong Kong, at Hei Ling Chau where boat people from northern Vietnam are held. These camps are referred to as closed centres because their inhabitants are not allowed out and must remain there until they are resettled in another country. Some have been there for nearly a decade.

You can walk down through the Chi Ma Wan Peninsula to the beaches at Yi Long and Tai Long, but arm yourself with a map. You can also get there by kaido from Cheung Chau.

Penny's Bay & Yam O Wan 竹篙灣，陰澳灣
Penny's Bay is home to the main yard of one of Hong Kong's most famous boatyards, which specialises in building sailing cruisers for the export market.

The biggest log ponds in Hong Kong are at Yam O Wan. Here timber from all over South-East Asia is kept in floating storage. Large rafts of logs are often seen being towed by tug towards Tsuen Wan.

Access to both of these areas is difficult unless you have your own boat.

Places to Stay
The cheapest accommodation on Lantau is at the government-run campsites near Pui O, Nam Shan, Pak Fu Tin, Chi Ma Wan and many places along the south coast. The *Countryside* map or the HKTA *Hostels, Campsites & Other Accommodation in Hong Kong* leaflet will tell you where they are. There is no camping charge at most of these sites.

A 10-minute walk to the east of the Lantau Tea Gardens at Ngong Ping is the YHA's *S G Davis Youth Hostel* (☎ 9855610), which has dormitory beds and a campsite. It costs HK$25 a night and you have to be a YHA member to stay here. The hostel is open on weekends and public holidays only. To get there, take a ferry from the Outlying Islands Ferry Pier to Mui Wo, then catch a bus to Ngong Ping.

The *Po Lin Monastery* (☎ 9855113) at Ngong Ping has separate dormitories for men and women. A bed costs HK$150 a night, which includes three vegetarian meals. To make a booking, call the monastery.

Also at Ngong Ping are the *Lantau Tea Gardens* (☎ 9855161). Accommodation for two persons on weekdays/weekends costs HK$150/190; for three persons it costs HK$180/230; for four persons HK$200/260.

You can also stay at the *Trappist Haven Monastery* (☎ 9876286), but applications have to be made in advance to the Grand Master, Trappist Haven, Lantau Island, PO Box 5, Peng Chau, Hong Kong, or try telephoning. Men and women must sleep in segregated dorms.

The HKYHA also operates a beach-side hostel called *Mong Tung Wan* (☎ 9841389) in the south-east corner of the island. Beds cost HK$25 and camping is permitted. From Mui Wo, take the bus to Pui O, then walk along the road to Ham Tin. At the junction of Chi Ma Wan Rd and the temple, take the footpath to Mong Tung Wan, about a 45-minute walk. An alternative route is to take a ferry to Cheung Chau Island, and hire a sampan to the jetty at Mong Tung Wan – a sampan carries about 10 people.

At Mui Wo, turn to your right as you exit the ferry pier – the beach and all places to stay are in this direction along Tungwan Tau Rd. The best deal around is the *Hoi Shuen Beach House* (☎ 9841603) where doubles run from HK$130 to HK$280, but the price doubles on weekends. The *Mui Wo Inn* (☎ 9847225, fax 9841916) has doubles from HK$191 to HK$313 on weekdays, and HK$391 to HK$487 on weekends. There's a place with no English sign, but it's No 23 Tungwan Tau Rd and offers good beachside accommodation starting from HK$160 for a double. *Sea House* (☎ 9847757) has rather dumpy-looking rooms starting from HK$160 on weekdays, HK$250 on weekends. Top of the line is the *Silvermine Beach Hotel* (☎ 9848295, fax 9841907), which has doubles from HK$560, minus 10% from Sunday to Thursday.

The *Cheung Sha Resort House* rents flats. You can book through Wah Nam Travel Service (☎ 8911161, 3320367). The smaller flats are for six people and rent for HK$180 on weekdays or HK$400 on weekends. From Mui Wo, take bus Nos 1, 2 or 3 to Cheung Sha and get off after the YWCA sign on the right.

Tong Fuk has mostly expensive beachside villas, but some reasonably priced flats. No signs in English, so look for prominent displays of bedroom-photographs posted outside the restaurants.

Top-end accommodation includes the *Sea Breeze Hotel* (☎ 9847977) at Pui O Beach on the south coast. Double rooms cost from HK$200 to HK$250 on weekdays and from HK$350 to HK$450 on weekends and public holidays. From Mui Wo you can get there on bus No 7.

Places to Eat

Apart from the Po Lin Monastery and the Lantau Tea Gardens, another place to eat is the more up-market *Silvermine Bay Restaurant* (☎ 9848267), 1 Chung Hau St, Mui Wo.

There is a decent Chinese restaurant in Tai O. There's no English sign, but to get there, cross the creek on the hand-pulled boat, then go straight up to the end of the road. The restaurant will be directly in front of you at the T-intersection.

Getting There & Away

The easiest access by far is to take a ferry from Central to Mui Wo. You can also take ferries from Peng Chau to Mui Wo via Chi Ma Wan, or take a kaido from Peng Chau to the Trappist Monastery on the east coast of Lantau.

The Hong Kong to Mui Wo ferries provide the most frequent service and depart from the Outlying Islands Ferry Pier at Central on Hong Kong Island. The first departure is at 7 am and the last is at 11.15 pm. There are 19 ferries on weekdays, 20 on weekends. From Mui Wo, the first ferry for Hong Kong departs at 6.10 am and the last is at 10 pm.

From Monday till noon on Saturday, adult fares are HK$6.50 ordinary class and HK$10 deluxe class. Weekends and public holidays, adult fares are HK$10 ordinary class and HK$18 deluxe class.

There are two boats daily on Saturday, Sunday and holidays to Tai O on the other end of the island. The boats run from Tuen Mun in the New Territories to Tai O via Sha Lo Wan on the northern side of Lantau.

Getting Around

Bus Services run by the New Lantau Bus Company all leave from the car park by the ferry pier in Mui Wo. Bus No 2 runs very

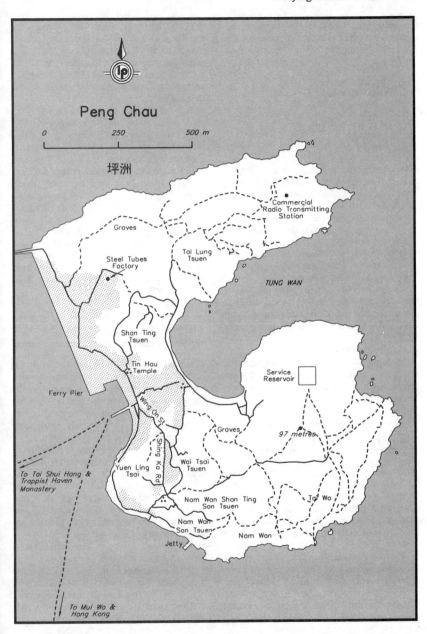

Peng Chau

0   250   500 m

坪洲

Graves

Commercial
Radio Transmitting
Station

Steel Tubes
Factory

Tai Lung
Tsuen

TUNG WAN

Shan Ting
Tsuen

Tin Hau
Temple

Service
Reservoir

Ferry Pier

Wing On St

Graves

97 metres

To Tai Shui Hang &
Trappist Haven
Monastery

Shing Ka Rd

Wai Tsai
Tsuen

Yuen Ling
Tsai

Tai Wo

Nam Wan Shan Ting
San Tsuen

Nam Wan
San Tsuen

Nam Wan

Jetty

To Mui Wo &
Hong Kong

frequently, but the others are just plain inadequate – they often fill up and you could find yourself waiting for hours. The seven bus routes are:

No 1 – Mui Wo to Tai O
No 2 – Mui Wo to Ngong Ping
No 3 – Mui Wo to Tung Chung
No 4 – Mui Wo to Tong Fuk
No 5 – Mui Wo to Shek Pik
No 6 – Student Bus
No 7 – Mui Wo to Pui O

Taxi If you think the bus service is rotten, just wait until you try Lantau taxis. In supposedly free-market Hong Kong, Lantau taxi drivers are a protected lot. The number of taxis is inadequate, they will not pick you up along country roads where you desperately need them and they are generally hostile to customers. It's easiest to find taxis in Mui Wo and occasionally in Tong Fuk – elsewhere, they are a rare item indeed.

Taxis are prohibited from taking you all the way to Ngong Ping – they will drop you off at the bottom of the access road, from where you have a steep climb up the mountain.

Hitching Forget it. I tried it accompanied by a Chinese woman who certainly looked totally harmless – we didn't have a crumb of success.

Peng Chau 坪洲

This quiet little island, just under one sq km in area, is inhabited by people who earn a living from fishing, farming and making matches, furniture and metal tubes. The population is a little more than 8000, making this small island crowded compared to nearby Lantau.

There are no cars on Peng Chau and you can walk around it with ease in an hour. There's been a drift of middle-class Hong Kong Chinese to this island, much as there has been a drift of Westerners to Cheung Chau and Lamma.

Peng Chau is also the place to depart for the Trappist Haven Monastery on Lantau. The monastery's boat meets every ferry and takes passengers over the short stretch of water to Lantau. The island is also popular with Hong Kongers who head straight for the seafood restaurants.

A land reclamation project on the west side of the island will undoubtedly bring more development. Only time will tell if this is done in good taste or in more typical concrete-box fashion.

Ferries to Peng Chau leave from the Outlying Islands Ferry Pier on Hong Kong Island. The first ferry departs at 7 am and the last at about 11.30 pm. There are 17 ferries a day, Monday to Saturday, with slightly fewer on Sunday and public holidays.

The first ferry from Peng Chau to Hong Kong Island departs at about 6.35 am and the last at about 10.20 pm. A few ferries go from Hong Kong to Cheung Chau via Peng Chau. Get the HYF timetable.

Tap Mun Chau 塔門

This small island is in the north-east of the New Territories where Tolo Harbour empties into Mirs Bay. The island has an old-world fishing village atmosphere and is noted for its **Tin Hau temple** where whistling sounds occur at the altar when easterly winds roar. The Tin Hau Festival is very big here.

Other main attractions are the **Tap Mun Cave** on the eastern side of the island and the beautiful **beaches**.

Many visitors claim that Tap Mun Chau is the most interesting island of all those around Hong Kong. Unfortunately, the beach is carpeted with beer cans, plastic bags and other detritus. Plus getting there is na bit of a hassle and few travellers bother. There is no accommodation on the island.

The easiest way is to take a kaido from Wong Shek Pier, which is at the last stop of bus No 94. The kaidos run once hourly.

Alternatively, there are supposedly two ferries a day to Tap Mun Chau from Ma Liu

Tap Mun Chau (Grass Island)

塔門

CHEK CHAU HAU (MIDDLE CHANNEL)
° Cham Pai (Channel Rock)

0   0.5   1 km

Pak Wan

Kung Chau

Hau Tsz Kok

Mau Ping Shan (Wintz Hill)

Che Wan

Hau Tsz Kok Pai

Lung Keng Lok

To Ma Liu Shui

Chung Mei Kok

Sheung Wai

Chau Tsai Kok

Tin Hau Temple

Chung Wai

Junk Rock

Tap Mun

New Fishermens Village

Balanced Rock

° Tit Shue Pai (Warburg Rock)

Yaumati Ferry Company (☎ 5423081), 1st floor, Central Harbour Services Pier, Pier Rd, Central.

Ping Chau 平洲

This small island is in Mirs Bay in the far north-east of the New Territories. It's very close to the coast of China and it used to be one of the most popular destinations for people who wanted to leave China by swimming – braving the sharks and Mao's patrol boats.

At one time the island supported a population of 3000, but now it is uninhabited. The mass exodus started in the 1960s when everyone suddenly decided that life in a Hong Kong factory was preferable to life on a peaceful fishing isle. There are several abandoned buildings on the island, but visitors are advised to bring camping equipment.

The island's highest point is only about 30 metres, but it has unusual rock layers in its cliffs, which glitter after a night of rain. There are beautiful white-sand beaches, especially **Lai Tau Wan**. The island is also good for swimming, though some of the beaches are slate.

Getting to Ping Chau is practically an expedition. Unless you have your own yacht, you must take the ferry from Ma Liu Shui (near the Chinese University) in the New Territories. The ferry runs only on weekends, departing on Saturday and returning on

Shui (near the Chinese University) in the New Territories. I say 'supposedly', because they don't always stop at Tap Mun even though the schedule says they do. The first at 7.25 am is a direct ferry and the second, at 3.15 pm, makes several stops along the way. Departing from Tap Mun, there is one indirect ferry at 8.40 am and a direct one at 5.50 pm. The ferries are run by the Hong Kong &

Sunday, so a visit to Ping Chau involves a mandatory camping trip.

Depart from Ma Liu Shui on Saturday at 11.15 am and return on Sunday from Ping Chau at 1.10 pm. Check these times since the schedule can change and you certainly don't want to miss the boat back to Hong Kong. Only round-trip tickets are sold.

Tickets for this ferry can be bought at the head office of the Hong Kong & Yaumati Ferry Company (☎ 5423081), 1st floor, Central Harbour Services Pier, Pier Rd, Central, or at the pier in Ma Liu Shui on the day of travel. They only sail if the weather is good.

Poi Toi 蒲台

This is one of the least visited islands – it's not even crowded on Sunday! That fact alone might make it worth the journey.

Poi Toi is a rocky island off the south-eastern coast of Hong Kong Island. There are a small number of permanent residents, but who knows how much longer before they will finally give up their peaceful outpost and migrate to the sin and glitter of the city just beyond their shores?

Ferries depart from Aberdeen on Tuesday, Thursday and Saturday at 9 am. They return from Poi Toi at 10.30 am, which means that if you want to explore the island, you must stay overnight. However, on Sunday there are three boats, so you can go and return the same day. The earliest Sunday boat departs from Aberdeen at 8 am. There are two Sunday boats departing from Stanley at 10 am and 11.30 am. Going the other way, there are Sunday departures from Poi Toi at 9.15 and 10.45 am, and 3, 4.30 and 6 pm.

A reservation is needed for all these boats. This can be booked by phone (☎ 5544059), but they don't speak English. Locals pay HK$14 for a one-way journey, but nonresi-

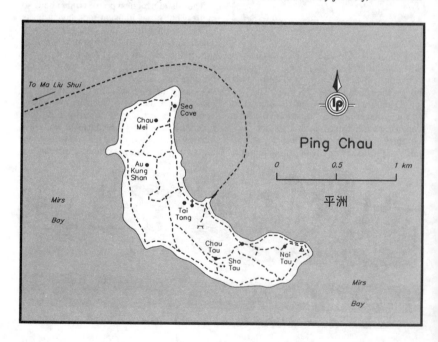

Top: Small vessel, Lantau (TW)
Bottom: Building junks, Cheung Chau (TW)

Top, Left & Right: Ruins of Sao Paulo, Macau Peninsula (TW)

dents of Poi Toi pay HK$28 for the round-trip if returning on the same day. If staying overnight, the fare jumps to HK$48 for the round-trip. The Aberdeen-Poi Toi trip takes 70 minutes, but only 35 minutes from Stanley.

Ma Wan 馬灣

Ma Wan is a flat and forested island off the north-eastern tip of Lantau. It was once famous as the 'Gate to Kowloon', where foreign ships would collect before entering Chinese waters.

The island was once a charming place to visit but these days it's hardly worth bothering. The two beaches where swimming is possible – Tung Wan and Tung Wan Tsai – have become polluted. Swimming, however, is still allowed and a lifeguard is present. The view on the eastern side of Ma Wan has been hopelessly marred by the construction of oil storage tanks on nearby Tsingyi Island.

The view on the western side of the island, looking towards Lantau, is OK but it's no place for swimming. This is the notorious Kap Shui Mun (Rapid Water Gate) where dangerous currents have been known to push back unmotorised junks.

Legend has it that a treasure junk, belonging to the pirate Cheung Po Tsai, sank in this channel as it had become impossible to recover in the deadly current.

About the only thing you can do is sit on the pier and watch the hoverferries rush by on their way to Tuen Mun (New Territories) and China.

The Chinese like to come to Ma Wan on weekends to eat seafood. There are several seafood restaurants on the islands and prices are reasonable. On weekdays, the restaurant owners have little to do and pass the time playing mahjong.

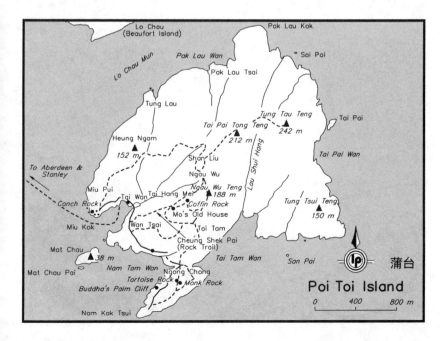

The island will be affected by the new airport development project on Lantau Island. The Lantau Fixed Crossing (a bridge) will connect Ma Wan to both Lantau Island and the New Territories. Having already been colonised by the British, the island of Ma Wan is destined to be 'Kowloonised' by the bridge.

Adding injury to insult, Ma Wan has many unleashed dogs who have a special antipathy to peculiar-looking foreigners. Keep in mind the advice of the former US president, Theodore Roosevelt, who said: 'Speak softly and carry a big stick'.

If you really want to visit Ma Wan, the only boat is a kaido from the Ma Wan Pier *(Ma Wan Matou)* just to the north of the island in the New Territories. To get there, take the MTR to Laichikok Station. After exiting the·MTR station, cross the street to Cheung Shun St and catch bus No 52 which takes you to the Ma Wan Pier (ask the bus driver where to get off). The kaido runs every hour.

MACAU

Facts about Macau

Only 65 km from Hong Kong but predating it by 300 years, Macau is the oldest surviving European settlement in Asia and Portugal's last colony. It is a city of cobbled side streets, baroque churches, Portuguese fortresses and unpronounceable Portuguese street names. Macau's culture, cooking and people are a hybrid of Portuguese and Chinese.

Most of the interesting historical buildings are in the central and southern parts of the peninsula. The southern part (near the Penha Church) is the most affluent area of town, with expensive homes perched on the hillsides with views of the sea. There are several Chinese temples and restored colonial villas, and it is the final resting place of many European seamen and soldiers. You will also find casinos, discos, high-rises and five-star hotels.

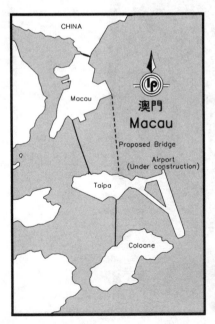

Tourism has had a shot in the arm in recent years with several large luxury hotels being built on the mainland and on the islands. Yet apart from the Chinese gamblers, most tourists who go to Macau spend just a few whistle-stop hours there. Many who visit Hong Kong don't bother going to Macau at all – a pity because it is one of those curious places where something new can be found on every visit.

HISTORY
Macau means the 'City of God' and takes its name from A-Ma-Gau, the Bay of A-Ma. At Barra Point stands the A-Ma Temple which dates back to the early 16th century.

According to legend, A-Ma, a poor girl looking for a passage to Canton, was turned away by the wealthy junk owners, so a fisherman took her on board. A storm blew up and wrecked all the junks except the boat carrying the girl. When it landed in Macau the girl disappeared, only to reappear later as a goddess on the spot where the fisherman built her temple.

Portuguese Exploration & Colonisation
Macau is an oddity which has managed to cling to the Chinese coast since the mid-16th century, despite attempts by the Chinese, the Spanish and the Dutch to brush it off. For more than a hundred years previously the Portuguese had been pushing down the west African coast in their search for a sea route to the Far East. But they were delayed by the attractions of slaves and gold from Guinea which brought immediate material rewards, and by their ambition to find the mysterious Christian king Prester John who would join them in a crusade against the Muslims.

When, in 1498, Vasco da Gama's ships rounded the southern cape of Africa and arrived in Calicut (Calcutta) in India, the Portuguese suddenly got a whiff of the enormous profits to be made from the Asian trade. Also, because the trade was almost exclusively in the hands of Muslims, they had the added satisfaction (and excuse) that any blow against their commercial rivals was a blow against the infidels.

There had never been any real intention to conquer large tracts of territory, colonise foreign lands or convert the native populations to Christianity en masse. Trade was always first and foremost in Portuguese minds. To this end, a vague plan was devised to bring all the important Indian Ocean trading ports under Portuguese control and to establish the necessary fortifications to protect their trade.

Thus, the Portuguese captured Goa on the west coast of India in 1510, and then Malacca on the Malay Peninsula in 1511 (their first ships having arrived there in 1509). They then attempted to subdue the Spice Islands of the Moluccas, in what is now Indonesia, and thus control the lucrative spice trade.

The Portuguese never did manage to monopolise the trade. As the years rolled by their determination and ability to do so declined. By the end of the 16th century their efforts were brought to a close by the arrival in Indonesia of powerful Dutch fleets also bent on wresting control of the spice trade.

More encouraging for the Portuguese was the trade with China and Japan. On their earliest voyages to India the Portuguese had heard of a strange, light-skinned people called the Chin, whose huge ships had once visited India but whose voyages had suddenly ceased. (From 1405 to 1433 the second Ming Emperor Yong Le had dispatched several enormous maritime expeditions which had made contact with many parts of Asia and Africa.)

When the Portuguese arrived in Malacca in 1511 they came upon several junks with Chinese captains. Realising that the Chins were not a mythical people and concluding that they had come from the 'Cathay' of Marco Polo's travels, a small party of Portuguese were sent northwards to find out what they could and possibly to open trade with the Chinese.

The first Portuguese set foot on Chinese soil in 1513 at the mouth of the Pearl River, near what is now Macau and Hong Kong. They reached Japan by accident in 1542, their ship having been blown off course.

By and large, initial Portuguese contact with China did not go well, and for years their attempts to gain a permanent trading base on the China coast met with little success. But in the early 1550s they reached some sort of agreement with Cantonese officials to settle on Sanchuang, a small island about 80 km to the south-west of the mouth of the Pearl River. Sanchuang's exposed anchorage led the Portuguese to abandon the island in 1553, moving to another island closer to the Pearl River.

To the north-east was a peninsula of land where the Portuguese also often anchored. It

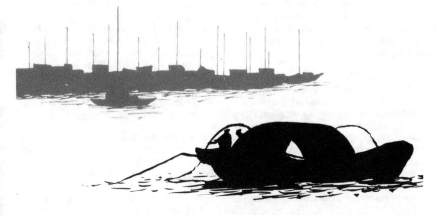

had two natural harbours – an inner harbour on the West River and an outer harbour in a bay facing the Pearl River – and to its south were some sheltering islands. In 1556 or 1557 the Portuguese and some Cantonese officials made an agreement which allowed the Portuguese to rent this peninsula of land – known variously as A-Ma-Gao, Amacon, Aomen and Macau – apparently in return for ridding the area of marauding pirates who plagued this stretch of the coast. However, the peninsula was never formally ceded to the Portuguese.

Macau grew rapidly as a trading centre, largely because the Chinese wanted to trade with foreign countries but were forbidden to go abroad on penalty of death. The most lucrative trade route for the Portuguese was the long circuit from the west of India to Japan and back, with Macau as the essential link. Acting as agents for Chinese merchants, they took Chinese goods to the west coast of India, exchanging them for cotton and textiles which they took to Malacca and sold to local merchants in exchange for spices and aromatic woods. The Portuguese then continued to Japan where they sold their Malacca cargo for Japanese silver, swords, lacquerware and fans, returning to Macau to exchange them for more Chinese goods.

The Japanese were forbidden to enter Chinese ports and the trade of other Asian nationals with China was largely insignificant. The Portuguese displaced the Arabs and, with no other Europeans yet on the scene, they became the carriers of all large-scale international commerce with China and Japan.

17th-Century Macau

By the start of the 17th century Macau supported several thousand permanent residents, including about a thousand Portuguese. The rest were Chinese Christian converts, mixed-race Christians from Malacca, Japanese Christians and a large number of African, Indian and Malay slaves. Large numbers of Chinese citizens worked in the town as hawkers, labourers and servants. There were many Chinese traders too.

Trade was the most important activity of the new town, but Macau was also fast becoming a centre of Christianity in the Far East. Priests and missionaries accompanied Portuguese ships, although the offensive was not jointly planned and the interests of traders and missionaries frequently conflicted. Among the earliest missionaries was Francis Xavier (later canonised) of the Jesuit order, who had spent from 1549 to 1551 in Japan attempting to convert heathens, before turning his attention to China. Xavier was stalled by Portuguese who feared the consequences of his meddling in Chinese affairs, but he made it as far as Sanchuang, where he died in December 1552. In the years to follow it was Jesuit missionaries, not traders, who were able to penetrate China beyond Macau and Canton.

The Portuguese who stayed in Macau, along with their Macanese (mixed-blood) descendants, succeeded in creating a home away from home with luxurious rococo houses and splendid baroque churches, paid for with the wealth generated by their monopoly on trade with China and Japan. These structures included the Basilica of Sao Paulo, hailed as the greatest monument to Christianity in the East.

Apart from traders and priests, this odd little colony attracted some colourful adventurers, madmen, artists and poets. Among them was the 16th-century poet Luis de Camoes, who was banished from Portugal to Goa and then to Macau, although some say he was never in the colony. He is said to have written in Macau at least part of his epic poem *Os Lusiadas*, which recounts the voyage of Vasco da Gama to India. British artist George Chinnery spent a quarter of a century in Macau, from 1825 until his death in 1852, and is remembered for his paintings of the place and its people.

Portuguese Decline

The Portuguese decline was as rapid as its success. In 1580 Spanish armies occupied Portugal, then in the early years of the 17th century, the Dutch began making their presence felt in the Far East. In response, the

Portuguese at Macau began building fortresses in anticipation of Dutch attacks. The Dutch made several forays on Macau, including major but unsuccessful attacks in 1607 and 1627.

Next the Japanese became suspicious of Portuguese (and also Spanish) intentions, and began persecuting Japanese Christians, eventually closing the country to foreign trade in 1637. In 1641 the Dutch took Malacca in Malaysia by force from the Portuguese.

Although Portugal regained its independence from Spain in 1640, all trade connections with China and Japan were cut off. The Portuguese could no longer provide the Chinese with the Japanese silver they wanted in exchange for their silk and porcelain, nor with spices since the spice trade was now in the hands of the Dutch. Macau was no longer of any use to the Chinese and by 1640 they had closed the port of Canton to the Portuguese, leaving Macau to deteriorate rapidly into an impoverished settlement in danger of extinction.

But Macau managed to survive by other means. From the mid-18th century – as the French, Dutch, Danes, Swedes, Americans and Spanish all profited from trading with China via Canton – restrictions and regulations concerning non-Portuguese residing in Macau were lifted. In effect the colony became an outpost for all of Europe in China, a position which it held until the British took possession of Hong Kong in 1841 and other Chinese ports were forced open to foreign trade in the years following.

Until the middle of the 19th century the history of Macau was a long series of incidents – incitements, standoffs, threats, disputes and attacks, which involved the Portuguese, Chinese and British – as the Portuguese attempted to maintain their grasp. The Portuguese even made plans around 1850 to attack Canton as the British had done during the Opium Wars, in order to dictate a Chinese-Portuguese treaty. A series of disasters, including the intended flagship of the fleet blowing up off Taipa Island, meant that this plan never came to fruition.

The Portuguese were once again forced to settle their differences with China through negotiation, although it was not until 1887 that a treaty was signed in which China effectively recognised Portuguese sovereignty over Macau. As for the problem of keeping Macau financially afloat, that had been more or less solved by Governor Isidoro Francisco Guimaraes (1851-1863), who introduced what has become the best known feature of the colony – licensed gambling.

19th-Century Macau

Macau had turned into something of a decaying backwater by the late 19th century, although it continued to serve as a place of refuge for Chinese who were fleeing war and famine in the north.

When the Sino-Japanese War erupted in the 1930s, the population swelled to a formidable 500,000. Europeans also took refuge in Macau during WW II because the Japanese honoured Portuguese neutrality and did not take Macau as they did Hong Kong. More people came in 1949 when the Communists took power in China, and from 1978 until about 1980 Macau was a destination for Vietnamese boat people. Somehow the tiny place managed to contain them all.

Macau's last great convulsion occurred in 1966 when China's Cultural Revolution spilled over into the colony. Macau was stormed by Red Guards and there were violent riots in which a few Red Guards were shot dead by Portuguese troops. The then governor reportedly proposed that the troubles could be ended if Portugal simply left Macau forever, but fearing the loss of foreign trade through Macau and Hong Kong, the Chinese backed off.

In 1974 a military coup in Portugal brought a left-wing government to power which proceeded to divest Portugal of the last remnants of its empire (including Mozambique, Angola and East Timor), yet the Chinese told the Portuguese that they preferred to leave Macau as it was.

Until 1975, Portugal maintained a 'touch-base' policy regarding Chinese immigrants. That is, any Chinese reaching Macau could obtain residency, even if they reached it by swimming. From 1975 on the policy was changed and all Chinese sneaking into Macau are now regarded as illegal immigrants.

Macau Today

Once the Joint Declaration over Hong Kong was signed by Britain and China, it was inevitable that China would also seek a similar agreement with Portugal on Macau's future. That agreement was finally inked in March 1987.

Under the Sino-Portuguese pact, Macau will become a Special Administrative Region (SAR) of China for 50 years after 20 December 1999. Like Hong Kong, Macau is to enjoy a 'high degree of autonomy' in all matters except defence and foreign affairs.

An important change occurred in 1982 regarding the status of Macau's Chinese majority. Prior to 1982, any person born in Macau could have full Portuguese citizenship. Partly due to pressure from China, and partly due to a scandal involving the selling of Portuguese passports to Hong Kongers, the rules were changed. Now, one parent must be a Portuguese citizen, though he or she need not be of Portuguese descent. Less than one-fifth of Macau's ethnic Chinese population holds Portuguese passports. Nevertheless, China continues to raise objections, claiming that anyone of Chinese descent is a Chinese citizen. In other words, race should be the deciding factor, not place of birth.

China has threatened to revoke the Portuguese citizenship of Macau's ethnic Chinese, which has caused much anxiety. However, so far there has not been a massive flight of people and capital as there has been in Hong Kong. The reason may have more to do with the fact that few Chinese have the financial resources to flee Macau.

The pro-democracy demonstrations in 1989 that swept through China before being brutally suppressed, also caught on in Macau. Shortly before the tanks started rolling over students in Beijing, a huge pro-democracy rally was held in Macau and attracted over 100,000 participants, more than one-fifth of the population.

All in all, 1990 was not a good year for Macau. Tourism was already down because of the Beijing massacre, but China's leadership shook everyone's confidence even further by interfering in Macau's internal affairs. Lu Ping, deputy director of China's Hong Kong & Macau Affairs Office, launched a verbal barrage against the Macau government. Lu insisted that the Macau government should tear down the statue of former governor Joao Ferreira do Amaral because it's 'too colonial'. He then went on to condemn the opening of a Taipei Trade & Tourism Office in Macau, and insisted that the government should move faster to make Mandarin Chinese *(Putonghua)* the official language of Macau, and that all Portuguese laws should be translated into Chinese. He also wanted Macau's civil service to be controlled by local Chinese, rather than Portuguese and Macanese as is presently the case.

Macau's governor Carlos Melancia launched a verbal counterattack, but he soon had serious problems of his own. He was forced to resign as the result of a scandal involving kickbacks for construction contracts on Macau's new airport, although the evidence against him was weak and many believe the accusations were politically motivated.

Tourism and foreign investment are both picking up again, but Macau enters its final decade under Portuguese rule with a bad case of the jitters. Nervousness about China's intentions has already hurt the economy, but many also believe that China wouldn't dare to harm Macau. As for the illegal immigrants, they have no doubts – despite the official policy of returning them to China, they continue to swim to what they hope will be a better life.

GEOGRAPHY

Macau is divided into three main sections – the Macau Peninsula which is attached to China at the northern tip, and the two islands of Taipa and Coloane. Taipa, directly to the

Temperature & Rainfall

Month	Jan	Feb	Mar	Apr	May	Jun	Jul	Aug	Sep	Oct	Nov	Dec
Temp °C	14.5	14.9	18	21.9	25.8	27.5	28.5	28.2	27.2	24.5	20.5	16.3
Rain mm	30	57	73	174	335	362	240	326	235	107	36	24

south of Macau, is attached by a two km bridge. Coloane is south of Taipa and connected to it by a causeway.

Macau is small: it has a total land area of 16 sq km, only 1.6% of Hong Kong's land total. The Macau Peninsula is just 5.5 sq km, while the islands of Taipa and Coloane occupy 3.3 sq km and 7.2 sq km respectively. However, due to land reclamation, the place is gradually getting bigger.

The northern tip of the Macau Peninsula, near the Chinese border, is the newer part of town where many high-rise apartments have been built, mostly on reclaimed land.

CLIMATE

Macau's climate is almost the same as Hong Kong's, but with one nice difference – the cool sea breeze is delightful on summer nights and acts as natural air-conditioning.

GOVERNMENT

Officially, Macau is not considered a colony. Instead, the Portuguese government regards Macau as a piece of Chinese territory under Portuguese administration. The difference is largely a matter of semantics.

The colony/Chinese territory has a governor who is appointed by the president of Portugal. The governor appoints five under secretaries, each with a specific field of administration. There is also a legislative assembly with 23 members. Eight of them are directly elected, another eight are elected by various 'economic interest groups', and seven are appointed by the governor. The assembly then elects its own president. There are three mayors: one for the Macau Peninsula and one each for the two islands, Taipa and Coloane.

ECONOMY

Macau's main industry, gambling, is mono polised by a small but wealthy Chinese business syndicate which trades under the name of STDM – Sociedade de Turismo e Diversoes de Macau (Macao Travel & Amusement Company). It was STDM that introduced the hydrofoils to Macau and built the Hotel Lisboa. This group won monopoly rights on all licensed gambling in Macau in 1962.

Although Macau has had a reputation for centuries as a gambling centre, casino gambling only got under way in 1934 when a Chinese syndicate called the Tai Hing obtained monopoly rights from the colonial government. Monopoly rights were renewed every five years and the monopoly went to whichever company would pay the most tax. The story goes that the original owners of the Tai Hing were able to pay a puny tax sum, but held on to the monopoly by paying off competitors. It wasn't until after the death of the two founders of the Tai Hing that the STDM gained a monopoly on the gambling industry.

About one-third of government revenue comes from gambling, another third from

"Ci dade do Santo Nome de Deus" - MACAU

direct and indirect taxes and the rest from land rents and service charges.

Macau entertains almost six million tourists a year, or more than 12 times the local population. Over 80% of the tourists come from Hong Kong, with most of the remainder from Japan, the UK, Taiwan, USA, Thailand and South Korea. Gambling and tourism provide about 25% of gross domestic product. The colony has various light industries, such as fireworks, textile and garment production, and wages are much lower than in Hong Kong.

The main reason that wages have remained low despite a labour shortage is that Macau has an agreement with China which allows a large number of Chinese workers to cross the border daily from Zhuhai. The agreement is controversial since it weakens the position of Macau's workers so they cannot demand better wages, but it also greatly benefits workers living in Zhuhai. The cheap supply of labour is attracting foreign investment. Taiwan, which suffers from its own labour shortage, is reportedly keen to invest heavily in Macau.

Macau closely follows the economic success formula employed in Hong Kong. It is a duty-free port and the maximum rate of taxation is 15%, as in Hong Kong.

The biggest news for Macau's economy is the construction of an international airport on the east side of Taipa Island at an estimated cost of US$625 million. This requires reclaiming land from the sea, and so far the project has moved slowly because of a dispute with the neighbouring city of Zhuhai in China.

Zhuhai's complaint is that the airport will create considerable noise pollution. For its part, Macau denies the problem, but a quick look at the map indicates that Zhuhai might find itself right under the flight path of approaching aircraft. Zhuhai officials successfully delayed the project for over six months by refusing to supply sand which was necessary to construct the runway. Macau finally broke the impasse by appealing directly to Beijing, which overruled Zhuhai officials and resumed shipments of

landfill material. To appease Zhuhai, Macau says it will share the airport with China. This will be accomplished by setting up a separate customs terminal so passengers heading to or from China will not have to pass through Macau customs.

The airport isn't the only big news for Macau's economy. A project is also under way to build a deep-water port on the northeast side of Coloane Island. Ironically, nearby Hong Kong has one of the finest natural deep-water harbours in the world, while Macau's shallow harbour is constantly choked with mud flowing down from China's Pearl River. In order to develop export-oriented industries like electronics, some way must be found to accommodate container ships. At present, Macau does not have a container terminal and all freight is handled inefficiently in crates.

The third major project is the construction of Taipa City, a large high-rise housing development on Taipa Island. In order to handle an expected increase in motor vehicle traffic, a second bridge is planned between Taipa and the Macau Peninsula. And on the Chinese side of the border, a new freeway is being built between Zhuhai and Canton, which will connect with the freeway being built from Hong Kong to Canton. There is even talk of extending the railway from Canton down to Zhuhai and maybe into Macau as well.

Not everyone is enthusiastic about all this development. It will certainly change the peaceful character of Macau, already badly battered by cars and new high-rise buildings. Nevertheless, there is no denying that these projects will benefit the economy. With Hong Kong's crowded airport close to saturation point, foreign airlines are already falling over themselves trying to secure landing rights in Macau.

POPULATION

Officially, 453,000 people live in the colony, but there are an estimated 40,000 illegal immigrants. About 98% live on the Macau Peninsula, making it one of the most crowded areas in the world. Ironically, the two islands have remained essentially rural, but this is due to change soon with the construction of Taipa City, a new high-rise development on Taipa Island.

PEOPLE

The population consists of about 95% Chinese and about 3% Portuguese and Macanese (Macau-born Portuguese and Eurasians). Nearly 1% of the population is from Thailand, mostly female, and employed in what is loosely called the entertainment industry.

EDUCATION

Macau University on Taipa Island is the main institute of higher learning. The school was once the small, privately-owned University of East Asia, but has been renamed, taken over by the government and now has a student body of 5000. The school is still rapidly expanding and even attracts students from Hong Kong and overseas.

The only other tertiary schools in Macau are a hotel catering academy and an industrial training centre.

ARTS

Chinese art is covered in the Facts about Hong Kong chapter. As for the Portuguese, their art is most apparent in the old churches and cathedrals which grace Macau's skyline. It's here that you'll see some fine examples of painting, stained-glass windows and sculpture.

CULTURE

About 95% of the population is Chinese and is culturally indistinguishable from Hong Kong. See the Facts about Hong Kong chapter for details.

Of course, the Portuguese minority has a vastly different culture, which they have kept largely intact. Although mixed marriages are not uncommon in Macau, there has been surprisingly little assimilation between the two ethnic groups – most Portuguese cannot speak Chinese and vice versa.

RELIGION

For the Chinese majority, Taoism and Buddhism are the dominant religions. However, nearly 500 years of Portuguese influence has definitely left an imprint, and the Catholic church is very strong in Macau. Many Chinese have been converted and you are likely to see Chinese nuns.

For more detailed information on religion see the Facts about Hong Kong chapter.

LANGUAGE

Portuguese is the official language, though Cantonese is the language of choice for about 95% of the population. English is regarded as a third language, even though it's more commonly spoken than Portuguese. Mandarin Chinese, or *pǔtōnghùa* as it's officially called, is understood (with some difficulty) by about half the Chinese population

Within the Macau educational system, English is now the main language of instruction and starts at elementary school. So, if you're having trouble communicating, your best bet is to ask a young person.

Although there is no compelling reason for you to learn Portuguese while in Macau there are a few words which are useful (and fun) to know for reading street signs and maps. The most important ones are:

admiral	*almirante*
alley	*beco*
avenue	*avenida*
bay	*baía*
beach	*praia*
big	*grande*
bridge	*ponte*
building	*edifício*
bus stop	*paragem*
cathedral	*sé*
church	*igreja*
courtyard	*pátio*
district	*bairro*
fortress	*fortaleza*
friendship	*amizade*
garden	*jardim*
guesthouse	*hospedaria* or *vila*
guide	*guia*

hill	*alto* or *monte*	police station	*esquadra da polícia*
hotel	*pousada*	post office	*correio*
island	*ilha*	restaurant (small)	*casa de pasto*
lane	*travessa*	path	*caminho*
library	*biblioteca*	road	*estrada*
lighthouse	*farol*	rock, crag	*penha*
lookout point	*miradouro*	school	*escola*
market	*mercado*	small hill	*colina*
moneychanger	*casa de câmbio*	square	*praça*
museum	*museu*	square (small)	*largo*
of	*da, do*	steep street	*calçada*
pawn shop	*casa de penhores*	street	*rua*
pier	*ponte-cais*	teahouse	*casa de chá*

Facts for the Visitor

VISAS & EMBASSIES

For most visitors, all that's needed to enter Macau is a passport. Everyone gets a 20-day stay on arrival. Visas are not required for the following nationalities: Australia, Austria, Belgium, Brazil, Canada, Denmark, France, Germany, Greece, Hong Kong, Ireland, Italy, Japan, Luxemburg, Malaysia, Netherlands, New Zealand, Norway, Philippines, Singapore, South Korea, Spain, Sweden, Switzerland, Taiwan, Thailand, UK and USA.

All other nationalities must have a visa, which can be obtained on arrival in Macau. Visas cost M$145 for individuals, M$290 for married couples and families, M$72 for children under 12 and M$72 per person in a bona fide group of at least 10 people. People holding passports from countries which do not have diplomatic relations with Portugal must obtain visas from an overseas Portuguese consulate before entering Macau. The Portuguese consulate (☎ 5225488) in Hong Kong is on the 10th floor, Tower Two, Exchange Square, Central.

Visa Extensions

After your 20 days are up, you can obtain a one-month extension from the Immigration Office. A second extension is not possible, although it's easy enough to go across the border to China and then come back again. The Immigration Office (☎ 577338) is on the 9th floor, Macau Chamber of Commerce Building, 175 Rua de Xangai, which is one block to the north-east of the Hotel Beverly Plaza.

Foreign Embassies in Macau

There are no foreign embassies in Macau, but China has plans to establish a visa office. This is partly in response to a move by Taiwan which already has a representative office in Macau.

Even more intriguing is the North Korean visa office which opened in Macau in January, 1991. See Lonely Planet's *North-East Asia on a shoestring* for more details about making the North Korea trip.

The addresses of these two representative offices are:

DPR Korea-Macau International Tourism Company, 23rd floor, Nam Van Commercial Centre, 57-9 Rua da Praia Grande (☎ 333355)
Taipei Trade & Tourism Office, Edificio Commercial Central, 150 Andar, Avenida Infante D Henrique No 60-64 (☎ 306282)

CUSTOMS

Customs formalities are few and it's unlikely you'll be bothered by them. There are no export duties on anything bought in Macau, and this includes antiques. You're allowed to bring in a reasonable quantity of tobacco, alcohol and perfumes.

Like Hong Kong, Macau Customs takes a very dim view of drugs. Weapons aren't allowed, so leave your AK-47 behind.

MONEY

There are no money changing facilities at the Jetfoil Pier, so make sure you have some Hong Kong dollars or you'll have difficulty getting from the pier to town!

The casino moneychangers are more convenient than the banks as they operate 24 hours a day, but banks give a better exchange rate. The best place to change money is the Taifung Bank. The Bank of China also gives a very good exchange rate. Both of these banks have branches all over Macau, including the arcade of the Hotel Lisboa. The Taifung Bank in the Lisboa Arcade stays open late into the evening.

The worst place to change money is the Hongkong Bank, which not only gives a poor exchange rate, but also hits you with a M$25 service charge for each transaction involving travellers' cheques.

There are also private moneychangers. Like the casinos, they keep longer hours but give poorer exchange rates. To find a moneychanger, look for a sign that says 'casa de cambio'. Big hotels offer moneychanging services if you are staying there, but banks are still your best bet.

If you have a Hong Kong Electronic Teller Card (ETC), it will work in Macau ETC machines. You can find an ETC machine at the Hongkong Bank branch at Rua do Praia Grande and Rua Palha. However, if you merely have a bank book from Hongkong Bank, you cannot make withdrawals at their Macau branch.

Currency

Macau's currency is called the *pataca*, normally written as M$, and one pataca is divided into 100 *avos*. Coins come as 10, 20 and 50 avos and one and five patacas. Notes are M$5, M$10, M$50, M$100 and M$500. Commemorative gold M$1000 and silver M$100 coins have been issued, although it's hardly likely you'll see them used as currency. There are no exchange control regulations and money can be freely transferred into and out of Macau. All major credit cards are accepted in big hotels, car rental agencies, etc.

Exchange Rates

You'll find that Hong Kong dollars, including coins, are readily accepted everywhere in Macau just as if they were patacas. However, patacas are worth 3% less than Hong Kong dollars, so by converting into patacas you get a 3% discount on everything you buy in Macau.

Unfortunately, patacas are not so well-received in Hong Kong. Moneychangers in Hong Kong will not accept patacas. Even worse, most Hong Kong banks won't take your patacas either! The only place that will change patacas for Hong Kong dollars is the Hang Seng Bank at their main branch at 18 Carnarvon Rd, Tsimshatsui. You lose a little bit by changing them in Hong Kong rather than in Macau. At the time of writing, Macau banks were trading HK$97 for M$100, whereas the Hang Seng Bank offered HK$95

for M$100. You would be wise to use all your patacas before departing Macau.

A$1	=	$M6.25
C$1	=	$M6.96
HK$1	=	$M1.03
NZ$1	=	$M4.72
UK£1	=	$M13.98
US$1	=	$M8.02
Y100	=	$M5.81

Costs

As long as you don't go crazy at the roulette wheel or slot machines, Macau is cheaper than Hong Kong. To help keep costs down, avoid spending weekends there.

Tipping

Classy hotels and restaurants will automatically hit you with a 10% service charge, which is supposedly a mandatory tip. Just how much of this money actually goes to the employees is a matter for speculation.

You can follow your own conscience, but tipping is not customary among the Chinese. Of course, porters at expensive hotels have become accustomed to hand-outs from well-heeled tourists.

Bargaining

Most stores have fixed prices, but if you buy clothing, trinkets and other tourist junk from the street markets, there is some scope for bargaining.

It's a different story at the pawn shops. Bargain ruthlessly! See the Things to Buy section at the end of this chapter for more details.

Consumer Taxes

There is a Macau government 5% tourist tax which affects the price of hotel rooms and up-market restaurant meals. However, this tax isn't applied to the real cheapie hotels and hole-in-the-wall restaurants.

WHEN TO GO

While most times of the year are OK as far as weather is concerned, there are certain times you should definitely avoid. Weekends and holidays will always create accommodation and transport problems. The Macau Grand Prix (third week of November) is a real crunch time.

WHAT TO BRING
Macau is a perfectly modern place and you'll be able to buy whatever you need.

TOURIST OFFICES
Local Tourist Offices
The Macau Government Tourist Office (☎ 315566) is at Largo do Senado, Edificio Ritz No 9, next to the Leal Senado building in the square in the centre of Macau. This office is open Monday to Friday from 9 am to 1 pm, and 3 to 5.30 pm. It's also open on Saturday from 9 am to 12.30 pm.

There is a small but very helpful tourist information counter right at the Jetfoil Pier. They can answer questions and issue maps and other brochures.

Overseas Reps
On Hong Kong Island there's an excellent Macau Government Tourist Office (☎ 5408180) at Room 305, Shun Tak Centre, 200 Connaught Rd, next to the Macau Ferry Pier. If you're taking the jetfoil or ferry to Macau, you can collect all the MGTO literature and read it while you're on the boat. The MGTO is closed for lunch from 1 to 2 pm. Macau also maintains overseas tourist representative offices as follows:

Australia
  Macau Tourist Information Bureau, 449 Darling St, Balmain, Sydney, NSW 2041 (☎ (02) 5557548)
Canada
  Macau Tourist Information Bureau, Suite 305, 1530 West 8th Ave, Vancouver, BC V6J 1T5 (☎ (604) 7361095
  5059 Yonge St, Toronto, Ontario (☎ (416) 7338768)
France
  Portuguese National Tourist Office, 7 Rue Scribe, 75009 Paris (☎ 7425557)

Germany
  Portuguese National Tourist Office, Kaiserstrasse 66-IV, 6000 Frankfurt/Main (☎ (0611) 234094)
Japan
  Macau Tourist Information Bureau, 4th floor, Toho Twin Tower Building, 5-2 Yurakucho 1-chome, Chiyoda-ku, Tokyo 100 (☎ (03) 35015022)
Singapore
  Macau Tourist Information Bureau, 11-01A PIL Building, 140 Cecil St, Singapore 0106 (☎ 2250022)
Thailand
  Macau Tourist Information Bureau, 150/5 Sukhumvit 20, Bangkok 10110, or GPO Box 1534, Bangkok 10501 (☎ 2581975)
UK
  Macau Tourist Information Bureau, 6 Sherlock Mews, Paddington St, London W1M 3RH (☎ (071) 2243390)
USA
  Macau Tourist Information Bureau, 3133 Lake Hollywood Drive, Los Angeles, CA, or PO Box 1860, Los Angeles, CA 90078 (☎ (213) 8513684, (800) 3317150)
  Suite 316, 70A Greenwich Ave, New York, NY 10011 (☎ (212) 2066828)
  630 Green Bay Rd, PO Box 350, Kenilworth, IL 60043-0350 (☎ (708) 2516421)
  PO Box 22188, Honolulu, HI 96922 (☎ (808) 5887613)

BUSINESS HOURS & HOLIDAYS
The operating hours for most government offices in Macau are weekdays from 8.40 am to 1 pm and 3 to 5 pm, and Saturday from 8.40 am to 1 pm. Private businesses keep longer hours and some casinos are open 24 hours a day.

Banks are normally open on weekdays from 9 am to 4 pm, and on Saturdays from 9 am until noon.

Chinese in Macau celebrate the same religious festivals as their counterparts in Hong Kong, but there are several Catholic festivals and some Portuguese national holidays too. The tourist newspaper *Macau Travel Talk*, available from the Macau Tourist Office, has a regular listing of events and festivals. Here are some of the more important holidays in Macau. See the Hong Kong Facts for the Visitor chapter for details about Chinese holidays.

New Year's Day – the first day of the year is a public holiday.

Chinese New Year – as in Hong Kong, this is a three-day public holiday in late January or early February.

Lantern Festival – not a public holiday, but a lot of fun, this festival occurs two weeks after the Chinese New Year. See the Hong Kong Facts for the Visitor chapter.

Procession of Our Lord of Passion – not a public holiday, but interesting to watch. The procession begins in the evening from St Augustine's Church and goes to the Macau Cathedral. The statue is kept in the cathedral overnight and the procession returns to St Augustine's the following day.

Feast of the Earth God Tou Tei – a minor holiday for the Chinese community in March or April.

Ching Ming Festival – a major public holiday in April. See the Facts about Hong Kong chapter.

Easter – a four-day public holiday starting on Good Friday and lasting through Monday.

Anniversary of the 1974 Portuguese Revolution – this public holiday on 25 April commemorates the overthrow of the Michael Caetano regime in Portugal in 1974 by a left-wing military coup.

Procession of Our Lady of Fatima – celebrated on 13 May, this commemorates a miracle that took place at Fatima, Portugal, in 1917. It is not a public holiday. The procession begins from Santa Domingo Church and ends at Penha Church.

A-Ma Festival – this is the same as the Tin Hau Festival in Hong Kong and occurs in May. It's not a public holiday.

Festival of Tam Kong – a relatively minor holiday usually celebrated in May.

Camoes & Portuguese Communities Day – held on 10 June, this public holiday commemorates 16th-century poet Luis de Camoes.

Dragon Boat Festival – as in Hong Kong, this is a major public holiday held in June.

Procession of St John the Baptist – the procession for the patron saint of Macau is held on 10 June.

Feast of St Anthony of Lisbon – this June event celebrates the birthday of the patron saint of Lisbon. A military captain, St Anthony receives his wages on this day from a delegation of city officials, and a small parade is held from St Anthony's Church. This is not a public holiday.

Battle of 13 July – celebrated only on the islands of Taipa and Coloane, this holiday commemorates the final defeat of pirates in 1910.

Ghost Month – this festival, in August or September, is an excellent time to visit temples in Macau. See the Hong Kong Facts for the Visitor chapter.

Mid-Autumn Festival – a major public holiday in September. See the Facts about Hong Kong chapter.

Portuguese Republic Day – a public holiday on 5 October.

Cheung Yeung Festival – a public holiday in October. See the Hong Kong Facts for the Visitor chapter.

All Saints' Day – held on 1 November. Both All Saints' Day and the following day *(All Souls' Day)* are public holidays.

Portuguese Independence Day – celebrated on 1 December, this is a public holiday.

Winter Solstice – not a public holiday, but an interesting time to visit Macau. Many Macau Chinese consider the winter solstice more important than the Chinese New Year. There is plenty of feasting and temples are crammed with worshippers.

Christmas – both the 24 and 25 December are public holidays.

CULTURAL EVENTS

Find out about cultural events, concerts, art exhibitions and other such activities from the tourist newspaper *Macau Travel Talk*. Free copies are available from the tourist office.

The Dragon Boat Festival is a Chinese holiday well known for its exciting dragon boat races. Similar races are held in Hong Kong and Taiwan. The Dragon Boat Festival is scheduled according to the lunar calendar, but usually falls sometime during June.

The Miss Macau Contest is held every August. Whether this a cultural or anticultural event depends on one's point of view.

The International Music Festival is held during the third week of October.

POST & TELECOMMUNICATIONS

The postal service is efficient and the clerks can speak English. Apart from a few main post offices, there are also numerous mini-post offices throughout Macau. These are little red booths that sell stamps.

	China	Portugal	Zone 1	Zone 2
Grams				
10	1.70	3.00	3.50	4.20
20	2.70	4.70	4.80	6.10
30	3.70	6.40	6.10	8.00
40	4.70	8.10	7.40	9.90
50	5.70	9.80	8.70	11.80
Aero-grams	1.30	1.90	2.50	3.20

Postal Rates

Domestic letters cost M$0.80 for up to 20 grams. As for international mail, Macau divides the world into zones. Zone 1 is east Asia, including Korea, Taiwan, etc. Zone 2 is everything else. There are special rates for China and Portugal. The rates for letters are as follows:

Sending Mail

The GPO on Leal Senado is open from 9 am to 8 pm, Monday to Saturday. Large hotels like the Lisboa also sell stamps and postcards and can post letters for you.

Receiving Mail

The General Post Office is in Leal Senado Square on Avenida de Almeida Ribeiro. The GPO has an efficient poste-restante service and English-speaking postal clerks.

Telephone

Macau's telephone monopoly is Companhia de Telecomunicacoes (CTM). For the most part service is good, but public pay phones can be hard to find, being mostly concentrated around the Leal Senado. Most large hotels have one in the lobby, but this is often insufficient and you may have to stand in line to use it. However, once you find a phone, it generally works OK.

Local calls are free from a private or hotel telephone. At a public pay phone, local calls cost M$1 for five minutes. All pay phones permit international direct dialling (IDD). The procedure for dialling to Hong Kong is totally different than for all other countries. You first dial 01 and then the number you want to call − you must *not* dial the country code.

The international access code for every country *except* Hong Kong is 00, after which you must dial the country code, the area code and then finally the number you wish to reach. If the area code begins with a zero, omit the first zero. To call into Macau from abroad, the country code is 853.

You can call home collect or use a credit card by using the 'home direct' system. This method only works for a few countries. You need to dial an access code, and then an operator from your home country will come on the line and ask which number you want to reach and how you want to charge the call. The access codes are as follows:

Country	Code
Australia	0800-610
Canada	0800-100
Holland	0800-310
Hong Kong	0800-852
Japan	0800-810
Portugal	0800-351
Singapore	0800-650
South Korea	0800-820
USA	0800-111

You'll need a big pocket full of change to make an IDD call unless you buy a telephone card from CTM. These are sold in denominations of M$50, M$100 and M$200.

Phones which accept these cards are numerous around Leal Senado, the Jetfoil Pier and at a few large hotels.

Yet another way is to make a call from the telephone office at Leal Senado, next to the GPO. The way to do it is to leave a deposit with a clerk and they will dial your number. When your call is completed the clerk deducts the cost from the deposit and refunds the balance. The clerks speak English and the office is open 24 hours. There is another telephone office north of the Lisboa Hotel on Avenida do Dr Rodrigo Rodriques, but this one is open only from 9 am to 8 pm, Monday to Saturday.

Fax, Telex & Telegraph

Unless you're staying at a hotel that has its own fax, the easiest way to send and receive faxes is at the GPO (not the telephone office) on Leal Senado. The number for receiving faxes at this office is ☎ (853) 550117, but check because the number can change. The person sending the fax must put your name and hotel telephone on top of the message so the postal workers can find you. The cost for receiving a fax is M$7.50 regardless of the number of pages.

Telex messages are sent from the telephone office next to the GPO. The telephone office also handles telegrams (cables).

TIME

Like Hong Kong, Macau is eight hours ahead of Greenwich Mean Time and does not observe daylight savings time.

When it is noon in Macau it is also noon in Singapore, Hong Kong and Perth; 2 pm in Sydney; 8 pm the previous day in Los Angeles; 11 pm the previous day in New York; and 4 am in London.

ELECTRICITY

Macau's electricity system is the same as in Hong Kong and China – 220 V AC, 50 Hz. The electric outlets are the same as Hong Kong's, that is, they accept three round pins. There are still a few old buildings wired for 110 V, but as long as you see three round holes on the outlets you can be assured it's 220 V.

Macau supplies 90% of its own power while the rest comes from China.

WEIGHTS & MEASURES

Macau subscribes to the international metric system. As in Hong Kong, street markets and medicine shops sell things by the *leung* (37.5 grams) and the *catty* (600 grams). There is a metric/imperial conversion chart at the back of the book.

BOOKS & MAPS

Books about Macau are scarce. Much of what's been published is in Portuguese, but there are a few good books in English.

People & Society

There are several pictorial coffee-table books about Macau. One such book, simply called *Macau*, is by Jean-Yves Defay. Another, also called *Macau*, is by Leong Ka Tai & Shann Davies and is part of the Times Editions series. It's an excellent hardback pictorial and history of the colony.

A good coffee-table sketchbook of the colony is *Old Macau* by Tom Briggs and Colin Crisswell, published by South China Morning Post.

A Macao Narrative (Oxford University Press) is by Austin Coates, a well-known Hong Kong magistrate, who also wrote *City of Broken Promises*.

Another good book with the title of *Macau* is by Cesar Guillen-Nuñez (Oxford University Press).

Novels set in Macau are rare, but there is one, also entitled *Macau* (Corgi Books) by Daniel Carney.

History

Historic Macau (Oxford University Press, Hong Kong, 1984) by C A Montalto de Jesus was first published in 1902 as a history of the colony. In 1926 the author added extra chapters in which he suggested that the Portuguese government cared so little about the colony and did so little to meet its needs that it would be better if Macau was administered by the League of Nations. The Portuguese government was outraged and copies of the book were seized and destroyed. The book can be bought at the Luis de Camoes Museum in Macau.

Travel Guides

Absolutely essential for anyone who is considering gambling at Macau's casinos is the *Macau AOA Gambling Handbook*. This comes as part of a set which includes the *Macau Pictorial Guide* and an excellent map of Macau. The whole package only costs HK$20 and is available from most of the main bookstores in Hong Kong. If not, you could try the Macau Tourist Office in Hong Kong or go directly to the publisher, AOA Ltd (☎ 3890352), 10th floor, 174 Wai Yip St, Kwun Tong, Hong Kong.

Behind the service counter at the Macau Government Tourist Office on Leal Senado, there is a small collection of books and other goods for sale. Check their list to see what is currently available. At the time this book was being researched, they had the following books for sale: *A Glimpse of Glory (M$50); Chronicles in Stone* (M$20); *Images in Asia* (M$55); *Seventeenth Century Macau* (M$70); *The Chinese Temple of Barra* (M$12); *The Church of St Paul* (M$7); *The Fortification of Macau* (M$15); *Macau in 50 Ways* (M$13); *An Illustrated Guide to Macau* (M$60).

Bookshops

There are few shops in Macau that carry English-language books, and those few only have a limited selection. The easiest to find is Livraria Sao Paulo, 115 Rua da Praia Grande. Most of the books are in Portuguese and oriented towards the Catholic Church, but they have some general interest English-language books and good maps of Macau. They also stock Lonely Planet guides.

The Portuguese Bookshop & Cultural Centre has some books in English as well as Portuguese. It's on Rua Pedro Nolasco da Silva near the Cathedral.

Maps

The best map of Macau I've seen is the *Map of Macau & Zhuhai* published by Universal Publications Ltd. These are more easily obtained in Hong Kong than in Macau. Main Hong Kong bookstores such as Swindon's should have it. The map has a complete street index on the back, shows the bus routes and has streets labelled in both Chinese characters and Portuguese.

Finally, you can get a free *Mapa Turistico* from the Macau Tourist Office. It's a fairly basic map but includes all the essential sights. Unfortunately, it lacks bus routes.

Another good map is the *Tourist Map of Macau* (Carta Turistica de Macau). It's easily obtained in Macau and the map has both English and Chinese characters and shows bus routes. Unfortunately, it does not have a street index.

Another is *Streetwise Macau* by Eric Stone. It shows the location of restaurants, hotels, casinos and other things of interest to tourists. Not bad, but it would be nice if it were more detailed.

Many bookstores in Macau sell the *Map of Macau, Shenzhen, Zhongshan*. Unfortunately, this map is mostly in Chinese characters.

MEDIA

Newspapers & Magazines

Other than the monthly tourist newspaper *Macau Travel Talk*, there is no English-language newspaper published in Macau. However, both the *South China Morning Post* and *Hong Kong Standard* are readily available from big hotels and some bookstores. It's also easy to buy foreign news magazines.

Radio & TV

Macau has three radio stations, two of which broadcast in Cantonese and one in Portuguese. There are no local English-language radio stations, but you should be able to pick up Hong Kong stations.

Teledifusao de Macau (TdM) is a government-run TV station which broadcasts on two channels. Shows are mainly in English and Portuguese, but with some Cantonese programmes. It's easy to pick up Hong Kong stations in Macau (but not vice versa) and you can also receive stations from China. Hong Kong newspapers list Macau TV programmes.

FILM & PHOTOGRAPHY
You can find most types of film, cameras and accessories in Macau, and photo processing is of a high standard. The best store in town for all photographic services is Foto Princesa (☎ 555959), 55-59 Avenida Infante D Henrique, one block east of Rua do Praia Grande. This is also the best place to get quickie visa photos.

HEALTH
Vaccinations and inoculation certificates are not normally required unless cholera has been detected in Hong Kong or Macau or if you're arriving from an infected area.

About 90% of Macau's water supply is pumped from a reservoir 13 km away in China. The water is purified and chlorinated and is probably OK to drink. Nevertheless, the Chinese always boil it (more out of custom than necessity). Hotel rooms are always supplied with a thermos filled with hot water, so you might as well take advantage of it just to be on the safe side. Distilled water is widely available from grocery stores.

For more details on health see the Health section in the Hong Kong Facts for the Visitor chapter.

EMERGENCY
The emergency telephone number for fire, police and ambulance is ☎ 999.

There are two government-run hospitals. English is mainly spoken at the Government (Centro) Hospital (☎ 514499, 313731), just on Estrada Sao Francisco, north of the Hotel Lisboa. Chinese-speaking people are usually treated at the Kiang Vu Hospital (☎ 371333) on Estrada do Repouso and Rua Coelho do Amaral.

WOMEN TRAVELLERS
Wearing a skimpy bikini at the beach will elicit some stares, but travel in Macau is as safe for women as in any Western country.

DANGERS & ANNOYANCES
In terms of violent crime, Macau is pretty safe, but residential burglaries and pick-pocketing are problems. Most hotels are well-guarded, and reasonable care with your valuables should be sufficient to avoid trouble.

Traffic is heavy and quite a few tourists have been hit while jaywalking. Macau police have been cracking down on jaywalking, and although they go light with foreigners, you can still get fined. Be especially careful at rush hour when the traffic (and the police) comes out in force.

Cheating at gambling is a serious criminal offence, so don't even think about it.

WORK
Unless you hold a Portuguese passport, you can pretty much forget it. Most Portuguese speak excellent English, so there is little need to import foreign English teachers. Most of the foreigners employed in Macau are Thai prostitutes and Filipino musicians. Unskilled labour is supplied by Chinese workers from nearby Zhuhai, who are paid a pittance.

ACTIVITIES
Windsurfing is possible at Hac Sa Beach on Coloane Island, and equipment is readily available for rent. There are two good swimming beaches on Coloane, Hac Sa and Cheoc Van. Cheoc Van Beach also has a yacht club.

Bicycles are available for hire on the two islands of Taipa and Coloane.

HIGHLIGHTS
Although gambling is what draws most people to Macau, the fine colonial architecture is what makes this place unique. Highlights include the Ruins of Sao Paulo, Fortaleza do Monte, Guia Fortress, Leal Senado and the Penha Church. St Michael Cemetery is a fascinating place to walk through, and many visitors are impressed by

Ma Kok Miu (A-Ma Temple). Taipa Village on Taipa Island is unique, and there is no better way to round off a trip to Macau than a fine meal at a Portuguese restaurant.

ACCOMMODATION
Hostels
There is one youth hostel in Macau, and a very nice one too, but you're not likely to get much use of it. For one thing, it's not on the peninsula, but out by Cheoc Van Beach near the southern end of Coloane Island. See the following Macau Islands chapter.

Hotels
Really cheap accommodation is a little harder to find in Macau than in Hong Kong. If you're looking for dirt-cheap dormitories, then you'll be disappointed. Nevertheless, with some effort you can find low to middle-priced single and double rooms in Macau during weekdays.

Weekends and holidays are another matter. Room prices double and accommodation of any kind is difficult to get. For definition purposes, 'weekend' means both Saturday and Sunday nights. Friday night is usually not a problem unless it's also a holiday. Also, during special events like the Macau Grand Prix, rooms can be impossible to obtain.

Another way to save money is to avoid the peak season (summer). Peak-season prices are quoted in this book because that's when most travellers will visit, but be aware that you can get substantial discounts in winter (except during Chinese New Year). For example, the Hotel Estoril quoted M$330 for a double when I visited in August but was asking only M$150 for weekdays in January.

The problem with tight accommodation has created a false impression that many hotels do not rent to foreigners. We have received several letters from travellers advising us that certain hotels recommended in this book no longer allow non-Chinese. This is not so. The problem here is the language barrier. What happens is that you show up at the door, and the manager comes out waving his arm while saying 'No, no!' This means 'no rooms', not 'no foreigners'. Unfortunately, for many of Macau's non-Portuguese majority, the only English sentences they've learned are 'No!' and 'Give me the money!'.

Most hotels in the mid-price range and above charge a 5% government room tax plus a 10% service charge.

FOOD
For some travellers, eating is the most rewarding part of a trip to Macau. Given its cosmopolitan past, it's not surprising that the food is an exotic mixture of Portuguese and Chinese cooking. There is also a little influence from other European countries and Africa.

The most famous local speciality is African chicken baked with peppers and chillies. Other specialties include *bacalhau*, which is cod, served baked, grilled, stewed or boiled. The cod is imported and rather salty. Sole, a tongue-shaped flatfish, is another Macanese delicacy. There's also ox tail and ox breast, rabbit prepared in various ways, and soups like *caldo verde* and *sopa a alentejana* made with vegetables, meat and olive oil. The Brazilian contribution is *feijoadas*, a stew made of beans, pork, potatoes, cabbage and spicy sausages. The contribution from the former Portuguese enclave of Goa on the west coast of India is spicy prawns.

Apart from cod and prawns, there's other seafood aplenty – shrimp, crab, squid and white fish. You won't find Macau's baked crab or huge grilled and stuffed king prawns anywhere else. There are lots of little seafood restaurants where you can pick your meal from the tank at the front of the shop.

If you're going out for a meal, it's worth remembering that people eat early in Macau – the dining room is clear and the chef has gone home by 9 pm. The Macau Tourist Office publishes a useful free leaflet called *Eating Out in Macau* which lists the more established restaurants in the city.

DRINKS
The Portuguese influence is most visible in the many fine imported Portuguese red and

white wines, port and brandy. Wines are cheap. Mateus Rose is the most famous and you can buy it for about M$23 a bottle in the wine shops. Even cheaper is a bottle of red or white wine, drinkable for those not heavily into chateau wines.

Spirits and beer are cheaper in Macau than in Hong Kong – even cheaper than at duty-free stores. Wine prices vary in the restaurants but are usually not too expensive. Many people leave the place with a bottle of Mateus tucked under their arm.

ENTERTAINMENT
Gambling

I once worked in a Las Vegas casino as a slot machine mechanic and later as a slot machine attendant. During that time I saw humanity at its worst.

Although the games in Macau are somewhat different from Las Vegas, the same basic principles apply. The most important principle to remember is this – if you want to win at gambling, buy a casino. In every game, the casino enjoys a built-in mathematical advantage. The casinos don't cheat the players because they don't have to. In the short-term, anyone can hit a winning streak

and get ahead, but the longer you play, the more certain it is that the odds will catch up with you. There is no system that can help you win. I know of one Las Vegas casino that caught a woman with a portable computer in her handbag, but they let her go because, as the manager said, 'a computer won't help'.

Your best bet is to gamble for fun only. Don't bet more than you can afford to lose and don't think you can 'make up your losses' by gambling more. If you win, consider yourself lucky – this time.

The most popular form of gambling in Macau is mahjong, played not in the casinos but in private homes. You can hear the rattle of mahjong pieces late into the night if you walk through any side street.

The legal gambling age in Macau is 18 for foreigners and 21 for Macau residents. Photography is absolutely prohibited inside the casinos.

If you want to play casino games which are more sophisticated than the slot machines, it's essential that you track down a copy of the *Macau AOA Gambling Handbook*.

Slot Machines These are the classic sucker games in any casino. Maybe the reason why slot machines are so popular is because it takes no brains to play – just put the coin in the slot and pull the handle. Some machines allow you to put in up to five coins at a time, which increases your chance of winning by five times (but costs you five times as much, so you're no better off). Contrary to popular belief, how hard or gently you pull the handle has no influence on the outcome. There are many small payoffs to encourage you to keep playing, but the goal of every slot player is to hit the grand jackpot (or megabucks as it is called in Macau).

The odds for winning on a slot machine are terrible. Usually machines are designed to give the casino a 25% advantage over the player. It's easy to win small payoffs, but the odds of hitting the grand jackpot are very small indeed. It's like spinning five roulette wheels at once and expecting them all to land on number seven. The more reels on the machine, the more unlikely they will line up for the ultimate payoff. Three-reel machines give you one chance in 8000 of hitting the jackpot. You have one chance in 160,000 of lining up four reels. If you play a five-reel machine, your chances of lining up all five winning numbers is one in 3.2 million.

Contrary to popular belief, slot machines are not controlled by computers, magnets or any other sophisticated device. The machines are as simple as a pair of dice. Another popular myth is that the machines will eventually fill up with money and then pay out. Neither is this true. When the machine is full, coins overflow down a tube into a bucket placed under the machine. The buckets are inside the cabinets that the machines rest on. The cabinets are unlocked and the buckets are emptied at about 4 am when the casino is nearly deserted.

Buckets filled with coins are heavy – one was dropped on my foot and broke my big toe. To this day, the toenail has not grown back.

If you do hit a jackpot, don't move away from the machine. Bells will ring, lights will flash, and a slot machine attendant will come running over to pay you in bills because the machine cannot possibly hold enough coins to pay a large jackpot.

Some customers attempt to cheat the machines by inserting metal wires or pouring Coca-Cola into the coin slot hoping that the machine will malfunction and pay out. This is illegal, but creates employment for slot machine mechanics.

Blackjack Also known as 21, this card game is easy to play, although it requires a little skill. The dealer takes a card and also gives one to the player. Each card counts for a particular number of points. The goal is to get enough cards to add up as close as possible to 21 without going over. If you go over 21, then you 'bust' which means you lose. If both you and the dealer go bust at the same time, the dealer still wins and this is what gives the casino the edge over the player. If the dealer and player both get 21, it's a tie

and the bet is cancelled. If the player gets 21 (blackjack) then he or she gets even money plus a 50% bonus.

Dealers must draw until they reach 16 and stand on 17 or higher. The player is free to decide when to stand or when to draw.

You may occasionally see a book or newspaper article describing a system for beating the casinos at blackjack. Such a system does exist and is called card counting. To do it you need a good memory and a quick mind. Basically, if you can remember which cards have been dealt from the deck you will know which cards still remain. As the dealer nears the end of the deck, you can make very good guesses about which cards remain and therefore estimate your chances of going bust and know when to stand and when to draw. When you're sure that you can beat the dealer's hand, you bet heavily.

It sounds great. The problem is it no longer works because to defeat card counters the casino dealers play with multiple decks and reshuffle the cards frequently.

Roulette This is a very easy game to play and I don't know why it isn't more popular in Macau. The dealer simply spins the roulette wheel in one direction and spins a ball in the opposite direction. Macau roulette wheels have 36 numbers plus a zero, so your chance of hitting any given number is one in 37. The pay-off is 35 to one which is what gives the casino its advantage.

Rather than betting a single number, it's much easier to win if you bet odd or even, or red versus black numbers. If the ball lands on zero, everyone loses to the house (unless you also bet the zero). If you bet red or black, odd or even, the casino's advantage is only 2.7%.

Very similar to roulette is boule. In fact it's identical except that it's played with a large ball about the size of a billiard ball. There are fewer numbers too. In Macau, boule has 24 numbers plus a star. The pay-off is 23 to one on numbers. On all bets (numbers, red or black, odd or even) the casino has a 4% advantage over the players. The minimum bet for boule in Macau is M$10.

Craps This game is extremely popular in the West and I don't know why it's rare in Macau. In fact, on my last trip to Macau I didn't see a single craps table and I wonder if they've been done away with. Maybe the casinos prefer not to have this game because the house has such a small advantage – only about 1.4%.

Craps is played with a pair of dice which are tossed down a long and narrow table. The dice are thrown by the players, not the dealers, so there is more of a feeling of participation. The person tossing the dice, the shooter, is permitted to shoot until he or she loses, then the dice are passed to the next player at the table in a counter-clockwise direction.

This game is more complicated than most. On the first roll (the 'come-out' roll) the shooter automatically wins if he or she throws a seven or 11. If a two, three or 12 is thrown on the first roll, it's an automatic loss. Any other number results in a point. The shooter must continue to toss the dice until the point is thrown again. However, if a seven is rolled before the point is made, then it's a loss. This method of betting is called betting the 'come' or 'front line'.

There are other ways to play. You can also bet that the shooter will lose (don't come) or that a pair of fours (a hard eight) will be thrown before other combinations adding up to eight (a soft eight). The complexity of the game is one of its attractions. If a shooter gets hot (wins several rolls in succession) the game gets exciting with lots of players jumping up and down and yelling. The exhilaration probably explains why craps is a favourite with compulsive gamblers.

Baccarat Also known as chemin de fer, this has become the card game of choice for the upper crust. Baccarat rooms are always the most classy part of any casino and the minimum wager is high, at least M$50 and up to M$1000 in some casinos.

Two card hands are dealt at the same time – the player hand and the bank hand. The hand which scores closest to nine is the winner. Players can bet on either their own hand or the bank hand. Neither is actually the house hand. The casino deducts a percentage if the bank hand wins, which is how the house makes its profit.

If the player understands the game properly, the house only enjoys slightly better than a 1% advantage over the player.

Fan Tan This is an ancient Chinese game practically unknown in the West. The dealer takes an inverted silver cup and plunges it into a pile of porcelain buttons, then moves the cup to one side. After all bets have been placed, the buttons are counted out in groups of four. You have to bet on how many will remain after the last set of four has been taken out. You can bet on numbers one, two, three or four, as well as odd or even. The minimum bet is M$20.

Dai Siu This is Cantonese for 'big-small'. The game is also known as *sik po* (dice treasure) or *cu sik* (guessing dice). It's extremely popular in Macau.

The game is played with three dice which are placed in a covered glass container. The container is then shaken. You then bet that the total of the toss will be from three to nine (small) or from 10 to 18 (big). However, you lose on combinations where all three dice come up the same, like 2-2-2, 3-3-3, etc, unless you bet directly on three of a kind.

For betting 'big-small' the house advantage is 2.78%. Betting on a specific three of a kind gives the house a 30% advantage – a sucker bet.

Pai Kao This is Chinese dominoes and reminds me a lot of mahjong. One player is designated the role of banker and the other players individually compare their hands against the banker. The casino doesn't play, but deducts a 3% commission from the winnings for providing the gambling facilities.

Keno Although keno is played in Las Vegas and other Western casinos, it's believed to have originated in China more than 2000 years ago. Keno was introduced to North

America by Chinese railway workers in the 19th century.

Keno is basically a lottery. There are 80 numbers of which 20 are drawn in each game. You are given a keno ticket and the object is to list as many numbers as you think will be drawn. You can bet on four numbers and if all four are among those drawn in the game, you're a winner. You can play five numbers, six, seven and so on. You have about one chance in nine million of guessing all 20 winning numbers. With only about two drawings per hour, it's a slow way to lose your money. I consider keno to be the most boring game in the casino.

Dog Racing Macau has a canidrome – that's what they call it – for dog racing. It's off Avenida General Castelo Branco not far from the Barrier Gate. Bus Nos 1, 1A, 2, 3, 4, 5, 6, 8 and 9 stop nearby it. Greyhound races are held four times a week on Tuesday, Thursday, Saturday and Sunday starting at 8 pm. There are 14 races per night with six to eight dogs per race. Admission to the Canidrome costs M$2, or M$5 in the members stand, or there are boxes for six people costing M$80 per group.

Off-Course Betting Centres will accept bets starting from 5 pm. The centres are in the Hotel Lisboa, Kam Pek Casino and Casino Pelota Basca.

Horse Racing The Macau Jockey Club opened a track on Taipa Island in 1991. The five-storey grandstands can accommodate 15,000 spectators and are air-conditioned. Unlike the race tracks at Hong Kong's Happy Valley and Shatin, the Macau Jockey Club operates throughout the summer. Now Hong Kongers can lose their money any season of the year.

Horse racing has a long history in Macau. In the early 1800s horse races were held outside the city walls on an impromptu course. You may notice on the Macau map that there is a street called Estrada Marginal do Hipodromo in the extreme north-east corner of town near the Barrier Gate. This

was a popular race course in the 1930s, but the area has now been taken over by flats and factories.

Want to visit Macau for free? All you've got to do is buy HK$5000 worth of gambling chips and the Hotel Lisboa will provide you with a free jetfoil ticket. Buy HK$30,000 worth of chips and they'll give you a free night's accommodation as well. It doesn't stipulate that you actually have to lose the chips although I guess they'd like it if you did. The proliferation of pawnshops around the casinos would seem to indicate that some people do lose the lot.

Grand Prix
The biggest event of the year is no doubt the Macau Grand Prix. As in Monaco, the streets of the town make up the race track. The six-km circuit starts near the Hotel Lisboa and follows the shoreline along Avenida da Amizade, going around the reservoir and back through the city.

The Grand Prix consists of two major races – one for cars and one for motorcycles. Both races attract many international contestants. Pedicab races are included as a novelty event.

The race is a two-day event held on the third weekend in November. More than 50,000 people flock to see the Grand Prix, and accommodation, a problem on normal weekends, becomes as rare as a three-humped camel. Be sure to book a return ticket on the jetcat or jetfoil if you have to return to Hong Kong. If you don't book, you may still be able to squeeze on board one of the ferries. Otherwise, if you have a China visa, you might consider making your exit through the People's Republic and staying at a hotel in Zhuhai. Ferries connect Zhuhai to Shenzhen and Hong Kong.

Certain areas in Macau are designated as viewing areas for the races. Streets and alleyways along the track are blocked off, so it's unlikely you'll be able to get a good view without paying. Prices for seats in the Reservoir stand are M$175 for adults, M$88 for children; in the Lisboa stand, M$520; in the Mandarin Oriental stand, M$520; and in the Grandstand, M$575.

If, one week after the Grand Prix, you still

haven't managed to get out of Macau (a possibility), you can join the Macau Marathon. Like the Grand Prix, this race is attracting a lot of international attention. It's held in the first week of December.

THINGS TO BUY

Pawnshops are ubiquitous in Macau, and it is possible to get good deals on cameras, but you must be prepared to bargain without mercy. In Macau pawnshops, it's no holds barred. These guys would sell their own mother to a glue factory.

I saw a nice camera – a Ricoh KR-5 – in a pawnshop window with a M$850 price tag. That's about how much it cost new, and this camera was eight years old! After examining it, I found the automatic timer was broken. After an exhaustive bargaining session, I got the price down to M$600. I bought the camera and the next day had it appraised at a camera shop. They told me I shouldn't have paid more than M$200. Just for fun, I took it over to another pawnshop and asked how much they would give me for it. They said it was worth M$50.

The Macau Government Tourist Office has T-shirts for sale at the bargain price of M$25. They also sell a set of poster-size 'antique maps of Macau' (M$150), a set of postcards (M$5), umbrellas (M$30) and raincoats (M$35).

Getting There & Away

Macau has a very small land border with China and most arrivals are by sea from Hong Kong. You won't see any huge cruise ships in Macau simply because the harbour isn't deep enough to accommodate them. However, a wide variety of small craft use Macau's harbour. Some business consortiums have been talking about creating a deep-water port on the east side of Coloane Island. This would involve an expensive dredging project, but so far it's just talk.

AIR
To/From Hong Kong
Helicopter For people in a hurry to lose their money, East Asia Airlines runs a helicopter service between Hong Kong and Macau. Flying time from Hong Kong is 20 minutes at a cost of HK$830 on weekdays, M$930 on weekends – quite an expense just to save the extra 30 minutes required by boat. There are at least four flights daily, and departures are from the ferry piers in both Hong Kong and Macau. You can get the tickets in Hong Kong (☎ 8593359) at counter 8, Shun Tak Centre, 200 Connaught Rd, Sheung Wan, Hong Kong Island. In Macau, you can book at the Jetfoil Pier (☎ 572983).

LAND
To/From China
From Gongbei in the Zhuhai Special Economic Zone, simply walk across the border, which is open from 7 am until 9 pm.

There is a bus from Macau to Canton, but it's more hassle than it's worth. The bus stops at the border for over an hour while all the passengers go through immigration and custom formalities. It would be easier to take a bus to the border, walk across, and catch a minibus to Canton from the other side. However, if you prefer the 'direct' bus, tickets are sold at Kee Kwan Motors, across the street from the Floating Casino. Buses leave daily at 7 am and noon, taking about six hours. Tickets cost M$37.

SEA
To/From Hong Kong
Although Macau is separated from Hong Kong by 65 km of water, the journey can be made in as little as one hour. There is a variety of sea vessels plying this route, the fastest and smoothest being the jetfoils and jumbocats. There are frequent departures throughout the day from 7 am to 9.30 pm.

You have a wide selection of boats to choose from. There are jetfoils, hoverferries, jetcats (jet-powered catamaran), jumbocats (large jetcat) and high-speed ferries. There are still two old hydrofoils plying this route, but they are to be retired soon and will probably be out of service by the time you read this. The fastest and most popular boats are the jetfoils and jumbocats.

Most of the boats depart from the huge Hong Kong-Macau Ferry Terminal next to Shun Tak Centre at 200 Connaught Rd, Sheung Wan, Hong Kong Island. This is easily reached by MTR to Sheung Wan Station.

Hoverferries depart from the China-Hong Kong Ferry Terminal in Tsimshatsui. However, these are far less numerous than jetfoils, so if you can't get a seat, go to Shun Tak Centre on Hong Kong Island.

Luggage space on the jetfoils is limited to what you can carry. You'll be OK just carrying a backpack or one suitcase, but no way will they let you on with a trunk or something requiring two people to move it.

If you have to return to Hong Kong the same day as departure, you'd be wise to book your return ticket in advance because the boats are sometimes full, especially on weekends and holidays. Even Monday mornings can be difficult for getting seats back to Hong Kong. If you can't get on the jetfoil, you might have a chance with the high-speed ferries which have a lot more room.

Jetfoil tickets can be purchased up to 28 days in advance in Hong Kong at the Hong

Kong-Macau Ferry Terminal and at Ticketmate offices in some MTR stations, or booked by phone (☎ 8595696) if you have a credit card. Jumbocat bookings (☎ 5232136) can be made 35 days in advance by telephone if you pay with plastic. If you buy a ticket at any other place than the pier, be certain you understand which pier the boat departs from. You need to arrive at the pier at least 15 minutes before departure, but from my experience you'd be wise to allow 30 minutes because of occasional long queues at the immigration checkpoint.

There are different classes on the jetfoils and hi-speed ferries. All other boats have only one class. The Hong Kong government charges HK$20 departure tax which is included in the price of your ticket. There is no such tax when leaving Macau. The following prices do not include the tax:

In Hong Kong, tickets can be bought at the Hong Kong-Macau Ferry Terminal and at Ticketmate kiosks in the Tsimshatsui and Jordan Rd MTR stations.

In Macau, you can book tickets on all boats up at the Jetfoil Pier. You can also book tickets on the jetfoil and hi-speed ferry right in the lobby of the Hotel Lisboa. A couple of blocks west of the Hotel Central is a window for booking tickets on the jumbocats. Tickets for the hoverferry can only be booked at the pier.

To/From China

From Zhoutouzui Wharf in Canton you can take an overnight ferry directly to Macau. Buy tickets at the wharf or from the large hotels such as the White Swan.

Going the other way, pick up the ferry to Canton at the wharf near the Floating Casino (Macau Palace Casino) in Macau. Departures are at 8 am, arriving in Canton at 7.15 am the next day. Fares range from M$69 in 2nd class, for rooms with six to 22 beds, to M$100 in 1st class for a bed in a room with four beds, a shower and TV. Finally there's also special class, which costs M$147 for a cabin with just two beds, as well as a TV and shower.

There is also a once-daily ferry at 8.30 am from Macau to Shekou in the Shenzhen Special Economic Zone (north of Hong Kong). The fare is M$79.

To/From Taiwan

A ferry runs between Macau and the port of Kaohsiung in southern Taiwan. The name of the ship is the *Macmosa*, a combination of the words Macau and Formosa.

From Taiwan one-way 1st-class tickets cost NT$3700 and the 2nd-class fare is NT$3000. From Macau a one-way 1st-class fare is M$1060; 2nd class is M$860. Round-trip fares are exactly double. There is one boat weekly during the winter, but at least twice weekly during the summer months. The journey takes 24 hours. In winter, the ship leaves Kaohsiung at 4 pm on Wednesday. Departures from Macau are at 2 am on Tuesday. Check departure times – they can change.

In Taiwan you can buy tickets at the pier in Kaohsiung or from Kwanghwa Tour & Travel Service in both Taipei and Kaohsiung. The Taipei office (☎ (02) 5310000) is on the 7th floor, 72 Sungchiang Rd. The Kaohsiung ticket office (☎ (07) 2821166) is on the 6th floor, 79 Chunghua 3rd Rd. In Kaohsiung,

Timetable

Vessel	Travel Time	Weekday	Weekend	Night
Hi-Speed Ferry	90 mins	HK$48/62	HK$60/74	
Hoverferry	80 mins	HK$60	HK$73	HK$86
Hydrofoil	75 mins	HK$68	HK$75	
Jetcat	75 mins	HK$68	HK$75	
Jetfoil	60 mins	HK$72/82	HK$78/88	HK$95/108
Jumbocat	60 mins	HK$78	HK$85	

the boat departs from Pier 1 *(dìyī mătoú)* on Penglai Rd – take bus No 1 or a taxi to get there. In Macau, tickets are most easily purchased at the Jetfoil Pier. In Hong Kong, you can buy tickets at Kwanghwa Tour & Travel Service (☎ 5457071), Room 803, Kai Tak Commercial Building, 317-321 Des Voeux Rd, Central, Hong Kong Island. Taiwan charges a departure tax of NT$200. Macau has no departure tax.

The ticket price entitles you to three free meals. There is also a small shop selling a few snacks, but nothing outstanding. If there's something you particularly crave (chocolate, fruit, biscuits, etc) bring your own. It's wise to bring books or magazines to help pass the time. The only entertainment on board is the karaoke bar and the slot machines in the mini-casino.

Getting Around

It's possible and very pleasant to tour most of the Macau Peninsula on foot. If you want to explore the islands of Taipa and Coloane, you'll have to deal with public transport.

BUS

There are minibuses and large buses, and both offer air-con and frequent services. They operate from 7 am until midnight.

You'll find it easier to deal with the bus system if you buy a good map of Macau showing all the routes. For most tourists, the No 3A bus is the most important since it connects the Jetfoil Pier to the downtown area and Floating Casino.

Here are all the bus routes within the Macau Peninsula. For buses to Taipa and Coloane, see the Macau Islands chapter. The fare on all these buses is M$1.50.

No 1
Fai Chi Kei, Canidrome, Avenida do Almirante Lacerda, Rua do Almirante Sergio, Ma Kok Miu (A-Ma Temple)
No 1A
Jetfoil Pier, Avenida Amizade, Reservoir, Rua dos Pescadores, Canidrome, Rua do Almirante Sergio, A-Ma Temple
No 2
Iao Hon, Canidrome, Rua de Francisco Xavier Pereira, Rua do Campo, Avenida de Almeida Ribeiro, GPO, Floating Casino, A-Ma Temple
No 3
Jetfoil Pier, Avenida de Almeida Ribeiro, GPO, Hotel Grand, Avenida do Almirante Lacerda, Canidrome, Barrier Gate
No 3A
Jetfoil Pier, Avenida do Dr Rodrigo Rodrigues, Avenida Almeida Ribeiro, GPO, Floating Casino, Ponte Praca e Horta
No 4 (loop route)
Fai Chi Kei, Canidrome, Lin Fong Miu (Lotus Temple), Avenida de Horta e Costa, Rua do Campo, Avenida Almeida Ribeiro, GPO, Avenida do Almirante Lacerda, Lin Fong Miu (Lotus Temple), Fai Chi Kei

No 5
A-Ma Temple, Rua das Lorchas, Avenida de Almeida Ribeiro, GPO, Rua da Praia Grande, Rua do Campo, Avenida Horta e Costa, Avenida do Almirante Lacerda, Canidrome, Barrier Gate
No 6 (loop route)
Iao Hon, Avenida do Almirante Lacerda, Floating Casino, Ma Kok Miu (A-Ma Temple), southern tip of Macau Peninsula, Avenida da Republica, Rua da Praia Grande, Estrada de Sao Francisco, Government Hospital, Hotel Royal, Hotel Lisboa, Avenida de Almeida Ribeiro, Avenida do Almirante Lacerda, Canidrome, Iao Hon
No 7
Iao Hon, Rua de Francisco Xavier Pereira, Rua do Campo, Avenida de Almeida Ribeiro, GPO, Floating (Macau Palace) Casino, A-Ma Temple
No 8
Ilha Verde, Canidrome, Lin Fong Miu (Lotus Temple), Vasco da Gama Monument, Avenida de Almeida Ribeiro, A-Ma Temple
No 9 (loop route)
Barrier Gate, Lin Fong Miu (Lotus Temple), Canidrome, Avenida do Almirante Lacerda, Avenida do Ouvidor Arriaga, Vasco da Gama Monument, Hotel Lisboa, Rua da Praia Grande, Avenida da Republica, A-Ma Temple, Floating Casino, Avenida de Almeida Ribeiro, Rua do Campo, Avenida de Horta e Costa, Avenida do Almirante Lacerda, Canidrome, Barrier Gate
No 16 (loop route)
Bairro Tamagnini Barbosa (west of the Barrier Gate), Barrier Gate, Avenida do Almirante Lacerda, Rua do Almirante Sergio, Rua da Praia Grande, Rua do Campo, Avenida do Ouvidor Arriaga, Fai Chi Kei, Bairro Tamagnini Barbosa
No 28B
Ilha Verde, Avenida do Conselheiro Borja, Reservoir, Jetfoil Pier, Hotel Lisboa, Rua da Praia Grande, Penha Church, Pousada de Sao Tiago
No 28C
Jetfoil, Avenida do Dr Rodrigo Rodrigues, Hotel Lisboa, Lou Lim Loc Gardens, Barrier Gate
No 32
Fai Chi Kei, Lin Fong Miu (Lotus Temple), Avenida de Horta e Costa, tunnel (under Guia Fortress), Jetfoil Pier, Hotel Lisboa

TAXI

Macau taxis are black with cream roofs. They all have meters and drivers are required to use them. Flagfall is M$5.50 for the first 1.5 km, thereafter it's 70 avos every 250 metres. There is a M$5 surcharge to go to Taipa and a M$10 surcharge to go to Coloane; there is no surcharge if you're heading the other way back to Macau. There is also an additional M$1 service charge for each piece of luggage carried in the boot (trunk). Not many taxi drivers speak English, so it would be helpful to have a map with both Chinese and English or Portuguese. It can be difficult to get a taxi during rush hour, but otherwise it shouldn't be a problem.

You can hire a taxi and driver for a whole day or half a day. The price as well as the itinerary should be agreed on in advance. Large hotels can usually help you to arrange this.

CAR & MOTORBIKE

For exploring the islands of Taipa and Coloane, renting a car (or moke) is a convenient way to get around if you can afford it. As for driving on the Macau Peninsula, I think it's an insane idea. Taking a bus tour of the peninsula would be cheaper, faster and less aggravating than driving.

Apart from the bumper to bumper traffic, there is really no place to park a car in Macau. To stop to look at something, it's entirely possible that you'll spend more than 30 minutes searching for a parking place and wind up parking several hundred metres from your destination.

While driving on the Macau Peninsula cannot be recommended, a rented car (or moke) can be a convenient, although expensive, way to explore the islands. Dividing the cost amongst several travellers makes it more reasonable.

It appears that motorcycles are impossible to rent unless you have a Macau driver's licence.

Road Rules

Drivers must be at least 21 years of age and must have held a driving licence recognised in Portugal for not less than two years. Portugal recognises the licences of most countries in the world so this shouldn't be a problem. Hong Kongers must have an international driving licence.

As in Hong Kong, driving is on the left side of the road. Another local driving rule is that motor vehicles must always stop for pedestrians at a crosswalk if there is no traffic light. It's illegal to beep the horn. (If only Hong Kong had this rule!)

Police in Macau are strict and there are stiff fines for traffic violators, so obey the rules unless you want to contribute even more to Macau's economy.

Rental

Mokes can also be rented from Macau Mokes Group Ltd (☎ 378851), Avenida Marciano Baptist, just across from the Jetfoil Terminal in Macau. They also have a Hong Kong office (☎ 5434190) at 806 Kai Tak Commercial Building, 317-321 Des Voeux Rd, Sheung Wan, near the Macau Ferry Pier on Hong Kong Island. A moke costs M$280 on weekdays and M$320 on weekends and holidays.

If you're staying at the Mandarin Oriental Hotel, you can rent mokes from Avis Rent-a-Car (☎ 336789, 567888 ext 3004). It's probably not necessary on weekdays, but you can book in advance at the Avis Hong Kong office (☎ 5422189).

BICYCLE

Bicycle rentals are no longer available on the Macau Peninsula. You can still rent bikes on the islands of Taipa and Coloane. Forget about renting a bike on the islands and riding it back into the city – riding a bike on the Macau-Taipa Bridge is illegal, and it would be suicidal to attempt it.

WALKING

Macau is certainly small enough that most areas of interest can be reached on foot. However, it's going to be a long and exhausting day if you don't take to motorised transport, so at least start early if you're going to rely on foot power alone.

PEDICABS

These are three-wheeled bicycle rickshaws.

In many Third World countries, pedicabs are used as cheap taxis. In Macau, which is hardly the Third World, pedicabs are a tourist novelty which are actually more expensive than taxis. As pedicabs don't have meters, agree on the fare before getting in. A short ride will cost M$10 or from M$30 to M$40 for an hour of sightseeing. As pedicabs cannot negotiate hills, you'll be limited to touring the waterfront.

It's easiest to find the pedicabs near the Hotel Lisboa. You won't have to solicit the drivers. If you so much as look their way they'll come chasing after you.

TOURS

Tours offer a fast way to see everything with minimum hassle and can easily be booked in Hong Kong, or in Macau after arrival. Tours booked in Macau are generally much better value as those booked in Hong Kong usually cost considerably more (yet include transportation to and from Macau and a side-trip across the border to Zhuhai in China). These are usually one-day whirlwind tours departing for Macau in the morning and returning to Hong Kong the same evening – they cost about HK$500.

A typical city tour (booked in Macau) of the peninsula takes three to four hours and costs about M$70 per person, often including lunch. Bus tours out to the islands cost about M$20 per person. You can also book a one-day bus tour across the border into Zhuhai, China, which usually includes a trip to the former home of Dr Sun Yatsen in Zhongshan County.

There is an exhausting one-day tour that departs Hong Kong at 7 am, takes you to Shekou (in the Shenzhen Special Economic Zone north of Hong Kong), then onto Zhuhai Special Economic Zone north of Macau by boat, then to the home of Dr Sun Yatsen in Zhongshan County, then to Macau by bus, and finally by jetfoil back to Hong Kong by 7.30 pm. This trip costs HK$760, not including the medical treatment you might need for seasickness or cardiac arrest.

If you'd like a slower pace, a three to four-day tour from Hong Kong to Macau, Zhuhai, Cuiheng (home of Dr Sun Yatsen), Shiqi, Foshan, Canton and then back to Hong Kong by train, costs about HK$1500.

Finding these tours is not difficult. In Hong Kong, the ubiquitous moneychangers often have a collection of free pamphlets offering tours to Macau. The Macau Tourist Office at Shun Tak Centre (Macau Ferry Pier) has piles of information on tours and this is probably the best place to go. Most Hong Kong travel agencies can also book tours.

In Macau, contact the tourist office or go directly to one of these tour agencies:

Able Tours
    5-9 Travessa do Padre Narciso (☎ 89798, HK 5459993)
China Travel Service
    2nd floor, Hotel Beverly Plaza, Avenida do Dr Rodrigo Rodrigues (☎ 388922, HK 5406333)
Estoril Tours
    Mezzanine floor, New Wing, Hotel Lisboa, Avenida da Amizada (☎ 573614, HK 5591028)
Guangdong Macau Tours
    37-E Rua da Praia Grande (☎ 588807, HK 8329118)
Hi-No-De Caravela
    6A-4C Rua de Sacadura Cabral (☎ 338338, HK 3686181)
H Nolasco, Lda
    20 Avenida Almeida Ribeiro (☎ 76463)
International Tourism
    9 Travessa do Padre Narciso, Loja B (☎ 86522, HK 5412100)
Lotus
    Edificio Fong Meng, Rua de Sao Lourenco (☎ 81765)
Macau Mondial
    74-A Avenida do Conselheiro Ferreira de Almeida (☎ 566866)
Macau Star Tours
    Room 511, Tai Fung Bank Building, 34 Avenida Almeida Ribeiro (☎ 558855, HK 3662262)
Macau Tours Ltd
    9 Avenida da Amizade (☎ 85555, HK 5422338)
MBC Tours
    7-9 Rua Santa Clara, Edificio Ribeiro, Loja D (☎ 86462)
F Rodrigues
    71 Rua da Praia Grande (☎ 75511)
Sintra Tours
    Hotel Sintra, Avenida Dom Joao IV (☎ 86394, HK 5408028)

Top: Rickshaws in Central Macau (TW)
Bottom: Cannon in Forteleza do Monte, Macau (RH)

Top: Lotus Mountain, Canton (RS)
Bottom: Backstreet scene, Canton (GI)

South China
    1st floor, 15 Avenida Dr Rodrigo Rodrigues, Apt
    A-B (☎ 87211, HK 5449053)
TKW
    4th floor, 27-31 Rua Formosa, Apt 408
    (☎ 591122, HK 7237771)

Vacations International
    Mandarin Oriental Hotel, Avenida da Amizade,
    (☎ 567888 ext 3004)
Wing On
    3rd floor, 303-4 Edificio Tai Fung, 32 Avenida
    Almeiro (☎ 77701)

Macau Peninsula 澳門半島

CENTRAL MACAU

Avenida de Almeida Ribeiro is the main street of Macau and is as good a place to start your tour as any. It crosses Rua da Praia Grande just up from the waterfront and effectively divides the narrow southern peninsula from the rest of Macau. It continues down to the Hotel Lisboa under the name of Avenida do Infante D Henrique (Macau's streets may not be very big but their names certainly are). A good place to start is the Hotel Lisboa, that grotesquely distinctive building which dominates the waterfront of Macau.

Jorge Alvares Statue 歐維士石像

The monument is at the corner of Rua da Praia Grande and Avenida da Amizade. Alvares is credited with being the first Portuguese to set foot on Chinese soil when he and his party landed on the island of Lin Tin, halfway between Macau and Hong Kong.

Governor Joao Ferreira do Amaral Statue 雅馬拉銅像

Between the entrance of the Hotel Lisboa and the Macau-Taipa Bridge is a statue to Joao Ferreira de Amaral, a governor of Macau in the mid-19th century. He was responsible for the expulsion of the Chinese customs officials from Macau, the declaration of the colony as a free port and the annexation of Taipa Island. The statue was erected in 1940 and is one of the most photographed monuments in Macau.

Amaral, who had lost his right arm in a battle several years before, was set upon by Chinese assassins one day near the border and was beheaded. The statue shows him on horseback with a whip in his left hand fighting off the attackers.

It may not be his last battle. The Chinese government has decided to assert its control over Macau long before 1999, and has insisted that the statue must go because it's 'too colonial'. It may even be gone by the time you read this. Many now believe that

China – the new colonial power – will dismantle other Portuguese monuments.

Leal Senado 市政廳

Across the street from the GPO on Avenida de Almeida Ribeiro is the Leal Senado which houses the municipal government offices.

The Leal Senado (Loyal Senate) is the main administrative body for municipal affairs, but it once had much greater power and dealt on equal terms with Chinese officials in the last century. It's called the Loyal Senate because it refused to recognise Spanish sovereignty over Portugal when the Spanish marched into Portugal in the 17th century and occupied it for 60 years. When Portuguese control was re-established, the city of Macau was granted the official name of 'Cidade do Nome de Deus de Macau, Nao ha Outra Mais Leal' or 'City of the Name of God, Macau, There is None more Loyal'.

Above the wrought-iron gates leading to the garden, inside the main building, is an interesting bas-relief, the subject of some dispute. Some say the woman depicted is the Virgin Mary sheltering all those in need of mercy. Others hold that it represents the Portuguese Queen Leonor of the 16th century.

Also inside the Leal Senado is the **public library**, open on weekdays from 9 am to noon and from 2 to 5.30 pm, and on Saturdays from 9 am to 12.30 pm. In front of the Leal Senado is the **Largo do Senado**, the Senate Square.

Sao Domingo Church (Church of St Dominic) 玫瑰堂

This is the most beautiful of Macau's baroque churches. The huge 17th-century building has an impressive tiered altar with images of the Virgin and Child and of Our Lady of Fatima, which is carried in procession during the Fatima Festival. There is a small museum at the back full of church regalia, images and paintings. The church is only open in the afternoon. To get in, ring the bell by the iron gates at the side. It is on Rua do Sao Domingos, at the northern end of Largo do Senado.

Luis de Camoes Museum
賈梅士博物院

A few blocks to the north of Sao Domingo is the modern **Sao Antonio Church**. The church is memorable for having been burnt to the ground three times.

To the left is the entrance to the Luis de Camoes Museum, a historically interesting building that was once the headquarters of the British East India Company in Macau. The museum has an extensive collection that includes early Chinese terracotta, enamel ware and pottery, paintings, old weapons, religious objects and a collection of sketches and paintings of old Macau and Canton. However, the building itself (which dates back to the 18th century) is of the most interest. It's open from 11 am to 5 pm daily, except Wednesday and public holidays. Admission is M$1.

Camoes Grotto & Gardens
白鴿巢花園

Behind the museum in the Camoes Grotto & Gardens is another memorial to Luis de Camoes, the 16th-century Portuguese poet who has become something of a local hero, although his claim is not all that strong. He is said to have written his epic *Os Lusiadas* by the rocks here, but there is no firm evidence that he was ever in Macau. A bust of him in the gardens is said to look rather better than the man.

A pleasant, cool and shady place, the gardens are popular with the local Chinese and you may find old men sitting here playing checkers. They don't mind an audience. There are good views from the top of the hill.

Old Protestant Cemetery
舊基督教墳場

Beside the Luis de Camoes Museum is the Old Protestant Cemetery – the resting place

of numerous non-Portuguese who made their way to Macau.

The cemetery was needed because ecclesiastical law forbade the burial of Protestants on Catholic soil – which meant the whole of Macau, at least inside the city walls. Beyond the walls was Chinese soil, and the Chinese didn't approve of foreigners desecrating their pitch either. The unhappy result was that Protestants had to bury their dead either in the nearby hills and hope the Chinese wouldn't notice, or else beneath the neutral territory of the city walls.

Finally the governor allowed a local merchant to sell some of his land to the British East India Company – despite a law forbidding foreign ownership of land – and the cemetery was established in 1921. A number of old graves were then transferred there, which explains the earlier dates on some of the tombstones. The gate shows the date 1814, which was when the cemetery committee was set up.

Among the better known people buried here is artist George Chinnery, noted for his portrayals of Macau and its people in the first half of the 19th century. Also buried here is Robert Morrison, the first Protestant missionary to China, who, as his tombstone records, 'for several years laboured alone on a Chinese version of the Holy Scriptures which he was spared to see completed'. Morrison is buried beside his wife Mary who became one of the cemetery's first burials after dying in childbirth – 'erewhile anticipating a living mother's joy suddenly, but with a pious resignation, departed this life after a short illness of 14 hours, bearing with her to the grave her hoped-for child'. Also buried here is Lord John Spencer Churchill, an ancestor of Sir Winston Churchill.

Other inscriptions on the tombstones indicate that ships' officers and crew are well represented. Some died from accidents aboard, such as falling off the rigging, while others died more heroically, like Lieutenant Fitzgerald 'from the effects of a wound received while gallantly storming the enemy's battery at Canton'. Captain Sir Humphrey Le Fleming Senhouse died 'from the effects of fever contracted during the zealous performance of his arduous duties at the capture of the Heights of Canton in May 1841'.

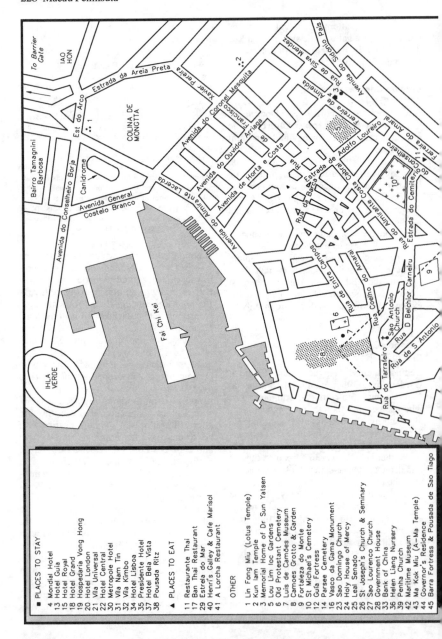

■ PLACES TO STAY

4 Mondial Hotel
13 Hotel Guia
15 Hotel Royal
18 Hotel Grand
19 Hospedaria Vong Hong
20 Hotel London
21 Vila Universal
22 Hotel Central
30 Metropole Hotel
31 Vila Nam Tin
32 Vila Kimbo
34 Hotel Lisboa
35 Presidente Hotel
37 Hotel Bela Vista
38 Pousada Ritz

▲ PLACES TO EAT

11 Restaurante Thai
17 Ban Thai Restaurant
29 Estrela do Mar
40 Henri's Galley & Cafe Marisol
41 A Lorcha Restaurant

OTHER

1 Lin Fong Miu (Lotus Temple)
2 Kun Iam Temple
3 Memorial Home of Dr Sun Yatsen
5 Lou Lim Ioc Gardens
6 Old Protestant Cemetery
7 Luis de Camões Museum
8 Camoes Grotto & Garden
9 Fortaleza do Monte
10 St Michael's Cemetery
12 Guia Fortress
14 Parsee Cemetery
16 Vasco da Gama Monument
23 Sao Domingo Church
24 Holy House of Mercy
25 Leal Senado
26 St Joseph's Church & Seminary
27 Sao Lourenco Church
28 Government House
33 Bank of China
36 Helen Liang Nursery
39 Penha Church
42 Maritime Museum
43 Ma Kok Miu (A-Ma Temple)
44 Governor's Residence
45 Barra Fortress & Pousada de Sao Tiago

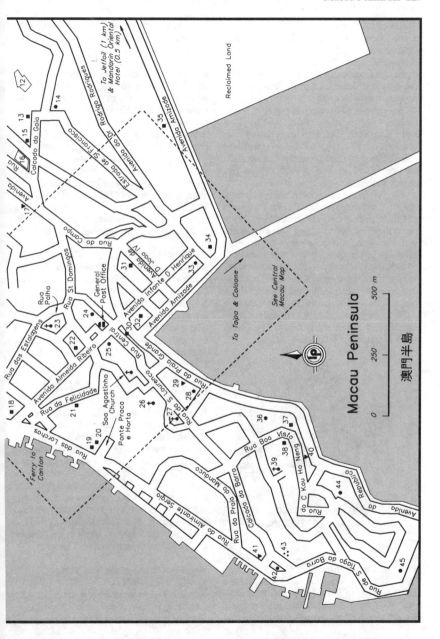

Macau Peninsula

澳門半島

0   250   500 m

To Taipa & Coloane

See Central
Macau Map

Reclaimed Land

To Jetfoil (1 km)
& Mandarin Oriental
Hotel (0.5 km)

Ferry to
Canton

Rua das Lorchas

Avenida Almeida Ribeiro

Rua da Felicidade

Rua dos Estalagens

Rua St Dominges

Rua do Campo

Estrada de St Francisco

Av. do Rodrigo Rodrigues

Calçada do Gaio

Avenida Amizade

Avenida Infante D Henrique

Avenida Amizade

Rua Central

Rua da Praia Grande

Rua de S Lourenço

Sao Agostinho
Church

Ponte Praca
e Horta

Rua do Almirante Sergio

Rua da Praia do Barra

Calçada da Barra

Rua da Praia do Manduco

Rua Boa Vista

Rua do C Kou Ho Neng

Rua da Republica

Avenida da Republica

Rua de S Tiago do Barra

General
Post Office

Avenida do Ap.

Rua Palha

14 13 15 16 17 35 34 31 33 23 24 22 25 30 29 28 27 26 21 20 19 18 36 37 38 39 40 44 45 41 42 43 12

Ruins of Sao Paulo 大三巴牌坊

Some say the ruins of the Cathedral of Sao Paulo are the greatest monument to Christianity in the east. The cathedral was finished in the first decade of the 17th century, and the crowned heads of Europe competed to present it with its most prestigious gift.

Built on one of Macau's seven hills, it was designed by an Italian Jesuit and built by early Japanese Christian exiles. All that remains is the facade, the magnificent mosaic floor and the impressive stone steps leading up to it. The church caught fire during a disastrous typhoon in 1835.

The facade has been described as a sermon in stone, recording some of the main events of Christianity in the various carvings. At the top is the dove, representing the Holy Spirit, surrounded by stone carvings of the sun, moon and stars. Beneath the dove is a statue of the infant Jesus surrounded by stone carvings of the implements of the crucifixion. In the centre of the third tier stands the Virgin Mary, with angels and two types of flowers – the peony representing China and the chrysanthemum representing Japan. The fourth tier has statues of four Jesuit saints.

Ruins of Sao Paulo

Fortaleza do Monte 大炮台

The fortress of Sao Paulo do Monte is on a hill overlooking the ruins of Sao Paulo and was built by the Jesuits around the same time. The first Portuguese settlers in Macau built their homes in the centre of the peninsula and the fort once formed the strong central point of the old city wall of Macau. The cannons on the fort are the very ones that dissuaded the Dutch from further attempts to take over Macau. In 1622 a cannon ball hit a powder keg on one of the invader's ships, which exploded, blowing the Dutch out of the water. Since this event occurred on St John the Baptist's Day, 24 June, he was promptly proclaimed the city's patron saint.

Now the old building is used as an observatory and a museum. From it there are sweeping views across Macau. Enter the fort from a narrow cobbled street leading off Estrada do Repouso near Estrada do Cemiterio. There is also a path from the fortress down to the ruins of Sao Paulo.

St Michael Cemetery 西洋墳場

This Catholic cemetery, almost exactly in the centre of the Macau Peninsula on Estrada do Cemiterio, is certainly Macau's most beautiful cemetery. Although a few of the tombs are plain to look at, most are works of art. The whole cemetery is adorned with statues of angels. This is the largest cemetery on the peninsula, though there is an even bigger Chinese cemetery on Taipa Island.

Lou Lim Loc Gardens 盧廉若花園

The restful Lou Lim Loc Gardens are on Ferreira de Almeida. The gardens and the ornate mansion with its columns and arches, now the Pui Ching School, once belonged to the wealthy Chinese Lou family. The gardens are a mixture of European and Chinese plantings, with huge shady trees, lotus ponds, pavilions, bamboo groves, grottoes and strangely shaped doorways. The twisting pathways and ornamental mountains are built to represent a Chinese painting and are said to be modelled on those in the famous gardens of Suzhou in eastern China.

Memorial Home of Dr Sun Yatsen
孫中山先生紀念館

Around the corner from the Lou Lim Loc Gardens, at the junction of Avenida da Sidonio Pais and Rua de Silva Mendes, is the

Memorial Home of Dr Sun Yatsen. Sun practised medicine in Macau for some years before turning to revolution and seeking to overthrow the Qing Dynasty. A rundown on Sun's involvement with the anti-Qing forces and later with the Kuomintang and Communist parties is in the History section of the Facts about Canton chapter.

The memorial house in Macau was built as a monument to Sun and contains a collection of flags, photos and other relics. It replaced the original house which blew up while being used as an explosives store. The house is open every day except Tuesday. Opening hours are Monday, Wednesday, Thursday and Friday from 10 am to 1 pm, and Saturday and Sunday from 10 am to 1 pm and 3 to 5 pm.

Guia Fortress 松山燈塔

The fortress sits on the highest point in Macau. The 17th-century **chapel** here is the old hermitage of Our Lady of Guia. The **Guia Lighthouse** (*guia* means 'guide' in Portuguese) is the oldest on the China coast and was first lit in 1865.

Parsee Cemetery 白頭墳場

The cemetery is at the junction of Estrada de Cacilhas and Estrada de Sao Francisco. Opposite it is the **Precious Blood Building** which was built at the end of the second decade of this century for a wealthy Macanese lawyer. Next to it and built about the same time is the palatial **Leng Nam School**.

Vasco da Gama Monument
華士古紀念銅像

This monument is at the corner of Rua Ferreira do Amaral and Calcada do Gaio, just to the west of the Parsee Cemetery and Guia Lighthouse. Da Gama's was the first Portuguese fleet to round the southern cape of Africa and make its way to India.

Military Club Building 陸軍俱樂部

The Military Club Building (one block north of Hotel Lisboa) was built in 1872 and is one of the oldest examples of Portuguese architecture still standing in Macau. Behind it are the **Sao Francisco Barracks** which house a military museum, open to the public daily from 2 to 5 pm.

THE SOUTH

There are a number of interesting sights on the peninsula – once known to the Chinese as the Water Lily Peninsula – south of Avenida de Almeida Ribeiro. A good way to start exploring this region is to walk up the steep Rua Central near the Leal Senado.

Dom Pedro V Theatre 岡頂戲院

To the right, off Rua Central, is the Dom Pedro V Theatre, a cream-coloured, colonnaded building which dates back to 1872.

Sao Agostinho Church
(Church of St Augustine) 聖奧斯定堂

Around the corner from the Dom Pedro V Theatre, in the Largo de Sao Agostinho, is the Sao Agostinho Church, which has foundations dating from 1586, although the present church was built in 1814. Among the people buried here is Maria de Moura, who in 1710 married Captain Antonio Albuquerque Coelho after he had lost an arm through an attack by one of Maria's unsuccessful suitors. Unfortunately, Maria died in childbirth and is buried with her baby and Antonio's arm.

Sao Lourenco Church
(Church of St Lawrence) 魯靈佐堂

Heading back down to and continuing along Rua Central, you'll find yourself on Rua de Sao Lourenco. On the right is the Sao Lourenco Church with its twin square towers. Stone steps lead up to the ornamental gates, but if you want to go in, use the side entrance. The original church is thought to have been built on this site at the time the Portuguese first settled in Macau, but the present church only dates from 1846.

Seminary of St Joseph 聖若瑟修院

Behind the Church of St Lawrence on Rua Do Seminario is the Church & Seminary of St Joseph. Enter the church through the seminary and across the courtyard. The church

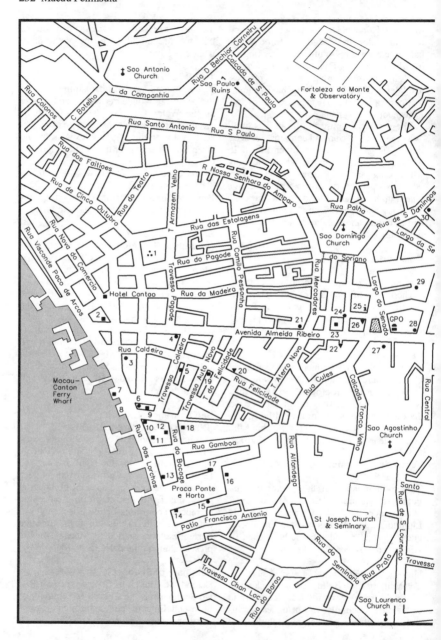

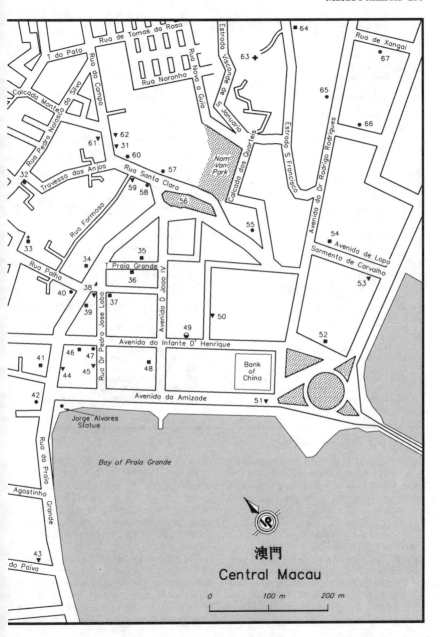

澳門
Central Macau

0   100 m   200 m

■ PLACES TO STAY

2   Hotel Grand
3   Hoi Keng Hotel
5   Hotel Man Va
7   Peninsula Hotel
9   Hotel Hou Kong
10 Hotel San Hou
11 Hospedaria Namkio
12 Hotel Ung Ieong
13 Hospedaria Vong Hong
14 Vila Hoi Von
16 Vila Kuan Heng
17 Hotel London
18 Vila Veng Va
19 Vila Universal
23 Hotel Central
34 Vila Nam Kok
35 Vila Nam Tin
36 Pensao Nam In
37 Vila Nam Loon
39 Vila Loc Tin
41 Metropole Hotel
46 Vila Kimbo
48 Sintra Hotel
52 Hotel Lisboa & Casino
54 Vila San Vu
64 Vila Tak Lei

▼ PLACES TO EAT

20 Fat Siu Lau Restaurant
22 Café Safari
26 Restaurant Long Kei
31 Maxim's
38 Algarve Sol Restaurant
43 Estrela do Mar
44 Solmar Restaurant

45 Restaurant Ocean
50 Dai Pai Dong
51 Esplanade Macau
53 Pizza Hut
59 Pizzeria Toscana
61 McDonald's
62 Portugues Restaurant

OTHER

1   Hong Kung Miu Temple
4   Casino Kam Pek
6   Kee Kwan Motors (Buses to Canton)
8   Floating Casino
15 Park 'n Shop
21 Taifung Bank
24 Sao Domingo Market
25 Tourist Office
27 Leal Senado
28 CTM Telephone Office
29 Holy House of Mercy
30 Portuguese Bookshop
32 Capitol Theatre
33 Cathedral
40 Hongkong Bank
42 Days & Days Supermarket
47 Foto Princesa
49 Bus Stop to Taipa & Coloane
55 Military Club
56 St Francisco Gardens
57 Cineteatro Macau
58 Bookstore
60 Watson's Drugstore
63 Centro Hospital
65 Telephone Company
66 Main Police Station
67 Immigration Office

dates from the mid-18th century and has a central dome, three altars and an arched corridor which leads to a pleasant courtyard. A gallery of religious art in the seminary is planned.

Harbour Office 港務局

Rua de Sao Lourenco leads into Rua da P E Antonio and Calcada da Barra. Near the end of Calcada da Barra is the peculiar Harbour Office, originally built in 1874 to accommodate Indian troops. Thus the distinctive arches.

Ma Kok Miu (A-Ma Temple) 媽閣廟

At the end of Calcada da Barra is the Ma Kok Miu at the base of Penha Hill. It is otherwise known as the A-Ma Temple and is dedicated to the goddess A-Ma (or Mother). A-Ma is more commonly known by her Hong Kong pseudonym Tin Hau, which means Queen of Heaven.

The original temple on this site was probably already standing when the Portuguese arrived, although the present building may only date back to the 17th century. A-Ma became A-Ma-Gao to the Portuguese and they named their colony after it. The temple consists of several shrines dating from the Ming Dynasty. The boat people of Macau come here on pilgrimage each year in April or May. The temple is actually a complex of temples, some dedicated to A-Ma and others to Kun Iam.

There are several stories about A-Ma, one of which is related in the Religion section in the Facts about Hong Kong chapter, but in Macau the tale goes that she was a beautiful young woman whose presence on a Canton-bound ship saved it from disaster. All the other ships in the fleet, whose rich owners had refused to give her a passage, were destroyed in a storm.

Maritime Museum 海事博物館
This museum was undergoing a major expansion during my last visit, so it's difficult to predict the outcome.

The Maritime Museum, which is opposite the Ma Kok Miu (A-Ma Temple), has a collection of boats and other artefacts related to Macau's seafaring past. It has a dragon boat which is used in races held during the Dragon Boat Festival, one of the most important traditional Chinese holidays, and there is also a flower boat, a tugboat and a Chinese fishing vessel.

The old Maritime Museum was good and the new one promises to be better, so try not to miss it.

Barra Fortress 媽閣古堡
From the Ma Kok Miu you can follow Rua de Sao Tiago da Barra around to the Barra Fortress at the end of Avenida da Republica. This fortress had great strategic importance when it was built in 1629, as ships entering the harbour had to come very close to the shore. The **Pousada de Sao Tiago Hotel** has been built within the walls of the fortress and is worth seeing even if you can't afford to stay there.

Governor's Residence 總督私邸
On the east side of the tip of the Macau Peninsula is Rua da Praia Grande, one of the most scenic streets in the city. Here you'll find the pink Governor's Residence, built in

the 19th century as a residence for a Macanese aristocratic family. Slightly further to the north is the **Bela Vista Hotel**, Macau's equivalent to Singapore's Raffles, built at the end of the 19th century.

Penha Church 西望洋聖堂
On a hill above the Bela Vista is the Bishop's Residence and Penha Church. From here you get an excellent view of the central area of Macau. You can also see across the Pearl River into China. In front of the church is a **replica of the Grotto of Lourdes**.

Government House 澳督府
The Government House on Rua da Praia Grande is pink like the Governor's Residence. Originally built for a Portuguese noble in 1849, it was acquired by the government at the end of the 19th century.

THE NORTH
The northern part of the peninsula has been more recently developed than the southern and central areas. Nevertheless, there are a few interesting historical sites in this region of Macau.

Kun Iam Temple 望厦觀音堂
The Kun Iam Temple on Avenida do Coronel Mesquita is really a complex of temples, the most interesting in Macau, and is dedicated to the goddess Kun Iam (Kuanyin), the Queen of Heaven and the Goddess of Mercy. The temple dates back about 400 years, though the original temple on the site was probably built more than 600 years ago.

The first treaty of trade and friendship between the USA and China was signed here in 1844. These days it's a place for fortune-telling rather than treaties and gets quite a lot of visitors.

Lin Fung Miu (Lotus Temple) 蓮峯廟
Near the Canidrome is Estrada do Arco where you'll find the Ling Fung Miu or Lotus Temple. The main hall of this temple is dedicated to Kun Iam. Another shrine is for A-Ma, the Goddess of Seafarers, and another is for Kuanti, the God of War,

Riches, Literature & Pawnshops. The temple complex probably predates the arrival of the Portuguese in Macau.

Barrier Gate 關閘

Once a popular tourist spot, the Barrier Gate, or Portas do Cerco, is the gate between Macau and China. In Portuguese, Portas do Cerco literally means Gate of Siege. Before 1980, when 'China-watching' was meant literally, Macau's Barrier Gate and Hong Kong's Lok Ma Chau attracted many curious visitors simply because it was the border, and that was as close as any foreigner ever got to the People's Republic. These days the Barrier Gate is just a busy border crossing, but if you want to see it, head straight up Istmo Ferreira do Amaral from the Ling Fung Temple.

Macau-Seac Tin Hau Temple
馬交石天后廟

From the Barrier Gate (Portas do Cerco) you can loop back down to the Hotel Lisboa along the eastern perimeter of the city. Head east along Avenida de Venceslau de Morris. At its extremity by the sea and the Macau Reservoir is the Macau-Seac Tin Hau temple. From there you can walk to the Casino Pelota Basca and the jetfoil pier, and from there catch bus No 3 back down to the Hotel Lisboa.

PLACES TO STAY
Places to Stay – bottom end

The cheapest hotels in Macau are mostly clustered near the Floating Casino. There are also several cheap and cheapish hotels between the Hotel Lisboa and Rua da Praia Grande, a somewhat nicer part of town. Finding them is easy as all the hotels have signs written in Portuguese. Cheap hotels usually call themselves *vila*, but sometimes they are called *hospedaria* or *pensao*.

The key to finding a good, cheap room is patience. If one place waves you off or charges too much, then try another. As long as you haven't arrived on a weekend, you should find something acceptable in half an hour or so after beginning your search.

Rua das Lorchas is a happy hunting ground for cheap hotels. There are two numbering systems on this street, which causes some confusion. The cheapest hotel I found was the *Hospedaria Vong Hong* on Rua das Lorchas. Depending on which numbering scheme you believe, it's either No 45 or 253, but it's on the north side of Praca Ponte e Horta (the square) and south of the Floating Casino. Tiny single rooms cost M$25 and larger rooms are M$50.

Nearby at 175 Rua das Lorchas is *Hospedaria Namkio* where singles cost M$37. It's a rather run-down sort of place, but it has character. Next to it is the *Hotel San Hou* at No 159 Rua das Lorchas, where singles/doubles are M$64/88. All rooms have shared bath, but the double rooms are huge with twin beds. Rooms with a balcony are the same price, so ask for one.

Just around the back is an alley called Rua do Bocage. At No 17 you'll find *Hotel Ung Ieong*, although a sign on the door says 'Restaurante Ung Ieong'. The rooms are so huge you could fit an army in there! Auditorium-sized doubles go for M$67 with bath, but look the place over before you pay because it's quite run-down.

Just opposite the Floating Casino and a few doors to the north is *Hoi Keng Hotel* (☎ 572033) where singles/doubles are M$130 or M$138 with private bath. The address is 153 Rua do Guimaraes but you enter just around the corner on Rua Caldeira.

Continuing one block north on Rua do Guimaraes, cross Avenida Almeida Ribeiro (the main drag of Macau) and look behind the Hotel Grand to find the *Hotel Cantao* where rooms cost M$60. The walls are paper thin but it otherwise looks OK.

Two blocks to the south of the Floating Casino, on Rua das Lorchas, is a large square called Praca Ponte e Horta. It looks like it might once have been a park, but now it's just a car park (most of Macau's open space is buried under cars these days). Anyway, there are several vilas around the square. On the east end of the square I recommend *Vila Kuan Heng* (☎ 573629) where rooms are clean and cost M$150 with private bath. On the west side of the square, on the corner with Rua das Lorchas, is the tattered-looking *Vila Hoi Von* where singles are M$100, but they're not really worth it.

Moving a few blocks to the east of the Floating Casino, the very clean and friendly *Vila Universal* (☎ 573247) is at 73 Rua Felicidade. The manager's English is good and singles/doubles cost M$184/276. The price is amazingly cheap for the high standard of the rooms, but it's often full because it offers such good value.

The *Vila Veng Va*, at the corner of Travessa das Virtudes and Travessa Auto Novo, has singles and doubles for M$150. The rooms are attractive and the manager is friendly.

Moving to the eastern side of the peninsula, the area between the Hotel Lisboa and Rua da Praia Grande is fertile ground for finding budget accommodation, although prices are somewhat higher than by the Floating Casino. One good place to try is the *Va Lai Vila* at 44 Rua da Praia Grande. Singles cost M$180, the rooms look clean and the management is friendly. On the opposite side of the street at 93 Rua da Praia Grande is *Vila Nam Kok* where singles are M$188.

Intersecting with Rua da Praia Grande is a small street called Rua Dr Pedro Jose Lobo where there's a good range of accommodation, including *Vila Nam Loon* which has singles for M$150. Around the corner on Avenida Infante D Henrique, near Rua da Praia Grande, is *Vila Kimbo* where singles cost M$130.

On Rua Dr Pedro Jose Lobo, the *Vila Loc Tin* has comfortable doubles for M$180. In the same building is the *Vila San Sui* which costs M$150 for a double.

Running off Avenida D Joao IV is an alley called Travessa da Praia Grande which has several good places. Among the best is the bright, airy and friendly *Vila Nam Tin* (☎ 81513) where singles/doubles with private bath cost M$150/175. On the same alley is *Pensao Nam In* (☎ 81002), where singles cost M$110, or M$230 for a pleasant double with private bath.

Behind the Hotel Lisboa on Avenida de Lopo Sarmento de Carvalho is a row of vilas. The *Vila San Vu* is friendly and has nice rooms for M$160.

Places to Stay – middle

The *Hotel London* (☎ 83388) on Praca Ponte e Horta has singles/doubles for M$200/240. The square is two blocks south of the Floating Casino.

True to its name, the *Hotel Central* (☎ 373888) is in the centre of town at 28-26 Avenida Almeida Ribeiro, west of the GPO. Rather dumpy-looking double rooms with private bath cost from M$220.

Just on the north side of the Floating Casino, on Rua das Lorchas, is the *Peninsula Hotel* (☎ 318899). Singles/twins are M$250/300. This is a new hotel, clean and well air-conditioned.

A few doors to the south of the Floating Casino you'll find an alley called Travessa das Virtudes. On your left as you enter the alley is the *Hotel Hou Kong* which has singles/doubles for M$230/322.

Just a block to the north of the Floating Casino, at 146 Avenida Almeida Ribeiro, is the *Hotel Grand* (☎ 579922) where singles/doubles cost M$228/288.

One block to the east of the Floating Casino is a street called Travessa Caldeira where you'll find the *Hotel Man Va* with doubles at M$287. Nearby at 71 Rua de Felicidade, close to Travessa Auto Novo, is *Hotel Ko Wah* (☎ 75599) which has doubles for M$195.

One more place to look around is the area north of the Hotel Lisboa on a street called Estrada Sao Francisco. You have to climb a steep hill to get up this street, but the advantage is that the hotels have good sea views. Just past the expensive Matsuya Hotel you'll find the *Vila Tak Lei* at 2A Estrada Sao Francisco, where doubles cost M$350. However, bargaining is entirely possible. As I was walking out the price dropped to M$200!

Places to Stay – top end

Macau's booming tourist industry has given rise to several new five-star hotels and more are planned. Yet in spite of the building boom, rooms are not always easy to get. During the summer travel season many of these places are often solidly booked, even during weekdays. Accordingly, weekday discounts, once a standard practice in Macau, are no longer so easily obtained at the higher-priced hotels.

The *Beverly Plaza* (☎ 337755, fax 308878), Avenida do Dr Rodrigues, is a new, luxurious place and home to China Travel Service where you can get a visa for China. Twin rooms range from M$680 to M$740.

The *Guia Hotel* (☎ 513888, fax 559822), Estrada do Eng Trigo 1-5, is relatively small with twins from M$420 to M$520, while triples cost M$620.

The *Hotel Lisboa* (☎ 577666, fax 567103) is Macau's most famous landmark. It's difficult to find the right adjective to describe the unique architecture (orange background with white circles), but it certainly is memorable. Regardless of what you think of the external design, the interior is first rate. The Lisboa has the best arcade in Macau, which is filled with shops, restaurants, banks, a billiard room and bowling alley. Even if you

don't stay here, it's worth a look. Single rooms are fairly cheap at M$260, but there are very few available. Twins range from M$340 to M$650.

The *Mandarin Oriental* (☎ 567888, fax 594589) is another five-star resort. Double rooms start at M$880. This hotel is on Avenida Amizade (the Grand Prix race course), south of the jetfoil pier.

The *Matsuya* (☎ 577000, fax 568080), owned by the People's Republic, is a small but luxurious place on a hillside at 5 Calcada de Sao Francisco. Most rooms have a sea view. Singles cost M$330/358, while doubles range from M$390 to M$490.

The *Metropole* (☎ 88166, fax 330800) has a choice location at 63 Rua da Praia Grande. The few single rooms are M$300. All the other rooms are twins costing M$430.

The *Modial* (☎ 566866) is on a side street called Rua de Antonio Basto, on the eastern side of Lou Lim Loc Gardens. Doubles range from M$330 to M$550.

A new, flashy place is the *Pousada Ritz* (☎ 339955, fax 317826), 2 Rua da Boa Vista. It has twins for a mere M$1000 to M$1200.

On the east side of the Lisboa is the *Pre-*

Hotel Lisboa

sidente (☎ 553888, fax 552735), Avenida Da Amizade. It's a first-rate place where doubles start at M$620.

Also at the top end is the *Royal* (☎ 552222, fax 563008) at 2-4 Estrada de Vitoria, across from the Vasco da Gama Monument. Doubles start at M$660.

The *Sintra* (☎ 85111, fax 510527) is on the waterfront on Avenida Dr Mario Soares, west of the Lisboa. Doubles start at M$420.

If I could afford it, the place I'd choose to live it up at in Macau would be the *Pousada de Sao Tiago* (☎ 378111, fax 552735). The location on Avenida da Republica at the very southern tip of the peninsula is dramatic enough, but the architecture has to be seen to be appreciated. The hotel blends into the hillside overlooking the harbour. It's worth coming here to have a drink at the bar and take a look. Originally, the hotel was a fortress, the Fortaleza da Barra, which was built in 1629. Doubles start at M$980 and are frequently booked solid.

The *Hotel Bela Vista* is one of Macau's most famous hotels. This grand colonial building is more than 100 years old and overlooks the waterfront on the south-east corner of the peninsula on Rua Comendador Kou Ho Neng. This is Macau's answer to Hong Kong's Peninsula or Singapore's Raffles. The hotel is now closed for renovation but should be open again during the life span of this book. Expect prices to be high.

On Taipa Island there is the *Hyatt Regency* and on Coloane there are two top-end hotels. See Places to Stay in the Macau Islands chapter.

PLACES TO EAT
Portuguese & Macanese
Henri's Galley (☎ 556251), also known as Maxims (not the Hong Kong fast-food chain), is right on the waterfront at 4 Avenida da Republica, the southern end of the Macau Peninsula. Henri's Galley is known for its African chicken, spicy prawns and prawn fondue. They also serve Chinese food.

Right next door is *Cafe Marisol* where food is both cheap and excellent. They set up

outdoor tables so you can take in the view across to the islands.

Also adjacent to Henri's Galley is *Ali Curry House*, which also has outdoor tables and a wide menu of curry dishes (M$25 to M$35) and steaks (M$30 to M$40) with a Portuguese flavour.

For good, cheap Portuguese and Macanese food, the *Estrela do Mar* (☎ 81270), at 11 Travessa do Paiva off the Rua da Praia Grande, is the place to go, as is the *Solmar* (☎ 74391) at 11 Rua da Praia Grande. Both places are famous for their African chicken and seafood.

Fat Siu Lau (☎ 73580), or 'House of the Smiling Buddha', serves Portuguese and Chinese food. It's at 64 Rua da Felicidade, once the old red-light Street of Happiness. Turn left opposite the Central Hotel in Avenida de Almeida Ribeiro. It's supposed to be the oldest restaurant in Macau or at least the oldest Macanese restaurant in the colony, dating back to 1903. The speciality is roast pigeon.

Another place known for good Portuguese food is *Portugues* (☎ 75445) at 16 Rua do Campo. Known for its good food and fine Spanish decor is *Algarve Sol* (☎ 89007), at 41-43 Rua Comandante Mata e Oliveira, two blocks west of the Hotel Lisboa between Rua da Praia Grande and Avenida D Joao IV.

An excellent place to eat is *Café Safari* (☎ 574313) at 14 Patio do Cotovelo near the Leal Senado. It has good coffee-shop dishes as well as spicy chicken, steak and fried noodles. This is a good place to eat breakfast.

High honours also go to *A Lorcha* (☎ 313193), a Portuguese restaurant near the A-Ma Temple at the south-west tip of the Macau Peninsula.

Chinese
Budget travellers should head to *Esplanade Macau* which sits on the traffic island on Avenida Amizade in front of the Hotel Lisboa and adjacent to the Bank of China. It's in an outdoor pavilion and opens only in the evening. They serve good Cantonese dishes like fried noodles for M$7 and drinks

are also very cheap. Not much English is spoken, but they have an English-language menu.

The Rua da Praia Grande is home to several dim-sum places. At No 11-B is *San Kong* (☎ 81618) and at No 35 is *Tung Hoi* (☎ 75515).

The *Restaurant Long Kei* (☎ 573970) on Leal Senado Square is a straightforward Cantonese place with bright overhead lights and sparse surroundings, but it also has topnotch Cantonese food and amiable waiters.

The *Restaurante Jade* (☎ 75126), a one-minute walk west of Leal Senado Square at 30 Avenida Almeida Ribeiro, is a large place with a good reputation for morning and afternoon dim sum. Nearby at 21 Avenida Almeida Ribeiro is *Golden Crown* (☎ 76666).

A standard seafood place is the *Restaurant Tong Kong* (☎ 77364) at 32 Rua da Caldeira (near the corner of Travessa de Caldeira), where your meal is swimming in the tanks at the front windows. It's known for its Hakka food.

Restaurant Ocean (☎ 371533), 4th floor, 11 Avenida da Amizade and Rua Dr Pedro Jose Lobo, is another standard dim sum and Cantonese restaurant.

Street Stalls

As in other Chinese cities, the evening street markets are about as cheap as cooking for yourself.

Seafood is the local speciality. Eating the sea snails takes a little practice. The idea is to use two toothpicks to roll the organism out of its shell, then dip it in sauce and devour.

One of the most conveniently located dai pai dongs is Rua da Escola Commercial, a tiny lane one block west of the Hotel Lisboa, just next to a sports field. There are also many cheap Chinese restaurants setting up chairs outdoors at night near the Floating Casino on Rua das Lorchas.

In the somewhat unlikely event that you find yourself near the Barrier Gate at night, there is a good dai pai dong on Estrada do Arco, a small street in front of the Lin Fong Miu (Lotus Temple).

Other Places to Eat

Fast Food *Pizzeria Toscana*, 28B Rua Formosa (near McDonald's), is a nice little place good for a coffee and pizzas from M$30 to M$50.

At M$8.60, Macau's Big Macs are the cheapest in the world. You can find them at McDonald's, 17-19 Rua do Campo.

On the opposite side of the street is *Maxim's Cake Shop*, a good place to grab a quick takeaway breakfast.

Pizza Hut plies its pies on Avenida de Lopo Sarmento de Carvalho, just behind the Lisboa Hotel. You can enter through the Hotel Lisboa shopping arcade.

Korean If you have a craving for bulgogi (marinated strips of beef) and kimchi (the Korean national dish, made up of cabbage, garlic and chilli), you can find them and other good Korean food at *Hoi Fu Garden* (☎ 566402) at 25 Estrada de Cacilhas (the street running along the east side of the Guia Fortress). *Hotel Presidente* on Avenida da Amizade (just east of Hotel Lisboa) also has a Korean restaurant.

Vietnamese *Kam Ngau Un* (☎ 309883) at 57-67 Avenida da Amizade offers good Vietnamese meals.

Thai *Restaurante Thai* (☎ 573288) has the usual fiery-hot dishes. It's at 27E Rua Abreu Nunes, a narrow street one block west of the Vasco da Gama Monument. At the intersection of Calcado do Gaio and Rua do Campo is *Restaurant Ban Thai* (☎ 552255).

Japanese If you can afford the ticket, there are Japanese restaurants in the Hotel Royal *(Ginza)* and Hotel Lisboa *(Furusato)*.

ENTERTAINMENT
Cinemas

The Cineteatro Macau is on Rua Santa Clara, down the street from Watson's Drugstore. The main theatre often has good quality films in English, as well as some Hong Kong movies.

To the left of the main theatre is the *Centro*

Cultural Shalom, a mini theatre seating about 30 people, which often shows excellent foreign films. Admission is M$25.

Billiards & Pinball
The shopping arcade at the Hotel Lisboa also includes a video-games centre to keep the kids busy, and a billiards room for grown-up kids.

Discos
The most popular with the locals is the *Mondial Disco* at the Hotel Mondial, Rua da Antonio Basto. There is no cover charge, but you are obliged to buy two drinks for M$70.

The Hotel Presidente is home to the *Skylight Disco*. There is no cover charge here, but you must buy one drink for M$80.

Nightclubs
The *Mikado Nightclub* in the Hotel Lisboa is a huge place. They have no trouble keeping the place packed in spite of the M$200 cover charge (which includes two drinks). The club features a Filipino band and floor show.

The Crazy Paris Show, performed nightly in the *Mona Lisa Hall* of the Hotel Lisboa, is very similar to the revue-style shows in Las Vegas. Basically, you get to watch several dozen European women dance on stage wearing nothing but a bunch of feathers. There's lots of bright lights and music. Some people find it glamorous, while others are somewhat less impressed. One visitor who saw the show concluded that the performers were transsexuals. Shows scheduled from Sunday to Friday are at 8.30 and 10 pm. On Saturday, shows are at 8.30, 10 and 11 pm. Admission is M$90 on weekdays or M$100 on weekends. There is no admittance for anyone under 18.

The *China City Nightclub* is at the Casino Pelota Basca near the Jetfoil Terminal. This is basically a male-oriented club, with hostesses who circulate and keep the clientele smiling. There is even a scantily clad hostess in the men's washroom who opens the water tap and hands paper towels to the customers. Admission is M$200 and there may be additional charges for time spent with the hostesses.

Prostitution
Besides gambling Macau is well known for prostitution, though many tourists remain blissfully unaware of it. Efforts are made to keep the sex trade low key to preserve Macau's family image.

Nevertheless, the prostitutes are there and are not difficult to find if you make inquiries. Most of the activity takes place at the saunas which are found in many hotels. Most of the women are from Thailand. As in Thailand, they often have a number pinned to their blouse and prospective customers choose a number. Many of the 'hostesses' are just teenagers.

If you want to pursue this form of entertainment, you'll have to do your own research. Rumour has it that, in these days of the AIDS epidemic, some places are turning away foreigners.

Casinos
None of the casinos in Macau offer the atmosphere or level of service considered minimal in Las Vegas. There are no seats for slot machine players and no cocktail waitresses offering free drinks to gamblers. Incredibly, they don't even have 'change girls' who walk the casino floor giving change to slot players so they can keep playing. There are no windows, the dealers don't talk to the customers and no one smiles. Perhaps smiling is against the rules?

Nevertheless, the casinos have no trouble attracting customers. Indeed, they are jam-packed. One thing they do have in common with Las Vegas is that there are no clocks in the casinos – no sense letting people know how late it is, lest they be tempted to stop playing and go to bed. Here are a few casinos to try:

Lisboa Casino Although it's by no means the newest casino in town, the Lisboa is still the largest and liveliest. It's a 24-hour casino and the action is nonstop. It has a more comfortable feel about it than the others –

maybe because it is just so much more spacious. The adjacent hotel offers the comforts of a good but overpriced shopping arcade, fine restaurants and a video arcade to keep the kids busy while mum and dad lose their life savings at the blackjack tables.

There is a big meter in the casino which shows how much will be paid if you hit the grand jackpot on the five-reel slot machines. The total shown on the meter increases until someone hits 'megabucks', then the meter is reset to zero and starts again. Of all the gambling halls in Macau, this one comes closest to matching the grandeur of a Las Vegas casino, though it still falls far short.

Floating Casino Officially the name is Macau Palace, but everyone calls it the Floating Casino. I admit, the concept sounds good. Anchored on the west side of Macau, the name 'Floating Casino' conjures up romantic images of riverboat gambling, but the reality is somewhat different. Apart from being earthquake-proof, the casino has little to recommend it. Inside, it's a crowded, windowless, smoke-filled box where players climb over each other to get at the tables. It's one of Macau's oldest casinos and looks it.

Kam Pek Casino The original Kam Pek Casino used to look like a Salvation Army soup kitchen, but the new one near the Floating Casino has been considerably improved. It's still smaller than the Lisboa, but it's often jam-packed with players who are oblivious to all else but the next roll of the dice.

Mandarin Oriental Hotel Casino This place appeals to the upper crust and the hotel is south of the Jetfoil Pier.

The first time I visited I wasn't allowed in because I was wearing shorts. On the other hand, women are permitted to wear shorts inside the casino, so I guess my legs just weren't beautiful enough. I changed clothes, but when I finally did get in I was still the worst dressed person in the casino (not intentionally). Even the hotel lobby looks like a museum. I could swear the toilet paper was perfumed.

Casino Pelota Basca Opposite the Jetfoil Pier is the Casino Pelota Basca. The name derives from the fact that this used to be the venue of jai alai (pronounced hi-a-lie) games. Jai alai, reputed to be the world's fastest ball game, is popular in many Latin American countries, particularly Cuba and Mexico. The game is similar to handball, racquetball or squash. The ball is three-quarters the size of a baseball and harder than a golf ball. Each player alternatively catches it and throws it with his *pletora* – an elongated wicker basket with an attached leather glove that is strapped to his wrist. As with horse racing and dog racing, jai alai is something else for gamblers to wager on.

Sadly, the jai alai games are no more. The game just never caught on with Hong Kongers, and the present-day Casino Pelota Basca just has the standard table games and slots.

THINGS TO BUY

The Sao Domingo Market is in the alley just behind the Hotel Central and next to the Macau Government Tourist Office. It's a good place to pick up cheap clothing.

Macau Islands 澳門島

The islands of Taipa and Coloane have a completely different character from the crowded Macau Peninsula. The quiet rural environment and beautiful beaches stand in sharp contrast to Macau's glittering casinos and jam-packed streets. The islands were a haven for pirates until relatively recently – the last raid took place in 1910.

But the islands may not remain a peaceful paradise forever. One hotel-casino, the Hyatt Regency, has already sprung up on Taipa, and a new luxury resort with a golf course is being built on Coloane. The new airport is being built on the east side of Taipa, and plans for a deep-water port on Coloane could be the final nail in the coffin. Still, these islands have a long way to go before reaching the level of intense development seen on the peninsula.

GETTING THERE & AWAY

Bus Nos 21 and 21A go to Coloane. All the others only run as far as Taipa Island. The complete bus routes to the islands are:

No 11
> Praca Ponte E Horta, Floating Casino, Avenida Almeida Ribeiro, GPO, Hotel Lisboa, Hotel Hyatt Regency (Taipa), Taipa Village and the Macau Jockey Club. Fare: M$1.60

No 21
> Praca Ponte E Horta, Floating Casino, Avenida Almeida Ribeiro, GPO, Hotel Lisboa, Hotel Hyatt Regency (Taipa), Restaurante 1999 (Coloane) and Coloane Village. Fare: M$2.30

No 21A
> Praca Ponte E Horta, Floating Casino, Avenida Almeida Ribeiro, GPO, Hotel Lisboa, Hotel Hyatt Regency (Taipa), Taipa Village, Restaurante 1999 (Coloane), Coloane Village, Cheoc Van Beach and Hac Sa Beach. Fare: M$3

No 28A
> Jetfoil Pier, Hotel Lisboa, Hotel Hyatt Regency (Taipa), Macau University, Taipa Village and the Macau Jockey Club. Fare: M$2

No 33
> Fai Chi Kei, Lin Fong Miu (Lotus Temple), Avenida Almeida Ribeiro, Hotel Lisboa, Hotel Hyatt Regency (Taipa), Macau University, Taipa Village and the Macau Jockey Club. Fare: M$2

No 38
> Special bus running from the city centre to the Macau Jockey Club one hour before the races. Fare: M$3

GETTING AROUND
Bicycle
Bicycle rentals are available in both Taipa Village and Coloane Village. There are good 10-speed bikes as well as the heavyweight clunkers.

Walking is permitted on the Macau-Taipa Bridge, but bicycles are prohibited. However, bikes are allowed on the Taipa-Coloane Causeway, but it's not very safe as the causeway is narrow and traffic can be heavy. One false move and you may wind up staying in Macau a lot longer than you intended. It would make a lot more sense to rent a bicycle on each island. Otherwise you may find, as I did, that the buses and walking are perfectly adequate.

TAIPA ISLAND 氹仔
When the Portuguese first saw Taipa it was actually two islands, but during the past few hundred years the east and west halves have joined – one of the more dramatic demonstrations of the power of siltation. Tiny Macau is one part of the huge Pearl River Delta. The siltation process continues and, if the mud flats to the south of Taipa Village are any indication, Taipa and Coloane are destined to become one island unless the greenhouse effect submerges everything but the high-rises.

When you come over the bridge, the first large building you encounter is the Hyatt Regency. Apart from being the only hotel on the island, it also has Macau's newest casino. Apparently the rural location has not hurt

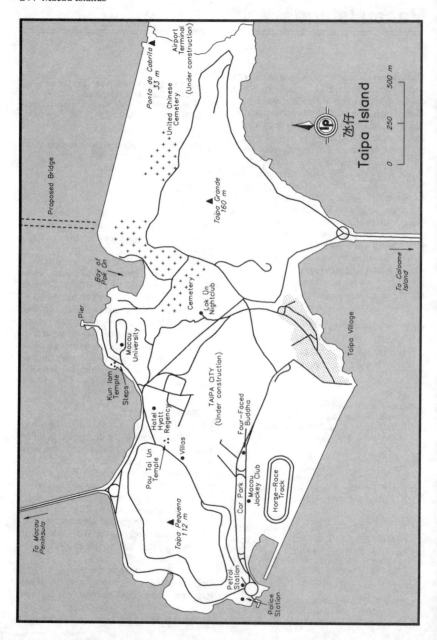

business, as when I was there the lobby was packed with new arrivals queuing to check in.

Macau University 澳門大學

Just a few hundred metres to the east of the Hyatt is a set of large modern buildings on a hill overlooking the sea. This is Macau University, the only university in this tiny enclave. It's worth dropping in for a quick look around and the cafeteria is a cheap place to eat. The vast majority of the students are from Macau and Hong Kong, but making conversation with them should be no problem since the language of instruction is English. The university is open seven days a week throughout the year, except for public holidays.

Kun Iam Temple 觀音廟

Walking downhill from the university (back towards the Hyatt Regency) you should find some stone steps off to your right going down towards the sea. Follow these a short distance and you'll soon reach the Kun Iam Temple. The temple is very small, and it's by the sea because Kun Iam is a goddess who protects sailors.

Pou Tai Un Temple 菩提園廟

Less than 200 metres to the west of the Hyatt Regency is the Pou Tai Un Temple, the largest temple on the island. It overlooks the tennis courts of the Hyatt. From here you can walk back to the Hyatt and catch a bus to Taipa Village at the south end of the island, or you could walk the 1.5 km to Taipa Village.

Taipa Village 氹仔市區

This is the only settlement on the island large enough to be called a village. The chief attraction is a street at the south-east corner of town called **Avenida da Praia**. This means Avenue of the Beach, but as you'll see, siltation has overwhelmed the beach and it has become a mud flat extending almost all the way to Coloane at low tide. Nevertheless, this is an attractive area with a tree-lined

promenade, wrought-iron benches and several old houses.

One of the houses has been preserved as the **Taipa House Museum** which is open to the public. Not much is known about the former residents of the house, but it's a good example of the architecture of the time (early 20th century). At the west end of the street and up a few steps is the **Our Lady of Carmel Church**.

The rest of the village is much more Chinese in its appearance. At the south-west corner of the village is a divided street called Largo Governador Tamagnini Barbosa where there is a small **Tin Hau temple**. It's very close to the main bus stop and bicycle rental shops.

Just around the corner on Rua do Regedor is the **Pak Tai Temple**. The only other sightseeing spot in town is a narrow alley called **Rua do Cunha** which has many tiny shops, though there isn't much that foreigners would be likely to want to buy.

Other Attractions

There are a few other spots that you might want to visit on Taipa, but you'll probably need to rent a bicycle unless you're a dedicated walker.

One spot is the **United Chinese Cemetery** on the north-east corner of the island. In the middle of the cemetery is a 30-metre high statue of Tou Tei, the Earth God.

The other big attraction on Taipa is the **Macau Jockey Club**. There's not much to see though, except when races are being held.

Outside the Macau Jockey Club is a **Four-Faced Buddha Shrine**. There are several similar statues located worldwide – one in Bangkok and another in (brace yourself) Las Vegas. Praying to the Buddha is supposed to bring good fortune, which is what one undoubtedly needs in Macau's casinos.

Places to Stay

The *Hyatt Regency* (☎ 3211234, fax 320595) offers everything you'd expect in a five-star hotel with prices to match. Twins range from M$860 to M$1180 and the hotel has it's own shuttle bus to the Macau Peninsula. There are plans to build other hotels on Taipa, but for now the Hyatt is the only place to stay.

Places to Eat

Taipa Village has several good and inexpensive restaurants. The best known for excellent Portuguese food is *Restaurante Panda* (☎ 327338) at No 4-8 Rua Direita Carlos Eugenio. On Rua do Cunha is a restaurant with the memorable name of *Cock Portuguese Food* (there is a picture of a rooster above the door). Also nearby is *Pinocchio* (☎ 327128) at 4 Rua do Sol, an obscure alley near the fire station.

For those on a budget, the best deal is the student cafeteria at Macau University.

Entertainment

Taipa has one of Macau's best nightclubs, the *Lok Ün*. It's popular with the local Portuguese, but tourists are few. Beer costs M$25 a glass and there is no cover charge. It's a bit hard to find (see the Taipa map) because it's down an obscure alley called Caminho das

Taipa Village

氹仔市區

Hortas, but at night there is a large, brightly lit sign which you can see from the main highway.

As you might imagine, the *Hyatt Regency* has an up-market casino. It's also fairly small and doesn't radiate that atmosphere of chaos that many gamblers enjoy. On the other hand, if you're attracted by the glitter of high-stakes gambling, this is the place to see it.

Casino Victoria is right inside the Macau Jockey Club. If you can't wait for the horse races to begin to start losing your money, the casino can accommodate you.

COLOANE ISLAND 路環

Of the two islands, Coloane is larger and is known for its beautiful beaches, one attraction Taipa is lacking. Coloane still lacks the high-rises which have invaded Taipa, but new hotels and villas have sprouted near the previously pristine beaches. The proposed deep-water port has the potential to turn Coloane into a jumble of factories, wharfs and warehouses. Still, the island is largely unspoiled and will probably remain that way for a few years longer.

Coloane Park 路環郊野公園

About one km south of the causeway, Coloane Park covers 20 hectares. There is a fountain and well-tended gardens, but the most notable feature is the aviary behind Restaurante 1999. The year 1999 holds the same ominous fascination for Macau residents that 1997 has for Hong Kong. All the buses to Coloane Village stop at Restaurante 1999. The restaurant is closed on Mondays except during public holidays.

The park is open from 9 am to 7 pm daily, and admission costs M$5. It costs another M$5 to visit the aviary, and M$20 if you want to rent a table in the picnic area.

Coloane Village 路環市區

The only real town on the island, this is largely a fishing village although in recent years, tourism has given the local economy a big boost. At the northern end of town are numerous building sheds for junks. You can walk there to see how the junks are built, but take along a big stick as several of the junk builders have nasty xenophobic dogs that are definitely hostile to foreigners!

If you arrive by bus, you'll be dropped off near the village roundabout. If you walk one short block to the west you'll see the waterfront. Here you'll get a good view of China. It's so close one could easily swim across the channel. In fact, many people used to do just that to escape from China.

A sign near the waterfront points towards the **Sam Seng Temple**. This temple is very small – not much more than a family altar. Just past the temple is the village pier.

Walking to the south along Avenida de Cinco de Outubro, you'll soon come to the main attraction in this village – the **Chapel of St Francis Xavier**. This interesting chapel was built in 1928 to honour St Francis Xavier who died on nearby Shang Ch'an Island in 1552. He had been a missionary in Japan and to this day Japanese come to Coloane to pay their respects.

Inside the chapel is a piece of the right arm bone of Xavier (other pieces of St Francis can be found in southern India). The bone fragment stands beside several boxes of bones of the Portuguese and Japanese Christians who were martyred in Nagasaki in 1597, Vietnamese Christians killed in the early 17th century and Japanese Christians killed in a rebellion in Japan in the 17th century. Near the chapel is a monument surrounded by cannon balls to commemorate the successful final battle against pirates in these islands in 1910. The battle is celebrated locally on July 13.

South of the chapel is a library and a sign pointing towards the **Kun Iam Temple**. This temple is also very tiny – not much more than an altar inside a little walled compound. Although there are no signs to indicate the path, if you walk just a little further past the stone wall you'll find the considerably larger and more interesting **Tin Hau Temple**.

At the very southern end of Avenida de Cinco de Outubro is the **Tam Kong Temple**. Inside is a whalebone, more than one metre long which has been been carved into a model of a ship with a wooden dragon head

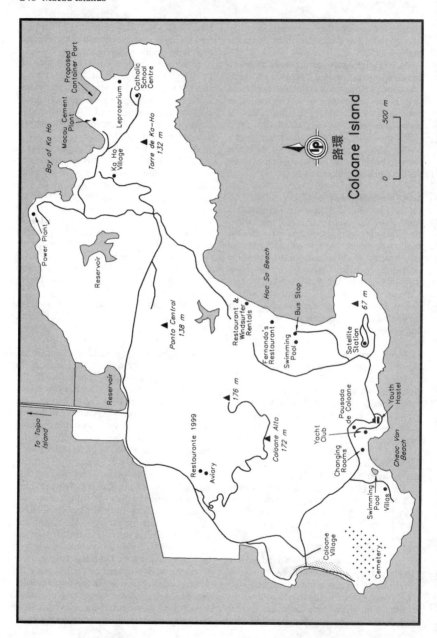

Coloane Island

路環

0   500 m

Bay of Ka Ho

Proposed Container Port

Macau Cement Plant

Leprosarium

Catholic School Centre

Torre de Ka-Ho 132 m

Ka Ho Village

Power Plant

Reservoir

Ponto Central 138 m

Reservoir

To Taipa Island

Restaurante 1999

Aviary

176 m

Coloane Alto 172 m

Restaurant & Windsurfer Rentals

Hac Sa Beach

Fernando's Restaurant

Swimming Pool

Bus Stop

Satellite Station

67 m

Pousada de Coloane

Yacht Club

Changing Rooms

Youth Hostel

Cheoc Van Beach

Swimming Pool

Villas

Coloane Village

Cemetery

and a crew of painted little men with Chinese pointed hats. The temple custodian enthusiastically welcomes foreigners and then holds up a little placard in English soliciting donations for the maintenance of the temple. Such donations are voluntary so let your conscience be your guide.

Cheoc Van Beach 竹灣

About 1.5 km down the road from Coloane Village is Cheoc Van Beach. The name means 'Bamboo Bay'. You can swim in the ocean for free (there are public changing rooms) or at the pool in **Cheoc Van Park** (for a fee). The pool is open from 9 am to 10 pm. Cheoc Van Beach also has a yacht club where you can inquire about boat rentals.

Hac Sa Beach 黑沙灣

The largest and most popular beach in Macau, the name Hac Sa means black sand. The sand does indeed have a grey to black colour and this makes the water look somewhat polluted, but actually it's perfectly clean and fine for swimming. The area is beautiful and on a clear day you get good

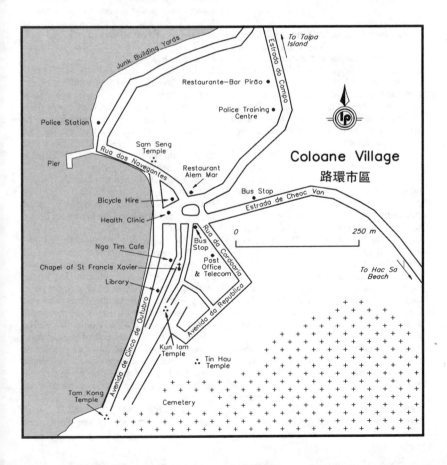

views of the islands south of Hong Kong, although you can't see Hong Kong itself.

Just near the bus stop is **Hac Sa Sports & Recreation Park**. Within the park is a large swimming pool, roller skating rink, playground and miniature golf course. It's open 9 am to 9 pm daily, and admission costs M$5. Use of the pool costs an additional M$15.

Behind Fernando's Restaurant is a place to rent horses. Further down the beach is a place to rent windsurfers.

Bus No 21A provides frequent service to Hac Sa. On weekends the buses are even more frequent.

Ka Ho 九澳村

At the eastern end of Coloane is Ka Ho, but it's not likely that you'll want to go there. It's not very attractive due to the shanties and the fact that the village sits right between a cement plant and power plant. There is a leprosarium here and the remains of a Vietnamese refugee camp. Perhaps the most interesting sight in town is the church called **Our Lady of Sorrows** which has a large bronze crucifix above the north door.

This is likely to change. Ka Ho is slated for development as a deep-water container port to accommodate the manufacturing industries Macau is hoping to attract.

Places to Stay

Youth Hostels The *Pousada de Juventude* youth hostel is at Cheoc Van Beach, but your chances of getting in are slim because it's nearly always full. There are only 30 beds, 15 each for men and women. Individual travellers can stay here if there is room, but normally big groups book the hostel far in advance, especially during summer and on weekends and holidays. To inquire, telephone ☎ 28024. If you want to make advance group bookings, write to Governo de Macau, Direccao dos Servicos de Educacao, Divisao de Actividades Juvenis (☎ 88151).

An International Youth Hostel Federation (IYHF) card is needed. The hostel is closed from 10 am to 3 pm and lights are out from 11 pm until 7 am. The cost for a dormitory bed is M$20 for foreigners and M$10 for Macau residents.

Hotels Very close to the beach at Cheoc Van Beach is a luxury hotel, the *Pousada de Coloane* (☎ 328143, fax 328251). Without a doubt it has the most relaxing atmosphere of any hotel in Macau. Twins range from M$480 to M$580. The hotel has its own sauna and swimming pool and is well known for its excellent Sunday lunch buffet.

Hac Sa Westin Hotel is a new resort complex on the far side of Hac Sa Beach. It was still under construction as this book was being researched, but plans call for a casino, luxury villas, a country club and an 18-hole golf course. Expect prices to be high.

Places to Eat

Right near the roundabout at Coloane Village is the *Choi Un Kei* which makes terrible sandwiches but has good soft drinks. The adjacent *Fai Kei Café* has lots of good cakes and drinks. On the other side of the roundabout is the relatively up-market *Restaurant Alem Mar* which serves Cantonese food. Right next to the St Francis Chapel is the small but good *Nga Tim Café*.

Walking out of town to the north, just past the Police Training Centre, is the *Restaurante-Bar Pirao* (☎ 328215), one of the best restaurants on the island for Portuguese food.

At Hac Sa Beach, *Fernando's* (☎ 328264) deserves honourable mention for some of the best food in Macau. The atmosphere is also pleasant, and it can get crowded in the evening. There are two main problems with this place. The first is that there is no sign above the door and it's possible to wander around for quite a while looking for it. The restaurant is at the far end of the car park, close to the bus stop. The other problem is that the menu is in Portuguese and Chinese only. Fernando himself (the manager) will gladly translate for you, and he recommends the clams.

Restaurante 1999 (☎ 328292) is in Coloane Park and serves fine Portuguese food.

CANTON

Facts about Canton

Step across the border from either Hong Kong or Macau and you're in Guangdong Province, the home of the Cantonese people and the most accessible part of China.

Canton is the traditional Western name for both the Chinese province of Guangdong, and also its capital city, Guangzhou. While Chinese names (Beijing, Nanjing, etc) are generally used in this book, the name Canton has been used because of its strong historical association with Hong Kong and Macau, and its greater acceptance, at least for the present, by Western readers.

The image of 'Chinatown' that most Westerners now have is based on the Cantonese. In Chinatowns from Melbourne to Toronto to London, Cantonese food is eaten and the Cantonese dialect predominates.

HISTORY

China is a sleeping giant. Let her sleep, for when she awakes, she will astonish the world.
Napoleon

It was the people of Guangdong who first made contact (often unhappy) with both the merchants and the armies of the modern European states, and it was these people who spearheaded the Chinese emigration to North America, Australia and South Africa in the mid-19th century. The move was spurred by gold rushes in those countries, but it was mainly the wars and growing poverty of the century which induced the Chinese to leave in droves.

The history of Guangdong Province over the past 2000 years is known to us in outline. While the Chinese were carving out a civilisation centred on the Yellow River region in the north, the south remained a semi-independent enclave peopled by native tribes, the last survivors of which are now minority groups.

It was not until the Qin Dynasty (221 BC to 207 BC), when the Chinese states of the north were for the first time united under a single ruler, that the Chinese finally conquered the southern regions. However, revolts and uprisings were frequent and the Chinese settlements remained small and dispersed among a predominantly aboriginal population.

Chinese emigration to the region began in earnest around the 12th century AD. The original native tribes were killed by Chinese armies, isolated in small pockets or pushed further south – like the Li and Miao peoples who now inhabit the mountainous areas of Hainan Island off the southern coast of China.

By the 17th century the Chinese had outgrown Guangdong. The pressure of population forced them to move into adjoining Guangxi Province and into Sichuan, which had been ravaged and depopulated after rebellions in the mid-17th century.

As a result of these multiple migrations, the people of Guangdong are not a homogeneous group. The term Cantonese is sometimes applied to all people living in Guangdong Province. More commonly, it refers to those who shared the language and culture of a group of counties during the last imperial dynasties. Other inhabitants of Guangdong are distinguishable from the Cantonese by their language and customs – such as the Hakka people who started moving southward from the northern plains around the 13th or 14th centuries.

What the migrants from the north found beyond the mountainous areas of northern and western Guangdong was the Pearl River Delta, cutting through a region which is richer than any in China, except for around the Yangtze and Yellow rivers.

The Pearl River Delta lies at the southeastern end of a broad plain stretching over both Guangdong and Guangxi provinces. Because of their fertility, the delta and river valleys could support a large population. The abundant waterways, heavy rainfall and warm climate allowed wet-rice cultivation of

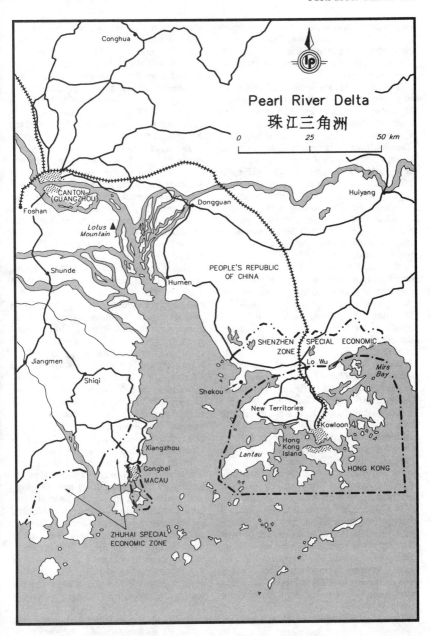

two crops a year (although in the past century the growth of the population and its heavy concentration in the Canton area was more than Guangdong could sustain, so grain had to be imported).

The first town to be established on the site of present-day Canton dates back to the Qin Dynasty, coinciding with the conquest of southern China by the north. Close to the sea, Canton became an outward-looking city. The first foreigners to come here were the Indians and the Romans as early as the 2nd century AD. By the time of the Tang Dynasty 500 years later, Arab traders were arriving regularly and a sizeable trade with the Middle East and South-East Asia grew.

Initial contact with modern European nations began in the early 16th century and resulted in the Portuguese being allowed to set up base downriver at Macau in 1557.

Next, Jesuits came and aroused the interest of the Imperial Court with their scientific and technical knowledge. This was mainly through their expertise in astronomy, which permitted the all-important astrological charts to be produced more accurately, though others worked as makers of fountains and curios or as painters and architects. In 1582 the Jesuits were allowed to establish themselves at Zhaoqing, a town north-west of Canton, and later in Beijing, but overall the Jesuit influence on China was negligible.

The first trade overtures from the British were rebuffed in 1625, but the imperial government finally opened Canton in 1685. British ships began to arrive regularly from the East India Company bases on the Indian coast and traders were allowed to establish warehouses (called 'factories') near Canton as a base from which to ship out tea and silk.

In 1757 a new imperial edict restricted all foreign trade to a single Canton merchants guild, the Co Hong, an indication of how little importance was placed on trade with the Western barbarians. The Europeans had a far greater interest in trade with China, and it was their pursuit of this interest which led to the Opium Wars (see the Facts About Hong Kong chapter).

Canton was always considered to exist on the edge of a wilderness, far from Nanjing and Beijing, which were the centres of power under the isolationist Ming (1368 to 1644) and Qing (1644 to 1911) dynasties. In the 19th century the Cantonese sense of independence, aided by the distance from Beijing, allowed Guangdong to become a cradle of revolt against the north. The leader of the anti-dynastic Taiping Rebellion, Hong Xiuquan (1814-1864), was born in Huaxian to the north-west of Canton, which was the centre of the early activities of the Taipings.

At the turn of the 20th century secret societies were being set up all over China and by Chinese abroad in order to bring down the crumbling Qing Dynasty. In 1905 several of these societies merged to form the Alliance for Chinese Revolution which was headed by Dr Sun Yatsen (who was born at Cuiheng village south-west of Canton).

The Qing Dynasty fell in 1911 when the court announced the nationalisation of the railways. The move was viewed by provincial governors and wealthy merchants as an attempt to restrict their autonomy. An army coup in Wuhan in central China seized control of the city and the heads of many other provinces declared their loyalty to the rebels. By the year's end, most of southern China had repudiated Qing rule and given its support to Sun Yatsen's alliance. On 1 January 1912 he was proclaimed president of the Chinese Republic, but it was a republic in name only since most of the north was controlled by local military leaders (warlords) left over from the Qing Dynasty.

In the wake of these events China underwent an intellectual revolution as its intelligentsia searched for a new ideology which could solve the country's social problems, end the warlordism and prevent further encroachments and demands on the Chinese by foreign powers. Study groups and other political organisations sprang up everywhere and included as members people such as Zhou Enlai and Mao Zedong. Then, in 1921, several Chinese Marxist groups banded together to form the Chinese Communist Party (CCP).

By this stage Sun Yatsen had managed to

secure a political base in Canton, setting up a government which was made up of surviving members of the Kuomintang – the party which emerged as the dominant revolutionary political force after the demise of the Qing Dynasty. In a shaky alliance with the Communists, the Kuomintang began training a National Revolutionary Army (NRA) under the command of Chiang Kaishek, who had met Sun in Japan some years before. Sun died in 1925 and by 1927 the Kuomintang was ready to launch its Northern Expedition – a military venture under the command of Chiang designed to subdue the northern warlords.

However, Chiang was also engaged in a power struggle within the Kuomintang. So, as the NRA moved in on Shanghai (then under the control of a local warlord whose strength had been undermined by a powerful industrial movement organised in the city by the Communists), Chiang Kaishek took the opportunity to put down both the Communists and his enemies in the Kuomintang.

Supported by Shanghai industrialists who were worried about the trade union movement, and by foreigners who feared the loss of trade and privileges, Chiang let loose a reign of terror against the Communists, their sympathisers and anyone who advocated revolutionary change in China.

With the help of Shanghai's underworld leaders, money from Shanghai bankers and the blessings of foreigners in Shanghai, Chiang armed hundreds of gangsters, dressed them in nationalist uniforms and launched an overnight surprise attack which wiped out the Communists in the city. This was quickly followed by the massacre of Communists and other anti-Chiang factions in Canton, Changsha and Nanchang.

By mid-1928 the Northern Expedition had reached Beijing and a national government was established with Chiang holding the highest political and military positions. Communists who survived the massacres retreated to the Jinggang Mountains on the Hunan-Jiangxi border and other mountainous areas of China, from where they began a war against the Kuomintang which lasted just over 20 years and which ended in victory for the Communists in 1949.

The dramatic revolutionary events around Canton in the early 20th century were nothing new. Centuries before the southerners had gained a reputation for independent thinking and rebellions and uprisings were a feature of Canton from its foundation. As early as the 10th century it became independent along with the rest of Guangdong Province.

The assimilation of southern China was a slow process, reflected in the fact that the southerners referred to themselves as the people of Tang (of the Tang Dynasty of 618 to 907 AD), while the northerners referred to themselves as the people of Han (of the Han Dynasty of 206 BC to 220 AD). Northerners regarded their southern compatriots with disdain, or as one 19th-century northern account put it:

The Cantonese...are a coarse set of people...Before the times of Han and Tang, this country was quite wild and waste, and these people have sprung forth from unconnected, unsettled vagabonds that wandered here from the north.

The traditional stereotype of the Cantonese – five million of whom live in the city of Canton and its surrounding suburbs – is of a proud people, frank in criticism, lacking in restraint, oriented to defending their own interests and not friendly. They are also regarded as shrewd in business and quick, lively and clever in catching on to new skills.

Of all the Chinese, the Cantonese have probably been the most influenced by the outside world. Almost everyone in southern Guangdong has relatives in Hong Kong who for years have been storming across the border loaded down with the latest hairstyles and gifts of cooking oil, TV sets or Sony cassette recorders – goods which the average Chinese either can't afford or which are in short supply in the People's Republic.

The Tiananmen Massacre

At the age of 73, Chinese reformist leader Hu Yaobang died suddenly from natural causes on 15 April 1989. Although not exactly a hero when he lived, his death served as a rallying point for reformists. On the weekend after his death, 22 April, China's leaders gathered at the Great Hall of the People for an official 'mourning for Hu'. Just outside, in Tiananmen Square, approximately 150,000 students and other activists held their own ceremony which soon turned into a massive pro-democracy protest.

It didn't end there. As the weather warmed up students flocked to Beijing to camp out in the square. By the middle of May, crowds of protesters in and around the square had swelled to nearly one million. Workers and even police joined in. Protests erupted in at least 20 other cities. Students from Beijing's Art Institute constructed the 'Goddess of Democracy' – a statue which bore a striking resemblance to New York's Statue of Liberty – in Tiananmen Square. The students made speeches demanding a free press and an end to corruption and nepotism. Huge pro-democracy demonstrations in Hong Kong, Macau and Taiwan supported the students. The arrival of the foreign press corps turned the 'Beijing Spring' into the media event of 1989.

Martial law was declared on 20 May. Zhao Ziyang was ousted from power because he had openly sympathised with the students. Li Peng assumed control of the party with the backing of Deng Xiaoping and Yang Shangkun.

Protests spread to other cities. Besides demonstrations on the Chinese mainland, 500,000 demonstrators in Hong Kong marched through the streets and held rallies. About 100,000 people took part in demonstrations in Macau.

As troops surrounded Beijing, enthusiasm began to shrivel. Crowds of students camped out in Tiananmen Square dwindled to around 10,000. The military assault came in the pre-dawn hours of 4 June. The number of deaths will never be known. While the government first claimed that there were no civilians killed in the square, some observers estimated the death toll at 3000. The truth probably lies somewhere in between. World

opinion quickly turned against China's government. Chinese students studying abroad staged large-scale protests and a number of Chinese diplomats defected.

No sooner had the blood been washed off the streets than the wave of arrests and executions began. The 'Beijing Spring' was abruptly followed by a severe 'winter' – those caught just speaking to a foreign journalist were immediately arrested for 'rumour mongering'. Chinese television showed 'hooligans' – their faces badly swollen from beatings – confessing to 'counterrevolutionary crimes'. While ordinary people were being arrested, a political purge was under way in the upper ranks of the Communist Party. Party Secretary General Zhao Ziyang was made the scapegoat. Zhao was replaced by Jiang Zemin, well-known as the 'weather vane' because of his ability to point in whatever direction the political winds are blowing.

The brutal suppression of the pro-democracy movement has had a major impact on China's economy. Tourism, foreign aid and investment have fallen off sharply. Hong Kong has also been badly affected – money and talent is rapidly fleeing the colony in anticipation of the Chinese takeover in 1997.

Many have feared that China would revert to its xenophobic past and close itself off from the outside world. This, at least, has not happened. A year after the protests, martial law was finally lifted and things more or less returned to normal. However, disillusionment and cynicism (both within and outside of China) remain deep. It is doubtful that the Communist Party will be able to regain the moral authority and respect it once commanded unless it is thoroughly reformed, and this seems unlikely until the old guard dies off. Many young reformists would like to take their place, but as the Chinese say, *Hǎo rén bù cháng shòu* – 'Good people don't live long'.

The goals of free enterprise, private business and individualism – things which are still anathema to the hardline Communists – represent the path which Guangdong is attempting to follow. In spite of constant interference from the Beijing bureaucrats, Guangdong continues to drag China – kicking and screaming – into the capitalist age.

GEOGRAPHY

Guangdong Province lies on the south-east coast of China and occupies just 2.2% of China's total land area. The dominant feature is the Pearl River Delta, a fertile plain which supports a huge population and provides a natural harbour. The river provides a natural transport system and is a chief reason for Canton's existence as a major economic hub. Not surprisingly, the Cantonese have a much closer affection for Hong Kong than Beijing – Canton is a mere 120 km from Hong Kong and 2300 km from the national capital.

CLIMATE

Most of Guangdong Province has a subtropical climate, though temperatures tend to be more extreme as one moves inland. Average monthly temperatures and rainfall for Canton are as follows:

universities, government and industries. Real authority is exercised by Communist Party representatives at each level in these organisations. They, in turn, are responsible to the party officials in the hierarchy above them, thus ensuring strict central control. Democracy in a Western sense doesn't exist.

Throughout the entire system, there are various antagonistic factions. Governing the country seems to be a delicate balancing act between these rival factions, and as a result the government is often too paralysed to make any significant policy decisions. This has been especially true since the 1989 Tiananmen massacre – conservatives (the hard-line Communists) and liberals (capitalist-style reformers) are at each others throats. The conservatives had the upper hand right after the massacre – presently, both sides seem to have each other checkmated.

Things are a little different in Guangdong Province, of which Canton is the capital. While paying lip service to the party's official line taken in Beijing, Guangdong officials from the governor on down have

Temperature & Rainfall

Month	Jan	Feb	Mar	Apr	May	Jun	Jul	Aug	Sep	Oct	Nov	Dec
Temp °C	13.6	14.2	17.2	21.6	25.6	27.3	28.8	28.2	27.2	24	19.7	15.7
Rain mm	27	65	101	185	256	292	264	248	149	49	51	34

GOVERNMENT

Every revolution evaporates, leaving behind only the slime of a new bureaucracy.
Franz Kafka

Precious little is known about the inner workings of the Chinese government, but Westerners can make educated guesses.

The highest authority rests with the Standing Committee of the Communist Party Politburo. Below it is the 210-member Central Committee, made up of younger party members and provincial Party leaders. At grass roots level the party forms a parallel system to the administrations in the army,

continued to push their own programme of economic liberalisation, although political liberalisation is not at present possible. Officials here have a much more relaxed attitude and are much less interested in controlling people's lives than elsewhere in China.

At the grass roots level the basic unit of government organisation is the work unit (dānwèi). Every Chinese is a member of a work unit, wherever he or she works – in a hospital, school, office, factory or village. Many Westerners may admire the cooperative spirit that this system is supposed to engender, but they would cringe if their own lives were so intricately controlled. Nothing can proceed without the work unit. It issues ration coupons for grain, oil, cotton and coal, and it decides if a couple may marry or divorce and when they can have a child. It assigns housing, sets salaries, handles mail, recruits party members, keeps files on each unit member, arranges transfers to other jobs or other parts of the country, and gives permission to travel abroad.

Work unit members are also compelled to attend endless, fruitless meetings which are held primarily to explain the wisdom behind the government's half-baked policies. The work unit's control extends into every part of the individual's life, but in Guangdong the work unit's role is somewhat played down.

Through the work units, the government has conducted an intensive programme of 'political education' since the Tiananmen massacre. Every workplace is required to display portraits of Mao, Marx, Engels, Stalin and Lenin. Workers and peasants are once again being forced to study the thoughts of Chairman Mao. Predictably, this has alienated the masses even further.

Intriguingly, in this newly repressive atmosphere, people have found a safe way to protest. Photos of Mao can be seen everywhere in Canton – pasted to the windows of taxis, on T-shirts and hanging up on the wall of many restaurants. However, this is not because the masses have suddenly decided they are sentimental for Maoist economics. Rather, it should be remembered that Mao obliterated other members of the ruling politburo when he launched the Cultural Revolution. One of Mao's political slogans has suddenly be come very popular again – 'Sweep away the vermin'.

ECONOMY

China's economic policies have undergone a radical change since the death of Mao Zedong. Under Mao, China had largely isolated itself from the economies of the rest of the world, apprehensive that economic links with other countries would make China dependent on them.

The Cultural Revolution, launched by Mao in the 1960s, put an end to even the most basic forms of private enterprise – free markets, simple food stalls and privately owned restaurants were regarded as examples of bourgeois capitalism. All aspects of the economy, from restaurants to steel mills to paddy fields, came under state ownership and rigid state control. Schools were closed and intellectuals were sent to labour in the countryside, depriving China of properly trained economists, managers and people with high-technology skills.

As the state tightened its grip, the economy reeled. Farmers were told to plant unprofitable crops and were paid a pittance for their labour, so production fell. As food shortages developed, peasants spent hours every day standing in long queues with ration coupons to buy their basic staples and factories produced shoddy goods which nobody wanted.

The Red Guards, who produced nothing, roamed the countryside terrorising the populace, burning schools and libraries and destroying temples. Many innocent people were denounced as 'capitalist roaders' and were killed, tortured or persecuted. Deng Xiaoping's son, Deng Pufang, was crippled for life when Red Guards threw him out of a 4th-floor window. Sometimes Red Guard factions battled each other. The country seemed to be moving towards civil war and financial collapse.

Mao died in 1976. Soon thereafter, members of the so-called Gang of Four led by Mao's wife, Jiang Qing, were arrested. Jiang Qing remained imprisoned until 1991, when she committed suicide.

The Maoist policies of isolation were reversed and China opened up to the West. Under the leadership of Deng Xiaoping, China turned away from the narrow path of centralised planning, state ownership and control of all facets of the economy.

The official slogan says that China will develop 'socialism with Chinese characteristics'. Another Deng cliche – 'to get rich is glorious' – is much more popular with the masses. Slogans aside, China is slowly returning to capitalism – in fits and starts rather than all at once.

Trying to reconcile the conflict between socialist theory and the reality of the free-market reforms (which are capitalist) has been a problem for the Communist Party. The official explanation is that China is still in the 'primary stage of socialism' and that the reforms are a temporary measure to help the country out until a purer form of socialism can evolve. In no way does the party admit that the country could be moving towards capitalism, or that capitalism could be more efficient than socialism. Indeed, it is just the opposite. When China was hit by severe floods in 1991, party officials publicly declared that the way they handled relief efforts proved 'the superiority of the socialist system', even though they had to go begging to Hong Kong and Taiwan for help.

Problems

China's economic progress of the past decade has been encouraging, yet the road to reform is not without its potholes. Criminal activity is on the upsurge – from burglaries to white-collar crimes such as fraud and embezzlement. One reason is that now there is more wealth worth stealing. Another reason for the increase in crime is that China is much less of a police state than in the time of the Cultural Revolution. Not that they've done away with the firing squads – indeed, public executions of criminals are still performed. But there is more freedom to move around and somebody with unexplained wealth isn't automatically arrested as in the old days.

The more relaxed atmosphere has also brought an upsurge in prostitution, which the Communists once claimed to have stamped out. Aside from any moral objections, prostitution poses a real danger of spreading AIDS.

Corruption has increased dramatically in recent years. The presence of cash-rich foreign investors creates more opportunities for officials to demand bribes. Corruption has also increased as a result of the country's dual-price system – the government sub-sidises about 40% of raw materials while the rest are sold at higher prices in the free market. Some individuals and state enterprises simply engage in the business of buying up cheap, subsidised materials and reselling them in the black market.

As the Maoist concept of the 'iron rice bowl' is being shattered, unemployment has raised its ugly head. Unprofitable state-run enterprises are being forced to shed their unneeded (and unproductive) workers in order to compete in a free market, but the result is rising joblessness. Not that the state sector has really learned to be efficient yet – about one-third of all state enterprises loses money and must be bailed out by the government, and many of the other two-thirds are only marginally profitable. The high cost of subsidising the unprofitable state companies has stretched the resources of the government, resulting in annual budget deficits.

Urban drift is another growing problem. Chinese people can now travel the country freely and are flooding into the cities in search of instant wealth, only to live on the streets because of the cities' inability to accommodate the human tidal wave. Housing and jobs are in short supply in China, especially in the cities, where you cannot rent a house or get a job without a residence permit. Authorities are understandably reluctant to issue urban residence permits to everybody who wants one.

Around Canton Railway Station you can see many drifters who have no other place to go. Ironically, the richer Canton becomes, the poorer it looks because of the abundance of new arrivals who sleep in the streets and turn to begging when they cannot find work. Those who are desperate enough may resort to crime. Many would probably be better off if they returned to the countryside, but few are willing to do so. However, the unemployed are being encouraged to start their own businesses, as evidenced by the numerous street vendors now seen in China.

Problems of infrastructure continue to plague China. Economic growth causes people to consume more. New roads, railways, power stations, telephone lines and container ports are being built, but demand continues to outstrip supply.

Then there is the brain drain. Many Chinese have correctly perceived that they would be far better off economically if they moved abroad. With the opportunity to go abroad to travel and study, more and more people are simply not returning to China. The USA is by far the favourite destination, although Australia and a few other places are also high on the list. A visitor or student visa to USA is widely regarded as an immigrant visa by most Chinese. Americans teaching English or studying in China often find themselves targeted for marriage, since getting married to a foreigner is the easiest way to get out of China.

China's geriatric leaders enjoyed their brief reassertion of power in 1989 after the Tiananmen massacre, but reality soon set in. As much as the hardliners would like to return to the 1950s, the fact is that the reforms have gone too far. Once China swung open the door and let in tourists, traders, foreign investment and capitalist reforms, the old revolutionaries found they could no longer 'put the toothpaste back in the tube'. When the old men in Beijing tried to reassert socialist orthodoxy during 1989 and 1990, the economy plunged into recession. Now the reforms are slowly getting back on track, especially in Guangdong where officials typically ignore edicts from Beijing anyway. Practically no one under the age of 80 believes in socialism any longer, and China's wheelchair leadership consists of mere mortals with little time left to shape the country's destiny.

One consequence of the Tiananmen massacre has been the souring of relations with the USA which has harshly criticised China's human rights violations. In 1991, the US Congress almost revoked China's status as a Most Favoured Nation (MFN). Having MFN status is crucial to China's export industries which have become greatly dependent on the US market. Loss of MFN status would be a crippling blow to Guangdong's economy, as well as to Hong Kong. Although MFN status was renewed

(barely), some US representatives have vowed to revoke it in the future if China's human rights record does not improve.

When you're touring the country remember that, for all the reforms, China is still not a capitalist country even though it is moving in that direction. Canton and neighbouring the Special Economic Zones (SEZs) like Shenzhen and Zhuhai are hardly representative of the rest of China as most Chinese cities and towns are far less prosperous. However, the Canton area is an indication of the direction in which the rest of China seems to be heading. You'll get at least a glimpse of some of the successes, pitfalls, fallacies and curious results of the new economic policies.

POPULATION

Nationwide there are more than 1.1 billion people. Guangdong Province has about 65 million people, or 6% of the nation's total.

Although overpopulation is a problem that pre-dates the Communist takeover, Mao Zedong must share a lot of the blame for the present mess. Mao believed that birth control was a capitalist plot to weaken China. Like Marx, he was not impressed by arguments that overpopulation could outstrip agricultural and natural resources. Rather, he felt that more people meant more production. Accordingly, up until 1973 the Chinese were urged to have as many children as possible for the good of the nation.

These policies have been reversed and China now has the world's most stringent birth-control policies. The legal marriage age for men is 22 and for women it's 20. If a woman delays marriage until after the age of 25 she is entitled to extra maternity leave. Couples are urged to have one child only and those who violate this policy are subject to stiff fines and loss of privileges. The one-child family is fairly common in the large cities, but in rural areas many have continued to have two or more children, despite fines and threats of demotions, loss of employment and housing benefits. Many women have been known to hide until after they've given birth to a second or third child, and then, to avoid sanctions, will not register the child's birth. Such women are known as 'birth guerrillas'.

Furthermore, government officials, anxious to meet quotas set by Beijing, have been known to falsify figures and sometimes force women to have abortions. Although the forced abortions have made big headlines in the West, it does not seem to be a common practice.

More disturbing are cases of female infanticide. Again, it is not an official policy and indeed, is highly illegal. Nevertheless, China is definitely a rigidly male-oriented society and female children are considered worthless. Female infanticide has had a long history in China and did not start with the one-child per family policy, but the new restrictions on family size have no doubt aggravated the problem.

All methods of birth control are free. The most commonly used are IUDs, abortion and sterilisation, although condoms and birth-control pills are also available. Posters urging the masses to practise family planning are ubiquitous in China.

Although the growth rate has slowed as a result of the one-child policy, the average population is still very young, and China's population will continue to grow for the next two decades before declining. It is projected to reach 1.28 billion by the year 2000.

PEOPLE
More than 98% of inhabitants of Guangdong are Han Chinese while the rest belong to small minority groups such as the Miao and Li.

ARTS
Basically, it's the same as for Hong Kong, but there are a few differences. Communist poster art has experienced a revival since the Tiananmen massacre of 1989 – or rather, it should be said that the leadership is trying to ram it down everyone's throats. You can see these posters in Canton – bright, flaming red hammers and sickles with Chinese slogans in the background saying things like 'The socialist road leads to happiness'. Most people pay no attention.

Disco music is big with the hip young urban Chinese. Love songs and soft rock from Taiwan and Hong Kong is in vogue in Canton while in Beijing tastes run more towards heavy metal and punk. There are dance halls in all the major cities to cater for the craze – sometimes with taped music, often with live bands featuring batteries of horns and electric violins.

Attempts to tailor Chinese classical music, song and dance to Western tastes have resulted in a Frankenstein's monster of Broadway-style spectacular and epic theatre film score. Chinese rock star Cui Jian released a big hit 'Rock for the New Long March'. In an attempt to show that the geriatric leadership is also hip, government officials authorised a disco version of 'The East is Red'. There are orchestras organised on Western lines which substitute Chinese for Western instruments. Exactly where all this is leading no one knows.

RELIGION
The situation is similar to Hong Kong and Macau, the basic difference being that all forms of religion were harshly suppressed during the Cultural Revolution. Priests, nuns and monks were imprisoned, executed or sent to labour in the countryside while temples and churches were ransacked and converted into factories and warehouses. Since the early 1980s, temples have been restored, at least for the sake of tourism. There has been a religious revival of sorts, but the main feature you will note about temples in China is that they are usually devoid of worshippers. If you're really interested in pursuing the topic of Chinese religion, you'd do better to look for it in Hong Kong or Taiwan. Taiwan remains the best venue for seeing traditional Chinese temples and ceremonies.

LANGUAGE
What a difference a border can make. Cantonese is still the most popular dialect in Canton and the surrounding area, but the official language of the People's Republic is the Beijing dialect, usually referred to in the

West as 'Mandarin'. In China it's referred to as *pǔtōnghùa* or 'common speech' and the Chinese government set about popularising it in the 1950s.

Probably the first words you'll learn are *méi yǒu*, which means literally 'not have'.

> I've come to the conclusion that the Chinese word for 'hello' and 'greetings' is 'meiyou'. Meiyou is what you'll hear the most and learn the first. That despised word – meiyou – was said much more often to me upon entry into an establishment than any hello I ever heard!
>
> **Deborah Koons**

Pinyin
In 1958 the Chinese officially adopted a system known as *pīnyīn* as a method of writing their language using the Roman alphabet. Since the official language of China is the Beijing dialect, this pronunciation is used. The original idea was to eventually do away with characters completely and just use pinyin. However, tradition dies hard and the idea has gradually been abandoned.

Pinyin is often used on shop fronts, street signs and advertising billboards. The popularisation of this spelling is still at an early stage, so don't expect Chinese to be able to use pinyin. In the countryside and the smaller towns you may not see a single pinyin sign anywhere, so unless you speak Chinese you'll need a phrasebook with Chinese characters if you're travelling in these areas. Though pinyin is helpful, it's not an instant key to communication since Westerners usually don't get the pronunciation and intonation of the romanised word correct.

Since 1979 all translated texts of Chinese diplomatic documents and Chinese magazines published in foreign languages have used the pinyin system of spelling names and places. The system replaces the old Wade-Giles and Lessing systems of romanising Chinese script. Thus under pinyin, 'Mao Tse-tung' becomes *Mao Zedong*; 'Chou En-lai' becomes *Zhou Enlai*; and 'Peking' becomes *Beijing*. The name of the country remains as it has been generally written: 'China' in

English and German, and 'Chine' in French – in pinyin it's *Zhongguo (zhōnggúo)*.

Tones
There are four basic tones used in Mandarin, while other dialects can have as many as nine. For example, in Mandarin Chinese the word *ma* can have four distinct meanings depending on which tone is used:

high tone	*mā* is mother
rising tone	*má* is hemp or numb
falling-rising tone	*mǎ* is horse
falling tone	*mà* is to scold or swear

In some words, the tone is not important. This so-called neutral tone is usually not indicated at all. Mastering tones is tricky for the untrained Western ear, but with practice it can be done.

The following is a description of the sounds produced in spoken Mandarin Chinese. The letter **v** is not used in Chinese. The trickiest sounds in pinyin are **c**, **q** and **x**. Most letters are pronounced as in English, except for the following:

Vowels
a like the 'a' in 'father'
ai like the 'i' in 'I'
ao like the 'ow' in 'cow'
e like the 'u' in 'blur'
ei like the 'ei' in 'weigh'
i like the 'ee' in 'meet' or the 'oo' in 'book'*
ian like in 'yen'
ie like the English word 'yeah'
o like the 'o' in 'or'
ou like the 'oa' in 'boat'
u like the 'u' in 'flute'
ui like 'way'
uo like 'w' followed by an 'o' like in 'or'
yu like German umlaut 'ü' or French 'u' in 'union'
ü like German umlaut 'ü'

Consonants
c like the 'ts' in 'bits'
ch like in English, but with the tongue curled back

h like in English, but articulated from the throat

q like the 'ch' in 'chicken'

r like the 's' in 'pleasure'

sh like in English, but with the tongue curled back

x like the 'sh' in 'shine'

z like the 'ds' in 'suds'

zh like the 'j' in 'judge' but with the tongue curled back

*The letter **i** is pronounced like the 'oo' in 'book' when it occurs after c, ch, r, s, sh, z, zh.

Consonants can never appear at the end of a syllable except for **n, ng** and **r**.

In pinyin, apostrophes are occasionally used to separate syllables. So, you can write *(ping'an)* to prevent the word being pronounced as *(pin'gan)*.

Body Language

Hand signs are well used in China. The 'thumbs-up' sign has a long tradition as an indication of excellence or, in Chinese, *gūa gūa jiào*. Another way to indicate excellence is to gently pull your own earlobe between thumb and index finger.

The Chinese have a system for counting on their hands. If you can't speak the language, it would be worth your while to at least learn Chinese finger counting. The symbol for number 10 is to form a cross with the index fingers, but in many locations the Chinese just show a fist.

Courses

The Chinese Language Centre of Zhongshan University in Canton, at 135 Xingang Xilu, offers a course in Mandarin Chinese.

Phrasebooks

Lonely Planet's *Mandarin Chinese Phrasebook* includes common words, useful phrases and word lists in English, simplified Chinese characters and pinyin.

A good phrasebook, obtainable in Hong Kong, is the *Speechless Translator*, which has columns of Chinese characters and English translations that you simply string together to form sentences – no talking required. It's very popular among travellers.

Greetings & Civilities

Hello
nǐ hǎo
你好
Goodbye
zàijiàn
再见

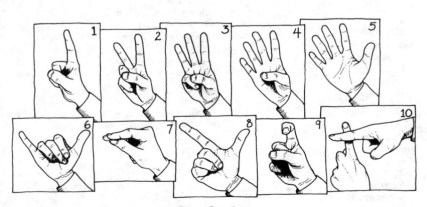

Finger Counting

Thank you
xièxie
谢谢

You're welcome
bùkèqì
不客气

no, don't have
méiyǒu
没有

no, not so
bù shì
不是

Emergency

Help!
jiùmìng a
救命啊

Thief!
xiǎo tōu
小偷

Fire!
hǔo zāi
火灾

I'm sick
wǒ shēng bìng
我生病

hospital
yīyùan
医院

pharmacy
yàodiàn
药店

laxative
xiè yào
泻药

anti-diarrhoeal drug
húang liǎn sù
黄连素

I'm lost
wǒ mí lù
我迷路

Necessities

toilet (restroom)
cèsǔo
厕所

toilet paper
wèishēng zhǐ
卫生纸

sanitary pads (Kotex)
wèishēng mián
卫生棉

How much does it cost?
dūoshǎo qián
多少钱

too expensive
tài gùi le
太贵了

post office
yóu jú
邮局

stamp
yóu piào
邮票

aerogramme
hángkōng yóujiǎn
航空邮简

poste restante
cún jú hòu lǐng lán
存局候领栏

Places

China International Travel Service (CITS)
zhōngguó gúojì lüxíngshè
中国国际旅行社

Bank of China
zhōngguó yínháng
中国银行

Public Security Bureau
gōng'ān jú
公安局

Foreign Affairs Branch
wài shì kē
外事科

CAAC
zhōnggúo mínháng
中国民航

Hotel

tourist hotel
bīngǔan, fàndiàn, jiǔdiàn
宾馆，饭店，酒店

dormitory
dūo rén fáng
多人房

single room
dān rén fáng
单人房

double room
  shuāng rén fáng
  双人房
bathtowel
  yùjīn
  浴巾
hotel namecard
  lüguan de míngpiàn
  旅馆的明片

Transport

I want to go to...
  wǒ yào qù...
  我要去 ...
left-luggage room
  jìcún chù
  寄存处
buy a ticket
  mǎi piào
  买票
refund a ticket
  tùi piào
  退票
bicycle
  zìxíngchē
  自行车
long-distance bus station
  chángtú qìchē zhàn
  长途汽车站
train station
  hǔochē zhàn
  火车站
airport
  fēijīchǎng
  飞机场
ferry pier
  mǎtóu
  码头
taxi
  chūzū chē
  出租车

Numbers

0	*líng*	零
1	*yī, yào*	一
2	*èr, liǎng*	二，两
3	*sān*	三
4	*sì*	四
5	*wǔ*	五
6	*liù*	六
7	*qī*	七
8	*bā*	八
9	*jiǔ*	九
10	*shí*	十
11	*shíyī*	十一
12	*shí'èr*	十二
20	*èrshí*	二十
21	*èrshíyī*	二十一
100	*yìbǎi*	一百
101	*yìbǎi língyī*	一百零一
200	*liǎngbǎi*	两百
1000	*yìqiān*	一千
2000	*liǎngqiān*	两千
10,000	*yíwàn*	一万
20,000	*liǎngwàn*	两万
100,000	*shíwàn*	十万
200,000	*èrshíwàn*	二十万

Food

I'm vegetarian.
  wǒ chī sù
  我吃素
I can't eat spicy food
  wǒ bùnéng chī là
  我不能吃辣
plain white rice
  mǐ fàn, bái fàn
  米饭，白饭
fried rice
  chǎo fàn
  炒饭
noodles
  miàn
  面
fried noodles
  chǎo miàn
  炒面
dumplings
  jiǎozi
  饺子
soup
  tāng
  汤
beef
  niú ròu
  牛肉
chicken
  jī ròu
  鸡肉

duck
yā ròu
鸭肉

fish
yú
鱼

goat (mutton)
yáng ròu
羊肉

pork
zhū ròu
猪肉

egg
dàn
蛋

vegetables
shū cài
素菜

eggplant
qiézi
茄子

mushrooms
mógu
磨菇

tofu (bean curd)
dòufu
豆腐

salt
yán
盐

sugar
táng
糖

Drinks

beer
píjiǔ
啤酒

Coca-Cola
kěkǒu kělè
可口可乐

coffee
kāfēi
咖啡

tea
chá
茶

water
kāi shuǐ
水

Facts for the Visitor

VISAS & EMBASSIES

Visas for individual travel in China are easy to get. China will even issue visas to individuals from countries which do not have diplomatic relations with the People's Republic. However, citizens of South Africa can only visit China on an organised tour, and must make an application at least one month before their planned arrival in China.

Visas for individual travel to China are readily available in Hong Kong and Macau. Don't worry if you have a Taiwanese visa in your passport – plenty of Taiwanese now visit the People's Republic.

Chinese residents of Hong Kong and Macau can apply for a *húi xiāng zhèng* which entitles them to multiple visa-free entry to the People's Republic.

You'll normally be issued a one-month single-entry visa for HK$90. The visa is only good for one month from the date of issue, not one month from the date you arrive in China, so there is no point in applying for one until just before you want to go. It is usually easy to extend your visa once you are inside China by applying at the Public Security Bureau.

You can also obtain a dual-entry visa for HK$250, or a multiple-entry visa for HK$700. The multiple-entry visa allows unlimited entries and is valid for six months, but you are only permitted to stay for 30 days at a time and this cannot be extended inside China. It is usually easy to obtain the multiple-entry visa if you've been in China previously and have stamps in your passport to prove it.

It normally takes two days to process a visa application, but if you're in a hurry, you can obtain an express visa in one day for HK$250.

Visa applications require one photo. The application asks you to specify where you plan to go, but once inside China no one knows or cares what you wrote on your visa application. You're advised to have one entire blank page in your passport. You'll have to part with your passport while your visa application is processed, so be sure you have enough money since you need the passport for cashing travellers' cheques.

Any travel agency in Hong Kong can easily get the visa for you, but will charge for this service. If you don't mind queuing, the cheapest visas can be obtained from the Visa Office of the Ministry of Foreign Affairs of the PRC (☎ 893 9812), 5th floor, Low Block, China Resources Building, 26 Har bour Rd, Wanchai, Hong Kong Island. It's open Monday to Friday, from 9 am to 12.30 pm and 2 to 5 pm, Saturday from 9 am to 12.30 pm.

Chinese Embassies

Australia
    247 Federal Highway, Watson, Canberra, 2600 ACT
Austria
    A-1030 Vienna, Metterrichgasse 4
Belgium
    21 Boulevard General Jacques, 1051 Brussels
Canada
    411-415 Andrews St, Ottawa, Ontario KIN 5H3
Denmark
    25 Oeregaardsalle, DK 2900 Hellerup, Copenhagen 2900
France
    11 Avenue George V, Paris 75008
Germany
    5307 Wachtbergeriederbachen, Konrad Adenauer Str, 104, Bonn
Italy
    56 Via Bruxelles, Roma 00198
Japan
    15-30 Minami-Azabu, 4-chome, Minato-ku, Tokyo
Netherlands
    Adriaan Goehooplaan 7, Den Haag
New Zealand
    2-6 Glenmore St, Kelburn, Wellington
Spain
    Trafalgar 11, Madrid
Sweden
    Bragevagen 4, Stockholm
Switzerland
    Kalecheggweg 10, Berne

UK
  31 Portland Place, London WIN 3AG
USA
  2300 Connecticut Ave NW, Washington, DC 20008. Consulates: 3417 Montrose Boulevard, Houston, Texas 77006; 104 South Michigan Ave, Suite 1200, Chicago, Illinois 60603; 1450 Laguna St, San Francisco, California 94115; 520 12th Ave, New York, New York 10036

Visa Extensions

Visa extensions are handled by the Foreign Affairs Branch of the local Public Security Bureau (PSB, China's police force). The Chinese government travel organisation, CITS, has nothing to do with extensions. Extensions cost Y25. The general rule is that you can get one extension of one month's duration, though at an agreeable Public Security Bureau, you may be able to wangle more if you can make a strong case (illness, transport delays, a pack of Marlboros, etc).

CUSTOMS

Immigration procedures are so streamlined they're almost a formality these days. The third-degree at customs seems to be reserved for Seiko-smuggling Hong Kongers who are a bigger problem than the odd stray backpacker.

I've personally had problems carrying my laptop computer into China. It's perfectly legal to bring one in, but customs wanted me to pay a US$500 deposit, refundable only if I brought out the computer through the same border crossing where I entered. I got around this by claiming that I would exit the country by another route.

People with bicycles and other expensive equipment have encountered this problem too. If you run into this when crossing the border from Hong Kong, always claim that you will exit the country by another route, such as flying out from Beijing or taking the Trans-Siberian to Moscow.

Customs require you to indicate on the 'Baggage Declaration for Incoming Passengers' form how many cameras, bicycles and electronic goodies you're taking into China. This is to prevent you from selling these goods after arrival. When leaving China you'll be asked to show that you still have all the items listed. Don't lose the declaration form! If any of these goods get lost or stolen while you're in China, you need to visit Public Security and make out a loss report which will clear you with customs.

You're allowed to import 400 cigarettes or the equivalent in tobacco products, one bottle of alcohol, 915 metres of movie film (8 mm only) and a maximum of 72 rolls of still film. The importation of fresh fruit is prohibited. It's illegal to import any printed material, film or tapes 'detrimental to China's politics, economy, culture and ethics', but don't become paranoid about what you take to read. One thing which the Chinese really are touchy about is the importation of bibles, especially Chinese-language bibles.

Cultural relics, handicrafts, gold and silver ornaments and jewellery purchased in China must be shown to customs officials on leaving. You'll also have to show your receipts, otherwise the goods may be confiscated. Cultural relics must have an intact attached red seal or a certificate from the authorities.

Customs usually only check that you've still got your Walkman and camera with you − often they don't even bother to check. You're not supposed to depart with Chinese currency, but it's highly unlikely you'll be subjected to a body search. If you lose the declaration form but have all the goodies a foreigner is expected to be carrying, you probably won't be hassled. You are more likely to be scrutinised if you have a multiple-entry visa and numerous entry and exit stamps from China.

If you happen to be of Chinese descent, or at least look Chinese, you are allowed to bring in some big, expensive goodies for your relatives once a year, duty free. Items which fall into this category include motorbikes, TV sets, washing machines, video recorders, computers, etc. China Travel Service (CTS) in Hong Kong and Macau can make arrangements where you pay for the goods first and then pick them up in China −

after all, a washing machine doesn't easily fit into a backpack. Contact CTS for details.

Warning

Many travellers are approached by Chinese and asked to carry cartons of cigarettes, alcohol and other items across the border. This is particularly common at the Shenzhen and Zhuhai border crossings. People who carry such items for others are commonly known as 'mules'. There are several good reasons for politely refusing these offers.

The first is obvious – smuggling. At the Shenzhen border post, I actually saw a Chinese woman on the train slit open a cigarette carton, remove a few packs of cigarettes and stuff a small box inside and seal the carton with tape. Many items that are prohibited in China can be sold for high prices, a good example being pornographic video tapes. By doing someone a favour you could wind up in hot water.

Another reason for refusing to be a mule has to do with time. Chinese are searched much more rigorously than foreigners. At the Shenzhen border crossing, customs has separate lines for Chinese and foreigners. You could easily clear customs in less than a minute, then have to wait an hour for the Chinese person to retrieve the goods you carried. Should you put yourself through this inconvenience because someone you don't know wants to save a bit of money on cigarettes? Perhaps they should quit smoking.

MONEY
Currency

The basic unit of Chinese currency is the *yuan* (Y), which is divided into *jiao* and *fen*. Ten fen make up one jiao (pronounced *mao*), and 10 jiao make up one yuan.

China has an absurd dual-currency system. Renminbi (RMB, 'people's money') are for the masses. Foreign Exchange Certificates (FECs, 'tourist money') are for the use of foreigners, including Overseas Chinese (Chinese born outside China). Foreigners are supposed to pay for hotels and travel fares in FEC – in practice, you can sometimes use RMB even in places that normally require payment in FEC. Having two currencies is a real pain because some places demand FEC and give change in RMB, which means you can easily wind up with excess RMB. You

can, in fact, spend RMB in most restaurants and shops, but having to constantly fight off demands for FEC is a real hassle.

Crazy as it sounds, Hong Kong and US dollars have become the unofficial third and fourth currencies of China. Amazingly, some 20% of Hong Kong's currency is believed to be circulating in China, most of it in Guangdong Province. Hong Kong dollars are particularly common in Shenzhen and Zhuhai Special Economic Zones.

Foreign currency and travellers' cheques can be changed at border crossings, the main centres of the Bank of China, at tourist hotels and some Friendship Stores.

Credit cards are now becoming accepted in the big cities, but don't rely entirely on plastic – most places don't have machines to process cards. Also beware of hefty commissions tacked on to credit card transactions.

When you leave China you can convert FEC (not RMB) back to foreign currency, but you *must* have your exchange receipts with you to prove that you changed foreign currency in the first place. You are only permitted to exchange *half* the total amount indicated on your receipts. If you find yourself with leftover RMB, you can usually unload it in Hong Kong at some of the hostels because many travellers are heading for China.

It may have occurred to you by now that there is something inherently ridiculous about having a dual-currency economy. What other country in the world prints tourist money? This unwieldy system has created a black market in FEC, Hong Kong dollars and US dollars. However, it is strongly advised that you don't change money on the street, especially in Canton. First of all, the black market rate at the time of this writing was only Y108 RMB for Y100 FEC, which is hardly a huge difference. More importantly, the moneychangers who approach you on the street are nothing more than thieves. The moneychangers will often offer a good rate, like Y120 or more, but this is just to entice you into getting robbed. Many bad incidents involving moneychangers have occurred, especially on Shamian Island. If you really

want to change money on the black market, do it in small private shops.

Exchange Rates

A$1	=	Y4.08
C$1	=	Y4.54
HK$1	=	Y0.67
NZ$1	=	Y3.13
UK£1	=	Y10.05
US$1	=	Y5.23
Y100	=	Y3.87

Costs

Although China is cheaper than Hong Kong or Macau, it's not as cheap as you would expect given the low wage levels earned by most Chinese. The main reason is because of a deliberate government policy of squeezing as much as money as possible out of foreign tourists. Foreigners must pay double for train fares and about 20% more than locals for airfares. Accommodation is usually the biggest expense. If you get into a dormitory, then China is cheap – otherwise, your daily living expense could be higher than in Hong Kong.

Hotel restaurants in Canton have grown accustomed to charging high prices for food, but you can get around this by eating at hole-in-the-wall restaurants. If you manage your money properly, you can still live in China on US$10 per day, depending on what standard of living you require. For sake of comparison, it's worth noting that the average salary for Chinese workers is US$32 per month.

Tipping

Tipping is not normally a custom. Bribery is another matter. Don't be blatant about it, but if you need some special service, it's customary to offer someone a cigarette and just tell him/her 'Go ahead and keep the pack – I'm trying to quit'. In China, a 'tip' is given before you receive the service, not after.

Bargaining

There's a lot of room to bargain in China – for hotel rooms, in private stores (those not government owned) and even with the police if you are fined. Always be polite and smiling when bargaining – nastiness will cause the other party to lose face, in which case they'll dig in their heels and you'll come out the loser.

WHEN TO GO

Since the weather is tolerable almost any time of year, the main consideration will be avoiding the crowds. One rule to remember is to avoid travelling on weekends and (even more so) at holiday times such as Easter and Chinese New Year! At those times everything is booked out and the crowds stampede across the border from Hong Kong, leaving trampled backpackers in their wake.

Accommodation in Canton is impossible to find during the Canton Fair, held twice annually in April and October. However, it is quite alright to visit Shenzhen, Zhuhai, Foshan and other places close to Canton, as long as you don't need to spend the night in Canton itself.

WHAT TO BRING

If you acquired a heap of heavy junk in Hong Kong, put it in storage. Some travel agents and hotels in Hong Kong store luggage. Another option is the bonded baggage room at Kai Tak Airport.

Pharmaceuticals

The pharmaceutical items mentioned in this section can be purchased in any Watson's drugstore in Hong Kong.

If you need vitamins, it's best to bring them from Hong Kong as those sold in China aren't reliable. Ditto for prescription drugs. A simple pain killer/fever reducer like Panadol might come in handy, especially during the winter cold and flu season. Sticking plaster (adhesive tape) is useful for blisters and many travellers throw a thermometer into their first-aid kit.

Mosquito repellent will make your life more pleasant and guards against malaria. A very effective brand is Autan.

Lomotil and Imodium (used to control diarrhoea) can be bought across the counter

in Hong Kong, even though they are sold by prescription in most Western countries.

Constipation can be a problem in China during winter when fresh fruits and vegetables are scarce and you wind up living on white rice and noodles. Rather than resort to laxatives, consider eating bran, which can be made palatable by mixing with yoghurt, widely available in China. You won't find bran in Chinese markets, but some Friendship Stores have it, otherwise bring some from Hong Kong.

If you need tampons, bring them from Hong Kong. Chinese sanitary napkins are big and bulky. Birth-control pills and condoms are available in China, but you'll probably save yourself some trouble and be assured of better quality if you get a supply in Hong Kong.

Shaving cream is hard to come by in China. Chinese razor blades are improving, but the razors themselves are of the old style – shave slowly or risk cutting your throat. The nail clippers made in China are often of poor quality. The Chinese don't seem to know what deodorant is, so if you want to smell nice, bring your own.

If you wear contact lenses, bring your own cleaning solution, eye drops and other accessories.

Chinese-made toothpaste is as good as any, but the toothbrushes are usually too hard and are bad for the gums. Dental floss is hard to find and UV (sunblock) lotion doesn't seem to exist.

Reading Matter

To preserve your sanity, bring some reading material. Good books in English are scarce in China, though occasionally you may find a real collector's item.

Clothing

After Hong Kong, which resembles one big fashion show, you may actually find China to be a relief. Most people in China dress casually. Foreigners can get away with wearing almost anything as long as it isn't overly revealing.

In summer, shorts are OK. Many Chinese

men walk around outdoors bare-chested at this time. However, Western men with a lot of body hair should not try this, as displaying a hairy chest in public will attract a large crowd of enthusiastic onlookers. Children may actually pull your body hair to test if it's real!

Beachwear should be conservative. Men with hairy chests should wear a T-shirt when swimming and women should wear one-piece swimsuits. Bikinis will attract spectators and public nudity will get you arrested.

You can wear flip-flop sandals (thongs) inside your hotel room or in a youth hostel, but if you set foot outside with them on you can expect stares and rude remarks. You may see some Chinese wear flip-flops outdoors, but don't think that means it's OK – it's considered an extremely low-class thing to do, like begging.

Chinese seem to have a national grudge against flip-flops. Many big hotels employ guards whose main function is making sure that nobody wearing flip-flops enters the lobby or hotel restaurant. As in Hong Kong, sandals are OK if they have a strap across the back of the ankle.

If you have rain gear, bring it along. If not, buy it in China where it's very cheap.

Gifts

Foreign cigarettes and beer are especially popular. A bag of M&M candy-covered chocolates or other foreign chocolates will go down well.

For Chinese who speak English, foreign books, magazines and newspapers are greatly appreciated, but try to take care that you don't give your friends reading material which is way beyond their level of comprehension.

The duty-free shop at the Hong Kong-Shenzhen border is a good place to buy cigarettes. Alternatively, you can buy lots of foreign-made goodies at the Friendship Stores in Shenzhen and Canton.

Don't go overboard with gift giving. There's a thin line between being nice and corrupting someone. On the other hand,

don't do the opposite – giving away your old jacket as a gift will be taken as an insult. Foreign-made T-shirts of exotic design are much in demand, but make sure it's new (or looks new). A second-hand rag is not a suitable gift.

A Chinese with good manners is supposed to refuse (at least once, maybe twice) the gift you want to offer. You are supposed to insist. They will then 'reluctantly' accept it. To accept a gift too readily is considered greedy. If you receive a present that is gift-wrapped, it is customary not to open it in front of the giver. If you open it immediately, it makes you look greedy.

TOURIST OFFICES
Local Tourist Offices

Most mid-range and top-end hotels have a desk in the lobby supplying tour information, a service you can use without being a hotel guest. Often hotel information desks have timetables for aeroplanes and trains and staff can sometimes book tickets for public transport. Also they often sell tickets for opera and other events. If you want to sign up for a city tour, the information desk can usually arrange that too, and often has pamphlets explaining which tours are available. Sometimes the staff at these information desks can speak English well, but don't count on it. The only way to find out is to inquire.

CITS and CTS both exist in order to help travellers. Sometimes they are very helpful and sometimes they seem to try hard to get rid of you.

Either service can buy your train or air tickets (and some boat tickets), make hotel reservations, organise tours, get tickets for cinema, opera, acrobatics and other entertainment, organise trips to farms or factories and provide vehicles.

While CITS is supposed to deal with foreigners, CTS is supposed to handle Overseas Chinese as well as Hong Kong, Macau and Taiwan compatriots. Both are state-run companies.

You might wonder why CITS and CTS don't merge instead of duplicating services.

Besides the fact that individual bureaucrats like to fight for their own turf, another reason is language. CITS staff are supposedly able to speak English (don't count on it) while CTS staff speak putonghua and sometimes Cantonese as well. If you can speak putonghua well, CTS staff are usually willing to help you even if you aren't Chinese. In Hong Kong, CTS officers speak English and will arrange tickets for you. In Macau, the CTS office is the place to go for China visas.

Considering all the marvellous services that CITS and CTS provide, why do so many travellers wind up hating these organisations? A lot depends on the office you are dealing with. Some CITS agents provide good service, while others couldn't care less. In China, state employees can almost never be fired, and they have little incentive to work. Some seem to derive perverse pleasure out of making sure that things don't work.

In Beijing, I went to CITS to get on a tour to the Great Wall. After keeping me waiting for 45 minutes, staff promptly closed the door. 'Out to lunch,' they explained. 'Come back in two hours.' I surprised them by actually coming back. So they told me they no longer arranged tours to the Great Wall and sent me to a big hotel five km down the road which they were sure had bus trips to the Great Wall. I found the hotel but they never had such bus trips. Fuming, I went back to CITS and demanded that they tell me how to get to the Great Wall. Their reply was to 'take a taxi'. When I did finally get to the Great Wall, I encountered the CITS tour bus, which had just arrived from Beijing.

Besides poor service, there are other reasons why travellers are fed up with CITS and CTS. Blatant overcharging is one good reason. Sometimes you will be told that you can only visit a certain area if you sign up for an expensive CITS tour, when in fact it's wide open and you can easily go yourself. CITS has been known to book 10-day tours and then only give eight days. And so on.

Fortunately, individual travellers don't have to deal a lot with CITS, especially in the Canton area where there is readily available transport and accommodation.

Overseas Reps

China International Travel Service The main office of CITS in Hong Kong has a particularly good collection of pamphlets about China, all in English. Outside of China and Hong Kong, CITS is usually known as China National Tourist Office (CNTO).

Australia
    CNTO, 11th floor, 55 Clarence St, Sydney NSW 2000 (☎ (02) 299 4057, fax 299 1958)
France
    CNTO, 51 Rue Saint-Anne, 75002, Paris (☎ 42 96 95 48, fax 42 61 54 68)
Germany
    CNTO, Eschenheimer Anlage 28, D-6000 Frankfurt am Main-1 (☎ (069) 55 5292, fax 597 3412)
Hong Kong
    Main Office, 6th floor, Tower Two, South Seas Centre, 75 Mody Rd, Tsimshatsui East, Kowloon (☎ 732 5888, fax 721 7154)
    Central Branch, Room 1018, Swire House, 11 Chater Rd, Central (☎ 810 4282, fax 868 1657)
    Mongkok Branch, Room 1102-1104, Bank Centre, 636 Nathan Rd, Mongkok, Kowloon (☎ 388 1619, fax 385 6157)
    Causeway Bay Branch, Room 1104, Causeway Bay Plaza, 489 Hennessy Rd, Causeway Bay (☎ 836 3485, fax 591 0849)
Japan
    China National Tourist Office, 6F Hachidal Hamamatsu-cho Building, 1-27-13 Hamamatsu-cho Minato-ku, Tokyo (☎ (03) 3433 1461, fax 3433 8653)
UK
    China National Tourist Office, 4 Glentworth St, London NW1 (☎ (071) 935 9427, fax 487 5842)
USA
    China National Tourist Office, Los Angeles Branch, 333 West Broadway, Suite 201, Glendale CA 91204 (☎ (818) 545 7505, fax 545 7506)
    New York Branch, Lincoln Building, 60E, 42nd St, Suite 3126, New York, NY 10165 (☎ (212) 867 0271, fax 599 2892)

China Travel Service In Hong Kong, the Kowloon and Mongkok branch offices of CTS are open on Sunday and public holidays.

Australia
    Ground floor, 757-759 George St, Sydney, NSW 2000 (☎ (02) 211 2633, fax 281 3595)

Canada
>PO Box 17, Main floor, 999 West Hastings St, Vancouver, BC V6C 2W2 (☎ (604) 684 8787, fax 684 3321)

France
>10 Rue De Rome, 75008, Paris (☎ (1) 45 22 92 72, fax 45 22 92 79)

Hong Kong
>Central Branch, China Travel Building, 77 Queens Rd, Central, Hong Kong Island (☎ 521 7163, fax 525 5525)
>
>Kowloon Branch, 1st floor, Alpha House, 27-33 Nathan Rd, Tsimshatsui (☎ 721 4481, fax 721 6251)
>
>Mongkok Branch, 2nd floor, 62-72 Sai Yee St, Mongkok (☎ 789 5970, fax 390 5001)

Japan
>Nihombashi-Settsu Building, 2-2-4, Nihombashi, Chuo-ku, Tokyo (☎ (03) 3273 5512, fax 3273 2667)

Macau
>2nd floor, Hotel Beverly Plaza, Avenida do Dr Rodrigo Rodrigues (☎ 38 8922, HK 540 6333)

Philippines
>489 San Fernando St, Binondo, Manila (☎ 47-41-87, fax 40-78-34)

Singapore
>Ground floor, Sia Building, 77 Robinson Rd, Singapore 0106, (☎ 224 0550, fax 224 5009)

Thailand
>460/2-3 Surawong Rd, Bangkok 10500 (☎ (2) 233 2895, fax 236 5511)

UK
>24 Cambridge Circus, London WC2H 8HD (☎ (071) 836 9911, fax 836 3121)

USA
>2nd floor, 212 Sutter St, San Francisco, CA 94108 (☎ (415) 398 6627, fax 398 6669)
>
>Los Angeles Branch, Suite 138, 233E, Garvey Ave, Monterey Park, CA 91754 (☎ (818) 288 8222, fax 288 3464)

Guangdong Overseas Travel Corporation

This organisation is mostly geared towards group tours rather than individuals.

Canada
>CITA Travel, 1450 TD Bank Tower, 700 West Georgia St, Vancouver, BC V7Y 1A1 (☎ (604) 683 7122, fax 603 7747)

Hong Kong
>Guangdong Co-International Travel Service, 2nd floor, Guangdong Hotel, 18 Prat Ave, Tsimshatsui, Kowloon (☎ 367 7016, fax 721 7232)

UK
>1st floor, 78 Shaftesbury Ave, London (☎ (071) 439 8888, fax 26 2775)

USA
>China International Travel Service – Guangdong, 138B World Trade Centre, San Francisco, CA 94111 (☎ (415) 362 7477, fax 989 3838)

USEFUL ORGANISATIONS
Public Security Bureau

The Public Security Bureau (PSB, *gōng'ān jú*) is China's police force. It has a special section to deal with foreigners called the Foreign Affairs Branch *(wài shì kē)* whose members can usually speak passable English, some quite fluently. If you need a visa extension, these are the people to see.

You'll also need to see them if your passport gets lost or stolen. If any of the goods which you marked on your customs declaration are stolen (such as your camera), you should report to the PSB to get some documentation to customs so that you won't be hassled when leaving the country.

Sometimes the PSB can be amazingly efficient. It has been known to recover stolen items that travellers had given up for lost, and it can help in serious disputes, such as when a restaurant is trying to charge you an outrageous price for a meal you've just eaten, or a taxi driver who tries to rip you off.

Generally, the PSB is kindly disposed towards foreigners and it's important to keep them that way. Some travellers have abused this hospitality by pestering them with trivia or by using them to 'get even' with someone they didn't like. As is no doubt the case in your own country, it's not wise to call the cops unless you think you've got a legitimate grievance that cannot be settled by reasonable negotiation.

If you approach the PSB in the right way (offering a cigarette is a good start) they will often be helpful and friendly, and will give good advice on places to stay and things to see.

BUSINESS HOURS & HOLIDAYS

Banks, offices, government departments and

Public Security Bureaus are open Monday to Saturday. As a rough guide only, they open around 8 to 9 am, close for two hours in the middle of the day, and then reopen until 5 or 6 pm. Sunday is a public holiday, but some businesses are open Sunday morning but make up for this by closing on Wednesday afternoon. CITS offices, Friendship Stores and the foreign-exchange counters in the tourist hotels and some of the local branches of the Bank of China have similar opening hours, and are generally open on Sunday as well, at least in the morning.

Many parks, zoos and monuments have similar opening hours, and are also open on Sundays and often at night. Shows at cinemas and theatres end between 9.30 and 10 pm.

Government restaurants are open for early morning breakfast (sometimes as early as 5.30 am) until about 7.30 am, then open for lunch and again for dinner around 5 to 8 or 9 pm. Chinese eat early and go home early – by 9 pm you'll probably find the chairs stacked and the cooks gone home. Privately run restaurants are usually open all day, and often late into the night especially around railway stations.

Long-distance bus stations and railway stations open their ticket offices around 5 or 5.30 am before the first trains and buses pull out. Apart from a one or two-hour break in the middle of the day, they often stay open until about 11 or 11.30 pm.

The Chinese work six days a week and rest on Sunday. The nine national holidays during the year are as follows:

New Year's Day – 1 January
Chinese New Year – the first day of the first lunar month, this holiday usually falls in the first half of February but sometimes occurs during the last week of January. Also known as the Spring Festival, the actual holiday lasts three days but many people take a week off. It's a bad time to travel as all accommodation and transport is full. Most businesses are closed as this is a family holiday. If you have to be in China at this time, settle down in a nice quiet place with some books and try not to go anywhere until the chaos ends.
International Working Women's Day – 8 March
International Labour Day – 1 May

Youth Day – 4 May, commemorates the Beijing student demonstrations of 4 May 1919 when the Versailles Conference gave German 'rights' in the city of Tianjin to Japan.
Children's Day –1 June
Anniversary of founding of Communist Party of China – 1 July
Anniversary of the founding of the Chinese People's Liberation Army – 1 August
National Day – 1 October celebrates the founding of the People's Republic of China in 1949.

POST & TELECOMMUNICATIONS
Postal Rates
The ordinary postal rates for international mail (other than to Hong Kong or Macau) follow. A slightly reduced postage rate exists for letters and postcards sent to certain countries.

For letters, surface mail costs Y1.50 up to 20 grams, and Y3 above 20 grams and up to 50 grams. Air mail letters are an additional Y0.50 for every 10 grams or fraction thereof.

Postcards are Y1.10 by surface mail and Y1.60 by air mail to anywhere in the world.

Aerogrammes are Y1.90 to anywhere in the world.

For printed matter, surface mail costs Y1 up to 20 grams, Y1.60 above 20 grams and up to 50 grams, Y2.80 above 50 grams and up to 100 grams, Y5.40 above 100 grams and up to 250 grams, Y10.20 above 250 grams and up to 500 grams, Y16.20 above 500 grams and up to one kg, Y27 above one kg and up to two kg, and for each additional kg or fraction thereof the charge is Y11.40.

Air mail for printed matter is an additional Y0.40 for every additional 10 grams or fraction thereof.

For small packets, surface mail charges are Y3.60 up to 100 grams, Y7.20 above 100 grams and up to 250 grams, Y13 above 250 grams and up to 500 grams, Y21.60 above 500 grams and up to one kg. Air mail for small packets is an additional Y0.40 for every 10 grams or fraction thereof.

Parcels are yet another category. Rates vary depending on the country of destination. Charge for a one-kg parcel sent surface mail from China to the UK is Y52, to the USA Y30.60, and to Germany Y35.60. The charge for a one-kg parcel sent air mail to the UK is Y82, to the USA Y77, and to Germany Y70.60.

Post offices are very picky about how you pack things. Don't finalise your packing until the thing has got its last customs clearance. If you have a receipt for the goods, then put it in the box when you're mailing it, since it may be opened again by customs further down the line.

The registration fee for letters, printed matter and packets is Y1. Acknowledgement of receipt is Y0.80 per article.

Sending Mail
China's international postal service is efficient. Letters sent by air will probably take from five to 10 days to reach their destination. An international express mail service operates in many Chinese cities. If possible, write the country of destination in Chinese in order to speed the delivery.

Receiving Mail
There are poste restantes in just about every city and town, and they seem to work, though less reliably in the small backwaters. I have never seen a poste restante window in any post office in China. Letters are not sorted in alphabetical order, but are usually kept in the order in which they were received. In large cities, the GPO will assign numbers to letters as they are received and post the number and names on a notice board. You have to find your name and write down the number(s) of your letters, then tell the clerk at the counter.

I've seen some strange names on the notice boards – 'Par Avion, General Delivery', and 'Hold Until Arrival'.

Telephone
Many hotel rooms are equipped with phones from which local calls are free. Local calls can be made from public phones (there are some around – not many). A recent innovation has been telephone cards which are available in denominations of Y20, Y50, Y100 and Y200. There are only a few places which have card phones, mostly big hotels and airport terminals.

Direct dialling for international calls is gradually being introduced at top hotels in the major cities. You can also call from the main telecommunications offices, but these are usually less convenient and mostly used by the locals. Lines are a bit faint but usually OK and you generally don't have to wait more than half an hour before you're connected. On the other hand, calling from rural areas can be difficult and you might have to wait all day to get a line, if you get one at all.

Rates for station-to-station calls to most countries in the world are Y18 per minute.

Hong Kong is slightly cheaper at Y12 per minute. There is a minimum charge of three minutes. If you go over your three minutes by even one second, you get charged for another three minutes. Collect calls are cheaper than calls paid for in China. Time the call yourself – the operator will not break in to tell you that the end of your three minutes is approaching. After you hang up, the operator will ring back to tell you how much it cost. There is no cancellation fee for calls.

If you are expecting a call – either international or domestic – try to advise the caller beforehand of your hotel room number. The operators frequently have difficulty understanding Western names, and the hotel receptionist may not be able to locate you.

In major cities, the local directory assistance number is ☎ 114; the long-distance (domestic) information number is ☎ 113. However, operators only speak Chinese.

Practically nobody in China has a telephone in their own home. To phone someone, you must call their place of work. In rural areas they shut off the phone system at night – since nobody works at night, who could you possibly call if the phone system was on?

The phone system has improved but Li Binsheng, a well-known cartoonist, once drew a satirical cartoon which depicted an old man standing with a telephone receiver in his hand while his son and grandson waited beside him. The caption for the old man said: 'If I fail to get through, my son will follow; if he fails too, he has his son to follow'.

Fax, Telex & Telegram

Fax messages, telexes and telegrams can be sent from some of the major tourist hotels and from the central telegraph offices in some of the bigger cities.

International fax and telexes (other than those to Hong Kong or Macau) cost around Y18 per minute with a three-minute minimum charge. International telegram rates are usually around Y3.50 per word, and more for the express service. Rates to Hong Kong are less.

TIME

All of China is on the same time, eight hours ahead of GMT (London) and 13 hours ahead of Eastern Standard Time (New York). China uses a system of daylight saving (nine hours ahead of GMT) from the third Sunday in April to the second Sunday in September. However, not every city follows it even though they are supposed to. Shenzhen and Canton use daylight saving, but Zhuhai does not.

Whatever advantages are supposed to be derived from daylight-saving time, they are negated by the fact that China adjusts its boat, bus and flight schedules one hour later during this time. However, trains continue to run on standard time.

ELECTRICITY

As in Hong Kong, China uses AC 220 V, 50 Hz. The only difference is in the design of the electrical outlets. In Hong Kong, three round prongs is standard, while in China there are three flat prongs. A few hotels also have two round prongs of the European type. If you need plug adaptors, buy them in Hong Kong.

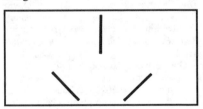

LAUNDRY

Most hotels have a laundry service, but check the prices first – some places charge so much you could buy new clothes cheaper.

WEIGHTS & MEASURES

The international metric system is in use. Local Chinese units of weight are still used in markets: the *liang* (37.5 grams) and the *jin* (16 liang).

BOOKS & MAPS

There are numerous books about China but

rather few dealing specifically with Canton or Guangdong Province. One of the few is *Kwangtung or Five Years in South China* (Oxford University Press, London, 1982) by the English Wesleyan minister Reverend John Arthur Turner, who worked as a missionary in China from 1886 to 1891. His book was originally published in 1894.

Another early account of Western contact with China comes from the Jesuit priest and missionary Matteo Ricci, who was permitted to take up residence at Zhaoqing near Canton in the late 16th century and in Beijing in 1601. An English translation of his diaries has been published under the title *China in the 16th Century – the Journals of Matteo Ricci 1583-1610*. This book is not easy to find.

Other rare books about Canton include *Canton in Revolution – The Collected papers of Earl Swisher, 1925-1928* (Westview Press, USA, 1977). Also, Ezra F Vogel's *Canton Under Communism* (Harvard University Press, 1969) covers the history of the city from 1949 to 1968.

More general books about China are easier to find and usually more interesting. *The Chinese* (Penguin Books) by David Bonavia helps remove some of the mystery about China. Bonavia also wrote *Seeing Red; Personal Encounters with Communism*.

One very popular book is *Life and Death in Shanghai* by Nien Cheng. In spite of the title, it's not specifically about Shanghai. Instead, it gives a gut-gripping account of the horrors of the Cultural Revolution. Along similar lines is *Son of the Revolution* by Ling Heng and Judith Shapiro.

Also worth reading is *China, Alive in the Bitter Sea* by Fox Butterfield. Butterfield was a New York Times reporter who lived in Beijing in 1980. His book paints a highly negative picture of the country, but gives a good view of life in China in 1980. Many of the problems he mentions still plague China.

Perhaps the best book to read about China has nothing to do with China – *The Trial* by Franz Kafka dramatises the helplessness of individuals against the bureaucracy, which is just the kind of nightmare that most Chinese have lived through.

Finding maps of Canton and other Chinese cities is easy enough if you don't mind one printed in Chinese characters only. To find one in English, look in the gift shops of the major hotels. The maps of Canton (Guangzhou) and Shenzhen by Universal Publications of Hong Kong, which indicate places in both Chinese and English, are especially recommended. You cannot buy these in China, but they are readily available from most Hong Kong bookstores. In Hong Kong, the best selection of maps on China can be found at the Peace Book Company (☎ 367 2201), 35 Kimberly Rd, Tsimshatsui, Kowloon.

MEDIA
Newspapers & Magazines
China publishes various newspapers, books and magazines in several European and Asian languages. The papers you're most likely to come across are *China Daily*, the English-language daily newspaper which began publication in mid-1981; *Beijing Review*, a weekly magazine on political and current affairs; and *China Today*, a monthly magazine.

Some Western journals and newspapers are sold in the large tourist hotels in the main cities. The *Herald Tribune* and the Asian edition of the *Wall Street Journal* are sold in Canton. In big hotels, it's easy to find *Time*, *Newsweek*, the *Far Eastern Economic Review* and the *Economist*.

Radio & TV
Despite attempts to tear down their TV antennas and jam foreign broadcasting, many Cantonese receive Hong Kong's transmission of the latest bourgeois and subversive episodes of Western programmes which the authorities believe have ruinous influences on the people's moral and ideological uprightness.

In the border areas of Shenzhen and Zhuhai it is easy to pick up English-language broadcasts from Hong Kong. In Canton, some hotels have good enough antennas to pick up Hong Kong TV stations.

Chinese TV is broadcast in either Cantonese or Mandarin. The only English-language programmes are occasional old foreign movies or educational shows that attempt to teach English. Most foreigners find Chinese TV dull, but it has at least one redeeming feature – there are very few advertisements.

FILM & PHOTOGRAPHY

Most major brands of film are available in the Canton area. It's more expensive than in Hong Kong, but not outrageous. The Chinese mostly take colour prints, so slide film can be hard to come by and is usually past its expiration date. Kodachrome seems to be especially hard to find in China.

Chinese-made black-and-white film is available in some department stores, but the quality (graininess) may not be as good as film from Western countries. Department stores usually have a good selection of camera accessories (tripods, cable releases, etc).

Chinese people react about the same as Westerners when it comes to getting their photo taken – in general, they don't like strangers photographing them. On the other hand, with a little friendly persuasion, many people will be happy to pose for you, especially if you can arrange to send them a copy of the photograph. They especially like photographs of their children. Many Chinese will also like to have a photograph of you, their new foreign friend. Unposed photographs are best taken from far away with a long telephoto lens.

The Chinese have different ideas than Westerners about what makes a good photograph. They almost never take pictures of scenery. Instead, they mostly take pictures of each other. A Chinese family making a trip from Hong Kong to the Great Wall will typically take hundreds of photos of each other – at Hong Kong Airport, in the plane, at Beijing Airport, in their hotel, in the restaurant, inside the tour bus going to the Great Wall, standing in front of the tour bus and in

the Great Wall souvenir shop. Yet they may never get a picture of the Great Wall by itself.

Many Chinese are perplexed as to why foreigners take pictures of street scenes, markets, old buildings, farmers working the fields and other such 'boring' scenes.

In Canton's Qingping Market, one old vendor asked me why foreigners like to take pictures of dead, butchered dogs. 'It's just dog meat. What is so interesting about it?' he demanded. I tried to give him the best explanation I could, but thinking about it later, I suppose it makes as much sense for foreigners to photograph dog meat as for Chinese to visit a Western country and take pictures of hot dogs.

HEALTH
Vaccinations

Vaccinations against cholera are required if you arrive in China within five days of leaving an infected area. Yellow fever vaccinations are required if you're arriving within six days of leaving an infected area. If you're coming from a 'clean' area, inoculations against cholera, yellow fever, typhoid and smallpox are not required.

Diarrhoea Travellers' diarrhoea has afflicted visitors to China since the time of Marco Polo. It's usually not serious and will often clear up without treatment. The main cause is unfamiliar bacteria in food and water, but sometimes it's caused by a sudden change in diet, such as eating a lot of spices, oil, etc. The best advice regarding water in China is not to drink it from the tap. Even the cheap hotels provide vacuum flasks of boiled water in the rooms and dormitories. However, if you find yourself choosing between drinking unboiled water or dying of thirst, I suggest you choose the former option – China's water is not as bad as in most tropical countries.

Should you suffer from travellers' diarrhoea, first try a simple cure by switching to a light, roughage-free diet for a few days. Yoghurt, white rice, bananas, pudding and boiled eggs will usually see you through. Dehydration (a common result of diarrhoea) makes you feel worse, so it would be wise to increase your intake of salt and liquids.

Further relief can be obtained by chewing tablets of activated charcoal – not widely available in China and, unfortunately, somewhat inconvenient to carry.

More serious cases can be treated with prescription drugs such as Lomotil and Imodium. Use such drugs with caution as they can cause side-effects, so only take the minimum dosage needed to control the diarrhoea. Don't take so much that you get plugged up, as your body is trying to expel the unwanted bacteria.

If you still continue to suffer, you may have a serious infection that requires medical attention. Some forms of severe, chronic diarrhoea are extremely serious, such as amoebic dysentery. Fortunately, you are not likely to catch such an ailment in China. You may, however, get it elsewhere in Asia, especially southern Asia.

The 'China Syndrome' Next to diarrhoea, this is the most common ailment to afflict visitors to China. Elsewhere it's called influenza or even the common cold, but it's uncommonly bad in China. You may have heard of the 'Shanghai flu', or various other influenza strains named after Chinese cities. The fact is that China is one vast reservoir of influenza viruses and practically the entire population is stricken during the winter.

What distinguishes this from the Western variety is the severity and the fact that the condition persists for months rather than days. Like any bad case of the flu, it starts with a fever, chills, weakness, sore throat and a feeling of malaise normally lasting a few days. After that, a prolonged case of coughing and bronchitis sets in, characterised by coughing up large quantities of thick green phlegm, occasionally with little red streaks (blood). The bronchitis makes sleep almost impossible, and this exhausting state of affairs can continue for as long as you stay in the country.

Why is bronchitis so common in China? The condition is aggravated by cold weather, poor nutrition and China's notorious air pollution. Smoking definitely makes it worse, and many people in China smoke. Over-crowded conditions increase the opportunity for infection. But the main reason is that Chinese people spit a lot, thereby spreading the disease. It's a vicious circle: they're sick because they spit and they spit because they're sick.

During the initial phase of influenza, bed rest, drinking warm liquids and keeping warm are helpful. The Chinese treat bronchitis with a powder made from the gall bladder of snakes – of questionable value but there's probably no harm in trying it. If you continue to cough up green phlegm, run a fever and can't seem to get well, it's time to roll out the heavy artillery – you can nuke it with antibiotics. Tetracycline (250 mg) taken orally four times daily for a minimum of five days is usually highly effective. Once you start on a course of antibiotics, it's important to continue until the pills are all gone, not just for three days until you feel better. Otherwise, a complete relapse is likely.

Antibiotics are often not readily available in China. While they can sometimes be obtained in hospitals, it wouldn't be a bad idea to bring some with you for emergency use. They can often be bought cheaply across the counter in many countries in South-East Asia (Taiwan and Thailand are good places to stock up). Antibiotics can have unpleasant side effects, especially on women since it makes them prone to yeast infections. In both sexes, antibiotics can upset the balance of intestinal flora. Therefore, this should be a measure of last resort.

Finally, if you can't get well in China, leave the country and take a nice holiday on a warm beach in Thailand.

Malaria Malaria exists in China, though it's not nearly so serious as in tropical parts of Asia. Malaria is spread by mosquitoes which transmit the parasite that causes the disease. Protection is simple – a daily or weekly tablet which kill the parasites if they enter your bloodstream. You usually have to start taking the tablets about two weeks before entering the malarial zone (to get you used to the routine) and must continue taking them for several weeks after you've left. Resistance to two types of antimalarial tablets (Chloroquine and Fansidar) has been reported in China. Fansidar should not in any case be used as a preventative – it is a powerful drug with possible side-effects, and should only be used as a cure, preferably under medical supervision.

Whether or not you decide to take antimalarial drugs, you should at least try to avoid getting bitten in the first place. Take some rub-on mosquito repellent and coils with you and sleep under the nets provided by many Chinese hotels. Rubbing White Flower Oil or Tiger Balm on your body helps to keep mosquitoes away too.

Hepatitis There are two kinds of hepatitis – infectious (A) and serum (B). Hepatitis A makes you very sick but complete recovery is the norm, while hepatitis B can cause liver cancer many years later.

There is no vaccine against hepatitis A. Gamma globulin injections have been used in the past to build up short-term resistance, but the effectiveness of this has been hotly debated. However, there is an effective vaccine against hepatitis B, but it is not always widely available in Western countries and is rather expensive. It is available and cheaper in Hong Kong and many countries in South-East Asia.

Hepatitis A is an infectious viral disease which is spread by poor sanitary conditions. Contaminated food (especially seafood), water and eating utensils are the most likely sources of infection. Swimming at a polluted beach is another way to contract this disease. Additionally, the Chinese custom of everybody dipping their chopsticks into a single dish, rather than using a serving spoon, is the another reason why the disease is so prevalent in China and Hong Kong. Using disposable chopsticks or carrying your own chopsticks is one way to reduce the chances of infection.

Hepatitis B is spread the same way as the AIDS virus: sexual contact, contaminated needles (including acupuncture needles) and from mother to child in the womb. About 20% of the population of China is believed

to be carrying hepatitis B. There is no cure, but most carriers are symptomless.

The hepatitis virus mainly affects the liver. The symptoms include fever, loss of appetite, nausea, depression, total lack of energy and pain near the bottom of the rib cage where the liver is. An attack of hepatitis A turns the skin and whites of the eyes yellow and urine turns a deep orange colour. If you contract hepatitis, then rest and good food are vital. Also steer clear of alcohol, non-prescribed drugs and tobacco.

Don't be overly paranoid about hepatitis. If you're careful about what you eat and drink, you should be OK. On the other hand, don't take it too lightly. I was in Shanghai during a large epidemic when about 100,000 people became infected with the disease in just a few months as the result of eating contaminated food.

Tuberculosis The tuberculosis bacteria (tubercle bacillus or TB) is transmitted by inhalation. Coughing spreads infectious droplets into the air. In closed, crowded spaces with poor ventilation (like a train compartment, for example) the air can remain contaminated for some time. In overcrowded China, where the custom is to cough and spit in every direction, it's not hard to see why infection rates remain high.

Many carriers of tuberculosis experience no symptoms, but the disease stays with them for life. The infection is opportunistic – the patient feels fine, but the disease suddenly becomes active when the body is weakened by other factors such as injury, poor nutrition, surgery or old age. People who are in good health are less likely to catch TB. Tuberculosis strikes at the lungs and the fatality rate is about 10%.

There are good drugs to treat tuberculosis, but prevention is the best cure. If you're only going to be in China for a short time there is no need to be overly worried. Tuberculosis is usually contracted after repeated exposures. Budget travellers – those who often spend a long time staying in cramped dormitories and travelling on crowded buses and trains – are at greater risk than tourists who remain relatively isolated in big hotels and tour buses.

The effective vaccine for tuberculosis is called BCG and is most often given to school children (a high-risk group). The disadvantage of the vaccine is that, once given, the recipient will always test positive with the TB skin test.

Public Toilets

Toilet paper is never provided in the toilets at bus and railway stations or other public buildings (mainly because people steal it), so you'd be wise to keep a stash of your own with you at all times. Only in big modern hotels can you hope to find toilet paper.

In hotels, the toilets are clearly labelled in English, but in most public buildings only Chinese is used. To avoid embarrassment, try to remember:

men 男

women 女

In China, as in most Asian countries, you can expect to encounter squat toilets. For the uninitiated who don't know what I'm talking about, a squat toilet has no seat for you to sit on while reading the morning newspaper – in other words, it's a hole in the floor but it flushes (usually).

At other times, instead of finding a hole you might encounter a ditch with water running through it. Both the hole and the ditch take some getting used to. It takes skill to balance yourself over this device, all the while taking care that your comb, passport and other valuables in your pockets don't fall into the abyss. It's not made any easier by the fact that most public toilets don't have doors, so all the world can watch as you try to deal with this particular aspect of culture shock.

If it's any consolation, you may be pleased to know that the squat position is considered more natural and better for your body's digestive system. Also, many Westerners consider it more sanitary since no part of the body touches the toilet.

Apparently, many Chinese do not care for the sit-down toilets used in the West. In China's big hotels where Western-style toilets are available, you'll often find big black footprints on the seats, as it seems that many Chinese stand on the toilet seat and then squat – they really do make a mess out of it.

In many places, the plumbing system cannot adequately handle toilet paper. In that case, you should toss the paper into a waste basket provided for that purpose.

Traditional Medicine

Chinese herbal medicine and acupuncture is discussed in the Hong Kong section.

You may encounter another form of Chinese traditional medicine known as *qìgōng*. *Qi* represents life's vital energy, and *gong* is from kung fu *(gōng fū)*, the Chinese martial arts. Qigong can be thought of as energy management and healing. Practitioners try to project their qi to heal others.

It's interesting to watch them do it. They typically place their hands above or next to the patient's body without actually making physical contact. To many foreigners this looks like a circus act, and indeed even many Chinese suspect that it's nothing but quackery. However, there are many who claim that they have been cured of serious illness without any other treatment but qigong, even after more conventional doctors have told them that their condition is hopeless.

Denounced as another superstitious link to the bourgeois past, the Red Guards nearly obliterated qigong and its practitioners during the Cultural Revolution. It is only recently that qigong has made a comeback, but many of the highly skilled practitioners are no longer alive.

Does qigong work? It isn't easy to say, but there is a theory in medicine that all doctors can cure one-third of their patients regardless of what method is used. So perhaps qigong gets its one-third cure rate too.

WOMEN TRAVELLERS

Women report relatively little sexual harassment in China, though it is probably not wise to wear overly revealing clothing. However, shorts are acceptable for women, though it's better to wear the longish variety rather than the fashionable 'hot pants' favoured by Hong Kong women.

Women may need to take special precautions with their health. For example, if you're prone to yeast infections, bring your own medication (Nystatin suppositories). See also the What to Bring section earlier.

DANGERS & ANNOYANCES

Visiting any country involves hassles and some culture shock. China is not the worst for this, but there are certain aspects of the culture that set Westerners on edge. It does little good to get overly upset and lose your temper. The best advice is to learn to laugh it off. Among the things you will have to learn to live with are:

Staring Squads

You'd better get used to it. Getting stared at is a common feature of travel in Asia, but in China it's a national sport. Pity the poor travellers who came to China 10 years ago when very few Chinese had ever seen a foreigner. It wasn't unusual for a visitor to be quickly encircled by a congregation of gaping onlookers. Walk down the street and the crowd would follow. Stop a while and the crowd would wait, never growing tired and never making any attempt to communicate with the extra-terrestrial being. Staring back never seemed to help. Indeed, the crowd would love it. Some people would run and get their children so they could enjoy the show too.

The good news is that things have improved, especially in Canton where foreigners are plentiful. The audience is beginning to show signs of staring fatigue, but it depends partly on how foreign you look. Tall, blond-haired blue-eyed travellers can still attract a larger crowd than the monkeys at the Canton Zoo. Black people seem to get it worst – some Black travellers have said they would never go back to China for just this reason.

The best way to avoid being stared at is to keep moving. Stopping on the street to read a map or to write something is particularly inviting. People will come to stare over your shoulder to see what you're reading.

Spitting

Clearing your throat and discharging the phlegm on the floor or out the window (to the peril of those below) is perfectly acceptable in China. Everyone does it – any time, any place. It's not as bad in summer, but in winter – when many people are afflicted by the notorious 'China Syndrome' – you'll have a hard time trying to keep out of the crossfire!

Littering

The environmental movement has not reached China. Rather than carry the trash down the stairs once a day to the rubbish bins, many Chinese find it more convenient to dump it out the window. (You get a hint of this in Hong Kong at Chungking Mansions – just look in the light-wells in the centre of the building.) The sewer grates are also convenient garbage dumps. Restaurants and street vendors usually dump all uneaten food down the sewer, much to the joy of the rats who inhabit the underworld.

I once took a boat cruise on the Pearl River in Canton, and while sitting on the lower deck, I watched in astonishment as it literally rained garbage from the upper deck. Unable to bring myself to toss trash in the river, I deposited my garbage in a rubbish bin near the ship's snack bar. About an hour later, I saw an employee take the rubbish bin and dump the contents overboard.

Nevertheless, the streets in China are reasonably clean, but not because civic-minded citizens are careful with their rubbish. The government employs a small army of people who do nothing all day but sweep up the continual mess. Otherwise the country would be quickly buried in it.

Push & Shove

When Mao was alive, leftists in Western countries pointed to China as a model of harmony and happiness, where smiling peasants joined hands and worked together in a cooperative effort to build a better society.

Undoubtedly, many of them were dismayed when they finally did get to visit the Peoples' Republic and saw what the Chinese go through to get on a bus. No cooperative effort, just panicked mobs frantically pushing, shoving and clawing to be first. Those who want to get off the bus are shoved right back inside by those who want to get on. In a few notorious incidents (mostly involving overcrowded ferries), people have actually been trampled to death.

When it comes to buying train tickets, the same situation exists – mobs of people battle for a limited number of seats. Only the fit survive. Foreign tourists can be spared this. CITS will buy train and aeroplane tickets for you, or you can get them from special ticket offices in the train stations which only serve foreigners and high-ranking cadres.

Crime

China is safer than most Western countries and the police do not normally carry guns. One of the notable accomplishments of the Communists has been the eradication of opium addiction and the criminal gangs responsible for it. So there is little danger from knife-wielding street junkies – many Western countries should be envious.

Unfortunately, Canton is the worst city in China when it comes to crime. It's usually not violent crime, but pickpockets are common and foreigners, who are always assumed to be rich, are prime targets. Some pickpockets have become quite professional, working in groups in which one person diverts your attention while another slits open your bag or pocket with a razor blade and empties the contents.

There is no foolproof defence, but keeping your passport and travellers' cheques deeply buried under your clothes in a moneybelt is wise. Be especially careful on buses and other crowded places.

Price Gouging

Overall, China is one of the more honest countries that I've travelled in, but price gouging does occur, and the Cantonese have the worst reputation for this among the Chinese. It probably wouldn't matter if they only charged visitors double, but I've seen attempts to charge foreigners 100 times the going price for services such as doing laundry or a simple shoe repair.

It's a good idea to agree on a price before using a service. Barring that, if you're absolutely sure that somebody is trying to rip you off, the best defence is to start making a lot of noise. A crowd will immediately gather, and this tends to intimidate the person who is trying to cheat you. Furthermore, many Chinese are likely to intervene on your behalf if they see that someone is trying to cheat you. Cheating is not, as some foreigners believe, culturally acceptable in China.

WORK

China is a low-wage country, so don't come here expecting to get rich. However, living and working in China is an experience and an education. Some work opportunities exist, mostly in teaching English. The jobs are usually offered through universities, and some sort of long-term commitment (usually one year) is expected. Salaries are about US$200 a month, most likely paid in nonconvertible RMB. Accommodation is usually provided. To find out about such jobs, inquire at Chinese embassies or directly at universities.

People with technical skills and the ability to speak Chinese can sometimes land very lucrative jobs with large foreign companies, but this is not accomplished so easily. Such jobs are often advertised in the *China Daily*.

ACTIVITIES

If you don't mind getting up at the crack of dawn, you can join the Chinese in the park for an early morning taichi session.

Sauna and massage have really caught on, but tend to be expensive, though still cheaper than Hong Kong. You can find these at the large hotels, though there are now some small, privately run spas. Unlike in Macau, saunas in China are not generally connected with prostitution.

HIGHLIGHTS

The Canton area does not have any spectacular scenery – for that you must go to Tibet or Sichuan. The main attraction is the feeling of being in China – the street markets, temples, the food, the chaos, surprising prosperity amidst crushing poverty, etc. Still, there are some things that I found particularly enjoyable: cruising on the Pearl River, relaxing on a beach in Zhuhai, walking in the White Cloud Hills, Lotus Mountain and Canton's Yuexiu Park. Many travellers find the Qingping Market in Canton to be a real experience, but it's not for animal lovers. The Nanyue Museum in Canton gets good reviews from travellers.

ACCOMMODATION

The PSB prohibits foreigners from staying in the dirt-cheap Chinese hotels. Privately run guesthouses, such as Hong Kong's Chungking Mansions, are also forbidden. As a result, travellers are forced into more up-market accommodation.

This is a real problem for budget travellers, who would prefer a dormitory costing no more than Y25 per night. At the present time, there is only one real budget hotel remaining in Canton, the Guangzhou Youth Hostel on Shamian Island, and this place often fills up.

Fortunately, there are a few tricks to keeping the hotel bill down. The simplest way is to share a room – double rooms usually cost the same as singles in China. Triple rooms are only slightly more, and most hotels will even install a fourth bed in your room for Y30 extra. With four travellers sharing a room, a mid-range hotel should cost no more than a dormitory. If you hang out near the door of the Guangzhou Youth Hostel when it's all full, you can probably solicit some other travellers to be your roommates.

A mid-range hotel in China costs about Y80 (US$15) to Y130 (US$25) for a double room. If this is in your price range, then China is a real bargain. Most mid-range hotels are quite luxurious for the price, with large rooms, twin beds, air-con, private bath, colour TV and telephone.

Accommodation in Shenzhen is somewhat more expensive than Canton, while Zhuhai is slightly cheaper.

FOOD

The food is similar to what you'll find in Hong Kong, except that there's a good deal of wildlife on the menu. Snake, monkey, pangolin (an armadillo-like creature), bear, giant salamander and raccoon are among the tastes that can be catered for, not to mention more mundane dog, cat and rat dishes.

One look at the people fishing in the sewage canals around Canton might dull your appetite for Pearl River trout.

DRINKS

Besides tea, China is also well known for beer. Brands made in China are excellent, the most popular being Tsingtao, now a major export. It's actually a German beer – the town where it is made, Tsingtao (Qingdao) was once a German concession. The Chinese inherited the brewery when the Germans were kicked out.

ENTERTAINMENT

Overall, China is not renowned for its nightlife. Discos and karaoke bars at the big hotels are popular with Hong Kongers.

THINGS TO BUY

Although it's not like Hong Kong, China does offer some opportunities for interesting shopping and there are many unusual goods available, often at low prices.

Department stores are almost always run by the government and prices are uniformly cheap.

In large cities you can also find Friendship Stores which are government-owned enterprises stocking imported goods and Chinese-made goods designed for export. Friendship Stores are definitely worth visiting although prices are somewhat higher than other department stores. You'll find luxuries such as imported chocolate, herbal medicines, silk panties and Chinese artwork. They have more mundane items too, such as clothing and tea. All department stores will accept RMB, but in Friendship Stores sometimes they will and sometimes they won't, and at other times they will accept RMB but charge you extra.

In government-run stores you get what you pay for. Prices may be a little higher, but jade is really jade, antiques are antiques and brand-name goods are authentic.

It's a different situation in the free market which has low quality fake goods everywhere. You can find fake herbal medicines, fake jewellery and even fake brand name cigarettes and fake Coca-Cola. There are even fake Friendship Stores (the real ones are run by the government). Counterfeit merchandise is becoming a serious enough problem to deter shoppers, but the government has done little to crack down on it. The best advice is to always carefully examine the goods you buy and don't shell out large sums of money for famous brand-name labels.

You can't bargain in government-owned stores and every item has a price tag. In privately owned stores there is usually room for bargaining. To get an idea of prices, first take a look in the department stores.

Wherever you buy, if you're getting something mechanical or electrical (like a clock or hairdryer), always test it before you leave the store. If buying a clock, make sure the alarm works. With clothing, examine the garment carefully for bad zippers and missing buttons. Defective merchandise is the norm in China and every sales clerk expects you to test the goods before you pay

for them. It's difficult to return defective items, though you can sometimes exchange them.

In capitalist countries, items which don't turn over quickly are taken out of stock so as not to use up valuable floor space. Apparently this isn't the case in China.

The Nanfang Department Store in Canton has a big, ancient-looking street lantern for sale. It's been sitting in the middle of the store, occupying valuable floor space, for at least five years. I saw it on my first trip to Canton and thought it would make a great collector's item, but I couldn't figure out how I would get it home and what I would do with it anyway. It's rather expensive, but perhaps in another few years it will be put on sale.

A lot of discarded 1950s technology is still alive and well in China. Nostalgia buffs will find shiny new goods on sale which would be collector's items in the West. Check out the treadle sewing machines, wind-up alarm clocks and Box Brownie cameras. Strolling through the department stores in China is rather like rummaging through your grandmother's attic.

Hand tools are a bargain in China. Of course, carrying home all this heavy metal won't be easy, but the prices are too good to pass up if you need them. Power tools are also good value if your home country uses 220 V, but always test them before taking them out of the store.

Ditto for photographic equipment. You may not want to use a Chinese camera for anything but a paperweight, but check out camera accessories (tripods, flashes, etc) and equipment for processing your own film.

Advertising & Marketing

Advertising and marketing for the foreign market is one area of economics and finance that the Chinese are still stumbling with. The Chinese have come up with bizarre brand names such as Flying Baby and White Elephant, and one factory gave a new ginseng product the fatal name of Gensenocide. You can start your morning with a can of 'Billion Strong Pulpy C Orange Drink', or finish your meal with a glass of 'Imperial Concubine Tea'. An alarm clock, once marketed under the name Golden Cock, has since been renamed. A perusal of the billboards along Canton's Renmin Beilu comes up with such space-age products as Moon Rabbit batteries, Flying Pigeon bicycles, Shaolin tonic water and the undoubtedly durable Long March car tyres. ■

Black-and-white photographic paper is incredibly cheap.

Rubber rain boots are durable and dirt cheap in Canton. Always try them on to make sure they fit, as Chinese sizes are tricky.

The blue Mao caps or People's Liberation Army (PLA) caps can be bought in the street markets and make good souvenirs.

China issues quite an array of beautiful stamps which are generally sold at post offices in the hotels. Outside many post offices you'll find amateur philatelists with books full of stamps for sale. These are worth checking.

Getting There & Away

One rule to remember is to avoid travelling on weekends and (even more so) at holiday times such as Easter and Chinese New Year! At those times everything is booked out and the crowds pour across the border into China from Hong Kong, leaving trampled backpackers in their wake.

In most cities, there are left-luggage rooms at the long-distance bus stations and train stations.

For specific details for getting to Canton, Shenzhen and Zhuhai from Hong Kong or Macau, see the relevant Getting There & Away sections for each of those cities.

AIR
To/From Hong Kong

There are international flights from Hong Kong and, more rarely, from other countries. On international flights, there are some alternatives to the Civil Aviation Administration of China (CAAC). Hong Kong's flag carrier, Cathay Pacific, provides excellent service and flies from Hong Kong to Canton as well as several other Chinese cities. Cathay is a popular airline and their flights into China often fill up far in advance.

Dragonair, a joint venture between Cathay Pacific and the People's Republic, flies from Hong Kong to a few destinations in China, although not yet to Canton. Within China, Dragonair tickets can be bought from CITS. In Hong Kong, their office (☎ 8108055) is on the 19th floor, Wheelock House, 20 Pedder St, Central, Hong Kong Island.

Hong Kong travel agents can book flights on Cathay Pacific and Dragonair, but most won't deal with CAAC.

On domestic and international flights the free baggage allowance for an adult passenger is 20 kg in economy class and 30 kg in 1st class. You are also allowed five kg of hand luggage, though this is rarely weighed.

CAAC The CAAC is China's domestic and international carrier. CAAC publishes a combined international and domestic timetable in both English and Chinese in April and November each year. These can be bought at most CAAC offices in China or from the CAAC offices in Hong Kong. The timetable could also serve as a useful phrasebook of Chinese place-names, but it's filled with misspellings.

Trying to book a flight on CAAC is often a frustrating experience – you can stand in a queue for an hour just to find out all flights are full. Telephoning to get information seems to be impossible. In Hong Kong flights can be booked at either of the CAAC offices, but both tend to be very crowded with long queues, so go at 9 am when they first open. After 10 am, the crowds increase substantially. Hong Kong travel agents cannot make bookings on CAAC via telephone or computer but have to go down there in person, just as you would, and most are unwilling to do so.

CAAC Overseas Outside China, CAAC maintains the following ticket sales offices:

Australia
> Suite 11, 6th floor, 422 Collins St, Melbourne 3000 (☎ (03) 6421555)
> Level 4, 70 Pitt St, Sydney (☎ (02) 2327895, airport 6936956)

Burma (Myanmar)
> 67 Prome Rd, Rangoon (☎ 21927, airport 40113)

Canada
> Unit 15, 131 Bloor St, West Toronto, Ontario (☎ (416) 9683300)
> 1040 West Georgia St, Vancouver, BC (☎ (604) 6850921)

France
> 10 Boulevard Malesher-bes 75008 Paris (☎ 42 66 16 58, airport 48 62 72 50)

Germany
> Duesseldorfer Str 4, D-6000 Frankfurt/M. 1, (☎ (069) 133038, airport (069) 6905214)
> Room 4004, Clara Zetkin Strasse 97 1080, Berlin (☎ 2291964)

Hong Kong

Ground floor, Gloucester Tower, des Voeux Rd, Central, Hong Kong Island (☎ 5216416)

Kowloon Branch, ground floor, Hankow Centre, 4 Ashley Rd, Tsimshatsui, Kowloon (☎ 7390022)

Italy

Corso D'Italia 29 00198, Rome (☎ (000396) 862249, airport 60123924)

Japan

A01 Building, 2-7 Akasaka 3 Chome Minato-Ku, Tokyo (☎ (03) 505-2021, Narita Airport (0476) 323941)

1st floor, Asako Hakata Building, 11-5, Hakata-Eki Higashi 1 Chome, Hakata-ku, Fukuoka (☎ (092) 4728383)

1st floor, Uchilhonmachi Green Building, 54 Uchihonmachi 2 Chome, Higashi-ku, Osaka (☎ (06) 946-1702, airport (06) 856-7116)

1st floor, Sumitomoseimei Building, 7-1 Manzaimachi, Nagasaki (☎ (0958) 28-1510)

Malaysia

Ground floor, Wisma On-Tai 161-B, Jalan Ampang 50450, Kuala Lumpur (☎ (03) 2613166)

Pakistan

25/C, 24th St, Block 6, PECHS Karachi (☎ (021) 435570)

Philippines

1493 Carissa St Dasmarinas Village, Makati, Manila (☎ 8172750, airport 8310643)

Singapore

01-53 Anson Centre, 51 Anson Rd (☎ 2252177, airport 5428292)

Sweden

Kungsgation 64, ITR S-III 22, Stockholm (☎ 46-8-216146)

Switzerland

Nuscheler Strasse 35 8001, Zurich (☎ (01) 2111617, airport 8163090)

Thailand

134/1-2 Silom Rd, Bangkok 10500 (☎ 2356510, 2351880)

Turkey

Cumhuriyet Cad 235/1 Harbiye, Istanbul (☎ (901) 1327111, airport 5746040)

UK

41 Grosvenor Gardens, London SWIW OBP (☎ (071) 630910)

Gatwick Airport, Room 601, North Roof Office Block (☎ (081) 567525)

USA

2500 Wilshire Blvd, Suite 100, Los Angeles, CA 90057 (☎ (213) 3842703, airport 6468104)

51 Grant Ave, San Francisco, CA 94108 (☎ (415) 3922161, airport 8770750)

45 East 49th St, New York City, NY 10017

4230E Pan Am Terminal Building, JFK Airport (☎ 3719898, airport (718) 6564722)

Russia

Leninskye Gory UL, Druzhby 6, Moscow (☎ 143-15-60, airport 578-27-25)

LAND

To/From Hong Kong

Bus A consortium of Hong Kong companies and the Chinese government are constructing a six-lane 240-km super highway from Hong Kong to Canton to Zhuhai. The bus service will improve, and it will also be possible to bring your own vehicle. There is also no doubt that trade, tourism and commerce will benefit.

Just when all this is going to happen is uncertain. For nearly 10 years now, driving to Canton has been a frustrating experience – slow going over bad roads which are eternally 'under construction'. The construction often brings traffic to a complete halt for hours at a time. The Chinese have a theory that it's better to create employment by hiring thousands of low-wage workers to build a road by hand, rather than use machinery which could complete the project much faster. Not much thought is given to the economic benefits which could be derived from getting the transport system up and running.

Train There is one international train line from Hong Kong to Canton. For details, see the Getting There & Away section in the Canton chapter.

TOURS

If time is more important than money, then the brief tours to China from Hong Kong are worth considering. Although expensive, you will never be able to complain about not being shown enough on a tour. Itineraries are

invariably jam-packed with as much as can possibly be fitted into a day, and the Chinese expect stamina from their guests.

Nor could you complain about the quantity of food – you may complain about the quality or degree of imagination involved in the cooking, but there is no way the Chinese will let you starve.

There are innumerable tours you can make from Hong Kong or Macau. The best information on tours is available from Hong Kong travel agents, CITS or CTS. They all keep a good stock of leaflets and information on a range of tours to China. You usually have to book tours one or two days in advance.

There is an endless variety of China tours, from one-day trips across the border to Shenzhen to a Long March across the country. The trips to Shenzhen are popular. These are usually daily, except on Sundays and public holidays, and cost from HK$188 to HK$495. Depending on the price, the tour includes a visa, transport, lunch and entry fees. Inquire about discounts for children. Some of these tours visit Shenzhen Reservoir (from which Hong Kong gets most of its water), the Shenzhen art gallery, a kindergarten, a commune and the local arts and crafts shop, a market and China's new tourist trap, Splendid China (see the Shenzhen chapter later for details). Some trips include the Shekou port district from where you can return to Hong Kong by hovercraft.

Day trips from Hong Kong also go to Zhuhai, north of Macau. The cost is about HK$500 and you're taken by jetfoil to Macau and then by bus to Zhuhai. These tours include a visit to Cuiheng village, the birthplace and former residence of Sun Yatsen.

Day tours to Canton are available for about HK$800 – travelling by hovercraft or jetcat to Canton in the morning and returning by train in the evening, with some tours stopping at Shenzhen along the way.

There are also two-day tours which visit Canton, Zhongshan, Zhuhai, Zhaoqing and Foshan for about HK$1700; and three-day tours to Canton and Foshan for about HK$1500. There are combined Hong Kong,

New Territories and Canton tours, and combined Macau and Canton tours...and so on.

Essentially the same tours can be booked in Macau at China Travel Service (CTS) in the Hotel Beverly Plaza. An enthusiastic one-day visitor described her tour as follows:

The tour starts in Macau at 9.30 am...Chinese customs are no problem...Our whole bus group (about 20 people) crossed the border in just 15 minutes.

The programme then was a 20-minute visit to the Dr Sun Yatsen Memorial Middle School followed by a half-hour visit (with a tea break) to the late founder of the Republic of China's residence. We had an excellent 1½-hour lunch in Shiqi with prawns, fish soup, chicken, pork, duck and real beer...We then had a half-hour walk around Shiqi, a short visit to a farmer's house in a small village and tea back at the border before we crossed into Macau.

The Chinese guide would stop the bus while we were driving through the country if we wanted to take pictures. He was very well informed and to me he seemed very open. It was a well-organised, friendly and helpful tour – money well spent.

Marian Yeuken

Warning

Judging by the mail we receive at Lonely Planet, many people who have booked extended tours through CTS and CITS have been less than fully satisfied. Although the one-day tours seem to be OK, tours further afield frequently go awry. The biggest complaints have been about the ridiculous overcharging for substandard accommodation and tours being cut short to make up for transport delays. Some people have booked a tour only to find that they were the only person on the tour. No refunds are given if you cancel – you forfeit the full amount. Other travellers report additional charges being tacked on which were not mentioned in the original agreement.

CITS drivers have been known to show up with all their relatives who want to tag along for free. One traveller reported booking a week-long tour – the female driver showed up with her boyfriend and asked if he could come along. The traveller foolishly agreed. At the first lunch stop, the driver and her boyfriend took off and left the foreigner behind – the couple then apparently spent the rest of the week enjoying a honeymoon at the traveller's prepaid hotel rooms!

LEAVING CHINA
Departure Tax
Airport departure tax is Y40, but there is no departure tax if you leave by boat.

Money
It is important to remember that you have to change money before entering immigration and customs. This applies to the airport, wharf, railway station (for international trains) or the land border crossings at Shenzhen and Zhuhai. At Zhoutouzui Wharf, the Bank of China opens two hours before departure.

Getting Around

AIR
Local Air Services
CAAC's flights cover about 80 cities and towns throughout China. Foreigners pay a surcharge at least 20% higher than Chinese, and foreigners must also purchase tickets in FEC rather than RMB. There are occasionally people outside the CAAC office peddling black-market air tickets, but I don't recommend that you buy these. The airlines can tell a Chinese-priced ticket from a foreign one, and if you have a Chinese ticket you will not be permitted to board the aircraft.

Taxi drivers meet incoming flights and try to charge foreigners about three times the going rate and will often ask for payment in US dollars. Don't accept any of this nonsense – either bargain a decent rate or insist they use the meter, and pay in RMB.

It is possible to buy all of your domestic CAAC tickets from the CITS in Hong Kong, and even from some non-Chinese airlines that have reciprocal arrangements with CAAC. However, this is generally *not* a good idea. First of all, it saves you no money whatsoever. Secondly, the tickets issued outside China need to be exchanged for a proper stamped ticket at the appropriate CAAC offices in China – a few of these offices get their wires crossed and refuse to honour 'foreign' tickets. Furthermore, CAAC flights often cancel, but you'll have to return the ticket to the seller in order to get a refund.

Stand-by tickets do exist on CAAC flights. Some seats are always reserved in case a high-ranking cadre turns up at the last moment. If no one shows up it should be possible to get on board.

CAAC was supposedly 'broken up' a few years ago into 'competing airlines'. This was supposed to stimulate competition and improve service. For the most part, this has proven to be a joke. CAAC now includes Air China, Shanghai Airlines, Xinjiang Airlines, Xiamen Airlines, China Eastern, China Southwest, China Northwest, Universal Airlines and others. All these airlines are listed in the CAAC timetable, sell tickets through CAAC offices and even have the CAAC logo on the tickets. Perhaps service will improve someday, but for now the 'new' airlines are just old medicine in new bottles.

Tales of the Unexpected
CAAC is an unusual airline – the first time I tried to check in, I was told that my luggage was too large, so I'd have to carry it on board! After take-off, the stewardess entertained us by proudly describing the scenic wonders we would find at our destination – coal mines, oil refineries, petrochemical plants, steel mills and brick factories.

CAAC also stands for China Airlines Always Cancels (the usual excuse is bad weather). CAAC is responsible for your meals and hotels whenever a flight is delayed beyond a reasonable amount of time. Just what constitutes 'reasonable' may be subject to interpretation. I was on a flight which was delayed for over 12 hours, but CAAC did not consider this a reasonable delay. After some bitter arguments, CAAC finally dished out hotel rooms to foreigners but the Chinese passengers were left to sleep in the waiting room. Delays are so common that almost every airport has a CAAC-run hotel.

Delays are inconvenient, but more worrisome is that CAAC also stands for China Airlines Almost Crashes. The airline's safety record appears to be a poor one – but no information on crashes or incidents is released unless there are foreigners on board.

The basic problem with CAAC is old technology. For the international runs they use nice, relatively new Boeings. But on the domestic runs it's sometimes old Russian turbo-props (like the Antonovs) designed and built back in the 1950s. The worst models are relegated to the lesser-known runs and may have no seat-belts, oxygen masks, life jackets or fire extinguishers, and sometimes the freight blocks the emergency exits. Finding parts and skilled mechanics to maintain such a wide variety of vintage aircraft remains a serious problem.

International flights must conform to IATA standards and are therefore considered safer than domestic ones. Those who are injured or killed in CAAC domestic crashes aren't likely to receive much in the way of financial compensation. The CAAC timetable states that the maximum amount paid for accidental injury or death will be Y20,000 (less than US$3800)

– though you may qualify for a ticket refund too. This isn't to scare you off flying CAAC, but to let you know that problems persist although service is slowly improving and new planes are being purchased.

A classic: amused passengers watched the pilot (returning from the toilet) locked out of the cockpit by a jammed door. The co-pilot opened the door from within, then both men fiddled with the catch and succeeded in locking themselves out of the cockpit. As passengers stared in disbelief the pilot and co-pilot attacked the door with a fire-axe, pausing for a moment to draw a curtain between themselves and the audience.

Hijackings have added a new dimension to the fire-axe routine. In January 1983 a hijacker fatally shot a pilot after ordering a diversion to Taiwan; the hijacker was then axed by the navigator. Heroics in the air is the Chinese way of dealing with the menace of pirates aloft – the motherland does not like to lose planes, especially to Taiwan. In July 1982 a Shanghai-bound plane was hijacked by five Chinese youths armed with sticks of dynamite, who ordered the plane to go to Taiwan. The pilot's response was to fly around in circles until the fuel was almost exhausted, whereupon the crew led passengers in an attack on the pirates with umbrellas and mop handles. The CAAC version of this near-calamity reads, 'The heroic deeds of the crew...showed the firm standpoint of their love for the Party and our socialist motherland...they feared no sacrifice...' The captain of the flight was awarded a special title created by the State Council – 'anti-hijacking hero'. Similar honours were bestowed on the crew of a plane hijacked to South Korea on 5 May 1983.

CAAC's worst reported crash occurred in October 1990 at Canton's Baiyun Airport – 127 passengers were killed. The cause was an abortive hijacking. As a result, Taiwan's government announced that hijackers would no longer receive political asylum and would be immediately returned to the mainland – where they would most likely receive the customary bullet in the back of the head. However, Taiwan still offers large rewards (paid in gold) to defecting Chinese air force pilots because the Communists still make verbal military threats against Taiwan.

Try to score a copy of CAAC's glossy in-flight magazines (produced in Japan) – these could be a collector's item someday. They're full of heroic folk tales about air crews and their flawless safety records, doctored folk tales, how the attendant at a CAAC hostel in Beijing found a million yen and rushed after the passenger to whom it belonged. There are even some safety tips.

BUS
Classes
There are two kinds of buses. The east side of the Canton bus station (closest to the Liu Hua Hotel) is where the big government-run buses are. These are cheaper but definitely more crowded, slower and less comfortable. You can get minibuses on the west side of the station. These are privately run and have amenities such as air-con, which are much appreciated during the sweatbox conditions of June to October. All buses and minibuses accept payment in RMB and – unlike the train – there is no additional charge for foreigners.

The company that runs the minibuses employs a big guy with a bamboo pole to make sure nobody jumps the queue.

When I was there, everyone lined up as they were supposed to. Then someone pulled the usual trick of shoving their way to the front. The big guy yelled *Pai dui!* ('Stand in line!'). The other guy continued to shove, so was promptly knocked halfway across the car park! I like this bus company.

TRAIN
Trains in China are reasonably fast, frequent and convenient. Trains also have the great advantage of being safer than buses. See the Getting There & Away sections of the Canton and Shenzhen chapters for details.

Canton 广州

Orientation

Known to the Chinese as Guangzhou, Canton is the sixth largest city in China and one of the oldest cities in the country. It's also the capital of Guangdong Province and for more than a thousand years was one of the main gateways to China. The city occupies a key position on the Pearl River Delta, 120 km north-west of Hong Kong.

Canton was originally three cities. The inner city was enclosed behind sturdy walls and was divided into the new and old cities. The outer city was everything outside these walls. The building of the walls began during the 11th century and was completed in the 16th century. The walls were eight metres high, between five and eight metres thick and 15 km in circumference,.

Canton's main thoroughfares, now called Jiefang Lu (Liberation Rd) and Zhongshan Lu, run north-south and east-west respectively. They divided the old walled city and met the walls at the main gates.

The city began to take its present form in the early 1920s. The demolition of the walls was completed, the canals were filled in and several km of motorways were built. This paralleled an administrative reorganisation of the city government that produced China's first city municipal council.

Outside the city walls to the west lies Xiguan, the western quarter. Wealthy Chinese merchants built their residences the same distance from the centre of the city as the foreign enclave of Shamian Island. The thoroughfare, still known as Shibapu, became the street of millionaires in the 19th century and remained the exclusive residential district of the well-to-do class. It was these people who patronised the famous old restaurants of the area.

In the north-east of the city is the Xiaobei (Little North) area. During the late dynastic times it was inhabited mainly by out-of-town officials because it was close to the offices of the bureaucracy. It was later developed into a residential area for civil servants, which it remains.

At the eastern end of Zhongshan Lu is a residential district built in the 1930s using modern town planning. It's known as Dongshan (East Mountain). Part of the Dongshan residential area is called Meihuacun (Plum Blossom Village) – a model village laid out in the 1930s with beautiful residences constructed for officials of high rank..

Before the Communists came to power, the waterfront on the south side of the Pearl River was notorious for its gambling houses and opium dens. The area became increasingly integrated with the city when it was developed as a site for warehouses and factories after the completion of the first suspension bridge in 1932.

Canton is now a large, sprawling city. The streets are usually split into sectors, each with a number or, more usually, labelled according to their position relative to the other sectors. For example, Zhongshan Lu (Zhongshan Rd) might be split into an east and a west sector – the east sector designated Zhongshan Donglu and the west sector called Zhongshan Xilu.

Information

Tourist Office There is a well-staffed CITS office (☎ 6677151) at 179 Huanshi Lu next to the main railway station. They have English-speaking staff and can sell you tickets for trains, planes, hovercraft and ships. The office is open from 8.30 to 11.30 am and 2 to 5 pm.

Though they deal mostly with Chinese speakers, you can get assistance from CTS (☎ 3336888), 2 Qiaoguang Lu, Haizhu Square, next to the Huaqiao Hotel.

The Guangdong Overseas Travel Corporation (☎ 6666277) is in the same building as CITS, but they mostly deal with tour groups.

Public Security The Public Security Bureau (☎ 3331060) is at 863 Jiefang Beilu, opposite the road which leads up to the Zhenhai Tower – a 15-minute walk from the Dongfang Hotel.

Money You can change money at branches of the Bank of China in most of the large tourist hotels, including the White Swan and Liu Hua.

Post & Telecommunications Just about all the major tourist hotels have post offices where you can send letters and packets containing printed matter. The post office in the White Swan Hotel is convenient if you're staying on Shamian Island.

If you're posting parcels overseas you have to go to the post office at 43 Yanjiang Xilu near the riverfront and Shamian Island. You have to get the parcel contents checked and fill out a customs form.

The GPO is locally known as the Liuhua Post Office *(liú huā yóu jú)*. It's next to the railway station in the large building with the Seiko sign on top. You can collect post restante letters here, despite there being no post restante window. Names are written on a notice board and you are supposed to see if your name is there and then find someone (but who?) to get the letter for you.

The telecommunications office is across from the railway station on the east side of Renmin Beilu.

The tourist hotels have direct-dial service to Hong Kong which is quite cheap. All main tourist hotels have telephone and fax facilities.

Foreign Consulates There are several consulates which can issue visas and replace stolen passports. The Polish Consulate is useful is you want to do the Trans-Siberian.

Japan
    Garden Hotel Tower, 368 Huanshi Donglu (☎ 3338999)

Poland
    Near the White Swan Hotel, Shamian Island
Thailand
    Rooms 309-310 & 303-316, White Swan Hotel, Shamian Island (☎ 8886968)
USA
    1 Shamian Nanjie, Shamian Island

Bookshops Try the Foreign Language Bookstore at 326 Beijing Lu, almost directly opposite the Seiko Store. They stock translations of Chinese books, as well as foreign magazines.

The Classical Bookstore, at 338 Beijing Lu, specialises in pre-1949 Chinese string-bound editions.

The Xinhua Bookstore, at 336 Beijing Lu, is the main Chinese bookstore in the city. It has a good collection of maps, often better than those you can buy on the street, but still mostly in Chinese characters (although some maps have both Chinese characters and pinyin). It also has lots of wall posters as well as reproductions of Chinese paintings.

Medical Services If you get sick you can go to one of the hospitals or to the medical clinic for foreigners – Guangzhou No 1 People's Hospital (☎ 3333090) *(dì yī rén mín yī yuàn)*, 602 Renmin Beilu.

If you're staying on Shamian Island or the riverfront, nearby is the Sun Yatsen Memorial Hospital (☎ 8882012) *(sūn yì xiān jì niàn yī yuàn)* at 107 Yanjiang Xilu, next to the Aiqun Hotel. Not much English is spoken here but medical facilities are pretty good and prices low.

Just next to Shamian Island and the Qingping Market is the Traditional Chinese Medicine Hospital *(zhōng yī yī yuàn)* on Zhuji Lu. If you want to try acupuncture and herbs, this is the place to go. Many foreigners come here to study Chinese medicine rather than to be patients.

Dangers & Annoyances Canton is easily the most dangerous city in China. Because Canton is widely perceived as the richest place in China, a large number of immigrants

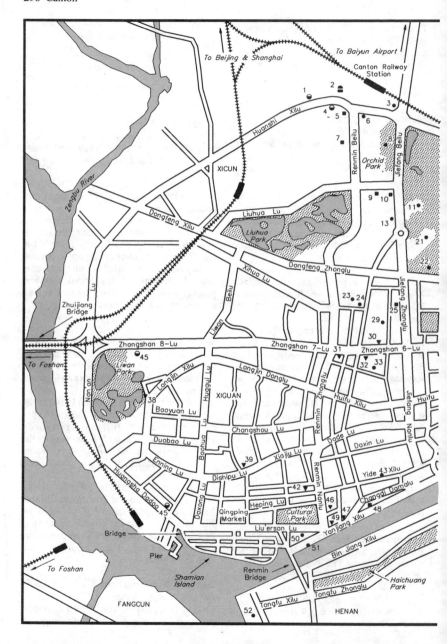

To Beijing & Shanghai

To Baiyun Airport

Canton Railway Station

Huanshi Xilu

XICUN

Renmin Beilu

Orchid Park

Jiefang Beilu

Liuhua Lu

Liuhua Park

Dongfeng Xilu

Lu

Zengbu River

Xihua Lu

Dongfeng Zhonglu

Liwan Beilu

Jiefang Zhonglu

Zhuijiang Bridge

To Foshan

Nan an Lu

Zhongshan 8-Lu

Zhongshan 7-Lu

Zhongshan 6-Lu

45

Liwan Park

Longjin Xilu

Longjin Donglu

Renmin Zhonglu

Huifu Xilu

Jiefang Nanlu

Huifu

XIGUAN

Huagui Lu

38

Baoyuan Lu

Changshou Lu

Dade Lu

Daxin Lu

Duobao Lu

Baohua Lu

39

Xiajiu Lu

Enning Lu

Dishipu Lu

Renmin Nanlu

Yide Xilu 43

Changdi Damalu

42

Heping Lu

Cultural Park

46

47

Huangsha Dadao

Daxiang Lu

45

Qingping Market

Liu'ersan Lu

49

Yanjiang Xilu

48

Bridge

50

Pier

51

Bin Jiang Xilu

To Foshan

Shamian Island

Renmin Bridge

Tongfu Zhonglu

Haichuang Park

FANGCUN

52

Tongfu Xilu

HENAN

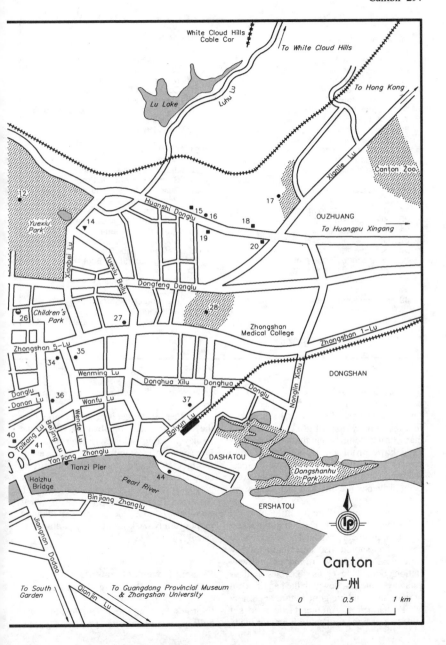

Canton
广州

■ PLACES TO STAY

5	Liu Hua Hotel
7	Hotel Equatorial
9	Dongfang Hotel
10	China Hotel
15	Baiyun Hotel
18	Holiday Inn
19	Garden Hotel
20	Ocean Hotel
25	Guangdong Guest House
40	Guangzhou Hotel
41	Huaqiao Hotel
48	Aiqun Hotel

▼ PLACES TO EAT

14	Beiyuan Restaurant
30	Xiyuan Restaurant
31	Muslim Restaurant
32	Caigenxiang (Veg) Restaurant
38	Banxi Restaurant
39	Guangzhou Restaurant
42	Snake Restaurant
46	Yan Yan Restaurant
47	Timmy's
49	Datong Restaurant

OTHER

| 1 | Long-Distance Bus Station |

2	GPO
3	CAAC/CITS
4	Minibus Station
6	Telecom Building
8	Mohammedan Tomb
11	Sculpture of the Five Rams
12	Zhenhai Tower
13	Public Security Bureau & Nanyue Museum
16	Friendship Store
17	Mausoleum of the 72 Martyrs
21	Sun Yatsen Monument
22	Sun Yatsen Memorial Hall
23	Bright Filial Piety Temple
24	Guangdong Antique Store
26	Buses to White Cloud Hills
27	Peasant Movement Institute
28	Memorial Garden to the Martyrs
29	Temple of the Six Banyan Trees
33	Huaisheng Mosque
34	South China Specialties Store
35	Canton Antique Store
36	Foreign Language Bookstore
37	Buses to Conghua
43	Sacred Heart Church
45	Buses to Foshan
50	Nanfang Department Store
51	No 1 Pier
52	Zhoutouzui Ferry Terminal (Boats & Jetcats to Hong Kong & Macau/ Boats along the Chinese Coastline)

from the countryside have poured into the city in search of instant wealth. Needless to say, most become disillusioned when they find that money doesn't grow on trees, and many turn to begging and theft. Canton taxis have knife-proof plastic shields or wire screens separating the driver from the passengers. Before these became mandatory, many drivers were attacked and some were killed.

For foreigners, there is little physical danger walking the streets, but pickpocketing is a problem, especially on crowded buses. You should also be cautious of bag snatchers, especially around the railway station. Some thieves use bicycles as their getaway vehicle – they grab the bag right out of your hand and are gone before you know what's happened. Another tactic is to slit your bag or pocket open with a razor blade

and remove the contents. The police are useless.

Another big danger is changing money on the black market. On Shamian Island, the moneychanging industry is controlled by a large gang. Almost without exception, every foreigner who changes money on the streets of Shamian Island gets ripped off. The only way to avoid this is never change money on the street. There are several shops on or near Shamian Island where you can change money safely. Ask around if you are interested.

Peasant Movement Institute
(nóng mín yùn dòng jiǎng xí sǔo)
农民运动讲习所
Canton's Peasant Movement Institute was built in 1924 on the site of a Ming Dynasty

Confucian temple. In the early days of the Communist Party, its members (from all over China) were trained at the institute. It was set up by Peng Pai, a high-ranking Communist leader who believed that if a Communist revolution was to succeed in China then the peasants must be its main force. Mao Zedong, who held the same opinion, took over as director of the institute in 1925 or 1926. Zhou Enlai lectured here and one of his students was Mao's brother, Mao Zemin. Peng was executed by the Kuomintang in 1929, and Mao Zemin was executed by a warlord in Xinjiang Province in 1942.

The buildings were restored in 1953 and they're now used as a revolutionary museum. There's not a great deal to see: a replica of Mao's room, the soldiers' barracks and rifles, and old photographs. The institute is at 42 Zhongshan 4-Lu.

Memorial Garden to the Martyrs
(liè shì líng yuán) 烈士陵园

This memorial is within walking distance of the Peasant Movement Institute, east along Zhongshan 4-Lu to Zhongshan 3-Lu. It was officially opened in 1957, on the 30th anniversary of the December 1927 Canton uprising.

In April 1927, Chiang Kaishek ordered his troops to massacre Communists in Shanghai and Nanjing. On 21 May the Communists led an uprising of peasants on the Hunan-Jiangxi border, and on 1 August they staged another in Nanchang. Both uprisings were defeated by Kuomintang troops.

On 11 December 1927 the Communists staged another uprising in Canton, but this was also bloodily suppressed by the Kuomintang. The Communists claim that over 5700 people were killed during or after the uprising. The memorial garden is laid out

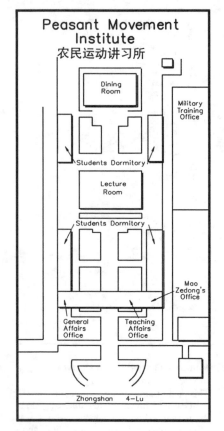

Peasant Movement Institute
农民运动讲习所

Dining Room

Military Training Office

Students Dormitory

Lecture Room

Students Dormitory

Mao Zedong's Office

General Affairs Office

Teaching Affairs Office

Zhongshan 4-Lu

victims of the unsuccessful Canton insurrection of 27 April 1911. (It was not until October 1911 that the Qing Dynasty collapsed and a Republic of China was declared in the south of the country.) The uprising had been planned by a group of Chinese organisations which opposed the Qing and which had formally united at a meeting of representatives in Tokyo in August 1905, with Sun Yatsen as leader.

The memorial was built in 1918 with funds provided by Chinese from all over the world, and was the most famous revolutionary monument of pre-Communist China. It's a conglomeration of architectural symbols of freedom and democracy used worldwide, since the outstanding periods of history in the rest of the world were going to be used as guidelines for the new Republic of China.

What that really means is that it's an exercise in architectural bad taste. In front, a small Egyptian obelisk carved with the words 'Tomb of the 72 Martyrs' stands under a stone pavilion. Atop the pavilion is a replica of Philadelphia's Liberty Bell in stone. Behind stands a miniature imitation of the Trianon at Versailles, with the cross-section of a huge pyramid of stone on its roof. Topping things off is a miniature replica of New York's Statue of Liberty. The Chinese influence can be seen in the bronze urns and lions on each side.

The monument stands on Yellow Flower Hill (Huanghuagang) on Xianli Zhonglu, east of the Baiyun and New Garden hotels.

Sun Yatsen Memorial Hall
(sūn zhōng shān jì niàn táng)
孙中山纪念堂
This hall on Dongfeng Lu was built in honour of Dr Sun Yatsen, with donations from Overseas Chinese and from Canton citizens. Construction began in January 1929 and finished in November 1931. It stands on the site of the residence of the governor of Guangdong and Guangxi during the Qing Dynasty, later used by Sun Yatsen when he became president of the Republic of China.

on Red Flower Hill (Honghuagang), which was one of the execution grounds.

There's nothing of particular interest here, though the gardens themselves are attractive. You'll also see the Pavilion of Blood-Cemented Friendship of the Sino-Soviet Peoples and the Pavilion of Blood-Cemented Friendship of the Sino-Korean Peoples.

Mausoleum of the 72 Martyrs & Memorial of Yellow Flowers
(húang hūa gāng qī shí èr liè shì mù)
黄花岗七十二烈士墓
This memorial was built in memory of the

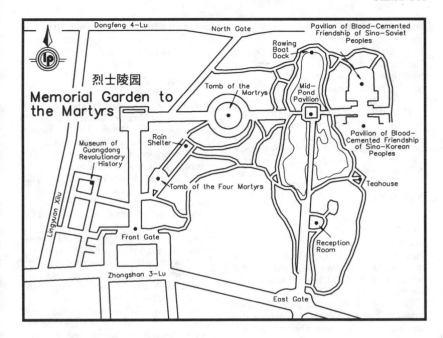

The Memorial Hall is an octagonal Chinese monolith some 47 metres high and 71 metres wide; seating capacity is about 4000.

Temple of the Six Banyan Trees
(liù róng sì hūa tǎ) 六榕寺花塔

The temple's history is vague, but it seems that the first structure on this site, called the Precious Solemnity Temple, was built during the 6th century AD, and was ruined by fire in the 10th century. The temple was rebuilt at the end of the 10th century and renamed the Purificatory Wisdom Temple since the monks worshipped Hui Neng, the sixth patriarch of the Zen Buddhist sect. Today it serves as the headquarters of the Guangzhou Buddhist Association.

The temple was given its name by Su Dongpo, a celebrated poet and calligrapher of the Northern Song Dynasty who visited the temple in the 11th or 12th century. He was so enchanted by the six banyan trees growing in the courtyard (no longer there) that he contributed two large characters for Six Banyans.

Within the temple compound is the octagonal **Flower Pagoda**, the oldest and tallest in the city at 55 metres. Although it appears to have only nine storeys from the outside, inside it has 17. It is said that Bodhidharma, the Indian monk considered to be the founder of the Zen sect, once spent a night here, and owing to the virtue of his presence the pagoda was rid of mosquitoes forever.

The temple is on Liurong Lu, just to the west of Jiefang Beilu, in central Canton. Until a few years ago the three large buddha statues stood in the open courtyard. The main hall was rebuilt in 1984. The buddhas have been painted and several other shrines opened. One shrine houses a statue of the monk, Hui Neng. The temple complex is now a major tourist attraction.

Bright Filial Piety Temple
(gūang xiào sì) 光孝寺

This temple is one of the oldest in Canton. The earliest Buddhist temple on this site possibly dates as far back as the 4th century AD. The place has particular significance for Buddhists because Hui Neng was a novice monk here in the 7th century. The temple buildings are of much more recent construction, the original buildings having been destroyed by fire in the mid-17th century. The temple is on Hongshu Lu, just west of the Temple of Six Banyan Trees. A section of the complex now houses the Guangdong Antique Store.

Five Genies Temple
(wǔ xiān gūan) 五仙观

This Taoist temple is held to be the site of the appearance of the five rams and celestial beings in the myth of Canton's foundation – see the section on Yuexiu Park for the story.

The stone tablets flanking the forecourt commemorate the various restorations that the temple has undergone. The present buildings are comparatively recent, as the earlier Ming Dynasty buildings were destroyed by fire in 1864.

The large hollow in the rock in the temple courtyard is said to be the impression of a celestial being's foot; the Chinese refer to it by the name of Rice-Ear Rock of Unique Beauty. The great bell was cast during the Ming Dynasty. It weighs five tons, is three metres high, two metres in diameter and about 10 cm thick, and is probably the largest bell in Guangdong Province. It's known as the 'calamity bell', since the sound of the bell, which has no clapper, is a portent of calamity for the city.

At the rear of the main tower stand life-size statues with archaic Greek smiles; these appear to represent four of the five genies. In the temple forecourt are four statues of rams, and embedded in the temple walls are inscribed steles.

The temple is at the end of an alleyway off Huifu Xilu. Huifu Xilu runs westward from Jiefang Zhonglu. The opening hours are daily from 8.30 to 11.30 am and 2.30 to 5.30 pm. Next door is Tom's Gym whose equipment dates back to the Stone Age!

Sacred Heart Church
(shí shì) 石室教堂

This impressive edifice is known to the Chinese as the House of Stone, as it is built entirely of granite. Designed by the French architect Guillemin, the church is an imitation of a European Gothic cathedral. Four bronze bells suspended in the building to the east of the church were cast in France; the original coloured glass was also made in France, but almost all of it is gone.

The site was originally the location of the office of the governor of Guangdong and Guangxi provinces during the Qing Dynasty, but the building was destroyed by British and French troops at the end of the second Opium War in the 19th century. The area was leased to the French following the signing of the Sino-French Tianjin Treaty. Construction of the church began in 1863 and was completed in 1888. It's on Yide Lu, not far from the riverfront, and is normally closed except on Sundays when masses are celebrated. All are welcome.

Another church you may find interesting is the **Zion Christian Church** at 392 Renmin Zhonglu. The building is a hybrid with a traditional European Gothic outline and Chinese eaves. It's an active place of worship.

Huaisheng Mosque
(húai shèng sì gūang tǎ) 怀圣寺光塔

The original mosque on this site is said to have been established in 627 AD by the first Muslim missionary to China, possibly an uncle of Mohammed. The present buildings are of recent construction. The name of the mosque means 'remember the sage', in memory of the prophet. Inside the grounds of the mosque is a minaret which is known as the Guangta (Smooth Tower) because of its flat, even appearance. The mosque stands on Guangta Lu, which runs eastwards off Renmin Zhonglu.

Mohammedan Tomb & Burial Ground

(mù hǎn mò dé mù) 穆罕默德墓

Situated in the Orchid Garden at the top of Jiefang Beilu, this is thought to be the tomb of the Muslim missionary who built the original Huaisheng Mosque. There are two other Muslim tombs outside the town of Quanzhou on the south-east coast of China, thought to be the tombs of missionaries sent by Mohammed with the one who is now buried in Canton.

The Canton tomb is in a secluded bamboo grove behind the Orchid Garden; continue past the entrance to the garden, walk through the narrow gateway ahead and take the narrow stone path on the right. Behind the tomb compound are Muslim graves and a monumental stone arch. The tomb came to be known as the Tomb of the Echo or the Resounding Tomb because of the noises that reverberate in the inner chamber.

Pearl River

(zhū jiāng) 珠江

The northern bank of the Pearl River is one of the most interesting areas of Canton; filled with people, markets and dilapidated buildings. A tourist boat ride down the Pearl River runs daily from 3.30 to 5 pm and costs Y10. Boats leave from the pier just east of Renmin Bridge. They take you down the river as far as Ershatou and then turn around and head back to Renmin Bridge.

Liu'ersan Lu

(liù èr sān lù) 六二三路

Just before you reach the south end of Renmin Lu, Liu'ersan Lu heads west. 'Liu er san' means '6 2 3', referring to 23 June (1925), when British and French troops fired on striking Chinese workers during the Hong Kong-Canton Strike.

Qingping Market

(qīng píng shì chǎng) 清平市场

A short walk down Liu'ersan Lu takes you to the second bridge which connects the city to the north side of Shamian Island. Directly opposite the bridge, on the city side, is Qingping Market on Qingping Lu – one of the best city markets in the whole country yet one of Canton's lesser known attractions.

If you want to buy, kill or cook it yourself, this is the place to come since the market is more like a takeaway zoo. Near the entrance you'll find the usual selection of medicinal herbs and spices, dried starfish, snakes, lizards, deer antlers, dried scorpions, leopard and tiger skins, bear paws, tree bark and unidentifiable herbs and plants.

Further up you'll find the live ones waiting to be butchered. Sad-eyed monkeys rattle at the bars of their wooden cages; tortoises crawl over each other in shallow tin trays; owls sit perched on boxes full of pigeons; fish paddle around in tubs aerated with jets of water. You can also get bundles of frogs, giant salamanders, pangolins, dogs and racoons, alive or contorted by recent violent death – which may just swear you off meat for the next few weeks.

The market spills out into Tiyun Lu which cuts east-west across Qingping Lu. Further north is another area supplying vegetables, flowers, potted plants and goldfish. There are small, very cheap food stalls in the streets on the perimeter of the market.

Shamian Island

(shā miàn) 沙面

Liu'ersan Lu runs parallel to the north bank of Shamian Island. The island is separated from the rest of Canton by a narrow canal to the north and east, and by the Pearl River to the south and west. Two bridges connect the island to the city.

'Shamian' means 'sand surface', which is all the island was until permission was given to foreign traders to set up their warehouses (factories) here in the middle of the 18th century. Land reclamation has increased its area to its present size: 900 metres from east to west, and 300 metres from north to south. The island became a British and French concession after they defeated the Chinese in the Opium Wars, and is covered with decaying

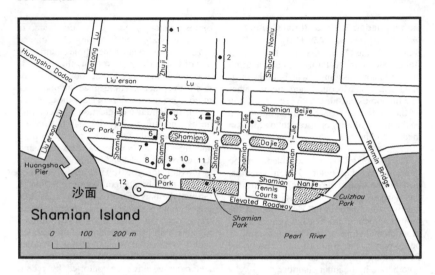

1 Traditional Chinese Medicine Hospital	8 Happy Bike Rental Station
2 Qingping Market	9 Guangzhou Youth Hostel
3 Victory Hotel	10 Shamian Hotel
4 Post Office	11 Pearl Inn
5 Economical Restaurant	12 White Swan Hotel
6 Li Qin Restaurant	13 Kiu Cun Restaurant
7 Polish Consulate	

1	中医医院	5	经济餐厅	9	广州青年招待所
2	清平市场	6	利群饮食店	10	沙面宾馆
3	胜利宾馆	7	波兰领事馆	11	夜明珠酒店
4	邮局	8	租自行车	12	白天鹅宾馆
				13	侨邨餐厅

colonial buildings which housed trading offices and residences.

The French Catholic church has been restored and stands on the main boulevard. The old British church at the western end of the island has been turned into a workshop, but is betrayed by bricked-up gothic-style windows. Today most of the buildings are used as offices or apartment blocks and the area retains a quiet residential atmosphere detached from the bustle across the canals.

Another 30,000 sq metres of land was added to the south bank of the island for the site of the 35-storey White Swan Hotel, which was built in the early 1980s. It's worth a walk along the north bank of Shamian

Island to get a view of the houses on Liu'ersan across the canal – seedy three and four-storey terrace houses probably dating to the 1920s and 1930s, but a pretty sight in the morning or evening sun. A few buildings of much the same design survive in the back streets of Hong Kong Island.

Just near the island, by the riverbank on Yanjiang Lu near the Renmin Bridge overpass, is the **Monument to the Martyrs of the Shaji Massacre** (as the 1925 massacre was known).

Cultural Park

(wén huà gōng yúan) 文化公园

The Cultural Park was opened in 1956. Inside are merry-go-rounds, a roller-skating rink, an aquarium with exhibits from Guangdong Province, nightly dance classes, acrobatic shows, films and live performances of Cantonese opera (sometimes in full costume).

One of the most breathtaking motorcycle stunt shows you'll ever see is held here in the evenings. Just as interesting is to watch the deadpan audience – no applause, no reaction. A foreigner walks down the street and all of China turns to stare, but a motorcycle stuntman performs a 360 degree mid-air flip and people act like it's nothing.

The Cultural Park is usually open until 10 pm and is worth dropping into. The main entrance is on Liu'ersan Lu.

Haichuang Park

(hǎi chúang gōng yúan) 海幢公园

Renmin Bridge stands just east of Shamian Island and connects the north bank of the Pearl River to the area of Canton known as Henan, the site of Haichuang Park. This would be a nondescript park but for the remains of what was once Canton's largest monastery, the **Ocean Banner Monastery**. It was founded by a Buddhist monk in 1662, and in its heyday the monastery grounds covered 2½ hectares. After 1911 the monastery was used as a school and soldiers' barracks. It was opened to the public as a park in the 1930s.

Though the three colossal images of the Buddha have gone, the main hall remains and is now used at night as a dance hall (live band). During the day the grounds are full of old men chatting, playing cards and chequers (draughts), and airing their pet birds.

The large stone which decorates the fish pond at the entrance on Tongfu Zhonglu is considered by the Chinese to be a tiger struggling to turn around. The stone came from Lake Tai in Jiangsu Province. During the Qing Dynasty the wealthy used these rare, strangely shaped stones to decorate their gardens. Many are found in the gardens of the Forbidden City in Beijing. This particular stone was brought back by a wealthy Cantonese merchant in the last century. When the Japanese took Canton in 1938 plans were made to ship the stone back to Japan, though this did not happen. After the war the stone was sold to a private collector and so disappeared from public view. It was finally returned to the park in 1951.

Yuexiu Park

(yùe xiù gōng yúan) 越秀公园

This is the biggest park in Canton, covering 93 hectares, and includes the **Zhenhai Tower**, the **Sun Yatsen Monument** and the large **Sculpture of the Five Rams**. The park also has a **sports stadium** with a seating capacity of 40,000, it's own **roller-coaster** and three **artificial lakes**: Dongxiu, Nanxiu and Beixiu – the last has rowboats which you can hire.

The Sculpture of the Five Rams, erected in 1959, is the symbol of Canton.

It is said that long ago five celestial beings wearing robes of five colours came to Canton riding through the air on rams. Each carried a stem of rice, which they presented to the people as an auspicious sign from heaven that the area would be free from famine forever. Guangzhou means 'broad region', but from this myth it takes its other name, City of Rams or just Goat City.

The Zhenhai Tower is east of the Sculpture of the Five Rams. The tower, also known as the Five-Storey Pagoda, is the only part of the old city wall that remains. From the upper

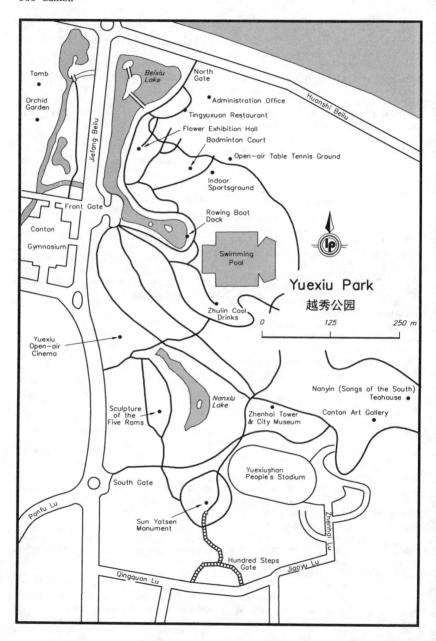

Tomb

Orchid Garden

Beixiu Lake

North Gate

Huanshi Beilu

Jiefang Beilu

Administration Office

Tingyuxuan Restaurant

Flower Exhibition Hall

Badminton Court

Open-air Table Tennis Ground

Indoor Sportsground

Front Gate

Canton Gymnasium

Rowing Boat Dock

Swimming Pool

Yuexiu Park

越秀公园

Zhulin Cool Drinks

0   125   250 m

Yuexiu Open-air Cinema

Nanyin (Songs of the South) Teahouse

Nanxiu Lake

Sculpture of the Five Rams

Zhenhai Tower & City Museum

Canton Art Gallery

South Gate

Yuexiushan People's Stadium

Panfu Lu

Sun Yatsen Monument

Zhenhai Lu

Hundred Steps Gate

Jigoyu Lu

Qingquan Lu

storeys it commands a view of the city to the south and the White Cloud Hills to the north. The present tower was built during the Ming Dynasty, on the site of a former structure. Because of its strategic location it was occupied by the British and French troops at the time of the Opium Wars. The 12 cannon in front of the tower date from this time (five of them are foreign, the rest were made in nearby Foshan). The tower now houses the City Museum with exhibits which describe the history of Canton from Neolithic times until the early part of this century.

The Sun Yatsen Monument is south of the Zhenhai Tower. This tall obelisk was constructed in 1929, four years after Sun's death, on the site of a temple to the goddess Guanyin (Kuanyin). The obelisk is built of granite and marble blocks and there's nothing to see inside, though a staircase leads to the top where there's a good view of the city. On the south side of the obelisk the text of Dr Sun's last testament, signed on the 11 March, 1925, is engraved in stone tablets on the ground:

For 40 years I have devoted myself to the cause of national revolution, the object of which is to raise China to a position of independence and equality among nations. The experience of these 40 years has convinced me that to attain this goal, the people must be aroused, and that we must associate ourselves in a common struggle with all the people of the world who treat us as equals. The revolution has not yet been successfully completed. Let all our comrades follow the principles set forth in my writings 'Plans for National Renovation', 'Fundamentals of National Reconstruction', 'The Three Principles of the People' and the 'Manifesto of the First National Convention of the Kuomintang' and continue to make every effort to carry them into effect. Above all, my recent declaration in favour of holding a National Convention of the People of China and abolishing unequal treaties should be carried into effect as soon as possible.

Orchid Park
(lán pǔ) 兰圃
Originally laid out in 1957, this pleasant little park is devoted to orchids – over a hundred varieties. Orchid Park is a great place in summer, but a dead loss in winter when all you will see are rows of flowerpots.

The Y2 admission fee includes tea by the small pond. The park is open daily from 7.30 to 11.30 am and 1.30 to 5 pm; closed on Wednesday. It's at the northern end of Jiefang Beilu, not far from the main railway station.

Nanyue Museum
(nán yùe wáng hàn mù) 南越王汉墓
Also known as the Museum of the Western Han Dynasty of the Nanyue King, the museum is built on the site of the tomb of the second ruler of the Nanyue Kingdom dating back to 100 BC. The Nanyue Kingdom is what the area around Canton was called back in the Han Dynasty. It's an excellent museum with English explanations. More than 500 rare artefacts are on display. Admission is Y3 for foreigners, Y1 for Chinese.

Liuhua Park
(liú huā gōng yúan) 流花公园
This enormous park on Renmin Beilu contains the largest artificial lake in the city. It was built in 1958, a product of the ill-fated Great Leap Forward. The entrance to the park is on Renmin Beilu.

Canton Zoo
(gǔang zhōu dòng wù yúan) 广州动物园
The zoo was built in 1958 and is one of the better zoos you'll see in China, which is perhaps not saying much. It's on Xianlie Lu, north-east of the Mausoleum of the 72 Martyrs.

Pearl River Cruise
(zhū jiāng yóu lǎn chúan)
珠江游览船
From April to October there are night cruises for tourists on the Pearl River. Departures are from Pier 2 (just south of the Nanfang Department Store). You can call ☎ 8861928, 4412629 or 8885188 for information about the cruise.

The White Swan Hotel also offers an evening cruise from 6 to 9 pm, including dinner on the boat.

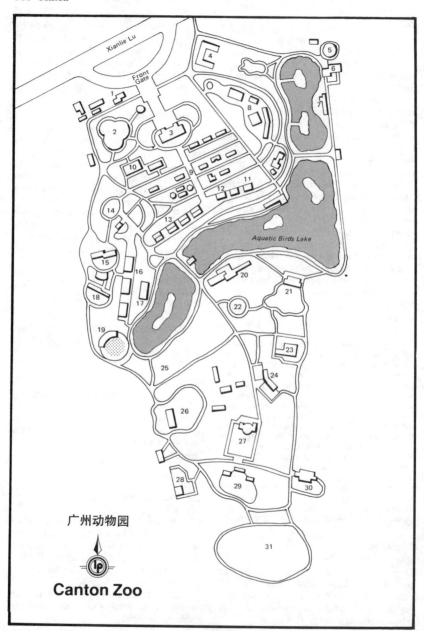

广州动物园

Canton Zoo

1	Broadcasting Room	1	广播楼
2	Baboon, Mandrill	2	山魈
3	Gorilla	3	大猩猩
4	Goldfish	4	金鱼
5	Boa House	5	蟒蛇楼
6	Snakes	6	蛇
7	Reptiles	7	爬行纲
8	Birds	8	鸟舍
9	Smaller Animals	9	小兽类
10	Gibbon	10	长臂猿
11	Lynx	11	猞猁
12	Bear	12	熊
13	Leopard	13	豹
14	Bear Hill	14	熊山
15	Tiger Hill	15	虎山
16	Herbivores	16	食草动物
17	Yak	17	牦牛
18	Lion Hill	18	狮子山
19	Hippopotamus	19	河马
20	Restaurant	20	饭店
21	Monkey Hill	21	猴子山
22	Lesser Panda	22	小熊猫
23	Panda	23	大熊猫
24	Kangaroo	24	袋鼠
25	Mexican Dog	25	墨西哥狗
26	Asian Elephant	26	亚州象
27	Giraffe	27	长颈鹿
28	Bactrian Camel	28	单蜂驼
29	Zebra	29	斑马
30	Bear	30	熊
31	Deer	31	鹿

Guangdong Provincial Museum

(gŭang dōng shěng bó wù gŭan)
广东省博物馆

The museum is on Yan'an 2-Lu on the south side of the Pearl River, and houses exhibitions of archaeological finds from Guangdong Province.

Zhongshan University

(zhōng shān dà xúe) 中山大学

Also on Yan'an 2-Lu, the university houses the Lu Xun Museum *(lŭ xùn bówùgŭan)*. Lu Xun (1881-1936) was one of China's great modern writers, and taught at the university in 1927. He was not a Communist though most of his books were banned by the Kuomintang.

Canton Fair

(zhōng gúo chū kŏu shāng pĭn jiāo yì hùi)
中国出口商品交易会

Apart from the Chinese New Year, this is the biggest event in Canton. The name implies that this is a fair with clowns and balloons for the kiddies. In fact, it's nothing of the kind. The Canton Fair is otherwise known as the Chinese Export Commodities Fair and is mostly of interest to business people who want to conduct foreign trade with China. The fair aims to promote China's exports, although it is a good place to make business contacts which could be helpful later in China. The fair is held twice yearly, usually in April and October (in spring and autumn) each time for 20 days.

The fair takes place in the large exhibition hall across the street from the Dongfang

Hotel, near the intersection of Liuhua Lu and Renmin Beilu. During the rest of the year, when there is no fair, the building sits unused. Unfortunately, the fair is not open to everybody who would like to attend. You must first receive an invitation from one of China's national foreign-trade corporations (FTCs).

Getting an invitation takes some effort. Those who have previously done business with an FTC should automatically receive an invitation. Those who have never done business with China should apply to China Travel Service (CTS) in Hong Kong. They need several days to process an application.

The Canton Fair is important to travellers for one reason – accommodation becomes a real problem when it's on. The fair is a very big event and, unless you are attending, Canton would be a good place to avoid at that time. If you're staying in youth hostels this should be less of a problem since few business people will stay in rock-bottom accommodation. However, transport will be more crowded than usual during the fair and taxi drivers will be even more arrogant than usual.

Places to Stay – bottom end

Canton has quite a number of hotels to choose from, but only a few provide relatively cheap rooms and there's not much in the way of cheap dormitory accommodation.

Shamian Island is almost a happy hunting ground for cheapish hotels. To get to them, take bus No 5 from Huanshi Xilu; the stop is on the opposite side of the road and just to the west of the railway station. The bus runs along Liu'ersan Lu on the northern boundary of the canal which separates Shamian Island from the rest of Canton. Four footbridges connect Shamian Island to the city.

Near the massive White Swan Hotel is the *Guangzhou Youth Hostel* (☎ 8884298) *(gǔang zhōu qīng nián zhāo dài sǔo)* at 2 Shamian 4-Jie. It's the most popular hotel in Canton with low-budget travellers, reasonably clean and quiet. Dormitory beds are Y20 to Y25 and double rooms Y50. There are no single rooms. The only negative is that

the plumbing occasionally blows up, sending travellers scurrying across the street to the nearby White Swan to use the toilets.

The only other place that might qualify as budget accommodation is the *CITS Hostel* (☎ 6664263) *(gúo lǚ zhāo dài sǔo)* right behind CITS and just east of the railway station. A dormitory bed costs Y20 in a four-bed room, but the catch is that you must supply your own roommates. So unless you can round up three friends, it will cost you Y80 to book the whole room *(bāo fáng)*, which is hardly worth it.

Places to Stay – middle

The *Shamian Hotel* (☎ 8888124, fax 8861068) *(shā miàn bīn gǔan)*, 50 Shamian Nanjie, is only a few steps to the east of the Guangzhou Youth Hostel on Shamian Island. Doubles with twin beds come in three standards costing Y79, Y89 and Y99. They seem to have a permanent 'all full' sign on the front desk, but ask anyway because they often have vacancies. Just because you manage to check in, don't think you can necessarily stay long. Big tour groups book this hotel in advance, so you might have a room today but be asked to move out the next day.

On the east side of the Shamian Hotel is the *Pearl Inn* (☎ 8889238) *(yè míng zhū jiǔ diàn)*, a fancy place known for its good restaurant, bar, sauna, disco and aggressive air-con. Standard/deluxe doubles are Y180/210.

Also on Shamian Island is the *Victory Hotel* (☎ 8862622, fax 8862413) *(shèng lì bīn gǔan)*. There's a lack of English signs, but the hotel is easily identified – it looks like a seafood restaurant with big fish tanks outside. It's at the corner of Shamian 4-Jie and Shamian Beijie. Doubles cost Y150 to Y165.

The *Aiqun Hotel* (☎ 6661445, fax 8883519) *(ai qún dà jiǔ diàn)* at 113 Yanjiang Xilu (at the corner with Changdi Damalu) is right on the riverfront. Singles/doubles are Y80/120, a bargain for the high standard of accommodation. Some travellers have even managed to pay RMB. Take bus

No 31 from the railway station; get off when you come to the river, turn left and walk up Yanjiang Lu for about 10 minutes.

The *White Palace Hotel* (☎ 8882313, fax 8889161) *(bái gōng jiǔ diàn)* is a good place to stay though the staff speaks little English. It's near the river at 17 Renmin Nanlu and doubles cost Y90.

Across the street from the White Palace is the *Xinya Hotel* (☎ 8884722) *(xīn yà jiǔ diàn)*, 10 Renmin Nanlu, where doubles are Y100. The hotel is a huge, elegant-looking place popular with Hong Kongers but rather few foreigners.

The *GD Hotel* (☎ 8883601) *(gǔang dōng dà jiǔ diàn)* is at 294 Changdi Damalu, one block north of the Aiqun Hotel. They charge Y130 for a double. No one here speaks English so they prefer foreigners who speak Chinese – otherwise they may claim to be full.

The *Guangzhou Hotel* (☎ 3338168, fax 3330791) *(gǔang zhōu bīn gǔan)* is at Haizhu (Sea Pearl) Square, east of the Aiqun Hotel. Singles/doubles are Y150/1650. Bus No 29 leaves from Huanshi Xilu, near the railway station, and goes past the hotel. Haizhu Square is a big roundabout with a giant statue in the middle.

Also on Haizhu Square is the *Huaqiao Hotel* (☎ 3336888) *(húa qiáo dà xià)*, a beautiful place to stay but more inclined to take Chinese than Westerners. Doubles are from Y90 to Y155. This hotel is just next to CTS (not to be confused with CITS).

Places to Stay – top end

The *Liu Hua Hotel* (☎ 6668800, fax 6667828) *(liú hūa bīn gǔan)* is a large tourist hotel at 194 Huanshi Xilu, directly opposite the railway station. It's easily recognisable by the big 'Seagull Watch' sign on the roof. Double rooms range from Y165 to Y210 and are very comfortable, though the cheaper ground-floor rooms can be very noisy.

The *Hotel Equatorial* (☎ 6672888, fax 6672582) *(gùi dū jiǔ diàn)*, 931 Renmin Beilu, is a short walk from the railway station and offers plush doubles for Y231.

The *Baiyun Hotel* (☎ 3333998, fax

3336498) *(bái yún bīn gǔan)*, 367 Huanshi Donglu, is a huge place east of the railway station. Doubles start at Y132. Bus No 30 from the railway station goes past the hotel.

Opposite the Baiyun Hotel is the *Garden Hotel* (☎ 3338989, fax 3350467) *(hūa yúan jiǔ diàn)* at 368 Huanshi Donglu, one of the most spectacular hotels in China. The hotel is topped by a revolving restaurant, and there's a snooker hall and a McDonald's-style fast-food joint on the ground floor. Doubles start at Y300.

Also in the same neighbourhood is the *Ocean Hotel* (☎ 7765988) *(yǔan yáng bīn gǔan)* at 412 Huanshi Donglu. It is an impressive luxury hotel with doubles from Y160 to Y220.

Immediately to the north-west of the Ocean Hotel is the *Holiday Inn* (☎ 7766999, fax 7753126) *(wén hùa jià rì jiǔ diàn)* at 28 Guangming Lu. Doubles start at Y270.

Guangdong Guest House (☎ 3332950, fax 3332911) *(gǔang dōng yíng bīn gǔan)*, 603 Jiefang Beilu, has doubles from Y190 to Y295. It's an exclusive-looking place with its own grounds and a wall around it. A sign by the lobby says that 'proper attire' is required at all times. It's a rather out of the way place.

The *Dongfang Hotel* (☎ 6669900, fax 6662775) *(dōng fāng bīn gǔan)*, 120 Liuhua Lu near Jiefang Beilu, is next to the China Hotel. It's a beautiful, well-situated hotel. Singles cost Y330 to Y380 and doubles are Y400 to Y460. It's about a 15-minute walk from the railway station and bus No 31 runs right by.

Towering over the Dongfang Hotel is the gleaming *China Hotel* (☎ 6666888, fax 6677014) *(zhōng gúo dà jiǔ diàn)* which boasts wall-to-wall marble, a disco and a bowling alley. Rooms start at Y397 singles and Y440 doubles. It's one of the top-rated hotels in China and has a good Friendship Store.

The *White Swan Hotel* (☎ 8886968) *(bái tiān é bīn gǔan)*, 1 Shamian Nanjie, certainly rates as one of the finest hotels in China. Apart from the waterfall in the lobby, there is a pool, sauna, disco and a great location on Shamian Island. Of course, it ought to be good given the price: Y370 for a 'standard' double, and Y477 for 'deluxe'. Furthermore, the price is doubled during the Export Commodities Fair, 14 to 29 April and 14 to 29 October. The White Swan is also popular with budget travellers for its post office, bank, ticket booking office (boats and aeroplanes) and for its toilets which come in handy when the plumbing blows up at the adjacent youth hostel.

You never know who you might run into at the White Swan. Whenever big shots from Beijing are in town they invariably stop here for a gourmet meal in the hotel restaurant (at government expense).

The very first time I went into the White Swan my jaw dropped in astonishment as none other than Deng Xiaoping walked out of the restaurant with an entourage of VIPs and security men.

Places to Eat

The Chinese have a saying that to enjoy the best in life, one has to be 'born in Suzhou, live in Hangzhou, eat in Canton and die in Liuzhou'. Suzhou is renowned for beautiful women, Hangzhou for scenery and Liuzhou for the finest wood for coffin-making. It's too late for me to be born in Suzhou, I don't like the weather in Hangzhou and I have no enthusiasm for dying in Liuzhou, but when it comes to eating, Canton is a pretty good place to stuff your face.

Bakeries One of the great delights of Canton is that you can get decent bread and pastries for breakfast or snacks. The bakery at the *White Swan Hotel* is cheap and very good. Ditto for the *China Hotel* and *Huaqiao Hotel*.

Chinese Food On Shamian Island, most budget travellers head for *Li Qun Restaurant (lì qún yǐn shí diàn)* on Shamian Dajie near the Victory Hotel (see the Shamian Island map). Prices are extremely low and the food is excellent.

The *Pearl Inn (yè míng zhū jiǔ diàn)* is just to your right as you face the Shamian Hotel on Shamian Nanjie. They have good and cheap dim sum on the ground floor restau-

rant. There is also a coffee shop serving Western breakfasts.

Also on Shamian Island is the *Victory Restaurant*, attached to the Victory Hotel. It has good Chinese food and prices are amazingly reasonable for such a high standard of service, although seafood can be expensive. An English-language menu is available.

The *Kiu Cun Restaurant (qiáo cūn cān tīng)* is in the park on Shamian Nanjie, Shamian Island. It's a pleasant place with outdoor tables, but prices are not especially cheap.

There are a couple of good places close to the riverfront. Foremost is the *Datong* (☎ 8888988) *(dà tóng jiǔ jiā)* at 63 Yanjiang Xilu, just around the corner from Renmin Lu. The restaurant occupies all of an eight-storey building overlooking the river. Specialities of the house are crisp fried chicken and roast suckling pig. The crisp-roasted pig skin is a favourite here. This is a great place for morning dim sum.

Close to the Datong Restaurant is the *Yan Yan Restaurant (rén rén cài guǎn)* on Xihao 2-Lu, a side-street which runs east from Renmin Lu. (Look for the pedestrian overpass which goes over Renmin Lu up from the intersection with Yanjiang Lu. The steps of the overpass lead down into a side-street and the restaurant is opposite them.) The Yan Yan is easily recognisable by the fish tanks in the entrance. Get your turtles, catfish and roast suckling pig here. It's also fantastically well air-conditioned.

The *Aiqun Hotel* has a great restaurant on the 14th floor. Apart from the food, it's worth coming up here just for the views overlooking the Pearl River.

One of the city's best known restaurants is the *Guangzhou* (☎ 8888388) *(guǎng zhōu jiǔ jiā)*, at 2 Wenchang Nanlu, near the intersection with Dishipu Lu. It boasts a 70-year history and in the 1930s came to be known as the 'first house in Canton'. Its kitchens were staffed by the city's best chefs and the restaurant was frequented by the most important people of the day. The four storeys of dining halls and private rooms are built around a central garden courtyard where potted shrubs, flowers and landscape paintings are intended to give the feeling (at least to the people in the dingy ground-floor rooms) of 'eating in a landscape'. Specialities of the house include shark-fin soup with shredded chicken, chopped crabmeat balls and braised dove. It does tend to be expensive and reservations are sometimes necessary.

The *Muslim Restaurant* (☎ 8888991) *(húi mín fàn diàn)* is at 325 Zhongshan 6-Lu, on the corner with Renmin Lu. Look for the Arabic letters above the front entrance. It's an OK place, but go upstairs since the ground floor is dingy.

North of Zhongshan Lu is Dongfeng Lu, which runs east-west across the city. At 202 Xiaobei Lu is the *North Garden Restaurant* (☎ 3330087) *(běi yúan jiǔ jiā)*. This is another of Canton's 'famous houses'. A measure of its success being the number of cars and tourist buses parked outside. Specialities of the house include barbecued chicken liver, steamed chicken in huadiao wine, stewed fish head with vegetables, fried boneless chicken (could be a first for China) and stewed duck legs in oyster sauce. The food here is good value.

In the west of Canton, the *Banxi* (☎ 8815718) *(bàn xī jiǔ jiā)*, 151 Longjin Xilu, is the biggest restaurant in the city. It's noted for its dumplings, stewed turtle, roast pork, chicken in tea leaves and a crabmeat-shark-fin consommé. Its famous dim sum is served from about 5 to 9.30 am, at noon and again at night. Dim sum includes fried dumplings with shrimp, chicken gizzards, pork and mushrooms – even shark-fin dumplings! You can try crispy fried egg rolls stuffed with chicken, shrimp, pork, bamboo shoots and mushrooms. Monkey brains are steamed with ginger, scallions and rice wine, and then steamed again with crab roe, eggs and lotus blossoms.

In the same general direction is the *Taotaoju* (☎ 8885769) *(táo táo jū)*, 288 Xiuli 2-Lu. Originally built as a private academy in the 17th century, it was turned into a restaurant in the late 19th century. Tao Tao was the name of the proprietor's wife. Dim

sum is the speciality here; you choose sweet and savoury snacks from the selection on trolleys that are wheeled around the restaurant. Tea is the preferred beverage and is said to be made with Canton's best water – brought in from the Nine Dragon Well in the White Cloud Hills.

Beijing Lu has two of Canton's 'famous' restaurants. The *Wild Animals Restaurant* *(yě wèi xiāng fàn diàn)*, at No 247, is where you can feast on dogs, cats, deer, bear paws and snake. Once upon a time they even served tiger.

Highly recommended is the *Taipingguan* (☎ 3332938) *(tài píng gǔan cān tīng)*, at 344 Beijing Lu, which serves both Western and Chinese food. Zhou Enlai fancied their roast pigeon.

South Garden Restaurant (☎ 4449211) *(nán yúan jiǔ jiā)* is at 142 Qianjin Lu and the menu features chicken in honey and oyster sauce or pigeon in plum sauce. Qianjin Lu is on the south side of the Pearl River; to get to it you have to cross Haizhu Bridge and go down Jiangnan Dadao. Qianjin Lu branches off to the east.

Just to the west of Renmin Lu, at 43 Jianglan Lu, is the *Snake Restaurant*

Location of Snake Restaurant

(☎ 8883811) *(shé cān guǎn)*, with the snakes on display in the window. The restaurant was originally known as the 'Snake King Moon' and has a history of 80 years. To get to the restaurant you have to walk down Heping Lu which runs west from Renmin Lu. After a few minutes turn right into Jianglan Lu and follow it around to the restaurant on the left-hand side. Creative snake recipes include fricasséed assorted snake and cat meats, snake breast meat stuffed with shelled shrimp, stir-fried colourful shredded snakes, and braised snake slices with chicken liver.

The Chinese believe that snake meat is effective in curing diseases. It is supposed to be good for dispelling wind and promoting blood circulation; and is believed to be useful in treating anaemia, rheumatism, arthritis and asthenia (abnormal loss of strength). Snake gall bladder is supposed to be effective in dispelling wind, promoting blood circulation, dissolving phlegm and soothing one's breathing. Way back in the 1320s the Franciscan friar Odoric visited China and commented on the snake-eating habits of the southern Chinese: 'There be monstrous great serpents likewise which are taken by the inhabitants and eaten. A solemn feast among them with serpents is thought nothing of'.

Cheap Eats The small government-owned dumpling *(jiǎo zi)* restaurants are cheap and the food is usually good, but the service leaves a lot to be desired. Before you get your food you must pay the cashier and obtain tickets which you take to the cook. Customers tend to be ignored, especially when they are busy, so if you want something to eat you have to be aggressive. Just watch how the Chinese do it. Join the push and shove match, or else come back later in the off-peak hours.

Innumerable street stalls are open at night in the vicinity of the Aiqun Hotel. If you walk around the streets, and particularly along Changdi Damalu on the north side of the hotel, you'll find sidewalk stalls dishing up frogs, toads and tortoises. At your merest whim these will be summarily executed, thrown in the wok and fried. It's a bit like eating in an abattoir, but at least there's no doubt about the freshness.

Adequate but mundane food is served in the little restaurants in Zhanqian Lu, a lane which runs alongside the Liu Hua Hotel. A few of these places are marginally better than the others; look around until you see something you like. Some of the restaurateurs have an aggravating habit of trying to snatch you off the street and charge ridiculous prices.

Vegetarian The *Caigenxiang Vegetarian Restaurant* (☎ 3344363) *(cài gēn xiāng sù shí guǎn)*, 167 Zhongshan 6-Lu, is one of the few places in Canton where you don't have to worry about accidentally ordering dogs, cats or monkey brains.

Fast Food Kentucky Fried Chicken has not spread its wings yet in Canton, nor have the golden arches arrived on the scene, but the China Hotel's *Hasty Tasty Fast Food* shop (which opens on to Jiefang Beilu) should make you feel at home. It looks and tastes exactly like any Hong Kong or US fast-food venue with banks of neon lights in the ceiling, laminex tables and unremarkable food.

Timmy's, near the Aiqun Hotel on Yan jiang Xilu, also serves its own variety of fast food.

Another place that serves a somewhat improved version of fast food is the *Friendship Cafe*, which is next to the Friendship Store and the Baiyun Hotel on Huanshi Donglu. The 'Friendship Sandwiches' are especially recommended.

It was a hot and steamy summer afternoon. I was sitting in Hasty Tasty, Canton's premier fast-food restaurant, enjoying the air-con and sipping a large Coke with ice. As I sat there contemplating where I would go next in this sizzling weather, a foreign tourist stepped up to the counter. His name was George.

George's wife was sitting at a table by the door. She wore a purple jump suit, gaudy fake jewellery, horn-rimmed sunglasses and enough perfume to be a fire hazard. Her hair – flaming orange and held rigid by hair spray – looked like two jiao worth of cotton candy. She was carefully explaining how she would break both their arms if they didn't shut up and stop fighting with each other.

As George approached the counter, the waitress grinned at him. Perhaps she did that to all the customers, or perhaps it had something to do with the way George was dressed – in pink shorts, a flowered shirt and a white sunhat embroidered with a picture of a fish and the words 'Sea World'.

'May I take your order?' the waitress asked. George looked relieved, obviously pleased that the waitress could speak English. 'Excuse me, I don't want to order anything right now, but could you tell me where's the nearest McDonald's?'

'Sorry sir' the waitress replied, 'we don't have McDonald's in Canton. I have never eaten there. But they have in Hong Kong – I saw on television'.

You might as well have hit him with a freight train. Shock, horror, disbelief – you could see it in his face. George turned his back on the waitress without saying another word and trudged fearfully towards the table where his wife and two charming children were sitting.

'Well George', she bellowed, 'where's the Mc-Donald's?'

'They haven't got one here', he answered coarsely. Immediately the two kids started yelling 'We want a Big Mac!'.

'Shut up!', George explained, 'We have to go back to Hong Kong!' I could see he was starting to panic. He slung his big camera over his shoulder, grabbed a shopping bag full of tourist junk purchased at the Friendship Store, and headed out the door with his wife and two children behind him. I watched from the window as they flagged down a taxi, and wondered if they were indeed heading for Hong Kong.

Things to Buy

The Chinese do produce some interesting items for export – tea, clothing, Silkworm missiles – the latter not generally for sale to the public.

The intersection of Beijing Lu and Zhong shan Lu is the top shopping area in the city. Here many excellent shops spread out along both streets. Another street that demands your attention is the bottom part of that long loop street (see map) in the south-west part of the city. I can't tell you the name of the street because it changes every few blocks. The section north of Shamian Island (near the Guangzhou Restaurant) is called Dishipu Lu. As you walk east from there the name changes to Xiajiu Lu, then Shangjiu Lu and finally Dade Lu. Whatever you want to call it, it's an excellent street for walking and shopping. The downtown section of Jiefang Lu is also good.

Department Stores You'll find practically everything you need in life in Canton's department stores. They have all the necessities such as clothing and appliances, plus plenty of luxury items too. But what most amazes me about these stores is the large amount of industrial goods that they stock. If you're in the market for a jackhammer or a 10,000-V transformer, then the local department store probably has what you need.

Canton's main department store is the Nanfang on Liu'ersan Lu, just to the east and opposite the main entrance to the Cultural Park. You can also enter the store from Yanjiang Lu by the river. The only other large store in the city is the Zhongshan Wulu Department Store, 250 Zhongshan 4-Lu.

Friendship Stores These stores usually want FEC money, but will also accept RMB after charging you 30% extra! After all, if there's going to be a black market, the government might as well be in on it too.

There are two Friendship Stores in Canton. The main one is next to the Baiyun Hotel on Huanshi Donglu. It's adjacent to the Friendship Cafe. This store has a particularly good supermarket, so if you have a craving for Cadbury chocolate bars or Swiss cheese, this is the place to come.

The other Friendship Store is next to the China Hotel on the corner of Liuhua Lu and Jiefang Beilu. Both Friendship Stores accept all major credit cards and can arrange shipment of goods back to your country.

Down Jackets If you're heading to north China in winter and don't already have a good down jacket, get one in Canton. Your life depends on it!

Down jackets are a bargain in China. With all the ducks and geese that the Cantonese eat, they have to do something with all those feathers. You can pick up a decent down jacket for a little more than Y100 at (*gōng nóng fú zhūang chǎng*) 310 Zhongshan 4-Lu, on the north side of the street and east of Beijing Lu and the Children's Park.

Always check zippers when you buy

clothing in China. Good down jackets should have some sort of elastic around the inside of the sleeves near the wrists. Otherwise the cold will travel up to your armpits. Make sure that the jacket has a hood.

Antiques The Friendship Stores have antique sections, but prices are high so don't expect to find a bargain. Only antiques which have been cleared for sale to foreigners may be taken out of the country. When you buy an item which is more than 100 years old it will come with an official red wax seal attached – this seal does not necessarily indicate that the item is an antique! You'll also get a receipt of sale which you must show to customs when you leave the country, otherwise the antique will be confiscated. Imitation antiques are sold everywhere. Some museum shops sell replicas of pieces on exhibit.

For antiques, try the Friendship Stores and that other main tourist trap, the Guangdong Antique Store at 696 Renmin Lu. There is also the Guangzhou Antique Shop at 170 Wende Beilu.

Arts & Crafts Brushes, paints and other art materials may be worth checking as a lot of this stuff is being imported by Western countries, so you should be able to pick it up cheaper at the source.

Scroll paintings are sold everywhere and are invariably very expensive, partly because the material on which the painting is done is expensive. There are many street artists in China who often sit on the sidewalk making on-the-spot drawings and paintings and selling them to passers-by.

Beautiful kites are sold in China and are worth getting, just to hang on your wall. Paper rubbings of stone inscriptions are cheap and make nice wall hangings when framed. Papercuts are sold everywhere and some are exquisite. Jade and ivory jewellery is commonly sold in China, but watch out for fakes. Remember that every ivory item bought brings the African elephant closer to extinction, and that countries such as Aus-

tralia and the USA prohibit the importation of ivory.

The Jiangnan Native Product Store, at 399 Zhongshan 4-Lu, has a good selection of bamboo and baskets and the Guangzhou Arts & Crafts Market is convenient at 284 Changdi Damalu, near the Aiqun Hotel.

No prizes for guessing the speciality at the Guangzhou Pottery Store, 151 Zhongshan 5-Lu.

Books, Posters & Magazines The gift shop at the White Swan Hotel might seem like a strange place to shop for books, but they have a decent collection of English-language maps, books and foreign magazines such as *Time, Newsweek, Far Eastern Economic Review* and the *Economist.* You must pay in FEC, but prices are not much higher than elsewhere in Canton.

Stamps Some travellers seem to think they can buy stamps cheaply in China and sell them for a profit at home, but it rarely works out that way. Nevertheless, China does produces some beautiful stamps, and if you are a collector, they're worth checking out. The Guangzhou Stamp Company is at 151 Huanshi Xilu, west of the railway station.

Getting There & Away
Air To give pilots a challenge, Canton's Baiyun Airport is right next to the White Cloud Hills, Canton's only mountains. It's 12 km north of the city centre.

The Airport Hotel (☎ 6661700) *(bái yún jī chǎng bīn gǔan)* is right next to the main terminal and is an excellent place to stay. In a nine bed dorm, beds are Y20; Y35 in a three bed dorm; Y65 for a single and Y85 for a double. All rooms have air-con and are reasonably clean.

There are three restaurants on the 2nd floor of the terminal building – one of them is excellent and the other two are best avoided. The one on the balcony overlooking the passenger waiting area is cheap but generally has awful food. The plush, nearly deserted restaurant is for cadres and doesn't welcome individuals. The big, crowded restaurant is fantastic – excellent dim sum or set meals for around Y3. It's one of the best bargains in Canton.

Airline Offices In Canton, CAAC is at 181 Huanshi Lu, to your left as you come out of the railway station. They have separate telephone numbers for domestic (☎ 6662969) and international (☎ 6661803). You can also book air tickets in the White Swan Hotel and China Hotel. The office is open from 8 am to 8 pm daily. There is an inexpensive bus that runs directly from the CAAC office to Baiyun Airport and back again.

Singapore Airlines (☎ 3358886) is in room 1056, Garden Tower, Garden Hotel, 368 Huanshi Donglu. Malaysian Airline System (☎ 3358828) is also in the Garden Hotel, Shop M04-05.

International Flights There are daily flights to Canton from Hong Kong on CAAC and Cathay Pacific for HK$320. Going the other way, it's Y215. The flight takes 35 minutes.

It is also possible to fly to Canton from a number of cities outside China including Manila and Singapore, though it is likely to be more expensive than first flying to Hong Kong. However, there may be times when all flights to Hong Kong are booked out but it's possible to fly into Canton.

Domestic Flights Check the CAAC timetable for current listings. Domestic flight destinations with airfares (in brackets) from Canton are as follows:

Beihai (Y208)	Meixian (Y110)
Beijing (Y633)	Nanchang (Y217)
Changchun (Y973)	Nanjing (Y412)
Changsha (Y192)	Nanning (Y182)
Changzhou (Y406)	Ningbo (Y393)
Chengdu (Y475)	Qingdao (Y626)
Chongqing (Y398)	Qinhuangdao (Y766)
Dalian (Y754)	Sanya (Y259)
Dandong (Y944)	Shanghai (Y414)
Guilin (Y154)	Shantou (Y127)
Guiyang (Y276)	Shashi (Y302)
Haikou (Y176)	Shenyang (Y876)
Hangzhou (Y369)	Shijiazhuang (Y612)
Harbin (Y1047)	Taiyuan (Y573)
Hefei (Y364)	Tianjin (Y663)

Hengyang (Y142)	Ürümqi (Y1220)
Hohhot (Y933)	Wuhan (Y285)
Huangshan (Y307)	Xiamen (Y196)
Ji'nan (Y548)	Xi'an (Y589)
Kunming (Y391)	Yantai (Y700)
Lanzhou (Y697)	Yichang (Y310)
Lianyungang (Y524)	Zhanjiang (Y130)
Liuzhou (Y176)	Zhengzhou (Y452)
Luoyang (Y463)	

Bus There are regular buses to Macau and to destinations within mainland China.

To/From Macau From Canton, buses to Macau leave at about 6.30 am daily from the Huaqiao Hotel in Haizhu Square.

If you want to go directly from Macau, Kee Kwan Motors, across the street from the Floating Casino, sells bus tickets to Canton. One bus takes you to the border at Zhuhai while a second bus takes you from there to Canton four hours later. The trip takes about five hours in all. On weekdays, buy your ticket the evening before departure.

This international bus is not necessarily the best way to make this journey. Having to get off the Macau bus, go through immigration and customs, wait for all your fellow passengers (and their enormous luggage), and then reboard another bus is a time-wasting and confusing exercise. It's usually faster to cross the Macau-Zhuhai border by foot and catch a minibus from Zhuhai to Canton. In Macau, bus No 3 runs between the Jetfoil Pier and the China border via the Hotel Lisboa, Avenida Almeida Ribeiro and the Floating Casino.

To/From Shenzhen From Canton to Shenzhen, minibuses operate from a bus station in front of the Liu Hua Hotel, which is across the street from the Canton Railway Station. The east side of the bus station (closest to the Liu Hua Hotel) is where the big government-run buses are. These are cheaper but slower and less comfortable. On the west side of this bus station is where you get the minibuses.

Privately owned air-con minibuses are lined up opposite the Shenzhen Railway Station near the Hong Kong border. The fare price is posted on a sign where the minibuses line up, and at the time of this writing was Y38. The drivers in Shenzhen often ask for Hong Kong dollars but will reluctantly accept RMB. Keep a calculator handy to see which works out cheaper. The trip takes five hours.

To/From Zhuhai From Canton, buses to Zhuhai depart from the bus station across the street from the railway station, west of the Liu Hua Hotel. There are two kinds of buses – minibuses and government-run buses. The minibuses are preferable and cost Y30.

From the Zhuhai Bus Station, which is to the west of the customs building, you can catch buses to Canton and other parts of Guangdong Province.

Train The KCR operates between Canton and Hong Kong and there is a local train to Shenzhen. You can also catch trains direct to Beijing, Shanghai or Guilin.

To/From Hong Kong The express train between Hong Kong and Canton is comfortable and convenient. The train covers the 182-km route in a little less than three hours.

Timetables change, but the current departure times from Hong Kong are at 8.18 and 9.03 am, and 12.28 and 2.28 pm. From Canton, departures to Hong Kong are at 8.30 and 10.20 am, and 4.28 and 6.30 pm. In Canton Railway Station, Hong Kong trains go from the end of the station, not from the main station building.

In Hong Kong, tickets can be booked up to seven days before departure at CTS or the Hunghom KCR Station for HK$163. Tickets booked the same day as departure cost HK$178. Return tickets are also sold, but only seven to 30 days before departure. You're allowed to take bicycles on the express train, and these are stowed in the freight car.

To/From Shenzhen The local train from Shenzhen to Canton is cheap and reasonably fast, but there are often long queues for tickets and seats can be difficult to come by at peak times. Hard seats (the Chinese equiv-

alent of 2nd class) are Y25. Soft seats (1st class) cost Y50. There are several trains per day from Shenzhen to Canton, but the schedules change so often that they're hardly worth quoting here. The trip takes between 2½ and three hours.

Many of the local trains from Shenzhen now stop at the new East Station. It may be nice and new, but it's also a long way from anywhere. Just follow the crowd to take a bus or minibus to the main railway station. The express trains all go to the main Canton Railway Station.

In Canton, you can buy train tickets from CITS several days in advance. Otherwise, you can join the queues at the railway station.

Whatever you do, be careful near the railway station. The whole area is a den of thieves – everything from pickpockets to bag slitters and purse snatchers. There are people selling black market (Chinese price) tickets outside the station, but the tickets are printed in Chinese so be sure you know what you're buying.

Boat Two types of ships ply the route between Hong Kong and Canton: jetcat (jet-powered catamaran) and a slow, overnight ferry. Between Macau and Canton there is a direct overnight ferry.

To/From Hong Kong The jetcat (named *Liwanhu)* takes three hours from Hong Kong to Canton. It departs Hong Kong once daily from China Hong Kong City, Tsimshatsui at 8.15 am and costs HK$154. In Canton, departures are from Zhoutouzui Wharf at 1 pm (2 pm during daylight saving time). Tickets can be bought from the CTS office at Haizhu Square, the White Swan Hotel or at the Liu Hua Hotel service desk, as well as the wharf. The ticket costs Y91.

There is also a hovercraft departing Hong Kong at 9 am, but this only goes as far as the port of Huangpu, 24 km east of Canton. This is not so convenient, so try to avoid getting on this one by mistake. On the rare chance you find yourself in Huangpu, the hovercraft returns to Hong Kong at 2.45 pm.

The Pearl River Shipping Company runs

two overnight ferries between Hong Kong and Canton – the *Tianhu* and the *Xinghu*. This is an excellent way to get to Canton from Hong Kong and saves you the cost of one night's accommodation. The ships are clean, fully air-con, have comfortable beds and a good Chinese restaurant. One ship departs Hong Kong daily from China Hong Kong City in Tsimshatsui at 9 pm and arrives in Canton the following morning at 7 am. In Canton the other ship departs at 9 pm (10 pm during summer daylight savings time) and arrives in Hong Kong at 7 am.

Ferry tickets to Canton can be bought most cheaply in China Hong Kong City. You can also buy them at CTS for an extra HK$20 service fee.

Second class has dormitory beds, which are quite comfortable and only cost HK$139. A 1st-class ticket costs HK$184 and gets you a bed in a four-person cabin with private bath. Special class is a two-person cabin with bath and costs HK$219. VIP class costs HK$600.

From Canton, tickets cost Y69 in 2nd class, Y100 in 1st class and Y123 in special class. On holidays there is an extra Y13 charge.

If you can't get a cabin or a bunk then buy a seat ticket and go to the purser's office as soon as you are on board. The purser distributes leftover bunks and cabins, but get in quick if you want one.

Bus No 31 (not trolley bus No 31) will drop you off near Houde Lu in Canton, which leads to Zhoutouzui Wharf (see map). To get from the wharf to the railway station, walk up to the main road, cross to the other side and take bus No 31 all the way to the station.

To/From Macau There are two ships which run on alternate days, the *Dongshanhu* and the *Xiangshanhu*.

In Canton, departures are from Zhoutouzui Wharf. The fare is Y37 in second class, Y57 in first class and Y87 in special class. There is an extra Y7 charge on holidays. From Canton, the boat departs at 8.30 pm, or 9.30 pm during daylight savings time.

In Macau, departures are from the pier near the Floating Casino (*not* the Jetfoil Pier). The boat leaves Macau at 8 pm and arrives in Canton the next morning at 7.15 am. Fares are M$69 in second class, M$100 in first class and special class costs M$147.

Getting Around

Canton proper extends for 60 sq km, with most of the interesting sights scattered throughout, so seeing the place on foot is impractical. Just the walk from the railway station to the hotels on Shamian Island is about six km – not recommended for beginning each day's sightseeing.

Bus Canton has an extensive network of motor and electric trolley buses which will get you almost anywhere you want to go. The problem is that they are almost always packed. Once an empty bus pulls in at a stop, a battle for seats ensues and a passive crowd of Chinese suddenly turns into a stampede.

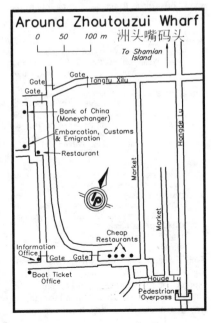

Even more aggravating is the tedious speed at which buses move, accentuated by the drivers' peculiar habit of turning off their motors and letting the bus roll to the next stop. You just have to be patient. Never expect anything to move rapidly and allow lots of time to get to the railway station to catch your train. Sometimes you may find you'll give up and walk. One consolation is that buses are cheap – you'll rarely pay more than two jiao per trip.

When boarding a bus, point to where you want to go on a map so that the conductor (who is seated near the door) will be able to sell you the right ticket. They usually tell you where you have to get off. In the early days of individual travel to China it was common for Chinese to offer their seats to foreigners. Sorry, but the novelty has worn off and these days you'll stand like everybody else.

Good Chinese maps of the city with bus routes are sold by hawkers outside the railway station and at some of the tourist hotel bookshops. Get one! There are too many bus routes to list here, but a few of the important routes are:

No 31

Runs along Gongye Dadao Bei, east of Zhou touzui Wharf, crosses Renmin Bridge and goes straight up Renmin Lu to the main railway station at the north of the city.

No 30

Runs from the main railway station eastwards along Huanshi Lu before turning down Nonglin Xia Lu to terminate in the far east of the city. This is a convenient bus to take if you want to go from the railway station to the Baiyun and Garden hotels.

No 5

Starting from the main railway station, this bus takes a similar route to No 31, but instead of crossing Renmin Bridge it carries on along Liu'ersan Lu, which runs by the northern side of the canal separating the city from Shamian Island. Get off here and walk across the small bridge to the island.

Taxi Taxis are available from the main hotels 24 hours a day. You can also catch a taxi outside the railway station or hail one in the street – a first for China. Demand for taxis is great, particularly during the peak hours:

from 8 to 9 am and during lunch and dinner hours.

Taxis are equipped with meters and drivers use them unless you've negotiated a set fee in advance. If you want to pay in RMB rather then FEC, Hong Kong dollars or US dollars, expect an argument about 50% of the time. In theory, the drivers are always supposed to accept RMB. Contrary to what some travellers will tell you, there is no such thing as an 'FEC taxi'.

The cost of a taxi varies depending on what type of vehicle it is. The cost per km (after flagfall) is displayed on a little sticker, usually on the right rear window. For the cheapest taxis, the sticker displays the number 1.40. Flagfall for these taxis is Y4.90 which takes you one km, after which you are charged at the rate of Y1.40 for every additional km, though the meter clicks Y0.70 every half-km interval. In the 1.40 taxis, a trip from the railway station to Shamian Island would cost slightly under Y10.

Taxis can be hired for a single trip or chartered on an hourly or daily basis. The latter is worth considering if you've got the money or if you're in a group which can split the cost. If you hire for a set period of time, negotiate the fee in advance and make it clear which currency you will pay with.

Minibus Minibuses seating 15 to 20 people ply the streets on set routes. If you can find out where they're going, they're a good way to avoid crowded buses. The front window usually displays a sign with the destination written in Chinese characters.

Bicycle Canton has at least two places to rent bicycles, but no doubt other rental shops will open. The Happy Bike Rental Station is on Shamian Island, near the White Swan Hotel and across the road from the Guangzhou Youth Hostel.

The Guangzhou Youth Hostel rents bicycles to their guests. A Y100 deposit is required unless you leave your passport. Bicycle theft is a problem, so you'd be wise to buy a cable lock (widely available) and try to leave the bike only in designated bicycle parks where it will be watched by attendants.

Around Canton

A few places around Canton make good day or half-day trips. Buses to some of these places depart either from the long-distance bus station on Huanshi Xilu, a 10-minute walk west of the main railway station, or from the provincial bus station across the road. For some destinations you must catch buses from smaller bus stations around the city.

WHITE CLOUD HILLS
(bái yún shān) 白云山
The White Cloud Hills, in the north-eastern suburbs of Canton, are an offshoot of Dayu Ling, the chief mountain range of Guangdong Province. The hills were once dotted with temples and monasteries, though no buildings of any historical significance remain. The hills are popular with the local people who come here to admire the views and slurp cups of tea. The Cloudy Rock Teahouse by a small waterfall on the hillside is recommended if you want to do the same.

At the southern foot of the hills is **Lu Lake**, also called Golden Liquid Lake, which was built for water storage in 1958 and is now used as a park.

The highest peak in the White Cloud Hills is **Star Touching Hill** *(mō xīng líng)*. It's only 382 metres, but anything higher than a sandcastle is a mountain in eastern China. On a clear day, you can see a panorama of the city – the Xiqiao Hills to one side, the North River and the Fayuan Hills on the other side, and the sweep of the Pearl River. Unfortunately, clear days are becoming a rarity in Canton.

The Chinese rate the evening view from **Cheng Precipice** as one of the eight sights of Canton. The precipice takes its name from a Qin Dynasty tale.

It is said that the first Qin Emperor, Qin Shi Huang,

heard of a herb which would confer immortality on whoever ate it. Cheng On Kee, a minister of the emperor, was dispatched to find it. Five years of wandering brought Cheng to the White Cloud Hills where the herb grew in profusion. On eating the herb, he found that the rest of it disappeared. In dismay and fearful of returning empty-handed, Cheng threw himself off the precipice, but having been assured immortality from eating the herb, he was caught by a stork and taken to heaven.

The precipice, named in his memory, was formerly the site of the oldest monastery in the area.

North of the Cheng Precipice, on the way up to Star Touching Hill, you'll pass the **Nine Dragons' Well**, the origins of which are also legendary.

One story goes that Canton officials worshipped twice yearly and in times of drought at the Dragon Emperor Temple that existed on the spot. During the 18th century, the governor of Canton visited the temple during a drought. As he prayed he saw nine small boys dancing in front of the temple, but they vanished when he rose from his knees. A spring bubbled forth from where he had knelt. A monk at the temple informed the amazed governor that these boys were in fact nine dragons sent to advise the governor that his prayers had been heard in heaven and the spring became known as the Nine Dragons' Well.

Getting There & Away
The White Cloud Hills are about 15 km from Guangzhou and makes a good half-day excursion. The express buses leave from Guangwei Lu, a little street running off Zhongshan 5-Lu to the west of the Children's Park, about every 15 minutes. The trip takes between 30 and 60 minutes, depending on the traffic. There is also a cable car from the bottom of the hill.

NANHU AMUSEMENT PARK
(nán hú lè yuán) 南湖乐园
As the name implies, this is geared for children rather than adults. However, even if you're no longer a toddler, this is still one way to kill half a day. Apart from the roller coaster, water slide, dodgem (bumper) cars, skating rink and go-carts, the park has a beautiful tree-shaded lake and a good restaurant.

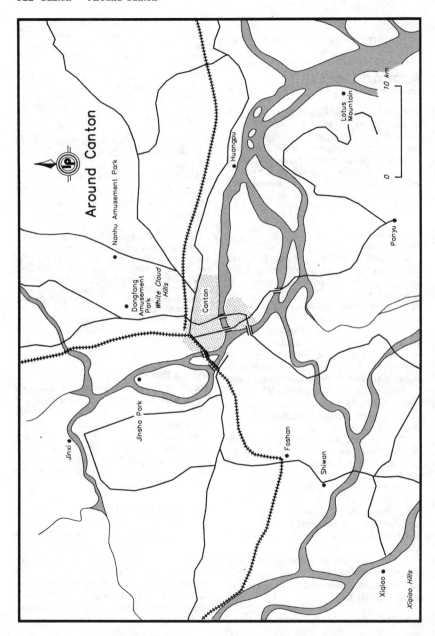

The park is north-east of the city in an area of rolling hills and is a good place to escape the crowds and noise of Canton. However, avoid this place on weekends when it is packed.

The restaurant staff try to play a little trick on you. When seated, a waiter will hand you a menu (in Chinese) which is basically a high-priced banquet that could feed an army. The waiter will try to tell you that this is all they serve. If you insist that you aren't interested in eating like a pig, you will finally be brought another menu (in English and Chinese) which includes many good dishes at cheap prices. The food is excellent.

Getting There & Away

Getting to Nanhu is easy. Air-con minibuses depart from near the main entrance of the railway station and go directly there. You can pay in RMB.

Another amusement park nearer to Canton is called Dongfang Leyuan, but it's not nearly as pleasant or scenic as Nanhu.

LOTUS MOUNTAIN
(lián hūa shān) 莲花山

This interesting and exotic place is only 46 km to the south-east of Canton and makes an excellent full-day trip. The name Lotus Mountain might conjure up images of some holy mountain like Emeishan or Huangshan. In fact, it's nothing like that.

Lotus Mountain is an old quarry site. Most people wouldn't think of a quarry as being attractive, but this place is an exception. The stonecutting ceased several hundred years ago and the cliffs have sufficiently eroded to a state where it looks almost natural.

Attempts to dress up the area by building pagodas, pavilions and stone steps have made the area into a sort of gigantic rock garden. Dense vegetation and good views of the Pearl River add to the effect. Overall, most of the buildings fit in well with the scenery and there are some nice walks. If only someone could persuade Chinese tourists to stop filling up the lotus ponds and gorges with bottles, cans and plastic bags, the area might become more popular with Westerners.

However, Lotus Mountain is now a popular weekend stop-off for tour groups from Hong Kong, which means that it would be best to visit on weekdays.

It's doubtful that you'd want to spend the night here, but there is one hotel, the *Lotus Mountain Villa (lián hūa shān zhuāng)*. There is one good restaurant on the mountain in the *Lotus Mansion (lián hūa lóu)*.

Getting There & Away

You can get there either by bus or boat, but the boat is more interesting. The once-daily boat leaves Canton at 8.45 am and takes about 2½ hours to reach Lotus Mountain, departing for Canton at 4.15 pm. That gives you about five hours on the mountain, which I found was about right for a relaxing hike and picnic.

The boat leaves from the Tianzi Pier *(tiān zì mǎ tóu)* on Yanjiang Lu, one block east of Haizhu Square and the Haizhu Bridge. It's not a bad idea to buy a ticket one day in advance. There are mahjong tables on the boat and you won't have any trouble finding partners if you want to participate.

Buses depart from the railway station area in Canton. In theory the bus should be faster than the boat, but with Canton's traffic jams it works out about the same. Soft drinks are available on the boat, but no food.

The major hotels in Canton also run tours to Lotus Mountain, though this will cost considerably more than doing it yourself. It also looks like they take all the fun out of the trip. I saw several of these tour groups, usually led by a young woman in uniform holding up a big flag and talking through a megaphone as the tourist troops marched in step leaving behind a trail of rubbish.

JINXI
(jīn xī) 金溪

If you love cruising on riverboats, you might want to have a look upstream from Canton. Jinxi is a small village of no particular interest in itself, but the boat trip is pleasant. Few foreign visitors come here, but it will give you a view of life in the countryside.

If you want to swim in the Pearl River, be sure you've had your hepatitis vaccination and get off the boat at **Jinsha Holiday Village** (jīn shā dù jià cūn). The holiday village isn't anything but a picnic ground and beach with a changing room, but it's popular with the Chinese (to be avoided on weekends). The boat from Canton will drop you off about noon and return at 3 pm. There is a restaurant and a place selling soft drinks near the beach. The river is muddy but cleaner than in Canton.

Getting There & Away

Catch the boat from the No 1 ferry pier, opposite the Nanfang Department Store on Yanjiang 1-Lu. A morning departure is at 10.30 am. Jinxi is the last stop. After a lunch break the boat is turned around and returns to Canton.

XIQIAO HILLS
(xī qiáo shān) 西樵山

Another scenic spot, these hills are 68 km south-west of Canton. Seventy-two peaks make up the area, the highest rising 400 metres. There are 36 caves, 32 springs, 28 waterfalls and 21 crags.

At the foot of the hills is the small market town of Xiqiao and around the upper levels of the hills are scattered several centuries-old villages. Most of the area is made accessible by stone paths. It's popular with Chinese tourists, but Westerners are rare.

Getting There & Away

Buses to the hills depart from the Foshan Bus Station on Daxin Lu, which runs west off Jiefang Nanlu.

CONGHUA HOT SPRINGS
(cōng huà wēn quán) 从化温泉

The springs are about 80 km north-east of Canton. Twelve springs have been found with temperatures varying from 30°C to 40°C, the highest being over 70°C. The water is supposed to help cure neuralgia (severe

spasmodic pain along the course of one or more nerves), arthritis, dermatitis and hypertension. One tourist leaflet even claims relief for 'fatigue of the cerebral cortex' (headache?) and gynaecological disease.

Unfortunately, there are no longer any outdoor pools. The water is piped into the private bathrooms of nearby hotels, so you'll have to enjoy the water without the benefit of natural scenery.

Getting There & Away

Buses to Conghua depart all day from the long-distance bus station on Hongyun Lu near Canton East Railway Station.

Buses also leave all day from the long-distance bus station on Huanshi Xilu. The first bus departs at about 7 am, the last at about 5.30 pm. As soon as you get to the springs, buy a ticket for the return journey to Canton as the buses are often full. The place is thick with bodies during weekends, so try to avoid going then.

FOSHAN
(fó shān) 佛山

Just 28 km south-west of Canton is the town of Foshan. The name means Buddha Hill.

The story goes that a monk travelling through the area enshrined three statues of Buddha on a hilltop. After the monk left, the shrine collapsed and the statues disappeared. Hundreds of years later, during the Tang Dynasty (618 AD to 907), the Buddha figurines were suddenly rediscovered, a new temple was built on the hill and the town was renamed.

Whether or not the story is true, from about the 10th century onwards Foshan became a well-known religious centre and, because of its location in the north of the Pearl River Delta (with the Fen River flowing through it) and its proximity to Canton, was ideally placed to thrive as a market town and trade centre.

Since the 10th or 11th century Foshan has been notable as one of the four main handicraft centres of old China. The other three were Zhuxian in Henan Province, Jingdezhen in Jiangxi Province and Hankou in Hebei Province. The nearby town of Shiwan

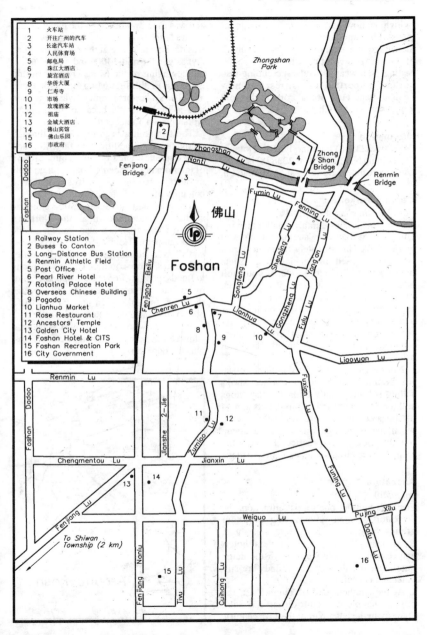

1 火车站
2 开往广州的汽车
3 长途汽车站
4 人民体育场
5 邮电局
6 珠江大酒店
7 旋宫酒店
8 华侨大厦
9 仁寿寺
10 市场
11 玫瑰酒家
12 祖庙
13 金城大酒店
14 佛山宾馆
15 佛山乐园
16 市政府

1 Railway Station
2 Buses to Canton
3 Long-Distance Bus Station
4 Renmin Athletic Field
5 Post Office
6 Pearl River Hotel
7 Rotating Palace Hotel
8 Overseas Chinese Building
9 Pagoda
10 Lianhua Market
11 Rose Restaurant
12 Ancestors' Temple
13 Golden City Hotel
14 Foshan Hotel & CITS
15 Foshan Recreation Park
16 City Government

佛山

Foshan

Zhongshan Park

Fenjiang Bridge

Zhong Shan Bridge

Renmin Bridge

Zhongshan Lu

Nanti Lu

Fumin Lu

Fenning Lu

Shenning Lu

Yong an

Foshan Dadao

Fenjiang Beilu

Chenren Lu

Songfeng Lu

Lianhua Lu

Congzheng Lu

Fulu Lu

Liaowan Lu

Renmin Lu

Fuxian Lu

Jianshe 2-Jie

Zumiao Lu

Jianxin Lu

Chengmentou Lu

Fenjiang Lu

To Shiwan Township (2 km)

Weiguo Lu

Pujing Xilu

Dafu Lu

Nonlu

Tiwu Lu

Cuihong Lu

(which is now virtually an extension of Foshan) became famous for its pottery, and the village of Nanpu (which is now a suburb of Foshan) developed the art of metal casting. Silk weaving and papercutting also became important industries and now Foshan papercuts are a commonly sold tourist souvenir in China.

Information

CITS (☎ 223338) is in the Foshan Hotel at 75 Fenjiang Nanlu. CTS (☎ 223828) is in the Overseas Chinese Building at 14 Zumiao Lu.

Lianhua Market

(lián hūa shì chǎng) 莲花市场

This market is considerably smaller than the Qingping Market in Canton, but it's still worth a look. Unfortunately, the main market is in an enclosed area which keeps some pretty powerful odours inside. If you can't handle it, the street in front of the market, Lianhua Lu, is also very interesting. Lots of small shops sell half-dead fish, turtles, dogs and snakes. If you're not in the market for something still moving, there are more mundane items such as biscuits and soft drinks.

Not every animal is for the dinner plate. It's getting more common to see shops selling pets, especially birds and fish (dogs still have a tough life in China). Pets almost disappeared during the Cultural Revolution when marauding Red Guards tried to stamp out this bourgeois practice. Perhaps the animals were mistaken for capitalist roaders.

Ancestors' Temple

(zǔ miào) 祖庙

Foshan's number-one tourist attraction, the Ancestors' Temple, is attracting large tour groups from Hong Kong and elsewhere. Recognising the opportunity, several hotels and restaurants have sprouted in the neighbourhood, but the temple grounds are still quiet and peaceful.

At the southern end of Zumiao Lu, the original temple was built during the Song Dynasty in the latter part of the 11th century,

and was used by workers in the metal-smelting trade for worshipping their ancestors. It was destroyed by fire at the end of the Yuan Dynasty in the mid-1300s and was rebuilt at the beginning of the Ming Dynasty during the reign of the first Ming Emperor Hong Wu. The Ancestors' Temple was converted into a Taoist temple because the emperor worshipped a Taoist god.

The temple has been developed through renovations and additions in the Ming and Qing dynasties. The structure is built entirely of interlocking wooden beams, with no nails or other metal used at all. It is roofed with coloured tiles made in Shiwan.

The main hall contains a 2500-kg bronze statue of a god known as the Northern Emperor (Beidi). He's also known as the Black Emperor (Heidi) and rules over water and all its inhabitants, especially fish, turtles and snakes. Since southern China was prone to floods, people often tried to appease Beidi by honouring him with temples and carvings of turtles and snakes. In the courtyard is a pool containing a large statue of a turtle with a serpent crawling over it, into which the Chinese throw one, two and five-fen coins, plus the odd drink can.

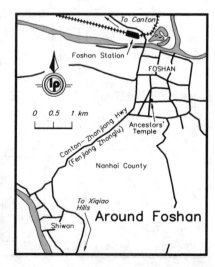

The temple also has an interesting collection of ornate weapons used on ceremonial occasions during the imperial days. The Foshan Museum is in the temple grounds, as is the Foshan Antique Store and an arts & crafts store. The temple is open daily from 8.30 am to 4.30 pm.

Shiwan

(shí wān) 石湾

Two km south-west of Foshan is Shiwan township, an area mostly known for its porcelain factories. Although there is nothing of outstanding scenic interest here you might want to take a look if you have an interest in pottery. Bus Nos 9 and No 10 go to Shiwan. You can catch bus No 9 in front of the Ancestors' Temple, or No 10 on Fenjiang Xilu. From the Ancestors' Temple, you could walk to Shiwan in 30 minutes.

Places to Stay

About the cheapest in town is the *Pearl River Hotel* (☎ 287512) *(zhū jiāng dà jiǔ diàn)* which has triples without air-con for Y45, and doubles for Y60. It's on Chenren Lu in

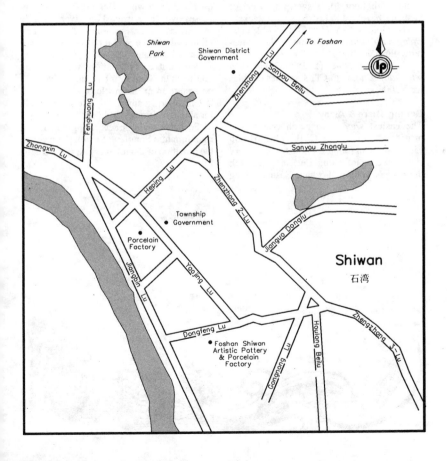

the centre of town, across the street from the post office.

Around the corner and just opposite the pagoda is the *Overseas Chinese Building* (☎ 223828) *(húa qiáo dà xià)* at 14 Zumiao Lu. Despite the misleading name it is indeed a hotel. Singles cost Y75 and doubles start at Y100.

The 16-storey *Rotating Palace Hotel* (☎ 285622) *(xúan gōng jiǔ diàn)*, is in the centre of town at Zumiao Lu and Lianhua Lu. A double room costs Y150. The rotating (revolving) restaurant is on the roof, and even if you don't eat there, you can pay a visit to the 16th floor for a sweeping view of Foshan's haze and industrial smokestacks.

The *Golden City Hotel* (☎ 357228) *(jīn chéng dà jiǔ diàn)*, 48 Fenjiang Nanlu, features plush doubles for Y195.

The *Foshan Hotel* (☎ 287923) *(fó shān bīn gǔan)* is home to CITS and has doubles for Y200.

Getting There & Away

The easiest way is to catch one of the minibuses near the Cultural Park on Liu'ersan Lu in Canton. These buses go very slowly westward along Liu'ersan Lu with the drivers yelling 'Foshan, Foshan'. Flag them down anywhere along the street. Once they fill up with passengers, they won't stop.

You can catch a bus at the terminal on Huangsha Dadao, one block to the west of Shamian Island. From the White Swan Hotel you can walk to the terminal in less than five minutes.

You can also catch buses to Foshan departing from the bus terminal next to the Liu Hua Hotel, near the railway station.

The bus from Canton heads into Foshan from the north. First stop is Foshan Railway Station (the railway line starts in Canton, passes through Foshan and heads west about 60 km to the town of Hekou). The bus then passes over the narrow Fen River, where a few decaying barges huddle, and a few minutes down the road it pulls into the long-distance bus station.

Walk out of the station, turn left and you're on the Canton-Zhanjiang Highway – no respite from the bustle of Canton! Turn left again down any of the side streets, walk for about 10 minutes and you'll come to one of Foshan's main streets, Songfeng Lu. A right turn into Songfeng Lu will point you in the direction of the town centre and Lianhua Lu.

Shenzhen 深圳

'The mountains are high and the emperor is far away', says an ancient Chinese proverb, meaning that life can be relatively free if one keeps far enough away from the central government. Shenzhen *(shēnzhèn)* – more than 2300 km from Beijing but within sight of Hong Kong – is a living example of the wisdom of this ancient proverb.

Shenzhen is a border town with Hong Kong and officially labelled a Special Economic Zone (SEZ). The Shenzhen SEZ came into existence in 1980. Three other SEZs were established at the same time: Zhuhai (near Macau), Shantou in the eastern part of Guangdong Province and Xiamen in Fujian Province.

But it soon became apparent that Shenzhen's location gave it major advantages over the others. A maximum tax rate of 15% and a minimum of bureaucratic hassles makes Shenzhen an attractive place to invest. Hong Kong investors can easily slip across the border to keep an eye on the factories they have set up in Shenzhen to exploit China's cheap land and labour. Hong Kong tourists find it cheap and convenient to make weekend excursions to the new luxury resorts, built by Hong Kong investors, that have sprung up in Shenzhen.

Another attraction is its open policy on housing. In China everybody needs a permit, called a *hukou*, to establish where they can live. Legally changing your place of residence is a difficult procedure in bureaucratic China, but anyone who buys a flat in Shenzhen can live there. Taking advantage of this, many Hong Kongers bought flats in Shenzhen's new high-rises and moved their relatives to the border area where they could be easily visited. Taking advantage of the fact that housing costs in Shenzhen are only about a third of the price in Hong Kong, many Hong Kongers have also moved themselves to Shenzhen and commute daily across the border.

Shenzhen even benefits from Hong Kong's waste. Many old taxis and buses were given or sold for scrap to Shenzhen where they now make up the bulk of the public transport. This accounts for the large number of vehicles in Shenzhen with the steering wheel on the right-hand side. It's also the reason why so many vehicles in Shenzhen look like they belong in the wrecking yard.

When travellers take the train from Hong Kong to China, the first view they get of the People's Republic is Shenzhen. For some, it's a dramatic entrance. For others, it's an anticlimax. With its towering skyscrapers Shenzhen looks so much like Hong Kong that you'll wonder if you didn't accidentally get on the wrong train.

After passing through customs most travellers board the first train for Canton, only stopping in Shenzhen long enough to change money and use the toilet. This is too bad, because Shenzhen is worth exploring, even if only for a day. True, the Chinese are trying to make Shenzhen into another Manhattan, but they haven't really succeeded, at least not yet.

Several unexpected problems have developed in Shenzhen and the other SEZs. While the SEZs originally expected to attract a great deal of foreign capital and technology, they have been more successful at attracting imported goods which are then smuggled to other parts of China. The SEZs were not meant to be a place for cadres to buy their Walkmans. Black marketeering in foreign currency and smuggled goods have become popular pastimes in Shenzhen. Yet another problem is that the Chinese government has discovered that its own enterprises don't compete very well against more efficient private companies.

The government now restricts access to the SEZs – Chinese citizens need a special permit to visit Shenzhen. Indeed, Shenzhen experiences the same problem that Hong Kong has with illegal immigrants. To stem the tide, an electrified fence has been

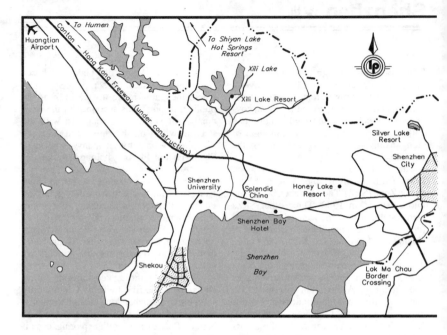

installed around the SEZ. Nevertheless, the population of one million is growing by an incredible 20% a year. Real economic growth is proceeding even faster.

It's not hard to understand why the immigrants keep coming. Typical salaries in Shenzhen are nearly Y1000 a month, more than five times the national average. Of course, the cost of living is also much higher than elsewhere in China, but employment in Shenzhen is relatively easy to find. There is no doubt that Shenzhen residents are better off than other Chinese.

Shenzhen is a bold experiment and a school. The Chinese are learning from their experience in Shenzhen just how a modern capitalist economy works. It's true that Shenzhen is not the real China – it's what China would be if it were not Communist.

Orientation

The name 'Shenzhen' refers to three places: Shenzhen City (opposite the border crossing at Lo Wu); Shenzhen SEZ; and Shenzhen County, which extends several km north of the SEZ. Most of the hotels, restaurants and shopping centres are found in Shenzhen City, along Renmin Nanlu, Jianshe Lu and Shennan Lu.

In the western area of the SEZ is the port of Shekou where you can get a hoverferry to Hong Kong. Shenzhen University is also in the west, as are the holiday resorts of Shenzhen Bay and Honey Lake. The main attraction in the eastern part of the zone is the beach at Xiaomeisha.

The northern part of the SEZ is walled off from the rest of China by an electrified fence to prevent smuggling and to keep back the hoards of people trying to emigrate illegally into Shenzhen and Hong Kong. There is a checkpoint when you leave the SEZ. You don't need your passport to leave but you will need it to get back in, so don't leave it in your hotel if you decide to make a day trip outside Shenzhen.

Chinese-character maps of Shenzhen are widely available from stalls near the railway station. English-language maps of Shenzhen are only readily available in Hong Kong.

Information

Tourist Office CITS (☎ 229403) has two offices. The most convenient one is on the 1st floor of the new railway station, but the main office is at 2 Chuanbu Jie, just west of Heping Lu.

Public Security The Foreign Affairs Office of the Public Security Bureau (☎ 226355) is on the west end of Jiefang Lu, on the north side of the street.

Money The good news in Shenzhen is that you can usually forget about FEC. RMB is much more readily accepted here than in Canton. However, in most places that deal with tourists, the Hong Kong dollar reigns supreme. Large tourist hotels will always ask

for payment in Hong Kong dollars, but mid-price hotels will take FEC and even RMB. If they accept RMB, they will sometimes, but not always, tack on an additional 15% (negotiable) to the charge.

Unless you are good at mathematics, bring a small pocket calculator with you. Many places that ask for Hong Kong dollars will accept RMB but 'accidentally' charge you the wrong exchange rate. A calculator will soon pay for itself.

You can convert Hong Kong dollars to RMB through the swarms of illegal money changers who approach you on the street and say *gǎng bì* (Hong Kong dollars). However, changing on the street is never recommended. If you're going to do black market dealing at all, it's safer in the shops and small restaurants. In Shenzhen everybody is a potential moneychanger.

When Shenzhen first came into existence as an SEZ, there was a serious plan floated to introduce a completely separate currency for the SEZ. Officials finally backed down after seeing what an uncontrollable mess the FEC fiasco had created.

If you have an Electronic Teller Card (ETC) from Hong Kong, you can use it to withdraw cash from the Hong Kong and Shanghai Bank, which has an auto-teller machine on the south-west corner of Cunfeng Lu and Renmin Nanlu.

Shenzhen City
(shēnzhèn shì) 深圳市
There isn't much in Shenzhen City to see, but it's still an interesting place to explore. The urban area near the border is a good place for walking. Most visitors spend their time exploring the shopping arcades and restaurants along Renmin Nanlu and Jianshe Lu.

On the north-east corner of Jiabin Lu and Renmin Nanlu is the International Trade Centre *(gúo jì mào yì zhōng xīn)* which has no English sign, but is easily recognised by its mammoth high-rise topped with a revolving restaurant. It's possibly the most interesting building in Shenzhen. At least the Chinese think so, as it's usually flooded with Chinese tourists taking photos of each other standing in front of the fountains. There is a supermarket and several good shops on the 3rd and 4th floor by the fountains (not in the high-rise section).

Splendid China
(jìng xiù zhōng húa) 锦绣中华
This is the mainland's answer to Taiwan's Window on China. The tourist brochure for Splendid China says 'visit all of China in one day'. You get to see Beijing's Forbidden City, the Great Wall, Tibet's Potala Palace, the Shaolin Temple, the gardens of Suzhou, the rock formations of Guilin, the Tianshan Mountains of Xinjiang and even some sights in Taiwan. The catch is that everything is reduced to one-fifteenth of life size.

Foreigners give this place mixed reviews. Some find it intriguing while others call it a 'bad Disneyland without the rides'. At least it's one way to get an overview of China's major scenic attractions. The Chinese are absolutely crazy about Splendid China – on weekends and holidays, Hong Kongers converge on the place.

Splendid China is in the western end of the SEZ, near Shenzhen Bay. From the railway station there are frequent minibuses. If you're entering Shenzhen by hoverferry, you could take a taxi from Shekou.

CTS in Hong Kong books full-day tours which take in Splendid China, along with a visit to a kindergarten, Dongmen Market, a traditional Hakka village, lunch and return to Hong Kong.

China Ethnic Culture Demonstration Villages
(zhōng gúo mín sú wén hùa cūn)
中国民俗文化村
Adjacent to Splendid China, the China Ethnic Culture Demonstration Villages seeks to do the same thing – give you a chance to see all of China in one day. In this case, rather than admiring miniaturised temples and mountains, you get to see full-sized ethnic minorities. To add to the effect, there are over 20 recreations of minority villages including a cave, Lama Temple, drum tower, rattan bridge and a statue of Guanyin (Kuanyin), the Goddess of Mercy. Just to remind you of China's claim to Taiwan, a Taiwanese aboriginal tribe is also represented. However, as of yet there are no representatives of Hong Kong's gwailo minority – could be an employment opportunity here!

The Resort Villages
(dù jià cūn)
Although the Shenzhen SEZ was originally meant to attract high-technology manufacturing, one of its chief sources of foreign exchange are the luxurious resort hotel-recreation complexes. These defy description, but are somewhat like Club Méditerranée, Disneyland, old European castles and just a touch of China all rolled into one. They offer discos, saunas, swimming pools, golf courses, horseback riding, roller coasters, supermarkets, palaces, castles, Chinese

pavilions, statues and monorails. The huge (and surprisingly cheap) dim sum restaurants become nightclubs in the evening, with Las Vegas-style floor shows.

Some travellers may find it all a bit too plastic, but some foreigners get into it – the Hong Kongers certainly do. Try not to have any preconceived notions. It's worth visiting these resorts if you have the time, even if just for a laugh. You don't have to spend a lot of cash either. Walking around and looking is pretty entertaining by itself and doesn't cost anything. You could also consider eating a dim sum lunch at the resorts, as prices are lower than in Hong Kong. Another possibility is to eat dinner and catch a floor show. Such an evening would cost about HK$100 for two people – a bargain when compared to Hong Kong entertainment prices.

The resorts are flooded on the weekends with free-spending Hong Kongers, so avoid visiting then unless you consider watching the crowd one of the amusements.

Honey Lake Resort *(xiāng mì hú dù jià cūn)*, west of Shenzhen City, is known for its amusement park, a miniature version of Disneyland called China Amusement City *(zhōng gúo yú lè chéng)* which is complete with monorail, roller coaster and castles. The resort is nice, but I didn't see much of a lake.

By contrast, **Shenzhen Bay Hotel** *(shēn zhèn wān dà jiǔ diàn)* is on the beach and offers great views across the bay to the New Territories in Hong Kong.

Xili Lake Resort *(xī lì hú)* has a nice lakeside view and good facilities. **Shiyan Lake Hot Springs Resort** *(shí yán hú wēn qúan dù jià cūn)*, five km to the north-west of Shenzhen outside the SEZ, has good country-club facilities.

Xiaomeisha Beach Resort *(xiǎo méi shā)* is the most beautiful of all. It's on the east side of the SEZ on the shore of Mirs Bay and has the best beach in Shenzhen.

Silver Lake Resort Camp *(yín hú)* is very close to Shenzhen City but is not as nice as the other resorts.

See Places to Stay for accommodation details.

Getting There & Away The easiest way to get to the resorts is to take a minibus from the railway station area in Shenzhen. These are operated by the hotels and only accept payment in Hong Kong dollars. The privately run minibuses that go up and down Shennan Lu are cheaper and accept payment in RMB, but you'll have to find out which minibus goes where.

Places to Stay

There is some good news and some bad news. The good news is that in Shenzhen you can get a much larger and more luxurious room than you could in Hong Kong for the same amount of money. In Shenzhen you can find a large deluxe double room with air-con, TV and private bath for between HK$200 and HK$300. In Hong Kong, this level of accommodation would cost five times as much.

The bad news for budget travellers is that there are no dormitories or dirt-cheap hotels. In Shenzhen, 'bottom end' means any hotel costing under Y100 for a double. Of course, there are some very cheap places for Chinese but it will be hard to persuade them to take you. If you're persistent (but remember to be friendly) it's conceivable you'll get into a dorm, but I rather doubt it. Otherwise, your best recourse is to find two or three other travellers to share with you. Remember, this situation occurs often in China, though Shenzhen is more expensive than the rest of the country.

Many of the top-end hotels will give you a 10% discount on weekdays. However, all of the better hotels have a 10% service charge as in Hong Kong. The cheaper places have no service charge, which is understandable since they don't give any service.

At one hotel I stayed in, the all-night security guard disappeared from his post at midnight and wasn't seen again until 7.30 am, before going off-duty at 8 am.

A lot of hotels in Shenzhen have a nasty habit of wanting to hold on to your passport, even though you pay for a room in advance. This is to make sure you don't run off with the

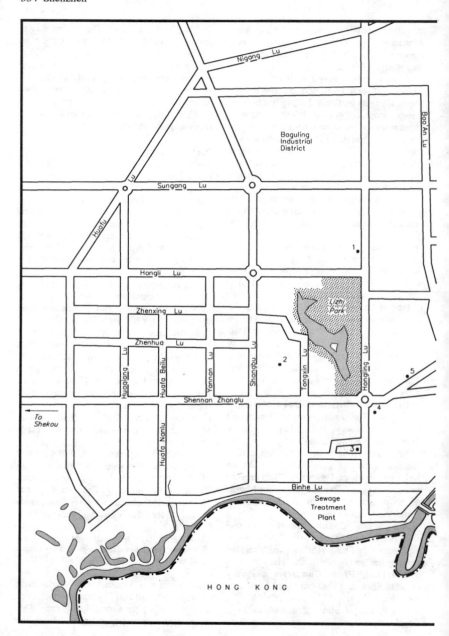

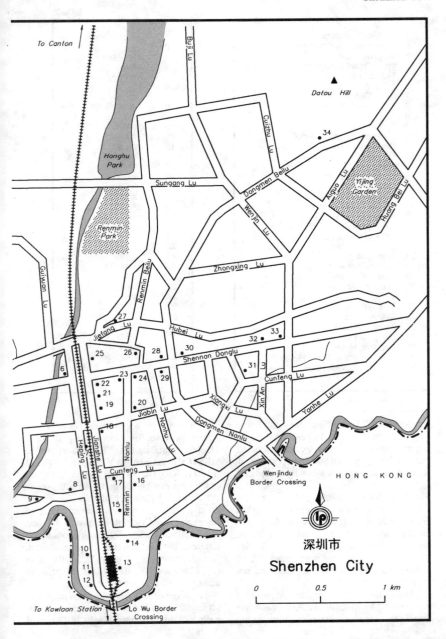

To Canton

Buji Lu

Datou Hill

Cuizhu Lu

● 34

Honghu
Park

Dongmen Beilu

Aguo Lu

Yijing
Garden

Huang Bei Lu

Sungang Lu

Wen Jin Lu

Renmin
Park

Guiwan Lu

Zhongxing Lu

Renmin Beilu

27 ●
Jiefang Lu

Hubei Lu

32 ● ● 33

25 ●   26 ●   28 ●

30 ●

Shennan Donglu

31 ●

Xin An Lu

Cunfeng Lu

6 ●

23 ●
22 ●
21 ●
19 ●

24 ●   29 ●

20 ●

Xiangxi Lu

Yanhe Lu

Jiabin Lu

Nanhu Lu

Dongmen Nanlu

18 ●

Nanlu

Heping Lu

Jianshe Lu

Cunfeng Lu

Wen jindu
Border Crossing

HONG KONG

8 ●

17 ●   ● 16

9 ●

15 ●

Renmin

深圳市

Shenzhen City

14 ●

10 ●

11 ●   ● 13

12 ●

To Kowloon Station

Lo Wu Border
Crossing

0   0.5   1 km

1	Xinhua Bookstore	1	新华书店
2	Shenzhen City Government	2	深圳市人民政府
3	Binjiang Hotel	3	滨江大酒店
4	Hotel Oriental Regent	4	晶都酒店
5	Public Security Bureau	5	公安局
6	Yatwah Hotel	6	日华宾馆
7	Shen Tieh Building	7	深铁大厦
8	CITS Main Office	8	中国国际旅行社
9	Heping Hotel	9	和平酒店
10	Forum Hotel	10	富临大酒店
11	Overseas Chinese Hotel	11	华侨大厦
12	Overseas Chinese Travel Service	12	华侨旅游部
13	Railway Station & CITS	13	火车站
14	Minibuses	14	小汽车出租点
15	Bank of China (small)	15	中国银行
16	Jinghu Hotel	16	京湖大酒店
17	Century Plaza Hotel	17	新都酒店
18	Panhsi Restaurant	18	洋溪酒家
19	Nanyang Hotel	19	南洋酒店
20	International Trade Centre	20	国际贸易中心
21	Bank of China (large)	21	中国银行
22	Shenzhen Hotel	22	深圳酒店
23	Wah Chung Hotel	23	华中国际酒店
24	Oriental Hotel	24	东方酒店
25	Post Office	25	邮局
26	Food Street	26	汇食街
27	McDonalds	27	麦当劳
28	Telecom Building	28	电信大楼
29	Airlines Hotel	29	航空酒店
30	Zhenhua Hotel	30	振华大厦
31	Fenghua Hotel	31	丰华酒店
32	Jingpeng Hotel	32	京鹏大厦
33	Nanfang International Hotel	33	南方国际大酒店
34	Bamboo Garden Hotel	34	竹园宾馆

furniture and TV set. Since they can't read English, you could easily give them an old expired passport if you have one. Otherwise, just tell them you need your passport to cash travellers' cheques – they usually accept this.

Places to Stay – middle

At the bottom of the barrel is the *Fenghua Hotel* (☎ 351168) *(fēng húa jiŭ diàn)*. The hotel entrance is on a small side-street called Nanji Lu, but there is a large sign in English that says 'FH'. Doubles range from Y75 to Y98. It's a rather run-down place and not especially recommended.

The *Binjiang Hotel (bīn jiāng dà jiŭ diàn)* on Hongling Lu looks like an American-style motel. You are much better off here paying in FEC since they give a ridiculously low exchange rate for Hong Kong dollars. Double rooms start at Y83 (but an absurd HK$168!), and go up to Y123 (HK$198) and Y150 (HK$300). As long as you're paying in Chinese money, it's good value.

The *Yatwah Hotel (rì húa bīn gŭan)* has a good location on the north-west corner of Shennan Lu and Heping Lu, just to the west of the railway tracks. The outside looks a bit tattered, but the interior is quite alright. Room prices are Y85 (HK$140), Y95 (HK$160) and Y130 (HK$210), plus an additional 10% on weekends.

The *Jinghu Hotel (jīng hú dà jiŭ diàn)* has no English sign but is easy to find and centrally located on Renmin Nanlu, just south of

Cunfeng Lu. Singles/doubles are Y88/170 (HK$130/250). This is about the best value you're going to find in Shenzhen if you're by yourself.

The *Shen Tieh Building* (☎ 234248) *(shēn tiĕ dà xià)* on Heping Lu is good value. Double rooms are Y100 (HK$150).

The *Shenzhen Hotel* (☎ 238000, fax 222284) *(shēn zhèn jiŭ diàn)* at 156 Shennan Donglu has doubles for Y118 (HK$198) and Y158 (HK$258). This place was recently renovated and is certainly reasonable for the high standard of accommodation.

Also recommended is the *Heping Hotel* (☎ 228151, 228149) *(hé píng jiŭ diàn)* on Chuanbu Jie near CITS. Really comfortable doubles start at Y120 (HK$190). The small dim sum restaurant on the first floor is not bad at all.

The *Jingpeng Hotel* (☎ 227190) *(jīng péng bīn gŭan)*, on Shennan Donglu, is an elegant-looking place that offers good value for money. Doubles with twin beds are Y115 (HK$170) and Y120 (HK$180). The hotel has its own billiard room, restaurant, gift shop and karaoke bar.

The *Zhenhua Hotel* (☎ 228501) *(zhèn húa dà xià)* on Shennan Donglu is definitely in the mid-range with doubles for Y120 (HK$180) and Y180 (HK$260).

Moving up in price and quality, there is the *Oriental Hotel* *(dōng fāng jiŭ diàn)* on the south-east corner of Renmin Nanlu and Shennan Donglu. A single room with private bath costs Y126 (HK$187), doubles are Y170 (HK$253) and triples are Y215 (HK$319). There are no discounts on weekdays and there is a 10% service charge. They also require a small refundable key deposit.

Across the street at 140 Shennan Donglu is the *Wah Chung Hotel* (☎ 238060) *(húa zhōng gúo jì jiŭ diàn)*. Spacious rooms cost Y148 (HK$198) and a triple room is Y185 (HK$245). There is a 10% service charge and rooms cost 10% more on weekends. You seem to get a better deal here if you pay in Hong Kong dollars.

The *Overseas Chinese Hotel* (☎ 223811) *(húa qiáo dà xià)* looks rundown, costs Y170 (HK$250) for a double and is not really

worth it. It's only real advantage is that it's location on Heping Lu is very close to the railway station.

The *Airlines Hotel* (☎ 237999, fax 237866) *(háng kōng dà jiŭ diàn)*, 130 Shennan Donglu, has singles/doubles for Y183/218 (HK$270/320). It's modern, clean and ruthlessly air-con.

Places to Stay – top end

The *Nanyang Hotel* (☎ 224968) *(nán yáng jiŭ diàn)* has doubles for Y192 (HK$240). This reasonably luxurious hotel is well known for its disco. It's on Jianshe Lu, north of Jiabin Lu.

The preceding is not to be confused with the similarly named *Nanfang International Hotel (nán fāng gúo jì dàjiŭ diàn)*. Rooms here cost Y204 (HK$301), Y228 (HK$336) and Y252 (HK$371).

The *Bamboo Garden* (☎ 533138, fax 534835) *(zhú yúan bīn gŭan)* is a little inconveniently located at Dongmen Beilu near the intersection with Aiguo Lu. However, it is a luxurious place and is known for its excellent restaurant. Many tour groups make a lunch stop here. You can book rooms from its Hong Kong office (☎ 3674127). Doubles cost Y238 (HK$350).

If you want to go first class, the *Century Plaza Hotel* (☎ 220888, fax 234060) *(xīn dū jiŭ diàn)* has it all. The hotel has a good spot on Cunfeng Lu, between Jianshe Lu and Renmin Nanlu. You can also make reservations in Hong Kong (☎ 8680638). Standard/deluxe doubles are Y374/428 (HK$550/630). The hotel accepts American Express.

The *Forum Hotel* (☎ 236333, fax 201700) *(fulin dà jiŭ diàn)* is at 67 Heping Lu, just to the west of the railway station. This place positively radiates luxury and has prices to match. Doubles cost a cool Y394 (HK$580) and Y435 (HK$640).

One of the newest places in town is the high-rise *Hotel Oriental Regent* (☎ 247000, fax 247290) *(jīng dū jiŭ diàn)* on the southeast corner of Shennan Zhonglu and Hongling Lu. This place has got everything from marble floors to perfumed toilet paper. Double rooms come in three standards costing Y353 (HK$520), Y394 (HK$580) and Y462 (HK$680).

For free-spending Hong Kongers, one of Shenzhen's big attractions are the holiday resorts outside the city. Obviously, budget travellers aren't going to spend the night in these places, but if you can afford mid-range hotels then the resorts are worth considering for a splurge. Actually, it's not horribly expensive. Weekday prices are about HK$350 for a double, which often includes a free breakfast and transportation to and from the Shenzhen border crossing (railway station area). They often throw in free use of their other facilities (sauna, disco, swimming pool) or else offer sizeable discounts to hotel guests. They usually give a 20% discount in their shopping centres if you stay at the resort.

You can book directly through the hotels or the resorts' Hong Kong offices. Hong Kong travel agents, including China Travel Service, can tell you about special package deals that the hotels won't bother to mention.

Honey Lake Resort (☎ 745061, fax 745045) *(xiāng mì hú dù·jià cūn)* West of Shenzhen City, it has doubles for HK$288 on weekdays or for up to HK$368 on weekends. Contact the two Hong Kong booking offices on ☎ 7989288 or ☎ 8656210. Hotel guests receive a 20% discount in the restaurant, amusement park, sauna and other facilities.

Shenzhen Bay Hotel (☎ 770111, fax 770139) *(shēn zhèn wān dà jiǔ diàn)* Doubles cost HK$368 on weekdays or HK$498 on weekends. Its Hong Kong booking office (☎ 3693368) is in the New World Office Building, Tsimshatsui. Hotel guests have free use of the swimming pool, night club shows and other facilities. Guests also receive a discount at the shopping centre.

Shiyan Lake Hot Springs Resort (☎ 960143) *(shí yán hú wēn qúan dù jià cūn)* Doubles range from HK$248 to HK$398 on weekdays or from HK$278 to HK$430 on weekends. This place is about five km north-west of Shenzhen, outside the SEZ.

Silver Lake Resort Camp (☎ 222827, fax 242622) *(yín hú)* Doubles range from HK$278 to HK$418 on weekdays or from HK$328 to HK$450 on weekends.

Xiaomeisha Beach Resort (☎ 550000) *(xiǎo méi shā)* Doubles cost HK$318 on weekdays or HK$398 on weekends, which includes breakfast and a 20% discount on other meals.

Xili Lake Resort (☎ 660022, fax 660521) *(xī lì hú)* Doubles range from HK$248 to HK$398 on weekdays or from HK$278 to HK$430 on weekends.

Places to Eat

Dim sum breakfast and lunch is available in all but the scruffiest hotels. Usually the dim sum restaurants are on the 2nd or 3rd floor rather than by the lobby. Prices are only slightly lower than in Hong Kong. You'll have to pay in Hong Kong dollars in the nicer hotels.

Food Street *(huì shí jīe)*, a small lane north of Renmin Nanlu and Shennan Donglu, has restaurants which mostly specialise in seafood and freshwater fish. Prices are generally low, but always ask first. You can pay in RMB and there is a sign in English at the front of the street.

The *Oriental Hotel*, on the corner of Renmin Nanlu and Shennan Donglu, has a Western-style restaurant on the ground floor. You have to pay in Hong Kong dollars, but prices are about as cheap as you can find in Shenzhen if you need Western food.

One of Shenzhen's best restaurants is the *Pan Hsi Restaurant* (☎ 238081) *(bàn xī jiǔ jiā)* at 33 Jianshe Lu.

Shenzhen is the site of China's first *McDonald's*, a major tourist attraction which draws Chinese from all over the country. If you want to join the crowd, it's on the north side of Jiefang Lu.

Entertainment

Hong Kong people (and the children of cadres) love nightlife, of which there is plenty in Shenzhen. Discos are especially popular and can be found at just about any large hotel.

The *Crystal Palace Disco* is in the Hotel Oriental Regent on the south-east corner of Hongling Lu and Shennan Zhonglu. It has bright lights and plenty of noise.

One of the best discos is the *33 Disco* (☎ 20388) in the Nanyang Hotel *(nán yáng jiǔ diàn)*. This place gets so crowded that you often need reservations. The cover charge is HK$40. It's on Jianshe Lu, north of Jiabin Lu.

If you want a first-class place to go, the *Century Plaza Hotel (xīn dū jiǔ diàn)* has a disco on the top floor. Ride the glass elevator and admire Shenzhen's night skyline. The cover charge is HK$70. It's on Cunfeng Lu between Jianshe Lu and Renmin Nanlu.

All the main hotels and resort areas have discos and nightclubs.

Getting There & Away

Air At the time of writing, Shenzhen was putting the final touches on Huangtian Airport and it should be open by the time you read this. The Chinese government claims that this will be an international airport and that Hong Kong may use it too. Plans call for setting up a separate customs and immigration terminal for China-bound passengers and Hong Kong-bound passengers.

At least that's China's plan – Hong Kong has shown little interest. Hong Kong is determined to build its own new airport on Chek Lap Kok Island (near Lantau), but this won't be completed until at least 1997. If Hong Kong's Kai Tak Airport hits the saturation point before then (very likely), Shenzhen's new airport could play an important role.

Bus From Hong Kong, there are bus services to Shenzhen run by: Citybus, Motor Transport Company of Guangdong & Hong Kong Ltd at the Canton Rd Bus Terminus, and CTS. For most travellers, buses are not a good option unless you are on a tour.

There are long-distance buses to Fuzhou, Xiamen and other coastal cities departing from the Overseas Chinese Travel Service *(húa qiáo lǚ yóu bù)*, next to the Overseas Chinese Hotel on Heping Lu.

Minibus There are frequent minibuses running between Canton and Shenzhen. In Canton, buses depart from next to the Liu Hua Hotel, across the street from the railway station. In Shenzhen, departures are just to the east of the railway station next to the

Hong Kong border crossing. The fare is Y38 and the ride takes five hours.

Train The Kowloon-Canton Railway (KCR) offers the fastest and most convenient transport to Shenzhen from Hong Kong. Trains to the border crossing at Lo Wu begin from the Hunghom KCR Station in Tsimshatsui East. Unless you want to walk to Hunghom, it's easiest to take the MTR to the Kowloon Tong Station, then change to the KCR. There are frequent departures throughout the day and the electric trains start at 6.40 am. The fare from Hunghom KCR Station to Lo Wu is HK$21.50 ordinary class or HK$37 first class. The last train from Hunghom to Lo Wu is at 8.50 pm. The border closes at 10 pm. Hunghom to Lo Wu is 34 km and the trip takes 37 minutes. Avoid taking this train on weekends when it's filled to overflowing and the stampede at the border crossing is incredible.

There are frequent local trains running between Canton and Shenzhen and the journey takes about three hours. The fare is Y35 in 2nd class and Y50 in 1st class, but the trains are often packed and there are long queues to buy tickets.

Car It is possible to drive across the Hong Kong-Shenzhen border, but I don't know why anyone would want to, given the convenience of public transport. The border crossing is at Man Kam To on the Hong Kong side and is called Wenjindu on the Chinese side. A new border crossing was opened at Lok Ma Chau in 1991.

On my first night in Shenzhen I saw a collision between a Shenzhen taxi and a car driven by a Hong Kong tourist. No one was seriously injured, but both cars were badly damaged. The accident occurred in front of my hotel at 7 pm. The police were called and the drivers were told to stay by their vehicles until the police arrived. By 11 pm the police had still not arrived. The Hong Kong tourist checked into my hotel and the taxi driver went home. The next morning I got up at 7 am and the police still hadn't come and the Hong Kong tourist and the taxi driver were playing mahjong together next to their wrecked vehicles. I ate breakfast then checked out of my hotel at 9 am. The police were still nowhere to be seen.

Boat Hoverferries run between Hong Kong and Shekou, a port on the west side of Shenzhen. There are three daily departures from the ferry terminal at China Hong Kong City on Canton Rd in Tsimshatsui, Kowloon, at 8, 10.15 am and 3.30 pm. There are four additional departures from the Macau Ferry Pier on Hong Kong Island at 8.20, 9.30 am, 2 and 4.30 pm. The fare is HK$69 and the trip takes 45 minutes. Departures from Shekou to Kowloon are at 9.15 am, 2.30 and 5 pm. Departures from Shekou to Hong Kong Island are at 8.15, 10.45 am, 3.15 and 4.45 pm. The fare is Y35.

There is a jetcat (jet-powered catamaran) once daily from Macau to Shekou. It departs Macau at 8.30 am and arrives in Shekou at 10 am. The cost is M$79.

There are three daily jetcats running between Shekou and Zhuhai SEZ (north of Macau).

Getting Around

Shenzhen has some of the best public transport in China. The city bus is OK. It's also dirt cheap and not nearly as crowded as elsewhere in China.

The minibuses are faster. These are pri-

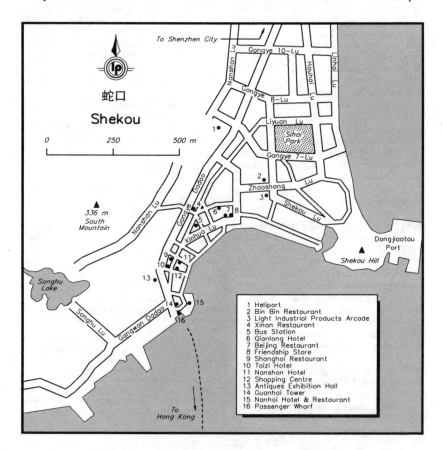

1 Heliport
2 Bin Bin Restaurant
3 Light Industrial Products Arcade
4 Xinan Restaurant
5 Bus Station
6 Qianlong Hotel
7 Beijing Restaurant
8 Friendship Store
9 Shanghai Restaurant
10 Taizi Hotel
11 Nanshan Hotel
12 Shopping Centre
13 Antiques Exhibition Hall
14 Guanhai Tower
15 Nanhai Hotel & Restaurant
16 Passenger Wharf

vately run and cheap, but if you can't read the destination in Chinese characters you will need help.

Taxis are abundant but not so cheap because their drivers have been spoilt by free-spending tourists. Negotiate the fare before you get in. When foreigners are passengers, drivers will usually ask for payment in Hong Kong dollars.

I couldn't find any bike rentals. The staff at the hotels just scratched their heads when I asked. They were puzzled that a foreigner would want to do an undignified thing like ride a bicycle. They offered to arrange a taxi and driver for me, which is what they normally do for tourists and cadres.

SHEKOU
(shé kǒu) 蛇口

A small city at the western end of the Shenzhen SEZ, Shekou is of only minor interest to tourists. Perhaps the most interesting thing about the town is its name, which means 'snake's mouth'. There are many factories here, and north of the city is Shenzhen University.

Many business travellers come here because of the factories, so for that reason there is an excellent hotel. The *Nanhai Hotel* (☎ 692888, fax 692440) *(nán hǎi jiǔ diàn)* has doubles which start at a breathtaking Y340 (HK$500).

There is a direct hoverferry service linking Shekou to Hong Kong Island. From Shenzhen City, you can reach Shekou by minibus.

AROUND SHENZHEN
Humen
(hǔmén) 虎门

The small city of Humen is north-west of Shenzhen on the Pearl River. It's only of interest to history buffs particularly curious about the Opium Wars that directly led to Hong Kong's creation as a British colony.

The **Bogue Forts** at Humen is the site of an impressive new museum which commemorates the destruction of the surrendered opium which sparked the first Opium War. There are many exhibits, including the large artillery pieces and other relics and the actual ponds in which Commissioner Lin Zexu had the opium destroyed. When the new museum opened, there was a special exhibition commemorating the 150th anniversary of the war.

The only problem with this place is getting there. No buses go directly to Humen, but buses and minibuses travelling from Shenzhen to Canton go right by. You could ask to be let off at the Humen access road, and then get a taxi, hitch or walk the five km into town.

Zhuhai 珠海

From any hilltop in Macau, you can gaze to the north and see a mass of modern buildings just across the border in China. This is the Zhuhai Special Economic Zone (SEZ). Like the Shenzhen SEZ, Zhuhai *(zhūhǎi)* has numerous elite resort playgrounds for Hong Kong, Macau and Overseas Chinese, as well as the occasional foreigner. Cadres also come to Zhuhai for 'meetings', usually returning to Beijing with a good suntan and a suitcase full of electronic goodies which are scarce up north.

Many travellers unfortunately conclude that having seen Shenzhen they will bypass Zhuhai – a big mistake. Zhuhai has its own character and in many ways is more attractive than Shenzhen.

The biggest attraction is the beach. Zhuhai has the atmosphere of a mediterranean resort but without the high prices. Zhuhai is a place to relax and enjoy yourself. There aren't many places like that in China.

Zhuhai is more laid-back than Shenzhen, much cleaner than Canton and definitely cheaper than Macau. True, it's not the real China, but since the real China puts many people off, that might be no great loss. Finally, there is one important historic site nearby – the former home of China's leading revolutionary, Dr Sun Yatsen.

It would probably be best to avoid Zhuhai on weekends when throngs of Hong Kong and Macau tourists flood across the border and hotel rooms become scarce.

Orientation

Zhuhai City is a municipality and SEZ which is divided into three main areas. The area nearest the Macau border is called Gongbei and is the main tourist area with lots of hotels, restaurants and shops. To the north-east is Jida, the eastern part of which is called Jiuzhou (where the port is). The Jida-Jiuzhou area has some large resort hotels as well as beautiful parks and beaches.

Finally, the northernmost section of the city is called Xiangzhou. There isn't much to see here. Xiangzhou is mostly an area of worker flats, factories and shops catering to the local Chinese population. It's only interest to travellers might be to get a glimpse of the everyday life of China's new entrepreneurial class.

The map called *Zhuhai Shi* (Zhuhai City) is widely available from bookstalls and hotel gift shops. These are all in Chinese characters but have bus routes and are useful for getting around. There are no useful English maps. The map entitled *Map of Macau & Zhuhai*, published by Universal Publications of Hong Kong, only covers the Xiangzhou area of Zhuhai, which isn't much use since most travellers stay in Gongbei.

Unlike most of China, Zhuhai does not use daylight saving time (but this could change), so if it's summer and you just arrived from Canton, set your watch back one hour.

Information

Tourist Office CTS (☎ 885777) is at 4 Shuiwan Lu, opposite the Gongbei Palace Hotel.

Public Security The Public Security Bureau (☎ 222459) is in the Xiangzhou district on the south-west corner of Anping Lu and Kangning Lu.

Money Hong Kong dollars are much in demand in Zhuhai, but few people show much interest in FEC. Most mid-range hotels accept RMB from foreigners without argument, though you could be charged a little bit more. The big resort hotels like Hong Kong dollars.

The Bank of China is a gleaming new building next to the towering Yindo Hotel on the corner of Yuehai Lu and Yingbin Dadao. You can also change money in most hotels, but another good place in Gongbei is the Nan Tung Bank on the corner of Yuehai Donglu and Shuiwan Lu.

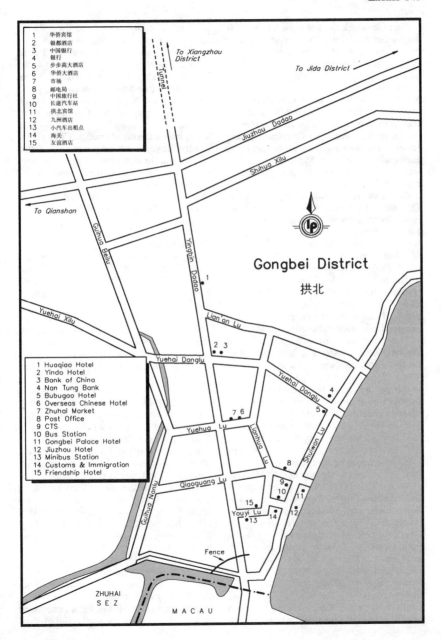

There are black market moneychangers at the border. As always, it is unwise to change money on the street. If you have to indulge in black marketeering try the small shops.

Things to See

Most visitors start their exploration of Zhuhai from the area near the Macau border. It's worth taking a look at the **Zhuhai Market** on Yuehua Lu, next to the Overseas Chinese Hotel. It's reasonably clean but not nearly as exotic as the Qingping Market in Canton – they keep the dog meat hidden when the tour buses come through.

Beaches are the top attraction in Zhuhai. Of course, if you visit in February the water won't look nearly so inviting as it does in July. Nevertheless, it's a scenic coastline with big boulders sheltering small stretches of white sand. There are only two beaches that are suitable for swimming.

The nicest stretch of beach is the bay in **Haibin Park** *(hǎi bīn gōng yúan)* near the Zhonglü Hotel at the northern end of the Jida district. If you stay in the Zhonglü Hotel, you can get the maximum benefit of this beach.

The other swimming beach is in the **Zhuhai Holiday Resort** at the south end of the Jida district and west of Jiuzhou Harbour. The walk along the coastline from Gongbei to this beach is very pleasant, and be sure to wander around the resort itself. You can't say it's not a beautiful place, though the statue of Mickey Mouse waving hello doesn't quite fit in with my idea of an idyllic beach resort. The Chinese apparently don't agree: carloads of them come to this place just to get their picture taken standing next to Mickey.

West of Haibin Park is an area called **Shijingshan Tourist Centre** *(shí jìng shān lü yóu zhōng xīn)*. The tourist centre itself is no big deal, just some gardens, an artificial lake, a supermarket and shops selling tourist junk. However, if you go inside the centre, head towards the back of the complex and you'll find some stone steps going uphill. Follow them up and up and you'll quickly find yourself in a forest with big granite boulders all around. Keep climbing to the top of the ridge and you'll be rewarded with outstanding views of Zhuhai City, Zhong shan and Macau.

On the south side of Shijingshan Tourist Centre is **Jiuzhou Cheng**. From the outside, you'll probably think it's some kind of restored Ming Dynasty village. Inside, you'll find that it's a high-class shopping centre where everything is priced in Hong Kong dollars.

On the south side of Jiuzhou Cheng is the **Zhuhai Resort** *(zhū hǎi bīn gǔan)*, another playground for rich Hong Kongers on holiday. It's worth stopping for a brief look.

There are several other interesting things to see in the area north of Zhuhai City in Zhongshan County. See the Around Zhuhai section later.

Places to Stay

There is good news and bad news. The bad news is that there is no real bottom-end accommodation in Zhuhai. Chinese hotels have cheap dormitories but do not accept foreigners.

The good news is that mid-range hotels are amazingly cheap in Zhuhai, and if you can find another foreigner to share with you, the cost is not much higher than a dormitory. For Y75 you can get a large double room with twin beds, private bath, air-con and colour TV. Most mid-range hotels will accept RMB on an equal rate with FEC, so if you have black market cash to unload, this is a good place to use it up.

Living it up in Zhuhai for a couple of days before crossing the border into Macau, where hotels cost at least three times as much, is a good way to end a trip to China.

The area near the Macau border crossing has a lot of hotels, restaurants, markets and activity, so it's a good place to start looking if you like nightlife. If you would prefer a little serenity, stay some place several blocks to the north.

Places to Stay – middle

Close to the border is the *Jiuzhou Hotel* (☎ 868851) *(jiǔ zhōu jiǔ diàn)* where doubles start at Y85. It's on the waterfront on Shuiwan Lu near Qiaoguang Lu and south of

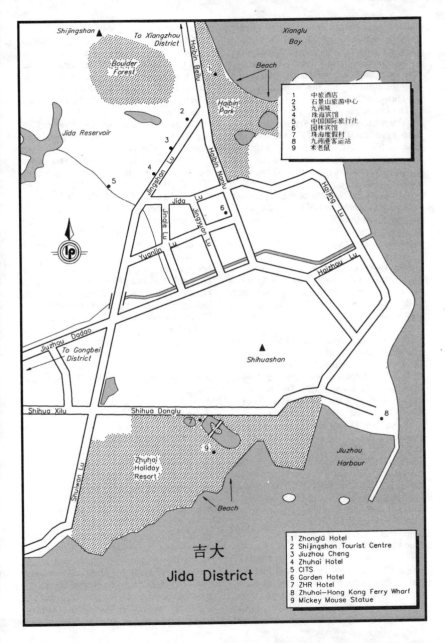

Shijingshan

To Xiangzhou
District

Xianglu
Bay

Boulder
Forest

Beach

Haibin Beilu

Haibin Park

1 中旅酒店
2 石景山旅游中心
3 九洲城
4 珠海宾馆
5 中国国际旅行社
6 园林宾馆
7 珠海度假村
8 九洲港客运站
9 米老鼠

Jida Reservoir

Jingshan Lu

Haibin Nanlu

Haijing Lu

Jida

Jinde Lu

Jingyuan Lu

Yuanlin

Haizhou Lu

Jiuzhou Dadao

To Gongbei
District

Shihuashan

Shihua Xilu

Shihua Donglu

Shuiwan Lu

Zhuhai
Holiday
Resort

Jiuzhou
Harbour

Beach

吉大
Jida District

1 Zhonglü Hotel
2 Shijingshan Tourist Centre
3 Jiuzhou Cheng
4 Zhuhai Hotel
5 CITS
6 Garden Hotel
7 ZHR Hotel
8 Zhuhai–Hong Kong Ferry Wharf
9 Mickey Mouse Statue

the Gongbei Palace Hotel, a few minutes walk from the border. Across the street is CTS, and although you may not have any use for its travel services, it does operate a hotel. Not especially recommended, rooms cost Y50 for a double and the building is called the Huaqiao Daxia.

The *Friendship Hotel (yǒu yí jiǔ diàn)* is on Youyi Lu (Friendship St) near the border gate between Lianhua Lu and Yingbin Dadao. Singles/doubles cost Y75/85, and you must leave a refundable Y50 deposit to ensure that you don't run off with the TV or toilet.

A little further from the border is the *Overseas Chinese Hotel (☎ 885183) (húa qiáo dà jiǔ diàn)*, on the north side of Yuehua Lu between Yingbin Dadao and Lianhua Lu, right next to the Zhuhai Market. Doubles are Y75.

The *Huaqiao Hotel (☎ 885123) (húa qiáo bīn guǎn)* on Yingbin Dadao, one block north of Yuehai Donglu, has three standards of double rooms for Y84, Y95 and Y106. It's a good, quiet place to stay with an excellent restaurant.

The *Bubugao Hotel (☎ 886628) (bù bù gāo dà jiǔ diàn)* is at 2 Yuehai Donglu, on the corner with Shuiwan Lu near the waterfront. Double rooms come in three flavours from Y70, Y100 and Y150. This is quite an attractive hotel on the inside and seems quite a bargain for the lower-priced rooms.

If you would like to stay in a beautiful peaceful place by the beach, a great deal is the *Zhonglü Hotel (☎ 332208) (zhōng lü jiǔ diàn)*. Double rooms are Y90, a bargain given the spacious, forested grounds and beach. It's in Haibin Park which is in the Jida district north-east of Gongbei. It's within walking distance of the Shijingshan Tourist Centre and luxurious Zhuhai Hotel.

Places to Stay – top end

The *Gongbei Palace Hotel (☎ 886833) (gǒng bèi bīn guǎn)* is the most luxurious place close to the border. It's by the waterfront on Shuiwan Lu near Qiaoguang Lu, about a one-minute walk from the border crossing. Among the facilities are a disco,

video game arcade, sauna and swimming pool (including water slide). Unfortunately, the beach is too rocky for swimming. The hotel runs bus tours of the surrounding area. Like most top-end places in Zhuhai, they ask for payment in Hong Kong dollars but will reluctantly accept FEC. Twin rooms start from Y226 (HK$328).

The ultra-modern *Yindo Hotel (☎ 883388, fax 883311) (yín dū jiǔ diàn)* is a gleaming high-rise dominating Zhuhai's skyline. Standard twins start at Y207 (HK$300), or you can rent the presidential suite for a mere Y6130 (HK$8888). The hotel is on the corner of Yuehai Lu and Yingbin Dadao.

The *Zhuhai Holiday Resort (☎ 332038, fax 332036) (zhū hǎi dù jìa cūn)*, or ZHR, is a five-star resort with good beaches and amenities such as a bowling alley, roller rink, tennis courts, club house, go-cart racing, horse riding, sauna and the 'Texas Bar & Lounge'. This is a place to wrap yourself in luxury if you can afford it and don't mind the fact that it doesn't look or feel much like China. It more closely resembles the south of France. The resort is on the shoreline north-east of Gongbei near Jiuzhou Harbour. Double rooms in the main hotel start from Y212 (HK$308), and a villa for two people is slightly cheaper at Y164 (HK$238). There is a 15% surcharge.

Zhuhai Hotel (☎ 333718, fax 332339) (zhū hǎi bīn guǎn) is another playground for the upper crust. However, it doesn't have the benefit of a beach, which makes it much less worth the expense in my opinion. Nevertheless, it caters to every whim and has a sauna, tennis courts, billiard room, swimming pool, nightclub and even mahjong rooms. Double rooms range from Y219 (HK$318) to Y274 (HK$398), while suites are Y509 (HK$738). There is also a 10% surcharge. Children under 12 are free if sharing the same accommodation. You can book in Macau (☎ 552275).

Garden Hotel (☎ 333968, fax 333497) (yúan lín dà jiǔ diàn), on Haibin Nanlu, is a luxurious hotel which is geared towards tour groups. However, the location is not particularly special so do not come here for the

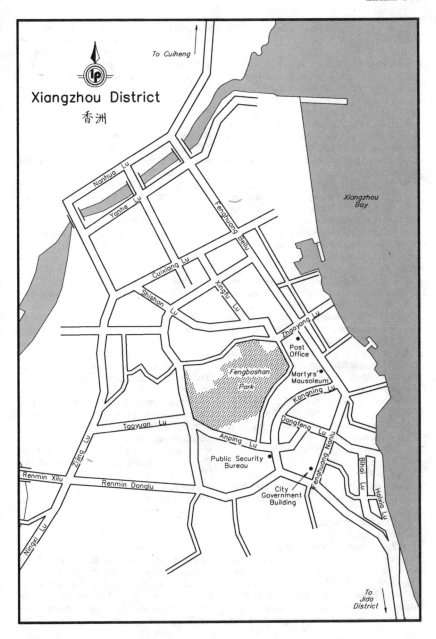

scenery. Double rooms begin at Y138 (HK$200).

Places to Eat

The area near the Macau border crossing has the most of everything – restaurants, bakeries, night markets and street vendors. It also has the most pickpockets! Little kids who approach you as beggars will sometimes try to relieve you of your wallet. They work in groups and practically glue themselves to foreigners. Their mothers can be equally aggressive.

Hang on to your wallet and you'll find plenty to spend your money on. Right next to the bus station is *Maxim's*, the Hong Kong fast-food chain famous for its cakes. It's a good place to catch a quick breakfast, though the Chinese bakeries are cheaper. You'll see many other restaurants around the border area.

The north-east corner of Youyi Lu and Yingbin Dadao has a good sidewalk restaurant, particularly in the evening.

If you haven't already made the discovery, dim sum restaurants are to be found in most hotels, usually on the 2nd or 3rd floors. Prices are low. I really liked the dim sum restaurant on the 2nd floor of the *Huaqiao Hotel* on Yingbin Dadao (north of Yuehai Donglu).

The 8th floor of the *Friendship Hotel* has a small, pleasant and cheap restaurant with good views of the harbour. The menu is in Chinese but the staff is friendly, and you can always just point at something.

Things to Buy

Zhuhai really isn't a great place to shop. You'll find more variety in Macau and Hong Kong.

Jiuzhou Cheng is an exclusive shopping mall next to the Zhuhai Hotel on Jingshan Lu in the Jida district. Obviously it is not for the local people, because everything is priced in Hong Kong dollars and you have to pay admission to get in. The mall looks like an ancient Chinese palace from the outside. Inside, you'll find numerous shops, well-manicured gardens, fountains, pavilions and

fish ponds. The shops sell many imported goods such as electrical appliances, pharmaceuticals, and stereos. It's open from 10 am to 6 pm. One good thing about this place is the supermarket. You can stock up on imported Hong Kong delicacies such as Watson's Cola and No Frills Dried Lemon Peel.

Getting There & Away

To/From Macau Simply walk across the border. In Macau, bus Nos 3 and 5 lead to the Barrier Gate, from where you make the crossing on foot. The Macau-Zhuhai border is open from 7 am to 9 pm.

To/From Canton Buses to Zhuhai depart from the bus station across the street from the railway station, just west of the Liu Hua Hotel. The large government buses are cheaper, but less frequent, slower and more crowded. Minibuses have air-con and cost Y30. All buses and minibuses accept payment in RMB.

Going the other way, buses from Zhuhai to Canton depart from the main bus station on Youyi Lu, directly opposite the customs building (the border checkpoint). The minibus station is also on Youyi Lu, one block to the west of the customs building.

To/From Hong Kong Jetcats between Zhuhai and Hong Kong do the trip in about 70 minutes. Departure times are 7.45, 11 am and 2.30 pm. Boats depart from the ferry terminal at China Hong Kong City on Canton Rd in Tsimshatsui, Kowloon and cost HK$100 on weekdays and HK$110 on weekends.

Going the other way, departures are from the Jiuzhou port district in Zhuhai at 9.30 am, 1 and 4.45 pm. The fare is Y47 weekdays, Y54 on weekends.

To/From Shenzhen A high-speed ferry operates between the Shekou port district in Shenzhen and the Jiuzhou port district in Zhuhai. There are five departures daily in each direction. From Shenzhen, the first boat is at 9 am and the last is at 4.30 pm. From

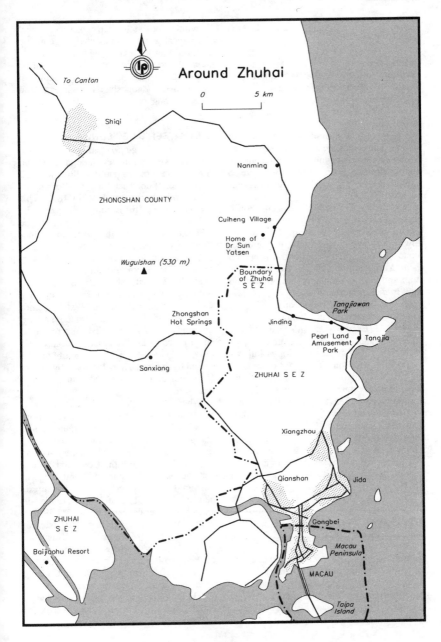

To Canton

Shiqi

ZHONGSHAN COUNTY

Nanming

Cuiheng Village

Home of
Dr Sun
Yatsen

Wuguishan (530 m)

Boundary
of Zhuhai
S E Z

Tangjiawan
Park

Zhongshan
Hot Springs

Jinding

Pearl Land
Amusement
Park

Tangjia

Sanxiang

ZHUHAI S E Z

Xiangzhou

Qianshan

Jida

ZHUHAI
S E Z

Gongbei

Baijiaohu Resort

Macau
Peninsula

MACAU

Taipa
Island

Around Zhuhai

0   5 km

Zhuhai, the first departure is 8.20 am and the last is at 3 pm.

Getting Around

Travelling around Zhuhai is a relief after Canton. No more elbowing your way into a bus, fighting with a taxi driver over FEC versus RMB or sitting in traffic that moves slower than a bicycle.

Zhuhai has a decent public transport system. The routes are clearly shown on the Zhuhai city map and you shouldn't have any trouble figuring it out. You might have to stand, but the buses aren't nearly as packed-out as in Canton.

Even better is the minibus system. You'll never have to wait more than 30 seconds for one of these to come along. To flag one down, just wave and they will come screeching to a halt regardless of other traffic behind them. Minibuses will stop in the public bus stops and most other places, but cannot stop right in major intersections.

On minibuses, the destination is written in Chinese characters and displayed on the windshield. Even if you can't read Chinese it hardly matters because there are only two basic routes. One route runs along Shuiwan Lu by the waterfront. The other route goes up Yingbin Dadao and terminates in Xiangzhou. Actually, there are variations of these routes, but all you have to do is tell the driver where you want to go (before you get in). If he doesn't go there, he'll just wave you off and drive away. If you can't pronounce the Chinese, point to it on a map or write it down.

The fare for minibuses is Y2 for any destination within the city limits, payable in RMB.

Around Zhuhai

North of Zhuhai City is Zhongshan County, the south of which has several very interesting places to visit. By starting in the morning you can travel by minibus and visit all of these places in one day and be back in Zhuhai in time for dinner.

A quick look at the map makes it clear that the logical way to do this is to make a loop trip. Starting from Gongbei, take a minibus along the coast to the former residence of Dr Sun Yatsen, then up to Shiqi, southward again to the Zhongshan Hot Springs and back to Gongbei.

SUN YATSEN'S RESIDENCE

(sūn zhōng shān gù jū) 孙中山故居

China's most famous revolutionary, Dr Sun Yatsen was born in a house on this site on 12 November 1866. That house was torn down after a new home was built in 1892. This second house is still standing and open to the public. The site also has a museum, but the Chinese have turned the place into something of a circus. Admission is Y1.

Sun Yatsen dedicated his life to the overthrow of the corrupt and brutal Qing (Manchu) Dynasty. His goal was to do away with dynasties altogether and establish a Chinese republic based on Western democratic principles. He organised several uprisings, all of which failed. As a result, he spent much of his life in exile because of a price on his head. There is no doubt that he would have faced a horrible death by torture if the emperor had succeeded in capturing him.

When the actual revolution came in 1911, Sun Yatsen wasn't in China. Still, there is no denying his role as a major organiser and instigator of the revolution. He is widely regarded as the father of his country and has been deified by both the Communist Party and the Nationalist Party (Kuomintang) in Taiwan. He briefly served as the first president of the Republic of China. He died in 1925 from liver cancer at the age of 59. His wife was Soong Chingling, the sister of Soong Mayling (Madame Chiang Kaishek).

Sun Yatsen's house is in the village of Cuiheng, north of the city limits of Zhuhai. There are frequent minibuses to Cuiheng departing from Gongbei near the border checkpoint. The fare was Y8 last time I went and the bus wasn't in good shape – the door fell off.

Just before you reach the Zhuhai City limits, you pass Pearl Land *(zhēn zhū lè yúan)*, another Chinese amusement park, which isn't worth stopping for unless you're really into roller coasters.

In Cuiheng there are two hotels – the huge Cuiheng Hotel *(cùi hēng bīn gǔan)* and the smaller Cuiheng Jiudian. It's doubtful you'll want to spend the night here unless you're a Sun Yatsen-ophile.

SHIQI

(shí qí) 石岐

The administrative centre of the county, Shiqi is often referred to as Zhongshan City. An industrial city, it bears no resemblance to Zhuhai and could hardly be called a main tourist attraction. Still, you must pass through here if doing the circuit from Cuiheng to Zhongshan Hot Springs. The city is worth perhaps 45 minutes of time to walk around.

The one and only scenic spot in town is **Zhongshan Park** which is heavily forested and dominated by a large hill topped with a pagoda. It's visible from most parts of the city so it's easy to find. It's nice and quiet in the park (except on Sunday) and a climb to the top of the pagoda will reward you with a sweeping view of the city's factories.

There is a large **Sun Yatsen Memorial Hall** *(sūn zhōng shān jì niàn táng)* on Sunwen Zhonglu to the east of Zhongshan Park. The car park is often jammed with tour buses from Macau, though there is nothing special about this place. The most worthwhile sight is the old, rusting MIG fighter parked on the lawn, a relic of the Korean War.

Apart from the pagoda in Zhongshan Park, the other dominant feature on the skyline of Shiqi is the Fu Hua Hotel, a huge golden building that's topped with a revolving restaurant. The hotel has a disco, sauna, bowling alley, billiard room and swimming pool.

You might be curious as to why anybody would build this stunning resort hotel in the middle of an industrial wasteland such as Shiqi. I asked numerous Hong Kongers this

question and the answer was always the same – everyone is here on business.

The quickest way out of town is to catch a minibus from the car park of the Tiecheng Hotel.

Places to Stay

Should you be so taken with Shiqi that you want to stay, about the cheapest place accepting foreigners is the *Tiecheng* (Iron City) *Hotel* (☎ 823803, fax 821103) *(tiě chéng jiǔ diàn)* at the corner of Zhongshan Lu and Sunwen Xilu. Doubles range from Y60 to Y95, plus a 10% service charge.

Across the street is the *International Hotel* (☎ 824788, fax 824736) *(gúo jì jiǔ diàn)*, 1 Zhongshan Lu, where doubles/twins cost Y198/228 (HK$288/330).

Top of the line is the *Fu Hua Hotel* (☎ 822034, fax 828678) *(fù húa jiǔ diàn)*, which has doubles for Y227 (HK$330). If you want to spend your honeymoon here, there are honeymoon suites for Y380 (HK$550) and the presidential suite goes for a trifling Y3310 (HK$4800). There is a 10% service charge.

Most likely, you won't want to stay in Shiqi unless you decide to open a factory there.

ZHONGSHAN HOT SPRINGS

(zhōng shān wēn qúan) 中山温泉

On the way back to Gongbei, it's easy to make a stop-off at this hot springs resort north of the Zhuhai City limits. The hot springs are not such a big attraction – they are piped into the hotel. More attractive is the surrounding resort area with its manicured gardens, hills, trees and ponds. You can clearly see Wuguishan, which at 530 metres is the highest peak in the area. Like other Chinese resorts, this place has some of that amusement-park atmosphere, with a disco and video game arcade, but thankfully there are no statues of Mickey Mouse or roller coasters. Basically, it's a pleasant place to stroll.

Apart from the mineral baths, the resort is famous for its golf course, which is one of

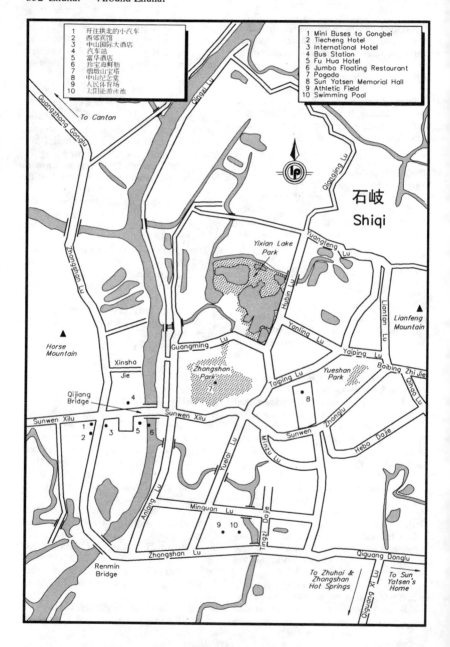

1	开往拱北的小汽车
2	西郊宾馆
3	中山国际大酒店
4	汽车站
5	富华酒店
6	珍宝海鲜舫
7	烟墩山宝塔
8	中山纪念堂
9	人民体育场
10	太阳能游泳池

1	Mini Buses to Gongbei
2	Tiecheng Hotel
3	International Hotel
4	Bus Station
5	Fu Hua Hotel
6	Jumbo Floating Restaurant
7	Pagoda
8	Sun Yatsen Memorial Hall
9	Athletic Field
10	Swimming Pool

To Canton

Guangzhong Gonglu

Qiaoxi Lu

Qiangjing Lu

石岐
Shiqi

Zhongshan Lu

Yixian Lake Park

Yuangfeng Lu

Lianton Lu

Lianfeng Mountain

Horse Mountain

Xinsha Jie

Hubin Lu

Yanling Lu

Guangming Lu

Yaiping Lu

Baibing Zhi Jie

Qijiang Bridge

Zhongshan Park

Taiping Lu

Yueshan Park

Qihao Lu

Sunwen Xilu

Sunwen Xilu

Zhonglu

Sunwen

Hebo Dajie

Anlong Lu

Yuetai Lu

Minzu Lu

Minquan Lu

Tugzi Dajie

Zhongshan Lu

Qiguang Donglu

Renmin Bridge

To Zhuhai & Zhongshan Hot Springs

Qiguang Xi Lu

To Sun Yatsen's Home

the best in China. The first professional golf championship ever held in China, the 1988 Dunhill Cup Pacific, took place here. Until recently, the golf course attracted many players from Macau. However, with Macau's new golf course recently completed, Zhongshan Hot Springs now has serious competition.

If you're a real hot springs or golfing enthusiast, you might want to spend a night here. Otherwise, you'll probably just want to look around briefly and then head back to Gongbei. Considering the palatial surroundings, the Zhongshan Hot Springs Hotel (☎ 683888, fax 683333) isn't horribly expensive, but they like Hong Kong dollars. Double rooms are Y137 (HK$200) to Y220 (HK$320). There is also a 10% service charge.

A minibus drops you by the entrance to the resort, then it's nearly a half-km walk to the hotel. For Y1 you can hire someone to carry you on the back of a bicycle. You won't have to look for them as they'll be looking for you. To get back to Gongbei, flag down any minibus you see passing the resort entrance. A minibus from the hot springs to Gongbei costs Y4.

Index

ABBREVIATIONS

Kowloon – Kow
Hong Kong Island – HKI
The New Territories – NT

Outlying Islands – OI
Macau Peninsula – MP
Macau Islands – MI

Canton – Can
Shenzhen – Shn
Zhuhai – Zhu

MAPS

TEXT

Map references are in **bold** type

Lonely Planet Guidebooks

Lonely Planet guidebooks cover every accessible part of Asia as well as Australia, the Pacific, South America, Africa, the Middle East and parts of North America and Europe. There are four series: *travel survival kits*, covering a country for a range of budgets; *shoestring guides* with compact information for low-budget travel in a major region; *walking guides*; and *phrasebooks*.

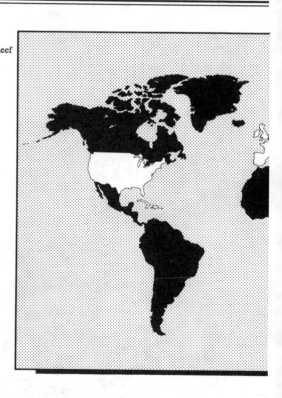

Australia & the Pacific
Australia
Bushwalking in Australia
Islands of Australia's Great Barrier Reef
Fiji
Micronesia
New Caledonia
New Zealand
Tramping in New Zealand
Papua New Guinea
Papua New Guinea phrasebook
Rarotonga & the Cook Islands
Samoa
Solomon Islands
Sydney
Tahiti & French Polynesia
Tonga
Vanuatu

South-East Asia
Bali & Lombok
Burma
Burmese phrasebook
Indonesia
Indonesia phrasebook
Malaysia, Singapore & Brunei
Philippines
Pilipino phrasebook
Singapore
South-East Asia on a shoestring
Thailand
Thai phrasebook
Vietnam, Laos & Cambodia

North-East Asia
China
Mandarin Chinese phrasebook
Hong Kong, Macau & Canton
Japan
Japanese phrasebook
Korea
Korean phrasebook
North-East Asia on a shoestring
Taiwan
Tibet
Tibet phrasebook

West Asia
Trekking in Turkey
Turkey
Turkish phrasebook
West Asia on a shoestring

Middle East
Egypt & the Sudan
Egyptian Arabic phrasebook
Israel
Jordan & Syria
Yemen

Indian Ocean
Madagascar & Comoros
Maldives & Islands of the East Indian Ocean
Mauritius, Réunion & Seychelles

Mail Order

Lonely Planet guidebooks are distributed worldwide and are sold by good bookshops everywhere. They are also available by mail order from Lonely Planet, so if you have difficulty finding a title please write to us. US and Canadian residents should write to Embarcadero West, 112 Linden St, Oakland CA 94607, USA and residents of other countries to PO Box 617, Hawthorn, Victoria 3122, Australia.

Europe
Eastern Europe on a shoestring
Eastern Europe phrasebook
Iceland, Greenland & the Faroe Islands
Trekking in Spain
USSR
Russian phrasebook

Indian Subcontinent
Bangladesh
India
Hindi/Urdu phrasebook
Trekking in the Indian Himalaya
Karakoram Highway
Kashmir, Ladakh & Zanskar
Nepal
Trekking in the Nepal Himalaya
Nepal phrasebook
Pakistan
Sri Lanka
Sri Lanka phrasebook

Africa
Africa on a shoestring
Central Africa
East Africa
Kenya
Swahili phrasebook
Morocco, Algeria & Tunisia
Moroccan Arabic phrasebook
Zimbabwe, Botswana & Namibia
West Africa

Mexico
Baja California
Mexico

South America
Argentina
Bolivia
Brazil
Brazilian phrasebook
Chile & Easter Island
Colombia
Ecuador & the Galápagos Islands
Latin American Spanish phrasebook
Peru
Quechua phrasebook
South America on a shoestring
Trekking in the Patagonian Andes

Central America
Central America on a shoestring
Costa Rica
La Ruta Maya

North America
Alaska
Canada
Hawaii

The Lonely Planet Story

Lonely Planet published its first book in 1973 in response to the numerous 'How did you do it?' questions Maureen and Tony Wheeler were asked after driving, bussing, hitching, sailing and railing their way from England to Australia.

Written at a kitchen table and hand collated, trimmed and stapled, *Across Asia on the Cheap* became an instant local bestseller, inspiring thoughts of another book.

Eighteen months in South-East Asia resulted in their second guide, *South-East Asia on a shoestring*, which they put together in a backstreet Chinese hotel in Singapore in 1975. The 'yellow bible' as it quickly became known to backpackers around the world, soon became *the* guide to the region. It has sold well over half a million copies and is now in its 7th edition, still retaining its familiar yellow cover.

Today there are over 80 Lonely Planet titles – books that have that same adventurous approach to travel as those early guides; books that 'assume you know how to get your luggage off the carousel' as one reviewer put it.

Although Lonely Planet initially specialised in guides to Asia, they now cover most regions of the world, including the Pacific, South America, Africa, the Middle East and Eastern Europe. The list of *walking guides* and *phrasebooks* (for 'unusual' languages such as Quechua, Swahili, Nepalese and Egyptian Arabic) is also growing rapidly.

The emphasis continues to be on travel for independent travellers. Tony and Maureen still travel for several months of each year and play an active part in the writing, updating and quality control of Lonely Planet's guides.

They have been joined by over 50 authors, 40 staff – mainly editors, cartographers, & designers – at our office in Melbourne, Australia, and another 10 at our US office in Oakland, California. Travellers themselves also make a valuable contribution to the guides through the feedback we receive in thousands of letters each year.

The people at Lonely Planet strongly believe that travellers can make a positive contribution to the countries they visit, both through their appreciation of the countries' culture, wildlife and natural features, and through the money they spend. In addition, the company makes a direct contribution to the countries and regions it covers. Since 1986 a percentage of the income from each book has been donated to ventures such as famine relief in Africa; aid projects in India; agricultural projects in Central America; Greenpeace's efforts to halt French nuclear testing in the Pacific and Amnesty International. In 1991 $68,000 was donated to these causes.

Lonely Planet's basic travel philosophy is summed up in Tony Wheeler's comment, 'Don't worry about whether your trip will work out. Just go!'